HISTORICAL DICTIONARY
of the
ELIZABETHAN
WORLD

Britain, Ireland, Europe, and America

by John A. Wagner

Oryx Press
1999

The rare Arabian Oryx is believed to have inspired the myth of the unicorn. This desert antelope became virtually extinct in the early 1960s. At that time, several groups of international conservationists arranged to have nine animals sent to the Phoenix Zoo to be the nucleus of a captive breeding herd. Today, the Oryx population is over 1,000, and over 500 have been returned to the Middle East.

© 1999 by The Oryx Press
4041 North Central at Indian School Road
Phoenix, Arizona 85012-3397

Cover portrait of Elizabeth I by Nicholas Hilliard, 1575, by courtesy of the
National Portrait Gallery, London.
Cover photograph of the author by JoAnne Reed.

Published simultaneously in Canada
Printed and bound in the United States of America

∞ The paper used in this publication meets the minimum requirements of
American National Standard for Information Science—Permanence
of Paper for Printed Library Materials, ANSI Z39.48, 1984.

Library of Congress Cataloging-in-Publication Data
Wagner, John A., 1954–
    Historical dictionary of the Elizabethan world : Britain, Ireland, Europe,
and America / by John A. Wagner.
        p.   cm.
    Includes bibliograpical references and index.
    ISBN 1-57356-200-9 (alk. paper)
    1. Great Britain—History—Elizabeth, 1558–1603 Encyclopedias.
    2. America—Discovery and exploration—English Encyclopedias.
    3. Ireland—History—1558–1603 Encyclopedias.   4. Europe—History—
1517–1648 Encyclopedias.   I. Title.
DA357.W34   1999
942.05'5'03—dc21   99-31109
                                                                                      CIP

To Paul, Courtney, Ray,
Katie, Patrick, Emma,
Peter, Haley, and Matthew

CONTENTS

GUIDE TO SELECTED TOPICS

Desmond Rebellion
Devise (for the Succession)
Dudley, John, Duke of
    Northumberland
Essex's Rebellion
Fitzgerald, Gerald, Earl of
    Desmond
Fitzgerald, James Fitzmaurice
Fitzmaurice's Rebellion
Gowrie conspiracy
Grey, Jane
Howard, Thomas, Duke of
    Norfolk
Lopez, Roderigo
Lopez plot
Northern rebellion
Northumberland's Coup
Pole conspiracy
Ridolfi plot
Ruthven raid
Seymour, Thomas, Lord
    Seymour of Sudeley
Stuart, Mary, Queen of Scots
Stukeley, Sir Thomas
Throckmorton plot
Wyatt's Rebellion

Religion

admonition controversy
advowson
Anabaptists
anticlericalism
benefice
Bible, English
"bill and book" episode
Black Rubric
Challenge Sermon
Convocation
Cranmer, Thomas
Davies, Richard
Huguenots
Jews
Marian exiles
Marian martyrs
Morgan, William
Protestantism
Reformation, English
Reformation, Irish
Reformation, Scottish
Reformation, Welsh
Salesbury, William
separatists
subscription crisis
tithes

Anglican

Anglican Church
Anglican settlement
Aylmer, John
Book of Common Prayer
catechism
Chapel Royal
church courts
Grindal, Edmund
High Commission, Court of
Hooker, Richard
Hutton, Matthew
Jewel, John
Laws of Ecclesiastical Polity
Parker, Matthew
Paul's Cross
Piers, John
Sandys, Edwin
supremacy, royal
Thirty-nine Articles
Whitgift, John
Young, Thomas

Roman Catholic

Allen, William
archpriest controversy
Blackwell, George
Campion, Edmund
Catholic League
Catholicism, English
Counter-Reformation
Garnet, Henry
Gerard, John
Gregory XIII
Jesuit Mission
Mary I
Mass
Parsons, Robert
penal laws
Pius V
priest holes
recusants
Regnans in Excelsis
seminary priests
Southwell, Robert
transubstantiation

Puritan

Barrow, Henry
"Book of Martyrs"
Browne, Robert
Calvin, John
Calvinism
Cartwright, Thomas
classical movement

Congregationalists
Foxe, John
Knox, John
lectureships
Lever, Thomas
Marprelate Tracts
Norton, Thomas
Nowell, Alexander
Penry, John
presbyterian movement
prophesyings
Puritans
vestiarian controversy
Whittingham, William

Royal Residences

Greenwich Palace
Hampton Court Palace
Nonsuch Palace
Oatlands Palace
palaces
Richmond Palace
St. James's Palace
Tower of London
Westminster Palace
Whitehall Palace
Windsor Castle

Science, Astrology, and Medicine

Bacon, Sir Francis
Borough, William
Dee, John
epidemic disease
Forman, Simon
Gilbert, William
medicine
plague

Scotland

Berwick, Treaty of (1560)
Berwick, Treaty of (1586)
Carberry, Battle of
casket letters
chaseabout raid
Darnley murder
Douglas, Margaret, Countess
    of Lennox
Edinburgh
Edinburgh, Treaty of
Gowrie conspiracy
Guise, Marie de
Hepburn, James, Earl of
    Bothwell

PREFACE

The *Historical Dictionary of the Elizabethan World* provides its users with clear and concise basic descriptions and definitions of people, events, ideas, and terms relating in some significant way to the Elizabethan period of British history. The *Dictionary* was written primarily for students and other nonspecialists who have interest—but little background—in this period of history. Besides providing a resource for quickly looking up names and terms encountered in reading or during study, the *Dictionary* offers an excellent starting point for classroom or personal research into Elizabethan subjects. The entries provide the basic information required to choose or hone a research topic, to answer small but vital questions of fact, and to identify further and more extensive information resources. The *Dictionary* also serves as a useful reader's companion for those whose Elizabethan reading—whether fiction or nonfiction—is more for enjoyment than for study.

The "Elizabethan Period"

Although the reign of Elizabeth I of England lasted from 17 November 1558 to 24 March 1603, the *Dictionary*, like most modern historians, views the "Elizabethan period" more broadly. Many of the defining characteristics of the era were products of events in earlier periods, particularly the reign of Elizabeth's father, Henry VIII (1509–1547). For example, one can make little sense of the religious upheaval of Elizabeth's reign without knowing about the origin and course of the English Reformation that Henry VIII somewhat unwittingly initiated in the 1530s. Thus, the *Dictionary* offers entries both on "Henry VIII" and on "Reformation, English," as well as on "Thomas Cromwell," the king's chief agent in the break with the Roman Catholic Church, and on the "*Book of Common Prayer*," an important change in the form of English worship that emerged from the English Reformation and influenced the liturgy of the Elizabethan Anglican Church.

On the other hand, many of the political themes, economic trends, and social or cultural movements of Elizabeth's time had their completion or fulfillment during the Jacobean period, that is, during the reign of her successor, James I (1603–1625). Thus, ending coverage abruptly in 1603 would do a disservice to those studying such topics as Elizabethan literature. The flowering of English poetry and drama that began in the 1570s and 1580s with the work of George Gascoigne and Sir Philip Sidney, among others, intensified spectacularly in the 1590s with the emerging careers of Christopher Marlowe and William Shakespeare, and then reached its maturity in the 20 years after Elizabeth's death with the later career of Shakespeare, the work of Ben Jonson, and the proliferation around London of theatres like the Globe. The "golden age" of English literature had an Elizabethan beginning, but a Jacobean ending, and the *Dictionary* recognizes this by including these later figures, as well as such broad cultural developments as "art," "architecture," and "dance" that trace major trends beyond 1603.

Geographic Scope

The *Dictionary* takes a similarly broad geographical approach. As queen of England, Elizabeth I's actions and decisions, as well as those of the English people themselves, had consequences far beyond the borders of England, a country roughly equal in size to Wisconsin. England shared the island of Britain with Wales (which Elizabeth ruled) and with Scotland (which she did not), and personalities and events in both countries affected the course of history in Elizabeth's England. Beyond the English coastline, France and the rest of Western Europe lay just 21 miles to the southeast, and the large neighboring island of Ireland lay little more than 100 miles to the west. England's political, commercial, and religious contacts with Europe, particularly France, Spain, and the Netherlands, increased dramatically in the late sixteenth century, while England's centuries-long attempt to impose its political control on Ireland acquired a new edge under Elizabeth, whose government sought also to impose a new religious regime on the Irish people. Besides increasing trade with its familiar European markets, Elizabethan England also made vigorous efforts to initiate trade with new markets, such as Asia, Russia, and Spanish America. Beyond this, the English under Elizabeth first began to give serious attention to exploring and colonizing North America. Thus, the "Elizabethan world," as defined by this *Dictionary*, encompasses not only England in the later sixteenth century, but the rest of the British Isles, America, and Western Europe, as well as selected sites of Elizabethan activity further afield.

Criteria for Inclusion

To be included in the *Dictionary*, a topic, event, or person had to have a role in some significant element of Elizabethan life or activity. Broad topics, such as "education," and narrower related topics, such as "grammar school," were included to give readers both general overviews and specific information on particular aspects of the Elizabethan world. Biographical entries were carefully chosen to provide a mix of well-known, highly important figures, like Robert Dudley, Earl of Leicester, the queen's long-time favorite and a figure of great political significance, and less well-known people who nonetheless contributed in interesting ways to Elizabethan life, such as Richard Topcliffe, the notorious torturer of imprisoned Catholics, and Elizabeth Hardwick, the outspoken Countess of Shrewsbury and the builder of magnificent Hardwick Hall. Drawn from a wide variety of respected reference and monograph sources, and from my own archival research in Great Britain, the information in these entries will provide readers with the fundamental grounding in Tudor history that will allow them to more effectively pursue their own reading and study of the Elizabethan world.

Structure of Entries

The *Dictionary*'s 497 entries, 218 of which are biographical, average 400 words in length. The entries are augmented by a chronology and 9 maps, placed at the beginning of the text section for easy reference. Each entry contains cross-references to related entries (which appear in SMALL CAPITALS) and concludes with one or more recommendations for additional reading. The additional reading recommendations include both scholarly works and useful popular treatments. In some cases, older books have been included if no more recent study has been published or if the older work remains the accepted scholarly standard on the subject, as is the case, for instance, with biographies of some lesser-known figures. All works appearing at the ends of entries as further reading are listed in the general bibliography, which also contains numerous other worthwhile books not found among the entry recommendations. A reader interested in further reading on a particular person or topic should check both the general bibliography and the further reading listings at the ends of relevant entries.

Except in a few cases where birth dates are unknown, life dates are supplied for all biographical entries. When exact birth years are not known, the *c.* notation, meaning "circa" or "at or about that time," precedes the date to indicate that the year given is approximate. When a single year is preceded by *d.,* the year given is the death date, and the birth year is totally unknown. The date ranges supplied for ruling monarchs are birth and death dates, not the years of their reign, which are given in the text of the entry. Finally, the spelling for all titles of Elizabethan publications has been modernized.

Additional Features

By using the Guide to Selected Topics and by following the cross-references in the text of the entries, the reader can trace a broad theme, such as religion, American exploration, or Elizabethan Ireland, through all its most important events, ideas, and personalities—and thus quickly acquire a sound, basic understanding of the subject. Because Elizabeth I's name appears in the vast majority of entries, it has not been cross-referenced, but the queen's own entry is a good place to start any information search on an Elizabethan topic. Where appropriate, the entries also contain cross-references to relevant illustrations, maps, and genealogical charts.

The *Dictionary*'s appendixes contain 8 genealogical charts, and listings of Elizabethan Archbishops of Canterbury and York, Elizabethan Roman Catholic popes, sixteenth-century European monarchs, historical fiction with Tudor and Elizabethan characters and settings, motion pictures with Tudor and Elizabethan characters and settings, sound recordings of Tudor and Elizabethan music, and Web sites for Tudor and Elizabethan topics.

An extensive bibliography of some of the most important and accessible popular and scholarly works on Elizabethan history is provided, as well as a detailed subject index to give access to names and terms mentioned in the entries which do not have separate entries of their own.

ACKNOWLEDGMENTS

I am deeply indebted to many people for helping bring this volume to publication. I want to thank the staff members of the following institutions for the time and help they gave me in identifying and obtaining photographs to illustrate this book: the British Library, the British Museum, and the National Portrait Gallery in London; the National Maritime Museum in Greenwich; and the Folger Shakespeare Library in Washington, D.C. I also wish to express appreciation to Tom Brennan for his creative and effective book and cover designs and for his outstanding work preparing maps and genealogical charts, to JoAnne Reed for her excellent photography, and to Michael Bronski for so willingly supplying much-needed computer assistance. At Arizona State University, I wish to thank the staff of Hayden Library for assisting me in obtaining necessary and sometimes obscure research materials, and the members of my British and Tudor history classes for helping me hone ideas and definitions with their questions and comments. At The Oryx Press, I am grateful to Barbara Flaxman and the Production staff, especially Linda Vespa and Chris Crites, for the time and care they lavished on the production of the book; to Liz Welsh, my editor, for her usual skillful and meticulous work; to Jennifer Ashley for her careful proofreading; and to Anne Thompson and Susan Slesinger for their encouragement on this and many other projects over the years. Finally, nothing would have been possible without my wife, Donna, whose invaluable help in tracking down useful Web sites pales before the support she gave me through her patience, understanding, and love.

CHRONOLOGY

1485	22 August	Henry Tudor (Henry VII), future grandfather of Elizabeth I, wins the English Crown at the Battle of Bosworth Field
1491	28 June	Birth of Prince Henry (later Henry VIII), second son of Henry VII and Elizabeth of York; future father of Elizabeth I
1501?		Birth of Anne Boleyn, future mother of Elizabeth I
1509	21 April	Death of Henry VII; accession of Henry VIII
1516	18 February	Birth of Princess Mary (later Mary I), daughter of Henry VIII and Catherine of Aragon; half sister of Elizabeth I
1520	13 September	Birth of William Cecil (later Lord Burghley), secretary of state and lord treasurer under Elizabeth I
1532/33?	24 June	Birth of Robert Dudley (later Earl of Leicester), favorite of Elizabeth I
1533	25 January	Henry VIII marries Anne Boleyn
	7 September	Birth of Princess Elizabeth (later Elizabeth I)
1536	19 May	Execution of Anne Boleyn for treason
1537	12 October	Birth of Prince Edward (later Edward VI), son of Henry VIII and Jane Seymour; half brother of Elizabeth I
1542	8 December	Birth of Princess Mary of Scotland, daughter of James V and Marie de Guise; cousin of Elizabeth I
	14 December	Six-day-old Princess Mary becomes queen of Scotland on the sudden death of her father
1547	28 January	Death of Henry VIII; accession of Edward VI
1553	6 July	Death of Edward VI
	10 July	Lady Jane Grey, cousin of Elizabeth I and her half siblings, is proclaimed queen
	19 July	Queen Jane is deposed; accession of Mary I; Princess Elizabeth becomes heir presumptive to the English Crown
1554	January/February	Sir Thomas Wyatt leads an unsuccessful rebellion against Mary I's proposed marriage to Prince Philip (later Philip II) of Spain
	18 March	Princess Elizabeth, suspected of supporting Wyatt's Rebellion, is imprisoned in the Tower of London

	19 May	Princess Elizabeth is removed from the Tower and confined at the royal manor of Woodstock
	25 July	Mary I marries Prince Philip (later Philip II) of Spain
1555	June	Princess Elizabeth is allowed to return to court but remains confined to her apartments
	October	Princess Elizabeth is allowed to withdraw from court to her house at Hatfield
1558	24 April	Mary, Queen of Scots, marries the Dauphin Francis (later Francis II)
	17 November	Death of Mary I; accession of Elizabeth I
	20 November	Elizabeth I appoints Sir William Cecil principal secretary
1559	10 January	Philip II of Spain, husband of the late Queen Mary I, proposes marriage to Elizabeth I, who refuses him
	15 January	Coronation of Elizabeth I
	23 January	First parliamentary session of Elizabeth I's reign opens (Parliament passes [29 April] the Act of Supremacy, severing England from the Roman Catholic Church, and the Act of Uniformity, giving England a Protestant Church)
	5 June	Elizabeth I rejects marriage proposal of Charles, the Catholic Archduke of Austria
	7 July	Scottish Protestants occupy Edinburgh, beginning civil war between Protestant lords of Scotland and French-backed Catholic regency government of Marie de Guise, mother of Mary, Queen of Scots
	10 July	Death of Henri II of France; accession of Francis II and his wife Mary, Queen of Scots, to the French throne
	17 July	Shane O'Neill succeeds to earldom of Tyrone in northern Ireland
	24 September	Scottish Protestants appeal to Elizabeth I for help in Scottish civil war
	17 December	Matthew Parker becomes Elizabeth I's first Archbishop of Canterbury
1560	12 January	Irish Parliament passes Act of Uniformity, giving Ireland a Protestant Church
	22 February	Elizabeth signs Treaty of Berwick with Scottish Protestants
	6 July	Conclusion of Treaty of Edinburgh
	24 August	Scottish Parliament establishes a Protestant Church
	8 September	Amy (Robsart) Dudley, wife of Robert Dudley, favorite of Elizabeth I, dies under mysterious circumstances, and rumors spread that Dudley murdered his wife to marry the queen
	5 December	Death of Francis II of France widows Mary, Queen of Scots; accession of Charles IX to French throne
1561	13 July	Elizabeth I refuses Mary, Queen of Scots, safe passage to Scotland because Mary refuses to ratify the Treaty of Edinburgh
	19 August	Mary, Queen of Scots, returns to Scotland from France
1562	24 August	Recoinage of debased English currency restores European confidence in English money

	20 September	Elizabeth I concludes treaty with French Protestants, providing military assistance in exchange for English possession of Le Havre
	October	Elizabeth I falls seriously ill with smallpox, raising fears of civil war should she die without a clear successor; Elizabeth names Robert Dudley protector in event of her death
	October	John Hawkins launches the first English slaving expedition to Africa and the first trading expedition to Spanish America
	November/ December	Shane O'Neill rises in rebellion in Ulster in northern Ireland
1563		Publication of John Foxe's *Acts and Monuments*, known popularly as "The Book of Martyrs"
	11 January	Second parliamentary session of Elizabeth's reign opens (Parliament unsuccessfully petitions Queen Elizabeth to marry and settle the succession and passes an Act of Artificers, which regulates wages and conditions of employment)
	April	Parliament orders a Welsh translation of the *Book of Common Prayer*
	11 September	Shane O'Neill, the Earl of Tyrone, submits to the queen's deputy in Ireland and ends his rebellion
1564	March	Elizabeth proposes Robert Dudley as husband for Mary of Scots
	11 April	Calais, lost to France by Mary I in 1558, is officially recognized as a French possession in the Anglo-French Treaty of Troyes
	23 April	Birth of William Shakespeare
	28 September	Elizabeth raises Robert Dudley to peerage as Earl of Leicester
	October	Riots occur in Ireland protesting the plantation of English colonists in the Irish counties of Offaly and Leix (renamed by the English Queen's and King's Counties)
	18 October	John Hawkins launches his second voyage to Spanish America
1565	25 July	Mary, Queen of Scots, marries Henry Stuart, Lord Darnley
	Summer	Elizabeth I visits Coventry on her summer progress
	6 October	Mary, Queen of Scots, defeats pro-English, pro-Protestant forces under her half brother, James Stuart, Earl of Moray
1566	March	Various London clergy are suspended for refusing to wear prescribed vestments
	9 March	A group of Protestant Scottish lords, with the support of Henry Stuart, Lord Darnley, seize and murder David Rizzio, the French secretary of Mary, Queen of Scots; Mary is placed under arrest
	20 March	Mary, Queen of Scots, resumes control of the Scottish government with the support of Lord Darnley
	19 June	Birth of Prince James of Scotland (later, James VI of Scotland and James I of England), son of Mary, Queen of Scots, and Henry Stuart, Lord Darnley
	August/September	Elizabeth I's summer progress takes her to Stamford and Oxford
	30 September	Third parliamentary session of Elizabeth's reign opens (Parliament

		unsuccessfully petitions Queen Elizabeth to marry and settle the succession and seeks unsuccessfully to make Protestant alterations in the Anglican settlement of 1559)
1567	10 February	The husband of Mary, Queen of Scots—Henry Stuart, Lord Darnley—is murdered at Kirk o'Field outside Edinburgh
	24 April	James Hepburn, Earl of Bothwell, abducts and imprisons Mary, Queen of Scots, at Dunbar Castle
	15 May	Mary, Queen of Scots, marries James Hepburn, Earl of Bothwell
	2 June	Death of the Irish rebel Shane O'Neill, Earl of Tyrone
	15 June	Scottish nobles defeat Mary, Queen of Scots, at Carberry Hill; Bothwell flees Scotland
	24 July	Mary, Queen of Scots, imprisoned at Lochleven, abdicates the Scottish Crown in favor of her son, James
	22 August	James Stuart, Earl of Moray, proclaimed regent of Scotland
	2 October	John Hawkins launches his third voyage to Africa and Spanish America
1568	2 May	Mary, Queen of Scots, escapes from Lochleven
	13 May	Mary, Queen of Scots, defeated at Langside
	16 May	Mary, Queen of Scots, flees into England and is imprisoned by Elizabeth I
	21 September	John Hawkins is routed by Spaniards at San Juan d'Ulloa, Mexico
	December	Elizabeth I orders seizure of Spanish coin onboard ships driven by privateers into Plymouth and Southampton
1569	June	James Fitzmaurice Fitzgerald leads a rebellion against English rule in southern Ireland
	1 November	Thomas Howard, Duke of Norfolk, is arrested for conspiring to wed Mary, Queen of Scots
	14 November	Earls of Northumberland and Westmoreland lead Northern Rebellion
1570	23 January	James Stuart, Earl of Moray, the Scottish regent, is assassinated
	February	Pope Pius V issues the bull *Regnans in Excelsis*, which declares Elizabeth I excommunicated and removed from her throne
	August	Thomas Howard, Duke of Norfolk, is released from the Tower
	September	Elizabeth I considers marriage proposals from Archduke Charles of Austria and Henri, Duke of Anjou (later Henri III of France)
1571	25 February	Elizabeth raises Sir William Cecil to the peerage as Lord Burghley
	April	The Ridolfi plot is uncovered
	2 April	Fourth parliamentary session of Elizabeth's reign opens (Parliament, reacting to the Northern Rebellion and Queen Elizabeth's excommunication, makes publishing a papal bull or calling the queen a heretic treason, but is frustrated by the queen in attempts to compel Catholics to attend Anglican services—or to pay ruinous fines for not attending)

	3 September	Thomas Howard, Duke of Norfolk, is reimprisoned for involvement in the Ridolfi plot
	December	Sir John Perrot begins an anglicization program in southern Ireland
1572	1 March	Elizabeth I closes English ports to the Dutch sea beggars
	1, 22 April	Sea beggars capture the Dutch ports of Brill and Flushing
	21 April	Treaty of Blois with France provides for mutual assistance in case of attack and an Anglo-French effort to settle the ongoing conflict between pro- and anti-Mary factions in Scotland
	8 May	Fifth parliamentary session of Elizabeth's reign opens (Parliament works unsuccessfully for the execution of Mary, Queen of Scots, and successfully for the execution of Thomas Howard, Duke of Norfolk, and Puritan members seek unsuccessfully to alter the 1559 Anglican settlement and establish a presbyterian church structure)
	2 June	Execution of Thomas Howard, Duke of Norfolk
	Summer	Queen Elizabeth visits Warwick on her summer progress
	24 August	Saint Bartholomew's Day Massacre of Protestants occurs in France
	29 August	Francis Drake seizes Spanish treasure ships in the West Indies
1573	9 July	Elizabeth grants Walter Devereux, Earl of Essex, right to colonize Ulster in northern Ireland
	9 August	Francis Drake returns from America with treasure taken from Spaniards
	December	Sir Francis Walsingham, a strong Puritan, is made secretary of state
1574		Arrival of first Roman Catholic seminary priests in England
	30 May	Death of Charles IX of France; accession of Henri III
	Summer	Queen Elizabeth visits Bristol and the western counties on her summer progress
1575	17 May	Death of Archbishop of Canterbury Matthew Parker
	Summer	Elizabeth visits Reading and Windsor on her summer progress
	26 July	Essex's army in Ireland massacres the inhabitants of Rathlin Island
	24 December	Edmund Grindal becomes Archbishop of Canterbury
1576	8 February	Sixth parliamentary session of Elizabeth's reign opens (Parliament again petitions Queen Elizabeth to marry, and Puritan members again seek unsuccessfully to alter the 1559 settlement of religion)
	15 March	Peter Wentworth, a Puritan member of Parliament, is imprisoned for criticizing the queen and demanding Parliament's right to freedom of speech
	7 June	Martin Frobisher launches his first voyage of exploration to America
	20 December	Archbishop of Canterbury Edmund Grindal refuses to suppress prophesyings as ordered by Queen Elizabeth
1577		James Burbage opens The Theatre in London
	25 May	Martin Frobisher launches his second voyage to America

	June	Archbishop of Canterbury Edmund Grindal is suspended from his office for his refusal to suppress prophesyings
	13 December	Francis Drake launches his voyage of circumnavigation
1578	4 April	James Hepburn, Earl of Bothwell, the last husband of Mary, Queen of Scots, dies in a dungeon in Denmark
	31 May	Martin Frobisher launches his third voyage to America
	June	Queen Elizabeth entertains a marriage proposal from Francis, Duke of Alençon, brother of Henri III of France
	Summer	Elizabeth I visits Norwich and eastern England on summer progress
	21 September	Robert Dudley, Earl of Leicester, marries Lettice (Knollys) Devereux, Countess of Essex, without Elizabeth's knowledge or consent
	26 September	Sir Humphrey Gilbert launches his first voyage to America
1579	July	James Fitzmaurice Fitzgerald and a papal force land in southern Ireland at Smerwick
	August	Francis Valois, Duke of Alençon, arrives in England to woo Elizabeth
	18 August	Death in battle of the Irish rebel James Fitzmaurice Fitzgerald
1580	June	Jesuit missionaries Edmund Campion and Robert Parsons arrive in England
	26 September	Francis Drake enters Plymouth harbor, completing his three-year circumnavigation of the globe
	10 November	English forces capture the Irish rebel fortress at Smerwick
1581	16 January	Seventh parliamentary session of Elizabeth's reign opens (Parliament imposes ruinous fines on Catholic recusants and makes converting or being converted to Catholicism treason)
	4 April	Elizabeth knights Francis Drake on the deck of the *Golden Hind*
	2 November	Francis Valois, Duke of Alençon, arrives in London to finalize marriage agreement with Elizabeth
	1 December	Execution of the Jesuit priest Edmund Campion
1582	February	Francis Valois, Duke of Alençon, leaves England after Elizabeth backs out of marriage
1583	11 June	Sir Humphrey Gilbert launches his second voyage to America
	July/August	Sir Humphrey Gilbert discovers and explores Newfoundland
	9 September	Sir Humphrey Gilbert is lost at sea
	23 September	John Whitgift becomes Elizabeth's third Archbishop of Canterbury
	November	Discovery of the Throckmorton plot
1584	25 March	Sir Walter Raleigh, half brother of Sir Humphrey Gilbert, obtains a patent from the queen to plant English colonies in America
	27 April	Sir Walter Raleigh sends out an exploratory mission to America under Philip Amadas and Arthur Barlowe
	10 July	Assassination of the Dutch Protestant leader, William of Orange

	23 November	Eighth parliamentary session of Elizabeth's reign opens (Parliament banishes all Catholic priests, recalls all Englishmen in Catholic seminaries in Europe, and prescribes death for anyone conspiring to overthrow or assassinate the queen)
	October	Formation of the Bond of Association
1585	9 April	Sir Walter Raleigh sends out a colonizing expedition to Virginia; the expedition establishes the first English colony at Roanoke
	May	War begins between England and Spain
	7 June	John Davis launches his first voyage of exploration to America
	10 August	Elizabeth concludes a treaty of alliance with the Dutch
	7 September	Drake sets sail on a raid of Spanish America
	December	Robert Dudley, Earl of Leicester, sails to the Netherlands with an army of over 6,000
1586	7 May	John Davis launches his second voyage of exploration to America
	June	Sir Francis Drake evacuates the English colonists from Roanoke
	20 September	Execution of Anthony Babington and six others for their involvement in the Babington Plot to replace Elizabeth with Mary, Queen of Scots
	14 October	Mary, Queen of Scots, found guilty of treason for her involvement in the Babington Plot
	15 October	Ninth parliamentary session of Elizabeth's reign opens (Parliament, reacting to the Babington Plot and the trial and condemnation of Mary, Queen of Scots, petitions Queen Elizabeth to go forward with Mary's execution)
1587	8 February	Execution of Mary, Queen of Scots
	21 April	Francis Drake attacks Cadiz
	8 May	Sir Walter Raleigh sends out a second colonizing expedition to Virginia under John White
	19 May	John Davis launches his third voyage of exploration to America
	18 August	Birth at Roanoke Colony of Virginia Dare, the first English child born in America
	24 December	Peregrine Bertie, Lord Willoughby, replaces Robert Dudley, Earl of Leicester, as commander of the English forces in the Netherlands
1588	20 May	Spanish Armada leaves Lisbon for England
	June	Preparations begin in England and around London to repel the Spanish Armada
	19 July	Spanish Armada is sighted
	28 July/8 August	English fleet meets Armada in a series of naval battles in the English Channel culminating in the Battle of Gravelines, after which the Armada is driven north by storms
	4 September	Death of Robert Dudley, Earl of Leicester
	11 September	Storms off Ireland destroy many of the remaining Armada vessels
	October	Marprelate Tracts begin to circulate in London

	24 November	Royal thanksgiving service held at Saint Paul's Cathedral for England's delivery from the Armada
1589	4 February	Tenth parliamentary session of Elizabeth's reign opens (Parliament again unsuccessful in altering the religious settlement of 1559)
	8 April	Drake and Sir John Norris launch the ultimately unsuccessful Portugal Expedition against Spain
	22 July	Murder of Henri III of France; Henri of Navarre, a Protestant, is proclaimed king as Henri IV
1590		Edmund Spenser publishes the first three books of *The Faerie Queen*
	6 April	Death of Sir Francis Walsingham; Robert Cecil (son of William Cecil, Lord Burghley) succeeds Walsingham as secretary of state
	17 August	John White's relief expedition to Roanoke finds no trace of the colonists of 1587
1591	13 May	Puritans associated with the Marprelate Tracts are charged with sedition
	3 August	Robert Devereux, Earl of Essex, leads an English military expedition to France to assist Henri IV
	3 September	Death of Sir Richard Grenville and loss of the *Revenge*
1592	25 February	The lord mayor of London petitions Archbishop John Whitgift to stop the corrupting influence plays and playhouses are having on the apprentices and servants of the city
	7 August	Sir Walter Raleigh imprisoned for seducing Elizabeth Throckmorton
	September	Fears of a new Spanish invasion sweep the southern coast of England; William Shakespeare is working as an actor and playwright in London
1593	19 February	Eleventh parliamentary session of Elizabeth's reign opens (Parliament passes a measure punishing Puritans and other Protestants who refuse to conform to the Church of England)
	6 April	Radical Protestants Henry Barrow and John Greenwood are hanged for sedition
	30 May	Death of Christopher Marlowe in a mysterious tavern brawl
	31 May	John Penry hanged for his role in publishing the Marprelate Tracts
	June/July	Severe visitation of the plague
	July	Henri IV of France converts to Catholicism
1594	Summer	Three-year period of rainy summer weather and bad harvests begins
1595	25 January	Beginning of Irish rebellion led by Hugh O'Neill, Earl of Tyrone
	6 February	Sir Walter Raleigh launches a voyage of American exploration to search for El Dorado
	22 February	Execution of Robert Southwell, a Jesuit priest
	28 August	Sir Francis Drake and John Hawkins raid the Spanish West Indies
1596	29 January	Sir Francis Drake dies at sea off Panama
	17 March	Spaniards raid the English coast near Plymouth

	6 July	Hugh O'Neill, Earl of Tyrone, raises rebellion in southern Ireland
	20 June	Robert Devereux, Earl of Essex, captures Cadiz
	5 July	Sir Robert Cecil is made principal secretary
	July/August	One of England's worst harvests of the century leads to food riots in Kent and elsewhere
	October	Second Spanish Armada is wrecked by storms
1597	July	Sir Walter Raleigh and Robert Devereux, Earl of Essex, launch the ultimately unsuccessful Islands Voyage against Spain
	October	Third Spanish Armada is wrecked by storms
	24 October	Twelfth parliamentary session of Elizabeth's reign opens (Parliament petitions the queen for redress of monopolies and passes a new Act for Relief of the Poor)
1598	4 August	Death of William Cecil, Lord Burghley
	14 August	Irish rebels under Hugh O'Neill, Earl of Tyrone, defeat the English at the Battle of Yellow Ford in northern Ireland
	13 September	Death of Philip II of Spain
	November	Hugh O'Neill, Earl of Tyrone, and other Irish rebels raid Dublin
1599		Richard Burbage builds the Globe Theatre
	12 March	Robert Devereux, Earl of Essex, is made lord lieutenant of Ireland
	8 September	Robert Devereux, Earl of Essex, arranges a truce with Hugh O'Neill, Earl of Tyrone, in Ireland
	24 September	Robert Devereux, Earl of Essex, returns from Ireland to England without the queen's permission
1600	May	Charles Blount, Lord Mountjoy, the new lord deputy of Ireland, arrives in Dublin
	5 June	Elizabeth pardons Robert Devereux, Earl of Essex, but deprives him of most of his offices and places him under house arrest
1601	8 February	Robert Devereux, Earl of Essex, raises a rebellion in London
	25 February	Execution of the Robert Devereux, Earl of Essex
	April	Sir Robert Cecil opens a secret correspondence with James VI of Scotland, Elizabeth I's likely heir
	September	Spanish fleet lands at Kinsale in Ireland
	27 October	Thirteenth and last parliamentary session of Elizabeth's reign opens (Parliament again petitions Queen Elizabeth to reform monopolies)
	30 November	Elizabeth delivers the "Golden Speech"
	24 December	Charles Blount, Lord Mountjoy, wins a resounding victory over Hugh O'Neill, Earl of Tyrone, and the Irish rebels at Kinsale
1602	2 January	Spanish commander at Kinsale in Ireland surrenders to Charles Blount, Lord Mountjoy
1603	24 March	Death of Elizabeth I; accession of James VI of Scotland

MAPS

Counties of England and Wales, 1603

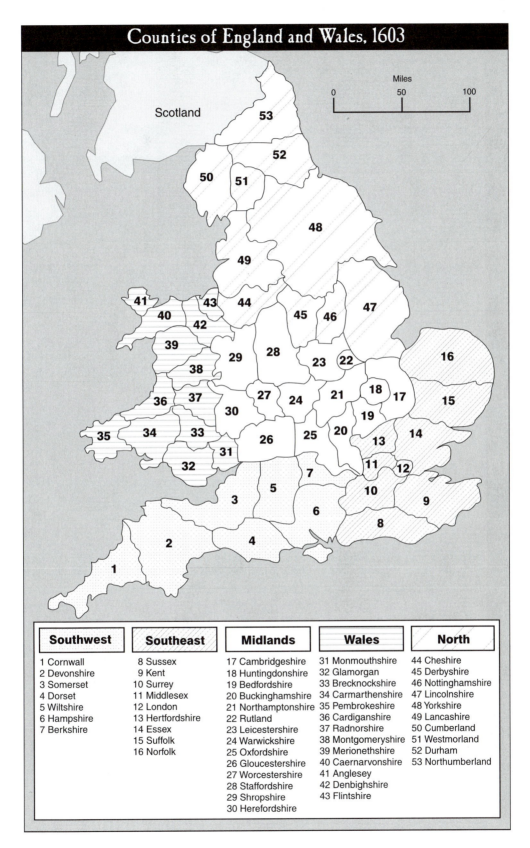

Southwest	**Southeast**	**Midlands**	**Wales**	**North**
1 Cornwall	8 Sussex	17 Cambridgeshire	31 Monmouthshire	44 Cheshire
2 Devonshire	9 Kent	18 Huntingdonshire	32 Glamorgan	45 Derbyshire
3 Somerset	10 Surrey	19 Bedfordshire	33 Brecknockshire	46 Nottinghamshire
4 Dorset	11 Middlesex	20 Buckinghamshire	34 Carmarthenshire	47 Lincolnshire
5 Wiltshire	12 London	21 Northamptonshire	35 Pembrokeshire	48 Yorkshire
6 Hampshire	13 Hertfordshire	22 Rutland	36 Cardiganshire	49 Lancashire
7 Berkshire	14 Essex	23 Leicestershire	37 Radnorshire	50 Cumberland
	15 Suffolk	24 Warwickshire	38 Montgomeryshire	51 Westmorland
	16 Norfolk	25 Oxfordshire	39 Merionethshire	52 Durham
		26 Gloucestershire	40 Caernarvonshire	53 Northumberland
		27 Worcestershire	41 Anglesey	
		28 Staffordshire	42 Denbighshire	
		29 Shropshire	43 Flintshire	
		30 Herefordshire		

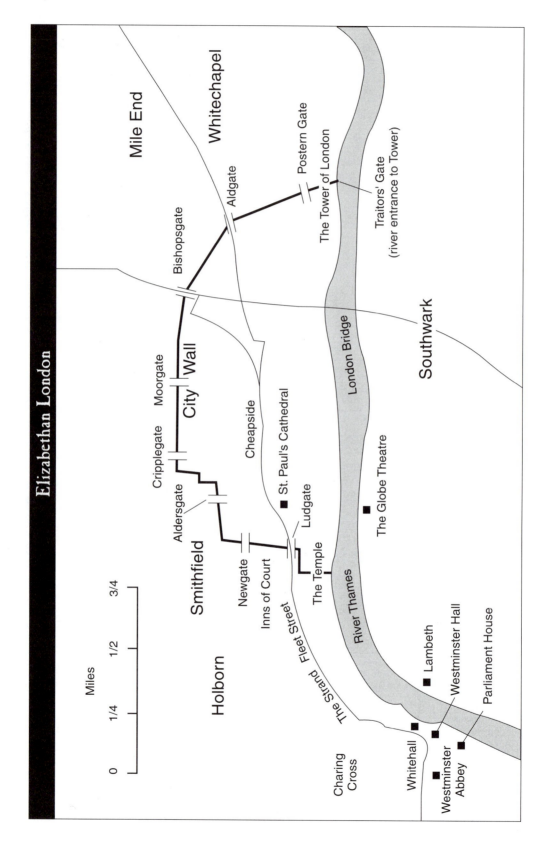

Elizabethan London

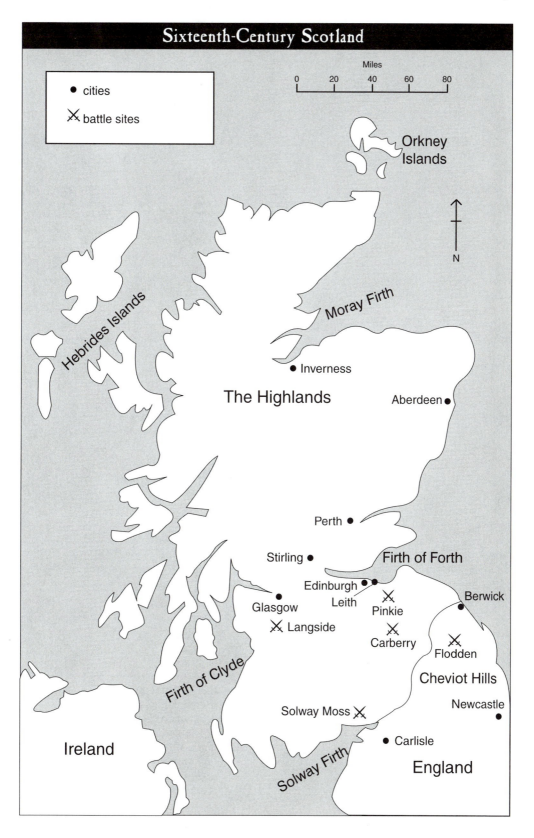

Sixteenth-Century Scotland

cities
battle sites

Miles
0   20   40   60   80

N

Orkney
Islands

Hebrides Islands

Moray Firth

Inverness

The Highlands

Aberdeen

Perth

Stirling

Firth of Forth

Edinburgh
Leith

Pinkie

Glasgow

Langside

Carberry

Berwick

Flodden

Cheviot Hills

Firth of Clyde

Solway Moss

Newcastle

Ireland

Carlisle

Solway Firth

England

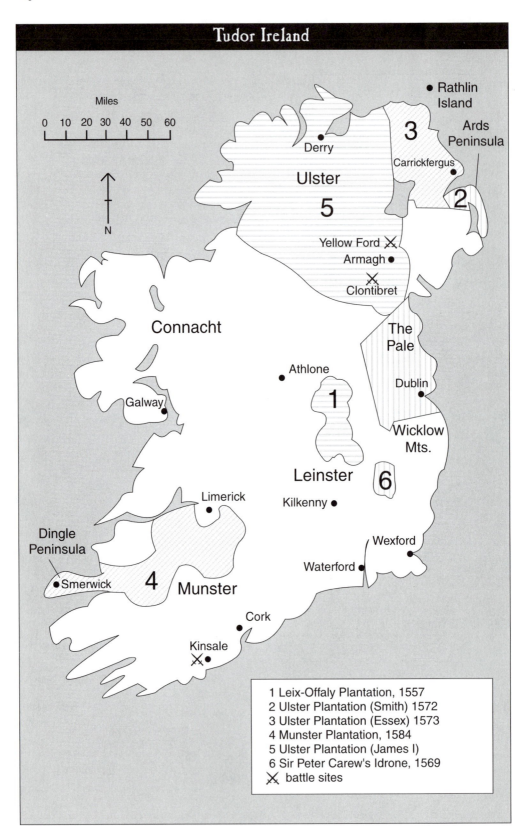

Tudor Ireland

Miles

0 10 20 30 40 50 60

N

Rathlin Island

Ards Peninsula

3

Derry

Ulster

Carrickfergus

2

5

Yellow Ford ✗

Armagh

Clontibret ✗

Connacht

The Pale

Athlone

Dublin

1

Galway

Wicklow Mts.

Leinster

6

Limerick

Kilkenny

Dingle Peninsula

Wexford

Waterford

Smerwick

4

Munster

Cork

Kinsale ✗

1 Leix-Offaly Plantation, 1557
2 Ulster Plantation (Smith) 1572
3 Ulster Plantation (Essex) 1573
4 Munster Plantation, 1584
5 Ulster Plantation (James I)
6 Sir Peter Carew's Idrone, 1569
✗ battle sites

Netherlands, 1590s

Miles

0   50   100

N

NORTH
SEA

Groningen

Amsterdam
●Leiden
Hague   Utrecht   ●Zutphen

Brill   United Provinces
of the Dutch
Flushing   Republic

Calais   ●Bruges   ● Antwerp
Ghent   Holy
Roman
Empire
●Boulogne   Spanish   ● Brussels
Netherlands

France

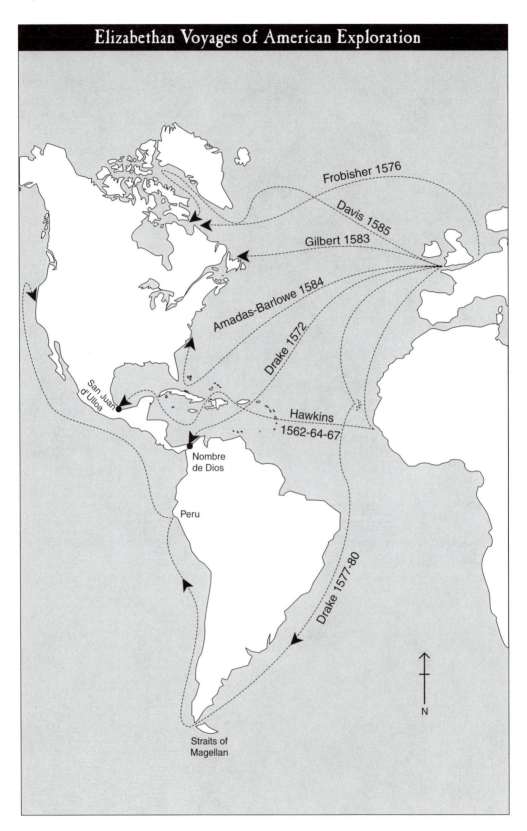

Elizabethan Voyages of American Exploration

Frobisher 1576

Davis 1585

Gilbert 1583

Amadas-Barlowe 1584

Drake 1572

Hawkins 1562-64-67

San Juan d'Ulloa

Nombre de Dios

Peru

Drake 1577-80

Straits of Magellan

N

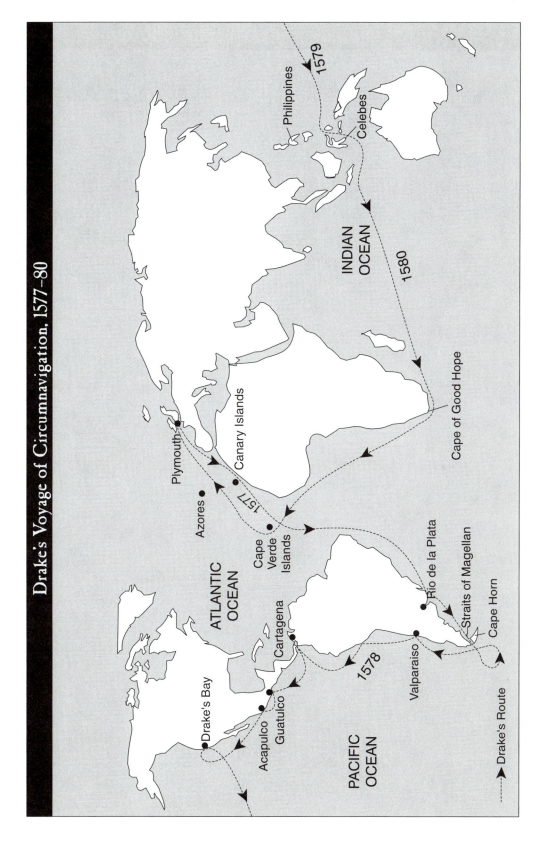

Drake's Voyage of Circumnavigation, 1577–80

Maps

PACIFIC OCEAN

ATLANTIC OCEAN

INDIAN OCEAN

Plymouth

Azores

Canary Islands

Cape Verde Islands

1577

Drake's Bay

Acapulco

Guatulco

Cartagena

Valparaiso

Rio de la Plata

Straits of Magellan

Cape Horn

1578

Cape of Good Hope

1580

Philippines

Celebes

1579

Drake's Route

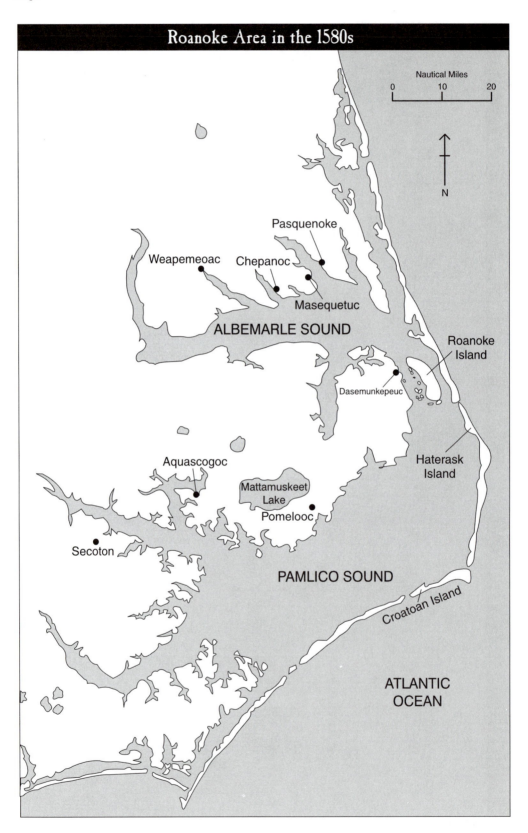

Roanoke Area in the 1580s

Nautical Miles

0   10   20

N

Pasquenoke

Weapemeoac   Chepanoc

Masequetuc

ALBEMARLE SOUND

Roanoke
Island

Dasemunkepeuc

Haterask
Island

Aquascogoc

Mattamuskeet
Lake

Pomelooc

Secoton

PAMLICO SOUND

Croatoan Island

ATLANTIC
OCEAN

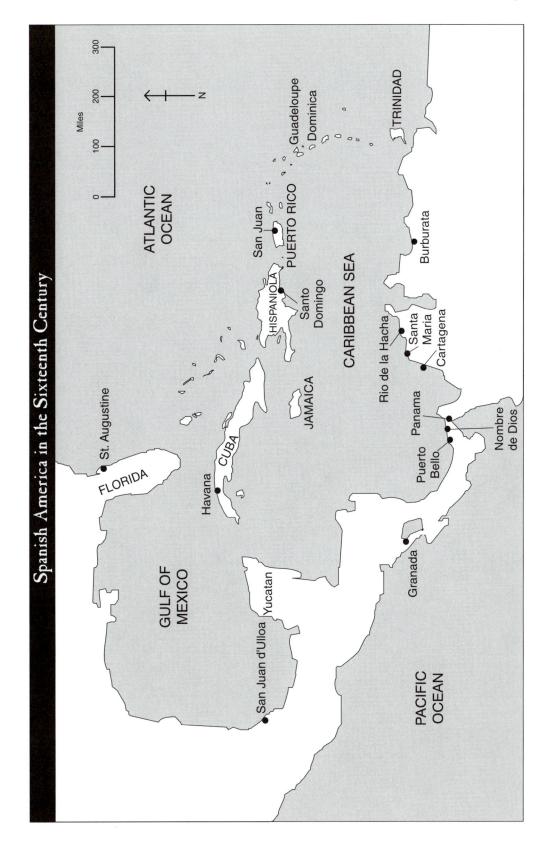

Spanish America in the Sixteenth Century

Miles
0 100 200 300

N

St. Augustine

FLORIDA

GULF OF
MEXICO

Havana

CUBA

Yucatan

San Juan d'Ulloa

JAMAICA

HISPANIOLA

Santo
Domingo

San Juan

PUERTO RICO

ATLANTIC
OCEAN

Guadeloupe
Dominica

TRINIDAD

CARIBBEAN SEA

Burburata

Rio de la Hacha

Santa
Maria

Cartagena

Panama

Puerto
Bello

Nombre
de Dios

Granada

PACIFIC
OCEAN

HISTORICAL DICTIONARY
of the
ELIZABETHAN
❧ WORLD ❧

Britain, Ireland, Europe, and America

Accession Day

The anniversary of Elizabeth I's accession to the throne on 17 November 1558 was one of the few truly secular HOLIDAYS in the English CALENDAR. In the first decade of Elizabeth's reign, Accession Day, also known as Queen's Day or Coronation Day, was celebrated with the ringing of bells and the building of bonfires. After the defeat of the NORTHERN REBELLION in 1570, the anniversary became a day of national thanksgiving and festival. The Accession Day tilts, elaborate tournaments held before thousands of spectators at the Westminster tilt-yard, allowed young courtiers to display their martial prowess and their devotion to queen and country (see COURT; VIRGIN QUEEN). After the start of the war with SPAIN in 1585, the holiday became a patriotic celebration of Protestant England and its glorious queen (see PROTESTANTISM). Accession Day celebrations were revived under Elizabeth's successor, JAMES I, when her reign began to be seen as a golden age of national greatness. The date remained emotionally significant and was an occasion for patriotic celebrations well into the eighteenth century. *See also* CHRISTMAS; EASTER; WESTMINSTER PALACE.

Further Reading: David Cressy, *Bonfires and Bells: National Memory and the Protestant Calendar in Elizabethan and Stuart England*, London: Weidenfeld and Nicolson, 1989.

Acts and Monuments of These Latter and Perilous Days. See "BOOK OF MARTYRS."

admiral. *See* OFFICERS OF STATE.

admonition controversy

The admonition controversy was an acrimonious pamphlet debate between English Protestants over the best form of church governance and the proper relationship of church and state. The controversy began in 1572 when Elizabeth suppressed a parliamentary bill that would have allowed Anglican bishops to exempt ministers from using sections of the *BOOK OF COMMON PRAYER* to which they objected.

After the queen killed the measure, two Puritan preachers in LONDON, John Field and Thomas Wilcox, published a pamphlet entitled *Admonition to the Parliament*. Although cast in the form of an address to PARLIAMENT, the *Admonition* was a vehicle for presenting the authors' views to the general public. The pamphlet was well received, going through several editions by the end of 1572. Wilcox's portion of the work was moderate and restrained, but Field castigated the ANGLICAN CHURCH in no uncertain terms, denouncing its practices and the Prayer Book as "popish" (i.e., Roman Catholic) and attacking its bishops as ungodly. Field's harsh tone led many PURITANS, including John FOXE and Thomas LEVER, to denounce the pamphlet.

In November 1572, after city authorities had imprisoned Wilcox and Field, an anonymous *Second Admonition* appeared in London. Archbishop Matthew PARKER commissioned John WHITGIFT, vice-chancellor of Cambridge (see UNIVERSITIES), to respond to the second pamphlet. Whitgift's *Answer to a Certain Libel Instituted, an Admonition to the Parliament* prompted a reply from Thomas CARTWRIGHT, a former divinity professor at

Cambridge who had been deprived of his position by Whitgift in 1570 for his criticisms of the Anglican Church. Cartwright's *Reply to an Answer Made of M Doctor Whitgift against the Admonition* was published in April 1573, only a year after he had returned from European exile. Although Cartwright fled again in December 1573 when a warrant was issued for his arrest, the pamphlet war continued, with Whitgift publishing his *Defense of the Answer to the Admonition* in 1574, and Cartwright publishing his *Second Reply* in 1575 and his *The Rest of the Second Reply* in 1577. In his writings, Whitgift supported the royal supremacy by making no distinction between the English Church and a Christian commonwealth (see SUPREMACY, ROYAL), while Cartwright advocated a presbyterian church distinct from a state whose officials would be subordinate to church leaders in spiritual matters. The admonition controversy split the Puritans and demonstrated the depth of some Puritans' opposition to the ANGLICAN SETTLEMENT of 1559. *See also* CATHOLICISM, ENGLISH; PRESBYTERIAN MOVEMENT; PROTESTANTISM.

Further Reading: Patrick Collinson, *The Elizabethan Puritan Movement,* Oxford: Clarendon Press, 1990; Donald Joseph McGinn, *The Admonition Controversy,* New Brunswick, NJ: Rutgers University Press, 1949.

advowson

An advowson was the right to appoint a clergyman to a BENEFICE. The right could be held by church officials, such as bishops, or by laypeople, from the monarch to town corporations and individual property owners. Laypeople began acquiring rights of advowson in the Middle Ages when landholders built churches on their own property and appointed the priests to serve those churches. Also, after the dissolution of the English monasteries in the 1530s (see REFORMATION, ENGLISH), many advowsons passed to the Crown or to the lay purchaser of the former monastic lands. An advowson was treated under the law as a piece of property, the ownership of which could be transferred by sale or grant. Patrons who were unwilling to sell their advowson outright could sell the right to make a one-time appointment to the benefice they controlled. In this way, many Elizabethans of even relatively small means could provide positions in the English Church for relatives or friends or could appoint a clergyman who upheld their particular doctrinal views.

The Reformation made control of advowsons extremely important. For example, under Elizabeth, Puritan clergymen were sometimes dismissed from their benefices by their bishops for refusing to conform to the doctrine or practice of the ANGLICAN CHURCH as established by the queen and PARLIAMENT. Puritan nobles and gentlemen (see GENTRY) could use their advowsons to appoint these dismissed ministers and preachers to positions under their control, thereby circumventing both the Crown and the ecclesiastical hierarchy and maintaining the propagation of Puritan thought and practice. *See also* ANGLICAN SETTLEMENT; COMMON LAW; LECTURESHIPS; PURITANS.

Further Reading: Patrick Collinson, *The Elizabethan Puritan Movement,* Oxford: Clarendon Press, 1990; A. G. Dickens, *The English Reformation,* 2nd ed., University Park: Pennsylvania State University Press, 1989; Rosemary O'Day and Felicity Heal, eds., *Princes and Paupers in the English Church 1500–1800,* Leicester: Leicester University Press, 1981.

agriculture

Agriculture was the heart of the Elizabethan economy, employing a far greater percentage of the English POPULATION than any other industry or occupation. Except for fish, wine, spices, and certain fruits, Elizabethan England grew or produced all the food and most of the raw materials the English people required, including hides for leather, wool for the CLOTH INDUSTRY, hemp for naval supplies, tallow for candles and soap, and horses for transport.

The most important feature of agriculture in the Elizabethan era was its transformation from production mainly for the subsistence of the farmer or the local community to production for sale to wider markets. This change was the result of a rapidly growing population, which caused a steep rise during the Elizabethan period in both the demand for food and in its price. Small peasant farmers gave way to gentleman and yeoman farmers (see GENTRY; SOCIAL HIERARCHY) whose larger acreages allowed them to produce grain surpluses that could be sold in LONDON and other parts of the kingdom where demand outstripped supply.

Enhancing this demand was the growth of the English cloth industry, which thrived on the increased production of English wool-growers. As more rural workers engaged in the manufacture of cloth, they joined the growing populations of London and other towns in swelling the percentage of English people who relied on others to grow their food. As a result of this demand, new farming methods (such as better crop rotation techniques) were devised to improve yields, and marginal lands, some of which had been out of production since the Black Death depopulation of the fourteenth century (see PLAGUE), were brought back under cultivation.

Many gentleman and yeoman farmers practiced enclosure, whereby land that had been pasture for common use by a village was enclosed with a hedge or fence and given over by the landlord to the production of grain for the commercial market. Enclosure sometimes added to the economic hardship of husbandmen or cottagers, who often lost the land they rented when their gentry landlords realized that it would be more profitable to grow grain and hire workers than to rent out the land. As the price of grain rose, the government increased its regulation of the market to ensure adequate supplies, for even small local shortages could lead to disorder. Except for the 1590s, when bad harvests required grain imports, English agriculture supplied the ordinary needs of the nation during the Elizabethan period.

Further Reading: C. G. A. Clay, *Economic Expansion and Social Change: England 1500–1700*: Vol. 1: *People, Land and Towns,* New York: Cambridge University Press, 1984; Penry Williams, *Life in Tudor England,* New York: G. P. Putnam's Sons, 1964; Joyce Youings, *Sixteenth-Century England*, New York: Penguin Books, 1984.

Alba, Duke of. *See* ALVAREZ DE TOLEDO, FERNANDEZ, DUKE OF ALVA.

Alençon, Duke of. *See* VALOIS, FRANCIS (HERCULES), DUKE OF ALENÇON.

Allen, William (1532–1594)

William Allen, an English scholar, polemicist, and priest, was instrumental in founding and directing the mission for the reconversion of Protestant Elizabethan England to the Roman Catholic Church. Allen's promising career in the English Catholic Church under MARY I

was cut short by the accession of Elizabeth in 1558 and the restoration of a Protestant English Church and the royal supremacy in 1559 (see ANGLICAN SETTLEMENT; CATHOLICISM, ENGLISH; SUPREMACY, ROYAL). Allen refused to take the oath of supremacy enjoined upon English clerics by PARLIAMENT and fled to Europe in 1561. He returned the following year to Lancashire, where he worked to bring lapsed Catholics back to the faith.

In 1565, he left England again, never to return. He founded an English college at Douai in the NETHERLANDS in 1568 for training English missionary priests and for educating the sons of English Catholic families (see SEMINARY PRIESTS). Allen established similar institutions in Rome in 1575 and in Valladolid, SPAIN, in 1589. He also organized the first JESUIT MISSION to England in 1580. Pope Sixtus V made him a cardinal in 1587.

Allen was deeply involved in Catholic plots against the Protestant English government and urged PHILIP II of Spain to launch the ARMADA against England. When the Armada finally sailed in 1588, Allen published *An Admonition to the Nobility and People of England and Ireland, Concerning the Present Wars . . .*, which urged English Catholics to rise up against Elizabeth and support the Spanish invaders. In several other works published in the 1580s, some in response to tracts published by the English government, Allen developed and refined an ideology for the politically aggressive faction within English Catholicism. Allen's death in Rome in 1594 left the English Catholic mission without a leader and led to the controversial appointment by the pope of an archpriest (see ARCHPRIEST CONTROVERSY). *See also* BLACKWELL, GEORGE; CAMPION, EDMUND; PARSONS, ROBERT; PROTESTANTISM; SOUTHWELL, ROBERT.

Further Reading: John Bossy, *The English Catholic Community 1570–1850,* New York: Oxford University Press, 1976; Arnold Pritchard, *Catholic Loyalism in Elizabethan England,* Chapel Hill: University of North Carolina Press, 1979.

Alleyn, Edward (1566–1626)

Edward Alleyn was one of the most popular actors on the Elizabethan stage and a shareholder in several important LONDON theatres. Born in London, Alleyn began acting in the

1580s, becoming a member of the Earl of Worcester's Company (known as Worcester's Men) in 1583 and the Lord Admiral's Company (known as the Admiral's Men) in 1589. In 1592, the Lord Admiral's Company joined with Lord Strange's Men (see CHAMBERLAIN'S MEN), a troupe that included William SHAKESPEARE. Alleyn was the combined company's leading actor at Philip HENSLOWE's Rose Theatre in Southwark, a London suburb on the south bank of the Thames, and on tour in the shires during the London PLAGUE of 1593.

In 1592, Alleyn joined Henslowe in running the Rose and in the management of several bear gardens (see ANIMAL SPORTS). He retired from acting in 1597 but returned to the stage in 1600 to perform at the new Fortune Theatre that he and Henslowe had built in London. He retired from the Admiral's Men in 1604, his last public appearance being in the coronation procession of JAMES I. Alleyn retained, however, his interest in the Fortune and in other Henslowe theatres. During his acting career, Alleyn, who was known for his roles in tragedies, played Tamburlaine and Faustus in Christopher MARLOWE's plays, Orlando in Robert GREENE's *Orlando Furioso,* and Hieronimo in Thomas KYD's *The Spanish Tragedy.* Alleyn was also famous as a musician (see MUSIC). He remained an active and generous patron of English DRAMA until his death in 1626. *See also* GLOBE THEATRE.

Further Reading: G. B. Harrison, *Elizabethan Plays and Players,* Ann Arbor: University of Michigan Press, 1956; Aileen Reid and Robert Maniura, eds*., Edward Alleyn: Elizabethan Actor, Jacobean Gentleman,* London: Dulwich Picture Gallery, 1994; A. P. Rossiter, *English Drama from Early Times to the Elizabethans: Its Background, Origins, and Development,* Folcroft, PA: Folcroft Library Editions, 1977; A. D. Wraight, *Christopher Marlowe and Edward Alleyn*, Chichester, England: Adam Hart, 1993.

Alva, Duke of. *See* ALVAREZ DE TOLEDO, FERNANDEZ, DUKE OF ALVA.

Alvarez de Toledo, Fernandez, Duke of Alva (1508–1582)

As PHILIP II's governor-general of the NETHERLANDS from 1567 to 1573, Fernandez Alvarez de Toledo, Duke of Alva (or Alba), crushed the first stage of the NETHERLANDS REVOLT, driving thousands of Protestant artisans and craftspeople to emigrate from the Netherlands to England. Governor of a Spanish province at 17, Alva so distinguished himself at the battle of Pavia in Italy in 1525 and against the Turks in Hungary and North Africa in the early 1530s that CHARLES V made him a general in 1534 and commander-in-chief of the imperial armies four years later, when Alva was only 30. In 1547, he was instrumental in helping Charles V defeat the German Protestants at Mühlberg, and in the late 1550s, Alva conducted successful campaigns in Italy for Charles's son, Philip II of SPAIN.

Philip sent Alva to the Netherlands in 1567 to restore Spanish authority after the violent outbreak there of Protestant iconoclasm (i.e., destruction of Catholic religious art and imagery) in the previous year. His Spanish troops defeated the rebel military forces, driving WILLIAM, PRINCE OF ORANGE, the rebel leader, into exile in Germany. Through the vigorous use of his so-called Council of Blood, a ruthless judicial tribunal, Alva established a repressive military regime in the Netherlands that restored order by summarily executing rebels and heretics and driving many Protestants, especially from the urban merchant and artisan classes, to flee to Protestant England.

In 1572, when Elizabeth I ordered all SEA BEGGARS (bands of Dutch rebels who had been committing indiscriminate acts of piracy in the English Channel) to leave English ports, they fell suddenly on the Dutch ports of Flushing and Brill (see CAUTIONARY TOWNS), thus reviving the Netherlands rebellion against Spanish rule in the northern provinces of Holland and Zeeland. In 1573, unable to crush the new uprising, and faced with the destruction of his fleet by rebel forces, Alva, then in his mid-60s, asked to be recalled to Spain. From there, he led a successful invasion of Portugal in 1580, thereby giving Philip control of the Portuguese Crown and fleet and making possible the attempted naval invasion of England in 1588 (see ARMADA). Alva died in Spain in 1582.

Further Reading: Geoffrey Parker, *The Dutch Revolt,* Ithaca, NY: Cornell University Press, 1977.

John White's map of Virginia (now coastal North Carolina) shows the islands of Hatarask (Hatteras) and Roanoac (Roanoke), which were both explored by the Amadas-Barlowe expedition in 1584. © *The British Museum.*

Amadas-Barlowe expedition

In March 1584, Walter RALEIGH secured a six-year patent from Queen Elizabeth to establish an English colony in North AMERICA. The patent, like the one given earlier to Raleigh's half brother, Sir Humphrey GILBERT, granted Raleigh's colonists "all the privileges of free Denizens and persons native of England" as if "they were born and personally resident within our said Realm of England." Before sending out colonists, Raleigh decided to reconnoiter the North American coast to find a likely settlement site and to learn something of the natives, climate, and products of the area.

On 27 April 1584, two small vessels left Plymouth under the command of Philip Amadas and Arthur Barlowe, two young gentlemen (see GENTRY) in Raleigh's household. Arriving in the West Indies in June, the expedition took on fresh water and then sailed north along the coasts of the present-day states of Georgia, South Carolina, and North Carolina. In July, they landed on Hatteras Island, where they observed fruit trees and an abundance of wildlife. After claiming the area for England, Amadas and Barlowe made contact with the Roanoke Indians, whose main village lay on nearby Roanoke Island. By trading clothing, wine, and meat for fish, the Englishmen established friendly relations with Wingina, the local chief. A small party of Englishmen then visited Wingina's village, where they were warmly welcomed and treated to a great feast. On 23 August, accompanied by Manteo and Wanchese, two young Roanoke men who volunteered to go to England, Amadas and Barlowe set sail for home, reaching England by 15 September.

Barlowe wrote a glowing account of the Roanoke region where, he declared, "the earth brings forth all things in abundance, as in the first creation, without toil or labor," and of the natives, who were "most gentle, loving, and faithful, void of all guile and treason." Raleigh quickly distributed Barlowe's report to stimulate interest in his colonial venture. To attract the queen's financial participation, Raleigh requested and received permission to name the newly claimed area Virginia in honor of the VIRGIN QUEEN. Although Elizabeth's investment was not forthcoming, Barlowe's report of the expedition's experiences helped make possible the establishment of Raleigh's first Roanoke Colony in 1585. *See* Maps, "Elizabethan Voyages of American Exploration" and "Roanoke Area in the 1580s." *See also BRIEF AND TRUE REPORT OF THE NEW FOUND LAND OF VIRGINIA*; HARRIOT, THOMAS; ROANOKE COLONY (1585); ROANOKE COLONY (1587).

Further Reading: Karen Ordahl Kupperman, *Roanoke: The Abandoned Colony,* New York: Barnes and Noble, 1993; Robert Lacey, *Sir Walter Ralegh*, New York: Atheneum, 1974; David B. Quinn, *Set Fair for Roanoke: Voyages and Colonies, 1584–1606*, Chapel Hill: University of North Carolina Press, 1984.

America

Before 1558, English interest in America waxed and waned, but after Elizabeth's accession to the throne, the growing desire to compete with SPAIN for trade and colonies stimulated increased American exploration. In the late 1480s, Christopher Columbus sent his brother Bartholomew to ask HENRY VII, Elizabeth's grandfather, to fund a voyage of westward exploration. Henry was interested, but he waited too long to act and Columbus concluded an agreement with Ferdinand and Isabella of Spain. In place of that lost opportunity, Henry backed another Italian navigator, John Cabot, whose expedition left England in May 1497. Agreeing to pay the Crown 20 percent of the profits derived from trade with the peoples of any new lands he might discover, Cabot reached what he called the "New Found Land" (Newfoundland, Canada) in late June. Convinced that he had reached Cipango (Japan), Cabot proposed that a trading fleet be outfitted and was enthusiastically supported by the king and the merchant community. Five ships filled with trade goods for Asia left England in 1498 but never returned, the fate of Cabot and his second expedition remaining a mystery to this day. Having realized that Cabot's discovery was a new land, not Japan, Henry VII in 1501 chartered the short-lived Company Adventurers to the New Found Land to conduct trade and colonization in the region, and in 1509, he sent Cabot's son Sebastian to seek a NORTHWEST PASSAGE to Asia. Sebastian Cabot found his way into Hudson's Bay, where the great icebergs frightened his crew and forced his return to England.

English interest in America faded under HENRY VIII, who was more interested in dominating the Old World than in exploring the New World. The governments of EDWARD VI, Henry VIII's successor, were too poor to support much EXPLORATION. Under MARY I, English explorers sought a Northeast Passage to Asia, with England's first JOINT-STOCK COMPANY funding the venture. Under Elizabeth, however, American exploration gathered momentum. The great success of John HAWKINS's unauthorized trade voyages to SPANISH AMERICA stimulated interest in American colonies, while the continuing desire to reach Asia revived interest in a Northwest Passage.

In the 1570s and 1580s, Martin FROBISHER and John DAVIS expanded English knowledge of northeastern North America while seeking the Northwest Passage. In the 1580s, Sir Humphrey GILBERT and his half brother Walter RALEIGH tried unsuccessfully to establish an English colony on the east coast of North America to supply England with both needed commodities and a base for raiding Spanish America (see LOST COLONY; ROANOKE COLONY [1585]; ROANOKE COLONY [1587]).

In England, the work of Richard HAKLUYT and other writers in publicizing and promoting exploration and colonization efforts kept interest in America high and greatly facilitated the successful English colonization of North America in the seventeenth century. *See* Maps, "Elizabethan Voyages of American Exploration," "Roanoke Area in the 1580s," and "Spanish America in the Sixteenth Century."

Further Reading: Samuel Eliot Morison, *The European Discovery of America: The Northern Voyages,* New York: Oxford University Press, 1971; A. L. Rowse, *The Elizabethans and America,* New York: Harper, 1959; Carl Ortwin Sauer, *Sixteenth Century North America,* Berkeley: University of California Press, 1971.

Anabaptists

The term "Anabaptist" technically meant "rebaptizer"; it described religious groups that practiced the rebaptism of adults who had received traditional infant baptism. In the sixteenth century, both Roman Catholics and mainstream Protestants (e.g., Lutherans and Calvinists) applied the term loosely to a wide variety of radical reform groups. Because Anabaptists often held principles and followed practices that sixteenth-century European society found unacceptable, they were persecuted in both Catholic and Protestant countries.

Anabaptism originated in Zurich, Switzerland, in the 1520s and slowly spread into England, Germany, FRANCE, and the NETHERLANDS in the following decades. Besides adult baptism, Anabaptist groups often advocated pacifism, religious tolerance, and community ownership of goods. Many Anabaptists also preached unitarianism, the denial of the Christian doctrine of the trinity, which they regarded as unscriptural. Because unitarianism often led to a repudiation of the divinity of Christ, both Catholics and Protestants (including John CALVIN himself) put Anabaptists to death for heresy (see CALVINISM; CATHOLICISM, ENGLISH; PROTESTANTISM).

Although never numerous, English Anabaptists began to appear in the 1530s. Most were members of the Family of Love, a Dutch Anabaptist group founded by Hendrik Niclaes that gained a foothold in England during the religious changes initiated by the reforming governments of EDWARD VI. Believing themselves pure and in union with God, Family of Love members felt free to deceive nonmembers about their true beliefs and denied any connection to the sect so as to blend more easily into the official English Church, whether it was Roman Catholic, as under MARY I, or Protestant Anglican, as under Elizabeth (see ANGLICAN CHURCH). Like every English monarch of the sixteenth and early seventeenth centuries, Elizabeth punished the open practice of Anabaptism, although she tolerated secret Anabaptism among her personal servants. Because they despised Anabaptists for their unitarianism, their radical social arrangements, and their toleration of Catholicism, PURITANS urged the queen to stronger and more consistent persecution of Anabaptists. Through their preaching of complete religious independence from the state, Anabapists influenced the development of the Brownists (see BROWNE, ROBERT) and other early English Separatist groups (see SEPARATISTS).

Further Reading: William R. Estep, *The Anabaptist Story,* Grand Rapids, MI: William B. Eerdmans, 1975.

Anglican Church

As established under Elizabeth in 1559, the Church of England, or Anglican Church, was Calvinist in doctrine, episcopal (i.e., under bishops) in structure, and governed by the Crown through PARLIAMENT (see ANGLICAN SETTLEMENT; CALVINISM; THIRTY-NINE ARTICLES). Although they disappeared from the Calvinistic churches of FRANCE, Germany, and the NETHERLANDS, bishops survived in the Anglican Church because they served as useful instruments of royal control (see SUPREMACY, ROYAL). The queen often allowed bishops to suffer Puritan criticism for actions she had privately urged them to take (see PURITANS).

Elizabeth was determined to have the Church of England serve the needs of the English state—as she herself defined those needs. Thus, she insisted on conformity to the manner of worship laid down by Parliament in the Act of Uniformity and the *BOOK OF COMMON PRAYER* but allowed a wide variety of beliefs and practices to exist within this mandated framework. Individuals could believe largely as they wished, so long as they outwardly conformed and kept their unapproved opinions to themselves. The Anglican Church was thus based on the idea that matters of worship and church government not specifically outlined in the Bible and authorized by the state could be left to local practice and national custom as things indifferent to salvation and true belief. Conversely, Puritans maintained that almost all religious practices were strictly prescribed in scripture and could not be left to local or national tradition (see BIBLE, ENGLISH).

At the Anglican Church's creation in 1559, doctrine and liturgy were vaguely defined, in part because the government sought to include as many people as possible, whether conservatives or advanced reformers. But the parameters of Anglicanism became sharper during the course of Elizabeth's reign as Roman Catholics fell away (see CATHOLICISM, ENGLISH) and Puritans began to distinguish themselves from the national church through disputes over vestments, governance, and liturgy (see CLASSICAL MOVEMENT; PRESBYTERIAN MOVEMENT; SEPARATISTS; VESTIARIAN CONTROVERSY). Anglicanism also defined itself through the writings of its chief thinkers, such as in Bishop John JEWEL's *Book of Homilies* (1571) and his *Apologia Ecclesiae Anglicanae* [*Apology for the Church of England*] (1562), and Richard HOOKER's *LAWS OF ECCLESIASTICAL POLITY* (1593, 1597). By Elizabeth's death in 1603, her Anglican Church had won the allegiance and devotion of a majority of her subjects. *See also* "BOOK OF MARTYRS"; FOXE, JOHN.

Further Reading: Patrick Collinson, *The Elizabethan Puritan Movement,* Oxford: Clarendon Press, 1990; Patrick Collinson, *The Religion of Protestants: The Church in English Society 1559–1625,* Oxford: Clarendon Press, 1982; Claire Cross, *Church and People 1450–1660: The Triumph of the Laity in the English Church,* Atlantic Highlands, NJ: Humanities Press, 1976; John Foxe, *Fox's Book of Martyrs,* edited by William Byron Forbush, Grand Rapids, MI: Zondervan, 1980; William P. Haugaard, *Elizabeth and the English Reformation: The Struggle for a Stable Settlement of Religion,* Cambridge: Cambridge University Press, 1968; Norman L. Jones, *Faith by Statute,* London: Royal Historical Society, 1982; Patrick McGrath, *Papists and Puritans Under Elizabeth I,* New York: Walker and Company, 1967.

Anglican settlement

The term "Anglican settlement" describes the series of governmental and parliamentary actions taken in the early years of Elizabeth's reign, especially during the PARLIAMENT of 1559, to shape the governance, theology, and liturgy (i.e., form of worship) of the officially established Church of England, the ANGLICAN CHURCH. From her sister, MARY I, Elizabeth had inherited an English Catholic Church that recognized the authority of the pope. But because Elizabeth was the daughter of Anne BOLEYN, whose marriage to HENRY VIII had symbolized England's original break with Rome, and because the English Catholic Church under Mary had lost considerable popular support by burning heretics (see MARIAN MARTYRS), Elizabeth had few reasons to maintain her sister's Church.

Elizabeth's own theological views and liturgical preferences remain unclear even today, but she and her ministers wanted to satisfy as many people as possible by making as few changes as possible. While disliking papal authority, most English people in 1558 were not strong Protestants and probably would have been content with an English Church freed from papal control but essentially Catholic in doctrine and practice. Thus, the two main issues for the government and Parliament were determining a form of worship and defining the relationship between church and Crown. However, when even moderate changes proposed by the government were vigorously opposed in the House of Lords by Catholic bishops appointed by Mary and by the Catholic PEERAGE, and when groups of returning MARIAN EXILES began demanding a more radically Protestant Church, the government gave up on placating Catholics and proposed more Protestant religious legislation (see PROTESTANTISM). A new Act of Supremacy in 1559 abolished the authority of the pope, but it heeded complaints about a layperson and a woman heading the English Church and gave Parliament a larger role with the Crown in directing religious affairs (see SUPREMACY, ROYAL). The 1559 Act of Uniformity abolished the MASS and restored Edward VI's 1552 *BOOK OF COMMON PRAYER,* with some alterations in wording to appease Catholics and conservatives (e.g., the BLACK RUBRIC was removed).

By giving the Anglican Church a form of worship that was too radical for Roman Catholics and too conservative for Protestants, the queen and Parliament established a religious settlement that became known as the *via media,* the "middle way," an attempt to accommodate as many viewpoints as possible in the new Anglican Church. Although attacked throughout Elizabeth's reign by Catholics on one hand and PURITANS on the other, the Elizabethan Anglican Church slowly won the support and affection of the great majority of English subjects and saved England from the religious civil wars that tormented FRANCE.

Further Reading: Claire Cross, *The Elizabethan Religious Settlement,* Bangor, ME: Headstart History, 1992; William P. Haugaard, *Elizabeth and the English Reformation: The Struggle for a Stable Settlement of Religion,* Cambridge: Cambridge University Press, 1968; Norman L. Jones, *Faith by Statute,* London: Royal Historical Society, 1982.

Anglo-Irish

The term "Anglo-Irish" refers to the descendants of the Norman and English conquerors who overran and settled parts of IRELAND in the twelfth and thirteenth centuries. Referring to themselves as "Englishmen born in Ireland," the Anglo-Irish became known in the seventeenth century as the "Old English" to distinguish them from the "New English," settlers brought in by the Elizabethan plantations (see PLANTATIONS, IRISH). During the reign of Elizabeth, the New English gradually replaced the Anglo-Irish as the island's political elite.

In the fifteenth and early sixteenth centuries, the Anglo-Irish ruled Ireland for the Crown through their control of the Irish Parliament and the lord deputyship. Beginning in the 1550s, however, the lord deputyship was held by Englishmen, and the Anglo-Irish members of the Irish Parliament found themselves increasingly at odds with the English administration in DUBLIN. Because the Anglo-Irish tended to be Catholic, to speak Irish as well as English, and to practice many Irish customs, they were often denigrated by the Protestant New English, who had nothing but contempt for the Irish and their ways. Critics such as the English writer Edmund SPENSER condemned the Anglo-Irish as degenerate Englishmen who had been corrupted through intermarriage and long interaction with the native Irish. Sir Peter CAREW, Sir Richard GRENVILLE, Sir Humphrey GILBERT, and other Elizabethans who sought to settle English colonists in Ireland advocated strengthening English control of the island through a policy of thorough anglicization (i.e., importing English ideas and practices). Such a policy meant the uniform imposition in Ireland of English customs, especially as related to legal practice and land tenure, and the establishment of a strong Irish Protestant Church to eradicate Roman Catholicism (see CATHOLICISM, ENGLISH; PROTESTANTISM).

By the end of Elizabeth's reign in 1603, the Anglo-Irish had lost control of the government in Dublin and were caught in a dilemma not unlike the one facing Roman Catholics in Elizabethan England—how to remain loyal to the English Crown and the Catholic Church at the same time. *See also* Maps, "Tudor Ireland."

Further Reading: Steven G. Ellis, *Tudor Ireland,* London: Longman, 1985; Colm Lennon, *Sixteenth-Century Ireland: The Incomplete Conquest,* Dublin: Gill and Macmillan, 1994; Margaret MacCurtain, *Tudor and Stuart Ireland,* Dublin: Gill and Macmillan, 1972; David B. Quinn, *The Elizabethans and the Irish,* Ithaca, NY: Cornell University Press, 1966.

animal sports

Three popular and violent forms of Elizabethan ENTERTAINMENT were the animal sports of cockfighting, bearbaiting, and bullbaiting. In cockfighting, specially bred fighting roosters were pitted against one another. Cockfighting occurred in small round arenas surrounded by wooden benches for spectators. Although most were temporary structures, some permanent cockpits existed, such as one constructed at WHITEHALL PALACE. For bearbaiting, a bear was chained in the middle of a large circular arena into which one or more large mastiffs was sent. These mastiffs—large dogs trained to fight—would lock their jaws onto the nose or ears of the bear and attempt to pull it to the ground. The bear would try to shake the dogs free, sometimes killing them with its claws. Bullbaiting simply replaced the bear with a bull that tried to gore its canine tormentors to death. Bullbaiting was more widely practiced because bulls were more common and the beef from a bull that had been baited was thought to be more flavorful. Bears, having no value as meat, usually survived to perform again. In all three sports, spectators crowded around the arena, betting on the outcome of the contest.

Animal sports were enjoyed by all levels of society. Sometimes the programs would include novel or comic variations, such as a blinded bear or a pack of dogs chasing a free-running horse with an ape on its back. Bull- and bearbaiting performances were also staged at Whitehall for the diversion of Elizabeth and her COURT; on one occasion in 1599, the queen even attending a bearbaiting staged at a LONDON bear garden. In the 1590s, several permanent bull- and bearbaiting arenas stood on the south side of the Thames across from London in Southwark, near where the GLOBE THEATRE was built. London theatre manager Philip HENSLOWE and his business partner, the actor Edward ALLEYN, acquired an interest in one of these bear gardens in 1594. In 1604, the two men were made joint masters of the "royal game of bears, bulls, and mastiff dogs," an entertainment monopoly that made them enough money to demolish one of the bear gardens and replace it with the Hope, a structure that was used for both animal sports and plays (see DRAMA). PURITANS condemned bull- and bearbaiting, not only for their cruelty, but also because such events usually occurred on Sundays when the greatest number of potential spectators were available.

Further Reading: F. J. Fisher, *London and the English Economy 1500–1700*, London: Hambledon Press, 1990; Martin Holmes, *Elizabethan London*, New York: Frederick A. Praeger, 1969; Gamini Salgado, *The Elizabethan Underworld*, Stroud, England: Alan Sutton Publishing, 1992.

Annales Rerum Anglicarum et Hibernicarum Regnante Elizabetha

Historians consider the *Annales* by William CAMDEN to be the best contemporary account of the reign of Elizabeth I. In English, the full title of the work is *The Annals or the History of the Most Renowned and Victorious Princess Elizabeth, Late Queen of England, Containing All the Most Important and Remarkable Passages of State, Both at Home and Abroad (So Far as They Were Linked with English Affairs) during Her Long and Prosperous Reign.*

Begun in 1608, only five years after Elizabeth's death, the first part of the Latin

Annales, which carried the story of the reign to the end of 1588, appeared in 1615. Camden completed the second part in 1617, but it was not published in LONDON until 1627, four years after Camden's death. A complete English translation first appeared in 1630. Popular interest in recent English history grew during the Elizabethan period, as evidenced by the sales of HOLINSHED'S *CHRONICLES* and other contemporary histories. Written for a large and uncritical audience, chronicles largely reprinted the works of earlier authors and made little attempt to test the credibility of sources. Arranged by years so new editions could be easily updated, the chronicles' political coverage consisted largely of what was already general public knowledge, and their social history tended toward a catalog of scandal and gossip, natural disasters, and unnatural occurrences.

Although Camden retained the year-by-year arrangement used for chronicles, the *Annales* is solidly based on official sources, both written and oral, not on gossip and hearsay. Camden, who had himself witnessed important events of the reign, had access to the royal archives, to the papers of William CECIL, Lord Burghley, and to many still-living Elizabethan officials and courtiers. Although Camden's goals were to pay tribute to the queen's memory ("which among Englishmen ought ever to be . . . sacred") and to teach the lessons of the past, he sought to be impartial, believing that the sources would speak for themselves to the reader about the glories of Elizabeth's reign (see VIRGIN QUEEN). Thus, although Camden was a staunch Anglican, his work is largely free of the anti-Catholic bias that permeates much Elizabethan writing. *See also* ANTIQUARIANISM.

Further Reading: William Camden, *The History of the Most Renowned and Victorious Princess Elizabeth, Late Queen of England*, edited by Wallace T. MacCaffrey, Chicago: University of Chicago Press, 1970 [selected chapters from the 1688 English edition of the *Annales*]; F. J. Levy, *Tudor Historical Thought*, San Marino, CA: Huntington Library, 1967.

Anne of Cleves (1515–1557)

Anne of Cleves, daughter of the ruler of a small Protestant state in Germany, was the fourth wife of HENRY VIII. After the death of Jane SEYMOUR in October 1537, Henry embarked almost immediately upon a search for a new wife. In 1539, changing political conditions in Europe made a Protestant marriage alliance attractive. The Roman Catholic powers of SPAIN and FRANCE had made peace, leaving both free to deal with the heretical king of England; in the Treaty of Toledo, both agreed not to negotiate separately with England. Also in 1539, the pope issued a bull (i.e., a papal edict) absolving English subjects from their obedience to Henry. Fearing Catholic invasion from abroad and Catholic revolt at home, Henry turned to Protestant Germany to find a wife who could bring him a useful political alliance.

The king's chief minister, Thomas CROMWELL, who had been pushing for a Protestant connection, negotiated the Cleves marriage after Henry had studied and approved the likeness he saw in the Hans Holbein portrait of Anne (or Anna), the eldest daughter of the Duke of Cleves. However, having ridden to Rochester in disguise to surprise his future wife upon her landing in January 1540, Henry was bitterly disappointed to find her, at least in his opinion, plain in looks, dull in personality, unfashionable in dress, and harsh in voice. He told his attendants "I like her not," and is said to have later described her to Cromwell, whom he blamed for the match, as "a great Flanders mare." Bound by treaty, the king proceeded reluctantly with the marriage.

By April 1540, the king had turned his attentions to one of Anne's LADIES-IN-WAITING, Katherine HOWARD, whom he married in July after CONVOCATION had annulled his marriage to Anne. The renewal of war between Spain and France in 1540 soon destroyed the political need for a Protestant marriage and helped overthrow Cromwell, who was executed in July 1540. The failure of the Cleves marriage allowed Cromwell's many enemies at COURT to convince the king that his chief minister was working against his religious policies. Unlike CATHERINE OF ARAGON, Anne readily accepted the annulment of her marriage and lived happily in England as the king's "dear sister" until her death in 1557.

Further Reading: Mary Saaler, *Anne of Cleves,* London: The Rubicon Press, 1995.

anticlericalism

Distrust and dislike of the clergy by laypeople, especially in regard to clerical wealth and claims to regulate and control lay actions, is known as anticlericalism. To be anticlerical is not necessarily to be anti-Christian or anti-religious, but rather to be critical of the political, social, and economic pretensions of the clergy. The Lollards, a reformist sect in the English Church in the fourteenth and fifteenth centuries, were strongly anticlerical. Some historians argue that resentment of Church wealth, and anger over clerical interference in their economic and social lives, led many English laypeople, especially in the GENTRY and professional classes, to support HENRY VIII's attacks on the Roman Catholic Church and the clergy in the 1530s. The success of Henry's break with the Roman Church allowed PROTESTANTISM to spread slowly throughout England and paved the way for Elizabeth's establishment of the Protestant ANGLICAN CHURCH in 1559. *See also* ANGLICAN SETTLEMENT; CATHOLICISM, ENGLISH; REFORMATION, ENGLISH.

Further Reading: A. G. Dickens, *The English Reformation,* 2nd ed., University Park: Pennsylvania State University Press, 1989.

antiquarianism

Elizabethan England witnessed a rise of interest in collecting and cataloging artifacts of British history, as well as a growing enthusiasm for studying the history, natural and human, of the various counties and localities of Britain. This passion for preserving the literary and material artifacts of the British past was known as antiquarianism, and its practitioners as antiquaries.

Elizabethan antiquaries were generally amateur scholars, such as wealthy gentlemen (see GENTRY) and country clergymen, who had the money or leisure to collect, research, and write. Elizabethan antiquarianism is thought to have been stimulated by the destruction of medieval art and artifacts during the Reformation and the dissolution of English monasteries in the 1530s and 1540s. The loss of these antiquities combined with the accelerating pace of change in the Elizabethan world to generate an interest in preserving and understanding as much of the past as still remained. Because antiquaries could delve most easily into the past of their own neighborhoods, antiquarian studies rapidly developed a focus on local history, topography, and genealogy.

A Society of Antiquaries was founded in LONDON around 1573 and eventually included among its members William CAMDEN, Robert COTTON, John STOW, and Richard CAREW. Members discussed ideas at meetings, corresponded with one another about their research and discoveries, and wrote papers and dissertations on topics of mutual interest. The Society declined after the accession of JAMES I in 1603 because the king believed it to be a subversive political group. When Camden and others sought to revive it in 1614, the king made his disapproval known, and the Society did not meet again until formally refounded in 1707.

The work of Elizabethan antiquaries resulted in the creation of a new historical genre, the county survey. The best-known examples of this genre are William LAMBARDE's *Perambulation of Kent* (1576), Richard Carew's *SURVEY OF CORNWALL* (1602), and John HOOKER's unpublished but widely distributed "Synopsis Chorographical of Devonshire." Besides such histories as HOLINSHED'S *CHRONICLES* (1577, 1587), Elizabethan antiquarianism also produced broader studies of Britain and England, such as William Camden's *BRITANNIA* (1586), and studies of towns, such as John Stow's *Survey of London* (1598) and John Hooker's *Description of the City of Exeter* (1919). *See also* LUMLEY, JOHN, LORD LUMLEY; REFORMATION, ENGLISH.

Further Reading: Joan Evans, *A History of the Society of Antiquaries*, Oxford: Society of Antiquaries, 1956; F. J. Levy, *Tudor Historical Thought*, San Marino, CA: Huntington Library, 1967; Stanley G. Mendyk, *"Speculum Britanniae": Regional Study, Antiquarianism, and Science in Britain to 1700,* Toronto: University of Toronto Press, 1989.

architecture

The major architectural development of the Elizabethan period was the construction of the first PRODIGY HOUSES, the magnificent country homes of the wealthier PEERAGE and GENTRY. Such houses as Longleat in Wiltshire, Wollaton in Nottinghamshire, and Hatfield in Hertfordshire exhibited the growing economic power and political influence of their courtier owners, whose fortunes were made in the royal service. Because such houses often served as waystops for the COURT as it traveled with Elizabeth on her summer progresses (see PROGRESSES, ROYAL), they fueled competition among wealthy courtiers to build even larger and grander homes.

The reign of Elizabeth also saw the emergence of the first English designers to call themselves architects. Prominent among these professionals was John Shute (d. 1570), who in 1563 published *The First and Chief Grounds of Architecture.* Being also a limner (see LIMNING), Shute, who studied building design in Italy, described himself as a "painter and architect." Another important Elizabethan architect, especially in the construction of prodigy houses, was Robert SMYTHSON, who helped design both Longleat and Wollaton.

Perhaps the most familiar modern image of Elizabethan architecture is the black-and-white timber and plaster house. The ground floor of this mainly urban style was used for shop space, while the upper floors overhung the lower, thus providing more area in the living quarters. The frame of the house was wood, with joints secured by wooden pegs. The spaces between wall studs were usually filled with wattle and daub. "Wattle," a mesh made from vertical wooden stakes woven together with thin horizontal branches, was covered with "daub," a clay, mud, or lime plaster mixed with straw. The wattle and daub was painted white, which contrasted with the dark wood beams to produce the black-and-white appearance. In the West Country, exposed beams were painted with tar to protect them from the ocean air; elsewhere, beams were often decoratively carved. Roofs were constructed of thatch, tile, or slate.

A final feature of Elizabethan architecture was the increased use of stone, formerly reserved for castles and cathedrals, in gentry houses of all sizes and, where stone was plentiful, even in the cottages of the lower classes (see SOCIAL HIERARCHY).

Further Reading: Mark Girouard, *Robert Smythson and the Architecture of the Tudor Era,* South Brunswick, NJ: Barnes, 1967.

archpriest controversy

The death of Cardinal William ALLEN in 1594 left the Catholic mission and the Catholic community in England without a leader or a clear direction for the future (see CATHOLICISM,

ENGLISH). To solve this problem of leadership, the English Catholic authorities in Rome appointed an English priest named George BLACKWELL to the new office of archpriest and head of the English Catholic mission. Blackwell was closely associated with the Jesuit order (see JESUIT MISSION) and with the order's advocacy of political action to overthrow Elizabeth and its support for restoring Catholicism in England by military means. The mission's secular priests (see SEMINARY PRIESTS), those clerics not affiliated with the Jesuits or any other Catholic order, opposed Blackwell and the Jesuits' political agenda.

A group of these secular priests, some of whom were being held as prisoners by the English government, appealed to Rome to withdraw the appointment of Blackwell. These appellants, as they were called, published almost 20 books over the next two decades in support of their position, thus exposing the divisions in the English Catholic mission and community to an embarrassing public debate. The appellants sought to ease the dilemma of English Catholics by disassociating the Catholic community from the political activity of the Jesuits. Many English Catholics wanted to be loyal subjects of their Protestant queen and thus had little sympathy for plots hatched against her government by English Jesuits, popes, or foreign Catholic princes.

In the late 1590s, the appellants began negotiating with the English government in an effort to win toleration for English Catholics in return for a renunciation by Catholics of political action and a condemnation of the Jesuits and of all previous and future plots against the queen and the ANGLICAN CHURCH. Elizabeth, realizing that the majority of English men and women were fearful of and opposed to Catholicism, refused any such arrangement. In November 1602, the queen issued a PROCLAMATION denouncing both Catholic secular priests and Jesuits.

Further Reading: John Bossy, *The English Catholic Community 1570–1850,* New York: Oxford University Press, 1976; Arnold Pritchard, *Catholic Loyalism in Elizabethan England,* Chapel Hill: University of North Carolina Press, 1979.

Armada

In the summer of 1588, PHILIP II of SPAIN sent an armada of 130 ships under Alonso Perez de GUZMAN EL BUENO, Duke of Medina Sidonia, into the English Channel to pick up and transport Spanish troops from the NETHERLANDS for an attack on England. The "Enterprise of England," as the invasion was called, aimed to restore the English Catholic Church and to replace Elizabeth with a Roman Catholic monarch of Philip's choosing (as the former husband of MARY I, Philip had a claim to the English Crown).

The English had feared a Spanish invasion since 1570 when the pope excommunicated Elizabeth (see *REGNANS IN EXCELSIS*), but Philip rejected the idea as impractical when Alvaro de BÁZAN, Marquis of Santa Cruz, suggested it in 1583. Events in the mid-1580s caused the Spanish king to reconsider. After Philip's seizure of the Portuguese throne in 1580, Elizabeth gave sanctuary and military aid to Don Antonio, the Portuguese pretender (i.e., claimant to the throne). Elizabeth also supported Dutch Protestant rebels against Philip, and in 1585 she extended official English protection to the Netherlands. The activities of Sir Francis DRAKE and other English privateers in SPANISH AMERICA and along the coasts of Spain itself caused Philip to fear for the security of his colonies and his treasure fleets (see PRIVATEERING). The execution by the English of Mary STUART, Queen of Scots, in February 1587, when planning for the invasion had already begun, only strengthened Philip's resolve, for it removed the pro-French Scots queen from the succession and gave Philip the opportunity to make his own claim to the English throne.

Drake's April 1587 raid on Cadiz, which destroyed Spanish SHIPS and supplies (see CADIZ RAID [1587]), and the death of Santa Cruz in January 1588 combined with endless delays in procuring men, ships, and provisions to prevent the sailing of the Armada until May 1588. In the same month, Elizabeth authorized the English fleet to launch a preemptive strike on the Armada as it gathered in Lisbon harbor. Three attempts to reach Portugal were foiled by contrary winds, but the English learned that bad weather had also forced the Armada into port in mid-June. Thinking that the Spanish invasion attempt had failed, the English were surprised by the Armada's arrival in the Channel on 29 July.

The English fleet quickly gained the wind advantage and used the superior maneuverability of its ships and the greater range and rapidity of fire of its guns to outduel the Armada in skirmishes off Portsmouth (31 July), Plymouth (2 August), and the Isle of Wight (4 August). On 6 August, the Armada anchored off CALAIS, but poor planning and communications made conjunction with Spanish troops in the Netherlands impossible. English fireships dispersed the Armada in confusion on the night of 7 August, and the English had the better of a final skirmish off Gravelines the next day (see GRAVELINES, BATTLE OF). The wind then drove the Armada into the North Sea and forced Medina Sidonia to circumnavigate the British Isles to eventually bring about two-thirds of the fleet home. Some 40 ships were destroyed, mostly by gales and reefs during the journey around SCOTLAND and IRELAND.

Although Philip attempted other invasions of England in 1596 and 1597, the failure of 1588 was decisive, not because of its actual losses, but because of its moral impact. The English victory, which was solemnly celebrated with the queen's ACCESSION DAY in November, gave confidence to English Protestants, soured English Catholics on foreign invasion schemes, and shattered belief in Spanish invincibility. *See also* FARNESE, ALESSANDRO, DUKE OF PARMA; NAVY and illustrations for GOWER, GEORGE; GRAVELINES, BATTLE OF; NAVY.

Further Reading: Garrett Mattingly, *The Armada,* Boston: Houghton Mifflin, 1959; Colin Martin and Geoffrey Parker, *The Spanish Armada,* New York: Norton, 1988.

army

Elizabethan England had no permanent standing army and few professional soldiers. Its peacetime military forces consisted of 200 Yeoman of the Guard (the Beefeaters), which was a ceremonial palace guard, and small garrisons at Berwick on the Scottish border and Dover on the Channel coast. A small group of ordnance officers at the TOWER OF LONDON maintained the royal armory. Under HENRY VIII, a new royal bodyguard, the Band of Gentlemen Pensioners, was established as an elite force to fight alongside the king when he went to war. Since Elizabeth, as a woman, never led a field army, the Pensioners became an ornamental guard of courtiers after 1558.

To raise an army in time of war or invasion, the Elizabethan government could summon the feudal levy, relying on the PEERAGE and GENTRY to fulfill the ancient feudal obligation of levying (supplying) men and arms for the royal army. However, after 1560, the levy was no longer an effective method of raising a military force, being too slow and costly. The government could hire foreign mercenaries, especially to make up shortages of firearms and men experienced in their use, or it could contract by indenture with private citizens to supply a certain number of troops for a certain payment. However, the main element in most Elizabethan armies was the county MILITIA— forces mustered in, trained by, and paid for by their county.

In Elizabethan armies, the percentage of men carrying firearms was increasing, while the number carrying such older and less effective WEAPONS as longbows, pikes (long wooden shafts with pointed steel heads), and bills (seven-foot wooden shafts with metal points and blades) was declining. English armies were usually divided into large wards and subdivided into companies of about 200. The company contained both infantry and cavalry and was commanded by a gentleman captain who was usually an amateur soldier. The captain was responsible for keeping his men armed, clothed, and fed, and for distributing pay, a responsibility that led to much corruption. Captains often charged the government for "dead pays," 10 extra payments for every 100 men actually under the captain's command. Supply contractors also frequently engaged in fraud. Elizabethan warfare was always an expensive undertaking; at a time when the annual royal revenue from all sources was running at perhaps £400,000 to £600,000, the government spent almost £100,000 a year supporting troops in the NETHERLANDS after 1585, and almost £2 million to fight the NINE YEARS WAR in IRELAND. *See also* NAVY; REVENUE, ROYAL.

Further Reading: C. G. Cruickshank, *Elizabeth's Army,* 2nd ed., Oxford: Clarendon Press, 1966.

art

Although the reign of Elizabeth saw a greater flowering of English literature (see DRAMA; POETRY) and MUSIC than of the visual arts, the period is important for the arts because it witnessed fundamental changes in style, inspiration, and patronage. These changes were brought about by two powerful social forces—HUMANISM and the English Reformation (see REFORMATION, ENGLISH). Both movements found artistic inspiration outside of religion and drew artistic patronage away from the English Church. By turning people to their Bibles and the BOOK OF COMMON PRAYER, the Protestant Church eliminated the demand for ornate altars, for statues of the Virgin, and for pictures of the saints. By stressing the beauty of the human body, humanism cultivated an interest in portraiture and the decorative arts within the English GENTRY and PEERAGE.

Eager to enhance the glory of his Crown, HENRY VIII imported artists from Italy to design and decorate his PALACES and to paint his family and COURT. The king's patronage of portrait painters like the German artist Hans Holbein the Younger encouraged his nobles and courtiers to commission private portraits and other works of art, something in which earlier English nobles had shown little interest. Holbein painted many English courtiers, including Sir Thomas More and Thomas CROMWELL. The king even commissioned Holbein to paint portraits of prospective brides, a task that caused the artist to fall from favor when his likeness of ANNE OF CLEVES proved too flattering.

In Elizabeth I's reign, art became the servant of the monarchy; artists produced allegorical works that glorified Elizabeth and embellished the growing myth of the VIRGIN QUEEN. Portraits of the queen were in high demand throughout the reign (see ELIZABETH I, PORTRAITS OF), and privately commissioned portraits of courtiers and their families followed the same theme, picturing individuals as loyal servants of Elizabeth.

The humanist focus on the individual and the Elizabethan preoccupation with the queen and the state joined in the popular art of LIMNING, or miniature painting (see HILLIARD, NICHOLAS; OLIVER, ISSAC). Miniatures were personal adornments worn as tokens of love or remembrance, or as romantic and allegorical symbols of devotion to the queen and to England. Through the interaction of humanism and PROTESTANTISM, the visual arts became the primary Elizabethan instrument for venerating the queen and celebrating the monarchy. (*Note:* For examples of Tudor and Elizabethan portraiture, see the various portraits of sixteenth-century figures reproduced throughout this volume.)

Further Reading: Eric Mercer, *English Art 1553–1625,* Oxford: Clarendon Press, 1960.

Ascham, Roger (1515–1568)

Roger Ascham's reputation as a humanist scholar of Latin and Greek classics earned him appointment as tutor to Princess Elizabeth, who later recalled him to the same post when she became queen. Born near York in 1515, Ascham spent his childhood in the household of Sir Anthony Wingfield, where he acquired a love of archery and of the classics. His passion for archery led him to publish an English treatise on the topic titled *Toxophilus* (1545). His love of the classics led him in 1529 to St. John's College, Cambridge (see UNIVERSITIES), where he became a reader in Greek by 1538 and a leading figure in the development of the university's program of Greek studies by the 1540s. He was appointed tutor to Princess Elizabeth in 1548, replacing William Grindal, a former pupil. Ascham was impressed with the princess's intellectual abilities, but not with the governors of her household, with whom he quarreled; he resigned his post in 1550 after various disputes with the princess's steward and with the princess herself.

After several years in Europe as secretary to the English ambassador to CHARLES V, Ascham returned to England to accept appointment as Latin secretary to EDWARD VI. At the king's death, Ascham was reappointed to his post by the Catholic queen, MARY I, an indication of his outstanding reputation as a scholar, for Ascham was a Protestant. At her accession in 1558, Elizabeth made him her private tutor, a position Ascham held until his death in 1568.

Ascham's most famous work, *Schoolmaster,* published by his widow in 1570, criticized the harsh discipline usually employed to keep sixteenth-century students at their books and advocated the use of gentle persuasion to motivate students to learn. Ascham's HUMANISM was colored with the English patriotism that became a hallmark of later Elizabethan society; he argued for the use of ENGLISH over Latin in scholarly writing, and he helped, with his own published works, to develop a distinctive English prose style. *Toxophilus,* he wrote, was a work on an "English matter in the English tongue for Englishmen." *See also* EDUCATION; GRAMMAR SCHOOL.

Further Reading: Lawrence V. Ryan, *Roger Ascham,* Stanford, CA: Stanford University Press, 1963.

Ashley, Katherine (d. 1565)

For almost 30 years, Katherine Ashley served Elizabeth Tudor as governess, teacher, confidant, and lady-in-waiting. Katherine, whom Elizabeth called "Kat," was born in Devonshire into the prominent GENTRY family of Champernowne. She married John Ashley, later Elizabeth's master of the jewel house, in 1545. A well-educated woman of increasingly Protestant sympathies, Ashley became Elizabeth's governess in 1537 when the princess was only four. She supervised the early education of the princess, working closely with William Grindal and Roger ASCHAM, Elizabeth's tutors in Latin and Greek.

After the death of HENRY VIII in 1547, Elizabeth was placed in the household of the dowager queen, Katherine PARR, and soon became a not-unwilling object of the romantic and political ambitions of Thomas SEYMOUR, Lord Sudeley, the dowager queen's new husband. Ashley foolishly encouraged Seymour's attentions to Elizabeth, which included playful romps in the garden and early morning invasions of the princess's bedchamber. Katherine Parr sent Elizabeth and Ashley from the house when she discovered the princess in her husband's arms. After Katherine Parr's death in 1548, Seymour worked through Ashley to persuade the princess to marry him. Already more politically astute than her governess, Elizabeth refused. Elizabeth's and Ashley's relations with Seymour came under investigation in 1549 when Seymour was arrested for TREASON. Ashley and Thomas PARRY, another of Elizabeth's servants, were interrogated in the TOWER OF LONDON, where they confessed all they knew. Elizabeth steadfastly refused to blame Ashley for her troubles, despite being urged to do so by the government's interroga-

tors. Ashley was eventually released and restored to Elizabeth's household.

In the 1550s, the governess suffered further periods of imprisonment and dismissal from the princess's service when the government of MARY I tried unsuccessfully to implicate Elizabeth in WYATT'S REBELLION. At her accession in 1558, Elizabeth appointed Ashley first lady of the bedchamber, despite some grumbling from the queen's new ministers, who remembered the former governess's past indiscretions. Elizabeth, who could be a capricious and ungrateful mistress, was a firm friend; she remained devoted to Ashley and deeply mourned her death in June 1565. *See also* LADIES-IN-WAITING; PARRY, BLANCHE.

Further Reading: Carolly Erickson, *The First Elizabeth,* New York: Summit Books, 1983; Christopher Hibbert, *The Virgin Queen,* Reading, MA: Addison-Wesley, 1991.

assizes. *See* COMMON LAW.

attainder

Attainder was a legislative act whereby medieval and Tudor Parliaments imposed penalties of property forfeiture or death on an individual for the commission of a serious crime, usually TREASON. In the fourteenth century, attainder was a parliamentary confirmation of conviction for such crimes in a COMMON LAW court. To be "attainted" also described the consequences of such conviction—forfeiture of property to the Crown and extinction of civil rights. Because PARLIAMENT was the highest and final court of the realm, acts of attainder prevented the heirs of the attainted from challenging the confiscation of their inheritance in a court of law. Only Parliament could reverse an act of attainder. The process was frequently used *in absentia* against persons charged with treason who had fled the realm and could not be apprehended for trial. In 1450, attainder was extended to the convicted traitor's heirs, who were declared "corrupt of blood" and therefore unable to inherit property or exercise certain civil rights. During the WARS OF THE ROSES in the fifteenth century, acts of attainder were passed by the regime in power against supporters of the previous regime—both those in custody and those in exile.

HENRY VIII took the use of attainder even further by having Parliament condemn someone by attainder as a way to avoid bringing the accused to trial in a court of common law. The person was, in effect, declared guilty of treason and therefore worthy of death by act of Parliament. In 1540, Henry VIII had his former chief minister, Thomas CROMWELL, condemned and executed under an act of attainder. In 1572, Parliament sought to proceed by attainder against Mary STUART, Queen of Scots, after the RIDOLFI PLOT, but Elizabeth quashed the effort. In the 1570s, Elizabeth signed acts that restored in blood (i.e., reversed the attainders of) the descendants of two of the men executed in 1536 with her mother, Anne BOLEYN. Attainder was finally abolished in England in 1870. Section 3, Article III, of the U.S. Constitution specifically forbids Congress from extending forfeiture or corruption in blood to the heirs of anyone convicted of treason against the United States.

Further Reading: John Bellamy, *The Tudor Law of Treason,* London: Routledge and Kegan Paul, 1979.

Aylmer, John (1521–1594)

As bishop of LONDON from 1577 until his death, John Aylmer was one of the most important and powerful officials of the ANGLICAN CHURCH. Born in Norfolk, Aylmer became in the 1540s chaplain to the Grey family (see GREY CLAIM), who had earlier paid for Aylmer's education at Cambridge (see UNIVERSITIES). As tutor to Jane GREY, eldest daughter of Henry Grey, Duke of Suffolk, Aylmer shared responsibility for the girl's Protestant upbringing. Aylmer became archdeacon of Stow in 1553, only months before the accession of the Catholic queen MARY I interrupted his ecclesiastical career. Aylmer fled with other MARIAN EXILES to Germany and then to Zurich, where he tutored English exile children and helped John FOXE prepare the initial Latin version of the work that would later be known as the "BOOK OF MARTYRS." While in Germany, Aylmer published *A Harbor for Faithful and True Subjects,* a work that later won him favor with Elizabeth because it refuted John KNOX's *The First Blast of the Trumpet against the Monstrous Regiment of Women,* a publication that deeply offended the queen.

After his return to England, Aylmer held various positions in the Elizabethan Church of England and was involved in CON-VOCATION's revision of English Church doctrine. Becoming bishop of London in March 1577, Aylmer rigorously enforced the Act of Uniformity, making enemies of all who sought to alter or circumvent the ANGLICAN SETTLEMENT of religion, whether Puritan or Catholic. As head of the most populous and most Puritan diocese in the country, Aylmer's insistence on conformity to official doctrine and his scandalous practice of playing bowls on Sunday angered PURITANS, who made him a target of ridicule in the MARPRELATE TRACTS. At the end of his life, Aylmer sought transfer to a smaller, quieter diocese, but he was still bishop of London when he died in June 1594.

Further Reading: Patrick Collinson, *The Elizabethan Puritan Movement,* Oxford: Clarendon Press, 1990; Felicity Heal, *Of Prelates and Princes,* Cambridge: Cambridge University Press, 1980.

Azores

The Azores are a group of islands in the mid-Atlantic, some 800 miles west of Portugal. The Portuguese colonized the Azores in the mid-fifteenth century, with thriving settlements established on the larger islands by 1460. The Azores became the base for early exploration of the northern and western Atlantic. After Christopher Columbus reached the New World in 1492, the Azores became a way station for trans-Atlantic voyaging.

The islands came under Spanish control in 1580 when PHILIP II seized the Portuguese Crown. As a mid-Atlantic haven for Spanish shipping, especially the treasure fleets from SPANISH AMERICA, the Azores saw frequent naval clashes between English and Spanish SHIPS. Almost every major English naval or PRIVATEERING effort against SPAIN after 1585 included an attack on the Azores as a main component. Sir Francis DRAKE, after wreaking havoc on the coast of Spain during his CADIZ RAID (1587), sailed to the Azores and captured a rich Spanish treasure ship from the East Indies. The failure of the 1589 PORTUGAL EXPEDITION was made worse by the fleet's inability to reach the Azores and attack Spanish shipping.

In 1591, the AZORES EXPEDITION under Lord Thomas Howard and Sir Richard GRENVILLE had as its objective the blockading of the islands to intercept treasure fleets from AMERICA. The ISLANDS VOYAGE of 1597 failed, in part, because the English allowed a Spanish treasure fleet to slip past them in the Azores. In the last decades of Elizabeth's reign, the Azores became a major flash point for hostilities between the English and Spanish fleets.

Further Reading: K. R. Andrews, *Elizabethan Privateering*, Cambridge: Cambridge University Press, 1964; James H. Guill, *A History of the Azores Islands*, Menlo Park, CA: n.p., 1972; A. L. Rowse, *Sir Richard Grenville of the Revenge*, London: Book Club Associates, 1977.

Azores expedition

In 1589, after the failure of the PORTUGAL EXPEDITION, Sir John HAWKINS proposed dividing the English fleet and using half of it to maintain a continuous blockade of the AZORES. The blockade could intercept treasure fleets from SPANISH AMERICA, thereby denying PHILIP II the funds required to rebuild the ARMADA and forcing him to make peace with England. Reassured that half the fleet would remain at home to protect England, and anxious to acquire some of Spain's American wealth, Elizabeth approved the project. Delayed by Spanish naval activity, Hawkins missed the 1590 treasure fleet, which reached SPAIN with a large shipment of silver for Philip's naval rearmament. When Hawkins and Sir Martin FROBISHER began blockading the Azores later in the year, Philip halted Spanish treasure shipments from AMERICA and Elizabeth recalled her fleet to support English forces in FRANCE (see BRITTANY EXPEDITIONS). The intermittent nature of the English blockade allowed small convoys to reach Spain and permitted Philip to gather a naval force to patrol the Azores.

In 1591, Elizabeth, disappointed by the lack of profit, sent out a refitted blockade squadron under Lord Thomas Howard and Sir Richard GRENVILLE. In August, the English SHIPS were surprised in the Azores by a Spanish fleet of 55 vessels. Howard escaped with most of the English vessels, but Grenville, protecting the rear of the squadron in the *Revenge*, was surrounded. For 15 hours on 9 and 10 September 1591, Grenville and his crew defended the *Revenge*, sinking two Spanish ships and damaging 15 others. Finally, ignoring their severely wounded captain's order to destroy the ship, the crew surrendered the *Revenge*. Shortly thereafter, Grenville died in Spanish custody and the *Revenge* sank in a cyclone that destroyed much of the Spanish fleet.

Although Grenville's heroics raised English confidence, the queen was disturbed that the *Revenge* had become the first English vessel to surrender to the enemy. Although the action in the Azores in 1591 had little effect on the course of the war, the fight of Grenville and the *Revenge* passed into legend, immortalized in the sixteenth century by Sir Walter RALEIGH in his *True Defense* and in the nineteenth century by Alfred, Lord Tennyson, in his poem "The *Revenge*." *See also* NAVY.

Further Reading: A. L. Rowse, *Sir Richard Grenville of the Revenge*, London: Book Club Associates, 1977.

B

Babington plot

In 1586, a young Catholic gentleman named Anthony Babington became involved in a Jesuit plot (see JESUIT MISSION) to assassinate Elizabeth, put Mary STUART on the English throne, and restore English Catholicism (see CATHOLICISM, ENGLISH). Babington, a former page of George TALBOT, Earl of Shrewsbury, Mary's first jailer in England, had probably seen Mary while in Shrewsbury's service, and certainly felt a romantic devotion to her. In 1580, while in Paris, he met Thomas Morgan, Mary's agent in FRANCE. On his return to England, Babington involved himself with a clandestine group of English gentlemen engaged in hiding members of the JESUIT MISSION in England. Babington's pro-Catholic activities caused John Ballard, a Jesuit priest, to recruit him for a plot against Elizabeth.

Babington and his co-conspirators secretly communicated with Mary, and on 12 July 1586, Babington wrote to the Queen of Scots, outlining for her the entire plan, including the murder of Elizabeth. Unbeknownst to Mary and the plotters, Sir Francis WALSINGHAM, Elizabeth's secretary of state and the head of an extensive government spy network, had discovered and tapped into Mary's secret system of correspondence in 1585 by means of a renegade Catholic spy named Gilbert Gifford. Walsingham thus knew of the plot and of Babington's involvement in it even before Babington wrote his letter to Mary. Sir Francis took no action, awaiting Mary's reply to the Babington letter, for the secretary's chief aim was to prove Mary's complicity in a plot to kill Elizabeth and to thereby force the queen to consent to her cousin's execution. He got his wish on 17 July, when Mary responded by endorsing the plan for her rescue and the murder of Elizabeth.

After his arrest, Babington confessed all and fully implicated Mary and Ballard in the plot. Babington and his co-conspirators were executed in September 1586. Mary was tried for TREASON the following month and executed in February 1587, largely as a result of her involvement with the Babington conspirators. *See also* BLOUNT, SIR CHRISTOPHER.

Further Reading: Wallace MacCaffrey, *Elizabeth I,* London: Edward Arnold, 1993; A. G. R. Smith, *The Babington Plot,* London: Macmillan, 1936; Jenny Wormald, *Mary, Queen of Scots,* London: Collins and Brown, 1991.

Bacon, Ann (1528–1610)

Ann Bacon was the wife of Sir Nicholas BACON, lord keeper of the Great Seal under Elizabeth I, and the mother of Sir Francis BACON, a prominent Elizabethan statesman, writer, and scientist. Ann Bacon was the second daughter of Sir Anthony COOKE, the tutor to EDWARD VI. The Cooke sisters were known as the most learned women in England, thanks to the excellent education given to them by their father (see CECIL, MILDRED; RUSSELL, ELIZABETH).

In the early 1550s, Ann accompanied her father to the court of Edward VI, and in 1553 she married Nicholas Bacon, a widower and friend of her sister Mildred's husband, William CECIL. Before her marriage, Ann had been a companion of Bacon's first wife and had cared for Bacon's young children. After losing two daughters in infancy, Ann and Nicholas

Bacon had two sons—Anthony, born in 1558, and Francis, born in 1561. While her husband rose in the queen's confidence, becoming lord keeper of the Great Seal and functioning as lord chancellor, the Crown's chief legal officer (see OFFICERS OF STATE), Ann Bacon quietly pursued her studies, translating Bishop John JEWEL's *Apologia Ecclesiae Anglicanae [Apology for the Church of England]* into English in 1564.

After her husband's death in 1579, the staunchly Protestant Ann spent much time worrying about her sons, particularly Anthony, who was in chronic poor health and whose circle of friends included many Catholics. In the 1590s, when Anthony became a close friend and follower of Robert DEVEREUX, Earl of Essex, Ann bombarded him with letters of advice that went largely unheeded. Anthony's death in 1601, shortly after (but unrelated to) his involvement in ESSEX'S REBELLION, undermined Ann's health and initiated a mental decline some years before her own death in 1610.

Further Reading: Catherine Drinker Bowen, *Francis Bacon,* Boston: Little, Brown and Company, 1963; Robert Tittler, *Nicholas Bacon,* Athens, OH: Ohio University Press, 1976.

Bacon, Sir Francis (1561–1626)

Sir Francis Bacon was the most influential philosopher and scientist of the Elizabethan period. The second son of Sir Nicholas BACON, Elizabeth's lord keeper, and Ann BACON, one of the highly educated daughters of Sir Anthony COOKE, Francis Bacon entered Cambridge (see UNIVERSITIES) with his brother Anthony in 1573. Because his father's death in 1579 left him in need of a livelihood, he enrolled in the INNS OF COURT and began a legal career by 1582. Having a high opinion of his own abilities, Bacon aggressively sought public office, but was largely ignored by the queen and thwarted by his uncle, William CECIL, Lord Burghley, who saw Bacon as a threat to the advancement of his own son, Sir Robert CECIL. Frustrated, Bacon joined the following of Robert DEVEREUX, Earl of Essex, hoping to gain office through the earl's influence. However, Bacon's unconcealed ambition and his imprudent opposition in PARLIAMENT to a government SUBSIDY bill cost him the posts of attorney general and solicitor. These failures taught Bacon to behave with greater circumspection; after 1597, he supported various government bills in Parliament and took a leading part in the 1601 prosecution of Essex, his former patron.

Although Bacon was knighted at the coronation of JAMES I in 1603 and became solicitor in 1607, his political career did not flourish until the death of his cousin Robert Cecil in 1612. Bacon became attorney general in 1613, lord keeper in 1617, and chancellor in 1618, and he was raised to the PEERAGE as Viscount St. Albans in 1621. Bacon's fall was as rapid as his rise was slow. Accused of taking bribes, he was impeached in the Parliament of 1621 and deprived of the chancellorship. He was also fined, sentenced to imprisonment, and forbidden to attend the COURT or sit in Parliament. Although spared confinement, Bacon never again held public office. He spent his last years in intellectual pursuits, dying, heavily in debt, in April 1626.

Sir Francis Bacon was a lawyer, historian, scientist, and courtier under both Elizabeth I and James I. *By courtesy of the National Portrait Gallery, London.*

Of Bacon's many influential writings, his most important were the *Essays* (1625); *The Advancement of Learning* (1605), which was dedicated to James I; the *Novum Organum [New Instrument]* (1620), a treatise on scientific method; the *History of the Reign of Henry the Seventh* (1622), an attempt to regain royal favor; and the *New Atlantis* (1627), a utopian fable. Bacon's brilliant essays and legal and scientific treatises led such later thinkers as Immanuel Kant, David Hume, and John Stuart Mill to acknowledge him as the founder of modern British philosophy. His emphasis in his writings on experiment and inductive thinking have also made him one of the fathers of the modern scientific method. In the last two centuries, Bacon has even been proposed as the true author of the literary works attributed to William SHAKESPEARE, although most Shakespeare scholars dismiss the theory as highly unlikely.

Further Reading: Catherine Drinker Bowen, *Francis Bacon*, Boston: Little, Brown and Company, 1963; Lisa Jardine, *Francis Bacon: Discovery and the Art of Discourse*, London: Cambridge University Press, 1974; Julian Martin, *Francis Bacon, the State, and the Reform of Natural Philosophy*, Cambridge: Cambridge University Press, 1992; Paolo Rossi, *Francis Bacon: From Magic to Science*, translated by Sacha Rabinovitch, London: Routledge and K. Paul, 1968.

Bacon, Sir Nicholas (1509–1579)

Besides being the father of Sir Francis BACON, Sir Nicholas Bacon was Elizabeth's lord keeper of the Great Seal (i.e., the Crown's chief legal officer) and an influential member of her PRIVY COUNCIL. Bacon was educated at Cambridge (see UNIVERSITIES), where he began lifelong friendships with two fellow students, William CECIL, the future principal secretary to Queen Elizabeth, and Matthew PARKER, the future Archbishop of Canterbury. After leaving Cambridge, Bacon studied in Paris and then received legal training in LONDON at the INNS OF COURT. His first government office was a legal position with the Court of Augmentations, which handled the revenues derived from confiscated monastic lands. Bacon also served as a solicitor for Cambridge University and on a commission charged with dissolving various religious institutions. In 1546, Bacon was appointed attorney of the Court of Wards, which oversaw the management by appointed guardians of the estates of underage heirs (see FISCAL FEUDALISM).

A convinced Protestant who had acquired numerous monastic properties, Bacon was retained in his post by EDWARD VI. Despite his religion, Bacon also remained in office during the reign of MARY I. Thanks to his friendship with Cecil, Bacon came into political prominence at the accession of Elizabeth in 1558. The queen knighted him, appointed him to the Privy Council, and named him lord keeper of the Great Seal to act in place of Mary's Catholic lord chancellor. In these offices, Bacon worked closely on religious issues with Cecil and with Archbishop Parker. In April 1559, the queen authorized Bacon to hear cases in the Court of Chancery and to exercise all the powers of the lord chancellor, the Crown's most important legal officer (see CHANCERY, COURT OF; OFFICERS OF STATE).

An excellent attorney and administrator, and a strong Protestant voice in the Council, Bacon enjoyed the favor of the queen, who visited his house on several occasions, including a six-day stay in 1577 that cost Bacon £600 (a substantial gentleman's annual income might only have been one-third that sum). Bacon

This portrait of Lord Keeper Sir Nicholas Bacon was painted by an unknown artist in 1579, the year of Bacon's death. *By courtesy of the National Portrait Gallery, London.*

grew increasingly fearful of Catholic plots in behalf of Mary STUART, Queen of Scots, and drew Elizabeth's anger when he hinted in 1570 that it might eventually become necessary to execute the captive queen (see RIDOLFI PLOT). Bacon's consistently Protestant stance made him a favorite target of Catholic propagandists, both in England and in Europe. Bacon died at York House, his London residence, in February 1579.

Further Reading: Robert Tittler, *Nicholas Bacon,* Athens, OH: Ohio University Press, 1976.

Barrow, Henry (1550–1593)

Through his passionate writings advocating the freeing of local churches from state control, Henry Barrow became one of the most important leaders of the Elizabethan separatist movement (see SEPARATISTS) and a founder of English and American CONGREGATIONAL-ISM. Born in Norfolk, Barrow was a distant relative of both Sir Francis BACON and Sir William CECIL. He was educated at Cambridge (see UNIVERSITIES) and in 1576 became a member of Gray's Inn (see INNS OF COURT). By the mid-1580s, Barrow had become a follower of Robert BROWNE, founder of the first English separatist congregation, whose members became known as Brownists.

Where PURITANS sought to "purify" the ANGLICAN CHURCH of its Catholic and non-scriptural elements, the separatists sought to withdraw from the English Church altogether and to form their own autonomous congregations. The Brownist ideal of church government, which was readily adopted and promoted by Barrow, called for the complete separation of local congregations from government authority—from any exercise of control over doctrine or practice by monarch, bishops, or PARLIAMENT.

Arrested in November 1586 by order of John AYLMER, Bishop of LONDON, Barrow was closely interrogated and imprisoned when he refused to recant his opinions. While in confinement, Barrow, along with fellow separatist John Greenwood and Puritan writer John PENRY, the probable author of the MARPREL-ATE TRACTS, wrote several works defending their views and describing the treatment they had received from the authorities. Smuggled out on small strips of paper, these tracts, in-cluding Barrow's *A True Description, Out of the Word of God, of the Visible Church* (1589) and *A Brief Discovery of the False Church* (1590), were published in Europe and widely distributed in England. These publications increased Barrow's influence among the English separatist community, but also led in March 1593 to the conviction and condemnation of Barrow and Greenwood for circulating seditious books.

The two men were executed at Tyburn (a notorious London execution site) on 6 April 1593. The executions and continuing government persecution caused many of Barrow's followers, called Barrowists, to flee to the NETHERLANDS and eventually to AMERICA, where their descendants put many of Barrow's ideas into practice among the Puritan congregations of the New England colonies.

Further Reading: Patrick Collinson, *The Elizabethan Puritan Movement,* Oxford: Clarendon Press, 1990; B.R. White, *The English Separatist Tradition,* London: Oxford University Press, 1971.

Barrowists. *See* BARROW, HENRY; CONGREGATIONALISTS.

Bazán, Alvaro de, Marquis of Santa Cruz (1526–1588)

Alvaro de Bazán, Marquis of Santa Cruz, was Spain's most experienced naval commander and a leading advocate of the "Enterprise of England." Santa Cruz fought in various naval actions in the Mediterranean, particularly distinguishing himself in JOHN OF AUSTRIA's victory over the Turks at Lepanto in 1571. He again served with distinction in Portugal in 1580, giving vital naval support to Fernandez ALVAREZ DE TOLEDO, Duke of Alva, the commander of Spanish land forces and former governor-general of the NETHERLANDS. Santa Cruz sealed Spain's conquest of Portugal by defeating a French naval force off the AZORES in 1582, a victory that gave Spain's PHILIP II control of the magnificent harbor of Lisbon and the large Portuguese fleet. With this great increase in his naval capabilities, Philip had the wherewithal to attack England.

Appointed captain-general of the ocean sea, Spain's chief naval commander, in 1583, Santa Cruz declared himself ready to clear the sea of English pirates and to invade England itself. Asked to estimate the requirements for such an invasion, Santa Cruz requested over 500 SHIPS; 30,000 seamen; 64,000 soldiers; and huge quantities of powder, shot, and food. He put the cost at the staggering sum of 3.8 million ducats. Because Santa Cruz's plan would have stripped the harbors of SPAIN, Portugal, and Italy of shipping, and was well beyond even Philip's financial capabilities, the king shelved the scheme. However, in 1587, after the execution of Mary STUART, Queen of Scots, Philip resurrected Santa Cruz's plan, scaling it down and combining it with an alternative scheme proposed by Alessandro FARNESE, Duke of Parma, the governor-general of the Netherlands. Parma had suggested transporting Spanish troops in the Netherlands across the Channel to invade England.

Santa Cruz was given command of the ARMADA that would sail from Spain to hold back the English fleet and escort Parma's forces to England. Prevented from departing in 1587 by Sir Francis DRAKE's Cadiz Raid, which destroyed vital naval supplies, Santa Cruz was within a week of sailing when he died in January 1588. The marquis's death delayed the sailing of his successor in command, Alonso Perez de GUZMAN EL BUENO, Duke of Medina Sidonia, until the summer of 1588. *See also* CADIZ RAID (1587); NAVY.

Further Reading: Garrett Mattingly, *The Armada,* Boston: Houghton Mifflin, 1959; Colin Martin and Geoffrey Parker, *The Spanish Armada,* New York: Norton, 1988.

bearbaiting. *See* ANIMAL SPORTS.

Beaufort family

The Beaufort family's claim to the English throne, which passed eventually to the TUDOR FAMILY, derived from the marriage in 1396 of John of Gaunt, Duke of Lancaster (1340–1399), to his long-time mistress, Katherine Swynford (d. 1403). Gaunt was the third son of Edward III (r. 1327–1377), and the uncle of Richard II (r. 1377–1399). Although all Gaunt's children by Swynford were born before their parents' marriage, Richard II granted them legitimate status under the name Beaufort. When Henry IV (r. 1399–1413), Gaunt's eldest son by a previous marriage, replaced his cousin Richard on the throne in 1399, he added a proviso to his half siblings' legitimation that

barred the Beauforts from the succession because of their originally illegitimate status. Thus, although related to the ruling Lancastrian dynasty, the Beauforts' right to the throne was tainted by their family origins.

When Gaunt's great-grandson, John Beaufort, Duke of Somerset, died in 1444, he left his wealth and his possible place in the succession to his only child, Margaret Beaufort (1443–1509). In 1456, Henry VI (r. 1422–1461, 1470–1471) wed Margaret's lands, and her claims to the throne, to his maternal half brother, Edmund Tudor, Earl of Richmond. Margaret transmitted the claims to her only child, Henry Tudor, who was born in January 1457, three months after his father's death. Although Henry Tudor's claim was distant, tainted by illegitimacy, and transmitted through the maternal line, the WARS OF THE ROSES had destroyed both the male line of Lancaster and the direct male line of Beaufort (Margaret's cousins, Henry and Edmund Beaufort, successively Dukes of Somerset, were executed in 1464 and 1471, respectively). Following these deaths, 14-year-old Henry Tudor became, in 1471, the only living male holder of both the Lancastrian and Beaufort claims to the Crown.

When Richard III usurped the throne of his nephew, Edward V, in 1483, thereby damaging national support for continuance of Yorkist rule (see YORKIST CLAIM), Henry Tudor seized his opportunity and made good the Beaufort claim by winning the Crown in battle against Richard in August 1485. Through his Beaufort blood, HENRY VII was able to initiate the rule of the Tudor dynasty and make possible the eventual reign of his granddaughter, Elizabeth I. *See* the genealogical chart in Appendix 1: "Houses of Lancaster, Beaufort, and Tudor."

Further Reading: Ralph A. Griffiths and Roger S. Thomas, *The Making of the Tudor Dynasty,* New York: St. Martin's Press, 1985.

Bedford, Earl of. *See* RUSSELL, FRANCIS, EARL OF BEDFORD.

Bedingfield, Sir Henry (1511–1583)

Sir Henry Bedingfield was the jailer specially appointed by MARY I to keep Princess Elizabeth confined in the TOWER OF LONDON and at Woodstock in 1554–55. Bedingfield was born in Norfolk, the son of Sir Edmund Bedingfield, the jailer of CATHERINE OF ARAGON during the last years of her life. In July 1553, Bedingfield, a staunch Catholic, was among the first gentlemen (see GENTRY) to acknowledge Princess Mary as queen, and to rally to her cause in opposition to the rival claim of Jane GREY (see NORTHUMBERLAND'S COUP). As a reward, Mary named Bedingfield to the PRIVY COUNCIL and granted him an annual pension of £100. When Mary's first PARLIAMENT met in October 1553, Bedingfield sat as MP (i.e., member of Parliament) for Suffolk; in 1554 and 1557, he was MP for Norfolk.

Mary committed Princess Elizabeth to the Tower in March 1554 for suspected complicity in WYATT'S REBELLION. In May, the queen appointed Bedingfield keeper of the princess, with a special guard of 100 men in blue liveries (i.e., uniforms). Because he treated her with a harsh lack of deference, Elizabeth feared that Bedingfield meant to quietly murder her. Bedingfield, however, had no such intention, and though firm with his royal charge, he kept her safe, giving strict orders that no one be allowed to visit her when he was absent. These orders may have prevented Simon Renard, the Spanish ambassador, and Lord Chancellor Stephen Gardiner from sending assassins to secretly kill the princess, something both men were suspected of plotting. Shortly after assuming his position as jailer, Bedingfield conducted Elizabeth to the royal manor at Woodstock, where he kept her in custody until ordered to bring her to court in June 1555.

After Elizabeth's accession in 1558, Bedingfield presented himself at COURT with apologies for his previous conduct; the queen is said to have dismissed him by snapping, "If we have any prisoner whom we would have sharply and straitly kept, we will send for you." Until his death in 1583, Bedingfield lived quietly in Norfolk, coming occasionally to the notice of the government as a recusant and a stubborn adherent to Catholicism (see CATHOLICISM, ENGLISH; RECUSANTS).

Further Reading: David Loades, *The Reign of Mary Tudor,* 2nd ed., London: Longman, 1991; Paul Johnson, *Elizabeth I,* New York: Holt, Rinehart and Winston, 1974.

benefice

A benefice is an ecclesiastical office in the ANGLICAN CHURCH that imposed on its holder certain prescribed duties in return for specified revenues, known as the "temporalities" of the benefice. For instance, a prebendary performed certain duties as a cathedral official in return for the income generated by a particular piece of land. A parish priest met the spiritual needs of his parishioners in return for the parish TITHES. Tithes originally referred to one-tenth of the yearly harvest of the local parish community, which was set aside for use by the priest; by Elizabethan times, however, this payment in kind had usually been transformed into a fixed annual cash payment.

The right to appoint to a benefice, known as an ADVOWSON, was a property right under the law and could be held by an ecclesiastical official (e.g., a bishop) or by a layperson (e.g., the monarch or a local member of the GENTRY). Because the Reformation (see REFORMATION, ENGLISH) and the dissolution of the monasteries placed more advowsons into lay hands, many Elizabethan patrons kept all or most of the tithes and other temporalities of benefices for themselves, thus eliminating or severely degrading the spiritual care available to many local parishioners. Disputes over revenues from benefices often soured relations between the Elizabethan clergy and laity, and between local parishioners and the lay holder of the local parish advowson.

Further Reading: Rosemary O'Day and Felicity Heal, eds., *Princes and Paupers in the English Church 1500–1800,* Leicester: Leicester University Press, 1981.

Bertie, Peregrine, Lord Willoughby de Eresby (1555–1601)

For his exploits in the NETHERLANDS, Peregrine Bertie, Lord Willoughby, became one of the most famous Elizabethan military heroes. Born in Germany, where his Protestant parents were living as MARIAN EXILES, Bertie was named to commemorate his family's enforced "peregrination" in foreign lands. On the family's return to England in 1559, Bertie's education was supervised by Sir William CECIL, who also helped arrange a marriage for him with the daughter of the Earl of Oxford.

Bertie's mother, Katherine Willoughby, had been the widowed Duchess of Suffolk when she married Richard Bertie, her horse master. Because Katherine had been Baroness Willoughby de Eresby in her own right, Peregrine inherited his title from her upon her death in 1580.

In 1585, Elizabeth sent the new Lord Willoughby to Denmark to negotiate for Danish help against SPAIN in the Netherlands. He then joined the English forces of Robert DUDLEY, Earl of Leicester, in Flanders, where Willoughby was named governor of Bergen (see NETHERLANDS EXPEDITION; NETHERLANDS REVOLT). He fought at Zutphen in September 1586, where he witnessed the mortal wounding of his friend Sir Philip SIDNEY. In 1587, he led Leicester's cavalry, and then succeeded Leicester as commander of all English forces when the earl was recalled to England. Caught between the military needs of the Dutch and the political and financial restrictions imposed by the queen, Willoughby's position in the Netherlands became increasingly difficult. In 1588, the government ordered him to send part of his force to England to help meet the ARMADA threat, but his own urgent requests to return home were denied. Willoughby repelled a Spanish attack on Bergen later in the year, a victory that made him the subject of several late-sixteenth-century ballads.

Willoughby's failing health finally led the queen to approve his recall from the thankless Dutch command in March 1589. In September, Willoughby led an unsuccessful English expedition to FRANCE to help HENRI IV against the CATHOLIC LEAGUE. To restore his health, Willoughby spent the early 1590s traveling in Europe, especially in Italy. In 1596, the queen named him governor of Berwick on the border with SCOTLAND, and he spent his last years sending the government regular reports on Scottish affairs. Willoughby died in Berwick on 25 June 1601.

Further Reading: Wallace T. MacCaffrey, *Elizabeth I: War and Politics 1588–1603,* Princeton, NJ: Princeton University Press, 1992; Geoffrey Parker, *The Dutch Revolt,* Ithaca, NY: Cornell University Press, 1977; Jane West, *The Brave Lord Willoughby: An Elizabethan Soldier,* Edinburgh: Pentland Press, 1998.

Berwick, Treaty of (1560)

The 1560 Treaty of Berwick constituted an agreement between Elizabeth I and rebellious Scottish Protestants to act in concert against the expansion of French influence in SCOTLAND. In 1559, when Mary STUART, Queen of Scots, also became queen of FRANCE, rumors began to spread of the French king's intention to send 3,000 additional troops to Scotland to support the pro-French regency government of Mary's mother, Marie de GUISE. Fearing that the French would eventually use their military forces in Scotland to invade England and place Mary on the throne, Elizabeth decided to assist the Lords of the Congregation, the leaders of the Protestant opposition to the Catholic regency regime.

In December 1559, the English admiral William WINTER succeeded in turning back most of the French reinforcements that sailed into the Firth of Forth. In February 1560, Elizabeth's agent, Thomas HOWARD, Duke of Norfolk, met with representatives of the Lords of the Congregation in Berwick on the Scottish border to conclude an offensive and defensive alliance against the Scottish regent. By the 1560 Treaty of Berwick, Elizabeth agreed to send an army into Scotland to assist the Protestants against the regent's French forces. In return, the Lords promised to send Scottish troops to the assistance of their English allies should the French invade England. Based on a shared PROTESTANTISM, this Anglo-Scottish alliance broke the centuries-old anti-English alliance between Scotland and France.

In accord with the agreement, an English army of over 6,000 men entered Scotland in March 1560 and joined Scottish forces in besieging the French fortress at Leith. The Berwick agreement was one of the first major foreign policy initiatives of Elizabeth's reign. The queen entered into it reluctantly, being as unwilling to support subjects in rebellion against their lawful queen as she was to see French power in Scotland increase. The military intervention begun by the Treaty of Berwick led in the summer of 1560 to the conclusion of the Treaty of Edinburgh, whereby Elizabeth achieved her goal of removing the French from Scotland (see EDINBURGH, TREATY OF).

Further Reading: Caroline Bingham, *The Stewart Kingdom of Scotland 1371–1603*, New York: St. Martin's Press, 1974; Gordon Donaldson, *Scotland: James V to James VII,* New York: Praeger, 1965; J. D. Mackie, *A History of Scotland*, 2nd ed., New York: Dorset Press, 1985; Fitzroy Maclean, *A Concise History of Scotland*, New York: Beekman House, 1970; Rosalind Mitchison, *A History of Scotland*, 2nd ed., London: Routledge, 1982; Jenny Wormald, *Court, Kirk, and Community: Scotland, 1470–1625*, Toronto: University of Toronto Press, 1981.

Berwick, Treaty of (1586)

The 1586 Treaty of Berwick created an Anglo-Scottish alliance, made possible the 1603 accession of the Scottish king to the English throne, and laid the foundation for the 1707 union of the two kingdoms. Signed at Berwick on 5 July 1586, the treaty bound each country to provide military assistance to the other in the case of attack by a third power. Each country also pledged not to enter into an agreement with a third country that would be harmful to the other. Finally, Elizabeth I and Scotland's James VI (see JAMES I) agreed to maintain the religion of their countries as it currently existed, a clause that ensured a Protestant successor to the English throne and gave James implicit assurance that he would be that successor. Although Elizabeth's experience as the unwilling focus of rebellion during her sister's reign (see MARY I) made her refuse ever to openly declare a successor, she did signal her intentions in May 1586 by providing the Scottish king with a regular subsidy to strengthen his position with the independent-minded Scottish nobility.

Negotiated for England by Sir Francis WALSINGHAM, the 1586 Treaty of Berwick used the unstated promise of succession to the English throne to convince James to ignore French offers of friendship and to cooperate with Elizabeth's government in reducing the age-old disorder that plagued the Anglo-Scottish border. Although the Scottish king later complained that his English pension was too small, the treaty proved its worth in February 1587 when James withstood enormous pressure to respond militarily to the English execution of his mother, Mary STUART, Queen of Scots. Although affronted by the act, James limited himself to an angry protest, being unwilling to risk the English throne for a mother he never knew. The 1586 Treaty of Berwick

destroyed any possibility that the old French-Scottish alliance would be revived, and it tied SCOTLAND more closely to England. It also helped ensure that the English and Scottish Crowns would be united in the person of King James upon Elizabeth's death.

Further Reading: J. D. Mackie, *A History of Scotland*, 2nd ed., New York: Dorset Press, 1985; D. Harris Willson, *King James VI and I*, New York: Henry Holt and Company, 1956.

Bible, English

Because PROTESTANTISM in general, and English Puritanism (see PURITANS) in particular, placed tremendous emphasis on the authority of scripture, the availability of an accurate ENGLISH translation of the Bible was of great importance. William Tyndale completed the first English translation of the New Testament in 1525. Although immediately popular in England, the Tyndale translation was banned by HENRY VIII in 1530. Beyond the standard Roman Catholic opposition to laypeople reading and interpreting the Bible for themselves without the guidance of the Church, the king and the bishops also objected to Tyndale's

The frontispiece of the Bishops' Bible of 1569 shows Elizabeth enthroned, surrounded by the virtues Justice, Mercy, Fortitude, and Prudence. *By permission of the British Library, No. 1105.f.1.*

Lutheran commentary and to his reformist word selection; e.g., translating "church" as "congregation."

Miles Coverdale published the first English translation of the entire Bible in 1535. Although reformist in tone, the unauthorized Coverdale translation found favor with Elizabeth's mother, Anne BOLEYN, who joined Archbishop Thomas CRANMER in urging Henry VIII to place an English Bible in every church, something the king finally ordered in September 1538. Because none of the available translations had been produced under Church direction, all were unsatisfactory in some way, and the need for an authorized version was widely recognized. Under the supervision of Thomas CROMWELL and the editorship of Coverdale, the Great Bible appeared in November 1539. Although shorn of Lutheran commentary and some reformist word choices, the Great Bible was based largely on the work of Tyndale and Coverdale. Backed by royal and episcopal authority, the Great Bible spread throughout England in the reigns of Henry VIII and EDWARD VI and was soon found in most English churches.

During the reign of MARY I, the MARIAN EXILES in Geneva, led by William WHITTINGHAM, produced their own translation of the Bible. The Geneva Bible appeared in 1560 and immediately superseded the Great Bible. Printed in a smaller and cheaper size, and in more readable type (see PRINTING), the Geneva Bible contained helpful marginal notes and strongly Calvinistic (see CALVINISM) alternative translations. It went through 140 editions and was far more popular than the less radical Bishops' Bible that the ANGLICAN CHURCH published in 1568 in an unsuccessful attempt to replace the Geneva edition. The Geneva Bible was the most widely read version in Elizabethan England, and remained so until after the publication of the new Authorized Version (i.e., the King James Version) in 1611.

Further Reading: F. F. Bruce, *History of the Bible in English,* New York: Oxford University Press, 1987.

"bill and book" episode

The term "bill and book" describes two unsuccessful Puritan attempts in the Parliaments of the late 1580s to pass bills giving the ANGLICAN CHURCH a presbyterian system of governance (see PRESBYTERIAN MOVEMENT; PURITANS). In the 1584 session of PARLIAMENT, Peter Turner, member for LONDON, submitted a bill that vested the government of the English Church in councils of ministers and elders in each county, instead of in bishops under the Crown and Parliament. Turner's bill also replaced the *BOOK OF COMMON PRAYER* with the more Calvinistic liturgy devised by John KNOX in the 1550s for use by his Geneva congregation of MARIAN EXILES (see CALVINISM). Led by Sir Christopher HATTON, who expressed the queen's opposition to the measure, the House of Commons refused to consider Turner's bill.

The Presbyterians, who were strongly represented within the clergy of London and the surrounding counties, tried again in the next session. In February 1587, Anthony Cope, the member for the Oxfordshire borough of Banbury, submitted a bill abolishing all existing laws for the government and liturgy of the English Church. The bill also would have replaced the Anglican Prayer Book with a revised form of the liturgy used in John CALVIN's Geneva, a system that gave ministers a central role in governing the Church. Unlike Turner, Cope had strong support from a group of Presbyterian members, including Job Throckmorton, who was later implicated in the publishing of the anonymous MARPRELATE TRACTS. Because Elizabeth had previously ordered the Commons not to meddle with matters of religion, she stopped all debate on the Cope initiative by directing the speaker to deliver the proposal (the "bill") and the Geneva liturgy (the "book") to her.

When Peter WENTWORTH and several other members of Parliament protested this action as a violation of the Commons's freedom of speech, the queen sent Wentworth, Cope, and three other members of Parliament to the TOWER OF LONDON. Government spokesmen in the Commons then denounced the bill, which many members had not yet studied in detail, as a radical destruction of the traditional structure and liturgy of the Anglican Church. The government members especially emphasized the disastrous social consequences that they believed would follow its passage. By raising the possibility of using Parliament to alter the ANGLICAN SETTLEMENT of 1559, the "bill and book" episode strengthened the Puritan desire for reform of the Church of England and aggravated the divisions between conservative Anglicans and Puritans.

Further Reading: Patrick Collinson, *The Elizabethan Puritan Movement,* Oxford: Clarendon Press, 1990.

Black Rubric

The Black Rubric was an explanatory footnote inserted into the Second BOOK OF COMMON PRAYER by order of the PRIVY COUNCIL. The last-minute addition to the Prayer Book was meant to address Protestant objections to certain wording prescribed for use in the Communion service. In September 1552, in a sermon preached at COURT before EDWARD VI, the reformer John KNOX argued against a directive found in Archbishop Thomas CRANMER's newly authorized Second *Book of Common Prayer* for communicants to kneel when receiving the bread and wine. Knox felt that the kneeling posture indicated adoration of the wafer and wine and therefore implied the real presence of the body and blood of Christ, a Catholic doctrine to which Knox and other Protestants strongly objected (see MASS; TRANSUBSTANTIATION). When Cranmer refused to remove the directive, the Council, under John DUDLEY, Duke of Northumberland, inserted the Black Rubric into the Prayer Book. This clarifying commentary denied that the kneeling posture intended any adoration of the bread and wine or in any way implied the presence of the body and blood of Christ in the Eucharist, for such belief, declared the Rubric, "were Idolatry to be abhorred of all faithful Christians."

The Elizabethan Prayer Book of 1559 dropped the Black Rubric but broadened the wording used by the priest when presenting the wafer to communicants. The Elizabethan book also added an "ornaments rubric" that ordered church ornaments (e.g., candles, statuary, crucifixes) and priestly garb to conform to the standard usage of the second year of King Edward's reign. This vague prescription caused much confusion and led in part to the VESTIARIAN CONTROVERSY of the 1560s, a significant event in the development of the Puritan faction within the Elizabethan Church of England. Unlike Knox and the later PURITANS, Eliza-

beth was indifferent to church ornaments and vestments as matters of doctrine and belief; rather, she saw such things as important symbols of royal control over English Church structure and government (see SUPREMACY, ROYAL).

Further Reading: *The First and Second Prayer Books of Edward VI,* New York: E. P. Dutton and Co., 1949; Norman L. Jones, *Faith by Statute,* London: Royal Historical Society, 1982; Diarmaid MacCulloch, *Thomas Cranmer,* New Haven, CT: Yale University Press, 1996.

Blackwell, George (c. 1545–1613)

George Blackwell's turbulent leadership of the English Catholic mission exposed the divisions between Jesuits and secular priests and hindered attempts to win official toleration for English Roman Catholics from Elizabeth's Protestant government (see CATHOLICISM, ENGLISH; SEMINARY PRIESTS). Born in Middlesex, the son of a LONDON pewterer, Blackwell graduated from Trinity College, Oxford (see UNIVERSITIES), becoming a fellow of the college in 1565. A convinced Catholic, Blackwell resigned his fellowship and left England to enter William ALLEN's English Catholic college at Douai in the NETHERLANDS in 1574. Blackwell was ordained a priest in 1575 and returned to England as part of the Catholic mission in 1576. In constant hiding from the authorities, Blackwell was arrested and briefly imprisoned in 1578. After his release, he returned frequently to Europe and became well known in Rome.

To restore effective leadership and discipline to the English Catholic mission after the death of Cardinal Allen in 1594, Pope Clement VIII created the new position of archpriest (see ARCHPRIEST CONTROVERSY), to which Blackwell was appointed by Robert PARSONS, director of the English JESUIT MISSION. As archpriest, Blackwell had absolute authority over all secular priests in England and instructions to work closely with the Jesuits. Because most secular priests were more interested in saving Catholic souls than furthering the Jesuit political agenda, they immediately disputed Blackwell's appointment and authority. The new archpriest's rigid adherence to his papal instructions and his dictatorial manner further alienated secular priests from his leadership.

For over a decade, English secular priests bombarded Rome with appeals for Blackwell's dismissal and for abolition of the office of archpriest. These appellants, as they were called, published almost 20 books in support of their position, thus exposing the divisions in the English Catholic mission and community to an unseemly public debate. The appellants' attempts to win official toleration for Catholics in return for a rejection of Jesuit political action were rejected by Elizabeth in 1602. Blackwell, after his arrest and imprisonment in 1607, recommended that his priests follow his lead in subscribing to the oath of allegiance that JAMES I had imposed on Catholics. Having twice condemned the oath, the pope deprived Blackwell of his office in 1608. The former archpriest died in prison in January 1613.

Further Reading: John Bossy, *The English Catholic Community 1570–1850,* New York: Oxford University Press, 1976; Arnold Pritchard, *Catholic Loyalism in Elizabethan England,* Chapel Hill: University of North Carolina Press, 1979.

Blois, Treaty of

The 1572 Treaty of Blois created a defensive alliance between England and FRANCE. Relations between the two countries had been strained since the French capture of CALAIS in 1558. Although the 1559 Treaty of Cateau-Cambrésis committed France to restore Calais to England after eight years, the possibility of such a restoration was slight (see CATEAU-CAMBRÉSIS, TREATY OF). In 1562, Elizabeth, in hopes of regaining Calais, concluded the Treaty of Hampton Court with the French HUGUENOTS, who opened the port of Le Havre to the English in return for military aid (see HAMPTON COURT, TREATY OF). However, the Huguenots negotiated a separate peace with the French Crown and then joined the French army in besieging Le Havre and compelling the English garrison to surrender (see LE HAVRE EXPEDITION). Although the 1564 Treaty of Troyes restored peace, the French again refused to return Calais (see TROYES, TREATY OF). By the early 1570s, the growing power of SPAIN threatened both countries. By supplying the Catholic forces in the French civil war with funds, Spain weakened the French monarchy and endangered the French state. As proved by the RIDOLFI PLOT, Spain, angered by English raids on SPANISH

AMERICA, was willing to conspire with Mary STUART, Queen of Scots, to overthrow English PROTESTANTISM.

Negotiated for England by Sir Thomas SMITH and Sir Francis WALSINGHAM, and signed on 19 April 1572, the Treaty of Blois committed each country to supply the other with 6,000 troops and eight ships to assist in repelling an invasion by a third power. In a private letter of understanding that accompanied the treaty, Charles IX of France agreed to provide this aid even if an invasion were undertaken for religious reasons, a danger that was then far greater for England than for France. The French also agreed to open a port to English merchants, whose business had been damaged when the "TREASURE CRISIS" OF 1568 closed the Spanish NETHERLANDS to English trade. The Treaty of Blois gave England some measure of security against Spain and considerably improved relations with France. The agreement also led to an improvement of relations with SCOTLAND. By allying with England, the French implicitly abandoned the cause of Mary Stuart and so paved the way for the Anglo-Scottish Treaty of Berwick in 1586 (see BERWICK, TREATY OF [1586]).

Further Reading: Frederic J. Baumgartner, *France in the Sixteenth Century,* New York: St. Martin's Press, 1995; Mary Dewar, *Sir Thomas Smith,* London: University of London, Athlone Press, 1964.

Blount, Charles, Lord Mountjoy
(1563–1606)

By his successful campaigns against the rebel Hugh O'NEILL, Earl of Tyrone, Charles Blount, Lord Mountjoy, extended English authority throughout Elizabethan IRELAND. As the second son of a penurious baronial family, Blount came to COURT in 1583 to seek his fortune. A handsome young man, Blount attracted the attention of the queen, who sent him a token of her regard (see FAVORITES). Although this mark of favor excited the jealousy of the rising royal favorite, Robert DEVEREUX, Earl of Essex, the two young men soon became good friends. Blount, like another friend, Sir Philip SIDNEY, was also attracted to Essex's sister Penelope RICH, the wife of Lord Rich. After Sidney's death in the NETHERLANDS in 1586, Lady Rich became Blount's mistress, bearing him five children.

In 1587, Blount was knighted for his services with the English expeditionary force in the Netherlands under Robert DUDLEY, Earl of Leicester (see NETHERLANDS EXPEDITION). After seven years of almost continuous campaigning with English armies in the Netherlands and FRANCE, Blount returned home in January 1594 to become captain of Portsmouth. He succeeded his father as Lord Mountjoy later that year. In 1597, he sailed with Essex on the unsuccessful ISLANDS VOYAGE, but escaped later involvement in the earl's conspiracies (see ESSEX'S REBELLION) and succeeded Essex as lord deputy of Ireland in February 1600.

In December 1601, Mountjoy defeated the Irish forces sent by Tyrone to link up with 4,000 Spanish troops holding the fortress at Kinsale (see KINSALE, BATTLE OF). Mountjoy's victory forced the Spanish to withdraw from Ireland and allowed the deputy to launch a campaign against Tyrone in northern Ireland while Sir George CAREW launched one against rebels in the south. The combined success of these campaigns led to the submission of Tyrone to Mountjoy in DUBLIN on 30 March 1603, only a week after Elizabeth's death. JAMES I, the new king, created Mountjoy the Earl of Devonshire, but the new earl's marriage to his mistress in 1605, after her divorce from Lord Rich, offended the king and put the earl into disfavor during the last months of his life. He died in LONDON on 3 April 1606.

Further Reading: Cyril Falls, *Mountjoy: Elizabethan General*, London: Odhams Press, 1955; Frederick M. Jones, *Mountjoy, 1563–1606: The Last Elizabethan Deputy*, Dublin: Clanmore and Reynolds, 1958.

Blount, Sir Christopher (1556–1601)

As third and last husband of Lettice KNOLLYS, Sir Christopher Blount became the stepfather and loyal supporter of Robert DEVEREUX, Earl of Essex. Blount was born into a Catholic GENTRY family in Worcestershire. He served as master of horse to Robert DUDLEY, Earl of Leicester, during the earl's NETHERLANDS EXPEDITION in the late 1580s. In 1586, Blount was one of the government agents who helped bring Mary STUART, Queen of Scots, to trial by uncovering her involvement in the BABINGTON PLOT. Within weeks of Leicester's death in September 1588, Blount, who had been recently knighted, married Lettice Knollys, the earl's widow. Blount's marriage significantly advanced his career, both politically and militarily, for it made him the stepfather of the queen's young favorite, the Earl of Essex, the countess's eldest son by her first husband (see DEVEREUX, WALTER, EARL OF ESSEX; FAVORITES).

In 1593, Essex secured his stepfather's return as MP (i.e., member of PARLIAMENT) for Staffordshire. In 1596, the earl gave Blount a prominent place in the expedition to Cadiz (see CADIZ RAID [1596]), and in 1599, Blount served in IRELAND as master of the field for Essex's Irish expedition. The loss of influence and position that befell Essex as a result of his failure in Ireland also touched Blount, who had become completely identified with his stepson's cause. Blount was deeply involved in Essex's abortive rebellion of February 1601, and was arrested and tried for treason along with the earl (see ESSEX'S REBELLION). He was condemned and executed with Essex in February 1601.

Further Reading: Robert Lacey, *Robert, Earl of Essex,* New York: Atheneum, 1971.

Bodley, Sir Thomas (1545–1613)

Sir Thomas Bodley was the founder of Oxford University's Bodleian Library and the benefactor after whom it was named. Born into a Protestant family in Exeter in Devonshire, the young Bodley spent the years of MARY I's reign in religious exile in John CALVIN's Geneva (see MARIAN EXILES). After Elizabeth's accession in 1558, he returned to England and entered Oxford (see UNIVERSITIES), where he became a lecturer in Greek and Latin by 1564. In the 1570s, the queen made use of his proficiency with languages by sending him on various diplomatic missions to European courts, particularly to Denmark and FRANCE. From 1589 to 1596, he held the difficult and sensitive post of English ambassador to the NETHERLANDS (see DIPLOMACY). Bodley was knighted by JAMES I in 1603.

In 1598, Bodley offered to restore and expand Oxford University's fifteenth-century library. In less than a decade, Bodley more than tripled the size of the library's holdings by his own judicious purchases and by persuading his wealthy and influential friends to act as benefactors. Bodley's collection criteria reflected his religious prejudices—he rejected printed versions of stage plays (PURITANS saw the theatre as sinful and frivolous) and anything that seemed too Catholic (see CATHOLICISM, ENGLISH; DRAMA). He particularly strengthened the library's scientific collections. In 1610, Bodley persuaded the Stationers' Company to give a gift copy of every book it printed to the Oxford library, thus making that institution the nucleus of England's first national library. At his death in 1613, Bodley left his large personal fortune to the library for the purchase of books and for the construction of the quadrangle that has housed the library ever since. *See also* LIVERIED COMPANY; PRINTING; STATIONERS' REGISTER.

Further Reading: Ian Gilbert Philip, *The Bodleian Library in the Seventeenth and Eighteenth Centuries,* Oxford: Clarendon Press, 1983.

Boleyn, Anne (c. 1501–1536)

Anne Boleyn, the second wife of HENRY VIII, was the mother of Elizabeth I. Through her mother, Anne belonged to the powerful HOWARD FAMILY, whose members in the next two generations played important roles in Elizabeth I's reign. From 1515, Anne was educated at the French court, in the households of the wife and sister of FRANCIS I. Anne returned to England in 1521, fluent in French and accomplished in MUSIC, dancing (see DANCE), and the ways of the COURT.

In 1523, Anne's older sister Mary became Henry VIII's mistress. Sometime in 1525–26, Anne (then maid-of-honor to the queen, CATHERINE OF ARAGON) also attracted the amorous attention of the king. Having already begun to question the validity of his marriage to Catherine because it had produced no living sons, Henry saw Anne, with whom he was rapidly falling in love, as the new wife he needed to produce the male heir he desired. Catherine's refusal to accept the invalidity of her marriage to Henry and the bastardization of her daughter (see MARY I), and the pope's refusal, for political reasons, to grant the king an annulment, delayed the marriage of Henry and Anne until 25 January 1533. Because Anne was pregnant and the Aragon marriage was not yet formally dissolved, the wedding ceremony was held secretly at WHITEHALL PALACE. To free himself of his first wife, Henry was obliged to have PARLIAMENT break England's links with the Church of Rome and to have Thomas CRANMER, his new Archbishop of Canterbury, officially invalidate the Aragon marriage and confirm the Boleyn marriage. Anne was crowned queen on 1 June 1533 and gave birth to Elizabeth on the following 7 September. By 1535, Henry began to tire of his new queen, who was more outspoken and politically active than he liked, and who had not given him a son. He had also become interested in another woman, Jane SEYMOUR.

When Anne miscarried a son in January 1536, the king became determined to be rid of her, and she was arrested in May on charges of adultery. Shortly before her arrest, Anne is known to have protested her innocence to Henry with the child Elizabeth in her arms. Four gentlemen of the court, including Anne's brother, George Boleyn, and the queen's musician, Mark Smeaton, were arrested and charged with having had sexual relations with the queen. All were tried, found guilty, and executed. Anne was beheaded on Tower Green on 19 May 1536, two days after Cranmer pronounced her marriage to Henry invalid. Parliament shortly thereafter declared three-year-old Princess Elizabeth illegitimate and re-

Anne Boleyn, mother of Elizabeth I, was beheaded in 1536. *By courtesy of the National Portrait Gallery, London.*

moved her from the succession (see SUCCESSION, ACTS OF). Throughout her life, Elizabeth, who barely remembered her mother, was attacked and ridiculed by her political and religious opponents for her mother's role in England's break with the Church of Rome and the manner of her mother's death; as a result, the adult Elizabeth rarely mentioned Anne's name. *See* the genealogical chart in Appendix 1: "Howard Family in the Sixteenth Century—Elizabeth I's Maternal Relatives."

Further Reading: Eric W. Ives, *Anne Boleyn,* Oxford: Blackwell, 1986; Retha M. Warnicke, *The Rise and Fall of Anne Boleyn,* Cambridge: Cambridge University Press, 1989.

Boleyn family

Through her mother's family, the Boleyns, Queen Elizabeth was related to several important noble families of England and IRELAND (see the genealogical chart in Appendix 1: "Howard Family in the Sixteenth Century—Elizabeth I's Maternal Relatives"). In the fifteenth century, the Boleyns rose from being prosperous LONDON merchants—Elizabeth's great-great-grandfather, Sir Geoffrey Boleyn, was lord mayor of London in 1458—to being prosperous country GENTRY—Elizabeth's great-grandfather, Sir William Boleyn, held land at Blickling in Norfolk.

The queen's maternal grandfather, who died when she was six, was Thomas Boleyn, Earl of Wiltshire and Ormond (1477–1539). His marriage in the late 1490s to Elizabeth Howard, a daughter of the second Duke of Norfolk, connected his children and grandchildren to the large, powerful, and ambitious HOWARD FAMILY. Thomas HOWARD, fourth Duke of Norfolk, whom Elizabeth executed for treason in 1572, was thus a distant cousin. Thomas Boleyn's mother (Elizabeth's great-grandmother) was Margaret Butler, daughter of the Earl of Ormond; by this connection, Elizabeth was related to one of the most powerful noble families in Ireland. Thomas BUTLER, tenth Earl of Ormond, besides being a cousin of Elizabeth I, was a great favorite of the queen's and a strong supporter of the Crown throughout the period of political unrest that characterized Elizabethan Ireland.

Anne BOLEYN, Elizabeth I's mother, was the youngest of three children born to Thomas Boleyn and Elizabeth Howard. Anne's brother, George Boleyn, Lord Rochford, was implicated in Anne's fall in May 1536; accused of having sexual relations with his sister, the queen, he was charged with TREASON and incest and executed a few days before Anne. Anne's sister, Mary Boleyn, who served at the French court in her youth, had become a mistress of FRANCIS I of FRANCE; in the mid-1520s, just before Anne caught HENRY VIII's attention, Mary also became a mistress of the English king. Although Mary Boleyn married William Carey, a member of the king's household, her eldest son, Henry CAREY, Lord Hunsdon, was reputed to be a son of Henry VIII, and thus Elizabeth's half brother—not her first cousin. Whatever the truth, Hunsdon became one of Elizabeth's most faithful servants, the queen appointing him her lord chamberlain and to various important diplomatic missions (see DIPLOMACY).

Further Reading: Eric W. Ives, *Anne Boleyn,* Oxford: Blackwell, 1986; Wallace MacCaffrey, *Elizabeth I,* London: Edward Arnold, 1993.

Bond of Association

Shaken by the assassination of WILLIAM, PRINCE OF ORANGE, and alarmed at the continual plotting against Queen Elizabeth by the Catholic supporters of Mary STUART, Queen of Scots, the PRIVY COUNCIL in October 1584 took steps to ensure Queen Elizabeth's safety. Because all royal officials lost their commissions and their power to act for the government upon the monarch's death, Mary Stuart could arrange the murder of Elizabeth and then succeed her victim as heir, and none of Elizabeth's councilors would have any legal authority to act against Mary or to avenge Elizabeth. To avoid such a situation, Sir Francis WALSINGHAM and William CECIL, Lord Burghley, drafted a Bond of Association to protect the queen.

The first clause of the Bond pledged all who signed it to obey the queen's commands and to stand ready to resist, pursue, and destroy any persons who sought her life. Signers of the Bond also agreed that any attempt on the queen's life would bar from the royal succession the person for whom the attempt had been made, and all agreed to kill that person by any means available. Although the Bond never mentioned Mary, she would die for any attempt on Elizabeth's life, whether or not she had anything to do with it. The Bond was also interpreted to include the heirs of anyone benefiting from Elizabeth's assassination. Thus, if Elizabeth were attacked, signers of the Bond would also be free to kill Mary's Protestant son, James VI (see JAMES I) of SCOTLAND.

Copies of the Bond were sent throughout England, and thousands of people all over the country signed it enthusiastically. Some Protestants, although loyal to Elizabeth and opposed to Mary, refused to sign the Bond because they found its endorsement of murderous vengeance to be repugnant. When PARLIAMENT passed the QUEEN'S SAFETY ACT in 1585, the Bond was revised to remove the possibility of action against James unless it could be conclusively proven that he had been involved in the conspiracy. Although Elizabeth denied any knowledge of the Bond when its thousands of signatures were shown to her 1586, such ignorance is unlikely. She certainly disapproved of the inclusion of James and may not have seen the final version, but she was likely aware of the scheme.

Further Reading: J. E. Neale, *Elizabeth I and Her Parliaments 1584–1601,* New York: St. Martin's Press, 1958.

Book of Common Prayer

The *Book of Common Prayer* was the parliamentary sanctioned liturgy of the Protestant English Church during the reigns of EDWARD VI and Elizabeth I. The Elizabethan Prayer Book was the official service book of the ANGLICAN CHURCH; it contained the prescribed forms of all rites, rituals, and ceremonies used at Anglican worship services.

The First *Book of Common Prayer* was largely the work of Archbishop Thomas CRANMER. Issued in 1549, it replaced the Latin MASS with an ENGLISH service, a change that removed much of the mystery from the ritual and promoted greater participation by the congregation. In most other ways, however, the Prayer Book was similar to traditional Roman Catholic rites, especially in terms of the words used during the communion service. The question of whether or not Christ's actual body and blood were present in the bread and wine of communion was the most contentious theological issue of the age. This doctrine of "Real Presence" was central to the Catholic Mass (see

TRANSUBSTANTION), but utterly repudiated by Protestants. Although the wording of the First *Book of Common Prayer* was vague enough to encompass both positions, most parishioners cared little for theology, and opposition to the Prayer Book stemmed mainly from the unfamiliar look and sound of the English service. An Act of Uniformity required clergymen to use the Prayer Book, stipulating punishments ranging from fines and loss of BENEFICE to life imprisonment for refusal to do so. The act also forbade criticism of the Prayer Book and attempts to obstruct its use.

In 1552, a new Act of Uniformity enjoined use of the Second *Book of Common Prayer* on clergy and also imposed penalties on laypeople who refused to attend services (see RECUSANTS). Even though the new Prayer Book gave the communion service a more Protestant tone, many Protestants still believed the wording was too conservative, and the PRIVY COUNCIL inserted the explanatory BLACK RUBRIC into the text to meet their objections. In 1559, the Second Prayer Book, which had been swept away by the Catholic restoration under MARY I, was reinstated without the Black Rubric by a new Act of Uniformity. A moderate formulation increasingly unacceptable to PURITANS, the 1559 version of the Prayer Book remained the official liturgy of the Anglican Church throughout Elizabeth's reign. *See also* ADMONITION CONTROVERSY; "BILL AND BOOK" EPISODE; CATHOLICISM, ENGLISH; PARLIAMENT; PROTESTANTISM.

Further Reading: A. G. Dickens, *The English Reformation,* 2nd ed., University Park: Pennsylvania State University Press, 1989; *The First and Second Prayer Books of Edward VI,* New York: E. P. Dutton and Co., 1949.

"Book of Martyrs"

"Book of Martyrs" was the popular name given to John FOXE's *Acts and Monuments of These Latter and Perilous Days,* the most famous and widely read book in Elizabethan England. Published in 1563, *Acts and Monuments* was an expanded ENGLISH edition of *Rerum in Ecclesia Gestarum,* a Latin history of the martyrs of the English Protestant Church that Foxe, a MARIAN EXILE, wrote and published in Europe in 1559. After returning to England, Foxe studied the episcopal registers of LONDON and the southern dioceses, read the papers of Archbishop Thomas CRANMER (who had been

Powerful illustrations of Protestant martyrdom in John Foxe's "Book of Martyrs" had a strong effect on both literate and nonliterate Elizabethans. *By permission of the British Library, No. C.37.h.2.*

burned to death by MARY I's government), and interviewed survivors and eyewitnesses to learn all he could about the burning of Protestants under Mary. To create the "Book of Martyrs," Foxe incorporated his account of the Marian persecution into a history of Christianity that focused on the English Church in the previous three centuries. The book was an immediate success.

In 1571, the bishops ordered a copy to be placed in all cathedral churches, and many parish churches and Protestant GENTRY families also acquired copies, thereby increasing the fame and popularity of both Foxe and his work. The book gave the Elizabethan Protestant Church a resource for combating the propaganda attacks of foreign and English Catholics, and gave English Protestants a rousing and readable account of the heroes of their faith. By writing in English, and by including a large number of woodcuts to illustrate the text, Foxe made his stories accessible to almost every English man and woman, whether literate or not. By telling the stories of martyred artisans, tradespeople, and apprentices, as well as of

martyred bishops and gentlepeople, Foxe broadened the book's appeal to all classes of Protestant society.

Foxe spent his last years revising and expanding the book; his last edition appeared in 1583, but later versions with additions by other writers appeared throughout the seventeenth century. For generations, the "Book of Martyrs" kept fresh the memory of the MARIAN MARTYRS and reinforced English distrust of Catholicism. *See also* CATHOLICISM, ENGLISH; PROTESTANTISM. *See also* the illustration for FOXE, JOHN.

Further Reading: John Foxe, *Foxe's Book of Martyrs,* edited by William Byron Forbush, Grand Rapids, MI: Zondervan, 1980; J. F. Mozley, *John Foxe and His Book,* New York: Octagon Books, 1970.

Borough, Stephen (1525–1584)

An explorer and navigator, Stephen Borough was one of the first English subjects to explore the Arctic Ocean and to make contact with Russia. Stephen and his younger brother, William BOROUGH, were born in Northam Parish in Devon, but little else is known about either brother before 1553, when both joined the three-ship expedition that Richard Chancellor and Sir Hugh Willoughby led into the Arctic Ocean, seeking a northeast passage to Asia. As Chancellor's navigator on the *Edward Bonaventure,* Stephen Borough sailed the ship around the North Cape of Scandinavia and into the White Sea, where the vessel made port at Archangel. From here, the Englishmen opened trade negotiations with the government of Ivan IV ("Ivan the Terrible"), czar of Russia. The *Edward Bonaventure* then returned safely to England, the only one of the expedition's vessels to do so. The Chancellor expedition led to the formation in 1555 of the MUSCOVY COMPANY, a joint-stock venture intended to open English trade with Russia (see JOINT-STOCK COMPANY).

In 1556, Stephen Borough, again accompanied by his brother William, sailed as master of the *Searchthrift* on an Arctic expedition that discovered the islands of Novaya Zemlya and the opening south of those islands into the Kara Sea. The *Searchthrift* returned to England in the summer of 1557. In 1560, Borough, as master of the *Swallow,* led three ships to Russia to establish trade relations with the czar for the Muscovy Company. On his return, Borough brought back Anthony JENKINSON, an English explorer who reached Russia after completing a difficult journey across the Caspian Sea and Central Asia. When Borough returned to Russia in May 1561, Jenkinson, who had been named English ambassador to Persia by the queen, accompanied Borough to complete the first leg of the long journey to his new post. In January 1563, Elizabeth appointed Borough chief pilot of the royal SHIPS in the Medway, a river in southeastern England that flows into the Thames. Borough remained in royal service until his death in July 1584.

Further Reading: F. R. Dulles, *Eastward Ho: The First English Adventurers to the Orient,* Freeport, NY: Books for Libraries Press, 1969; A. L. Rowse, *The Expansion of Elizabethan England,* New York: Scribner, 1972.

Borough, William (1536–1599)

An explorer and seafarer, William Borough also wrote an important work on navigation. Born in Devon, William Borough was only 16 when he went to sea with his elder brother, Stephen BOROUGH, as a member of the expedition that Richard Chancellor and Sir Hugh Willoughby

led into the Arctic Ocean to discover a northeast passage to Asia. In 1556, Borough also accompanied his brother on the Arctic voyage that discovered the Novaya Zemlya islands. He later sailed on the MUSCOVY COMPANY's annual trade voyages to Russia, and in 1574–75 he traveled the Russian trade route as an agent for the company. From the careful notes he kept of his travels to and through Russia, Borough wrote *A Discourse of the Variation of the Compass, or Magnetical Needle* (1581), a work that described the worthlessness of navigational charts produced by cartographers who ignored or misunderstood compass variation.

By about 1580, Borough, like his brother Stephen, had entered royal service, becoming clerk of the SHIPS, an administrative post in the royal NAVY, in 1582. Borough sailed with Sir John HAWKINS on a largely unsuccessful PRIVATEERING expedition to the Spanish coast in 1586, and was second in overall command to Sir Francis DRAKE during the CADIZ RAID (1587). On the latter voyage, Borough quarreled violently with Drake, who had Borough placed in custody aboard his vessel. When the crew of Borough's ship mutinied, Drake had Borough court-martialed and sentenced to death. Upon the expedition's return, Admiral Charles HOWARD, Lord Howard of Effingham, overturned the sentence and restored Borough to command of his ship. To avoid further trouble with Drake, Howard transferred Borough to command of the supply fleet in the Thames, a post Borough held throughout the ARMADA crisis of 1588. Although Borough was somewhat involved in preparations for Sir Martin FROBISHER's AZORES EXPEDITION in 1589 and for Drake and Sir John NORRIS's PORTUGAL EXPEDITION in the same year, he was never given another naval command. During his last decade, Borough lived quietly, dying in 1599.

Further Reading: F. R. Dulles, *Eastward Ho: The First English Adventurers to the Orient,* Freeport, NY: Books for Libraries Press, 1969; A. L. Rowse, *The Expansion of Elizabethan England,* New York: Scribner, 1972.

boroughs

Boroughs were incorporated towns that held royal charters clearly defining their political and economic rights. Borough towns had the right to control their own markets and the right to restrict the activities of buying, selling, and producing within borough boundaries to their own residents. Outsiders had to pay handsomely for the right to conduct business in the town. The mayor or chief officer of the borough could hold a court to resolve disputes between citizens (although serious crimes were reserved for the royal COMMON LAW courts), and the larger boroughs had their own sheriffs and commissions of the peace (see JUSTICES OF THE PEACE) and held their own MILITIA musters. A borough was collectively assessed for taxes, with the collection left to a municipal official, who was responsible for making up any shortfall in the assessment (see TAXATION).

Boroughs also sent representatives (i.e., burgesses) to PARLIAMENT, although the qualifications for voting and for holding borough office varied widely and were spelled out in each town's charter. In some boroughs, the franchise was restricted to certain guilds or certain families, while in others, voting rights were more widely distributed among male citizens. At the end of Elizabeth's reign in 1603, England had 191 parliamentary boroughs, ranging in size from LONDON, with over 200,000 residents and considered a county in its own right, to small northern and Welsh boroughs of a few hundred people. After London, the next largest English borough towns were Norwich, Bristol, and York, with populations in 1600 of about 15,000, and Exeter, Coventry, Salisbury, and Newcastle, each with about 10,000 inhabitants. Although a fifteenth-century statute required that anyone sitting in Parliament for a borough constituency be a resident of the borough, most town representatives in Elizabethan Parliaments were outside gentlemen (see GENTRY) or the nominees of influential local peers (see PEERAGE). Smaller boroughs were willing to accept such arrangements because they were often too poor to pay the upkeep of a parliamentary representative who had to be lodged and fed for several weeks in London, while larger boroughs preferred to have their interests represented by a well-connected and articulate gentleman.

Although a number of smaller boroughs declined in population until they ceased to exist (like Old Sarum, the infamous "rotten borough" of the nineteenth century that still sent a representative to Parliament even though the town site was deserted), most larger towns grew in size, wealth, and political sophistication during the Elizabethan period. *See also* LOCAL GOVERNMENT.

Further Reading: Jonathan Barry, ed., *The Tudor and Stuart Town: A Reader in English Urban History, 1530–1688,* New York: Longman, 1990; C. G. A. Clay, *Economic Expansion and Social Change: England 1500–1700*: Vol. 1: *People, Land and Towns,* New York: Cambridge University Press, 1984; Sybil M. Jack, *Towns in Tudor and Stuart Britain,* London: Macmillan, 1996; David Loades, *Tudor Government,* Oxford: Blackwell Publishers, 1997; John Patten, *English Towns 1500–1700,* Hamden, CT: Archon Books, 1978; Robert Tittler, *The Reformation and the Towns in England: Politics and Political Culture, 1540–1640,* Oxford: Clarendon Press, 1998.

Bothwell, Earl of. *See* HEPBURN, JAMES, EARL OF BOTHWELL.

Brief and True Report of the New Found Land of Virginia

Because it was written by an Englishman who had actually lived in Virginia, the *Brief and True Report of the New Found Land of Virginia* was one of the most influential and persuasive pro-colonization tracts published in Elizabethan England. In 1585, Thomas HARRIOT, the author of the *Report,* was a member of the first colonial expedition sent to Virginia by Walter RALEIGH. The colonists established themselves on Roanoke Island (off what is now North Carolina), but lack of supplies and disputes with the local Indians led them to abandon their settlement and return to England with Sir Francis DRAKE in June 1586.

Harriot, who believed that North America promised to be more than simply a base for PRIVATEERING against SPANISH AMERICA, published the *Report* in 1588 to convince the English government and people that AMERICA would eventually return the investment of money and effort required to develop it. Illustrated with 23 drawings by fellow colonist John WHITE (see, for example, the illustration with AMADAS-BARLOWE EXPEDITION), the *Report* was divided into three sections covering foodstuffs, building materials, and "merchantable" commodities, those potentially profitable products needed to entice investment in colonization. Responding to allegations that the Roanoke colonists had left Virginia because they were starving, Harriot described the area's rich soil and the many crops the Indians cultivated, especially the beautifully colored maize that grew quickly and provided enormous yields.

In an attempt to dispel rumors that Virginia was nothing but a barren sandbar, Harriot used the section on building materials to describe Virginia's forests and varied landscape. As to profitable products, Harriot described rich native dyes, oils for soap and textile manufacture, giant walnuts and acorns, and fat grapes. He also believed that many medicinal plants could be found and that sugarcane and other valuable commodities of Africa and the West Indies could be grown. Eager to encourage long-term development and to discourage searches for quick wealth, Harriot downplayed mineral resources, saying only that iron was a possibility and that the Indians had small amounts of copper and silver. Widely read and reprinted, the *Report* even found its way into the library of the Virginia Company, the joint-stock enterprise that established Jamestown, the first permanent English colony in North America in 1607. *See also* JOINT-STOCK COMPANY; "LOST COLONY"; ROANOKE COLONY (1585); ROANOKE COLONY (1587).

Further Reading: Thomas Harriot, *A Brief and True Report of the New Found Land of Virginia,* facsimile ed., introduced by Randolph G. Adams, New York: History Book Club, 1951; Karen Ordahl Kupperman, *Roanoke: The Abandoned Colony,* New York: Barnes and Noble, 1993; J. W. Shirley, *Thomas Harriot,* New York: Clarendon Press, 1983.

Bristol, Treaty of

The 1574 Treaty of Bristol was temporarily successful in stopping the deterioration of relations between SPAIN and England that developed following the "TREASURE CRISIS" OF 1568. Each country had seized the other's shipping in 1569, and trade between England and Spain and between England and the Spanish-controlled NETHERLANDS had been disrupted, with serious economic consequences for both countries. Because neither Elizabeth nor PHILIP II of Spain was ready for war in the early 1570s, the two countries concluded the 1573 Treaty of Nymegen, a preliminary agreement that restored trade for two years (see NYMEGEN, TREATY OF).

In August 1574, representatives of the two countries met in the western English port of Bristol to negotiate a permanent settlement encompassing mutual compensation for the shipping losses each country had suffered at the other's hands since 1568. Signed on 21 August, the Treaty of Bristol restored full diplomatic and commercial relations between Spain and England and initiated a six-year period of relatively friendly and stable intercourse between the two. In the agreement, England admitted to being the debtor by estimating Spain was responsible for shipping losses totalling £70,000, while accepting Spanish claims against England of £90,000.

The treaty said nothing about the illegal trading and PRIVATEERING expeditions undertaken by John HAWKINS and Francis DRAKE in SPANISH AMERICA, and both countries continued to attack and seize each other's shipping, especially in American waters. In Europe, however, each monarch worked to maintain the new spirit of friendship. In 1575, Philip expelled English Catholic dissidents from the Netherlands, something England had long demanded. Elizabeth returned the favor by agreeing to refuse sanctuary in England to any rebels against the Spanish Crown, an especially important concession in the case of Dutch rebels. However, despite these efforts at peacemaking, religious differences, the ongoing NETHERLANDS REVOLT, and continuing English raids on Spanish America eventually nullified the Treaty of Bristol and brought the two countries to open war by 1585.

Further Reading: P. S. Crowson, *Tudor Foreign Policy,* New York: St. Martin's Press, 1973; J. H. Elliott, *Imperial Spain, 1469–1716,* New York: St. Martin's Press, 1967.

Britannia

William CAMDEN's *Britannia* was the first historical/topographical survey of the British Isles and was the inspiration for a new genre of descriptive writing on the counties and regions of England and Britain. In English translation, the full title is *Britain, or a Chorographical Description of the Most Flourishing Kingdoms of England, Scotland, and Ireland, and the Adjoining Islands from the Most Profound Antiquity.* "Chorography" refers to the practice of describing in detail the history, culture, and topography of a particular region, a type of historical/geographical writing uncommon in the twentieth century but popular in the sixteenth.

Designed "to restore Britain to its antiquities," *Britannia* is based on vast amounts of historical and archaeological material collected by Camden over more than a decade of traveling and researching throughout the British Isles. The first part of *Britannia* is a chronological survey of British history from earliest times to the Norman Conquest in 1066. Camden supplied little of his own narrative, but described (and liberally quoted from) other important sources. He was among the first English historical writers to critically examine and partially dismiss such myths of British origins as the story of Brutus (a descendant of Aeneas of Troy who supposedly came to Britain around 1100 B.C.) and the legends of Arthur. The second part of *Britannia,* a survey of each of the counties of England and WALES, provides the following kinds of information: "who were the ancient inhabitants, what was the reason of the name, what are the bounds of the county, the nature of the soil, the places of greatest antiquity, and most eminent at present; and lastly, who have been dukes or earls of them since the Norman Conquest."

Britannia was first published in LONDON in 1586 and was dedicated to William CECIL, Lord Burghley. Although written in Latin, the work was popular, going through five new editions by 1600 and appearing in an enlarged and revised sixth edition in 1607. Foreign editions were published in Germany in 1590 and 1616. The sixth edition contained maps and plates of coins and inscriptions collected by Camden. An ENGLISH translation, supervised by the author, appeared in 1610 and was reprinted in 1637. *See also* ANTIQUARIANISM.

Further Reading: Gordon J. Copley, ed., *Surrey and Sussex,* taken from the 1789 English edition of William Camden's *Britannia,* London: Hutchinson, 1977; F. J. Levy, *Tudor Historical Thought,* San Marino, CA: Huntington Library, 1967.

Brittany expeditions

The Brittany expeditions were a series of English military campaigns conducted in FRANCE between 1591 and 1595 to assist the French king in combating invading forces from SPAIN and the NETHERLANDS. PHILIP II of Spain sent troops into the Brittany Peninsula of northwest France in 1590 to assist the CATHOLIC LEAGUE against HENRI IV, the new Protestant king of France. Philip also ordered Alessandro FARNESE, Duke of Parma, his governor-general in the Netherlands, to invade northern France and break Henri IV's siege of Catholic Paris. Pressured to enter the conflict by young courtiers like Robert DEVEREUX, Earl of Essex, who longed for military glory, and fearing that a Spanish seizure of French ports on the English Channel might lead to an invasion of England, Elizabeth agreed to provide Henri with military assistance.

A force of 600 men commanded by Sir Roger WILLIAMS left England for Brittany in March 1591. A second force of 3,000 under Sir John NORRIS landed in Brittany in May. As punishment for his secret marriage, Elizabeth kept Essex at COURT until August, when he arrived in France at the head of 4,000 men. The earl participated bravely if ineffectively in the siege of Rouen before surrendering his command in January 1592 when the Spanish commander declined to resolve the siege by meeting Essex in single combat. Parma relieved the siege of Rouen in April, and the Spanish inflicted a severe defeat on Norris in May.

Unimpressed with English assistance, and suspicious of Elizabeth's desire for a French town (to replace long-lost CALAIS), Henri sought to end the war with Spain by converting to Catholicism in July 1593. Although this action angered Elizabeth, it did not immediately mollify Henri's French enemies, and the king could renew the English alliance only by agreeing to pay for a new English expedition to help carry on the war. This force, eight SHIPS and 4,000 men under the command of Norris and Sir Martin FROBISHER, landed in Brittany in September 1594. In November, Frobisher and Norris won a major victory at Crozon. Although England had lost thousands of men in France and had severely strained its financial resources, the Brittany campaigns were successful in that they frustrated Spanish efforts in France, stalled Spanish operations in the Netherlands, and limited Spanish opportunities to intervene in IRELAND.

Further Reading: Frederic J. Baumgartner, *France in the Sixteenth Century,* New York: St. Martin's Press, 1995; Mark Greengrass, *France in the Age of Henri IV,* New York: Longman, 1984; Desmond Seward, *The First Bourbon: Henri IV, King of France and Navarre,* Boston: Gambit, 1971; R. B. Wernham, *After the Armada,* Oxford: Clarendon Press, 1984.

Brooke, Lord. *See* GREVILLE, FULKE, LORD BROOKE.

Browne, Robert (c. 1550–c. 1633)

Robert Browne was an early English separatist (see SEPARATISTS). Born into a Rutland GENTRY family, Browne was educated at Cambridge (see UNIVERSITIES), where he completed his bachelor's degree in 1572. After graduation, Browne moved to LONDON and supported himself as a schoolmaster. Browne soon became disgusted with the entire governance structure of the ANGLICAN CHURCH, rejecting both bishops and the parish system in favor of independent congregations of like-minded believers. By 1581, he had moved to Norfolk and gathered around him a group of followers called Brownists, because they had elected him to be their pastor. Having chosen to separate themselves from the Anglican Church, the Brownists agreed to be governed only by the regulations set forth in the Bible. Such extreme nonconformity was unacceptable to the religious thinking of the age, and Browne was repeatedly imprisoned for his beliefs, winning release each time through the influence of his kinsman William CECIL, Lord Burghley.

Late in 1581, Browne and most of his congregation moved to Middelburg in the NETHERLANDS to escape Anglican persecution. But Browne's imperious manner combined with poverty and personal disputes among members to break up the congregation by late 1583. Traveling to SCOTLAND with a few followers, Browne angered the leaders of the Scottish Presbyterian Church with his vehement unauthorized preaching and was soon imprisoned. Browne returned to England in 1586 and underwent a mysterious change of heart; he gave up his unlicensed preaching and troublemaking and withdrew his support from English separatism. He then served for five years as master of a Stamford GRAMMAR SCHOOL. In about 1591, he obtained a BENEFICE in the Anglican Church through the influence of Burghley. Although Browne held this church living for more than 40 years, preaching to his congregation in full conformance with Anglican doctrine and policy, he is today hailed by modern CONGREGATIONALISTS as an early and important leader of their movement. Browne died in Northampton in about 1633.

Further Reading: Patrick Collinson, *The Elizabethan Puritan Movement,* Oxford: Clarendon Press, 1990; B. R. White, *The English Separatist Tradition,* London: Oxford University Press, 1971.

Brownists. *See* BROWNE, ROBERT; CONGREGATIONALISTS.

bullbaiting. *See* ANIMAL SPORTS.

Burbage, James (c. 1530–1597)

James Burbage was the owner and builder of the first theatre in Elizabethan England. By 1574, Burbage had left his original trade as a joiner to become a member of the Earl of Leicester's company of actors. He is therefore likely to have taken part in the famous series of entertainments that the company's patron, Robert DUDLEY, Earl of Leicester, provided for the queen at Kenilworth during her visit there on progress in 1575 (see ENTERTAINMENT; PROGRESSES, ROYAL). In April 1576, responding to the mayor of LONDON's opposition to the performance of plays in the courtyards of the city's inns, Burbage, with the financial assistance of his father-in-law, began construction of an enclosed wooden playhouse at a site on Holywell Street in Shoreditch that he leased for 21 years from Giles Allen. Soon known simply as The Theatre, the structure was the first to be built in England specifically for the performance of plays.

Opening in 1577, The Theatre was a great success, with its profits and popularity soon spawning the construction of a rival playhouse nearby, The Curtain. Besides managing the theatre, Burbage selected and trained its company of actors, which included his father-in-law, his son Richard BURBAGE, and the famous comic actor Richard TARLTON. Despite the growing opposition of PURITANS to the public performance of plays, Burbage continued to enjoy success, and he sought in 1596 to expand his business by turning part of the old Dominican monastery in London (known as Blackfriars) into an indoor playhouse called the Blackfriars Theatre. However, the strong opposition of neighboring residents forced the opening of the theatre to be delayed until after Burbage's death. In 1597, a dispute with Giles

Allen over the renewal of the lease on The Theatre led Burbage's sons to move the playhouse to the south shore of the Thames in Southwark, where they renamed it the GLOBE THEATRE. *See also* DRAMA.

Further Reading: Herbert Berry, *Shakespeare's Playhouses*, New York: AMS, 1987; John Orrell, *The Quest for Shakespeare's Globe*, New York: Cambridge University Press, 1983; Irwin Smith, *Shakespeare's First Playhouse*, Dublin: Liffey Press, 1981.

Burbage, Richard (c. 1567–1619)

Richard Burbage was one of the most popular dramatic actors in Elizabethan England. The son of theatre owner James BURBAGE, Richard was trained in acting by his father and made his stage debut at an early age. In 1587, when he was about 20 and already a popular performer, Burbage joined the Earl of Leicester's company of players and stayed with the group throughout the 1590s when it became first the Earl of Derby's Men, then the CHAMBERLAIN'S MEN, and finally, at the accession of JAMES I in 1603, the King's Men. From 1594, one of Burbage's closest associates in the acting company was the playwright and actor William SHAKESPEARE, in whose plays Burbage frequently performed leading roles.

On his father's death in 1597, Burbage and his brother inherited the two London playhouses at Shoreditch and Blackfriars. The Theatre at Shoreditch was closed in 1597 because of a dispute with Giles Allen, who had leased the site of the playhouse to James Burbage in 1576. Fearing that Allen might raze the structure, the Burbage brothers dismantled it themselves and had it reconstructed in Southwark, on the south side of the Thames. Shakespeare was among those loaning money for the difficult and costly move. Renamed the GLOBE THEATRE, the reconstructed playhouse opened in the autumn of 1599. At the Globe, Burbage's fame as an actor grew, and he was sought out by many playwrights for the leading roles in their works. He was, for instance, the first actor to play the roles of Richard III, Hamlet, Macbeth, Othello, King Lear, and Romeo in the plays of Shakespeare; Richard III was perhaps Burbage's most popular role (see SHAKESPEARE, WORKS OF).

As the majority shareholder in the Globe, Burbage acquired great wealth, and in 1609 he was able to buy out the lease of the acting company performing at the Blackfriars Theatre and install the King's Men there. The members of the company, including Shakespeare, were also shareholders in the Globe and the Blackfriars and shared in the profits of the two playhouses. The Globe burned to the ground on 29 June 1613 during a performance of Shakespeare's *Henry VIII*, Burbage barely escaping with his life. A rebuilt Globe opened in 1614 (see the illustration for GLOBE THEATRE), and Burbage continued to act there until his death in March 1619. *See also* DRAMA.

Further Reading: G. B. Harrison, *Elizabethan Plays and Players*, Ann Arbor: University of Michigan Press, 1956; Martin Holmes, *Shakespeare and Burbage*, Totowa, NJ: Rowman and Littlefield, 1978; John Orrell, *The Quest for Shakespeare's Globe*, New York: Cambridge University Press, 1983.

Burghley, Lord. See CECIL, WILLIAM, LORD BURGHLEY.

Burghley, Lady. See CECIL, MILDRED, LADY BURGHLEY.

Butler, Thomas, Earl of Ormond (1532–1614)

Known as the "black earl" for his dark hair and complexion, Thomas Butler, tenth Earl of Ormond, was one of the most important political figures in Elizabethan IRELAND. Brought to England at an early age, Butler was raised at the COURT of HENRY VIII as a Protestant English nobleman (see GENTRY). In 1546, after his father was poisoned, the 14-year-old Butler succeeded to the wealthy Irish earldom of Ormond. Returning to Ireland in 1554, the earl served the Irish government as lord treasurer and privy councilor. He worked to reconcile the Irish and ANGLO-IRISH nobility to the English administration; for instance, persuading the rebellious Shane O'NEILL to submit to the queen in 1561.

In the mid-1560s, Ormond reopened the ancient Butler-Fitzgerald feud by retaliating against attacks on Butler lands by Gerald FITZGERALD, Earl of Desmond, leader of the Fitzgerald family. To restore order, Elizabeth summoned both earls to England in 1565 and forced them to make peace. Because the queen was attracted to Ormond, who was her cousin on her mother's side (see BOLEYN FAMILY), she kept him at court. He finally returned to

Ireland in 1569 when his brothers supported the rebellion of James Fitzmaurice FITZ-GERALD, who opposed the Irish government's plans to settle English colonists in southern Ireland (see FITZMAURICE'S REBELLION). Ormond's brothers, particularly Sir Edmund Butler, joined the uprising mainly to attack Sir Peter CAREW, an Englishman whose claims to ancient family estates in Ireland threatened to deprive Butler of much of his property (see BUTLER WARS). To save his brothers, Ormond denounced Carew and Sir Henry SIDNEY, the lord deputy of Ireland, but otherwise continued to support the English administration against Irish rebels, helping Sir Humphrey GILBERT crush uprisings in southern and western Ireland in 1570–71.

After ending the Fitzgerald feud in 1583 by decisively defeating Desmond at Kerry, Ormond consistently supported the English government, capturing and killing shipwrecked Spaniards after the ARMADA in 1588 and working uneasily but loyally with Robert DEVEREUX, Earl of Essex, to suppress the rebellion of Hugh O'NEILL, Earl of Tyrone, in 1598–99 (see NINE YEARS WAR). For Ormond's services, Elizabeth granted him extensive lands in southern Ireland in 1602, and JAMES I named him vice-admiral of Ireland in 1612. The earl died at age 82 in November 1614.

Further Reading: Steven G. Ellis, *Tudor Ireland,* London: Longman, 1985; Colm Lennon, *Sixteenth-Century Ireland: The Incomplete Conquest,* Dublin: Gill and Macmillan, 1994; Margaret MacCurtain, *Tudor and Stuart Ireland,* Dublin: Gill and Macmillan, 1972; David B. Quinn, *The Elizabethans and the Irish,* Ithaca, NY: Cornell University Press, 1966.

Butler wars

The term "Butler wars" refers to an uprising led by the younger brothers of Thomas BUT-LER, tenth Earl of Ormond, that occurred in the Carlow region of southeastern IRELAND in the summer of 1569. Although the rising began in conjunction with FITZMAURICE'S REBELLION in Munster to the southwest, it had little to do with the religious and political grievances fueling that insurrection (see FITZGERALD, JAMES FITZMAURICE). The Butler wars arose almost solely from the dissatisfaction of Sir Edmund Butler with the outcome of a lawsuit initiated by Sir Peter CAREW to regain lands that his family had held in Ireland some 200 years earlier.

Carew had come from England with the queen's permission to seek recovery at law of his family's long-lost estates. Part of the property claimed by Carew was a Carlow district known as the Dullough, which formed the core of Butler's lands. When the Irish Council under Lord Deputy Sir Henry SIDNEY found Carew's claims to be valid and ordered that he be placed in possession of the Dullough, Butler used the outbreak of Fitzmaurice's Rebellion as a cover to begin his own campaign of revenge against Carew and Sidney in Carlow. Butler harried Carew's lands, harassed his tenants, and drove off his cattle. Given command of a troop of government soldiers, Carew responded by besieging Butler's castle at Clogrennan and by inflicting a costly defeat on Butler's force of GALLOWGLASSES and KERN near Kilkenny.

When word of his brother's actions reached Ormond in England, the earl, who was a favorite of Elizabeth's, obtained permission to return to Ireland. Having the queen's ear, Ormond was able to convince her that the uprising had been precipitated by Carew's high-handed attempts to dispossess ANGLO-IRISH landowners of long-held properties to which he had little right. Although Butler suffered a spell of imprisonment for his attacks on Carew, the queen also put a stop, at least for a time, to Carew's land suits. The Butler wars were a sign of the rising conflict between English settlers and Anglo-Irish landowners for political and economic control of Elizabethan Ireland (see PLANTATIONS, IRISH).

Further Reading: Steven G. Ellis, *Tudor Ireland,* London: Longman, 1985; J. A. Wagner, *The Devon Gentleman: The Life of Sir Peter Carew,* Hull, England: University of Hull Press, 1998.

Byrd, William (c. 1543–1623)

William Byrd is considered the greatest Tudor composer, now occupying in Elizabethan MUSIC the same position William SHAKESPEARE holds in Elizabethan literature. Byrd was born in Lincoln, where he was appointed cathedral organist in 1563. In 1572, he moved to LONDON, sharing the duties of organist in the CHAPEL ROYAL with the composer Thomas TALLIS. In 1575, Elizabeth granted Byrd and Tallis a monopoly on the printing, publishing, and sale of music, and on the sale of music paper (see MONOPOLIES). The partners' first publication was *Cantiones Sacrae,* a collection of their own motets (i.e., choral works on a sacred theme) dedicated to the queen.

About 1580, Byrd became a Roman Catholic, but retained his position in the Chapel Royal, even though he openly dedicated his compositions to Catholic noblemen and was listed by the government as a recusant after 1592 (see RECUSANTS). Because Byrd poured his faith into his music rather than into political activity, and because he continued to write music for Anglican services and to dedicate works to the queen, his loyalty was never questioned. After Tallis's death in 1585, Byrd published several collections of his own music, including *Psalms, Sonnets and Songs of Sadness and Piety* (1588), *Songs of Sundry Natures* (1589), and two additional volumes of *Cantiones Sacrae* (1589, 1591). A prolific composer who produced over 140 pieces for the keyboard and some 60 additional works, Byrd's last publications included a series of three Masses written in the 1590s and a later collection of *Psalms, Songs and Sonnets* (1611) (see MASS).

Byrd was a master of keyboard music, producing many works for the virginal (a small harpsichord popular in the sixteenth century). He was one of the first English composers to write songs for a solo voice with instrumental accompaniment, believing that "there is no music of instruments . . . as good as that . . . made by the voice of Man." Byrd was popular among contemporaries as both a composer and a performer, and he had a great influence on later English and European composers. He died at his Essex estate on 4 July 1623.

Further Reading: John Harley, *William Byrd: A Gentleman of the Chapel Royal,* Brookfield, VT: Ashgate Publishers, 1997; David Wulstan, *Tudor Music,* Iowa City: University of Iowa Press, 1986.

C

Cadiz raid (1587)

Sir Francis DRAKE's 1587 attack on the harbor of Cadiz, SPAIN's most important Atlantic port, delayed the sailing of Spain's great ARMADA for more than a year. As the threat of Spanish invasion mounted in the late 1580s, Elizabeth's naval commanders began clamoring for permission to launch a preemptive strike at Spain. In April 1587, the queen finally allowed Drake to put to sea with a large fleet capable of meeting any Spanish force on its way to England and strong enough to descend on Spain and "distress the ships within the havens." This Drake did immediately upon reaching Cadiz on 19 April; the English fleet sailed straight into the harbor before the Spanish could respond. Defying shore batteries and fireships, Drake held the harbor for three days, destroying some 30 vessels and great quantities of provisions being collected for the Armada, including the casks and barrel staves needed to load supplies on the Spanish SHIPS. Having thus "singed the king of Spain's beard," Drake then seized the fort and anchorage of Sagres near Cape Vincent on the southwestern tip of Spanish-controlled Portugal. From there, Drake raided the Portuguese coast for almost two months, inflicting further damage on the reputation and financial credit of PHILIP II.

When disease and lack of supplies began to weaken his crews, Drake abandoned Sagres and sailed into the Atlantic to the AZORES, where he captured an East Indian treasure ship with a rich cargo. This capture was enough to secure a financial profit for the expedition, which had been organized on the usual joint-stock basis and thus needed to satisfy investors as well as accomplish military goals (see JOINT-STOCK COMPANY). Although Drake's raid severely disrupted Spain's preparations for the invasion of England, Philip was undaunted and began again the long process of gathering ships and supplies. Thus, the sailing of the Armada was only delayed by the Cadiz raid of 1587, not averted. However, the extra year bought by the raid gave England much-needed time to prepare her defenses and strengthen her fleet. *See also* CADIZ RAID (1596); NAVY; PRIVATEERING.

Further Reading: John Cummins, *Francis Drake*, New York: St. Martin's Press, 1995; Harry Kelsey, *Sir Francis Drake: The Queen's Pirate*, New Haven, CT: Yale University Press, 1998; Christopher Lloyd, *Sir Francis Drake*, Boston: Faber and Faber, 1979; John Sugden, *Sir Francis Drake*, New York: Simon and Schuster, 1990.

Cadiz raid (1596)

Just as the Cadiz raid of 1587 enhanced the fame of Sir Francis DRAKE, the Cadiz raid of 1596 made a popular hero of Robert DEVEREUX, Earl of Essex. In 1596, when word reached LONDON that PHILIP II of Spain was preparing a new naval expedition against England (see ARMADA), the PRIVY COUNCIL again authorized a preemptive strike to be launched against Cadiz, Spain's main Atlantic port (see CADIZ RAID [1587]). When the Spanish attacked the French port of CALAIS, a former English possession, Essex wished to participate in the city's defense. However, Elizabeth, who had never reconciled herself to the loss of Calais, would only assist in the town's defense if HENRI IV agreed to return it to England. While the two monarchs dickered, Calais fell to Spain, and the English returned to their original plan.

Operating under the joint command of Essex and Charles HOWARD, Lord Howard of Effingham, the largest and best-equipped English fleet of the war left Plymouth early in June 1596. The force numbered nearly 150 ships and over 6,000 soldiers. The fleet arrived off Cadiz in late June to find the port undefended and a rich Indies fleet anchored outside the harbor. While Essex attacked the town by sea, Howard landed his troops and completed the capture of the city. Although Cadiz was subjected to a thorough sacking, the Indies fleet was destroyed before the English could seize it. Essex gallantly ordered that all churches remain unharmed and that all women, children, and religious be allowed to depart in safety. The earl then declared himself governor of Cadiz and knighted 68 of his men.

On 1 July, the English burned the town and sailed for the AZORES where they expected to find a treasure fleet from AMERICA. But no treasure ships materialized, and the fleet returned to England with little to show for its efforts. The English people hailed Essex as a conqueror, but the queen chastised him for the venture's lack of profit. Despite its military success, the raid began the earl's downfall. The popularity Essex won at Cadiz soon brought him into conflict with Elizabeth, who would share her special place in the hearts of the English people with no man (see VIRGIN QUEEN).

Further Reading: Robert W. Kenny, *Elizabeth's Admiral: The Political Career of Charles Howard, Earl of Nottingham,* Baltimore: The Johns Hopkins Press, 1970; Robert Lacey, *Robert, Earl of Essex,* New York: Atheneum, 1971.

Calais

Calais, a French port town on the Strait of Dover opposite England, was captured by Edward III in 1347 after a year-long siege. Considered a part of England rather than a foreign territory under English rule, the town became England's first line of defense and a vital center of English continental trade. After the English were expelled from FRANCE in 1453, the town was all that remained of England's continental possessions, and as such became an important symbol of the country's past glory. After 1455, Calais became an important factor in English politics as a haven and point of strength for the Yorkist party during the WARS OF THE ROSES. The fall of the town to France in 1558, although of little military importance, was a severe blow to the confidence and popularity of MARY I's government. Mary lost the town as a consequence of her entry into SPAIN's war against France, which she joined merely to support her husband, PHILIP II of Spain.

Elizabeth reluctantly ceded the town to France in 1559 to untangle England from both the war and the Spanish alliance (see CATEAU-CAMBRÉSIS, TREATY OF). In 1560, Elizabeth's intense desire to regain Calais complicated the negotiations among England, France, and SCOTLAND that culminated in the Treaty of Edinburgh (see EDINBURGH, TREATY OF). When France refused to restore Calais to English control, Elizabeth grudgingly accepted an agreement to have French troops and influence removed from Scotland, a concession that ultimately proved far more important to England than the return of Calais because it led to peace between the realms of England and Scotland. Nonetheless, the queen's desire to regain Calais complicated Anglo-French relations for the rest of her reign. *See also* BRITTANY EXPEDITIONS; HAMPTON COURT, TREATY OF.

Further Reading: P. S. Crowson, *Tudor Foreign Policy,* New York: St. Martin's Press, 1973; Wallace T. MacCaffrey, *The Shaping of the Elizabethan Regime: English Politics, 1558–1572,* Princeton, NJ: Princeton University Press, 1968.

calendar

In the sixteenth century, Europe still used the Julian calendar, devised in the first century B.C. by Julius Caesar. Because the Julian year was slightly longer than the solar year, the calendar had, by the sixteenth century, accumulated a surplus of 10 days. The vernal equinox, which in the first centuries of the Christian era had fallen on 21 March, was in the sixteenth century falling on 11 March. To rectify this problem, Pope GREGORY XIII ordered the suppression of 10 days in 1582. To prevent a recurrence of the problem, the pope declared that, thereafter, all years ending in "00" would not be leap years (i.e., years that added one day to total 366) unless they were divisible by 400. Thus, 1600 was to be a leap year, but 1700, 1800, and 1900 were not; the Julian calendar had considered all four years to be leap years. This reformed calendar, called the Gregorian calendar, was readily adopted by most of Catholic Europe, but only gradually accepted by Protestant countries, such as England, which retained the Julian calendar until 1752.

England's refusal to accept Gregory's reforms meant that crossing to FRANCE moved Elizabethan travelers forward 10 calendar days, and returning to England moved them back 10 days. If you left England on 20 August 1590 and experienced an average four-hour crossing of the English Channel, you would land in France on 30 August 1590. England's rejection of the Gregorian calendar also meant that Elizabethans started their new year on a different day from Catholic Europe. The Gregorian calendar begins years on 1 January, the start of the Roman new year, but in England the year began on 25 March, the feast of the Annunciation (see HOLIDAYS). Thus, the months of January and February 1595 in France were January and February 1594 in England. On 25 March, the year 1595 began in England, and the Elizabethans remained in line with Catholic Europe until the next 1 January. Elizabethans sometimes addressed this difference by writing the date as, for instance, 21 January 1594/5. The day 1 January was called New Year's Day in Elizabethan England and gifts were exchanged. The day was officially observed on the ecclesiastical calendar as the feast of the Circumcision of Christ.

Further Reading: David Cressy, *Bonfires and Bells: National Memory and the Protestant Calendar in Elizabethan and Stuart England*, London: Weidenfeld and Nicolson, 1989.

Calvin, John (1509–1564)

John Calvin was a French theologian and reformer whose ideas heavily influenced the theology and governance of the Protestant churches in England, SCOTLAND, FRANCE, and the NETHERLANDS. Born in Picardy in northern France, Calvin studied theology in Paris and law in Orleans before returning to Paris in 1531 to study Greek and Hebrew. He converted to PROTESTANTISM by 1530, and by 1534 was a leading figure in the French Protestant community. Persecuted for his religious views, Calvin fled France and eventually settled in the Swiss town of Geneva, where he began to lecture and was accepted as a minister.

In his *Institutes of the Christian Religion* (1536), Calvin had described a system of ecclesiastical and civil government based upon the

law of God as revealed in the Bible. However, when Calvin attempted to establish this system in Geneva, he aroused opposition and was expelled from the city in 1538. He spent three years in Strasbourg, where he wrote several new theological treatises and thoroughly revised the *Institutes*. In 1541, continuing religious turmoil convinced the Genevan authorities to recall Calvin, who established a theocratic government that, by 1555, directed the affairs of the city and the social and individual lives of the citizens. Through such MARIAN EXILES as John KNOX, who visited Geneva in the 1550s, Calvin had a great influence on both the English and Scottish Churches. His ideas (see CALVINISM), such as the superiority of a presbyterian church government, also formed the core of Puritan thinking (see PRESBYTERIAN MOVEMENT).

The godly commonwealth that English PURITANS and SEPARATISTS established in North America in the seventeenth century was an extension of the godly government Calvin established in Geneva in the sixteenth century. By systematizing Protestant doctrine in his *Institutes,* and by setting a pattern for Protestant church government and discipline in his theocracy in Geneva, John Calvin gave the reformed Churches of Britain and Western Europe the strength, organization, and adaptability to both survive and to shape the social, political, and economic changes of the seventeenth century. Calvin died in Geneva in 1564. *See also* HUGUENOTS.

Further Reading: William J. Bouwsma, *John Calvin,* Oxford: Oxford University Press, 1988; Alister E. McGrath, *A Life of John Calvin,* Oxford: Basil Blackwell, 1990; T. H. L. Parker, *John Calvin*, Philadelphia: Westminster Press, 1975.

Calvinism

The term "Calvinism" refers to the teachings of the French reformer John CALVIN and to the doctrines and practices that arose out of those teachings in the Protestant Churches of England, SCOTLAND, FRANCE, and the NETHERLANDS. At the core of Calvinist thought are the doctrines of predestination and election, ideas that go back to the early Christian Church but which were given their fullest expression by Calvin in the sixteenth century. According to predestination, all humans are sinful and worthy of damnation, but God "elects" some (the Elect) to be saved by freely extending to them the gift of grace. In this life, the Elect have an inner assurance of their salvation that is outwardly displayed in the godliness of their conduct. Unlike Roman Catholic doctrine, Calvinism denies humans any possibility of achieving salvation through their own actions. Righteous behavior is a sign of God's election, not a way to earn heaven. By emphasizing thrift, industry, sobriety, and responsibility, the hallmarks of a life lived by the Elect, Calvinism had an encouraging effect on the new capitalist economies arising in the sixteenth and seventeenth centuries out of the feudal, agricultural society of medieval Europe.

Because they believed the leadership of godly elders was sanctioned by scripture, Calvinistic Churches favored a presbyterian form of governance (see PRESBYTERIAN MOVEMENT) and considered communion a mere commemoration of the Last Supper, thus repudiating papal authority, the MASS, and the Catholic doctrine of TRANSUBSTANTIATION. In the late 1550s, the returning MARIAN EXILES brought Calvinistic ideas and practices to England from Europe. Although the ANGLICAN SETTLEMENT of 1559 resulted in an essentially Calvinist Church, the Crown and PARLIAMENT rejected presbyterianism in favor of the royal supremacy and somewhat modified the Calvinist view of communion and other rituals (see SUPREMACY, ROYAL).

By attempting to adhere more closely to Calvinist practice, English PURITANS often found themselves at odds with the queen and the bishops through whom she governed the English Church. Their failure to convince Elizabeth and JAMES I to undertake further reform led many Puritans to immigrate to AMERICA in the seventeenth century. Thus, Calvinism was practiced in its purest form in Scotland, thanks to the work of John KNOX, and in New England, where the ideas and institutions of the Puritan colonists eventually exercised great influence on the religious, social, and economic development of the United States. *See also* HUGUENOTS.

Further Reading: Arthur Dakin, *Calvinism*, Philadelphia: Westminster Press, 1946; John Thomas McNeill, *The History and Character of Calvinism*, New York, Oxford University Press, 1954; T. H. L. Parker, *Calvin: An Introduction to His Thought*, London: Geoffrey Chapman, 1995.

Cambridge University. *See* UNIVERSITIES.

Camden, William (1551–1623)

William Camden, an Elizabethan antiquary (see ANTIQUARIANISM) and historian, wrote the first topographical survey of the British Isles and what is considered the best contemporary account of the reign of Elizabeth I. Born in LONDON, the son of a painter, Camden was educated at Oxford (see UNIVERSITIES), which he left in 1571 to begin traveling about Britain on a study of the history, archaeology, and topography of the island.

In 1575, Camden's research slowed when he became second master at Westminster School (see GRAMMAR SCHOOL). In 1577, the Flemish cartographer Abraham Ortelius, then visiting England, urged Camden to publish the material he had collected during his travels. This encouragement launched Camden on almost another decade of travel and research, which culminated in 1586 with the publication of *BRITANNIA,* a Latin historical/topographical survey of Britain dedicated to William CECIL, Lord Burghley. The work was well received, running to five editions by 1600 and appearing in an enlarged sixth edition in 1607. Philemon Holland published the first English translation in 1610. Along with William LAMBARDE's work on Kent, *Britannia* inspired a whole series of county topographical surveys, such as Richard CAREW's *SURVEY OF CORNWALL* (1602).

Although he became headmaster of Westminster School in 1593, Camden continued to publish, including a Greek grammar in 1597, a list of epitaphs found in Westminster Abbey in 1600, and a collection of early English chronicles in 1603. After abandoning the writing of a general history of England as too ambitious, Camden undertook in 1608 to write a history of the reign of Elizabeth I. The first part of the *ANNALES RERUM ANGLICARUM ET HIBERNICARUM REGNANTE ELIZABETHA,* which was published in 1615, carried the story of the reign through 1588. Although Camden completed the second part of the *Annales* in 1617, it was not published in London until 1627, four years after his death. The first complete English translation of the *Annales* appeared in 1630.

Further Reading: William Camden, *The History of the Most Renowned and Victorious Princess Elizabeth, Late Queen of England,* edited by Wallace T. MacCaffrey, Chicago: University of Chicago Press, 1970; Gordon J. Copley, ed., *Surrey and Sussex,* taken from the 1789 English edition of William Camden's *Britannia,* London: Hutchinson, 1977; F. J. Levy, *Tudor Historical Thought,* San Marino, CA: Huntington Library, 1967.

Campion, Edmund (1540–1581)

Edmund Campion, who with Robert PARSONS initiated the JESUIT MISSION to England, was one of the English Jesuits executed for TREASON by Elizabeth's government. The son of a LONDON bookseller, Campion took his master's degree at Oxford (see UNIVERSITIES) in 1564. A talented speaker, Campion, when only 13, delivered a speech of welcome to MARY I on her entry into London in 1553. In 1566, he welcomed Elizabeth to Oxford with a speech that won him the praise and patronage of Robert DUDLEY, Earl of Leicester. Ordained a deacon in the ANGLICAN CHURCH, Campion taught at Oxford until 1570, when his conversion to Catholicism forced him to leave the university (see CATHOLICISM, ENGLISH).

Sheltered for a time in IRELAND by Lord Deputy Sir Henry SIDNEY, the father of his friend Philip SIDNEY, Campion wrote a verse *History of Ireland* that he dedicated to Leicester. Campion also began a prose history of Ireland, which was later completed by his student Richard STANYHURST and was included in the first edition of HOLINSHED'S *CHRONICLES.* In 1571, he fled to William ALLEN's English Catholic college at Douai in the NETHERLANDS. He then entered the Jesuit order in Rome, accepting appointment to a Jesuit college in Prague. In 1580, Allen chose Campion and Robert Parsons to become the first Jesuit missionaries in England. They arrived in June and began immediately to travel about the country saying MASS and ministering to lapsed and practicing Catholics. Campion moved through the western and northern counties, finding refuge in Catholic GENTRY homes, while Parsons stayed nearer London. In June 1581, Campion caused a stir in Oxford with the distribution by confederates of his secretly printed pamphlet *Decem Rationes* (*Ten Reasons*), which attacked the Anglican Church.

With spies and informers everywhere posing as Catholics, Campion's arrest in Berkshire in July 1581 was only a matter of time. Tortured three times on the rack, Campion finally divulged the name of a few of his Catholic protectors. When brought to trial at Westminster in November, he was too weak from torture to enter a plea (see WESTMINSTER PALACE). Campion was convicted of treason, and on 1 December 1581 was dragged through the streets of London to his execution at Tyburn. Because Campion had professed loyalty to the queen and had shown no interest in the Jesuit political agenda, his execution, which was witnessed by a large crowd, was unpopular.

Further Reading: Bernard Basset, *The English Jesuits from Campion to Martindale,* New York: Burns and Oates, 1968; E. E. Reynolds, *Campion and Parsons: The Jesuit Mission of 1580–1,* London: Sheed and Ward, 1980; Evelyn Waugh, *Edmund Campion,* London: Cassell, 1987.

Carberry, Battle of

The Battle of Carberry, which was really nothing more than an armed negotiation, set the stage for ending the rule of Mary STUART, Queen of Scots, and for initiating the reign of her son, James VI (see JAMES I). In the months following the murder of her husband, Henry STUART, Lord Darnley, in February 1567, Queen Mary showed increasing signs of unfitness to rule. Her refusal to observe even the conventions of mourning, and her stunning marriage in May 1567 to James HEPBURN, Earl of Bothwell, who was widely suspected of involvement in the DARNLEY MURDER, drove many of even her strongest supporters into opposition. Because Mary had been mysteriously seized and carried off by Bothwell about a month before the sudden marriage, a group of 12 earls and 14 lords bound themselves in early June in an alliance known as the Confederate Lords. Tired of Mary's weak leadership and unwilling to be subservient to Bothwell, the Confederate Lords announced their intention of freeing the queen from the earl's control and punishing the murderers of Darnley.

On 15 June 1567, the army of Mary and Bothwell faced the army of the Confederate Lords at Carberry, about eight miles west of EDINBURGH. Bothwell challenged several of the lords to single combat, but they refused, and the queen's army gradually dispersed during the long, hot day as the two sides negotiated a settlement. By evening, Bothwell agreed to leave SCOTLAND under a safe-conduct in return for the Lords' promise to treat Mary honorably. In a state of mental collapse, Mary was brought back to Edinburgh where the citizens greeted her with cries of "Burn the whore!" and "Kill her!" Imprisoned in Lochleven Castle, the queen miscarried twins in early July. On 24 July, the Confederate Lords forced her to abdicate in favor of her year-old son, James, who was crowned five days later at Stirling. Mary's half brother, James STUART, Earl of Moray, who had prudently absented himself from the events surrounding his sister's abdication, returned to Edinburgh in August to become regent for the young king. The negotiations at Carberry in 1567 illustrated clearly how little faith in Mary's ability to rule remained among the members of Scotland's political elite.

Further Reading: J. D. Mackie, *A History of Scotland,* 2nd ed., New York: Dorset Press, 1985; Jenny Wormald, *Mary, Queen of Scots,* London: Collins and Brown, 1991.

Carew, George, Earl of Totnes
(1555–1629)

As lord president of Munster, George Carew was instrumental in defeating the Irish rebel leader Hugh O'NEILL, Earl of Tyrone, and ending the NINE YEARS WAR. Educated at Oxford (see UNIVERSITIES), Carew and his elder brother Peter joined their cousin Sir Peter CAREW in IRELAND in 1574. Upon Sir Peter's death in 1575, Carew volunteered to serve in the Irish army under Lord Deputy Sir Henry SIDNEY. When his brother was killed by Irish rebels in 1580, George Carew succeeded him as constable of Leighlin Castle. In 1583, George murdered an Irishman who had boasted of killing his brother. Although condemned for this rash act, Carew rehabilitated himself by 1586, when Lord Deputy Sir John PERROT knighted him and sent him to England to report on the state of Ireland. In this duty, Carew favorably impressed both Elizabeth and William CECIL, Lord Burghley, and was appointed Irish master of ordnance. In 1591, he obtained the same post for England through the influence of his distant relative, Sir Walter RALEIGH. He participated in the CADIZ RAID (1596) and set out on the ISLANDS

VOYAGE in 1597, but a storm damaged his vessel and forced him to return.

An ally of Sir Robert CECIL, Carew won appointment as lord president of Munster in 1600 as a counterbalance to the new lord deputy, Charles BLOUNT, Lord Mountjoy, who was a supporter of Cecil's rival, Robert DEVEREUX, Earl of Essex. Despite their political differences, Carew was one of Mountjoy's chief lieutenants in crushing Tyrone's rebels during the Nine Years War, and especially distinguished himself in the successful action against the Spanish troops at Kinsale (see KINSALE, BATTLE OF). Through a skillful combination of ruthlessness and DIPLOMACY, Carew restored order to Munster by Elizabeth's death in 1603.

Carew found immediate favor with JAMES I, who created him Baron Carew of Clopton House in 1605. The king later appointed him councilor for the colony of Virginia, governor of Guernsey, and a member of the PRIVY COUNCIL. In 1610, James sent Carew back to Ireland to report on the state of the island. In 1618, Carew pleaded unsuccessfully for the life of Raleigh. Created Earl of Totnes by Charles I in 1626, Carew died in London in 1629. A man of antiquarian interests (see ANTIQUARIANISM), and a friend of William CAMDEN and

Sir George Carew, a successful soldier in Elizabethan Ireland, was painted by an unknown artist about 1620. *By courtesy of the National Portrait Gallery, London.*

Sir Robert COTTON, Carew carefully collected and organized his family papers, thus creating what is today an important archive of information on Elizabethan Ireland. *See also* CAREW, RICHARD.

Further Reading: Steven G. Ellis, *Tudor Ireland,* London: Longman, 1985; J. A. Wagner, *The Devon Gentleman: The Life of Sir Peter Carew,* Hull, England: University of Hull Press, 1998.

Carew, Sir Peter (c. 1514–1575)

Sir Peter Carew was an important figure in the Elizabethan colonization and conquest of IRELAND. Born into a Devonshire GENTRY family, Carew proved a poor student, and in 1526 traveled to FRANCE as a page for one of his father's acquaintances. For six years, Carew lived by his wits in France and Italy, losing contact with his family and attaching himself to the service of various noblemen. About 1532, he returned to England, stunning his parents, who had given him up for dead. Fluent in French and Italian, and full of current knowledge about continental fashions and military practices, Carew found a ready reception at the English COURT. HENRY VIII used him in various military and diplomatic capacities, and the governments of EDWARD VI employed Carew in Devon and Cornwall to suppress the 1549 Prayer Book Rebellion (which arose out of opposition to the First *BOOK OF COMMON PRAYER*) and to institute the king's Protestant policies.

In 1553, Carew, unhappy with MARY I's choice of a Catholic, Spanish consort, joined the conspiracy that led to WYATT'S REBELLION, an unsuccessful attempt to replace Mary with her half sister Elizabeth. Carew spent two years in European exile until captured in the NETHERLANDS in May 1556 by agents of Mary's husband, Prince Philip (see PHILIP II). After several months' confinement in the TOWER OF LONDON, Carew was pardoned, perhaps in part for informing on other antigovernment conspirators. For the first two years of her reign, Elizabeth employed Carew on various assignments, but after 1560 he withdrew from court, perhaps for financial reasons.

In 1568, he turned his attention to regaining at law various long-lost family estates in Ireland. With the queen's permission, Carew traveled to Ireland to institute legal proceedings that recovered a portion of these lands, but

severely disaffected the former landholders and triggered an uprising (see BUTLER WARS). The queen ordered Carew to desist, and when he came to England to plead his case, she refused him permission to return to Ireland. He spent his last years seeking to revive his Irish causes and arguing that peace and stability in Ireland required more English settlers, stronger military efforts, and more repressive government—views that gained greater favor in government circles after his death. Carew died in Ireland in November 1575. *See also* CAREW, GEORGE, EARL OF TOTNES; CAREW, RICHARD; HOOKER, JOHN; PLANTATIONS, IRISH.

Further Reading: J. A. Wagner, *The Devon Gentleman: The Life of Sir Peter Carew,* Hull, England: University of Hull Press, 1998.

Carew, Richard (1555–1620)

Richard Carew was a well-respected Elizabethan scholar and antiquary (see ANTIQUARIANISM). A distant cousin of Sir Peter CAREW; George CAREW, Earl of Totnes; and the seventeenth-century poet Thomas Carew, Richard Carew was born at Antony, his family's estate in Cornwall. He was educated at Oxford (see UNIVERSITIES), where he befriended William CAMDEN and held his own in a public disputation with Philip SIDNEY. In 1577, he returned to Cornwall, where he busied himself with learning languages and studying the natural and human history of the county.

He was appointed a justice of the peace in 1581 and sheriff of Cornwall in 1582. Carew served in PARLIAMENT for the town of Saltash in 1584 and for the town of St. Michael's in 1597. He was also deputy lieutenant of Cornwall under Sir Walter RALEIGH, whose son Carew Raleigh was Richard Carew's godson. Simply through reading, Carew taught himself French, German, Spanish, Italian, and Greek. He joined the Society of Antiquaries in 1589 and began a stimulating correspondence on various topics with Camden and other members. In 1605, Camden published one of Carew's letters, entitled *Excellency of the English Tongue;* this letter makes reference to William SHAKESPEARE as the equal of the Roman poet Catullus. Carew also translated various works from other European languages and produced a fantasy tale in verse entitled *A Herring's Tail* (1598).

Carew's most important work was his SURVEY OF CORNWALL (1602), a detailed study of his home county that he dedicated to Sir Walter Raleigh (see also BRITANNIA). The *Survey* was widely read and well received, but Carew's plans for a second edition were spoiled by his declining health. Carew died at Antony in 1620. His son, also named Richard, wrote an account of his father's life, and later published a work entitled *True and Ready Way to Learn the Latin Tongue,* which is often erroneously attributed to the elder Richard Carew.

Further Reading: F. E. Halliday, ed., *Richard Carew of Antony: The Survey of Cornwall,* London: Andrew Melrose, 1953.

Carey, George, Lord Hunsdon

(1547–1603)

George Carey was lord chamberlain of England and patron of the CHAMBERLAIN'S MEN, an acting company that included William SHAKESPEARE and Richard BURBAGE among its members. As a grandson of the queen's aunt, Mary Boleyn (see BOLEYN FAMILY), Carey was a cousin of Elizabeth I (see the genealogical chart in Appendix 1: "Howard Family in the Sixteenth Century–Elizabeth I's Maternal Relatives"). Educated at Cambridge (see UNIVERSITIES), Carey served under Thomas RADCLIFFE, Earl of Sussex, in campaigns against the NORTHERN REBELLION and on the Scottish border between 1569 and 1571. Knighted by Sussex in 1570, Carey became constable of Bamburgh Castle in 1574 and captain-general of the Isle of Wight in 1582. In the latter post, he was responsible for strengthening the island's defenses and for securing parliamentary representation for the borough of Newtown (see BOROUGHS), a service that earned him the right to nominate one of the town's MPs (i.e., members of Parliament) for life. Carey himself sat for Hertfordshire in the PARLIAMENT of 1571, and for Hampshire in 1584–85, 1586–87, 1589, and 1593. The queen sent him on diplomatic missions to SCOTLAND in 1582 and 1589 (see DIPLOMACY).

Carey succeeded his father, Henry CAREY, as second Lord Hunsdon in 1596, and as lord chamberlain (see OFFICERS OF STATE) in 1597. The chamberlainship gave Hunsdon the patronage of the Chamberlain's Men, an acting troupe whose members moved themselves, in 1598, to the new GLOBE THEATRE in Southwark. Hunsdon often presented the company in performances at COURT or at his residence at Hunsdon House. The company's last appearance before Elizabeth was on 2 February 1603, a few weeks before her death. Hunsdon was present at RICHMOND PALACE when the queen died on 24 March, and he assisted his younger brother, Robert Carey, in leaving the guarded palace to ride for Scotland to inform James VI (see JAMES I) of his accession. Hunsdon died a few months later, shortly after the Chamberlain's Men came under royal patronage and became the King's Men.

Further Reading: Paul Johnson, *Elizabeth I,* New York: Holt, Rinehart and Winston, 1974; Alan Palmer and Veronica Palmer, *Who's Who in Shakespeare's England,* New York: St. Martin's Press, 1981.

Carey, Henry, Lord Hunsdon

(1524–1596)

Henry Carey, first Lord Hunsdon, was lord chamberlain of England and cousin to Elizabeth I (see the genealogical chart in Appendix 1: "Howard Family in the Sixteenth Century—Elizabeth I's Maternal Relatives"). As the son of Elizabeth's aunt, Mary Boleyn (see BOLEYN FAMILY), Henry Carey was the queen's first cousin, although COURT rumors claimed he was the queen's half brother because his true father was HENRY VIII, who had been Mary Boleyn's lover before her marriage to William Carey. Elizabeth showed Carey immediate favor upon her accession in 1558, knighting him and raising him to the PEERAGE as Lord Hunsdon. By 1561, Hunsdon was a knight of the Garter and a member of the PRIVY COUNCIL. He became an important figure in Anglo-Scottish relations in 1568 when Elizabeth made him governor of Berwick. The post gave him partial responsibility for border defenses and sent him on diplomatic missions into SCOTLAND (see DIPLOMACY), but also involved him in a dispute with the queen over the untimely payment of his salary and official expenses.

Hunsdon took the field against the NORTHERN REBELLION in 1569, defeating the rebel earls in battle. Because Elizabeth had appointed him lord chamberlain (see OFFICERS OF STATE) in 1583, the company of actors that came under his patronage in the mid-1590s became known as the CHAMBERLAIN'S MEN, a troupe that included Richard BURBAGE and

William SHAKESPEARE. A commissioner at the 1586 trial of Mary STUART, Queen of Scots, Hunsdon in 1587 was given the unenviable assignment of explaining to James VI of Scotland (see JAMES I) why his mother's execution was necessary. Elizabeth next named Hunsdon lord warden of the Scottish marches (i.e., borders) and made him one of the commanders at the ARMY's main camp at Tilbury (see TILBURY SPEECH) during the ARMADA crisis of 1588. Hunsdon died in 1596 at Somerset House in LONDON, a royal residence the queen allowed him to use.

Further Reading: J. E. Neale, *Queen Elizabeth I,* Chicago: Academy Chicago Publishers, 1992; Alan Palmer and Veronica Palmer, *Who's Who in Shakespeare's England,* New York: St. Martin's Press, 1981.

Cartwright, Thomas (1535–1603)

Thomas Cartwright was the foremost Puritan advocate of presbyterianism in Elizabethan England (see PRESBYTERIAN MOVEMENT; PURITANS). The son of a Hertfordshire yeoman (i.e., small farmer), Cartwright was educated at Cambridge (see UNIVERSITIES), where he became a convinced Protestant. He spent the reign of the Catholic queen, MARY I, practicing law, but returned to Cambridge after the accession of Elizabeth in 1558 to teach, becoming Lady Margaret Professor of Divinity at St. John's College in 1569. Cartwright's lectures were tremendously popular, but his vocal opposition to a system of church government based on bishops, and his support for the presbyterian system of governance based on a hierarchy of representative church assemblies, brought him into conflict with the university administration.

Cartwright was convinced that a presbyterian system of church government was laid down in the Bible, and that the espiscopal system enjoined by PARLIAMENT and demanded by the queen was ungodly. Deprived of his professorship and forced to leave England, Cartwright departed in 1570 for Geneva, where John CALVIN had instituted a presbyterian church. Agreeing with Calvin that ministers should be chosen by the people, and that church members should be disciplined in their local congregations by the pastor and a popularly elected council of elders, Cartwright returned to England in 1572 to involve himself briefly in the ADMONITION CONTROVERSY,

a pamphlet war between English presbyterians and Anglican bishops and ministers.

Cartwright's activities soon forced him to flee again to Europe, where he spent some years in the NETHERLANDS as minister to the English congregation at Antwerp. He returned to England in 1585 to become master of an almshouse founded by the royal favorite, Robert DUDLEY, Earl of Leicester, a patron of Puritans. Cartwright soon renewed his attacks on the ANGLICAN CHURCH, and in 1590, two years after Leicester's death, Cartwright was arrested and imprisoned. Released in 1592, Cartwright spent his last years establishing Puritanism in the English Channel Islands. He died in December 1603.

Further Reading: Patrick Collinson, *The Elizabethan Puritan Movement,* Oxford: Clarendon Press, 1990; A. F. Scott Pearson, *Thomas Cartwright and Elizabethan Puritanism, 1535–1603,* Gloucester, MA: P. Smith, 1966.

casket letters

On 20 June 1567, George Dalgleish, servant to James HEPBURN, Earl of Bothwell, third husband of Mary STUART, Queen of Scots, surrendered a silver casket of documents to the Protestant lords then opposing Mary. The casket (or box) contained eight letters from Mary to Bothwell, a love sonnet written by the queen, and two contracts of MARRIAGE between the queen and the earl. Mary's opponents revealed the casket and its contents in 1568 to prove that the queen had plotted with Bothwell to murder her second husband Henry STUART, Lord Darnley. Led by James STUART, Earl of Moray, the regency government that had supplanted Mary in 1567 sought to prevent her return to SCOTLAND by persuading Elizabeth to keep Mary in captivity in England.

If genuine, the letters depicted a woman completely under the domination of Bothwell and fully involved in a conspiracy to murder Darnley. The letters exist today only in copies. The original documents and the casket disappeared in 1584 while in the possession of Mary's son, James VI (see JAMES I); no one has seen them since. Historians have long debated the authenticity of the letters, but most current opinion accepts them as genuine. The reluctance the regency government exhibited in producing the letters makes forgery by Mary's opponents unlikely—Moray revealed the documents only when Elizabeth demanded proof of Mary's complicity in the DARNLY MURDER, more than a year after the casket came into Moray's possession. Elizabeth did not publish the letters until after she learned of Mary's involvement in the RIDOLFI PLOT of 1571, which aimed, in part, at the murder of Elizabeth herself. Also, the speed with which James VI managed to "lose" the letters seems to indicate that he believed them to be genuine, and his mother's involvement in murder to be proved by them.

Further Reading: M. H. Armstrong Davison, *The Casket Letters,* London: Vision, 1965; Jenny Wormald, *Mary, Queen of Scots,* London: Collins and Brown, 1991.

Cateau-Cambrésis, Treaty of

Concluded in April 1559 during the first months of Elizabeth's reign, the Treaty of Cateau-Cambrésis made peace between FRANCE and SPAIN and ended English control of CALAIS. By allying herself with her husband, PHILIP II of Spain (see HABSBURG FAMILY), MARY I had involved England in a war that led in January 1558 to the French capture of Calais. By Elizabeth's accession in the following November, French, Spanish, and English commissioners had begun negotiations to end the war.

Bankrupt and war-weary, both Spain and France were eager to make peace; they quickly agreed to restore prewar conditions by mutually withdrawing from recently conquered territories. The great sticking point was Calais, which Elizabeth was determined to regain and France was equally determined to keep. Although Calais was expensive to maintain and of little military benefit, the town's symbolic importance was enormous. An English possession since 1347, Calais was the last remnant of England's once extensive European empire. To lose it was devastating to English pride and honor. Although Philip was bound, as an ally, to support England's demand for Calais, his need for peace eventually led him to abandon the issue. Without Spain's support, Elizabeth was forced to accept a face-saving scheme. The final treaty ceded Calais to France for eight years, at the end of which time it was to return to England. However, the return was so hedged with restrictions and conditions, including England's good behavior toward SCOTLAND, France's ally, that it was clear Calais would re-

main France's possession.

Elizabeth never reconciled herself to the loss of Calais; the LE HAVRE EXPEDITION in 1563 and negotiations with the Dutch and with HENRI IV of France in the 1590s were all complicated by Elizabeth's desire to regain the town. Besides the loss of Calais, the Treaty of Cateau-Cambrésis had an unexpected effect on Elizabethan foreign policy. HENRI II of France was killed in an accident that occurred during the treaty celebrations. His death made his daughter-in-law, Mary STUART, Queen of Scots—Elizabeth's presumed heir—the new queen of France, bringing to a crisis the issue of French influence in Scotland and Elizabeth's lack of an acceptable Protestant successor.

Further Reading: P. S. Crowson, *Tudor Foreign Policy,* New York: St. Martin's Press, 1973; G. R. Elton, *England under the Tudors,* 3rd ed., London: Routledge, 1991.

catechism

A catechism is a summary of church doctrine and practice that is used by a particular Christian denomination as its official manual of religious instruction. Catechisms often take the form of a series of questions and answers. The catechism of the ANGLICAN CHURCH was written by Alexander Nowell, the dean of St. Paul's Cathedral in LONDON (see illustrations for GRAMMAR SCHOOL; NOWELL, ALEXANDER). In 1562, CONVOCATION authorized Nowell, author of the first English Protestant catechism issued under EDWARD VI in 1549, to prepare a new catechism for the new English Protestant Church that emerged from the ANGLICAN SETTLEMENT of 1559. Like other Calvinist Churches in Europe, the Anglican Church recognized the need to create a clear and formal statement of its beliefs and practices to instruct English children and to clearly distinguish itself from Roman Catholicism (see CATHOLICISM, ENGLISH).

Issued in 1570 and later distributed in an abridged version, Nowell's catechism presented an Anglican statement of faith, described Anglican practice, explained Anglican sacraments, and outlined Anglican doctrine. As a former MARIAN EXILE, Nowell heavily emphasized John CALVIN's doctrines of predestination and election (see CALVINISM) and repudiated such Roman Catholic doctrines and practices as

TRANSUBSTANTIATION and the use of images in worship. In terms of church governance, Nowell was a strong supporter of the royal supremacy (see SUPREMACY, ROYAL), and his catechism demanded that Anglicans give strict obedience to civil authority, a feature that won the catechism the warm support of the government and the Anglican Church hierarchy. Nowell's catechism remained in use until the English Revolution of the 1650s.

Further Reading: Patrick Collinson, *The Elizabethan Puritan Movement,* Oxford: Clarendon Press, 1990.

Catherine of Aragon (1485–1536)

Catherine was the first wife of HENRY VIII and the mother of MARY I. The youngest child of Ferdinand and Isabella of SPAIN, Catherine, then 15, arrived in England in October 1501 to marry Prince Arthur, eldest son of HENRY VII. When Arthur died in April 1502, Catherine remained in England while her parents negotiated her marriage to Arthur's younger brother, Prince Henry. Although both parties agreed that the marriage between Catherine and Arthur had not been consummated (i.e., completed by sexual intercourse) and was thus not fully valid, the Spanish insisted on a papal dispensation allowing Catherine to marry her brother-in-law, a match otherwise prohibited by Catholic Church law. In 1504, Catherine's mother died and her father's political position weakened, leading Henry VII to delay his son's MARRIAGE and cut off Catherine's financial support. When her father also refused support, Catherine was left alone and destitute in a foreign country. She refused to return home, persevering until 1509 when the death of Henry VII and the changing foreign policy needs of the realm led to her marriage to the new king, Henry VIII.

The couple's marriage seems to have been happy, marred only by the failure of their children to live. Although pregnant at least six times between 1509 and 1518, Catherine bore only one child who survived infancy: Mary, born in 1516. By the mid-1520s, Henry, concluding that he would have no male heir with Catherine, sought a new marriage with Anne BOLEYN, a court lady who had attracted his attention. Catherine vigorously defended her marriage against the king's assertion that it was invalid; that she was only his brother's widow.

At a session of the special court convened in 1529 to consider the matter, Catherine dropped to her knees before the king and begged him to say whether or not she had been a virgin when she married him—Henry refused to answer. The king banished Catherine from COURT in 1531, and she never saw him or her daughter again.

In 1533, the English Church, newly separated from the Church of Rome, pronounced Catherine's marriage invalid and her daughter, Mary, illegitimate. The king's new wife, Anne Boleyn, was declared the true queen by PARLIAMENT, and Anne's daughter, Elizabeth, was declared Henry's heir. Catherine never accepted this verdict and, despite much ill treatment, continued to call herself queen until her death in January 1536.

Further Reading: Garrett Mattingly, *Catherine of Aragon,* Boston: Little, Brown, 1941.

Catholic League

The Catholic League was a sixteenth-century union of French Catholics who opposed the extension of civil rights and religious freedom to French HUGUENOTS. In the 1560s, as civil war between Catholics and Huguenots weakened the authority of the French Crown, Catholic nobles and churchmen in France formed small, local unions of believers to defend the Catholic faith. In 1576, after the government made political concessions to the Huguenots, these local groups united to form a national Catholic League under the leadership of the GUISE FAMILY.

Suspicious of King HENRI III, who seemed willing to compromise with Huguenots, the League looked to PHILIP II of SPAIN for financial and military assistance. In 1577, Henri suppressed the League by declaring himself its leader and then decreeing its dissolution. The League was revived in 1585, a year after the death of Henri's brother, Francis VALOIS, Duke of Alençon, made a Protestant succession likely. The new Catholic League centered not on the rural followers of wealthy nobles and bishops, but on the middle-class professionals, artisans, and clergymen of Paris and the larger towns. Denouncing the king for his tolerance of Huguenots, the new Catholic League replaced royal officers with League officials in municipal governments throughout FRANCE. In 1588, during the "Day of the Barricades," a League-inspired mob in heavily Catholic Paris drove Henri out of the city. After the assassination of the Duke of Guise in 1588, Paris and other towns renounced their allegiance to the Crown and established revolutionary governments. In Paris, a committee called The Sixteen seized power and created a Committee of Public Safety to arrest and execute traitors and Huguenots.

Frightened by the revolutionary fervor of their lower-class colleagues, most aristocratic members of the League accepted the Huguenot leader, Henri of Navarre, as King HENRI IV in 1589. However, civil war continued to rage between the Catholic League and the king until 1593, when Henri converted to Catholicism. In 1594, Henri finally entered Paris, and the power of the League began to decline as the influence of the monarchy revived. By prolonging the French wars of religion, the activity of the League isolated France and left Elizabethan England as the main counterbalance to Spain after 1560. Also, League resistance to Henri IV brought English troops to France on the king's side after 1589 (see BRITTANY EXPEDITIONS). *See also* VALOIS FAMILY.

Further Reading: Frederic J. Baumgartner, *France in the Sixteenth Century,* New York: St. Martin's Press, 1995; R. J. Knecht, *The French Wars of Religion, 1559–1598,* 2nd ed., London: Longman, 1996.

Catholicism, English

During the reign of Elizabeth, the number of English Roman Catholics—those English men and women giving allegiance to the pope—declined from perhaps a majority of the POPULATION to a small, despised, and politically restricted minority centered largely around a few noble and gentle families (see GENTRY). At her accession in 1558, Elizabeth inherited a Roman Catholic Church from her sister MARY I. With the ANGLICAN SETTLEMENT of 1559, Elizabeth broke with the Church of Rome and made herself the head of a moderately Protestant, anti-papal Church. Over the next 40 years, the Elizabethan government was highly successful in associating anti-Catholicism with patriotism, and in associating support of Roman Catholicism with TREASON against England.

As popes such as PIUS V, foreign Catholic princes such as PHILIP II of SPAIN, and English Catholic exiles such as William ALLEN and Robert PARSONS (see JESUIT MISSION) launched ever more sophisticated and dangerous plots to dethrone Elizabeth and restore England's state religion to Catholicism (see POLE CONSPIRACY; RIDOLFI PLOT; BABINGTON PLOT), the Elizabethan government gained further opportunities to identify English Catholics as spies and traitors and to convince PARLIAMENT and the English people to support further repression of their Catholic countrymen (see PENAL LAWS; RECUSANTS). Anti-Catholicism was also generated by John FOXE's widely read "BOOK OF MARTYRS," which reminded people of the persecution Mary I's Catholic government conducted against its own people (see MARIAN MARTYRS), and by the 1570 bull, *REGNANS IN EXCELSIS,* whereby the pope claimed the right to decide who held the English throne by depriving Elizabeth of her royal title and absolving her subjects of their allegiance to her.

As the Spanish ARMADA entered the English Channel in 1588 to overthrow Elizabeth and the ANGLICAN CHURCH, the connection between patriotism and PROTESTANTISM became dramatically clear, and most English Catholics supported the monarch of their country over the leadership of their Church. The work of Catholic SEMINARY PRIESTS, who generally avoided political activity, and the organization of the English Catholic community around the country households of Catholic gentlemen of some wealth and political influence, allowed English Catholicism to survive the Elizabethan persecution and enter the seventeenth century as a small but stable community, professing its loyalty to the English Crown and eschewing political activity.

Further Reading: John Bossy, *The English Catholic Community 1570–1850,* New York: Oxford University Press, 1976; David Lunn, *The Catholic Elizabethans,* Bath, England, Downside Abbey, 1998; Adrian Morey, *The Catholic Subjects of Elizabeth I,* Totowa, NJ: Rowman and Littlefield, 1978; Arnold Pritchard, *Catholic Loyalism in Elizabethan England,* Chapel Hill: University of North Carolina Press, 1979.

cautionary towns

The small Dutch ports of Flushing and Brill, which came to be known as the "cautionary towns," played important roles in the development of the NETHERLANDS REVOLT and in the formation of Elizabethan foreign policy.

Now known as Vlissingen and Brielle, sixteenth-century Flushing and Brill were located about 45 miles apart on the northeastern coast of the Spanish Netherlands (see Maps, "Netherlands, 1590s"). In April 1572, the towns became the focus of the faltering Dutch rebellion against PHILIP II of SPAIN.

On 1 April 1572, the SEA BEGGARS, an irregular naval force created by the Dutch rebels in 1568, fell suddenly upon the undefended town of Brill, where they seized the port, sacked Catholic churches, and drove out Catholic residents. Deprived of any safe port since July 1568, the beggars had taken to the open seas where they preyed upon the shipping of neutral states. Elizabeth gave them safe haven in English ports, but their continued attacks on merchant vessels forced the queen to order their expulsion on 1 March 1572. The beggars' capture of Brill one month later, and their occupation, on 22 April, of Flushing, where the citizens expelled the Spanish garrison and welcomed the beggars as protectors, gave the rebel naval force safe ports from which to operate, and revived the Netherlands Revolt by establishing beachheads from which it could expand.

In 1585, the ports again linked England and the Netherlands by becoming, as the so-called cautionary towns, the security guaranteeing the Treaty of Nonsuch, a political and military alliance between England and the United Provinces (see NONSUCH, TREATY OF). In return for English troops and money, the Dutch surrendered Flushing and Brill to English control as a gesture of good faith. In 1598, the two countries restructured the Treaty of Nonsuch, leaving the towns in English hands as pledges for the £800,000 the Dutch owed the queen. After Elizabeth's death in 1603, JAMES I made peace with Spain, but his efforts to settle the Dutch debt and withdraw from the cautionary towns were unavailing until 1616, when the English returned the towns to Dutch control for a payment of only some £200,000 of the original debt.

Further Reading: Geoffrey Parker, *The Dutch Revolt,* Ithaca, NY: Cornell University Press, 1977.

Cavendish, Thomas (1560–1592)

Thomas Cavendish, the second Englishman to circumnavigate the globe, was a famous Elizabethan seaman, adventurer, and pirate. Born in Suffolk, Cavendish inherited a substantial fortune but squandered it by riotous living and courtly extravagance. He took to a career of piracy, and in 1585 attached his ship to the colonizing expedition sent to North America by Walter RALEIGH (see ROANOKE COLONY [1585]). Upon returning from this voyage, Cavendish began planning for an expedition to duplicate Sir Francis DRAKE's famous circumnavigation of 1577–80 (see DRAKE'S CIRCUMNAVIGATION).

Leaving Plymouth in July 1586 with his flagship *Desire* and two other vessels, Cavendish sailed down the African coast and then crossed the Atlantic to Brazil. The fleet took 49 days to negotiate the Straits of Magellan, entering the Pacific on 24 February 1587. Cavendish attacked Spanish shipping and ports on the South American coast, capturing some rich prizes but also suffering many casualties and losing one ship. He lost another vessel when the crew mutinied over the division of plunder and sailed off on their own, never to be seen again. Cavendish continued across the Pacific in the *Desire,* reaching the Philippines in January 1588 and rounding the Cape of Good Hope by June. He sailed into Plymouth on 9 September 1588, barely a month after the defeat of the Spanish ARMADA. Only 28 years of age, Cavendish was the object of wide popular acclaim, celebrated in numerous songs and ballads. He was also warmly received at COURT by the queen and was significantly enriched by the proceeds of his adventure.

Eager to undertake another voyage, Cavendish used the prospect of finding a NORTHWEST PASSAGE from the Pacific side to persuade the explorer John DAVIS to join him on an expedition to Asia. A five-ship fleet left England in August 1591 but was scattered by severe storms in the Straits of Magellan in January 1592. Davis failed to run the Straits and returned to England. Cavendish also sailed back into the Atlantic, where he encountered contrary winds and an attack by the Portuguese. He never returned home, dying at sea in May 1592.

Further Reading: Philip Edwards, ed., *Last Voyages: Cavendish, Hudson, Ralegh, the Original Narratives,* Oxford: Clarendon Press, 1988; James A. Williamson, *The Age of Drake,* New York: World Publishing, 1965.

Cecil, Mildred, Lady Burghley
(1526–1589)

The wife of William CECIL, Lord Burghley, who was principal secretary and lord treasurer under Elizabeth I, Mildred Cecil was the eldest daughter of Sir Anthony COOKE, the tutor to EDWARD VI. The Cooke sisters were known as the most learned women in England, thanks to the excellent education given to them by their father (see BACON, ANN; RUSSELL, ELIZABETH).

As a young woman, Mildred undertook a number of scholarly works, including a translation from the Greek of the writings of St. Basil the Great. When her father was appointed tutor to Prince Edward in 1546, Mildred accompanied him to COURT, where she met William Cecil, who was then a widower with a young son. Sharing a love of learning and a growing PROTESTANTISM, Cecil and Mildred Cooke were married on 25 December 1546. The connection with the daughter of Sir Anthony Cooke, an increasingly important figure at court after 1547, perhaps helped to start Cecil's political career by winning him an introduction to Edward SEYMOUR, Duke of Somerset, then lord protector for the 10-year-old Edward VI. After losing several children in infancy, the Cecils had two daughters, Anne (who became the wife of Edward de VERE, Earl of Oxford) and Elizabeth, and one son, Robert CECIL, who succeeded his father as Elizabeth's secretary of state in the 1590s.

Mildred, who helped to educate her own children, as well as many sons of noblemen whom her husband brought into the household, became Lady Burghley upon her husband's elevation to the PEERAGE in 1572. A patron of St. John's College, Cambridge (see UNIVERSITIES), Lady Burghley also gave generous anonymous gifts for the upkeep of poor prisoners in LONDON. On her death in 1589, her husband published a written tribute to her scholarship. She was buried in Westminster Abbey.

Further Reading: B. W. Beckingsale, *Burghley: Tudor Statesman,* New York: St. Martin's Press, 1967.

Cecil, Sir Robert (1563–1612)

Robert Cecil, the son of Elizabeth's great minister William CECIL, Lord Burghley, was the queen's foremost advisor and minister of state in the last decade of her reign (see also CECIL, MILDRED). Cecil attended St. John's College, Cambridge (see UNIVERSITIES), and traveled for a time in FRANCE, studying briefly at the Sorbonne. From 1584, he served in PARLIAMENT and on various diplomatic missions, including an unsuccessful 1588 mission to the NETHERLANDS to negotiate peace with SPAIN (see DIPLOMACY). He was knighted and promoted to the PRIVY COUNCIL in 1591, and he became secretary of state in 1596, although he had been performing the duties of the office for several years before his appointment.

Cecil was a hard-working administrator like his father, who had groomed him for high office, but, being a small man and round-shouldered, he was generally less respected than his father, and less trusted by Elizabeth. He was a particular opponent of Robert DEVEREUX, Earl of Essex, who vied with Cecil for paramount influence with the queen both at COURT and in council. Although the queen was more attracted to the brilliant courtier Essex, Cecil won the contest by maneuvering

Robert Cecil, shown here in a 1602 portrait by John de Critz the elder, succeeded his father, William Cecil, as Elizabeth I's chief minister in the 1590s. *By courtesy of the National Portrait Gallery, London.*

Essex into taking the difficult lord deputyship of IRELAND, where Essex's ill-considered actions cost him the favor of the queen (see ESSEX'S REBELLION).

After Essex's execution in February 1601 for attempting a coup to restore his position at court, Cecil was indisputably the chief minister of the Crown. As such, he wrestled with the intractable problems of Ireland and royal finance, the Crown being unable to subdue the one because of deficiencies in the other. On the issue of finance, Cecil brought Elizabeth into serious conflict with Parliament by his vigorous exploitation of MONOPOLIES to increase royal revenues (see REVENUE, ROYAL). Never his father's equal in managing Parliament, Cecil and the queen had to bow to parliamentary pressure and promise to reform monopolies. Cecil was instrumental in securing the peaceful accession of JAMES I in 1603, having conducted a secret correspondence with James for some time before the queen's death. The new king retained Cecil as chief minister and created him Earl of Salisbury in 1605. Cecil died in 1612.

Further Reading: Algernon Cecil, *A Life of Robert Cecil, First Earl of Salisbury,* Westport, CT: Greenwood Press, 1971; P. M. Handover, *The Second Cecil,* London: Eyre and Spottiswoode, 1959; Alan Haynes, *Robert Cecil, Earl of Salisbury,* London: P. Owen, 1989.

Cecil, William, Lord Burghley

(1520–1598)

William Cecil, the son of a Northamptonshire GENTRY family, was Elizabeth's closest and most trusted advisor. As a young man, Cecil served in HENRY VIII's household; he was educated at Cambridge (see UNIVERSITIES) and at Gray's Inn (see INNS OF COURT). In 1544, Cecil married a daughter of Sir Anthony COOKE (see CECIL, MILDRED); Cooke may have introduced Cecil to Edward SEYMOUR, Duke of Somerset, EDWARD VI's uncle and lord protector. Cecil entered Somerset's service in 1547, becoming secretary to the duke in 1549. Cecil was imprisoned in the TOWER OF LONDON after the duke's fall, but was pardoned and named secretary of state and privy councilor in 1550 by John DUDLEY, future Duke of Northumberland and supplanter of Somerset as head of Edward's government. Although also knighted by Northumberland, Cecil did not support the duke's plan to put

Jane GREY on the throne and was among the first councilors to join Princess Mary (see MARY I) in July 1553 (see NORTHUMBERLAND'S COUP).

Mary did not re-employ Cecil as secretary, distrusting his PROTESTANTISM, but he continued to sit in PARLIAMENT and to serve the Marian government in various minor ways. Elizabeth named Cecil her principal secretary within days of her accession in November 1558. Holding a unique position of trust with Elizabeth, Cecil acted during her reign as a moderate counterbalance in matters of religion and foreign affairs to the more extreme Protestant and warlike policies of the royal favorite, Robert DUDLEY, Earl of Leicester (see FAVORITES). Cecil served the queen faithfully and well in many capacities—he coordinated the deliberations of the PRIVY COUNCIL, supervised the EXCHEQUER, managed Parliament, and advised on foreign policy. He believed the queen should marry as soon as possible to produce a clear Protestant heir and favored sterner measures against Mary STUART, Queen of Scots, but he had to endure the queen's procrastina-

This 1572 portrait of William Cecil, Lord Burghley, Elizabeth I's long-time minister of state, shows him holding the staff of office of the Lord Treasurer. *By courtesy of the National Portrait Gallery, London.*

tion on these and many other issues. In 1572, Elizabeth raised Cecil to the PEERAGE as Lord Burghley and named him lord high treasurer. He continued to serve the queen until his death in 1598, and was succeeded as the queen's chief minister, if not fully in the queen's trust, by his younger son, Robert CECIL.

Further Reading: B. W. Beckingsale, *Burghley, Tudor Statesman*, New York: St. Martin's Press, 1967; Conyers Read, *Lord Burghley and Queen Elizabeth*, New York: Alfred A. Knopf, 1960; Conyers Read, *Mr. Secretary Cecil and Queen Elizabeth*, London: Jonathan Cape, 1965.

cess

"Cess" was the term used for the traditional exactions of food and other supplies laid upon the landowners of the Irish PALE and surrounding districts by the English government in DUBLIN. The supplies gathered through the assessment and collection of cess were used to maintain the household of the lord deputy (i.e., the Crown's representative at the head of the Irish government) and to feed the enlarged military garrison required by the Elizabethan government to suppress rebellion and to extend its authority throughout IRELAND.

General cesses of grain, meat, and other commodities were conducted every autumn by cessors sent out from Dublin to collect these supplies from landowners in quantities determined by the amount of land held. The commodities gathered were to be paid for at fixed rates set well below the market rate, and government payment was often slow, incomplete, or not forthcoming. Besides reducing food supplies and distorting market prices, the cess system was also susceptible to bribery, extortion, and intimidation. When combined with government demands for transport (see PURVEYANCE) and for the billeting of troops, cess collection could cause great economic disorder and political unrest among the Pale population. The largest Elizabethan cesses were undertaken in 1559–60 and 1575, but the yearly exactions generated constant complaints and petitions to both the Dublin and LONDON governments.

Powerful ANGLO-IRISH landowners often sought and sometimes won freedom from cess exactions. In 1569, when the English adventurer Sir Peter CAREW regained control of large tracts of Irish land that had once belonged to his family, he vigorously sought but was continually denied exemption from cess. He then suggested a plan whereby he himself would be allowed to collect all supplies assessed on his property, a request the government was willing to consider.

In the 1560s and 1570s, the Dublin government experimented unsuccessfully with importing food from England by using private contractors. In the 1580s, the government attempted to commute cess exactions into a permanent monetary tax, but Irish landowners also balked at this plan. Cess was finally ended in 1585 when the property holders of the Pale agreed to payment of a lower fixed sum than originally stipulated by the government. *See also* COIGN AND LIVERY.

Further Reading: Steven G. Ellis, *Tudor Ireland*, London: Longman, 1985.

Challenge Sermon

John JEWEL's "Challenge Sermon" allowed the newly established ANGLICAN CHURCH to answer its Catholic critics, and it began a debate that helped the Church define its positions on various doctrines and practices. On 29 November 1559, only months after Elizabeth's first PARLIAMENT passed acts of supremacy and uniformity creating the new Protestant Church (see SUPREMACY, ROYAL), John Jewel, soon to be appointed Bishop of Salisbury, preached a sermon at PAUL'S CROSS in LONDON that attacked various Catholic practices—such as distributing only the communion bread and not the wine—as improper deviations from the form of worship laid down in scripture.

Jewel's oration soon became known as the Challenge Sermon because it challenged Catholics to provide evidence that these questionable practices had existed in the early Christian Church. If, said Jewel, Catholics could show him—out of the Bible, the writings of early Church fathers, or the decrees of Church councils—that these practices went back to the founding of Christianity, he "would give over and subscribe" to Catholicism. Jewel repeated the sermon at COURT in March 1560 and again at Paul's Cross, extending the challenge to cover 27 separate Catholic positions concerning the MASS. He hoped to put Catholics on the defensive and to counter the often successful Catholic argument that the Protestants were innovators and thus were obliged to defend their positions.

Because Catholics could not ignore Jewel's challenge, the sermon sparked a lively pamphlet debate. The Catholic dean of St. Paul's Cathedral in London, Henry Cole, sought to publish an immediate reply, but was imprisoned before he could do so. The challenge was then taken up by Catholic exiles in Europe, including Thomas Harding and John Rastell. Their pamphlets replied to Jewel's 1562 publication, *Apologia Ecclesiae Anglicanae [Apology for the Church of England]*, which was the first detailed explanation of Anglican positions on controversial topics. The *Apologia* eventually elicited more than 40 published responses from English Catholics, most of them in exile in the NETHERLANDS. Only the NETHERLANDS REVOLT in the 1570s put a stop to the debate. Through his sermon and the *Apologia*, Jewel laid a solid foundation for future efforts at shaping, refining, and defending the practices and doctrines of the Anglican Church. *See also* HOOKER, RICHARD; *LAWS OF ECCLESIASTICAL POLITY*.

Further Reading: J. E. Booty, *John Jewel as Apologist of the Church of England,* London: S.P.C.K., 1963; Norman Jones, *The Birth of the Elizabethan Age,* Oxford: Basil Blackwell, 1993.

chamberlain. *See* OFFICERS OF STATE.

Chamberlain's Men

The Chamberlain's Men was a LONDON acting company whose membership after 1594 included William SHAKESPEARE. In the early 1590s, Shakespeare was a member of Lord Strange's Men, a troupe under the patronage of Ferdinando STANLEY, Lord Strange. Lord Strange's Men performed at Philip HENSLOWE's Rose Theatre where, on 3 March 1592, it put on a successful performance of Shakespeare's *Henry VI, Part 2* (see SHAKESPEARE, WORKS OF). However, later that year, a virulent outbreak of the PLAGUE caused the city authorities to close all theatres and disband all acting companies. Lord Strange died in 1594, and when the theatres reopened later that year, his acting company came under the patronage of Henry CAREY, Lord Hunsdon, lord chamberlain of England (see OFFICERS OF STATE).

The new Chamberlain's Men severed their connection with Henslowe and the Rose and began performing at James BURBAGE's playhouse in London, known as The Theatre. Unlike the previous arrangement with Henslowe, whereby he paid and thus controlled the actors, the Chamberlain's Men was a partnership, with the company's six main actors, including Richard BURBAGE, William KEMPE, and William Shakespeare, receiving profits from the performances according to the amount of their investment in the company.

In 1599, the company moved to the GLOBE THEATRE in Southwark, in which the company's principals were also shareholders. The shareholders' investment bought and maintained costumes and props, while their profits came from a division of half the receipts from the gallery seats at the Globe. The other half of the gallery income went toward the costs and upkeep of the theatre, which included the hiring of actors for minor roles and the paying of watchmen, wardrobe keepers, copyists, and musicians.

Shakespeare remained a member of the company for the rest of his career, acting and writing an average of two plays per year until about 1608. The company performed frequently at COURT for the queen, and in 1603 came under the patronage of the new king, JAMES I, at which time it became known as the King's Men. By 1604, the number of shareholders in the company had increased to 12, and by Shakespeare's death in 1616, the King's Men had 26 permanent actors—a large number for the time and an indication of the company's success.

Further Reading: G. B. Harrison, *Elizabethan Plays and Players,* Ann Arbor: University of Michigan Press, 1956; Martin Holmes, *Shakespeare and Burbage,* Totowa, NJ: Rowman and Littlefield, 1978; Roslyn L. Knutson, *The Repertory of Shakespeare's Company, 1594–1613,* Fayetteville: University of Arkansas Press, 1991; John Orrell, *The Quest for Shakespeare's Globe,* New York: Cambridge University Press, 1983; Peter Thomson, *Shakespeare's Theatre,* London: Routledge and Kegan Paul, 1983.

chancellor. *See* OFFICERS OF STATE.

chancellor of the Exchequer. *See* OFFICERS OF STATE.

Chancery, Court of

The Court of Chancery was a PREROGATIVE court of EQUITY presided over by the lord chancellor, the medieval officer of state who supervised the monarch's writing office and the use of the Great Seal, which was used to authenticate official documents. Before 1500, the chancellorship was an important administrative and political position, not a judicial one. Chancery's judicial role developed in the fifteenth century out of the lord chancellor's issuance of writs to begin actions in the royal courts. When COMMON LAW courts could not reach a verdict or were unable to act, the parties could petition that the matter be brought before the lord chancellor personally. Chancery therefore compensated for deficiencies in the common law and provided an additional court to handle the increased volume of litigation during the Tudor period.

Because of his unprecedented authority and position, Thomas Wolsey, while serving as HENRY VIII's lord chancellor in the early sixteenth century, greatly increased the volume of business that came before the court. However, Chancery's procedures developed haphazardly and remained rather vague until after Wolsey's fall from power in 1529. The court began to acquire a more formal structure and procedure in 1530 when it started keeping records.

By the Elizabethan period, the lord chancellor was viewed solely as the government's chief legal officer, and the Court of Chancery had well-defined procedures, down to the quality of paper and ink required for court documents. The Court of Chancery was not an attempt to circumvent the common law or to place the monarch above the law; like other equity courts (see REQUESTS, COURT OF; STAR CHAMBER, COURT OF), it was a royal response to the growing volume of litigation in the sixteenth century and the need for additional courts with more flexible procedures.

Further Reading: W. J. Jones, *The Elizabethan Court of Chancery,* Oxford: Clarendon Press, 1967.

Chapel Royal

The Chapel Royal was a company of male singers and musicians maintained by the Crown to provide religious MUSIC for the monarch's various royal chapels. The Chapel Royal employed the finest musicians and singers in the country, and (with the occasional exception of boy trebles who were pressed into service) Chapel positions were highly coveted. Such leading Elizabethan musicians and composers as William BYRD and Thomas TALLIS, who both served as organists, were gentlemen of the Chapel Royal.

For a young boy, a position in the Chapel choir could lead to social advancement or economic security. Many Tudor bishops began as choirboys in the Chapel Royal, and many secular musicians and even some courtiers started there. When a boy's voice changed, he would be guaranteed royal patronage in finding new musical employment if his voice was still pleasing; if not, he would be sent to one of the UNIVERSITIES at royal expense or otherwise employed or rewarded.

Under Elizabeth, as under her father, HENRY VIII, the Crown also maintained a secular musical company that paralleled the Chapel Royal. Comprising both vocal and instrumental music, this secular company employed former Chapel Royal singers as well as some foreign musicians, including JEWS. Company members provided music for MASQUES, DANCES, and other ENTERTAINMENT and ceremonies at COURT; built and maintained the royal collection of musical instruments; and provided instruction in music to courtiers and their children. On grand occasions, such as coronations, royal weddings, and state funerals, the Chapel Royal and the secular music company performed together.

Further Reading: David Baldwin, *The Chapel Royal: Ancient and Modern,* London: Duckworth, 1990; David Wulstan, *Tudor Music,* Iowa City: University of Iowa Press, 1986.

Charles I. *See* CHARLES V.

Charles V (1500–1558)

Through a series of fortunate marriages and deaths, Charles Habsburg became ruler of much of Western Europe and AMERICA, thereby acquiring the power and wealth to significantly influence the political, religious, and economic history of sixteenth-century England. As the eldest son of Philip, Duke of Burgundy, and Joanna, Princess of SPAIN, Charles succeeded his maternal grandfather,

Ferdinand of Aragon, as king of Spain in 1516 and his paternal grandfather, Maximilian I, as Holy Roman emperor in 1519 (see the genealogical chart in Appendix 1: "Habsburg Dynasty in Spain and the Holy Roman Empire"). Charles therefore ruled Spain and its American and Italian possessions (as Charles I), Germany (as the Holy Roman Emperor), and the NETHERLANDS (as Duke of Burgundy). This combination of Habsburg territory nearly encircled FRANCE and led after 1520 to intense rivalry and warfare, particularly for control of Italy, between Charles and FRANCIS I of France.

In 1521, Charles rejected the doctrines of his German subject, the reformer Martin Luther. For the rest of his reign, Charles, a devout Catholic, fought to contain the spread of Lutheranism in his German possessions, while maintaining the war against France in the west and the struggle against the advancing Turkish empire in the east. As ruler of the Netherlands, the great trading partner of England, Charles's economic policies significantly affected the English economy. As ruler of Italy, Charles's success in imposing his political and military dominance on the pope complicated HENRY VIII's efforts to divorce his first wife, CATHERINE OF ARAGON, who was Charles's aunt. The emperor's pressure in his aunt's behalf forced the pope to deny Henry's request, which led the English king to break with the Roman Catholic Church and marry Anne BOLEYN, Elizabeth's mother.

For the rest of his life, Charles remained a staunch supporter of Catherine and her disinherited daughter Mary (see MARY I). In 1554, after Mary's accession to the English throne, Charles exercised great influence over the new regime and successfully promoted a marriage between Mary and his son Philip (see PHILIP II), to whom he abdicated the Spanish Crown and control of the Netherlands in 1556. English dissatisfaction with Mary I's Spanish marriage led to WYATT'S REBELLION, an unsuccessful rising to replace Mary with her half sister Elizabeth. The failure of the rebellion landed Elizabeth in the TOWER OF LONDON and nearly resulted in her execution. Tired and ill, Charles transfered all his lands to his son and his brother Ferdinand in 1556–57. Charles V died in a Spanish monastery in 1558. *See also* HABSBURG FAMILY.

Further Reading: Karl Brandi, *The Emperor Charles V,* London: Jonathan Cape, 1970; Otto Habsburg, *Charles V,* New York: Praeger, 1970; Royall Tyler, *The Emperor Charles V,* London: G. Allen and Unwin, 1956.

chaseabout raid

Beginning in August 1565, the royal army of Mary STUART, Queen of Scots, and the rebel forces of James STUART, Earl of Moray (Mary's Protestant half brother and former chief councilor) "chased" each other for some weeks around southern SCOTLAND in a farcically conducted dispute over who controlled the Scottish government. Moray, an illegitimate son of James V, had led the queen's government since Mary's return from France in 1561 (see STUART CLAIM). With Mary's acquiescence, Moray supported the Protestant Church of Scotland, yet tolerated the practice of Catholicism, both in the country and in the queen's household (see CATHOLICISM, ENGLISH). Nowhere else in Europe did a monarch treat religion as a purely private matter and refuse to impose religious uniformity on the country's subjects.

This tolerant policy collapsed in July 1565 when the queen wed her cousin Henry STUART, Lord Darnley, and began to hint that she would make Catholicism once again ascendant in Scotland. Moray, fearing that he would be displaced in the queen's counsels by Darnley and by the foreign and Catholic courtiers in Mary's household, rose in rebellion in August. Few of the Protestant nobles of Scotland joined Moray. Although they disliked the influence that Catholics like David RIZZIO, Mary's Italian secretary, had with the queen, they had no reason at that time to distrust Darnley. In early October 1565, Moray fled Scotland for England without ever coming into contact with the royal army. The "chaseabout raid" destroyed the relative political stability that Scotland had enjoyed in the previous four years and initiated a period of intense upheaval that would, within two years, lead to the murders of Rizzio and Darnley and the abdication and exile of Mary.

Further Reading: J. D. Mackie, *A History of Scotland,* 2nd ed., New York: Dorset Press, 1985; Jenny Wormald, *Mary, Queen of Scots,* London: Collins and Brown, 1991.

Christmas

Christmas, the birth of Christ, was one of the most important HOLIDAYS of the Elizabethan year. In England, the Christmas season extended from Christmas Eve to Epiphany (the celebration of the visit of the Wise Men to the infant Jesus) on 6 January. Epiphany was also called Twelfth Day, for it was the twelfth day after Christmas, and thus the last day of the 12-day Christmas season. In the Middle Ages, Twelfth Night, the eve of Epiphany, had been the most important midwinter celebration, but by Elizabethan times, 25 December, Christmas Day itself, was becoming an increasingly important day of feasting and merriment.

Like the modern holiday, an Elizabethan Christmas was celebrated with Christmas songs and MUSIC, as well as with dancing, plays, and games (especially card games) (see DANCE; ENTERTAINMENT). Homes were decorated with holly, ivy, and mistletoe, and meals included traditional Christmas foods, such as nuts, oranges, and special pies and cakes. Other holiday rituals included the burning of the Yule log, the lighting of Christmas candles, and the drinking of wassail, a spiced ale. New Year's Day, 1 January, did not mark the start of a new year in England as it did in Europe (see CALENDAR), but was instead a day for exchanging gifts, for visiting friends, and for general merriment and feasting.

Twelfth Night and Twelfth Day, 5 and 6 January, saw some of the most riotous celebrations of the Christmas season. Spiced fruitcake was a traditional food, and celebrations often included the selection of a lord and lady of misrule to preside over the dancing and other festivities. Wassail was also commonly drunk on New Year's Day and on Twelfth Night. Because the holiday retained so many traditions and rituals from the Catholic past, Puritan disapproval of Christmas increased throughout Elizabeth's reign (see PURITANS). For a time in the 1650s, when the monarchy was gone and England was a Puritan commonwealth, Christmas was declared a public fast day. However, most of the ancient Christmas traditions returned with the monarchy after 1660.

Further Reading: David Cressy, *Bonfires and Bells: National Memory and the Protestant Calendar in Elizabethan and Stuart England*, London: Weidenfeld and Nicolson, 1989; Ronald Hutton, *The Rise and Fall of Merry England: The Ritual Year, 1400–1700*, New York: Oxford University Press, 1994; Ronald Hutton, *The Stations of the Sun: A History of the Ritual Year in Britain*, New York: Oxford University Press, 1996.

chronicles. *See* ANNALES RERUM ANGLICARUM ET HIBERNICARUM REGNANTE ELIZABETHA *or* HOLINSHED'S *CHRONICLES.*

church courts

Existing since the Norman Conquest of the eleventh century, the English system of Church courts was entirely separate from the secular courts of COMMON LAW. Before the Reformation, the highest ecclesiastical court of appeal was the papal court, but HENRY VIII's break with Rome in the 1530s placed English Church courts under the Crown and PARLIAMENT. Although medieval Church courts had administered canon law, the law of the Church, the post-Reformation courts administered a combination of old canon law and new parliamentary statute (see REFORMATION, ENGLISH).

Church courts monitored clerical conduct, ensured lay church attendance, enforced payment of TITHES and fees, and dealt with the validity of marriages, the probate of wills, and charges of fornication, adultery, and heresy. Ecclesiastical courts could suspend attendance at services, excommunicate, and, in some cases, imprison, but they could not impose fines or capital punishment. Under MARY I, convicted heretics were handed over to the secular authorities for execution (see MARIAN MARTYRS). Unlike the common law courts, Church courts did not use juries; defendants cleared themselves through compurgation, the practice of swearing to their innocence and then bringing into court a certain number (according to the crime) of compurgators to swear to the truth of their oath.

The hierarchy of courts followed the ANGLICAN CHURCH structure, from the archdeaconries (at least two per diocese) to the dioceses (26 in Elizabethan England) to the provinces (Canterbury and York), with appeals rising from level to level until they reached the attention of the Crown, often, under Elizabeth, in the form of the Court of High Commission (see HIGH COMMISSION, COURT OF). At each level, consistory courts handled the great volume of routine work, such as probating wills and issuing licenses. The provincial consistory court of Canterbury, known as the Court of

Arches, sat in LONDON; the Archbishop of York's provincial court, the Court of Chancery, sat in York. More contentious issues, especially those involving the supervision and correction of clergy, were handled by visitation, a traveling diocesan tribunal conducted at regular intervals by bishops and their judicial officers. Jurisdictional disputes between Church courts and secular courts were common. Crown judges frequently issued writs of prohibition withdrawing from Church courts any case over which royal courts claimed jurisdiction.

Further Reading: Ralph Houlbrooke, *Church Courts and the People during the English Reformation,* Oxford: Oxford University Press, 1979.

Church of England. *See* ANGLICAN CHURCH.

classical movement

The classis was one of a hierarchy of courts that developed within the illegal presbyterian church structure that English PURITANS tried to establish inside the ANGLICAN CHURCH in the 1570s and 1580s (see PRESBYTERIAN MOVEMENT). A classis consisted of the ministers and representative elders of the churches within a given area. The primary goal of the classical movement was to define and impose a system of godly discipline on all ministers and congregations. In this way, the local classis maintained adherence to Puritan notions of worship and morality among the participating congregations.

The classical movement, like the PROPHESYINGS of the previous decade, ignored the authority of the bishops and had no royal or statutory sanction (see PARLIAMENT). The government uncovered and rooted out the movement in the 1590s when authorities began investigations to discover the authorship of the scurrilous MARPRELATE TRACTS, which attacked and discredited the bishops and other Church officials who opposed Puritan reforms. Many classis leaders were friends of the Marprelate authors, and this connection was enough to convince many people that the bishops were right when they claimed that an underground Puritan movement was attempting to subvert the established order. The bishops under Archbishop John WHITGIFT suppressed the classical movement by arresting and prosecuting classis leaders, as well as all advocates, such as Thomas CARTWRIGHT, of a presbyterian system of church government.

Further Reading: Patrick Collinson, *The Elizabethan Puritan Movement,* Oxford: Clarendon Press, 1990; Patrick McGrath, *Papists and Puritans under Elizabeth I,* New York: Walker and Company, 1967.

Clifford, George, Earl of Cumberland
(1558–1605)

George Clifford, third Earl of Cumberland, was one of the most active Elizabethan privateers (see PRIVATEERING). Through his mother, Eleanor Brandon, a younger daughter of Mary Tudor, the sister of HENRY VIII, Clifford was a distant cousin of Queen Elizabeth. In 1571, a year after inheriting his title at the age of 12, the young earl entered Trinity College at Cambridge (see UNIVERSITIES), where his tutor was the future Archbishop of Canterbury, John WHITGIFT. Having a great interest in seamanship and navigation, Cumberland focused his studies at Cambridge on mathematics. He earned a master's degree in 1576, and then went to Oxford to study geography. Cumberland acquired a great reputation as a jouster, and was frequently the queen's champion at the ACCESSION DAY tilts, where he challenged all comers and was well known for his gallant speeches.

Cumberland also became a noted English seaman. In 1588, he commanded Sir Francis DRAKE's old ship, the *Elizabeth,* during the running Channel fights against the ARMADA (see GRAVELINES, BATTLE OF). Between 1586 and 1598, Cumberland equipped and led 12 privateering expeditions designed to attack Spanish shipping and raid the ports of SPANISH AMERICA. On his final voyage in 1598, Cumberland sailed to Puerto Rico, where he captured the forts at San Juan that had withstood Drake's attack in 1595. Cumberland hoped to establish a permanent English settlement on the island, but lack of supplies and his own ill health prevented him from doing so. The heavy cost of his various expeditions, which he met out of his own resources, and his weakness for gambling put the earl in severe financial difficulties in the last years of his life. Cumberland died heavily in debt in 1605. *See also* NAVY; SHIPS.

Further Reading: Richard T. Spence, *The Privateering Earl,* Stroud, England: Alan Sutton Publishers, 1995.

clipping. *See* COINAGE.

cloth industry

Woolen cloth was the chief export and most important commercial product of Elizabethan England. Raw wool, sent primarily to large urban cloth manufacturers in the NETHERLANDS, had been the principal export of medieval England. By the start of Elizabeth's reign, however, when the country had almost 11 million sheep (nearly four times the human POPULATION), England had developed a cloth industry of its own that supplied most domestic needs and employed more people than any other occupation except AGRICULTURE.

Clothiers from LONDON and other towns (see BOROUGHS) bought wool from GENTRY and yeoman producers (see SOCIAL HIERARCHY) and sent it to rural peasant households, where the FAMILY supplied most of the labor to produce cloth. After the wool was washed, it was carded, a process that freed the fibers of knots and tangles. The carded wool was then spun into thread, and the thread was woven into cloth on a horizontal loom. The cloth was then fulled—a washing process to shrink it and felt it (i.e., to bind fibers more tightly together to make the cloth stronger and warmer). Although some cloth was then dyed, much was left its natural color, with most of the cloth exported to the Netherlands remaining undyed for Flemish cloth manufacturers to finish. The export of woolen cloth was largely controlled out of London by the MERCHANT ADVENTURERS, who bought the finished product from the clothiers and sold it in the Netherlands and Germany.

English efforts to find a northeast passage and to establish a commercial presence in the Middle and Far East were stimulated by a desire to sell English cloth to Russia, Persia, and India. The coarser types of woolen broadcloth, kerseys, and worsteds (the latter two special types of cloth developed in the villages of Kersey and Worsted) were known as "old draperies," while the lighter, finer types of cloth woven in East Anglia were known as "new draperies." These newer cloth types were developed by Flemish and Huguenot immigrants who had fled the religious turmoil in the Netherlands and FRANCE (see HUGUENOTS). Although the steady deterioration of relations with SPAIN, the ongoing NETHERLANDS REVOLT, and episodes like the "TREASURE CRISIS" OF 1568 disrupted English cloth exports to Europe, the growing domestic market and the development of new markets in Russia and elsewhere allowed the Elizabethan cloth industry to expand.

Further Reading: D. C. Coleman, *The Economy of England 1450–1750,* Oxford: Oxford University Press, 1977; G. D. Ramsay, *The English Woollen Industry, 1500–1750,* London: Macmillan, 1982.

cockfighting. *See* ANIMAL SPORTS.

coign and livery

Coign (or coyne) and livery referred to a system of billeting and exactions imposed by Irish and ANGLO-IRISH lords on the tenants or subordinates within their clans or territories in IRELAND. "Coign" derived from an Irish word for guest, and "livery" was an English term for the payment or allowance given by a lord to a servant or retainer. Under the coign and livery system, the lord send out his GALLOWGLASSES and KERN, his horses and their keepers, and even his hounds and huntsmen to be lodged in the homes of his tenants and subjects. The hosts were required to provide these "guests" not only with living quarters, but also with food and even wages. The necessity of providing feed and stabling for horses endowed the term livery with another meaning, as in "livery stable."

The operation of coign and livery varied from district to district. Sometimes a lord's military commander organized billeting on his own, using a letter of authorization from the lord to obtain cooperation. Sometimes a district was simply required to lodge and feed a certain number of men and horses. In other cases, especially by the Elizabethan period, the coign and livery requirement was transformed into a set money payment. Because of the lack of coinage in Ireland's subsistence economy, direct billeting of troops and exaction of supplies was the best way for a lord to maintain his troops and servants.

The system was open to numerous abuses, such as bribery, violence, and excessive demands, and was, therefore highly unpopular. Exactions demanded of PALE residents in time of war by Anglo-Irish nobles were particularly resented, and coign and livery was repeatedly attacked in the House of Commons of the Irish PARLIAMENT where, by the sixteenth century, numerous limitations on the practice had been enacted. However, such enactments had little force in the native Irish lordships outside the Pale and the authority of the DUBLIN government. *See also* CESS.

Further Reading: Steven G. Ellis, *Tudor Ireland,* London: Longman, 1985.

coinage

Money in Elizabethan England consisted of a series of silver and gold coins, the value of which was closely tied to the amount and current value of the gold and silver they contained. At Elizabeth's accession in 1558, the English coinage was in serious disarray. To raise funds for war, the governments of HENRY VIII and EDWARD VI debased the English coinage several times between 1542 and 1551. Debasement meant reducing the amount of actual gold and silver in coins while maintaining their face value. The government's profit came from the lowering of costs to acquire bullion and to mint coins, relative to a maintenance of the coins' old level of purchasing power. Thus, by 1551, the amount of gold and silver in certain coins was only one-fourth of what it had been before 1542, although the face value of the coins, as declared by the government, was the same as it had been in 1542. This practice netted the government over £1.3 million, but also destroyed public confidence in the coinage. Prices rose sharply, markets fell into disorder as the exchange rate fluctuated, and people began to hoard "good" coins and refuse to accept debased ones.

Elizabeth's government undertook a thorough reform of the coinage after 1559, calling in debased coins and issuing new coins of full weight and value. The main royal mint was in the TOWER OF LONDON. Most coins were hand-struck, although in 1560, Elizabeth tried to have coins milled by machine; this experiment failed because of resistance from the mint operators, who had contracts with the Crown to produce coins. The main operator early in the reign, the Frenchman Eloye Mestrelle, was hanged for forgery in 1578. Coin clipping, the illegal practice of shaving slivers of gold or silver from the edges of coins, was widespread. Clipping, which was easily done because Elizabethan coins, unlike modern ones, had

unmilled edges, drove good unclipped coin out of circulation by encouraging hoarding.

The main English denominations were the penny, the shilling, the crown, and the sovereign, although many other denominations, as well as foreign coins, were in circulation. Elizabethans had no paper money, although coinage could be deposited with a banker or merchant for a letter of credit. Large amounts of money were often calculated in "moneys of account": denominations such as the mark or the pound that did not exist as actual currency but only as a method of reckoning.

Elizabethan Coinage	Denomination (Abbreviation)	Relative Value
Silver Coins	halfpenny (ob.)	½d.
	penny (d.)	
	twopenny (half-groat)	2d.
	shilling (s.)	12d.
Gold Coins	half-crown	2s. 6d.
	quarter angel	2s. 6d.
	angelet	5s.
	crown	5s.
	sovereign	20s. (1 pound)
Moneys of Account	farthing (q.)	¼d.
	threepenny	3d.
	groat	4d.
	mark	13s.4d. (2/3 pound)
	pound (li.)*	20s.

* The pound symbol (£) is modern usage; the Elizabethans used li. following the number, e.g., 20li.

Further Reading: C. E. Challis, *The Tudor Coinage,* New York: Barnes and Noble Books, 1978.

College of Arms

The College of Arms, or Heralds' College, is a corporate institution established in 1484 and charged with the granting of coats of arms to families qualified to hold GENTRY status (see SOCIAL HIERARCHY). The College, which still functions today, supervises the work of the royal heralds, or officers of arms, who first appeared in the twelfth century as royal officials who understood the pictorial devices worn by armored knights, and so could identify each knight for the king.

In Elizabethan times, the chief function of the heralds was to determine who was and was not qualified to hold the rank of a gentleman. The heralds periodically toured the countryside to make such determinations. The "heralds' visitations," the records of these tours, were collections of genealogical tables confirming a family's gentry status. Heralds could admit new members to the gentry ranks by granting coats of arms to any lawyer, merchant, university instructor, or civil or military officer who possessed the required wealth and lifestyle.

The chief heralds are Garter King of Arms, established in 1417 and attached to the Order of the Garter, a prestigious fourteenth-century chivalric order of knighthood; Clarenceaux King of Arms, established about 1362 and responsible for determining gentry status in England south of the River Trent; and Norry King of Arms, established in the thirteenth century and responsible for England north of the River Trent. Norry King of Arms also assumed responsibility for IRELAND during EDWARD VI's reign. The College also directs the work of the six ordinary heralds—Richmond, Somerset, York, Lancaster, Chester, and Windsor, all instituted between the fourteenth and sixteenth centuries—and of the four lower-ranking pursuivants—Portcullis (the name derives from a Tudor badge), Bluemantle (from the blue background of the French royal arms), Rouge Croix (from the red cross of St. George), and Rouge Dragon (from the Welsh red dragon emblem of the Tudors). Today, the College of Arms in LONDON is the official repository of genealogical records for English, Welsh, Northern Irish, and Commonwealth families.

Further Reading: Felicity Heal and Clive Holmes, *The Gentry in England and Wales 1500–1700,* Stanford, CA: Stanford University Press, 1994; Anthony R. Wagner, *Heralds of England: A History of the Office and College of Arms,* London: H.M.S.O., 1967.

common law

The common law is the body of English legal principles evolved by judges from custom and precedent and administered, in Elizabethan times, in the main royal courts sitting at Westminster Hall in LONDON (see WESTMINSTER PALACE). Common law developed in the twelfth century as local and feudal courts administering various local and private systems of law declined and were replaced by a system of law administered by the king's justices on principles common to the entire kingdom. The king being the fount of all justice,

the chief common law courts developed out of the judicial function, exercised on the king's behalf, by his circle of nobles and advisors. As the volume of judicial business increased, royal law courts evolved firm structures, set procedures, and defined jurisdictions; they also ceased following the king about the realm and became permanently headquartered in Westminster.

The chief Elizabethan courts of the common law were the Court of Common Pleas, which dealt with civil disputes between subjects over a variety of causes; the Court of Queen's (or King's) Bench, which dealt with matters affecting the Crown and with criminal matters; and the EXCHEQUER, which handled cases involving royal finance; *see* COMMON PLEAS, COURT OF; KING'S (QUEEN'S) BENCH, COURT OF. During the Elizabethan period, the volume of litigation brought before the courts of common law increased dramatically. By the end of Elizabeth's reign in 1603, some 50,000 new cases were being commenced each year before Common Pleas and Queen's (King's) Bench, a tenfold increase over the volume of litigation in 1500.

Under Elizabeth, more litigation came into the common law courts in relation to the overall population of the kingdom than has been entertained by the courts at any time before or since. The work of the Elizabethan courts also touched a larger percentage of the population, reaching into almost all social classes (see SOCIAL HIERARCHY). About a third of all Elizabethan litigants were members of the landed gentry, but a growing two-thirds came from lower classes—yeoman farmers and husbandmen from the countryside, and merchants and artisans from the towns. By bringing an end to the foreign wars that had marked the last years of HENRY VIII, and to the intermittent internal strife that had characterized the reigns of EDWARD VI and MARY I, the reign of Elizabeth also saw the volume of cases originating outside London and the southern counties grow considerably as peace and prosperity encouraged litigants from the northern and especially the western counties to bring their cases before the courts of common law. The general increase in court activity was also in part the result of widespread social and economic changes, such as a more

The courts of common law in session in Westminster Hall, an early seventeenth-century view by an anonymous artist. © *The British Museum*.

active land market, a greater and more sophisticated use of credit, and the growth in wealth and numbers of the GENTRY class, and in part the result of the political stability and emphasis on the rule of law given to the country by Elizabeth and her Tudor predecessors (see TUDOR FAMILY).

Common law procedure was complex; it was based on the issuance of writs by the court of proper jurisdiction. A litigant in the shires wishing to initiate a legal action traveled to London to purchase the writ needed to begin the case. The writ summoned defendants to appear before the court and answer the pleas put in against them by plaintiffs. Many cases were settled at this point, but if the suit progressed, writs were issued returning the case to its original shire for trial by jury before the next court of assize in the shire. The assizes were judicial tribunals consisting of royal judges and serjeants-at-law (senior attorneys who specialized in pleading cases before the common law courts) that twice each year traveled a circuit through a group of shires (there were six such circuits) to hear civil and criminal cases. The assize sat for several days in the main town (see BOROUGHS) of the shire, hearing all cases awaiting trial. After hearing all civil suits returned by writ from Westminster, the assize judges heard all major criminal matters, such as murder and TREASON, and tried all prisoners in the local jail and all suspects bound over by the local JUSTICES OF THE PEACE (JPs) to appear before the assize. The assize judges tried all criminal cases (felonies) that involved the death penalty, while the local JPs handled less serious offenses (misdemeanors) at their quarterly sessions.

Common law was not the only type of law administered in Elizabethan England; other types included statute law (passed by PARLIAMENT), civil (Roman) law (used in CHURCH COURTS), and EQUITY (legal principles followed in the Court of Chancery and other new equity courts). *See also* CHANCERY, COURT OF.

Further Reading: C. W. Brooks, *Pettyfoggers and Vipers of the Commonwealth: The "Lower Branch" of the Legal Profession in Early Modern England,* Cambridge: Cambridge University Press, 1986; Arthur R. Hogue, *Origins of the Common Law,* Indianapolis: Liberty Fund, 1985; Wilfrid R. Prest, *The Inns of Court under Elizabeth I and the Early Stuarts, 1590–1640,* London: Longman, 1972; R. C. Van Caenegem, *The Birth of the English Common Law,* 2nd ed., Cambridge: Cambridge University Press, 1988.

Common Pleas, Court of

The Court of Common Pleas was the busiest and slowest of the Elizabethan COMMON LAW courts. Like the other principal law courts of the realm, the Court of King's (or Queen's) Bench and the EXCHEQUER, Common Pleas was a medieval common law court staffed by royal justices and permanently situated since the thirteenth century in Westminster Hall in LONDON; *see* KING'S (QUEEN'S) BENCH, COURT OF; WESTMINSTER PALACE. The Court of Common Pleas had jurisdiction over civil actions between subjects. It usually heard cases concerning matters of property, debt, and trespass, but its competence was wide, encompassing cases of nonpayment of rent, defamation of character, and even medical malpractice.

Common Pleas heard appeals from lower courts, and appeals from Common Pleas went to the Court of Queen's (King's) Bench. Because Common Pleas followed the slow, complicated, and often expensive procedures of the common law, and because it conducted business in medieval French rather than English, the court lost business in the sixteenth century to the newer PREROGATIVE courts of EQUITY (see CHANCERY, COURT OF; STAR CHAMBER, COURT OF; REQUESTS, COURT OF) that developed under the Tudors (see TUDOR FAMILY). These courts tended to be more flexible in procedure and were conducted in English. Nonetheless, the overall volume of business coming before Common Pleas, as before all common law courts, greatly increased under the Tudors, as Elizabeth and her predecessors broke down local jurisdictions and centralized the administration of the realm under the Crown.

Further Reading: C. W. Brooks, *Pettyfoggers and Vipers of the Commonwealth: The "Lower Branch" of the Legal Profession in Early Modern England,* Cambridge: Cambridge University Press, 1986; Margaret Hastings, *The Court of Common Pleas in Fifteenth Century England,* Ithaca, NY: Cornell University Press, 1947; Wilfrid R. Prest, *The Inns of Court under Elizabeth I and the Early Stuarts, 1590–1640,* London: Longman, 1972.

Condell, Henry (c. 1562–1627)

Henry Condell, a London stage actor and colleague of William SHAKESPEARE, was a co-editor of the first edition of Shakespeare's plays, known as the FIRST FOLIO. In 1598, Condell joined the CHAMBERLAIN'S MEN, an acting company based at the GLOBE THEATRE. The company included among its members William Shakespeare and Richard BURBAGE. When the company came under royal patronage in 1603 and was renamed the King's Men, Condell remained part of the troupe, his name being listed in the royal patent creating the new patronage arrangement.

Condell performed in both comedies and tragedies, and he is known to have played roles written not only by Shakespeare but by Ben JONSON and other Elizabethan dramatists. Condell's name disappeared from the company's cast lists about 1619, but he appears in the list of actors placed at the beginning of the First Folio in 1623 and in other official lists of the King's Men down to 1625. Condell became a shareholder in the Blackfriars Theatre in 1603 and in the Globe Theatre by 1612. After the playwright's death in 1616, Shakespeare's will left Condell and fellow actors John HEMINGES and Richard Burbage a small sum of money "to buy them rings."

With Heminges, Condell edited and oversaw the printing of the First Folio of Shakespeare's plays in 1623. In their preface to the volume, which they entitled "To the Great Variety of Readers," Condell and Heminges stated their aim in undertaking the project to be "only to keep the memory of so worthy a friend and fellow alive." They were probably also interested in preventing others from laying claim to Shakespeare's works and in presenting a good printed text for each play. Besides the preface, the two editors provided a list of players, including themselves, who had performed the works of Shakespeare at both the Globe and Blackfriars theatres and a dedication to the earls of Pembroke and Montgomery, both noted patrons of the theatre. Condell, who had apparently prospered in his profession, died at his country estate at Fulham in 1627. See also DRAMA.

Further Reading: Charles Connell, *They Gave Us Shakespeare: John Heminge and Henry Condell,* Boston: Oriel Press, 1982.

Congregationalists

Congregationalists were Protestant SEPARATISTS who believed that voluntarily formed local congregations constituted the proper structure for the Christian Church. Although basically Calvinists in doctrine (see CALVINISM),

Elizabethan congregationalists rejected all forms of church hierarchy, including bishops and presbyterian councils, and all claims to church oversight beyond the congregation, whether made by the Crown or PARLIAMENT. Their ideas were based on the concept that all believing Christians were members of the priesthood and that like-minded Christians could band together into a congregation to conduct worship according to the dictates of the Bible, not the mandates of Parliament or councils. These ideas were developed during the reign of Elizabeth by Robert BROWNE and Henry BARROW, whose followers formed the earliest Elizabethan separatist groups known as Brownists and Barrowists. By refusing to use the *BOOK OF COMMON PRAYER* and separating or withdrawing themselves from the ANGLICAN CHURCH, these groups provoked official persecution.

In the 1580s and 1590s, several separatist groups, including one led by Browne, moved to the NETHERLANDS, where they sought to worship as they chose. One such group is known to American history as the Pilgrims; they left the Netherlands for the New World in 1620 when they began to fear that their children were losing their English identity and becoming Dutch. In the seventeenth century, many separatists settled in the English colonies in North America, where congregationalism became the accepted form of church organization among the Puritan Churches of New England.

Seventeenth-century Congregationalists in England were known as independents, and came to form the chief political opposition to the Presbyterians during the civil war of the 1640s. In the 1650s, English Congregationalists secured full freedom of worship during the rule of Oliver Cromwell, who was himself an independent. The restoration of the monarchy in 1660 also restored the royal supremacy and the hierarchy of bishops, but English Congregationalists and other Protestant dissenters from the Anglican Church were granted freedom from persecution by the Toleration Act of 1689. *See also* BIBLE, ENGLISH; PRESBYTERIAN MOVEMENT; PROTESTANTISM; PURITANS; SUPREMACY, ROYAL.

Further Reading: Patrick Collinson, *The Elizabethan Puritan Movement,* Oxford: Clarendon Press, 1990; B R. White, *The English Separatist Tradition,* London: Oxford University Press, 1971.

Convocation

The term "Convocation" refers to legislative assemblies of the clergy that met in the two provinces of the English Church, Canterbury and York. The Convocation of Canterbury, the much larger and richer southern province of the English Church, usually met in LONDON at St. Paul's Cathedral at the same time as PARLIAMENT. The Convocation of York usually met sometime later in York at St. Peter's Cathedral (York Minster) to consider what the Canterbury assembly had initiated. By the Tudor period, the two bodies comprised an upper house of bishops and a lower house of lesser clergy. Convocation granted the Crown clerical TAXATION (taxes paid by members of the clergy) and debated and passed the laws or canons of the English Church.

In 1534, an act of Parliament, part of the legislative program that separated the English Church from the Roman Catholic Church, severely limited the legislative independence of Convocation, placing the deliberations of each body under the direction and oversight of the monarch as supreme head of the Church (see SUPREMACY, ROYAL). By Elizabeth's reign, Convocation was clearly controlled by the Crown, requiring the monarch's license to convene and to consider legislation, and the monarch's assent to any legislation passed. The Elizabethan Convocation was thus an excellent instrument for the queen, allowing her to frustrate any alterations in ANGLICAN CHURCH doctrine and practice of which she did not approve; conversely, Convocation was of little use to Elizabethan PURITANS and other reformers who wanted to change what they considered wrong with the English Church. As a result, Puritans often sought to initiate change through Parliament or through independent, unauthorized action in local congregations (see CLASSICAL MOVEMENT; CONGREGATIONALISTS; PROPHESYINGS).

Further Reading: A. G. Dickens, *The English Reformation,* 2nd ed., University Park: Pennsylvania State University Press, 1989.

Cooke, Sir Anthony (1504–1576)

A prominent scholar and educator, Sir Anthony Cooke served as tutor to EDWARD VI and was noted for the EDUCATION he gave his own children, especially his daughters. Born into an Essex GENTRY family, his great-grandfather having been lord mayor of LONDON in the 1460s, Cooke showed great academic promise and was educated by private tutors. An excellent student, he became highly skilled in Latin and Greek and extremely knowledgeable in POETRY, history, and mathematics. He fathered a large family of four sons and five daughters, who, under his instruction, acquired an excellent education; his daughters were acclaimed as the most learned women in Tudor England.

His daughter Mildred (see CECIL, MILDRED) married William CECIL, the future Elizabethan principal secretary; his daughter Ann (see BACON, ANN) married Nicholas BACON, the future Elizabethan lord keeper; his daughter Elizabeth (see RUSSELL, ELIZABETH) married Lord John Russell, the son of Francis RUSSELL, Earl of Bedford; and his daughter Katherine married Henry KILLIGREW, the future Elizabethan diplomat (see DIPLOMACY). Two prominent late Elizabethan politicians, Sir Robert CECIL and Sir Francis BACON, were his grandsons.

Cooke's educational success with his own children and with the son of Edward SEYMOUR, future Duke of Somerset (who was, for a time, resident at Gidea Hall, the Cooke home in Essex), won for Cooke appointment as tutor to Prince Edward. When his pupil became king in 1547, Cooke was knighted and won a seat in PARLIAMENT. A Protestant, Cooke also served on a number of commissions for overseeing reform of the English Church. In July 1553, he was briefly imprisoned in the TOWER OF LONDON by MARY I for suspected involvement in NORTHUMBERLAND'S COUP. By May 1554, he was a MARIAN EXILE living in Strasbourg. Cooke returned to England after Elizabeth's accession in 1558 and was once again named to a series of Church commissions, including one in October 1559 that was charged with hearing the oaths of clergymen who were required to swear to the new ANGLICAN SETTLEMENT of religion. In 1568, Cooke received Elizabeth I at Gidea Hall, where she stopped on one of her progresses (see PROGRESSES, ROYAL). He is known to have translated several scholarly and ecclesiastical works from the Latin and to have written several Latin verses. Cooke died on 11 June 1576.

Further Reading: B. W. Beckingsale, *Burghley: Tudor Statesman,* New York: St. Martin's Press, 1967.

Cotton, Sir Robert (1571–1631)

Robert Cotton was a leading Elizabethan antiquary (see ANTIQUARIANISM). Born into a Huntingdonshire GENTRY family claiming descent from King Robert the Bruce of SCOTLAND, Cotton was educated at Westminster School (see GRAMMAR SCHOOL), where he studied under the antiquary William CAMDEN, and at Cambridge (see UNIVERSITIES). A member of the Society of Antiquaries, Cotton used the money derived from his marriage to a wealthy heiress to build the most extensive collection of books and manuscripts in Elizabethan England.

In the late 1590s, Cotton became a client of the lord chamberlain of England, George CAREY, Lord Hunsdon, who introduced Cotton at COURT and helped him find a seat in the PARLIAMENT of 1601. A close friend of Ben JONSON, John Donne, and many leading scholars and writers of his day, Cotton opened his impressive library to any scholar who required access for his research. Cotton also gave many books to other collectors, including Thomas BODLEY and Robert CECIL. In 1616, Cotton spent five months in the TOWER OF LONDON for his involvement in certain political intrigues at the court of JAMES I. This episode led Cotton to align himself with the growing political opposition to the Crown and the court.

In 1622, Cotton purchased a large house in Westminster situated between the two Houses of Parliament. By virtue of its location, Cotton House became the unofficial library of Parliament, as opposition MPs (members of Parliament) searched Cotton's collection for historical precedents to use in their speeches. In 1629, Cotton's involvement in the circulation of an antigovernment pamphlet caused Charles I to imprison him and close the library. Although released the following year, Cotton was not allowed to use his own library unless supervised by a government clerk. Deeply distressed by this humiliating restriction, Cotton died in May 1631. Presented to the nation by Cotton's grandson in 1700, the Cotton collection has since become part of the British Library. *See also* WESTMINISTER PALACE.

Further Reading: Kevin Sharpe, *Sir Robert Cotton,* New York: Oxford University Press, 1979.

Counter-Reformation

The term "Counter-Reformation" describes the movement of reform and renewal that the Roman Catholic Church underwent during the second half of the sixteenth century. The Counter-Reformation movement allowed Rome to regain ground lost to the Protestant Reformation in the early decades of the century.

The recovery was initiated by the general council of the Church convened at Trent in northern Italy by Pope Paul III. Meeting in intermittent sessions from 1545 to 1563, the Council of Trent issued numerous decrees calling for reform of abuses within the Church and mapping a strategy for recovery of the Church's authority in areas of Europe lost to PROTESTANTISM. Although some German Lutherans attended the early sessions in hopes of arriving at a compromise with Rome, the Council ultimately rejected any accommodation with Protestantism. The Council of Trent came to be characterized by a fierce loyalty to the institution of the papacy and a determination to reinvigorate the Catholic religious orders. The most important new order was the Society of Jesus, the Jesuits, a highly trained and disciplined order founded by Ignatius Loyola in 1543; the Jesuits became the chief agents of Counter-Reformation activity throughout Europe.

The Counter-Reformation began to direct its attention to England in 1570, when Pope PIUS V issued the bull *REGNANS IN EXCELSIS* excommunicating Elizabeth and absolving her subjects of their allegiance to her. Pope GREGORY XIII implemented many of the Trent decrees and strongly supported the first JESUIT MISSION to England, which was initiated by Edmund CAMPION and Robert PARSONS in 1580. Recognizing the politically active Jesuits as the most dangerous element in the English Catholic clergy, the Elizabethan government passed various statutes to outlaw their work in England (see PENAL LAWS). The Jesuits and the Counter-Reformation helped preserve a small English Catholic community (see CATHOLICISM, ENGLISH; SEMINARY PRIESTS), but made little headway in restoring England (or SCOTLAND) to Roman Catholicism. However, in IRELAND, the Catholic Church, by identifying itself with resistance to English rule as well as to English Protestantism, was able to forge a strong and lasting bond between itself and the Irish people.

Further Reading: Edward McNall Burns, *The Counter Reformation*, Princeton, NJ: Van Nostrand, 1964; N. S. Davidson, *The Counter-Reformation*, Oxford: Blackwell, 1987; A. G. Dickens, *The Counter Reformation*, New York: Harcourt, Brace and World, 1969; G. W. Searle, *The Counter Reformation*, London: University of London Press, 1974.

court

The royal court was an ill-defined entity that comprised—in its widest sense—the royal household and the entire entourage of government ministers, royal officials, and personal servants surrounding the monarch. The court existed to serve the personal and political needs of the monarch, to display the wealth and power of the monarch to the kingdom and to foreign rulers, and to provide an arena for ambitious subjects to pursue wealth and power through royal favor.

Because sixteenth-century monarchies were personal, access to the ruler was all-important, and the court took its tone from the personality of the king or queen. Being an unmarried woman with no immediate family, Elizabeth presided over a less martial court than that of her father, HENRY VIII. However, the Elizabethan court offered writers, artists, and musicians an even wider stage than had the courts of previous Tudors (see ART; DRAMA; MUSIC; POETRY; TUDOR FAMILY). The court, which numbered between 1,000 and 1,500 people depending on the time of year and the residence, moved with Elizabeth as she traveled among her many PALACES (see also PROGRESSES, ROYAL). The household comprised some 20 departments responsible for acquiring supplies, preparing meals, and cleaning up afterward. Staffed by people of lower social rank (see SOCIAL HIERARCHY), the household departments were headed by serjeants, who had worked their way up the ranks and who answered to a staff of clerks working under the direction of the lord steward and the controller, prominent positions held by important GENTRY or noble courtiers.

The chamber, comprising those court servants who had access to the queen, was directed by the chamberlain and vice-chamberlain, also important court officials. The queen's most intimate servants, her LADIES-IN-WAITING, served in the privy chamber and came under Elizabeth's personal supervision. These women met the queen's most personal needs and served as conduits of royal access for ambitious or disgraced courtiers who needed to maintain or regain royal favor (see also FAVORITES). The master of the revels, a privy chamber official, arranged MASQUES and other court ENTERTAINMENT. The Elizabethan court also included two largely ceremonial guard units—the Yeoman of the Guard, established by HENRY VII, and the Band of Gentlemen Pensioners, established by HENRY VIII (see ARMY). Although Elizabeth wanted a large and magnificent court, she also wanted an inexpensive one, so cost-cutting measures, such as limiting the number of people who had a right to eat at royal expense, alternated with more elaborate entertainments.

Further Reading: David Loades, *The Tudor Court,* London: Batsford, 1986.

Court of Chancery. *See* CHANCERY, COURT OF.

Court of Common Pleas. *See* COMMON PLEAS, COURT OF.

Court of High Commission. *See* HIGH COMMISSION, COURT OF.

Court of King's (Queen's) Bench. *See* KING'S (QUEEN'S) BENCH, COURT OF.

Court of Requests. *See* REQUESTS, COURT OF.

Court of Star Chamber. *See* STAR CHAMBER, COURT OF.

Courtenay, Edward, Earl of Devonshire (c. 1526–1556)

Because he was English and had a clear claim to the throne, Edward Courtenay, Earl of Devonshire, became a strong candidate for marriage to MARY I, especially among those in the English political community who sought to prevent the queen from marrying outside the realm. As the son of Henry Courtenay, Marquis of Exeter and Earl of Devonshire, Courtenay was descended from a sister of Edward IV and thus had a YORKIST CLAIM to the English throne (see Appendix 1: "Yorkist Claim to the English Throne"). When HENRY VIII executed the Marquis of Exeter for TREASON in 1538 (a treason consisting mainly of having Yorkist blood), he imprisoned Exeter's 12-year-old son Edward in the TOWER OF LONDON, where the young man stayed until released in 1553 by Mary, a close friend of his mother.

Because of his Yorkist lineage and his ancient English name, Courtenay, who was restored to the earldom of Devonshire by Mary, quickly became the leading candidate of those councilors and MPs (members of PARLIAMENT) who favored an English husband for the queen. Because of his long imprisonment, Courtney was not well known and had no real enemies; he also had a strong supporter in Bishop Stephen Gardiner, Mary's lord chancellor and a fellow prisoner with Courtenay in the Tower during much of EDWARD VI's reign. Mary, however, found the young earl to be weak, foolish, and unstable, and she never seriously considered him for marriage.

After the queen decided to marry Prince Philip of SPAIN (see PHILIP II), the very decision many of Courtenay's supporters had sought to prevent, the earl involved himself in the plotting that led to WYATT'S REBELLION. The plotters agreed that Courtenay would make an equally suitable husband for Princess Elizabeth, with whom they hoped to replace Mary. In January 1554, as the government began to suspect treason, Courtenay confessed all he knew to Bishop Gardiner and was sent back to the Tower in February after Wyatt's Rebellion collapsed. In the spring of 1555, he went into exile in Europe, dying under somewhat mysterious circumstances in Italy in 1556.

Further Reading: D. M. Loades, *Two Tudor Conspiracies,* Cambridge: Cambridge University Press, 1965.

Cranmer, Thomas (1489–1556)

As HENRY VIII's Archbishop of Canterbury, Thomas Cranmer was instrumental in bringing about England's break with the Church of Rome and, after Henry's death, in establishing a Protestant Church in England. Born into a minor GENTRY family near Nottingham, Cranmer earned a degree in divinity at Cambridge, where he seems in the 1520s to have associated with a group of anti-papal, reformist scholars. He first came to the king's attention in 1530 when he wrote a treatise defending Henry VIII's attempt to annul his marriage to CATHERINE OF ARAGON. Cranmer suggested that the king canvass the UNIVERSITIES of Europe to marshal scholarly support for his position.

In 1533, Henry appointed Cranmer Archbishop of Canterbury, a choice confirmed by the pope, who was anxious to do whatever favors he could for Henry VIII. Cranmer, as a strong supporter of the royal supremacy, was a political ally of Thomas CROMWELL in subordinating the English Church to the Crown and in undertaking religious reform (see SUPREMACY, ROYAL). In 1533, Archbishop Cranmer declared the king's marriage to Catherine of Aragon invalid and his marriage with Anne BOLEYN lawful. These actions led to the recognition of Princess Elizabeth, for whom Cranmer stood as godfather, as heir to the throne. In 1536, he also invalidated Henry's marriage to Anne Boleyn, which led to the disinheriting of Princess Elizabeth. In 1540, Cranmer likewise presided over the dissolution of the royal marriage to Anne of Cleves. During the 1540s, Cranmer was a leader of the reform party at court and, despite efforts by the conservatives to bring him down, always retained the favor and affection of Henry VIII, who named him to Prince Edward's regency council.

After 1547, Cranmer became increasingly Protestant in his thinking; the two editions of the *BOOK OF COMMON PRAYER* issued under EDWARD VI were largely his work. He joined the unsuccessful attempt to exclude the Catholic MARY I from the throne and was imprisoned by Mary for heresy (see NORTHUMBERLAND'S COUP). He refused to recognize the return of papal jurisdiction and was condemned for heresy, dying at the stake on 21 March 1556 (see MARIAN MARTYRS). Many of his efforts during Edward's reign to devise a scriptural, Protestant Church for England became the basis for the ANGLICAN SETTLEMENT in 1559. *See also* PROTESTANTISM.

Further Reading: Diarmaid MacCulloch, *Thomas Cranmer,* New Haven, CT: Yale University Press, 1996.

Cromwell, Thomas (c. 1485–1540)

As HENRY VIII's chief minister in the 1530s, Thomas Cromwell engineered the parliamentary break with the Roman Catholic Church that freed the king to marry Elizabeth's mother, Anne BOLEYN. In his youth, Cromwell spent time as a soldier in Italy and as a merchant in the NETHERLANDS. He then took up law and was elected to PARLIAMENT in the 1520s. By 1525, he was in the service of Cardinal Thomas Wolsey, acting as the cardinal's secretary and undertaking the dissolution of several small monasteries, the revenues of which Wolsey applied to the new colleges he had founded (see UNIVERSITIES).

Cromwell is usually credited with suggesting to the king, in about 1531, that Henry make himself head of the English Church and thereby solve the dilemma caused by the pope's refusal to annul Henry's first marriage to CATHERINE OF ARAGON. By 1532, Cromwell was a member of the PRIVY COUNCIL, and by 1534 he was the king's secretary. He drafted and pushed through Parliament most of the key Reformation legislation (see REFORMATION, ENGLISH), and was the driving force behind the dissolution of the monasteries. He was made a baron in 1537 (see PEERAGE) and pushed a legislative program that increased the power of the king in Parliament in all areas of government. He was opposed by religious conservatives at COURT for his association with religious reform and for his low-class origins.

Cromwell advocated alliance with the Lutheran princes of Germany, and negotiated the king's 1540 marriage to ANNE OF CLEVES, the daughter of a German duke. The king's intense dissatisfaction with his new wife, and the alliance she represented, allowed Cromwell's enemies to persuade Henry that his minister was a heretic working against the royal wishes in religion. Cromwell was created Earl of Essex in April 1540, but two months later was arrested and imprisoned in the

TOWER OF LONDON for TREASON. He was condemned by ATTAINDER and executed in July 1540.

Further Reading: A. G. Dickens, *Thomas Cromwell and the English Reformation,* New York: Harper and Row, 1969; G. R. Elton, *The Tudor Revolution in Government,* Cambridge: Cambridge University Press, 1953.

Cumberland, Earl of. *See* CLIFFORD, GEORGE, EARL OF CUMBERLAND.

customs revenue

One major source of Crown revenue during Elizabeth's reign was customs duties, the taxes collected on the import and export of certain commodities (see REVENUE, ROYAL). The authority to collect customs duties was conferred on the Crown by PARLIAMENT. Since the time of Edward IV in the late fifteenth century, this authority was usually granted to the monarch for life by the first Parliament of the reign.

English FOREIGN TRADE was highly regulated, responding to the political, financial, and military needs of the government, and to social conditions. For instance, grain exports were suspended during periods of famine and food shortage, as in the 1590s, and all trade with the Spanish NETHERLANDS was halted in the early 1570s after the breakdown of relations with SPAIN caused by the "TREASURE CRISIS" OF 1568. The exportation of goods from England required a license from the Crown, and the exportation of certain items, such as livestock and hides, was forbidden, while other products, such as beer, copper, and herring, were restricted. Customs duties included such ancient taxes as tonnage, a charge levied at a fixed rate on a tun of wine imported from Europe, and poundage, a tax of 12 pence on each pound of assessed value levied on all commodities imported into England (see COINAGE). The major English exports subject to customs duties were wool, woolen cloth, and tin. Under MARY I, Lord Treasurer William PAULET, Marquis of Winchester, who retained his office under Elizabeth, reformed the collection of customs and raised the customs rates, thereby substantially augmenting Crown customs revenue.

At the start of Elizabeth's reign, income from the cloth customs alone amounted to £30,000 per year, and the total annual revenue from all customs was over £75,000, making the customs as important a component of royal revenue as the £50,000–£100,000 per year the queen obtained from the revenues of the royal estates. Because customs duties were difficult to collect, the Crown often contracted with private collectors who promised the government a fixed sum and kept as profit anything they collected over that amount. Although an increasingly important component of the royal income, customs duties were sensitive to political and environmental conditions, rising and falling with war and peace, famine and surplus, and strong or strained foreign relations. *See also* FISCAL FEUDALISM; SUBSIDY; TAXATION.

Further Reading: G. D. Ramsay, *English Overseas Trade During the Centuries of Emergence,* London: Macmillan, 1957.

D

dance

A popular pastime in Elizabethan England (see ENTERTAINMENT), dancing was a required skill for a courtier, who needed to keep abreast of the most fashionable new dances from Italy and FRANCE if he was to serve as a lively dancing partner for the queen. Elizabeth was so fond of dancing that a man's political career was said to depend on his ability to dance. Early in his career, Sir Christopher HATTON, the future chancellor of England, was accused by his rivals of owing his position at COURT to his skill as a dancer. Dancing schools became so common after 1560 that foreign ambassadors (see DIPLOMACY) commented on "the dancing English."

At Elizabeth's accession in 1558, court dances tended to be slower and more stately than the country dances of the lower classes (see SOCIAL HIERARCHY). Later in the reign, however, the trend, which Elizabeth encouraged, was for livelier dances, such as the jig. The MASQUE, a popular form of court entertainment, almost always included dancing, from relatively simple dances performed by the masque participants with members of the audience to complicated and elaborate performances given by the actors as part of the masque pageant. COURT dances often involved couples and could require intricate footwork and graceful movement. Country dances often involved groups of couples in round, square, or rectangular formations, and were generally simpler in footwork and more open and athletic in movement. Social divisions in dance were not rigid; Elizabeth encouraged her courtiers to learn popular country dances, while common people occasionally danced the simpler court dances.

Besides the social dances of court and country, numerous more formalized dances were common in Elizabethan England. The most popular of these was the morris dance, which usually involved male dancers attired in bells, ribbons, and otherwise colorful and outlandish attire. Morris dances were commonly performed at the summer holiday celebrations, such as those accompanying the Whitsunday festivities (see HOLIDAYS). Although PURITANS generally frowned on dancing as frivolous and tending to sexual license, their disapproval failed to dampen the Elizabethan love of dance. *See also* MUSIC.

Further Reading: Skiles Howard, *The Politics of Courtly Dancing in Early Modern England*, Amherst: University of Massachusetts Press, 1998; John Fitzhugh Millar, *Elizabethan Country Dances*, Williamsburg, VA: Thirteen Colonies Press, 1985.

Darnley, Lord. *See* STUART, HENRY, LORD DARNLEY.

Darnley murder

On 10 February 1567, Henry STUART, Lord Darnley, husband of Mary STUART, Queen of Scots, was murdered at the house of Kirk o'Field outside EDINBURGH. The murder represented a final solution to a difficult political problem. On 30 July 1565, Mary proclaimed Darnley, her new husband, king of SCOTLAND. Mary's PROCLAMATION drove her half brother James STUART, Earl of Moray, into rebellion (see CHASEABOUT RAID) with various other Protestant lords. Darnley, through his drinking, licentiousness, and irresponsibility, soon made himself obnoxious to the queen, who denied him any real power. To recover his position, Darnley, on the promise of being crowned king, joined the Protestant lords in the murder of Mary's hated Catholic advisor, David RIZZIO. Although disgusted by her husband's deed, Mary induced him to betray his Protestant confederates and help her retrieve her political position. When, after two betrayals, Darnley had still not achieved power, he began publicly insulting the queen, most notably by his refusal to attend the December 1566 baptism of his son James (see JAMES I), thereby casting doubt on the infant prince's legitimacy.

By the start of 1567, Darnley had become a complete political liability, detested by both the Protestant lords and the Catholic queen. Darnley's removal became imperative, but, because the queen refused divorce, it could be achieved only by his death. In January, Darnley returned to Edinburgh and lodged at Kirk o'Field, where Mary visited him on the evening of 9 February. Changing her mind about spending the night, Mary left to attend the marriage celebrations of a COURT official. At about 2 A.M. on 10 February, the house at Kirk o'Field exploded; Darnley escaped into the garden, but was smothered to death there by persons unknown. Suspicion immediately fell upon James HEPBURN, Earl of Bothwell, to whom Mary had shown marked favor. The murder became a European cause célèbre, but it need not have led to Mary's downfall, for Darnley's death removed an acknowledged political embarrassment. Both Elizabeth in England and Catherine de MEDICI in France advised Mary to maintain an appearance of innocence, to act within the law, and to allow the scandal to die down. In this way, Elizabeth had survived Amy DUDLEY's death in 1560 and Catherine de Medici was to survive the SAINT BARTHOLOMEW MASSACRE in 1572. However, Mary refused to go into mourning and continued to show favor to Bothwell, whom she married in May. Thus, Mary's shocking behavior after the murder, rather than the murder itself, led to her overthrow in 1567 by her outraged subjects.

Once Mary had been removed from power and was imprisoned in England, both Elizabeth and the new Scottish regime headed by

Moray used Mary's apparent complicity in Darnley's murder to keep her from returning to the throne. Although Moray and the Protestant lords were surely aware beforehand of the plan to kill Darnley, even if they were not directly involved, they used the damning evidence of the CASKET LETTERS to lay the blame solely on Bothwell (who likely *was* involved) and on Mary (who likely knew of the plan). Thus, in death, Darnley became a more effective political force than he ever was in life.

Further Reading: Caroline Bingham, *Darnley: A Life of Henry Stuart, Lord Darnley,* London: Constable, 1995; Jenny Wormald, *Mary, Queen of Scots,* London: Collins and Brown, 1991.

Davies, Richard (1501–1581)

Richard Davies, a leader of the Reformation in WALES (see REFORMATION, WELSH), helped translate the New Testament into Welsh. The son of a Welsh parish priest, Davies was educated at Oxford (see UNIVERSITIES), completing his degree in 1530. A strong Protestant, Davies was given two benefices in the diocese of Lincoln by EDWARD VI (see BENEFICE). On the accession of the Catholic monarch MARY I in 1553, Davies was deprived of his Anglican Church livings because of his reformed beliefs. He and his wife fled the country and settled for a time among the English exile community at Frankfurt before moving to Geneva in Switzerland, where they lived in great poverty (see MARIAN EXILES).

Upon the accession of Elizabeth in 1558, Davies returned to England and was appointed to the Welsh bishopric of St. Asaph in 1560. In the following year, Davies was promoted to the Welsh bishopric of St. David's, a position that allowed him to become the leading advisor to Archbishop Matthew PARKER and to Secretary William CECIL on issues pertaining to the Welsh Church. A sound scholar and capable linguist, Davies contributed to the preparation of the Bishops' Bible, which appeared in 1568 (see BIBLE, ENGLISH).

In 1563, Davies and Welsh reformer William SALESBURY promoted a private bill in PARLIAMENT authorizing the translation of the Bible and the *BOOK OF COMMON PRAYER* into Welsh. Both men believed that the success of PROTESTANTISM in Wales depended on the ability of Welsh children to read the Bible in their native tongue. Although the bill passed, it made no financial provision to support the work of translation. Davies and Salesbury therefore agreed to share the cost of producing both translations. Davies worked with Salesbury on the *Book of Common Prayer,* but Salesbury did most of the work on the Welsh New Testament, which was published in 1567. The two men also planned to produce a Welsh version of the Old Testament, but quarreled over the translation of certain words and the project was not successful. Translation of the complete Bible into Welsh was left to William MORGAN, the Bishop of St. Asaph, who published his work in 1588. Besides working to strengthen the ANGLICAN CHURCH in Wales, Davies was known as a leading patron of Welsh bards (see POETRY). He died in November 1581.

Further Reading: Glanmor Williams, *Renewal and Reformation: Wales c. 1415–1642,* Oxford: Oxford University Press, 1993.

Davis, John (c. 1550–1605)

John Davis (or Davys) was an accomplished navigator and a tireless searcher for the NORTHWEST PASSAGE. Born in Devon, Davis was a neighbor of the Gilbert and Raleigh families and grew up knowing the future Elizabethan explorers Sir Humphrey GILBERT and his half brother Sir Walter RALEIGH. Davis went to sea at an early age, and in 1583 proposed an expedition to discover the Northwest Passage to Elizabeth's secretary of state, Sir Francis WALSINGHAM. With the assistance of Adrian Gilbert, Sir Humphrey's brother, and the financial backing of LONDON and Devon merchants, Davis commanded a 1585 expedition that explored the east and west coasts of Greenland.

The next year, Davis led a three-vessel expedition that again explored Greenland and the east coast of Canada. He made friendly contact with Inuit (Eskimo) peoples and returned with a large haul of cod, but found no Northwest Passage. On a third expedition in 1587, Davis explored the waterway west of Greenland, now called Davis Strait, and entered Baffin Bay. He sailed far to the north, but still found no passage. In 1588, Davis commanded the *Black Dog* in the Channel battles against the ARMADA, and in 1591 he sailed with Thomas CAVENDISH's voyage to the Pacific via the southern tip of South America. Davis

During his American explorations, John Davis made friendly contact with the Inuit (Eskimo) peoples. This Inuit mother and her child were drawn by John White. © *The British Museum.*

agreed to join the venture as commander of the *Desire* when Cavendish promised him a chance to search for the Pacific end of the Northwest Passage. However, when storms separated the two men and prevented Davis from running the Straits of Magellan, he turned around and sailed home alone, discovering the Falkland Islands along the way.

In 1594, Davis published a work of navigation entitled *Seaman's Secrets.* In 1595, he published *The World's Hydrographical Description,* which attempted to prove the existence of a Northwest Passage. Davis sailed with Raleigh on the CADIZ RAID (1596), on the ISLANDS VOYAGE in 1597, and on a Dutch voyage to the East Indies in 1598. In 1601, he was a navigator on the first trading voyage sent to Asia by the EAST INDIA COMPANY. Davis joined the company's second expedition in 1604 and was killed in December 1605 when the expedition was attacked by Japanese pirates off Singapore.

Further Reading: John Davis, *The Voyages and Works of John Davis, the Navigator,* New York: B. Franklin, 1970; Samuel Eliot Morison, *The European Discovery of America: The Northern Voyages,* New York: Oxford University Press, 1971.

Davison, William (c. 1541–1608)

William Davison became the scapegoat for Queen Elizabeth's refusal to take responsibility for the execution of her cousin, Mary STUART, Queen of Scots. Davison's official career began in 1566 when he traveled to SCOTLAND as secretary to the English ambassador, Sir Henry KILLIGREW. In 1576, the queen sent Davison to report on the NETHERLANDS REVOLT, and in 1577 he became the English representative in Antwerp (see DIPLOMACY). Davison spent 1583–84 in EDINBURGH attempting to dissuade James VI (see JAMES I) from a French alliance. He returned to the NETHERLANDS in 1585, and by the end of 1586 his successful diplomatic work had won him appointment to the PRIVY COUNCIL and as assistant secretary of state (see OFFICERS OF STATE) under Sir Francis WALSINGHAM.

The commission appointed to try Mary Stuart condemned her to death on 25 October 1586, and PARLIAMENT petitioned the queen for her execution on 12 November. Elizabeth ordered William CECIL, Lord Burghley, to prepare the death warrant, and Burghley gave it to Davison to obtain the queen's signature. Because the French and Scottish ambassadors were petitioning for Mary's life, Elizabeth ordered Davison to hold the warrant until she requested it. Over the next few weeks, Elizabeth made several attempts to convince Sir Amias PAULET, Mary's jailer, to murder the Scottish queen quietly so as to relieve Elizabeth of responsibility for executing her cousin publicly. Horrified by these requests, Paulet refused.

On 1 February 1587, Elizabeth sent for Davison and signed the warrant, but bemoaned the necessity of executing Mary and hinted that Davison should arrange with Paulet to have Mary secretly killed. Davison showed the signed warrant to Burghley and Walsingham, who convened the Privy Council to issue letters ordering its implementation. Accordingly, Mary was beheaded on 8 February. Upon hearing the news, Elizabeth angrily declared that she had never ordered the execution and that it had been carried out against her wishes by the Privy Council acting under unauthorized instructions from Davison. Elizabeth arrested Davison and charged him with contempt and

misprision (improper performance of an official duty); he was convicted in Star Chamber, heavily fined, and imprisoned in the TOWER OF LONDON until 1589 (see STAR CHAMBER, COURT OF). Although Burghley and Robert DEVEREUX, Earl of Essex, defended Davison, the queen never readmitted him to her favor.

Further Reading: Paul Johnson, *Elizabeth I,* New York: Holt, Rinehart and Winston, 1974; Jenny Wormald, *Mary, Queen of Scots,* London: Collins and Brown, 1991.

Davys, John. *See* DAVIS, JOHN.

debasement. *See* COINAGE.

Dee, John (1527–1608)

Although known today primarily as an astrologer and alchemist, John Dee was also one of the finest geographers and mathematicians in Elizabethan England. Dee was born in LONDON, although his family came originally from WALES. He earned his baccalaureate degree at Cambridge (see UNIVERSITIES) in 1544 and two years later was appointed a fellow of Trinity College, Cambridge, by HENRY VIII. In the late 1540s, Dee left England to study in the NETHERLANDS at Louvain, where he met and befriended many of the leading geographers of Europe. By 1550, he was in Paris delivering a series of popular public lectures on Euclid. On his return to London, Dee brought back the first astronomical instruments ever seen in England.

After spending part of the reign of MARY I in prison for allegedly plotting against the queen, Dee won favor with Queen Elizabeth by using his astrological knowledge to calculate a propitious day for her coronation. Over the course of the reign, Dee became an important figure in the promotion of English exploration and the expansion of English trade. He strongly supported efforts to find a Northeast Passage to Asia and to discover the continent of "Terra Australis Incognita," which Dee was convinced existed in the southern hemisphere. A host of famous Elizabethan navigators and explorers, including Sir Martin FROBISHER, Sir Francis DRAKE, Stephen and William BOROUGH, and Sir Walter RALEIGH, sought out Dee for his mathematical and technical expertise. His extensive library and his fine collection of navigational and astronomical instruments were open to any seaman or scientist who wished to use them. The queen consulted Dee frequently on matters both scientific and astrological, even coming sometimes to his home at Mortlake.

In the 1580s, Dee's attempts to conjure spirits and to discover the "philosophers' stone," an object thought capable of converting base metals into gold, involved him with a disreputable spiritual medium named Edward Kelley. Kelley's obvious impostures hurt both Dee's reputation and his finances. In 1583, a mob, believing Dee to be a magician, attacked his house at Mortlake and destroyed many of his books and instruments. Dee spent the rest of his life attempting to refute the charge of sorcery. He died in poverty at Mortlake in December 1608. *See also* FORMAN, SIMON; WITCHCRAFT.

Further Reading: Richard Deacon, *John Dee,* London: Muller, 1968; Peter J. French, *John Dee,* New York: ARK Paperbacks, 1987.

"The Description of England"

William HARRISON's "The Description of England" is the most valuable source on Elizabethan life and customs available to modern historians. Part of the team of writers working with Raphael HOLINSHED on *The Chronicles of England, Scotland, and Ireland* (popularly known as HOLINSHED'S *CHRONICLES*), Harrison wrote a long treatise describing the island of Britain and its people as they existed in the 1570s. Titled "An Historical Description of the Island of Britain," Harrison's treatise became the introduction to the first edition of Holinshed's *Chronicles,* published in 1577. For the second edition of the *Chronicles* published in 1587 by an editorial team under John HOOKER, Harrison reordered the sections of his work, retaining the original title for Book I and using the title "The Description of England" for Books II and III.

Book I included topographical and historical descriptions of the whole island of Britain, including SCOTLAND. Some of the individual sections covered the languages of Britain; major rivers and waterfalls; the air, soil, and main commodities of the island; and important highways. The books comprising "The Description of England" (which also included WALES) described, among other things, the ANGLICAN CHURCH and its dioceses, the UNIVERSITIES, the shires (see LOCAL GOVERNMENT), the SOCIAL HIERARCHY, PARLIAMENT, the POOR LAWS, the punishment of criminals, ARCHITECTURE, towns (see BOROUGHS), castles and PALACES, the NAVY, the COINAGE, English pets and livestock, inns and fairs, the keeping of time, minerals, and antiquities (see ANTIQUARIANISM).

Harrison's work is important because of its interesting detail and its lively, readable style. For instance, in describing the lavish meals of the nobility, with their "great number of dishes and change of meat," Harrison credits their preparation mainly to "musical-headed Frenchmen." Harrison's descriptions of Elizabethan social classes are particularly useful—the gentry are "those whom their race and blood, or at the least, their virtues, do make noble and known," while townsmen are "those that are free within the cities and are of some likely substance to bear office in the same." Another service performed by Harrison is his preservation for modern readers of the natural vocabulary and language rhythms of Elizabethan ENGLISH, for, as Harrison complained, the printer's schedule denied him the scholarly notes and more formal style he thought proper, the work being "no sooner penned than printed." *See also* PRINTING.

Further Reading: William Harrison, *The Description of England,* edited by Georges Edelen, New York: Dover Publications, 1994.

Desmond, Earl of. *See* FITZGERALD, GERALD, EARL OF DESMOND.

Desmond Rebellion

The Desmond Rebellion was instrumental in opening the Munster region of southern IRELAND to more intensive English colonization. Although named for the man who ultimately became its leader, Gerald FITZGERALD, 14th Earl of Desmond, the Desmond Rebellion was begun by James Fitzmaurice FITZGERALD (often referred to simply as Fitzmaurice), leader of an earlier rising in southern Ireland (see FITZMAURICE'S REBELLION). Seeking to bring the COUNTER-REFORMATION to Ireland, Fitzmaurice landed in southern Ireland in July 1579 with a force of several hundred Spanish and Italian troops provided by Pope GREGORY XIII. The papal force built a fort at Smerwick and called upon all Irishmen to rise in defense of the Catholic religion (see SMERWICK, SIEGE OF). When Fitzmaurice was killed in August, leadership of the uprising passed to Desmond's younger brothers.

In November, Sir John Pelham, the English lord deputy, assuming that the actions of Desmond's brothers indicated the earl's support for the rebellion, proclaimed Desmond a traitor. This proclamation drove the earl into open revolt and angered Elizabeth, who had hoped to limit the spread of rebellion by negotiating with Desmond. In 1580, the queen appointed a new lord deputy, the strongly Protestant Lord Grey de Wilton. Faced with a second uprising centered in the PALE just 25 miles from DUBLIN, Grey attacked the rebels in the steep valley of Glenmalure and suffered a severe defeat. The action at Glenmalure and the arrival at Smerwick in September 1580 of another 700 papal troops encouraged the Desmond rebels to continue their rising. However, in November, Grey joined forces with Thomas BUTLER, Earl of Ormond, a staunch royalist and an enemy of Desmond, to lay siege to the Smerwick fort. The papal troops surrendered after four days, only to be massacred by Grey's men.

Desmond's Irish supporters, realizing that they could expect no more help from Rome, gradually abandoned the earl and submitted to the Dublin government. Between 1580 and 1583, Ormond devastated Munster in a campaign vividly described by Edmund SPENSER in *A View of the Present State of Ireland*. Both Spenser and Walter RALEIGH participated in the suppression of the uprising. Captured in November 1583, Desmond died shortly thereafter when his supporters tried to rescue him. Because over 30,000 inhabitants of Munster were dispossessed or otherwise driven from their lands, Desmond's Rebellion opened Munster to a subsequent plantation of English colonists (see PLANTATIONS, IRISH).

Further Reading: Steven G. Ellis, *Tudor Ireland*, London: Longman, 1985; Brian Fitzgerald, *The Geraldines: An Experiment in Irish Government, 1169–1601,* London: Staples Press, 1951.

de Vere, Edward, Earl of Oxford. *See* VERE, EDWARD DE, EARL OF OXFORD.

Devereux, Penelope. *See* RICH, PENELOPE, LADY RICH.

Devereux, Robert, Earl of Essex
(1567–1601)
Robert Devereux, Earl of Essex, was the most prominent courtier and most famous military leader of Elizabeth's last years. The son of Walter DEVEREUX, Earl of Essex, and Lettice KNOLLYS, Essex was already, by age 17, a favorite of the 50-year-old queen. Elizabeth's affection for the young earl stemmed in part from ties of blood (Essex was the queen's cousin through his mother) and in part from his mother's marriage to Robert DUDLEY, Earl of Leicester, the great love of Elizabeth's life.

Essex came to COURT in 1584, was knighted in 1586, and became master of horse, which had also been Leicester's first position at court, in 1587. After Leicester's death in 1588, the queen quickly transferred much of her affection for him to Essex. By 1593, she had named him Knight of the Garter and privy councilor. The relationship between aging monarch and young favorite was stormy. In

Robert Devereux, Earl of Essex, Elizabeth I's last royal favorite, was painted by an unknown artist about 1596. *By courtesy of the National Portrait Gallery, London.*

1589, Essex slipped away from court without permission to join the PORTUGAL EXPEDITION. This escapade brought down the queen's wrath on Sir Francis DRAKE and the other leaders of the expedition, but Essex himself was forgiven when he returned to court. The earl was a co-leader of the brilliantly successful CADIZ RAID (1596), an action that won him great military fame in England and Europe. Essex's involvement in the unsuccessful ISLANDS VOYAGE of 1597, however, hurt his reputation and his standing with the queen.

In 1599, he was named lord lieutenant of IRELAND, and sent to that island with a large army to put down the rebellion of Hugh O'NEILL Earl of Tyrone (see NINE YEARS WAR). Essex made little headway against O'Neill and settled instead for a truce. He returned to England without permission in September 1599. For this action, he was charged with dereliction of duty and treating with the enemy, and he was stripped of all favors and offices, including his monopoly on sweet wines, upon which his financial position depended (see MONOPOLIES). He was imprisoned until August 1600 but arrested again in February 1601 for leading a brief uprising in LONDON that aimed at taking the queen prisoner (see ESSEX'S REBELLION). For this plot, Essex was condemned for TREASON and executed on 25 February 1601.

Further Reading: Robert Lacey, *Robert, Earl of Essex,* New York: Atheneum, 1971; Lytton Strachey, *Elizabeth and Essex,* Oxford: Oxford University Press, 1981.

Devereux, Walter, Earl of Essex

(c. 1541–1576)

Walter Devereux, first Earl of Essex, led a major English colonization effort in Elizabethan IRELAND. In 1561, Devereux married Lettice KNOLLYS, daughter of Sir Francis KNOLLYS and second cousin to the queen; in 1572, Elizabeth made Devereux Earl of Essex and a Knight of the Garter. In 1573, Essex proposed a scheme for subduing and colonizing Ulster, a province of northern Ireland in which England had little cultural influence and even less political control (see ULSTER ENTERPRISE [ESSEX]). The formal agreement between Essex and Elizabeth made the venture a private effort; the earl was to receive no government commission or salary. Elizabeth recognized the earl's right to colonize a portion of Ulster, and she granted him freedom from CESS and certain rights over trade and the administration of justice. Essex and the queen agreed to jointly raise a force of 1,200 men and to share the costs of building fortifications. The earl mortgaged his lands in England in return for a royal loan of £10,000 to cover start-up costs; if the loan was not repaid in three years, the lands were forfeit to the Crown.

Essex and an enthusiastic group of volunteers, including such other proponents of Irish colonization as Sir Peter CAREW, left for Ireland in July 1573. From the outset, the expedition suffered from lack of supplies, bad weather, disease, and the hostility of the Irish lord deputy, Sir William FITZWILLIAM, who saw Essex's venture as a threat to his position. By 1574, Essex, facing financial ruin, asked to amend the agreement to convert the enterprise into a government project. Elizabeth was sufficiently agreeable to keep Essex campaigning in Ireland until 1575, when she withdrew her support.

Essex returned to England and negotiated with the government for assistance in meeting his extensive debts. An arrangement approved by the queen in May 1576 granted Essex lands in Ireland and appointed him earl marshal of Ireland, although the earl had to sell his English estates to satisfy his creditors. Essex then returned to Ireland where he died in September 1576. His sudden death at age 35 led to rumors that he had been poisoned by Robert DUDLEY, Earl of Leicester, who was suspected of having an affair with Essex's wife. Although Leicester married the widowed countess in 1578, murder was never proved and is unlikely. Essex's son and heir, Robert DEVEREUX, became Elizabeth's favorite in the 1590s (see FAVORITES).

Further Reading: Steven G. Ellis, *Tudor Ireland,* London: Longman, 1985; Colm Lennon, *Sixteenth-Century Ireland: The Incomplete Conquest,* Dublin: Gill and Macmillan, 1994; Margaret MacCurtain, *Tudor and Stuart Ireland,* Dublin: Gill and Macmillan, 1972; David B. Quinn, *The Elizabethans and the Irish,* Ithaca, NY: Cornell University Press, 1966.

Devise (for the Succession)

The *Devise* was a document that embodied the plans of EDWARD VI and his chief minister, John DUDLEY, Duke of Northumberland, to exclude Edward's half sisters, princesses Mary (see MARY I) and Elizabeth, from the succession (see SUCCESSION, ACTS OF). Edward feared that Mary, who was Catholic and next in line for the throne, would overturn the Protestant English Church and restore the authority of the pope. As Edward's health deteriorated in the spring of 1553, he and Northumberland agreed to a plan whereby the succession, as ordained by act of PARLIAMENT and the will of Edward's father, the deceased HENRY VIII, would be altered to exclude Mary and Elizabeth and to pass the Crown directly to the male heirs of Frances (Brandon) Grey, Duchess of Suffolk, who was the daughter of Henry VIII's sister Mary (see GREY CLAIM). These male heirs were nonexistent in 1553, for the duchess had only daughters, the eldest of whom, Jane GREY, was only about 15 and unmarried. To ensure the birth of male heirs, and to tie his family to the royal house, Northumberland arranged a marriage between Jane and his son Guildford.

When it became clear that the sickly Edward would die before a male heir could be born, Northumberland altered the *Devise* to pass the Crown on to Jane herself. Both the prospective queen and the royal judges had to be bullied into accepting the arrangement (see NORTHUMBERLAND'S COUP). Edward's death on 6 July 1553 was kept secret from the country and from Jane (who fainted on hearing of her accession) until 9 July. The reign of Queen Jane ended after only nine days, after which Jane, her husband, her father, and her father-in-law were arrested by Queen Mary and sent to the TOWER OF LONDON. Northumberland was executed in August 1553; the other three survived until February 1554 when they were executed in the aftermath of WYATT'S REBELLION.

Further Reading: W. K. Jordan, *Edward VI: The Threshold of Power*, Cambridge, MA: Harvard University Press, 1970; David Loades, *John Dudley, Duke of Northumberland*, Oxford: Clarendon Press, 1996; David Loades, *The Reign of Mary Tudor*, 2nd ed., London: Longman, 1991.

Devonshire, Earl of. *See* COURTENAY, EDWARD, EARL OF DEVONSHIRE.

diet

The respective diets of upper- and lower-class Elizabethans were characterized by the proportion of bread and meat consumed. Among the PEERAGE, GENTRY, and wealthier urban merchants, meals often consisted of several varieties of meat, including beef, pork, mutton, and capon (chicken), and such exotic fare (at least in the twentieth century), as woodcock, rabbit, venison, and even crane. For large feasts, a wide selection of meats would be available, with guests ordering a sampling of the dish they most favored; everyday meals had less variety. In the sixteenth-century, meat was usually slaughtered in the fall and, lacking refrigeration, had to be pickled or salted to be kept through the winter. Asian spices were in high demand because they hid the taste of salted meat or recently slaughtered meat that had passed its prime.

Artisans, yeoman, and rural laborers ate less meat and more bread, eggs, and cheese. While peasants sometimes ate peas and lentils, green vegetables and fruits were rarely eaten by any Elizabethan social class (see SOCIAL HIERARCHY). The type of bread eaten was a strong social indicator. The finest wheat bread, made from whole-meal flour and creamy yellow in color, was reserved for upper-class tables, while darker and coarser wheat breads and brown or black rye or barley breads were the fare of servants and peasants. During Lent, upper-class tables replaced meats with an equally wide variety of fish. Although the Reformation had overthrown many Catholic practices (see REFORMATION, ENGLISH), the government encouraged the tradition of refraining from meat during Lent because it maintained the fishing industry from which the NAVY drew sailors.

For drink, Elizabethans took such fermented beverages as wine, ale, and beer; water, frequently tainted by natural impurities and poor urban sanitation, was seldom drunk. Wine, which had to be imported from Europe, was an upper-class drink; lower-class beverages were ale (made of water, barley, and spices) and beer (brewed with hops and cheaper than ale because it could be stored longer). Although peasants occasionally faced famine, as occurred during the bad harvests of the 1590s, the traditional lower-class diet, being a better balance of foods, was probably more healthful than the high-protein, meat-heavy diet of the upper classes, which made such medical complaints as urinary infections and kidney and bladder stones common. *See also* MEDICINE and the illustration for ENTERTAINMENT.

Further Reading: J. A. Sharpe, *Early Modern England: A History 1550–1760,* 2nd ed., Oxford: Oxford University Press, 1997; Penry Williams, *Life in Tudor England,* New York: G. P. Putnam's Sons, 1964; Joyce Youings, *Sixteenth-Century England,* New York: Penguin Books, 1984.

diplomacy

Diplomacy, the art of maintaining relations and conducting negotiations between countries, was enormously complicated in the Elizabethan period by religious differences. The system of sending resident ambassadors to the COURT of a foreign power arose in Renaissance Italy, where the various city-states sought through war and alliance to maintain the balance of power. Because face-to-face meetings between rulers were difficult to arrange and risky to conduct, quiet negotiations undertaken by resident ambassadors who could also discreetly gather information proved a much better method of conducting diplomacy.

By the early sixteenth century, the Italian diplomatic system spread to northern Europe, where HENRY VII, Elizabeth's grandfather, was one of the first rulers to adopt it. Because envoys were the personal representatives of their monarchs, the precedence given to ambassadors on ceremonial occasions was of great importance, and was a sign of the state of the host monarch's current relations with each envoy's ruler. Latin was the diplomatic language for much of the century, although vernacular tongues, especially French, came into more common usage by the Elizabethan period. Cardinal Thomas Wolsey, chief minister of HENRY VIII, created the English diplomatic service, exchanging resident envoys with CHARLES V, the pope (until the break with Rome), the French and Scots kings, and the Republic of Venice. Envoys conducted negotiations over outstanding issues and kept their governments informed of events in foreign courts. Because communications were slow, ambassadors had great freedom of action in dealing with crisis situations. For instance, the

Spanish ambassador's overreaction to the "TREASURE CRISIS" OF 1568 led to an embargo of trade between England and the NETHERLANDS. Modern foreign departments did not develop until the seventeenth century.

Under Elizabeth, the direction of foreign affairs was increasingly centered in the hands of Sir Francis WALSINGHAM, one of the secretaries of state. Besides supervising English ambassadors at foreign courts, Walsingham also built and maintained a widespread intelligence network. Religion and the intrigues on behalf of Mary STUART, Queen of Scots, made English diplomatic relations difficult, particularly with SPAIN. The Catholic envoys of PHILIP II found dealing with heretics as distasteful as the Protestant envoys of Elizabeth found dealing with papists. In 1572, England expelled the Spanish ambassador for his involvement in the RIDOLFI PLOT. In 1584, another Spanish ambassador, Bernadino de Mendoza, was expelled for his involvement in the THROCKMORTON PLOT. *See also* FRANCE.

Further Reading: M. S. Anderson, *The Rise of Modern Diplomacy, 1450–1919,* London: Longman, 1993; Garrett Mattingly, *Renaissance Diplomacy,* Baltimore: Penguin, 1964.

Don Antonio Expedition. *See* PORTUGAL EXPEDITION.

Don John of Austria. *See* JOHN OF AUSTRIA.

Dorset, Earl of. *See* SACKVILLE, THOMAS, EARL OF DORSET.

Douglas, Margaret, Countess of Lennox (1515–1578)

Margaret Douglas was the granddaughter of one king of England and the grandmother of another. Douglas's mother was Margaret Tudor, eldest daughter of HENRY VII and widow of James IV of Scotland; her father was Margaret Tudor's second husband, Archibald Douglas, Earl of Angus. Margaret Douglas was thus the aunt of Mary STUART, Queen of Scots, the first cousin of Elizabeth I, and a claimant to the English throne (see STUART CLAIM). Because her parents separated in 1518 and divorced in 1527, Douglas passed from the custody of her mother to that of her father and spent the 1520s being shuttled among various residences in both SCOTLAND and England.

In 1528, her uncle, HENRY VIII, placed her in the household of his daughter, Princess Mary (see MARY I), with whom she formed a close friendship. In 1533, Douglas was named first lady-in-waiting to Princess Elizabeth (see LADIES-IN-WAITING), but became first lady in the realm in 1536 when the execution of Elizabeth's mother, Anne BOLEYN, caused both Elizabeth and Mary to be declared bastards. Douglas then stood next in the English succession after her half brother James V of Scotland, although some Englishmen considered Douglas's claim to be superior because she had been born in England (see SUCCESSION, ACTS OF). In the 1540s, Douglas went briefly to the TOWER OF LONDON for her politically unacceptable relationships with men of the powerful HOWARD FAMILY. In 1544, the king arranged a marriage for her with Matthew Stuart, Earl of Lennox, a union that resulted in two sons—Henry STUART, Lord Darnley, and Charles Stuart, Earl of Lennox.

Because Douglas was Catholic, Henry VIII barred her from the succession in his will. After Elizabeth's accession, this bar led Douglas to scheme for a marriage between her son Darnley and his cousin, Mary Stuart; when the marriage occurred in 1565, Elizabeth punished Douglas with imprisonment in the Tower until after Darnley's murder in 1567 (see DARNLEY MURDER). In 1574, Douglas arranged the marriage of her second son to the daughter of the ambitious Elizabeth HARDWICK; this union, unauthorized by Elizabeth, resulted in the imprisonment of both mothers-in-law and the birth of Arabella STUART. Released from the Tower in 1577, Douglas died in March 1578, too soon to see the accession to the English throne of her grandson, JAMES I, the son of Darnley.

Further Reading: Caroline Bingham, *Darnley, A Life of Henry Stuart, Lord Darnley*, London: Constable, 1995; David N. Durant, *Bess of Hardwick: Portrait of an Elizabethan Dynast,* New York: Atheneum, 1978; Antonia Fraser, *Mary, Queen of Scots*, New York: Delacorte Press, 1969; Jenny Wormald, *Mary, Queen of Scots*, London: Collins and Brown, 1991.

Drake, Sir Francis (c. 1543–1596)

Sir Francis Drake was the most famous seaman, explorer, and privateer of Elizabethan England. Born into a Devonshire yeoman family, Drake first went to sea in 1563 and again in 1566 with his cousin John HAWKINS, who led trading expeditions to Africa and SPANISH AMERICA. In 1567, on Hawkins's third trading expedition to the Spanish colonies in AMERICA, Drake held his first command, the 50-ton *Judith*. The disastrous end to this voyage, ambushed by Spaniards at SAN JUAN D'ULLOA, combined with Drake's PROTESTANTISM to instill in him an intense hatred of SPAIN and Spaniards.

In the 1570s, Drake commanded several PRIVATEERING expeditions against Spanish targets in the New World. In 1577, Drake, who was rapidly acquiring a romantic reputation in England and an evil one in Spain (the Spaniards called him "El Draque," "the Dragon") secretly received Elizabeth's permission to conduct raids against Spanish shipping. Drake's plan was to sail around Cape Horn (the tip of South America) and attack Spanish vessels in the Pacific, where English raiders would be unexpected. Drake was also to seek out the Pacific end of any NORTHWEST PASSAGE around North America. After a difficult trip through the Straits of Magellan, Drake plundered at will in the Pacific before sailing north to the California coast, which he claimed for England as Nova Albion. Not finding a Northwest Passage, Drake sailed across the Pacific, returning home in 1580 with a fabulous cargo of Spanish treasure and spices. Because the queen was a financial backer of the expedition (thus the need for secrecy), she realized a handsome return on the sale of Drake's booty. DRAKE'S CIRCUMNAVIGATION of the globe (only the second in history) and his exploits against Spain made him a hero in England and throughout Europe.

In 1581, Drake was knighted aboard his ship, the *Golden Hind*. In 1585, he led a damaging raid of the Spanish West Indies, capturing much armament and harming PHILIP II's ability to outfit the ARMADA. In 1587, Drake attacked Cadiz in Spain (see CADIZ RAID [1587]), destroying some 30 ships and great quantities of naval supplies and again delaying the sailing of the Armada. He participated in the naval battles that defeated the Armada in 1588, although his plan to sail out and meet the enemy in Spanish waters was rejected by

This portrait by M. Gheeraerts shows the famous seaman and circumnavigator Sir Francis Drake standing next to the globe. *National Maritime Museum, London.*

the queen as too risky (see GRAVELINES, BATTLE OF; NAVY). His undisciplined handling of SHIPS in the English attack on the ports of northern Spain in 1589 put him out of favor with the queen and somewhat diminished his reputation (see PORTUGAL EXPEDITION). He retired from naval service to become mayor of Plymouth and the town's representative in PARLIAMENT. In 1595, he joined Hawkins on another raid of Spanish America, but the venture was a disaster and Drake died at sea on 28 January 1596. *See also* BOROUGH, WILLIAM; OXENHAM, JOHN.

Further Reading: John Cummins, *Francis Drake,* New York: St. Martin's Press, 1995; Harry Kelsey, *Sir Francis Drake: The Queen's Pirate,* New Haven, CT: Yale University Press, 1998; Christopher Lloyd, *Sir Francis Drake,* Boston: Faber and Faber, 1979; John Sugden, *Sir Francis Drake,* New York: Simon and Schuster, 1990.

Drake's circumnavigation

Francis DRAKE'S voyage of circumnavigation made Drake a hero in England and Europe and contributed heavily to the deterioration of relations between England and SPAIN (see Maps, "Drake's Voyage of Circumnavigation, 1577–80"). In 1577, Elizabeth gave permission for a voyage to explore the coasts of South America for possible English settlement. A fleet of five ships *(Pelican, Elizabeth, Marigold, Swan,* and *Christopher)* carrying 160 men left Plymouth under Drake's command on 13 December 1577.

Drake sailed first to Africa, where he captured several Spanish and Portuguese vessels that yielded a cache of fish to enlarge his food stores and a Spanish pilot who knew the Africa-Brazil route. Arriving in South America in early April 1578, the fleet spent several months moving down the east coast before three ships—*Pelican, Elizabeth,* and *Marigold*—entered the Straits of Magellan on 20 August. They emerged into the Pacific on 6 September, but heavy storms destroyed *Marigold* and drove *Elizabeth* back into the Straits, from where it set sail for England three weeks later. On the *Pelican,* which he renamed the *Golden Hind,* Drake sailed up the west coast of South America, sacking the town of Valparaiso in December and capturing the rich silver ship, the *Cacafuego,* off the Peruvian coast in March 1579. After seizing several other treasure ships, Drake captured two Spanish pilots who knew the route to the Philippines. Continuing north, Drake looted several Mexican villages before finally landing at Drake's Bay, somewhere on the California coast, in mid-June.

Finding no likely NORTHWEST PASSAGE, Drake sailed south to catch the trade winds and came to the East Indies by October. Adding six tons of cloves to his cargo in the Indies, Drake landed on an island off Java to undertake repairs made necessary by storms and a collision with submerged rocks off Celebes. In March 1580, the *Golden Hind* began the crossing of the Indian Ocean, sailing around Africa's Cape of Good Hope in June and arriving in Plymouth on 26 September 1580. Of the 160 men who had left Plymouth almost three years earlier, about 100 came safely home. Drake's cargo, worth almost £500,000—equal to three years' normal income for the Crown—helped Elizabeth overlook the many complaints about Drake with which the Spanish government had bombarded her since 1578. *See also* PHILIP II; PRIVATEERING; SPANISH AMERICA.

Further Reading: Derek A. Wilson, *The World Encompassed: Francis Drake and His Great Voyage,* New York: Harper and Row, 1977.

drama

The last two decades of the reign of Elizabeth I (and the first two of JAMES I) witnessed the writing and production of some of the finest plays in the English language. In 1500, English drama consisted of medieval morality plays and cycles of mystery plays, religious drama performed by amateur actors on town streets during fairs and HOLIDAYS. Over the next century, a professional Elizabethan theatre developed from these beginnings. The Reformation and the political turmoil that attended it freed English drama from religious themes and provided playwrights with secular plots, while the English nationalism stimulated by the break with the Roman Catholic Church caused writers to mine English history for stories and characters (REFORMATION, ENGLISH). The development of English HUMANISM put Elizabethan writers in touch with classical Greek and Roman styles and imbued them with a love of drama and literature.

Wary of the political and religious purposes for which drama could be used, Elizabeth banned the performance of unlicensed plays in 1559 and suppressed religious play cycles in the 1570s. In 1572, she forbade anyone but PEERS to sponsor professional troupes of players, and in 1574 empowered her master of the revels to license all plays and acting companies. These actions placed the English theatre under royal control and accelerated the secularization of Elizabethan drama. Beginning with Leicester's Men, an acting troupe sponsored by Robert DUDLEY, Earl of Leicester, who used the stage to promote his political program and his hopes for a royal marriage (see DUDLEY MARRIAGE SUIT), numerous professional companies arose under the patronage of important courtiers. Along with the development of groups of professional players came the building of permanent theatres—the first being James BURBAGE's London playhouse, The Theatre, constructed in 1576. Patterned after the open-air arenas used for ANIMAL SPORTS, other theatres soon appeared in and around London, including Burbage's Blackfriars (1576), the Rose (1587), and the Swan (1595). Many company actors became shareholders in particular theatres; for example, William SHAKESPEARE and the other principals of the CHAMBERLAIN'S MEN were part owners of the GLOBE THEATRE (1599).

The development of a professional theatre meant that playwrights no longer had to attach themselves to a noble patron and limit themselves to the themes and forms the patron favored, but could do well by writing for a theatre or troupe on themes that interested them (within government guidelines). These developments opened the playwriting profession to many who otherwise might not have been able to develop their talents, such playwrights as John LYLY, George PEELE, Robert GREENE, Christopher MARLOWE, Ben JONSON, and William Shakespeare. *See also* ALLEYN, EDWARD; HENSLOWE, PHILIP; POETRY; SHAKESPEARE, WORKS OF; STATIONERS' REGISTERS and the illustration for GLOBE THEATRE.

Further Reading: Herbert Berry, *Shakespeare's Playhouses*, New York: AMS, 1987; Ernest A. Gerrard, *Elizabethan Drama and Dramatists: 1583–1603*, New York: Cooper Square Publishers, 1972; G. B. Harrison, *Elizabethan Plays and Players*, Ann Arbor: University of Michigan Press, 1956; A. P. Rossiter, *English Drama from Early Times to the Elizabethans*, Folcroft, PA: Folcroft Library Editions, 1977.

This drawing from the frontispiece of William Alabaster's *Roxana Tragaedia* (London, 1632) is one of the earliest surviving depictions of an English stage performance. *By permission of the Folger Shakespeare Library.*

Dublin

Dublin, the capital of the modern Republic of IRELAND, was the largest town and the seat of English government in Elizabethan Ireland. Located along the east central coast of Ireland at the mouth of the River Liffey, Dublin was first settled by Scandinavian raiders in the mid-ninth century. The town fell to Norman invaders from England in the 1170s, becoming thereafter the principal settlement and administrative center of English royal government in Ireland. In the early thirteenth century, King John made Dublin the capital of the English lordship by building Dublin Castle to house the Irish royal treasury and the Irish royal law courts. By the fourteenth century, Dublin had become the meeting site of the Irish PARLIAMENT. By the fifteenth century, the area of effective English rule in Ireland was reduced largely to the town of Dublin and the surrounding districts of the PALE, with control of the town government resting mainly with Dublin's ANGLO-IRISH merchant families.

Enriched by the city's former monastic properties, the Dublin merchant elite initially supported the Reformation (see REFORMATION, IRISH) imposed by the English Crown in the 1530s. However, the Elizabethan policy of extending a centralized English administration throughout Ireland alienated the Catholic Anglo-Irish citizens of Dublin by placing them under the control of Protestant lord deputies from England who had little sympathy with their religion or their Irish customs. By the end of Elizabeth's reign, Dublin had lost many of its civic privileges, and the city's old Anglo-Irish leadership, politically restricted under the PENAL LAWS as Catholic RECUSANTS, had been replaced in power in the city, as the Anglo-Irish were throughout Ireland, by Protestant English (and, later, by Scots). Although Dublin became the second most important city of the British Isles in the eighteenth century, its POPULATION at the start of Elizabeth's reign was probably under 5,000 and little more than 10,000 at the queen's death in 1603.

Further Reading: Steven G. Ellis, *Tudor Ireland,* London: Longman, 1985; Colm Lennon, *The Lords of Dublin in the Age of Reformation,* Dublin: Irish Academic, 1989.

Dudley, Ambrose, Earl of Warwick

(c. 1528–1590)

The third son of John DUDLEY, Duke of Northumberland, Ambrose Dudley, Earl of Warwick, was a prominent Elizabethan military figure and a leading Protestant peer (see PEERAGE). Like his brothers, Ambrose Dudley was given a careful humanist (see HUMANISM) education. He was knighted in 1549 after serving with his father against rebels in Norfolk. Dudley was prominent at the court of EDWARD VI and friendly with the king and his half sister Princess Elizabeth. In July 1553, he joined his father's attempt to put Jane GREY on the throne in place of Princess Mary (see MARY I) and was committed to the TOWER OF LONDON along with his brothers Henry and Robert (see DUDLEY, ROBERT, EARL OF LEICESTER) when the attempt failed (see NORTHUMBERLAND'S COUP). Although convicted of TREASON, Ambrose Dudley was pardoned and released with his brothers in October 1554. In 1557, all three brothers served in Prince Philip's (see PHILIP II) St. Quentin campaign against FRANCE, where Henry died in battle.

At Elizabeth's accession, Ambrose came into favor at COURT, although he did not elicit the queen's romantic interest as did his brother Robert. The queen named him master of ordnance in 1560 and created him Earl of Warwick in 1561. In October 1562, the queen appointed Warwick captain-general of the military expedition being sent to take possession of the French port of Le Havre, which was being handed over to Elizabeth by the HUGUENOTS in return for her assistance against the royalist Catholic forces. When the two parties in the civil war came to terms in April 1563, Elizabeth ordered Warwick to hold the town against the combined Catholic-Huguenot armies. Severely wounded during the siege, Warwick received royal permission in July to return home with the remnant of his army (see LE HAVRE EXPEDITION).

His health permanently damaged, Warwick served as a commissioner at the trial of Thomas HOWARD, Duke of Norfolk, in 1572, and at the trial of Mary STUART, Queen of Scots, in 1586. He was admitted to the PRIVY COUNCIL in 1573, where he advocated various Puritan causes (see PURITANS). Always interested in foreign trade and exploration, Warwick was a chief promoter of Martin FROBISHER's first expedition in 1576. Warwick died in February 1590 from the effects of a leg amputation made necessary by his old wounds.

Further Reading: Alan Haynes, *The White Bear: Robert Dudley, the Elizabethan Earl of Leicester,* London: Peter Owen, 1987; David Loades, *John Dudley, Duke of Northumberland,* Oxford: Clarendon Press, 1996.

Dudley, Amy (c. 1532–1560)

On 4 June 1550, in the presence of EDWARD VI, Amy Robsart, the daughter of a Norfolk gentleman, married Sir Robert DUDLEY, a younger son of John DUDLEY, then Earl of Warwick. The newlyweds, who were both about 18, resided in Norfolk, although Robert was often at COURT. On Edward's death in 1553, Robert was arrested for supporting the unsuccessful coup on behalf of Jane GREY (see NORTHUMBERLAND'S COUP). Until October 1554, Robert was imprisoned in the TOWER OF LONDON under sentence of death, although Amy was allowed to visit him occasionally.

The Dudleys' fortunes changed on the accession of Elizabeth in 1558. The new queen knew Robert Dudley from her brother's court and remembered that they both had experienced the Tower and the possibility of execution in her sister's time (see MARY I). Elizabeth made Dudley master of horse and named him to the PRIVY COUNCIL. The queen's obvious infatuation with Dudley (see FAVORITES) led, both in England and abroad, to all manner of rumors concerning their relationship and the imminence of their MARRIAGE. The Spanish ambassador called Dudley "the king that is to be," and numerous people were imprisoned for openly declaring that Elizabeth was pregnant by her lover. Meanwhile, Amy Dudley, an obvious obstacle to any marriage plans, lived mostly in the country and was almost never seen at court. When, on 8 September 1560, Amy was found lying dead with a broken neck at the foot of her stairs, Dudley came under immediate suspicion of murder.

The timing and manner of Amy's death seemed to confirm months of gossip; it was soon being openly stated that Dudley had ordered his wife thrown down the stairs to free himself to wed the queen. Although a coroner's jury returned a verdict of accidental death, ru-

mors continued to accuse the royal favorite of murder. At the hearing, household servants hinted at suicide; they reported that Amy had been overheard praying for deliverance from her "desperation." Amy's disturbed state of mind may have been a result of rumors concerning her husband and the queen, or of a painful illness she was said to be suffering. Amy's death cooled Elizabeth's passion, and though Dudley retained her special affection for the rest of his life, the possibility of marriage with him slowly disappeared. *See also* DUDLEY MARRIAGE SUIT.

Further Reading: Alan Haynes, *The White Bear: Robert Dudley, the Elizabethan Earl of Leicester,* London: P. Owen, 1987; Elizabeth Jenkins, *Elizabeth and Leicester,* New York: Coward-McCann, 1962; Derek A. Wilson, *Sweet Robin: A Biography of Robert Dudley, Earl of Leicester,* London: H. Hamilton, 1981.

Dudley, John, Duke of Northumberland (c. 1502–1553)

John Dudley was the virtual ruler of England during the last years of EDWARD VI and was the leader of the unsuccessful attempt to place Jane GREY on the throne (see NORTHUMBERLAND'S COUP). The son of Edmund Dudley, HENRY VII's unpopular financial minister, John Dudley became the ward of Sir Edward Guildford in 1510 when HENRY VIII executed Edmund Dudley as a scapegoat for the unpopular financial policies of the previous reign. Often in the company of his guardian's brother, Sir Henry Guildford, a friend and companion of Henry VIII and organizer of the king's tournaments, Dudley was trained as a soldier and courtier. Dudley was knighted in FRANCE in 1523, but he did not achieve significant office until the late 1530s when he became deputy governor of CALAIS.

Dudley was created Viscount Lisle in 1542, and in the years following he became lord admiral, Knight of the Garter, and member of the PRIVY COUNCIL. Dudley was a prominent military figure in the 1540s, leading the assault on Boulogne in 1544 and commanding the royal fleet against the French in 1545. Henry VIII's will named Dudley to Prince Edward's regency council, and Edward shortly afterward created Dudley Earl of Warwick and lord chamberlain of England. Dudley fought against the Scots in 1547 and led the mercenary forces that suppressed Kett's Rebellion in

1549. In October 1549, he led the coup that overthrew Protector Edward SEYMOUR, Duke of Somerset, and emerged as the leader of the new government in 1550. In 1551, the king created him Duke of Northumberland. His government continued the reform of the Church begun by Somerset, issuing the more Protestant Second *BOOK OF COMMON PRAYER* in 1552.

Northumberland's control of the government and his position with the king were unchallenged after he engineered the execution of Somerset in January 1552. Northumberland devised, with the consent of the dying Edward VI, a plan to remove Mary (see MARY I) and Elizabeth from the succession and pass the Crown to Jane Grey, to whom he married his son Guildford (see *DEVISE; SUCCESSION, ACTS OF*). The failure of this scheme in July 1553 led to Northumberland's execution for TREASON. Under Elizabeth, Northumberland's surviving sons, Ambrose and Robert DUDLEY, rose to the PEERAGE as earls of Warwick and Leicester, respectively; Leicester ultimately became the queen's great favorite and nearly her husband (see DUDLEY MARRIAGE SUIT, FAVORITES).

Further Reading: Barrett L. Beer, *Northumberland,* Kent, OH: Kent State University Press, 1973; David Loades, *John Dudley, Duke of Northumberland,* Oxford: Clarendon Press, 1996.

Dudley, Lettice, Countess of Leicester. *See* KNOLLYS, LETTICE.

Dudley marriage suit

Of all the courtships of Elizabeth I, the suit pressed by Robert DUDLEY, future Earl of Leicester, came closest to success and had the greatest affect on English politics. In January 1559, only weeks after her accession, Elizabeth named Dudley master of horse, a position that gave him access to the queen and made him a regular companion when Elizabeth rode or hunted. By April 1559, Dudley was in such high favor that gossip concerning the nature of his relationship with the queen was beginning to spread throughout the COURT and the country. Rumors began to circulate that Dudley planned to poison his wife and so free himself to marry the queen. When scurrilous rumors about Elizabeth and Dudley were heard at foreign courts, Elizabeth's reputation both at

home and abroad began to suffer.

Because people of the sixteenth century believed no woman could rule a kingdom, Elizabeth's husband was expected to rule for her. Intense opposition to the match arose among such powerful political figures as William CECIL, who feared for his own position should Dudley marry the queen. On 8 September 1560, at the height of these fears and rumors, Dudley's wife, Amy DUDLEY, was found dead at the foot of her stairs. The timing of this event was devastating to Dudley's ambitions and the queen's good name. Although a careful investigation led to an official verdict of accidental death, a conclusion accepted by most modern historians, rumors that Dudley was involved in the murder, or at least some sort of cover-up, dogged him for the rest of his life. The queen lessened the intensity of her relationship with Dudley after October 1560, but he remained the royal favorite until his death in 1588, and Elizabeth was clearly attracted more to him than to any other man (see FAVORITES).

After his wife's death, Dudley tried in various ways to convince the queen to marry him, including scheming with foreign ambassadors, creating a domestic political following, and commissioning plays and ENTERTAINMENT that set forward his merits as a husband. By the late 1560s, even a number of former opponents began to support the match as better than no MARRIAGE at all, but by that time Elizabeth had decided that even though she loved Dudley, she was unwilling to share her throne with him. *See also* MARRIAGE QUESTION; VIRGIN QUEEN.

Further Reading: Susan Doran, *Monarchy and Matrimony: The Courtships of Elizabeth I,* London: Routledge, 1996; Alan Haynes, *The White Bear: The Elizabethan Earl of Leicester,* London: Peter Owen, 1987.

Dudley, Robert, Earl of Leicester
(1532–1588)

Robert Dudley was the lifelong favorite of Queen Elizabeth, and the only man she seriously contemplated marrying. Dudley was the fifth son of John DUDLEY, Duke of Northumberland, the leader of EDWARD VI's PRIVY COUNCIL. Although imprisoned in the TOWER OF LONDON in 1553 for supporting his father's unsuccessful attempt to

Robert Dudley, Earl of Leicester, the great love of Queen Elizabeth's life, was painted by an unknown artist about 1575. *By courtesy of the National Portrait Gallery, London.*

put Jane GREY on the throne (see NORTHUMBERLAND'S COUP), Dudley was pardoned by MARY I in 1554. Because Dudley had been partially educated with Princess Elizabeth—both were tutored by Roger ASCHAM—and had shared the experience of Tower imprisonment with her, he became immediately intimate with the new queen upon her accession in November 1558.

In 1559, Elizabeth named Dudley master of horse, Knight of the Garter (a medieval order of chivalry), and privy councilor. Elizabeth, who gave all her FAVORITES nicknames, dubbed Dudley her "eyes," and thereafter many of his letters to her were signed with the symbol "OO." Although married to Amy DUDLEY since 1550, Dudley was rumored to be seeking MARRIAGE with the queen (see DUDLEY MARRIAGE SUIT). The rumors became particularly intense in September 1560 when Dudley's wife was found dead at the foot

of a staircase. Dudley was cleared of any involvement in the death, but the widespread rumors of murder were enough to convince the queen to cool their relationship, and by 1563 any possibility of marriage was gone. Created Earl of Leicester in 1563, Dudley remained a powerful force at COURT and in council, acting as a leader of the Protestant war faction in opposition to the more moderate religious and foreign policies advocated by William CECIL.

In 1563, Elizabeth offered Leicester as a husband to her cousin Mary STUART, Queen of Scots. Although Elizabeth was anxious to prevent Mary from taking a French or Spanish husband, the proposal was never taken seriously by either Leicester or Mary, who in 1565 rejected the English earl for Henry STUART, Lord Darnley. In 1578, Leicester's secret marriage to Lettice KNOLLYS, the widowed Countess of Essex, landed him briefly in the Tower when the queen learned of it. He eventually returned to favor, but his advice thereafter was rarely followed as closely as Cecil's. Leicester commanded two largely unsuccessful military expeditions to the NETHERLANDS in the 1580s and was, to the queen's fury, named governor-general of the Netherlands in 1586 (see NETHERLANDS EXPEDITION). He died in 1588 shortly after the repulse of the Spanish ARMADA. In love with him to the last, Elizabeth carefully wrote "His last letter" on the note Leicester sent from his deathbed, preserving it as a special keepsake. Leicester's stepson, Robert DEVEREUX, Earl of Essex, partially succeeded him in the queen's affections in the 1590s. *See also* DUDLEY, AMBROSE, EARL OF WARWICK.

Further Reading: Alan Haynes, *The White Bear: The Elizabethan Earl of Leicester,* London: Peter Owen, 1987; Elizabeth Jenkins, *Elizabeth and Leicester,* New York: Coward-McCann, 1962; Derek A. Wilson, *Sweet Robin: A Biography of Robert Dudley, Earl of Leicester,* London: H. Hamilton, 1981.

Dutch Revolt. *See* NETHERLANDS REVOLT.

E

East India Company

The East India Company was the most successful JOINT-STOCK COMPANY formed in the Elizabethan period. The Governor and Company of Merchants Trading into the East Indies received its charter from the queen on 31 December 1600. Given a trade monopoly that extended from East Africa across India to the East Indies, the East India Company intended to challenge Dutch-Portuguese dominance of the rich East Indian spice trade (see MONOPOLIES). The company's first trading voyage sailed in February 1601 and returned in the autumn of 1603. A second expedition, during which the noted Elizabethan navigator and explorer John DAVIS met his death, left England in 1604 and returned two years later. Despite the high costs of the long voyages, the first two expeditions proved immensely profitable, and the company's future and English trade with India were firmly established.

After 1607, the company sent annual expeditions to India. The work of Sir Thomas Rowe, who, as company emissary to the Moghul emperor between 1615 and 1619, won trade privileges for the company in India, and the Dutch massacre of English merchants at Amboina in the East Indies in 1623, focused English East Asian trade in India. The company thereafter established a series of factories (trading posts) in the Bay of Bengal and in 1640 acquired the site of the modern Indian city of Madras. After 1660, the company obtained charters that gave it rights in India to acquire territory, conclude alliances, make war and peace, raise troops, and coin money. In 1667, the company acquired the site of modern Bombay, and in 1690, it founded Calcutta.

In the eighteenth century, the company extended its territorial control throughout India and developed a triangular trade that sent Indian goods (including opium) to China for tea that was sold in England. The tea shipments that sparked the Boston Tea Party in 1773 were East India Company cargoes sent directly to the American colonies to help the company out of financial difficulties. The company lost its trade monopoly in India in 1813 and thereafter functioned solely as an administrative bureaucracy. The British Crown assumed full sovereignty over India in 1858 after the company's Indian army mutinied in 1857. *See also* REGULATED COMPANY.

Further Reading: K. N. Chaudhuri, *The English East India Company: The Study of an Early Joint-Stock Company, 1600–1640*, New York: Reprints of Economic Classics, 1965; Brian Gardner, *The East India Company*, New York: Dorset Press, 1990.

Easter

Being the celebration of Christ's resurrection from the dead, Easter was the most important feast on the English Church CALENDAR and one of the biggest HOLIDAYS of the Elizabethan year. Easter is a movable holiday, occurring on a Sunday in March or April. The calculation of the date of Easter was a major controversy in Anglo-Saxon England; adherents of the Church of Rome celebrated Easter on a different day than adherents of the Irish Celtic churches, a real difficulty if, for instance, the king and queen followed different Churches. By Elizabethan times, however, Easter fell on the first Sunday after the first full moon occurring on or after 21 March, meaning that

Easter could fall anywhere between 22 March and 25 April.

Easter was preceded by the 40 days of Lent, a season of fasting and abstinence that spiritually prepared the believer for the joyous celebration of the resurrection. Lent began on Ash Wednesday, which fell on the Wednesday before the sixth Sunday before Easter, sometime between 4 February and 10 March. The week before Easter, known as Easter or Holy Week, began on Palm Sunday. The Catholic custom of carrying palms into church on Palm Sunday was not permitted by the ANGLICAN CHURCH. Many similar Catholic rituals that had once been conducted during Easter Week, on Maundy Thursday, Good Friday, and Holy Saturday (Easter Eve), had also been suppressed, including certain acts of charity observed on Maundy Thursday and the ritual of "creeping to the cross" on Good Friday.

Easter itself was one of the three holidays each year when all good Anglicans took communion—the others being CHRISTMAS and Whitsun (the feast of Pentecost falling in May or June). After the Reformation, many parishes kept Easter books to record church attendance (see REFORMATION, ENGLISH). With the eating of meat once again permissible, Easter was a day of great feasting and revelry. The name Easter is thought to derive either from the pagan goddess *Eostre*, whose spring festival fell at about the same time as the Christian holy day, or from *Eosturmonath*, the fourth month of the Anglo-Saxon year. Like other Christian feasts, Easter had, by Elizabeth's reign, acquired a series of secular customs, some of which involved eggs and other fertility symbols from ancient times.

Further Reading: David Cressy, *Bonfires and Bells: National Memory and the Protestant Calendar in Elizabethan and Stuart England*, London: Weidenfeld and Nicolson, 1989; Ronald Hutton, *The Rise and Fall of Merry England: The Ritual Year, 1400–1700*, New York: Oxford University Press, 1994; Ronald Hutton, *The Stations of the Sun: A History of the Ritual Year in Britain*, New York: Oxford University Press, 1996.

Eastland Company

The Eastland Company was a REGULATED COMPANY chartered by the queen in 1579. The company was given a monopoly to trade with Scandinavia, Poland, and the Baltic towns of northern Germany (see MONOPOLIES). In the previous year, increasing rivalry with the English MERCHANT ADVENTURERS had led the English government to revoke the special trading privileges it had extended to the Hanseatic League. A trading organization comprising various towns of north Germany and the Baltic, the Hanseatic League or Hanse had dominated the trade of the Baltic and northern Europe for centuries. The formation of the Eastland Company was an attempt by the queen to improve English access to the timber and other naval commodities of the Baltic market (see NAVY; SHIPS).

After paying an entrance fee, Eastland Company members traded dyed and dressed English cloth for timber, hemp, tar, cordage, and other naval stores vital to the English fleet (see CLOTH INDUSTRY). Although Eastland Company traders had to share part of the Baltic market with the Merchant Adventurers, most of the Baltic was closed to English merchants who were not company members. The Eastland Company did a brisk business in the late sixteenth and early seventeenth centuries, but the closing of the Baltic market to other English traders, who had been able to do business there before 1579, caused some unrest in the LONDON merchant community. The company's monopoly was confirmed in the Navigation Acts of 1651 and 1660, but stiff competition from the Dutch and from English interlopers virtually destroyed the company's privileged position in the region in the late seventeenth century. Nonetheless, the Eastland Company continued to exist into the late eighteenth century. *See also* JOINT-STOCK COMPANY.

Further Reading: R. W. K. Hinton, *The Eastland Trade and the Common Weal in the Seventeenth Century*, Hamden, CT: Archon Books, 1975.

Edinburgh

Located in southeastern SCOTLAND on the south side of the Firth of Forth, Edinburgh was the capital and largest city of sixteenth-century Scotland. The earliest settlements on the site of Edinburgh go back to the sixth century, but the earliest historical references to the royal burgh or town of Edinburgh date to the early twelfth century. Although the administrative center of medieval Scotland, Edinburgh was not recognized as the capital of the country until the late fifteenth century, probably because it was not far from the English border and thus vulnerable to English attacks. The Scottish PARLIAMENT began meeting in Edinburgh during the reign of James III (r. 1460–1488), and the town's position as the seat of royal government solidified under James IV (r. 1488–1513), who built the palace of Holyroodhouse and located the royal courts in Edinburgh.

In Elizabethan times, Edinburgh was confined to the sweeping spine of rock that descended from the height of massive Edinburgh Castle along the "Royal Mile" to the elaborate royal residence at Holyroodhouse. Although the great central block of Edinburgh Castle had been built in the fifteenth century, with an ornate dining hall added by James IV in the early sixteenth century, buildings and fortifications had existed on the Castle height since the eleventh century, with the still-surviving St. Margaret's Chapel dating from around 1100. In the 1560s, during the reign of Mary STUART, Queen of Scots, Edinburgh witnessed the preaching of John KNOX, the murder of David RIZZIO at Holyroodhouse, and the murder of Henry STUART, Lord Darnley, at the house of Kirk o'Field (see DARNLEY MURDER). In June 1567, when the Confederate Lords brought Mary back to the capital after her defeat at the Battle of Carberry (see CARBERRY, BATTLE OF), Edinburgh mobs greeted the queen with shouts of "Burn the whore," burning being the prescribed punishment for a woman convicted of murdering her husband.

Under Mary's son, James VI (see JAMES I), Edinburgh grew to perhaps 20,000 inhabitants and acquired a university, Edinburgh College, in 1582. After the accession of James to the English throne in 1603, the Scottish monarch was no longer resident in Edinburgh and politically ambitious Scots were drawn to LONDON, although Edinburgh remained the administrative and legal capital of the Scottish monarchy.

Further Reading: David Daiches, *Edinburgh*, London: Hamish Hamilton, 1978; Allen Massie, *Edinburgh*, London: Sinclair-Stevenson, 1994.

Edinburgh, Treaty of

By ensuring the success of the Scottish Reformation, the Treaty of Edinburgh broke the ancient alliance between SCOTLAND and FRANCE and laid the foundation for a new understanding, based on a shared PROTESTANTISM, between Scotland and England (see REFORMATION, SCOTTISH). Concluded in July 1560, the Treaty of Edinburgh ended French and English military intervention in Scotland, and civil war between Scottish Protestants and Scottish Catholics for control of the regency government of Mary STUART, Queen of Scots.

French, Scottish, and English commissioners met in Edinburgh in June 1560 to resolve the military and political stalemate that had resulted from the death of Marie de GUISE, Queen Mary's mother and regent, and the defeat in May of an Anglo-Scots army besieging the regent's French forces at Leith. The English delegation was led by William CECIL, who was able to use French military weakness and English command of the seas to forge an agreement favorable to England (see WINTER, SIR WILLIAM). In the treaty, the English and the French agreed to withdraw all military forces from Scotland. The French agreed to dismantle their fortresses, to stop interfering in Scottish affairs, and to prevent any French subject from holding an official position in the Scottish government. The treaty also obligated Mary, the Catholic claimant to the English throne, to cease displaying the English royal arms along with her own. The treaty vested the government of Scotland in a council of 12, 5 to be named by the Protestant Scottish PARLIAMENT and 7 to be named by the Catholic queen, then resident in France as the wife of the French king.

Elizabeth was unhappy with the treaty because the French had refused to restore CALAIS, lost by her sister MARY I in 1558. Mary Stuart refused to ratify the treaty because Elizabeth would not formally recognize her as heir to the English throne. Despite the dissatisfaction of the two queens, the treaty began the process whereby England and Scotland, almost 150 years later, jointly agreed to a political union.

Further Reading: B. W. Beckingsale, *Burghley: Tudor Statesman,* New York: St. Martin's Press, 1967; J. D. Mackie, *A History of Scotland,* 2nd ed., New York: Dorset Press, 1985; Jenny Wormald, *Mary, Queen of Scots,* London: Collins and Brown, 1991.

education

Elizabethan England had no national system of education, and only a small fraction of Elizabethan children, mostly boys, received any formal schooling. Beginning at about age 6, boys and girls began to be taught the skills appropriate to their gender and social position. The sons of the nobility and wealthier GENTRY might receive training from private tutors and through service in another noble or gentle household. Cecil House, the home of William CECIL, Lord Burghley, became well known as an educational establishment; at times as many as 20 young men were in residence, learning manners, religion, and statecraft from tutors

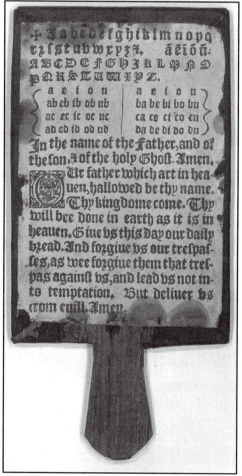

Elizabethan children learned their ABCs from a hornbook like this one. A hornbook consisted of paper printed in black ink mounted on wood, covered with a protective and transparent layer of animal horn. *By permission of the Folger Shakespeare Library.*

and from Burghley himself. The sons of prosperous urban merchants and craftsmen, and of less wealthy or less-well-connected gentlemen often began their education in petty schools, which might be private enterprises or establishments run by a town, guild, or parish. Some were attached to a local GRAMMAR SCHOOL.

Petty schools taught the fundamentals of reading and writing in ENGLISH, and perhaps some basic arithmetic. The alphabet was taught using a hornbook, a piece of wood on which was affixed a sheet of paper with a printed alphabet or reading text covered with a thin layer of horn to protect the paper. Although the Reformation had begun to free education from Church control, the petty school still had a strong religious component, with prayers and the CATECHISM used to teach reading (see REFORMATION, ENGLISH). Schoolmasters varied widely in their own education—some had little schooling, while about one-third had university training. Discipline in the petty schools was often harsh, with the birch rod used freely to correct misbehavior and academic failure, a practice that Elizabeth's tutor, Roger ASCHAM, severely criticized. Bright or high-placed students might proceed around age 10 to grammar school and from there to one of the UNIVERSITIES or to the INNS OF COURT for legal training.

Basic literacy was low in Elizabethan England but was expanding along with the number of petty and grammar schools. Perhaps 30 percent of men and 10 percent of women were literate by the end of Elizabeth's reign in 1603. Literacy was higher in the towns (see BOROUGHS), especially LONDON, and in the more populous southern and eastern parts of the kingdom, as well as in the more Puritan areas where great emphasis was placed on being able to read the Bible (see BIBLE, ENGLISH; PURITANS). *See also* the illustration for GRAMMAR SCHOOL.

Further Reading: David Cressy, *Education in Tudor and Stuart England,* New York: St. Martin's Press, 1976.

Edward VI (1537–1553)

Edward VI was the son and successor of HENRY VIII. The prince's birth on 12 October 1537 gave Henry the male heir he had long sought, and for whom he had dissolved two

William Scrots painted this portrait of Edward VI, half brother of Elizabeth I. *National Maritime Museum, London.*

marriages and all English connection with the Church of Rome. Edward's mother, Jane SEYMOUR, Henry's third queen, died of a puerperal fever just two weeks after her son's birth. Beginning in 1544, the prince was given an intensive humanist (see HUMANISM) EDUCATION directed by the foremost scholars in England, including John Cheke, professor of Greek at Cambridge (see UNIVERSITIES), and Roger ASCHAM, a future tutor of Edward's half sister Elizabeth. By 1552, Edward could speak, read, and write Greek, Latin, and French and was proficient in history, geography, political theory, music, mathematics, and rhetoric. He had even learned to use an astrolabe and other instruments of navigation.

Edward developed into a zealous Protestant. Henry had chosen reformist tutors for his son, and Edward favored Protestant COURT preachers, who repeatedly reminded the young king of his duty to defend the reformed Church of England from "papist" error. Edward was nine years old when he succeeded his father in January 1547. His government was first directed by his maternal uncle, Edward SEYMOUR, Duke of Somerset, himself a moderate Protestant. By 1550, the Council had overthrown Somerset for his arrogant and highhanded administration, and John DUDLEY, Duke of Northumberland, emerged as the new leader of the government. Northumberland engineered Somerset's execution for TREASON in 1552, a fact the king noted starkly in his diary—"The Duke of Somerset had his head cut off upon Tower Hill between eight and nine o'clock in the morning."

As Edward's health began to deteriorate in 1553, he and Northumberland devised a plan (see *DEVISE*) to prevent his Catholic sister Mary (see MARY I) from succeeding and to pass the Crown to his Protestant cousin Jane GREY, whom Northumberland had married to his son. Edward believed that Mary's accession would destroy his reformed English Church and throw England into civil war. Northumberland, fearing for his own position under a Catholic queen, encouraged the king in this belief. Edward died of pulmonary tuberculosis at age 15 on 6 July 1553. Northumberland's succession scheme failed, and Mary came to the throne eager to restore Catholicism (see CATHOLICISM, ENGLISH; NORTHUMBERLAND'S COUP). *See also* genealogical charts in Appendix 1: "Stuart Claim to the English Throne"; "Grey Claim to the English Throne"; "Houses of Lancaster, Beaufort, and Tudor"; "House of Tudor, 1485–1603."

Further Reading: W. K. Jordan, *Edward VI: The Young King,* Cambridge, MA: Harvard University Press, 1968; W. K. Jordan, *Edward VI: The Threshold of Power,* Cambridge, MA: Harvard University Press, 1970.

Effingham, Lord Howard of. *See* HOWARD, CHARLES, EARL OF NOTTINGHAM.

Elizabeth I (1533–1603)

The last Tudor monarch of England, Elizabeth I was the daughter of HENRY VIII and his second wife, Anne BOLEYN (see TUDOR FAMILY). Born on 7 September 1533 at GREENWICH PALACE, Elizabeth was proclaimed heir to the English throne at birth but was removed from the succession and declared a bastard in 1536 after the execution of her

John Bettes painted this portrait of Elizabeth I. *National Maritime Museum, London.*

NORTHUMBER-LAND'S COUP attempt, but her reluctance to accept Catholicism and her position as a Protestant alternative to Mary cost her the queen's favor. Mary imprisoned her sister in the TOWER OF LONDON in 1554 on suspicion of involvement in WYATT'S REBELLION, but nothing could be proved and Elizabeth was eventually released.

When Mary died childless on 17 November 1558, Elizabeth succeeded to the throne. Appointing William CECIL as her principal secretary, and showing marked favoritism toward Robert DUDLEY, her master of horse, Elizabeth turned to PARLIAMENT to restore the English Church to PROTESTANTISM (see ANGLICAN SET-

mother for TREASON and adultery (see SUCCESSION, ACTS OF). Under the guidance of Henry VIII's last queen, Katherine PARR, Elizabeth received an excellent education from such humanist scholars as William Grindal and Roger ASCHAM (see HUMANISM). On his death in January 1547, Henry left a will restoring Elizabeth to the succession behind her half siblings, Prince Edward (see EDWARD VI) and Princess Mary (see MARY I). Except for an improper flirtation with Thomas SEYMOUR, maternal uncle to Edward VI (see ASHLEY, KATHERINE), Elizabeth lived quietly during her brother's brief reign.

After Edward's death in July 1553, Elizabeth supported her half sister Mary against

TLEMENT). Two of the most pressing problems of the new reign were the MARRIAGE QUESTION and the succession. Because Elizabeth's most likely heir was her Catholic cousin, Mary STUART, Queen of Scots (whom many Catholics already considered rightful queen of England) and because the age expected a woman ruler to take a husband to help her govern, Elizabeth's ministers urged her to marry and produce a Protestant heir. Although for a time she seemed likely to marry Dudley, and although many other suitors appeared, including her former brother-in-law, PHILIP II of SPAIN, Elizabeth confounded expectations by remaining unmarried and refusing to formally name a successor (see VIRGIN QUEEN; ELIZABETH I, PORTRAITS OF).

Elizabeth also steadfastly maintained the moderate ANGLICAN CHURCH, frustrating Puritan hopes for religious reform but also sparing England the religious wars that savaged FRANCE. Catholic conspiracies to place Mary Stuart on her throne (see BABINGTON PLOT; RIDOLFI PLOT), and the threat of invasion from the Spanish, Catholic NETHERLANDS, forced Elizabeth to intervene militarily in the NETHERLANDS REVOLT in 1585 and threw England into war with Spain. In 1588, one year after Elizabeth reluctantly consented to the execution of Mary Stuart (who had been a prisoner in England since 1568), Philip launched the ARMADA against England. By 1590, William Cecil was old and Dudley was dead, and a series of new political leaders had arisen at COURT, including Robert DEVEREUX, Earl of Essex, and Robert CECIL. Although the years after the defeat of the Armada witnessed military failure and economic decline for England, they also saw the flowering of the greatest cultural renaissance in English history; remarkable developments in MUSIC, ARCHITECTURE, ART, DRAMA, and POETRY; as well as brilliant achievements in commerce and exploration, that made England's "Elizabethan Age" a period of confidence and progress. Elizabeth, in her 70th year, died at RICHMOND PALACE on 24 March 1603. She was succeeded by her kinsman, James VI of Scotland (see JAMES I).

Surprisingly little contemporary evidence survives as to the queen's physical appearance. A reasonable description of Elizabeth I would be that she was slightly above average height for an upper-class woman of her time, that she had fair skin and dark eyes, a long slightly hooked nose, reddish-gold hair that curled naturally, a slim figure, and beautiful hands with fine long fingers. She appears to have resembled her father more than her mother, and her paternal grandfather, HENRY VII, more than anyone else. In her old age, her hair thinned and turned gray and her teeth deteriorated, but her figure remained trim and her body erect, all features shared with her grandfather.

She also shared certain personality traits with Henry VII. Both monarchs were accused of financial rapacity, of being overly frugal to the point of meanness. Certainly neither showed the bluff open-handedness of Henry VIII when it came to distributing rewards for royal service. Both realized that England must be solvent to be strong, and both strove to obtain the maximum benefit from any expenditure of limited resources. Thus, though both Henry VII and Elizabeth had a taste for the regal and the opulent, all such displays—whether rich court finery for Elizabeth or lavish new palaces for Henry—were meant to impress foreigners with the glory of England or the Tudor dynasty, and never simply for show. Elizabeth and her grandfather also shared a strong sense of national responsibility, carefully weighing the benefits and risks of each action for the nation as a whole. In Elizabeth, this caution often seemed to exasperated ministers to be simply procrastination and indecision, and to reaffirm their own notions of the unfitness of women to rule a kingdom. However, over time, her ministers and most of her subjects came to appreciate her sound judgment and common sense, and in the less harmonious politics of her successor's reign, many English people came to look upon Elizabeth's time as a lost golden age.

Elizabeth never forgot the lesson of her sister's reign, when she had been the popular alternative to an unpopular queen. She always considered the love of the people to be her strongest asset in governing, and she strove all her life—with much success—to win and to retain that love. Even such political and religious enemies as Philip II, who approved and financed plans for her overthrow and murder, gave her grudging respect as an intelligent and worthy opponent. Historians today consider Elizabeth one of the greatest monarchs in English history and one of the greatest female rulers of all time. By refusing to be pressured into marrying, Elizabeth allowed England to survive as an independent power. By crafting and maintaining a broadly based religious settlement, by pursuing peace and financial prudence, and by inspiring achievement in others through competition for her favor, Elizabeth gave England a new national unity and a new outward-looking attitude.

Further Reading: Carolly Erickson, *The First Elizabeth*, New York: Summit Books, 1983; Christopher Haigh, *Elizabeth I*, London: Longman, 1988; Paul Johnson, *Elizabeth I*, New York: Holt, Rinehart and Winston, 1974; Wallace MacCaffrey, *Elizabeth I*, London: Edward Arnold, 1993; J. E. Neale, *Queen Elizabeth I*,

Chicago: Academy Chicago Publishers, 1992; Jasper Ridley, *Elizabeth I*, New York: Viking, 1988; Lacey Baldwin Smith, *Elizabeth Tudor*, Boston: Little, Brown and Company, 1975; Anne Somerset, *Elizabeth I*, New York: Alfred A. Knopf, 1991.

Elizabeth I, portraits of

Ranging in date from the late 1540s to just before the queen's death in 1603, about 135 contemporary portraits of Elizabeth I survive. Pictures of Elizabeth were in high demand from the beginning of the reign. A PROCLAMATION of 1563 declared that "all sorts of subjects and people both noble and mean [common]" desired to own and display the queen's image. The proclamation sought to regulate production of Elizabeth's likeness by proposing the distribution to painters of one portrait commissioned and approved by the queen as the pattern for all royal images. But Elizabeth's excommunication in 1570 (see PIUS V; *REGNANS IN EXCELSIS*), the start of war with SPAIN in 1585, and the ARMADA crisis in 1588 made displaying the royal likeness an act of patriotism, and the demand for royal portraits soon exceeded the time and talent needed to produce them in the form and quality demanded by the queen. In 1596, when the PRIVY COUNCIL ordered the destruction of poor-quality portraits that were causing Elizabeth "great offense," a large number were collected and burned.

One of the most famous surviving portraits of Elizabeth I is the richly colored "Armada Portrait"; painted by George GOWER about 1588, it shows the queen wearing an elaborate bow-covered gown and standing before a depiction of the English victory over the Armada. Traditionally attributed to Nicholas HILLIARD, the 1585 "Ermine Portrait" was commissioned by William CECIL, Lord Burghley. The portrait is named for the white ermine, a symbol of purity and chastity, that curls

The "Darnley Portrait" of Elizabeth I was painted about 1575 by an unknown artist. *By courtesy of the National Portrait Gallery, London.*

around the queen's left wrist. Another likeness of the VIRGIN QUEEN is the "Siena" or "Sieve Portrait" from the early 1580s; it depicts the queen holding a sieve, a symbol of chastity deriving from a story about a Roman vestal virgin.

The 1575 "Darnley Portrait" (accompanying this entry) shows the queen holding a multicolored feather fan that sets off the accent colors in her white gown. The "Ditchley Portrait" from 1592 is the largest surviving image of Elizabeth and one of the few to suggest her age. Almost all other portrayals of the queen, including the "Rainbow Portrait," painted in about 1600 when Elizabeth was nearing 70, give her the face of a young woman, a convention dictated by both the propaganda needs of the state and the queen's vanity. For various depictions of Elizabeth I, see the illustrations accompanying the following entries in this book: BIBLE, ENGLISH; ELIZABETH I; GOWER, GEORGE (Armada Portrait); HILLIARD, NICHOLAS; LIMNING; PARLIAMENT; VIRGIN QUEEN. *See also* ART; LIMNING.

Further Reading: Roy Strong, *The Cult of Elizabeth: Elizabethan Portraiture and Pageantry,* London: Thames and Hudson, 1977; Roy Strong, *Gloriana: The Portraits of Queen Elizabeth I,* London: Thames and Hudson, 1987.

enclosure. *See* AGRICULTURE.

English

In medieval England, the language of the law and the royal COURT was French, while the language of literature, scholarship, and, to some extent, DIPLOMACY, was Latin. English began to come into fashion at court and among the nobility (see PEERAGE) in the late fourteenth century, when the Hundred Years War with FRANCE encouraged a more self-conscious English nationalism. By Elizabeth's accession in 1558, English was the language of government and was becoming the language of literature and scholarship. Unlike the fourteenth-century English of Geoffrey Chaucer, which is unintelligible to a twentieth-century ear, the English of William SHAKESPEARE, Christopher MARLOWE, and other Elizabethan writers is close enough to modern English to be comprehensible.

Although some Elizabethan words had different meanings than they do today, and other words have today fallen out of use (e.g., "thee" and "thou" as familiar forms of address), the main difference between Elizabethan and modern English consists of variations in the pronunciation of certain vowels (e.g., the Elizabethan pronunciation of "weak" rhymed with "break"). Elizabethan pronunciation varied widely from region to region, and no standard pronunciation existed, although the LONDON dialect was beginning to achieve a certain dominance by the end of the reign.

Unlike the standard British English today associated with the BBC, the UNIVERSITIES, and the royal family (a fairly recent development), Elizabethan English had no official form, and widely varying dialects could even be heard spoken at court by nobles and gentlemen (see GENTRY) from different parts of the realm. Spelling also lacked consistency, and people tended to spell words as they pronounced them, with wide variations in pronunciation producing equally wide variations in spelling. This variety even affected proper names; Sir Peter CAREW's name, for instance, appears in Elizabethan documents in numerous spellings, including "Caroo," "Carowe," and "Care." Elizabethan English was a vigorous and flexible language that, through Elizabethan exploration and political and commercial expansion, extended itself into WALES, Lowland SCOTLAND, IRELAND, and AMERICA.

Further Reading: John H. Fisher, *The Emergence of Standard English,* Lexington: University of Kentucky Press, 1996; Robert McCrum, William Cran, and Robert MacNeil, *The Story of English,* rev. ed., Boston: Faber and Faber, 1992.

entertainment

Although common people labored from dawn to dusk in trade, AGRICULTURE, or some craft or industry (see CLOTH INDUSTRY), and members of the landowning classes served in government, managed their estates, or ran their local administration (see LOCAL GOVERNMENT), Elizabethans found ample time to pursue a wide variety of entertainments and pastimes. While PURITANS objected to people spending the Sabbath and HOLIDAYS engaging in activities they considered frivolous, the principal leisure times for Elizabethans, espe-

This early seventeenth-century miniature watercolor depicts Elizabethans at home, playing cards. *By permission of the Folger Shakespeare Library.*

cially the lower classes (see SOCIAL HIERAR-CHY), remained Sundays after church and holiday seasons.

In LONDON, the rise of theatres (see GLOBE THEATRE) and the flowering of English DRAMA and MUSIC led to the development of the first English entertainment industry, with both courtiers and ordinary Londoners attending various kinds of performances. DANCE, both at COURT and in the country, remained a popular pastime. Hunting was a favorite leisure activity of the PEERAGE and GENTRY, and ANIMAL SPORTS were enjoyed by all classes. The government, meanwhile, encouraged such activities as archery and fencing because of their military applications (see ARMY). Widely played outdoor sports included football, a somewhat more violent version of modern soccer; blindman's bluff and hoodman's blind, games in which a blindfolded person tries to catch or identify the people who are touching or hitting him or her; bowls, a game that involved the throwing of balls at a target; and ten-pins (or nine-pegs or skittles), which was similar to modern bowling. Tennis, introduced from FRANCE in the Middle Ages, was popular with the upper classes, while all classes enjoyed swimming, wrestling, and horseback riding.

The most popular indoor pastimes were chess, draughts (similar to modern checkers), dice, and card games of various kinds, including early versions of twenty-one, cribbage, whist, and poker. Elizabethan card decks were similar to modern decks, employing the same four suits, although the deck lacked a joker, and the king, queen, and knave (jack) had full-length images on them, not the modern mirror image. Except for chess, most indoor (and many outdoor) games involved gambling, itself one of the most popular Elizabethan leisure activities. The Elizabethan period also saw the introduction into England of billiards, which became an upper-class pastime, and a board game called "goose," which was the ancestor of many modern board games.

Further Reading: Muriel St. Clare Byrne, *Elizabethan Life in Town and Country*, 7th ed., Gloucester, England: A. Sutton, 1987; Marcia Vale, *The Gentleman's Recreations: Accomplishments and Pastimes of the English Gentleman, 1580–1630*, Totowa, NJ: Rowman and Littlefield, 1977; Keith Wrightson, *English Society, 1580–1680*, New Brunswick, NJ: Rutgers University Press, 1982.

epidemic disease

Like the rest of sixteenth-century Europe, Elizabethan England suffered outbreaks of epidemic disease. Ignorance about the causes of disease, ineffective medical treatment, poor sanitation, and the unchecked movement of infected people all contributed to the spread of epidemics. Like their medieval forebears, Elizabethans viewed epidemics as divine punishment for sin or for disobedience to God's will. Lacking any understanding of microorganisms, Elizabethan MEDICINE ascribed the spreading of epidemic disease to unusual celestial events, such as comets, or to the spread of a miasma, a foul, poisonous body of air thought to arise from rotting corpses or vegetation.

Several types of epidemic disease were present in Tudor England, claiming small numbers of lives almost continually, but erupting at irregular intervals into more deadly and widespread outbreaks. A mysterious illness known as the "sweating sickness," or simply "the sweat," caused great fear because it killed quickly and struck the wealthy and powerful as frequently as the poor. The sweat was less active during Elizabeth's reign, the last large eruption occurring in 1551. Elizabeth came to the throne in 1558 in the midst of a serious epidemic of what was called the "new ague," a fever that was probably some form of influenza. The new ague, along with famine caused by the bad harvests of the mid-1550s, killed almost 6 percent of the English POPULATION between 1556 and 1560. Although influenza continued to claim lives throughout the reign, particularly when harvests again turned bad in the 1590s, it never returned to the epidemic levels seen in the first two years of Elizabeth's rule.

In 1562, a serious smallpox epidemic swept England. The disease attacked the upper classes with surprising virulence, nearly carrying off the queen herself. The deadliest and most common epidemic disease in Elizabethan England was the bubonic PLAGUE, the horrible Black Death that ravaged England and much of Europe in the fourteenth century. Although less virulent than they had been 200 years earlier, small plague outbreaks occurred almost every year of Elizabeth's reign, and serious, widespread outbreaks hit England in 1563, 1578–79, 1582, 1592–93, and 1603.

Further Reading: Leslie A. Clarkson, *Death, Disease, and Famine in Pre-Industrial England,* New York: St. Martin's Press, 1976; Paul Slack, *The Impact of Plague in Tudor and Stuart England,* Oxford: Clarendon Press, 1985.

equity

Equity is the custom and practice of law that arose outside the COMMON LAW, notably in chancery—the office of the chancellor—to remedy deficiencies and inequities in the common law. In the fifteenth and sixteenth centuries, various new law courts developed to supplement the courts of common law. New procedures for more efficiently administering justice were developed rather haphazardly by the lord chancellor and the king's councilors as they handled petitions addressed to the monarch by subjects (see PRIVY COUNCIL). These new procedures gradually developed into a body of legal practice used in every new English court that evolved after 1400, including the Courts of Star Chamber, Requests, and Chancery (see CHANCERY, COURT OF; REQUESTS, COURT OF; STAR CHAMBER, COURT OF).

Some of the equity procedures unknown to the common law courts included the use of injunctions (enjoining parties to refrain from a particular action until the case was decided), the use of subpoenas (compelling a party to appear), and the practice of putting witnesses under oath. Also, all proceedings in equity courts were conducted in ENGLISH rather than in the French used in common law courts. Because the equity courts tended, at least at first, to be more flexible, speedier, and less costly than the tradition-bound common law courts, they were more popular with Tudor litigants.

Further Reading: W. J. Jones, *The Elizabethan Court of Chancery,* Oxford: Clarendon Press, 1967.

Essex, first Earl of. *See* DEVEREUX, WALTER, EARL OF ESSEX.

Essex, second Earl of. *See* DEVEREUX, ROBERT, EARL OF ESSEX.

Essex's Rebellion

A brief rebellion led by Robert DEVEREUX, Earl of Essex, the queen's young favorite, was the last great political upheaval of Elizabethan England. In 1599, Essex lost favor with the queen for concluding an unauthorized truce with the Irish rebel Hugh O'NEILL, Earl of Tyrone, and for returning to England without permission from his post as lord deputy of IRELAND. Elizabeth ordered the earl confined to his house but halted a Star Chamber inquiry into his activities in Ireland and released him from confinement when he wrote to her humbly begging forgiveness (see STAR CHAMBER, COURT OF). However, still denied access to COURT, Essex began plotting against the queen in November 1600 when she refused to renew his monopoly on the sale of sweet wines, an action that threatened the extravagant earl with bankruptcy (see MONOPOLIES). Supported by his stepfather, Sir Christopher BLOUNT; his friend, Henry WRIOTHESLEY, Earl of Southampton; and various other young noblemen and gentlemen, Essex planned to seize the queen and force her to remove his political enemies, especially Robert CECIL, from power.

On 6 February 1601, Essex's followers paid the CHAMBERLAIN'S MEN to perform William SHAKESPEARE's *Richard II* at the GLOBE THEATRE. Because the play depicted the deposition of an English monarch, Blount and the other Essex supporters in the audience next day hoped the performance would psychologically dispose Londoners, with whom Essex was popular, to accept the coup. Suspicious of Essex's activities, the PRIVY COUNCIL summoned the earl for questioning, but he refused to appear; having lost the element of surprise, he sought to rouse LONDON to his support by announcing throughout the city that the queen's pro-Spanish ministers sought to kill him.

On 8 February, Essex imprisoned four messengers who came to him at Essex House from the queen. He then led about 200 of his followers into London, but the Privy Council had already denounced Essex as a traitor to the city government, and few Londoners rallied to him. With his supporters melting away, he retreated to Essex House, where he found his hostages gone and Charles HOWARD, Earl of Nottingham, preparing to besiege the building. After burning all incriminating documents, Essex surrendered. Tried and condemned with his chief followers, Essex was beheaded at the TOWER OF LONDON on 25 February, with Blount and others suffering the same fate some weeks later. Southampton languished in the Tower until released by JAMES I in 1603. *See also* TREASON.

Further Reading: Robert Lacey, *Robert, Earl of Essex,* New York: Atheneum, 1971.

ex officio oath. *See* HIGH COMMISSION, COURT OF.

Exchange, Royal. *See* ROYAL EXCHANGE.

Exchequer

The Exchequer was the financial and accounting office of medieval England; it supervised sheriffs in their collection of royal REVENUES from land, feudal dues, and other taxes (see FISCAL FEUDALISM; TAXATION). The name came from the chequered table that Exchequer officials, known as the barons of the Exchequer, used as an abacus to tally accounts. The Exchequer developed out of the royal household, becoming by the thirteenth century a separate department of state headquartered at WESTMINSTER PALACE. The Exchequer also acted as a court of COMMON LAW with jurisdiction over a variety of cases, including the trying of corrupt or delinquent sheriffs, the levying of all fines imposed by the royal courts, the auditing of the accounts of royal officials, the recording of transfers of property held by the Crown, and the supervision of government execution of parliamentary statute.

Divided into the Upper Exchequer, the audit department, and the Lower Exchequer, the receipt department, the office was under the direction of the lord treasurer, who for much of Elizabeth's reign was William CECIL, Lord Burghley. Early in the sixteenth century, the Exchequer, like the other common law courts, was notorious for its slowness, inefficiency, and antiquated, inflexible rules and procedures. However, in the reign of MARY I and the first decade of Elizabeth I's rule, the government restructured the Exchequer and consolidated it with other revenue courts to improve its performance.

Further Reading: D. C. Coleman, *The Economy of England 1450–1750,* Oxford: Oxford University Press, 1977; G. R. Elton, "The Elizabethan Exchequer: War in the Receipt" in S. T. Bindoff, Joel Hurstfield, and C. H. Williams, eds., *Elizabethan Government and Society,* London: University of London, Athlone Press, 1961.

exploration

Seeking information to encourage further exploration, to promote the opening of new commercial markets, or to stimulate the establishment of English colonies, Elizabethan explorers traveled to many parts of the world never before seen by English subjects. John Cabot, an Italian in the employ of HENRY VII, Elizabeth's grandfather, launched the first English voyage of exploration in 1497. Seeking a NORTHWEST PASSAGE to Asia, Cabot convinced himself that the North American coast he discovered was Japan. With the enthusiastic backing of the king, Cabot sailed west again in 1498, intent on establishing trade with Asia. However, he never returned, the fate of his expedition remaining a mystery to this day. In 1509, Henry VII funded Sebastian Cabot, John's son, in a new search for the Northwest Passage. Cabot sailed into icy Hudson's Bay, but could find no route to Asia and returned to England to find that Henry VII had died.

The new king, HENRY VIII, was interested in expanding his NAVY but not in continuing the search for Asian trade routes. The major exploration effort of the reign was a private venture undertaken by William Hawkins in 1530. Hawkins founded the Atlantic triangular trade by obtaining ivory in Africa for trade in Brazil. The knowledge of lands, peoples, and sailing conditions that Hawkins acquired in Africa and AMERICA proved invaluable to later Elizabethan explorers. John DUDLEY, Duke of Northumberland and leader of the English government under EDWARD VI, did Elizabethan explorers a great service by employing the aging seaman Sebastian Cabot and the young mathematician John DEE as special advisors charged with framing a more coherent English exploration policy. Cabot shifted English efforts toward a search for a northeast passage, which resulted in the first English trade contacts with Russia during the last years of MARY I in the late 1550s.

Under Elizabeth, interest in Africa and America revived as John HAWKINS, son of William, led three trade voyages to SPANISH AMERICA in the 1560s. Hawkins carried slaves from West Africa to the Caribbean where he sold them to Spanish colonists for a handsome profit. In the East, the English explorer Anthony JENKINSON journeyed from Russia through Central Asia; although he established a profitable trade with Persia, Jenkinson found Central Asia too unsettled for the overland trade route to East Asia to be practicable. This discovery revived interest in a Northwest Passage and stimulated the American explorations of Sir Humphrey GILBERT and Martin FROBISHER in the 1570s, and of John DAVIS in the 1580s. Although the Northwest Passage was never found, the English desire to break Spain's trade monopoly with her colonies led Gilbert and his half brother Walter RALEIGH to propose the establishment of English colonies in America to provide England with valuable raw materials and to serve as bases for PRIVATEERING raids on Spanish America. Gilbert was lost at sea in 1583 after exploring the North American coast, but Raleigh was able to plant two short-lived colonies on Roanoke Island off the Virginia (now North Carolina) coast in 1585 and 1587 (see AMADAS-BARLOWE EXPEDITION; "LOST COLONY"; ROANOKE COLONY [1585]; ROANOKE COLONY [1587]).

In England, the work of Raleigh and other English explorers and colonizers was greatly furthered by the writings of Richard HAKLUYT. Beginning in 1579 with his *Discourse on the Strait of Magellan* and continuing through the 1580s with the *Discourse on Western Planting* and the monumental *PRINCIPAL NAVIGATIONS, VOYAGES AND DISCOVERIES OF THE ENGLISH NATION*, Hakluyt collected and disseminated accounts of voyages that aroused and maintained an interest in exploration and colonization in the English government and people. Although no successful English colony had been established by Elizabeth's death in 1603, new commercial markets had been opened in Russia, Africa, the Middle East, and East Asia by the work of English explorers, and the establishment of the first permanent English colony, Jamestown in Virginia, was only four years away.

Further Reading: F. R. Dulles, *Eastward Ho: The First English Adventurers to the Orient*, Freeport, NY: Books for Libraries Press, 1969; Samuel Eliot Morison, *The European Discovery of America: The Northern Voyages*, New York: Oxford University Press, 1971; George Bruner Parks, *Richard Hakluyt and the English Voyages*, New York: F. Ungar, 1961; A. L. Rowse, *The Elizabethans and America*, New York: Harper, 1959; Carl Ortwin Sauer, *Sixteenth Century North America*, Berkeley: University of California Press, 1971.

family

The patriarchal nuclear family was the core social and economic unit of Elizabethan England. Elizabethan society saw itself not as a collection of individuals but as an aggregation of male-headed households; POPULATION was reckoned as number of householders, to whom wives, children, and servants were subordinate. Although an average family contained four or five individuals, household size varied by social class (see SOCIAL HIERARCHY). Relatives beyond the nuclear family were more likely to be part of upper-class households than of lower-class ones. Upper-class couples also tended to marry earlier, to have more children as a consequence, and to have the wherewithal to ensure a higher survival rate among their offspring. Also, because infants in upper-class families were customarily fed by wet-nurses, noble and gentlewomen did not experience the contraceptive effects of breastfeeding—unlike women in lower-class families where mothers breastfed their own children.

Noble and gentle families also included retainers and servants, while the families of urban merchants and craftsmen included apprentices who lived with the family while learning the householder's trade or craft. Thus, a peer's household could number 30 to 40 people, and a gentleman's or wealthy merchant's 10 to 12 (see PEERAGE; GENTRY). The household was also the primary unit of production, with the family supporting itself by working together in AGRICULTURE or in some trade or craft, especially the production of cloth (see CLOTH INDUSTRY). Among the lower classes, most sons were expected to take up the occupation of their fathers when they married and started their own household, and most daughters were expected to marry a man of their father's social class. Among the upper classes, social expectations were less rigid, but family connections determined MARRIAGE prospects and influenced careers at COURT or in LOCAL GOVERNMENT.

Nicholas Hilliard's depiction of a mother and her child (perhaps James I's wife and son, Queen Anne and Prince Henry). Notice that the child is dressed as an adult. © *The British Museum.*

High mortality rates also left many families with only one parent and many children with stepparents and half siblings. Some historians have argued that relationships between parents and children, especially in upper-class families, were stiff and distant, characterized by strict discipline enforced by the father. Although the Elizabethan father's authority over his family is unquestioned, most historians agree that parent-child relationships in the Tudor period were as close and loving as such interactions are expected to be in modern families.

Further Reading: Lawrence Stone, *The Family, Sex and Marriage: In England 1500–1800,* New York: Harper and Row, 1977.

Family of Love. *See* ANABAPTISTS.

Farnese, Alessandro, Duke of Parma
(1546–1592)

As Spanish governor-general of the NETHERLANDS after 1578, Alessandro Farnese, Duke of Parma, so firmly reestablished Spanish authority in the southern provinces of the Netherlands that the country split eventually into the independent Dutch Republic in the north and the Spanish Netherlands in the south. Born in Rome, the son of Ottavia Farnese, Duke of Parma, and Margaret, the illegitimate daughter of CHARLES V, Alessandro Farnese was thus the nephew of PHILIP II of SPAIN. Serving under his uncle JOHN OF AUSTRIA (known as Don John), half brother of Philip II, Parma distinguished himself against the Turks in the naval battle of Lepanto in 1571. In 1577, after ably serving Philip as a diplomat and military commander in Italy and elsewhere, Parma accompanied Don John to the Netherlands, where he won a major victory over the Netherlands rebels at Gembloux (see NETHERLANDS REVOLT).

In 1578, after Don John's death, Parma succeeded his uncle as governor-general and began a campaign of reconquest that captured Antwerp in 1585 and led to the eventual restoration of Spanish authority throughout the southern provinces. The momentum of this campaign was broken in the 1580s by the need to prepare for the coming of the Spanish ARMADA, which was to ferry Parma's troops across the Channel to overthrow Elizabeth I and restore Catholicism to England, an action that Philip thought was a necessary prerequisite to finally crushing the Netherlands Revolt. Although skeptical of the claims made by Cardinal William ALLEN and others of the great numbers and enthusiasm of English Catholics, Parma readied his troops for a junction with the Spanish fleet. In August 1588, as the Armada sailed up the Channel, poor communications, shoal water, and the action of the English fleet prevented Parma from making contact, and, after 7 August, strong winds blew the Armada northward and ended any hope of its joining with Parma (see GRAVELINES, BATTLE OF).

After the failure of the Armada, Parma intervened, on Philip's orders, in the French civil war, forcing the new Protestant king of France, HENRI IV, to raise his siege of Catholic Paris in 1590. Parma also resumed his campaign of reconquest in the Netherlands, but made little progress after 1590, when rebel victories created a military stalemate that ensured the eventual independence of the north, just as Parma's earlier successes had ensured continued Spanish rule in the south.

Further Reading: Geoffrey Parker, *The Dutch Revolt,* Ithaca, NY: Cornell University Press, 1977; Giovanna Solari, *The House of Farnese,* Garden City, NY: Doubleday, 1968.

fashion, men

The Elizabethan period saw many long-used items and styles of men's clothing fall out of fashion, to be replaced with styles that were often more elaborate and eye-catching. Elizabethans, especially of the upper classes, were highly fashion conscious; being able to afford the latest, most fashionable attire was important for nobles and gentlemen seeking to make their fortunes and political careers at the COURT of a queen who loved rich and striking gowns. Clothes, as the SUMPTUARY LAWS show, were also an important indicator of class. Most of the fashions today associated with Elizabethans were worn by the upper classes and seem to modern eyes to be heavy and constricting. However, England has a cool, damp climate, and Elizabethans, lacking modern heating systems, relied more on their clothes for warmth than we do today. Also, the clothing of the lower classes, the great majority of the POPULATION, was less elaborate and more

This watercolor depicts fashionable court attire for men in about 1600. Note the breeches and the stiff lace collar. *By permission of the Folger Shakespeare Library.*

functional, allowing greater freedom of movement (see GENTRY; SOCIAL HIERARCHY).

Although gentlemen and commoners wore the same basic types and styles of clothing, fabrics, decorations, and colors varied greatly according to class. Common male garments included woolen hose or stockings over which were worn codpieces, trunkhose, or breeches. Codpieces were padded coverings for the crotch that acted like a trouser-fly, unbuttoning or untying to open. Trunkhose, a garment reaching from the waist to the thighs, gradually displaced the codpiece. Trunkhose could be simple or striking, with vertical slashes and contrasting colors. Late in the reign, men began to wear breeches—knee-length trousers with a fly opening that tied or buttoned (see illustration accompanying this entry).

Above the waist, men wore doublets—short, fitted jackets of wool, leather, or some finer fabric. During Elizabeth's reign, the doublet's waistline went from being cut straight to dipping downwards in a V shape (see illustration accompanying the entry for DUDLEY, ROBERT). Doublets closed with hooks, buttons, or laces, and sometimes had detachable sleeves. Over the doublet, a man might wear a jerkin or a coat. A jerkin was similar to a doublet but might be sleeveless, and a coat could be of many styles and fabrics depending on the social class of the wearer.

Shoes were generally square-toed, flat, and made of leather. Men also usually wore wool or linen caps or hats, doffing them as a mark of respect to superiors. Puritans tended to dress more somberly, both in style and color (see illustration accompanying entry for FOXE, JOHN). Boys generally wore the same types and styles of clothing worn by adult men of their social class. *See also* FASHION, WOMEN and the many portraits of Elizabethan men reproduced in this volume.

Further Reading: Jane Ashelford, *A Visual History of Costume*: Vol. 2: *The Sixteenth Century*, London: Batsford: 1983; J. A. Sharpe, *Early Modern England: A Social History 1550–1760*, 2nd ed., Oxford: Oxford University Press, 1997; Charles Hamilton Smith, *Ancient Costumes of England: From the Druids to the Tudors*, New York: Arch Cape Press, 1989.

fashion, women

Elizabethan women generally wore one of three basic clothing styles. The simplest garment was the kirtle, a long fitted dress that closely resembled medieval clothing. Upper-class women seldom wore a kirtle by itself, preferring to wear it under other garments. The most common Elizabethan style among all classes of women was the combination of the bodice for the upper body with a series of skirts (known as petticoats) for the lower body. The bodice was a stiff woolen garment that functioned like both a bra and a girdle. The style for the bodice neckline rose and fell several times during the reign—bodices were low-cut in the early and later years, and high in the middle years. A bodice could be sleeved or sleeveless, though the latter style was worn only as an undergarment by upper-class women. Bodice stiffening was supplied by whalebone, wood, or even metal, the degree of stiffening depending on how fashionable or practical the garment needed to be. Lower-class working women wore looser bodices that gave them greater ease of movement. Common women laced their bodices in the front, but COURT ladies fastened theirs with buttons or hooks and eyes.

The major change in petticoat styles during the Elizabethan period was the replacement of the flowing skirt of earlier decades with full skirts formed into cylindrical or bell shapes by various types of stiffened underskirts. The

This watercolor depicts fasionable court attire for women in about 1600. Note the effect of the farthingale, which pushes the skirt out at the waist and then allows it to drop straight down to the feet in a bell shape. *By permission of the Folger Shakespeare Library.*

farthingale (see illustration with this entry), an underskirt into which were sewn a series of wire, whalebone, or wooden hoops, originated in SPAIN, and became fashionable at the English court in the later decades of Elizabeth's reign. The wheel farthingale, which was often worn with a padded roll tied around the waist, pushed the skirt out from the hips and caused it to fall straight down to the feet. Lower-class women who wished to copy court styles favored the wheel farthingale because it pushed the skirt away from the legs and increased freedom of movement.

The richest form of women's garment was the gown, essentially a skirt and bodice sewn together and worn over a kirtle or underskirt. Court gowns could be highly decorated, with false sleeves and slashed skirts revealing contrasting underskirts. As portraits show, Elizabeth wore striking and colorful gowns (see illustrations with the entries for ELIZABETH I; ELIZABETH I, PORTRAITS OF; GOWER, GEORGE), her taste tending in her later years to increasingly elaborate styles. *See also* FASHION, MEN and the many portraits of Elizabethan women reproduced in this volume.

Further Reading: Jane Ashelford, *A Visual History of Costume*: Vol. 2: *The Sixteenth Century*, London: Batsford:

1983; J. A. Sharpe, *Early Modern England: A Social History 1550–1760*, 2nd ed., Oxford: Oxford University Press, 1997; Charles Hamilton Smith, *Ancient Costumes of England: From the Druids to the Tudors*, New York: Arch Cape Press, 1989.

favorites

The accession of a young woman to the English throne altered the political dynamic surrounding intimate royal relationships. The ill-defined role of royal "favorite," informally conferred by the court on anyone who held a position of special friendship or trust with the monarch, acquired sexual overtones when the monarch was a woman giving special favor to a man. In medieval England, the position of royal favorite was a male role because it carried an implication of political influence and power. A king's sexual relationships with women—while sometimes conferring influence—did not tend to raise the woman to the position of favorite because she could not exercise her influence directly as could a male friend of the king.

Thanks perhaps to the circumstances of her mother's death (see Anne BOLEYN) and to the uneasy nature of her relationship with her sister (see MARY I), Elizabeth's close friendships were with men. The queen's two great favorites were Robert DUDLEY, Earl of Leicester, and Leicester's stepson, Robert DEVEREUX, Earl of Essex. Leicester was the love of Elizabeth's youth, the man she would have married had not her position as queen made MARRIAGE such a complicated undertaking (see DUDLEY MARRIAGE SUIT; MARRIAGE QUESTION). The queen's affection and favor brought Leicester financial gain and political influence. Elizabeth forgave Leicester every indiscretion, including his secret marriage to Lettice KNOLLYS, which the queen took as betrayal, and for which she never forgave Knollys. However, the queen never allowed her passion for Leicester to give him the power his ambition craved, and he never replaced William CECIL as Elizabeth's most trusted advisor. Both her own and foreign courts assumed that the favor Elizabeth showed Leicester was based on sexual intimacy. Whether or not that was true is now unclear.

Elizabeth's relationship with the much younger Essex was based on his connection with Leicester and on the pleasure his lively company gave an aging woman. By the end of the reign, assumptions about the basis of Leicester's special position, and the queen's open use of sexual byplay to show favor, led most male courtiers to play the public role of Elizabeth's ardent suitor (see VIRGIN QUEEN). Although Essex achieved the status of favorite by playing this role more fully than most, Elizabeth consented to his execution when he rose in rebellion against the political limits that she imposed on him (see ESSEX'S REBELLION).

Further Reading: Susan Doran, *Monarchy and Matrimony: The Courtships of Elizabeth I*, London: Routledge, 1996; Alan Haynes, *The White Bear: The Elizabethan Earl of Leicester*, London: Peter Owen, 1987; Robert Lacey, *Robert, Earl of Essex*, New York: Atheneum, 1971.

First Folio

The first collected edition of the plays of William SHAKESPEARE, now known as the First Folio, appeared in 1623, seven years after Shakespeare's death. Although the title page

This engraving of William Shakespeare by Martin Droeshout appeared on the title page of the First Folio, a collection of Shakespeare's plays published in 1623. *By permission of the Folger Shakespeare Library.*

of the First Folio states that the volume was printed in London by Isaac Jaggard and Edward Blount, publication of the edition also involved Isaac Jaggard's father, William Jaggard, and the printers William Aspley and John Smethwick. The printers worked under the editorial direction of Shakespeare's two acting colleagues, John HEMINGES and Henry CONDELL, who provided a preface entitled "To the Great Variety of Readers," and a dedication offered to William, Earl of Pembroke, and Philip, Earl of Montgomery.

The First Folio contains 36 of Shakespeare's 37 plays, lacking only *Pericles, Prince of Tyre,* which, though recorded in the STATIONERS' REGISTER by Edward Blount in 1608, did not appear among Shakespeare's collected plays until the Third Folio edition in 1663–64. The First Folio represented the first appearance in print (and is today the sole authority for) 18 of Shakespeare's plays: *All's Well That Ends Well; Antony and Cleopatra; As You Like It; The Comedy of Errors; Coriolanus; Cymbeline; Henry VI, Part 1; Henry VIII; Julius Caesar; King John; Macbeth; Measure for Measure; The Taming of the Shrew; The Tempest; Timon of Athens; Twelfth Night; The Two Gentlemen of Verona;* and *The Winter's Tale* (see SHAKESPEARE, WORKS OF). For seven other plays that had appeared in earlier editions, the First Folio is today the most authoritative text*: Henry V; Henry VI, Part 2; Henry VI, Part 3; King Lear; The Merry Wives of Windsor; Othello;* and *Richard III.*

Although no manuscript of any Shakespeare play is today extant, Heminges, Condell, and their collaborators must have worked both from earlier printed versions of the plays and from Shakespeare's now-lost manuscripts. A Second Folio of the plays was published in 1632, a Third Folio in 1663–64, and a Fourth Folio in 1685, with each new volume printed from the edition immediately preceding it. With each seventeenth-century edition, spelling and punctuation were regularized and modernized, but, with the exception of some revisions in the Second Folio, few changes were made to the text until Nicholas Rowe published the first edited volume of Shakespeare in 1709. *See also* SONNET, SHAKESPEAREAN.

Further Reading: Charles Connell, *They Gave Us Shakespeare: John Heminges and Henry Condell,* Boston: Oriel

Press, 1982; A. L. Rowse, *William Shakespeare,* New York: Harper and Row, 1963; S. Schoenbaum, *Shakespeare's Lives,* Oxford: Clarendon Press, 1991.

fiscal feudalism

The Tudor monarchs' financial exploitation of ancient feudal obligations has become known as fiscal feudalism. The original basis of feudalism in medieval England was the granting of land by the king to a vassal in return for military service. To ensure continuous service, the king held certain rights, such as the right to arrange for the marriage of the vassal's widow or daughter, or the right to hold in ward the lands of an underage heir. The vassal also had certain monetary obligations, such as the duty to maintain the arms and armor of a knight or to contribute to the costs of knighting the king's eldest son or of marrying off the king's eldest daughter. By the Elizabethan period, the military obligation of vassals had largely disappeared, but these and other monetary obligations remained for the Crown to exploit when it wanted to raise money without going to PARLIAMENT. HENRY VII, Elizabeth's grandfather, and Thomas CROMWELL, HENRY VIII's chief minister in the 1530s, both exploited the Crown's feudal rights to the fullest.

The most valuable of the feudal dues was wardship, the right of the Crown to administer the estate of a tenant-in-chief—a wealthy noble or gentle landowner (see GENTRY; PEERAGE; SOCIAL HIERARCHY)—while the heir to the estate was a minor. The Crown also had the right to dispose of the heir's MARRIAGE, a particularly lucrative right since noblemen and gentlemen were always looking for suitable marriage partners for their children. Wardship brought Elizabeth almost £15,000 per year. The queen also received a sizable yearly sum from the collection of livery, a small fee paid by heirs upon entering into their landed inheritance.

The collection of these ancient obligations stemming from an obsolete system of land tenure caused much complaint, especially after the start of war with SPAIN in 1585, when efforts were undertaken to make collection more effective. Fiscal feudalism became a serious grievance under JAMES I and his son, who, lacking Elizabeth's parsimony, were always in need of money. Parliament abolished feudal dues when it set about to reform royal abuses in the 1640s.

Further Reading: F. C. Dietz, *English Public Finance, 1485–1641,* 2nd ed., London: F. Cass, 1964; Joel Hurstfield, *The Queen's Wards: Wardship and Marriage under Elizabeth I,* 2nd ed., London: Frank Cass, 1973.

Fitzgerald, Gerald, Earl of Desmond
(c. 1533–1583)

Gerald Fitzgerald, 14th Earl of Desmond, was an important ANGLO-IRISH nobleman in Elizabethan IRELAND. Because his father had usurped the Desmond title, the earl was not destined to hold his title from birth and so received little formal EDUCATION as a child. Lack of training put the adult earl at a severe disadvantage in his rivalry with Thomas BUTLER, Earl of Ormond, who, besides being Elizabeth's cousin (see BOLEYN FAMILY), had been educated in England and imbued with the social and political skills of an English courtier. Constant land and political disputes between Desmond and Ormond, whose families had long been at odds, led to a pitched battle at Affane in February 1565. Victorious in the encounter, Ormond paraded the humiliated Desmond through the streets of Waterford. Elizabeth summoned the two earls to England and put both under bonds to keep the peace, but only Desmond went to the TOWER OF LONDON.

After six years of confinement, he returned to his estates in Munster to find them devastated by the effects of FITZMAURICE'S REBELLION, which had begun in 1569 while he was imprisoned in England. Heavily in debt, Desmond attempted to restore his fortunes by working closely with the DUBLIN administration to promote order and reform. He abandoned the traditional exactions of COIGN AND LIVERY, which had caused much unrest, and even assisted some small-scale efforts at English colonization in Munster, one of the issues that had ignited the Fitzmaurice rising.

In 1579, James Fitzmaurice FITZGERALD, Desmond's cousin, returned to Ireland and renewed his revolt against the English government. When Fitzmaurice Fitzgerald was killed and the earl's brother, Sir John Fitzgerald, accepted leadership of the uprising, the Dublin government assumed that Desmond also was involved and proclaimed him a traitor, thus forcing him to join the rebellion (see DESMOND REBELLION; TREASON). After initial successes, Desmond was defeated and

Munster was subjected to a devastating scorched-earth policy, which caused a famine that decimated the local POPULATION. His estates confiscated, Desmond—pursued by Ormond, who was now acting under a government commission to suppress the rebellion—went into hiding. Ormond's forces captured and killed Desmond in November 1583. The seizure of Desmond's lands and the depopulation of war-torn Munster led to the establishment of a large-scale English plantation in Munster in the mid-1580s (see PLANTATIONS, IRISH).

Further Reading: Steven G. Ellis, *Tudor Ireland,* London: Longman, 1985; Brian Fitzgerald, *The Geraldines: An Experiment in Irish Government, 1169–1601,* London: Staples Press, 1951.

Fitzgerald, James Fitzmaurice (d. 1579)

James Fitzmaurice Fitzgerald (usually known as Fitzmaurice) led two rebellions against English political and religious control of IRELAND. Fitzmaurice was the cousin of Gerald FITZGERALD, Earl of Desmond. When Elizabeth imprisoned Desmond in the TOWER OF LONDON in 1565, Fitzmaurice claimed leadership of the Fitzgerald interest in southern Ireland. On poor terms with his cousin and angered by English attempts to colonize Desmond lands, Fitzmaurice allied himself with other disaffected Irish and ANGLO-IRISH chieftains and rose in rebellion against the English government in June 1569 (see FITZMAURICE'S REBELLION; PLANTATIONS, IRISH). Declaring his uprising a Catholic crusade to win support from Catholic Europe, Fitzmaurice laid siege to Cork and Kilkenny, demanding that the magistrates abolish Protestant worship within their towns. After spreading terror and destruction, Fitzmaurice was put to flight by troops commanded by Lord Deputy Henry SIDNEY and Captain Humphrey GILBERT.

In 1570, Fitzmaurice revived the rebellion, remaining at large until 1573, when he was forced to submit to Sir John PERROT, the lord president of Munster. When Desmond returned to Ireland later in the year, Fitzmaurice tried unsuccessfully to convince him to join in opposing English rule. In March 1575, accompanied by his family and a few supporters, Fitzmaurice sailed for Europe. In Paris, he unsuccessfully offered the Crown of Ireland to HENRI III in exchange for military and financial support in overthrowing English rule. In 1577, he offered Ireland to JOHN OF AUSTRIA, but PHILIP II of SPAIN declined to intervene on his half brother's behalf, being too heavily engaged in the NETHERLANDS and Portugal to risk war with England. With the help of the dissident Englishman Sir Thomas STUKELEY, Fitzmaurice finally persuaded Pope GREGORY XIII to provide troops for an invasion.

Landing in southwestern Ireland in June 1579, Fitzmaurice and his papal army established a fort at Smerwick and waited for the arrival of Stukeley with reinforcements (see SMERWICK, SIEGE OF). Fitzmaurice, meanwhile, sent urgent requests to Desmond and other Anglo-Irish leaders to join his forces. When no response came from Desmond, Fitzmaurice set off on pilgrimage to a nearby monastery. On his way there, he was slain in a skirmish with Anglo-Irish forces hostile to his enterprise. Because the rising begun by Fitzmaurice in 1579 came eventually under the leadership of Desmond, it became known as the DESMOND REBELLION.

Further Reading: Steven G. Ellis, *Tudor Ireland,* London: Longman, 1985; Colm Lennon, *Sixteenth-Century Ireland: The Incomplete Conquest,* Dublin: Gill and Macmillan, 1994; Margaret MacCurtain, *Tudor and Stuart Ireland,* Dublin: Gill and Macmillan, 1972; David B. Quinn, *The Elizabethans and the Irish,* Ithaca, NY: Cornell University Press, 1966.

Fitzmaurice, James. *See* FITZGERALD, JAMES FITZMAURICE.

Fitzmaurice's Rebellion

Fitzmaurice's Rebellion was an unsuccessful attempt by various Irish and ANGLO-IRISH chiefs to halt the imposition on IRELAND of a centralized English administration and a Protestant church. Led by James Fitzmaurice FITZGERALD (known as Fitzmaurice), who had assumed leadership of the Fitzgerald clans while his cousin, Gerald FITZGERALD, Earl of Desmond, lay prisoner in the TOWER OF LONDON, Fitzmaurice's Rebellion began in June 1569 in the Munster region of southern Ireland. Angered by English attempts to colonize Desmond lands, Fitzmaurice joined forces with other Irish dissidents to demand the end of English land-grabbing and the restoration of Catholic worship.

The uprising soon spread across southern Ireland, encompassing even members of the Butler family, the traditional enemies of the Fitzgeralds (see BUTLER WARS). The younger brothers of Thomas BUTLER, Earl of Ormond, had little interest in ending English rule or in overturning the Protestant Church of Ireland—they joined the rising solely to take revenge on Sir Peter CAREW, an English gentleman (see GENTRY) who had recently been awarded control of large tracts of Butler land by the lord deputy and his council. While the Butlers harried Carew's lands, Fitzmaurice besieged the towns of Cork and Kilkenny, demanding that the civic magistrates abolish Protestant services. By turning the rebellion into a Catholic crusade, Fitzmaurice hoped to win support from Catholic Europe. Fitzmaurice visited much terror and destruction on English landholders and town dwellers, but by the end of the year, he had been driven into hiding by forces under Lord Deputy Henry SIDNEY and Captain Humphrey GILBERT. Meanwhile, Ormond's arrival from England in August led to the submission of the Butlers. Although Fitzmaurice revived the rising in 1570, Gilbert and the new president of Munster, Sir John PERROT, ultimately crushed the rebellion by imposing a virtual reign of terror on Munster.

Between 1571 and Fitzmaurice's submission in 1573, Perrot executed more than 800 rebels and laid waste to the lands of many more. Desmond returned to Ireland from England in 1573 to find his lands devastated and his people impoverished. In 1575, Fitzmaurice fled to Europe, where he sought to interest the governments of FRANCE and SPAIN in backing an invasion of Ireland. The destruction and depopulation caused by Fitzmaurice's Rebellion and by the later DESMOND REBELLION (1579–1583) made possible the large-scale English plantation of Munster in the mid-1580s (see PLANTATIONS, IRISH).

Further Reading: Nicholas P. Canny, *The Elizabethan Conquest of Ireland: A Pattern Established 1565–76,* New York: Barnes and Noble Books, 1976; Steven G. Ellis, *Tudor Ireland,* London: Longman, 1985; Colm Lennon, *Sixteenth-Century Ireland: The Incomplete Conquest,* Dublin: Gill and Macmillan, 1994; Margaret MacCurtain, *Tudor and Stuart Ireland,* Dublin: Gill and Macmillan, 1972; David B. Quinn, *The Elizabethans and the Irish,* Ithaca, NY: Cornell University Press, 1966.

Fitzroy, Henry, Duke of Richmond (1519–1536)

As the illegitimate son of HENRY VIII and Elizabeth Blount, one of the LADIES-IN-WAITING to CATHERINE OF ARAGON, Henry Fitzroy was a half brother of Princess Elizabeth. Henry VIII gave his son a humanist education (see HUMANISM), and in June 1525, the king bestowed upon him numerous lands and offices and created him Duke of Richmond, HENRY VII's title before he won the throne. Conferral of the dukedom started rumors that the king meant to name Richmond heir to the throne, or even to marry him to his half sister Princess Mary (see MARY I). Because Fitzroy was never recognized as legitimate, such an intention is unlikely; the king probably sought only to make Fitzroy a more attractive MARRIAGE prospect.

In 1533, probably through the influence of Queen Anne BOLEYN, Fitzroy married Mary Howard, daughter of the Duke of Norfolk, one of the queen's Howard relatives (see HOWARD FAMILY). Because Richmond was only 14 and already in frail health, the marriage was never consummated (completed by sexual intercourse). The duke witnessed Anne Boleyn's execution in May 1536, and a month later attended the PARLIAMENT that declared Princess Elizabeth illegitimate. He died in July 1536 amid rumors that he had been poisoned by the late queen, although the cause of his death seems to have been tuberculosis.

Further Reading: Carrolly Erickson, *Great Harry,* New York: Summit Books, 1980; J. J. Scarisbrick, *Henry VIII,* Berkeley: University of California Press, 1968.

Fitzwilliam, Sir William (1526–1599)

Sir William Fitzwilliam served twice as lord deputy of IRELAND. Born into a Northamptonshire GENTRY family, Fitzwilliam was introduced to the COURT of EDWARD VI by his kinsman, John Russell, Earl of Bedford. Although a Protestant, Fitzwilliam supported the succession of the Catholic queen MARY I in 1553 (see NORTHUMBERLAND'S COUP) and was rewarded by an appointment as keeper of the great seal of Ireland. A client of Thomas RADCLIFFE, Earl of Sussex, lord deputy of Ireland, Fitzwilliam was named, after 1559, to various Irish posts, including treasurer for war and lord justice. He also sat in the Irish PAR-

LIAMENT. Fitzwilliam distinguished himself in campaigns against Shane O'NEILL in the 1560s and was several times put in charge of the Irish administration during absences in England of Sussex and the next lord deputy, Sir Henry SIDNEY.

In January 1572, Fitzwilliam succeeded Sidney as lord deputy. Through Sir John PERROT, lord president of the southern Irish province of Munster, Fitzwilliam dealt with the last phases of FITZMAURICE'S REBELLION. He also attempted to control the activities of Turlough Luineach O'NEILL in Ulster, a task made more difficult by the ultimately unsuccessful efforts of Sir Thomas SMITH and Walter DEVEREUX, Earl of Essex, to establish an English plantation in Ulster (see PLANTATIONS, IRISH; ULSTER ENTERPRISE [ESSEX]; ULSTER ENTERPRISE [SMITH]). Although ordered to assist both ventures, Fitzwilliam, jealous of his own authority, was slow to help either. In ill health and heavily criticized at court for the failures in Ulster and elsewhere, Fitzwilliam requested and received his recall in 1575, being replaced by Sidney.

Fitzwilliam lived quietly in England until 1588 when Elizabeth reappointed him to the Irish deputyship. He arrived in time to conduct the capture and execution of Spaniards from the retreating ARMADA who washed up on Irish shores. Becoming involved in the quarrels of Irish chieftains in Ulster, Fitzwilliam was later charged with being responsible for the NINE YEARS WAR. Recalled to England in July 1594, he was also accused of corruption by his Irish and English enemies, charges that Fitzwilliam vigorously denied. He died at his Northamptonshire home in 1599.

Further Reading: Steven G. Ellis, *Tudor Ireland,* London: Longman, 1985; Colm Lennon, *Sixteenth-Century Ireland: The Incomplete Conquest,* Dublin: Gill and Macmillan, 1994; Margaret MacCurtain, *Tudor and Stuart Ireland,* Dublin: Gill and Macmillan, 1972; David B. Quinn, *The Elizabethans and the Irish,* Ithaca, NY: Cornell University Press, 1966.

food. *See* DIET.

foreign trade

The Elizabethan era was a period of expansion and innovation in English foreign trade. Beginning in the fifteenth century, the European exploration and discovery of new lands in AMERICA and of new trade routes to Asia and the Middle East opened new markets, introduced new trade items, and reoriented European international trade from the Mediterranean to the Atlantic. Situated on the western edge of Europe, England was well placed to develop trade with America and to exploit the new Atlantic sea routes to Africa and Asia. Although supplying unfinished woolen cloth to the NETHERLANDS textile industry remained the largest and most lucrative component of English trade (see CLOTH INDUSTRY; MERCHANT ADVENTURERS), Elizabethans laid the groundwork for a massive expansion in trade in the next century by actively pursing new markets, new commodities, and new trading arrangements.

Starting in the 1550s, English voyages of exploration to Russia, the Middle East, and Asia were followed by the creation of joint-stock trading companies to establish trade in each region (see EAST INDIA COMPANY; JOINT-STOCK COMPANY; LEVANT COMPANY; MUSCOVY COMPANY). The joint-stock arrangement spread the risk and expense of opening new markets in unfamiliar regions among a larger number of investors. In America, a desire to find an English-controlled NORTHWEST PASSAGE to the spice and silk markets of Asia, and to exploit the growing markets in the Spanish colonies, drove forward English EXPLORATION of North America. In the 1560s, John HAWKINS's trade expeditions to SPANISH AMERICA demonstrated the Spanish colonists' growing appetite for many commodities, especially slaves, which could be readily obtained on one side of the Atlantic and profitably sold on the other. Although Spanish trade regulations inhibited this trade and further aggravated the already strained relations between England and Spain (see SAN JUAN D'ULLOA), the conflict with PHILIP II increased Elizabethan interest in American colonies as suppliers of needed metals and agricultural produce and as bases for PRIVATEERING raids on Spanish America.

The American explorations of Martin FROBISHER and John DAVIS in the 1570s and 1580s failed to find a practicable Northwest Passage to Asia, but added to English knowledge of North America and helped men like Humphrey GILBERT, Walter RALEIGH, and Richard HAKLUYT promote American colonization as a way to obtain raw materials and create new markets. By Elizabeth's death in 1603, English traders and trading companies were increasingly active in a host of new world markets, the value of English foreign trade was rapidly growing, and the number of English subjects engaged in some aspect of foreign trade was rising.

Further Reading: G. D. Ramsay, *English Overseas Trade During the Centuries of Emergence*, London: Macmillan, 1957.

Forman, Simon (1552–1611)

Simon Forman was noted throughout Elizabethan LONDON as an astrologer and healer, and he is well known today for his valuable diaries and case books. Born into a Wiltshire yeoman (peasant) family, Forman was only 11 when the death of his father put an end to his formal EDUCATION. In 1567, he apprenticed himself to a Salisbury grocer, but by the early 1570s he was at Oxford, acting as a servant for two cousins and picking up what education he could. He then held a number of teaching positions, and in his spare time began to dabble in astrology, magic, and necromancy (the conjuring of spirits). In 1579, he set himself up as a healer outside Salisbury, but this unauthorized medical practice led to his arrest and imprisonment (see MEDICINE).

After his release in July 1580, Forman moved to London, where he established a thriving but necessarily peripatetic medical practice, staying always one step ahead of the authorities. By 1588, Forman had acquired enough influential clients to allow him to practice medicine and astrology in relative safety. However, his fortune and his reputation were fully secured in 1592–93 when he successfully treated himself and many other Londoners during a severe visitation of the PLAGUE. After 1594, the Royal College of Physicians (the membership of which had fled London during the plague) repeatedly fined and imprisoned Forman for illegally practicing medicine, but he was speedily released each time through the intervention of highly placed friends.

In his diary, which he had kept since 1564, Forman recorded the many people, of all social classes, who consulted him on matters medical and astrological. He was frequently consulted by people seeking hidden treasure, lost or stolen property, or missing persons.

Many of his clients were WOMEN who wanted Forman to predict the commencement or course of a love affair; Forman began sexual relationships with many of them, faithfully recording the details in his diary. Although he married at age 47 in 1599, his sexual involvements with female clients continued. In 1603, he was finally granted a license to practice medicine by Cambridge (see UNIVERSITIES), and his practice, in both medicine and astrology, flourished until his death in September 1611.

Further Reading: A. L. Rowse, *Sex and Society in Shakespeare's Age: Simon Forman the Astrologer,* New York: Charles Scribner's Sons, 1974.

Foxe, John (1516–1587)

John Foxe, a Protestant scholar and cleric, was the author of the "BOOK OF MARTYRS," the most widely read volume in Elizabethan England. Born at Boston in Lincolnshire, Foxe became tutor in 1548 in the household of the widow of Henry FITZROY; among his pupils were Thomas HOWARD, the Elizabethan Duke of Norfolk, and Charles HOWARD, the future Lord Effingham and Elizabeth's lord admiral. In 1554, Foxe fled to Germany with other Protestants seeking to escape the Catholic regime of MARY I (see MARIAN EXILES). His

John Foxe, author of the "Book of Martyrs," was painted by an unknown artist about 1587. *By courtesy of the National Portrait Gallery, London.*

work as a proofreader for a Basel printer taught him the tremendous power of the press (see PRINTING). Hearing of the burnings of Protestants in England by Mary's government, Foxe augmented a Latin history of English martyrs that he had been writing with descriptions of the MARIAN MARTYRS. This work was published in August 1559, the same year Foxe returned to England to be ordained in Elizabeth's new ANGLICAN CHURCH.

Until 1564, Foxe lived in the household of his former student, the Duke of Norfolk, at whose execution for TREASON he was present in 1572. In 1563, Foxe republished his work in an expanded ENGLISH edition entitled *Acts and Monuments of These Latter and Perilous Days.* Soon known popularly as the "Book of Martyrs," the work traced the history of the Church since Christ, but focused on the recent history of the English Church and especially on the men and women martyred by Mary's regime. The book became widely known and read, especially after 1571 when the bishops ordered every cathedral church to own a copy. Many parish churches and Protestant GENTRY families also owned copies, bringing Foxe great fame.

Foxe spent the last decades of his life revising and expanding the "Book of Martyrs." He published his last edition in 1583, but new versions with additions by other writers continued to appear throughout the seventeenth century. For many generations, Foxe's sympathetic depiction of the Marian martyrs kept alive their memories and fostered hatred of Catholicism in the national consciousness (see CATHOLICISM, ENGLISH).

Further Reading: J. F. Mozley, *John Foxe and His Book,* New York: Octagon Books, 1970; V. N. Olsen, *John Foxe and the Elizabethan Church,* Berkeley: University of California Press, 1973.

France

Suffering from a succession of religious wars and weak kings, France came close to political disintegration in the Elizabethan period. In 1559, only months after Elizabeth's accession, HENRI II was killed during a tournament celebrating the Treaty of Cateau-Cambrésis that ended the long war between VALOIS France and HABSBURG Spain (see CATEAU-CAMBRÉSIS, TREATY OF). Henri's death passed the French Crown to Francis II, a sickly boy of 15 who was dominated by the Duke and Cardinal of GUISE, the maternal uncles of Francis's young queen, Mary STUART, Queen of Scots. The Guises were eager to suppress PROTESTANTISM in France, to maintain a Catholic and pro-French government in SCOTLAND, and to push their niece's claim to the Crown of England (see STUART CLAIM).

In 1560, the Treaty of Edinburgh and the death of Francis II ended any immediate French threat to Elizabeth from Scotland (see EDINBURGH, TREATY OF). Catherine de MEDICI, widow of Henri II, sent Mary Stuart back to Scotland and assumed control of the government of her second son, 10-year-old Charles IX. The weak regency government of Catherine, and the equally ineffective government of her third son, HENRI III, who came to the throne in 1574, could do nothing to stop the spread of CALVINISM throughout France or to control the violent Catholic reaction to Calvinism's growth. Catholics rejected the leadership of the French Crown when the monarchy seemed unable (and, at times, unwilling) to suppress the HUGUENOTS, and the Huguenots turned against the Crown after Catherine instigated the 1572 slaughter of Huguenot leaders known as the SAINT BARTHOLOMEW MASSACRE. Civil war between the Huguenots and the Guise-led CATHOLIC LEAGUE raged intermittently from 1562 to the 1590s, leaving a weak and distracted France unable to play any significant part in European affairs. England, not France, acted as the main counterbalance to the growing power of SPAIN, particularly in the NETHERLANDS.

The French monarchy began to revive in 1589 with the end of the Valois dynasty and the accession of HENRI IV of the House of Bourbon. Although he was a Protestant and had received military assistance from Elizabeth (see BRITTANY EXPEDITIONS), Henri converted to Catholicism in 1593 to secure the acquiescence of the Catholic League to his rule. By Elizabeth's death in 1603, Henri was just beginning the political rebuilding process that would make the French Crown the most powerful monarchy in seventeenth-century Europe.

Further Reading: Frederic J. Baumgartner, *France in the Sixteenth Century,* New York: St. Martin's Press, 1995; Robin Briggs, *Early Modern France, 1560–1715,* 2nd ed., Oxford: Oxford University Press, 1998; R. J.

Knecht, *The French Wars of Religion 1559–1598,* 2nd ed., London: Longman, 1996; J. H. M. Salmon, *Society in Crisis: France in the Sixteenth Century,* New York: St. Martin's Press, 1975.

Francis I (1494–1547)

Francis I of France was a contemporary and rival of HENRY VIII, father of Elizabeth I. Francis succeeded his uncle, Louis XII (see VALOIS FAMILY), in 1515. Flamboyant and cultured, Francis was a patron of Renaissance ART and learning, granting Leonardo da Vinci a pension in 1516. Within months of his accession, Francis invaded Italy, won a victory at Marignano, and gained control of the duchy of Milan. In 1519, he sought election as Holy Roman Emperor but lost to the Habsburg candidate, Charles I of SPAIN (see CHARLES V; HABSBURG FAMILY). In 1516, he and the pope signed the Concordat of Bologna, which gave Francis a degree of control over the French Catholic Church that Henry VIII was not to gain over the English Church until he broke with Rome in the 1530s. In June 1520, Francis and Henry tried to impress each other at the Field of Cloth of Gold, an elaborately staged meeting of the French and English courts near CALAIS.

From the early 1520s, Francis waged intermittent war with Charles V for dominance in Italy. After being defeated and taken prisoner at Pavia in 1525, Francis spent a year in captivity in Spain, and won his release only by agreeing to renounce his Italian possessions and to send his two eldest sons (see HENRI II) to Spain as hostages. Upon regaining his freedom, Francis repudiated the agreement, thereby sentencing his sons to three years of severe confinement.

In the late 1520s, Francis forged an alliance against Charles V that included England, the pope, and Venice; by 1529, he had won the release of his sons but was forced again to renounce his Italian holdings. He concluded a peace with Charles V in the late 1530s, which caused much nervousness in England, where Henry VIII and his ministers feared a Franco-imperial invasion to overthrow the anti-papal English king; however, the concord between Francis and Charles did not last long enough to seriously threaten Henry.

In the 1540s, Francis fought both Henry and Charles, losing Boulogne to Henry in 1544 but landing raiding parties in southern England in 1545. Francis died in 1547, seven months after Henry VIII. *See also* the genealogical chart in Appendix 1: "Valois and Bourbon Dynasties of France."

Further Reading: R. J. Knecht, *Francis I,* Cambridge: Cambridge University Press, 1982; R. J. Knecht, *French Renaissance Monarchy: Francis I and Henry II,* 2nd ed., London: Longman, 1996; Desmond Seward, *Prince of the Renaissance: The Golden Life of François I,* New York: Macmillan, 1973.

Frobisher, Sir Martin (1539–1594)

Martin Frobisher was one of the earliest Elizabethan explorers of North America. Born into a Yorkshire GENTRY family, Frobisher was sent to LONDON at an early age to be raised by a maternal uncle who was a merchant adventurer engaged in the Africa trade (see MERCHANT ADVENTURERS). Between 1553 and 1575, Frobisher served on numerous trading and PRIVATEERING expeditions, spending time in the 1560s as a soldier in IRELAND and as a prisoner in a Portuguese fortress on the West African coast.

In 1576, with the help of such powerful advocates as Sir Humphrey GILBERT, John DEE, and Ambrose DUDLEY, Earl of Warwick, Frobisher persuaded a group of London merchants to finance an expedition to discover a NORTHWEST PASSAGE around AMERICA to Asia. Frobisher's two SHIPS left the Thames on 7 June 1576, receiving a wave of send-off from the queen as they sailed under her window at GREENWICH PALACE. The expedition skirted Greenland before exploring what is today Baffin Island, where Frobisher discovered what he took to be gold-bearing rock. He also encountered groups of Inuit (Eskimo) peoples. Frobisher returned to England in October convinced that he had visited the eastern edge of Asia. The promise of gold spurred the formation of the Company of Cathay, a joint-stock venture to which the queen contributed a ship and £1,000 (see JOINT-STOCK COMPANY).

Leaving London on 25 May 1577, Frobisher's second expedition included three vessels and a company of miners, desire for gold having overshadowed the quest for a Northwest Passage. Frobisher once again explored the area of Baffin Island, excavating tons of rock and taking several Inuit captives. John WHITE, one of the expedition's members, made several

John White's drawing of Englishmen from Martin Frobisher's crew skirmishing with American Inuit (Eskimo) peoples in July 1577. © *The British Museum.*

still-extant watercolors of the captives. The fleet returned to England in September. Convinced by German assayers that Frobisher's ore contained gold, the company outfitted a third expedition of 15 ships, which sailed on 31 May 1578. This fleet survived an exceptionally cold and stormy summer to return, much reduced in men and ships, in October. The rock brought back from the three voyages eventually proved worthless, costing the investors nearly £20,000 and Frobisher any hope of a fourth expedition.

In 1585, Frobisher was part of Sir Francis DRAKE's raid on the Spanish West Indies (see SPANISH AMERICA), and in 1588 Frobisher distinguished himself in the Channel fighting against the ARMADA. He took part in other naval actions against SPAIN in the 1590s, dying in November 1594 of a wound received in an assault on a Spanish fort.

Further Reading: William McFee, *Sir Martin Frobisher,* London: J. Lane, Bodley Head, 1928; Samuel Eliot Morison, *The European Discovery of America: The Northern Voyages,* New York: Oxford University Press, 1971.

gallowglasses

The heavily armed bodies of infantry known as gallowglasses (from the Irish *galloglaigh,* "foreign warriors") formed the core of most Irish armies during the Elizabethan period. Gallowglasses were armored foot soldiers who entered battle wielding battle-axes, spears, and two-handed swords. They were used to form a solid defensive wall capable of beating off cavalry charges and protecting the lighter-armed Irish horsemen as they formed and regrouped before and after their own charges of the enemy.

The gallowglasses originated in the thirteenth century when northern Irish chieftains, particularly in Ulster, recruited mercenaries from the Hebrides Islands and other parts of northwestern SCOTLAND to serve as bodyguards. Paid for their services with grants of land from the Irish lords who employed them, the Scottish mercenaries settled in IRELAND in large numbers in the later Middle Ages. By the Elizabethan period, such families as the MacSweenys, the MacDonalds, and the MacLeods had become part of the hereditary nobility of Ireland, supplying the elite mercenary core of the military forces fielded by Irish leaders to fight English armies and menace English settlements.

All parties involved in the wars and rebellions of Elizabeth's reign, including ANGLO-IRISH nobles and even the English government in DUBLIN itself, employed gallowglasses during their campaigns. The turmoil of the period even stimulated a new wave of mercenaries, nicknamed the REDSHANKS by the English, to enter Ireland from the western isles of Scotland. Hugh O'NEILL, Earl of Tyrone, made effective use of gallowglasses in his victories over the English in the 1590s during the NINE YEARS WAR. However, when the defeat of Tyrone and his Spanish allies at the siege of Kinsale in 1601 led to more effective English government and heavier English settlement, especially in Ulster in the north, the use of gallowglasses gradually faded out. *See also* ARMY; KERN; KINSALE, BATTLE OF; PLANTATIONS, IRISH; WEAPONS; YELLOW FORD, BATTLE OF.

Further Reading: Steven G. Ellis, *Tudor Ireland,* London: Longman, 1985; Cyril Falls, *Elizabeth's Irish Wars,* London: Methuen, 1950; Colm Lennon, *Sixteenth-Century Ireland: The Incomplete Conquest,* Dublin: Gill and Macmillan, 1994; Margaret MacCurtain, *Tudor and Stuart Ireland,* Dublin: Gill and Macmillan, 1972; David B. Quinn, *The Elizabethans and the Irish,* Ithaca, NY: Cornell University Press, 1966.

Garnet, Henry (1555–1606)

Henry Garnet was leader of the English JESUIT MISSION from 1587 to 1606. Born into a GENTRY family in Derbyshire, Garnet was raised a Protestant. In the early 1570s, he moved to LONDON, where he worked as a proofreader for a printer of legal materials (see PRINTING). After two years in this position, Garnet abandoned his PROTESTANTISM and resolved to join the Catholic priesthood. He traveled to Italy in 1575 and entered the Jesuit college in Rome. Garnet eventually became professor of Hebrew at the college and for a time also served as professor of mathematics.

In 1586, he joined the Jesuit Mission to England, landing safely with fellow priest Robert SOUTHWELL on 7 July. In 1587, he became superior of the Jesuit province of England, a position he held until his death. Sheltering in the country homes of Catholic gentry, Garnet traveled around the kingdom ministering to Catholics (see CATHOLICISM, ENGLISH). He occasionally smuggled himself into London prisons to comfort Catholic prisoners, and in 1593 he successfully reconciled his dying mother to Catholicism. Under Garnet's leadership, both the number of Jesuits working in the country and the number of English Catholics slipping overseas to join the Jesuit order greatly increased.

In 1605, Garnet and fellow Jesuit John GERARD were implicated in the Gunpowder Plot, a conspiracy of Catholic gentlemen to blow up the king, the House of Lords, and the House of Commons when JAMES I came to open PARLIAMENT. The government tracked Garnet to a country house near Worcester where Garnet concealed himself in one of the mansion's PRIEST HOLES. After four days, cramped quarters and lack of air forced Garnet to surrender. Lodged in the TOWER OF LONDON and examined by the PRIVY COUNCIL, Garnet was threatened with torture but spared its application by order of the king. Garnet was not involved in devising the plot but learned of it through the confessional and tried to dissuade the conspirators from going forward. His knowledge of the conspiracy was enough to convict him at his trial. He was executed at St. Paul's Churchyard in London on 3 May 1606.

Further Reading: Philip Caraman, *Henry Garnet, 1555–1606, and the Gunpowder Plot,* London: Longmans, Green, and Company, 1964.

Gascoigne, George (c. 1525–1577)

George Gascoigne was a prominent poet and dramatist of the early Elizabethan period. Born into a Bedfordshire GENTRY family, Gascoigne entered Cambridge (see UNIVERSITIES) but left without a degree. He attended the INNS OF COURT in the 1550s and was a member of the Parliaments of 1557 and 1559. A failed romance sent Gascoigne traveling in Europe, where he lived so extravagantly and amassed so many debts that his father disowned him. At that point, he turned to writing POETRY. In 1566, two of his dramatic works were staged— *The Supposes,* the first English play adapted

from an Italian comedy, and *Jocasta,* the first English adaptation from a classical Greek tragedy of Euripides.

Although elected to PARLIAMENT again in 1568, Gascoigne fled the country when his stepchildren sued him for misuse of their inheritance and a group of his creditors asked the Commons to deny him his seat for his failure to pay debts. Gascoigne spent three years as a soldier in the NETHERLANDS, first under WILLIAM, PRINCE OF ORANGE, and then with Sir Humphrey GILBERT. He was captured by the Spanish and imprisoned for several months, an experience that produced *The Fruits of War* and *Gascoigne's Voyage into Holland.* Back in England by 1573, he discovered that an anonymous edition of his early poetry, *A Hundred Sundry Flowers,* had been published without his permission. In 1575, he issued a revised authorized edition of his work under the title *The Posies of George Gascoigne,* which was notable for including "Certain Notes of Instruction Concerning the Making of Verse," the first critical essay on poetry in English.

Gascoigne next wrote verses for the extravagant ENTERTAINMENT presented to Elizabeth I at Kenilworth during the summer progress of 1575 by Robert DUDLEY, Earl of Leicester (see PROGRESSES, ROYAL). During the next year, Gascoigne wrote his only original play, a tragedy entitled *The Glass of Government;* a blank verse satire titled *The Steel Glass,* for which Walter RALEIGH wrote some laudatory verses; and *The Spoil of Antwerp,* an eyewitness account of the Spanish sack of Antwerp in 1576. Gascoigne died in October 1577. His work was highly praised by his contemporaries, including Edmund SPENSER, and his innovative use of verse narrative was later adopted by William SHAKESPEARE, who also drew upon Gascoigne's *The Supposes* for part of the plot of *The Taming of the Shrew.*

Further Reading: Charles Tyler Prouty, *George Gascoigne,* New York: B. Blom, 1966.

gentry

As a social class, the Elizabethan gentry comprised those landowners who lacked titles of nobility but exercised extensive political and social influence in their localities. Standing below the royal family and the titled PEERAGE in the SOCIAL HIERARCHY, the gentry formed the bulk of the country's political, social, and economic elite. By the end of Elizabeth's reign in 1603, gentlemen and their families made up about 3 percent of the English POPULATION, and the actual number of gentlemen in England stood at about 16,000, four to five times the number of Englishmen who could claim gentry status in the 1520s.

The gentry were subdivided into knights, esquires, and mere gentry—categories based roughly on wealth and social status, with the parameters for each subdivision varying by locality. The status of knighthood had originally been conferred by the Crown for military service, but by the Tudor period it was reserved for gentlemen holding land that generated an income of at least £40–£50 per year. The untitled eldest sons of the titled nobility also carried the knighthood designation of "Sir" as a courtesy title. Officially, esquires were the untitled male heirs of the younger sons of the nobility, local officeholders such as sheriffs and JUSTICES OF THE PEACE, and the descendants of ancient landholding families who could prove that ancestors once held the rank. Unofficially, esquires in Elizabethan England required an appropriate level of landed wealth, a leisurely lifestyle free from the need for manual labor, participation in LOCAL GOVERNMENT, and a certain degree of respect from the local community. Mere gentlemen, who were originally the younger brothers and sons of knights and esquires, had become, by Elizabethan times, anyone who could to some degree fulfill the informal requirements of esquire status.

Gentlemen of all categories were entitled to a coat of arms, which served as a formal recognition of their social status. Heralds from the COLLEGE OF ARMS periodically toured the countryside to determine who was and was not entitled to gentry status. Heralds could enlarge the gentry ranks by granting coats of arms to lawyers, university instructors, and civil and military officers who possessed the required wealth and lifestyle. Throughout the sixteenth century, the numbers, wealth, and political sophistication of the gentry grew. By Elizabethan times, members of the gentry class filled the UNIVERSITIES, the House of Commons in PARLIAMENT, and the commissions of peace in the counties, as well as many seats on the PRIVY COUNCIL and positions throughout the royal government.

Further Reading: Felicity Heal and Clive Holmes, *The Gentry in England and Wales 1500–1700,* Stanford, CA: Stanford University Press, 1994.

Gerard, John (1563–1637)

John Gerard was a prominent member of the JESUIT MISSION to England. Born into a Lancashire GENTRY family, Gerard spent several years as a student at various English Catholic seminaries in Europe. In 1579, he entered Oxford (see UNIVERSITIES), but withdrew for religious reasons in 1580. In 1581, he entered Clermont College, a Jesuit institution in Paris, but was soon forced by ill health to return to England. After a brief imprisonment for attempting to leave England without license, Gerard entered the English College at Rome, where he was ordained a priest and admitted to the Jesuit order in 1588.

Immediately assigned to the English mission, Gerard traveled about the country ministering to English Catholics (see CATHOLICISM, ENGLISH) and successfully eluding all attempts to capture him. He was finally arrested on a trip to LONDON when a servant betrayed him to the government. He was lodged eventually in the TOWER OF LONDON and was subjected to torture by order of the PRIVY COUNCIL. According to his Latin autobiography, which provides a remarkable account of Jesuit activity in Elizabethan England, Gerard was suspended for hours by his wrists, a method of torture that nearly crippled him for life. In October 1597, Gerard engineered a daring escape, crossing the Tower moat by swinging himself out on a rope. Despite the danger, he stayed in England, returning to his missionary work.

On the accession of JAMES I in 1603, Gerard withdrew his support from various ongoing Catholic plots to overthrow the Protestant monarch in the belief that the new king could be persuaded to suspend the PENAL LAWS against Catholics. However, James proved a disappointment, and Gerard was (probably unfairly) implicated in the Gunpowder Plot of November 1605, a Catholic attempt to blow up the king and PARLIAMENT. Unable to remain in England, Gerard slipped out of the country in the entourage of the Spanish ambassador, leaving on 3 May 1606, the day his Jesuit colleague Henry GARNET was executed for his part in the Gunpowder conspiracy. Gerard spent most of the rest of his life in Rome, where he became spiritual director of the English College in 1627; he died there in July 1637.

Further Reading: John Gerard, *The Autobiography of a Hunted Priest,* translated by Philip Caraman, New York: Pellegrini and Cudahy, 1952.

Gilbert, Sir Humphrey (c. 1539–1583)

Sir Humphrey Gilbert, the maternal half brother of Sir Walter RALEIGH, was one of the first Elizabethans to advocate the colonization of North AMERICA (see Maps, "Elizabethan Voyages of American Exploration"). Gilbert attended Oxford (see UNIVERSITIES) and was briefly a page in the household of Princess Elizabeth. He was at the siege of Le Havre in 1563 (see LE HAVRE EXPEDITION) and campaigned for the Crown in IRELAND in the late 1560s. Convinced of the existence of a NORTH-WEST PASSAGE that would allow England to compete with the Iberian states for the Asian silk and spice trades, Gilbert wrote a treatise entitled *Discourse of a Discovery for a New Passage to Cathaia* (i.e., China), which he presented to the queen in 1566. Elizabeth was uninterested in seeking a Northwest Passage, but she did authorize Gilbert and others to plant English settlers in Ireland.

In 1570, Gilbert won a knighthood for ruthlessly crushing Irish rebels (see FITZMAURICE'S REBELLION), and in 1572 he wrote his *Discourse on Ireland,* which described the benefits to England of further colonization in Ireland. Later in 1572, he led a company of English volunteers to the NETHERLANDS to assist the Dutch rebels but accomplished little militarily. On his return, Gilbert helped organize Martin FROBISHER's American voyages of exploration, and also bombarded the government with proposals for seizing the New-foundland fishing fleets of SPAIN and FRANCE (see NEWFOUNDLAND FISHERY), for attacking the Spanish silver fleet, and for capturing Cuba.

In June 1578, Elizabeth granted Gilbert a six-year license to "inhabit and possess at his choice all remote and heathen lands" not actually held by a Christian ruler. With financial assistance from Raleigh and others, Gilbert launched a fleet of seven SHIPS in November, but by February 1579 he was back in England, the fleet having been dispersed by storms and poor discipline. Gilbert spent several years raising money from various sources, and in June 1583 he launched a second expedition of five ships from Plymouth. By August, the fleet reached Newfoundland, which Gilbert claimed for England and where he intended to establish a colony. Gilbert's explorations of the coastline were cut short by the wreck of one of his ships, and unrest among his men forced him to agree to return home. On 9 September 1583, a sudden storm swamped his vessel, and Gilbert and all aboard were lost. Shortly before this disaster, Gilbert, sitting at the stern of the ship with a book in his hand, had called out to his companions on the other ship, "We are as near to heaven by sea as by land," an indication that the book he was reading was Sir Thomas More's *Utopia.*

Further Reading: Donald Barr Chidsey, *Sir Humphrey Gilbert,* New York: Harper and Brothers, 1932; Samuel Eliot Morison, *The European Discovery of America: The Northern Voyages,* New York: Oxford University Press, 1971.

Gilbert, William (1540–1603)

William Gilbert was both an eminent physician and one of the leading men of science of the Elizabethan age. Born in Essex, Gilbert was educated at St. John's College, Cambridge (see UNIVERSITIES), completing a degree in MEDICINE in 1569. From his university days, when he began making meteorological observations, Gilbert was interested in scientific research and experimentation. After traveling for some years in Europe, Gilbert settled in LONDON in 1573, where he developed a flourishing medical practice. He also began conducting extensive research into magnetism, performing more than 300 different experiments on magnetic and electrical attractions. His work led in 1600 to the publication of *De Magnete,* a scientific treatise that criticized much previous work in the field and rejected outright many of the long-cherished theories of Aristotle.

In 1599, Gilbert was elected president of the Royal College of Physicians. He won appointment as personal physician to the queen in 1601 and attended Elizabeth during her last illness in 1603. At the accession of JAMES I, Gilbert retained his post as royal physician, but he died on 10 December 1603, only a few months into the new reign. Gilbert's other great scientific work, *De Mundo,* was published post-humously in 1651. A combination of two manuscripts describing Gilbert's views on the structure of the universe, *De Mundo* agreed with Nicolaus Copernicus's theory that the earth rotated on its axis and suggested that some form of magnetism kept the planets in their fixed orbits.

Further Reading: Leslie A. Clarkson, *Death, Disease, and Famine in Pre-Industrial England,* New York: St. Martin's Press, 1976; A. L. Rowse, *The Elizabethan Renaissance: The Cultural Achievement,* New York, Scribner, 1972.

Globe Theatre

Because it is closely associated with William SHAKESPEARE, the Globe has become the best-known theatre of Elizabethan LONDON. In 1596, James BURBAGE sought unsuccessfully to renew his lease on the land where he had built The Theatre, his London playhouse. When Burbage died in 1597, negotiations with the landowner remained at a standstill, prompting his sons Cuthbert and Richard

This eighteenth-century depiction of the Globe Theatre was based on a 1616 engraving. © *The British Museum.*

BURBAGE to take a novel approach to solving the problem. On 28 December 1598, only days before the lease was due to expire, the Burbages commissioned a carpenter named Peter Street to dismantle the entire theatre and move it across the Thames to the southern suburb of Southwark (see Maps, "Elizabethan London"). By autumn 1599, the new Globe Theatre was open for performances. Because the move was a costly undertaking, the Burbage brothers gathered a group of investors to finance the project. These new co-owners of the theatre included five members of the CHAMBERLAIN'S MEN acting company, one of whom was Shakespeare.

The Globe was a round wooden structure rising about 40 feet in height to accommodate three tiers of galleries that took up roughly 13 feet of the theatre's 80-foot diameter. Thrusting into the uncovered central auditorium, which was about 65 feet in diameter, was a raised rectangular stage, approximately 40 feet wide and partially covered by a thatched roof supported by two pillars. The stage could hold no more than 12 actors at a time, although the building, despite its cramped dimensions, could accommodate audiences of over 2,000. Actors' dressing rooms lay behind the stage, and rising above it were a gallery (see illustration for DRAMA), which could be used for the audience or as part of the stage (e.g., the balcony scene in *Romeo and Juliet*), and a balcony, from which elaborate machinery caused gods and angels to descend to the stage. A trapdoor in the stage floor allowed the appearance of demons and the staging of burials.

Adorned with a globe on its roof, the theatre had carved on its front a Latin quotation that translated roughly into Shakespeare's line, "All the world's a stage." When a play was in progress, the Globe flew a flag bearing its emblem. On 29 June 1613, a blank volley fired as part of a performance of Shakespeare's *Henry VIII* set the Globe's thatch roof on fire. No one died in the flames, and Richard Burbage opened a rebuilt Globe in 1614.

Further Reading: John Cranford Adams, *The Globe Playhouse: Its Design and Equipment,* 2nd ed., New York: Barnes and Noble, 1961; Bernard Beckerman, *Shakespeare at the Globe, 1599–1609,* New York: Macmillan, 1962; Herbert Berry, *Shakespeare's Playhouses,* New York: AMS, 1987; Leslie Hotson, *Shakespeare's Wooden O,* London: Hart-Davis, 1959; John Orrell, *The Quest for Shakespeare's Globe,* New

York: Cambridge University Press, 1983; Peter Thomson, *Shakespeare's Theatre*, 2nd ed., London: Routledge, 1992.

Golden Speech

On 30 November 1601, a deputation of the House of Commons came to WHITEHALL PALACE to thank Elizabeth for her PROCLAMATION promising to reform the abuse of MONOPOLIES. The speech she delivered that day, made poignant by the unspoken belief of her hearers that it was the last time the aging queen would address her people, was to be cherished for generations as the Golden Speech, for, said one member, it was worthy "to be written in gold."

The PARLIAMENT of 1601, Elizabeth's last, had angrily demanded that the queen keep her promise to the previous Parliament to reform monopolies. Because Parliament's demands touched the royal PREROGATIVE, constituting, in effect, an attempt to limit or modify the powers inherent in the Crown, the issue precipitated one of the few serious political breeches to occur between queen and Parliament during the reign. Realizing from the intensity of Parliament's anger how great was the outrage over monopolies throughout the kingdom, Elizabeth issued a proclamation promising remedy. This action transformed the angry mood of the Commons to joy; when the speaker tried to name a deputation to deliver the Commons's thanks to the queen, he was met by cries of "All! All! All!" The queen responded that all were welcome, and the speaker and 140 members came to Whitehall to hear Elizabeth give the following address:

Mr. Speaker. We perceive your coming is to present thanks to us. Know I accept them with no less joy than your loves can have desire to offer such a present, and do more esteem it than any treasure or riches; for those we know how to prize, but loyalty, love, and thanks, I account them invaluable. And though God hath raised me high, yet this I account the glory of my crown, that I have reigned with your loves. . . . I do not so much rejoice that God hath made me to be a queen, as to be a queen over so thankful a people, and to be the means under God to conserve you in safety and to preserve you from danger. . . . Of myself I must say this: I never was any greedy, scraping grasper, nor a strict fast-holding prince, not yet a waster; my heart was never set upon any worldly goods, but only for my subjects' good. What you do bestow on me, I will not hoard up, but receive it to bestow on you again; yea, my own properties I account yours, to be expended for your good, and your eyes shall see the bestowing of it for your welfare.

Mr. Speaker, you give me thanks, but I am more to thank you, and I charge you, thank them of the lower house for me; for, had I not received knowledge from you, I might have fallen into the lapse of an error, only for want of true information. . . . That my grants shall be made grievances to my people, and oppressions be privileged under color of our patents, our princely dignity will not suffer. When I heard it, I could give no rest unto my thoughts until I had reformed it. . . . To be a king and to wear a crown is a thing more glorious to them that see it, than it is pleasant to them that bear it. For myself, I was never so much enticed with the glorious name of a king, or royal authority of a queen, as delighted that God hath made me His instrument to maintain His truth and glory, and to defend this kingdom from peril, dishonor, tyranny, and oppression. . . . It is not my desire to live or reign longer than my life and reign shall be for your good. And though you have had, and may have, many mightier and wiser princes sitting in this seat, yet you never had, nor shall have, any that will love you better.

An official version of the speech, somewhat edited and elaborated by the queen, was quickly issued by the royal printer (see PRINTING). But an unofficial version, closer to the speech as delivered on 30 November because it was drawn from the rough notes the queen handed that day to Henry Saville, provost of Eton, was soon circulating under the title "The Golden Speech of Queen Elizabeth." This version was to be reprinted many times over the next century.

Further Reading: Paul Johnson, *Elizabeth I,* New York: Holt, Rinehart and Winston, 1974; J. E. Neale, *Queen Elizabeth I,* Chicago: Academy Chicago Publishers, 1992.

Gower, George (c. 1540–1596)

As serjeant-painter to the queen, George Gower was one of the most successful portrait painters in Elizabethan England. By the early 1570s, Gower, who began life as a Yorkshire gentleman, was one of the most sought-after portraitists in London. The queen appointed Gower her serjeant-painter in 1581, thus increasing the demand for his services among members of her COURT. In 1584, Gower and the famous miniaturist Nicholas HILLIARD tried unsuccessfully to obtain a monopoly on the production of royal portraits, a commodity that commanded a lucrative and growing mar-

The "Armada Portrait" of Elizabeth I, painted by George Gower about 1588. *By courtesy of the National Portrait Gallery, London.*

ket (see ELIZABETH I, PORTRAITS OF; MONOPOLIES). In 1593, however, Gower became official painter to the English NAVY.

Although only a few extant works, including a self-portrait from 1579, are known for certain to be Gower's, many portraits of Elizabethan nobles and courtiers, all painted between about 1570 and 1586, are attributed to Gower. The 1588 "Armada Portrait" (illustrating this entry) is perhaps Gower's best known surviving work. This portrait shows a richly gowned Elizabeth standing before a depiction of the English victory over the Spanish ARMADA. Gower died in August 1596. *See also* ART; LIMNING.

Further Reading: Eric Mercer, *English Art 1553–1625,* Oxford: Clarendon Press, 1962; Roy Strong, *The Cult of Elizabeth: Elizabethan Portraiture and Pageantry,* London: Thames and Hudson, 1977.

Gowrie conspiracy

In August 1600, attendants of James VI of SCOTLAND (see JAMES I) killed the Earl of Gowrie and his brother, allegedly to prevent the two men from carrying out a plot to kidnap or assassinate the king. The Gowrie conspiracy is one of the most mysterious episodes in Scottish history. John Ruthven, Earl of Gowrie, was a son of a leader of the 1582 RUTHVEN RAID, in which Protestant noblemen kidnapped and confined James to prevent him from embracing Catholicism, and a grandson of one of the murderers of David RIZZIO, the hated Catholic favorite of Mary STUART, Queen of Scots (see FAVORITES).

A strong Presbyterian like his father and grandfather, Gowrie was 22 in 1600 when he traveled from Italy to England, where he was well received by Queen Elizabeth. After returning to Scotland, Gowrie made himself conspicuous by opposing the king's demand for money in the current PARLIAMENT. On 5 August 1600, James and a small following left the COURT and rode with Gowrie's 19-year-old brother, the Master of Gowrie, to Gowrie House, the Ruthven family home in Perth. There, according to the king, the two brothers attempted to kidnap him, as their father had done 18 years earlier. The king was somehow able to alert his attendants, who burst into the house and slew both brothers in the ensuing fight.

James immediately ordered public rejoicing at his narrow escape, but many, both within the Scottish Church and throughout the kingdom, doubted the king's version of events. Rumors suggested that James had concocted the story to destroy the Ruthvens. The king's reasons were variously described as his jealousy over the favor Gowrie had found with James's wife, Queen Anne, his desire to avoid repaying a large debt he owed to the earl, and his desire to avenge the humiliation of the Ruthven raid and to prevent Gowrie from leading presbyterian opposition to his efforts to strengthen royal control of the Scottish Church. Whatever happened, the episode showed how fragile were relations between the king and the Scottish Church and how unsure James was of his support in Scotland as he waited for the aging Elizabeth to leave him the Crown of England.

Further Reading: J. D. Mackie, *A History of Scotland,* 2nd ed., New York: Dorset House, 1985; George M. Thomson, *A Kind of Justice: Two Studies in Treason,* London: Hutchinson, 1970; D. Harris Willson, *King James VI and I,* New York: Henry Holt and Company, 1956.

Grafton, Richard (c. 1513–c. 1572)

Richard Grafton was a prominent London printer and an important Elizabethan chronicler and historian. Although little is known of Grafton's early life, he was, by the 1530s, a member of the LONDON Grocers' Company (see LIVERIED COMPANIES). A strong supporter of the Reformation, Grafton moved to Paris in 1538 to oversee the printing of a revised version of Miles Coverdale's English Bible (see BIBLE, ENGLISH; REFORMATION, ENGLISH). When HENRY VIII granted permission for the PRINTING of a further revision of Coverdale's work, Grafton and Coverdale undertook the project in Paris where the work was already underway. Charged with heretical activities by the French government, Grafton fled to England, where the project, which later became known as the Great Bible, was published in 1539. With the government requiring each parish to own a copy, the Great Bible ran to seven editions.

In 1543, Grafton published an updated edition of *The Chronicle of John Hardynge;* he himself wrote the new section covering the period from the reign of Edward IV (1461–

1483) to 1543. In 1547, he published a new edition of *Hall's Chronicle,* updated to the death of Henry VIII. Appointed official printer to EDWARD VI in April 1547, Grafton printed Thomas CRANMER's first *BOOK OF COMMON PRAYER* in 1549 and an edition of the *Acts of Parliament* in 1552–53. During NORTHUMBERLAND'S COUP in 1553, Grafton printed the proclamation of Jane GREY as queen, an action that cost him his post as royal printer when MARY I won the throne. Briefly imprisoned, Grafton submitted to the queen and was released, but he seems to have given up his printing business.

In the 1560s, Grafton published three original works of English history—*An Abridgement of the Chronicles of England* (1562), *Manual of the Chronicles of England* (1565), and the two-volume *A Chronicle at Large and Mere History of the Affairs of England . . . to the First Year . . . of Queen Elizabeth* (1568). These projects involved Grafton in a bitter dispute with fellow historian John STOW, who attacked Grafton for garbling the works of Hall and Hardynge. Grafton responded by accusing Stow of "impudently" plagiarizing his works. The exact date of Grafton's death is unknown, but it appears to have been about 1572.

Further Reading: Annabel Patterson, *Reading Holinshed's Chronicles,* Chicago: University of Chicago Press, 1994.

grammar school

Elizabethan grammar schools were private educational foundations intended to give boys a basic grounding in the classics. Because the Reformation had wrested control of EDUCATION from the Church (see REFORMATION, ENGLISH), many such schools were established in the sixteenth century, especially in towns, where they served the sons of poorer families who could not pay for tutors. Many sons of the urban middle class and the lesser GENTRY, as well as a few lower-class boys who showed promise, received their education at the local grammar school.

Most boys entered the grammar school around the age of 8 or 9 and left around age 14 or 15, but the length of a student's training depended on his parents. Except for short two- or three-week vacations at CHRISTMAS and EASTER, school was in session year round, six days a week. In summer, the morning began at 6:00 A.M. and ran to 11:00 A.M., with the afternoon session running from 1:00 P.M. to 4:00 or 5:00 P.M. In winter, the day usually started an hour later and ended an hour earlier. In many schools, Thursday afternoon was granted as a holiday. Discipline was harsh, with the birch rod kept handy to punish infractions. Elizabeth's tutor, Roger ASCHAM, was exceptional in his belief that children could be "sooner allured by love, than driven by beating, to attain good learning."

The main grammar school subject—and sometimes the only one—was Latin. Students learned Latin grammar and vocabulary, translated ENGLISH into Latin, read the Latin Bible, and studied both classical authors and contemporary scholars, such as Erasmus. Although much instruction was oral, printed textbooks of Latin grammar appeared in the early Tudor period. Where the schoolmaster was able, study

The master and students of an Elizabethan grammar school are depicted on the title page of Alexander Nowell's catechism. Note the handy bundle of birch rods for enforcing discipline or administering correction. *By permission of the Folger Shakespeare Library.*

of Greek and Hebrew grammar supplemented work with Latin. Schools allowed some opportunities for recreation akin to modern recess. Boys were allowed to practice archery; to play chess; to run, wrestle, and leap; and were occasionally encouraged to act in yearly dramatic presentations put on by the school (see DRAMA). Many sixteenth-century grammar schools survived into the nineteenth century and were then absorbed into the state education system.

Further Reading: David Cressy, *Education in Tudor and Stuart England,* New York: St. Martin's Press, 1976.

Grand Tour

The term "Grand Tour" refers to the practice arising in Elizabeth's reign of young English gentlemen and noblemen spending an extended period of time traveling in Europe to broaden their experience and complete their EDUCATION (see GENTRY; PEERAGE). Specific reasons for undertaking such a tour varied greatly and included learning foreign languages, meeting important European figures, viewing famous historical sites, or undertaking a specific course of study, such as ART or civil law in Italy, astrology or gardening in Paris, or MEDICINE or MUSIC in FRANCE or the NETHERLANDS. Some young men took to touring for less exalted motives—to flee debt or scandal at home or simply for love of adventure and travel.

Most modern governments and societies accept the principle that certain aspects of a citizen's private life are beyond state concern, but in the Elizabethan era the government made no such distinction, especially when its citizens were residing in Catholic lands. France, Italy, and SPAIN, the most common destinations, were all Catholic societies. Through resident ambassadors and other travelers, the Elizabethan government kept careful watch on Englishmen traveling in those countries, both for fear that the travelers might be seduced by Catholicism and in hopes that they might become useful sources of intelligence. Sir Robert CECIL, secretary of state for Elizabeth in the 1590s and chief minister for JAMES I thereafter, closely followed the European activities of many traveling Englishmen, including his Cecil and Bacon relatives. His cousin Anthony Bacon, elder brother of Sir Francis BACON, was a particular concern, being given to extravagant living in France with homosexual and Catholic friends.

Travel to Spain was severely reduced by the start of hostilities in 1585, but English travel to the rest of Western Europe continued unabated even during the war years of the 1590s. While the government was wary of the possible consequences of travel on some young men, it also encouraged such tours for many others, seeing the experience as excellent training for future statesmen, diplomats, and civil servants (see DIPLOMACY). After the end of the Spanish war in 1604, travel to Spain revived, government restrictions and surveillance eased, and the Grand Tour developed into a standard component of the education of many young English gentlemen and noblemen in the seventeenth and eighteenth centuries.

Further Reading: John Stoye, *English Travellers Abroad 1604–1667,* rev. ed., New Haven, CT: Yale University Press, 1989.

Gravelines, Battle of

Fought on 8 August 1588, the naval Battle of Gravelines was the final Channel encounter between the Spanish ARMADA and the English fleet. The battle began about 7 A.M. off the Flemish village of Gravelines. The night before, the Armada had anchored in its tight crescent formation off CALAIS to the southwest. By launching fireships, the English forced the Spanish commander, Alonso Perez de GUZMAN EL BUENO, Duke of Medina Sidonia, to break formation. The next morning, when the English found the wind in their favor and the Armada scattered along the Flanders shore, the English admiral, Charles HOWARD, Lord Howard of Effingham, ordered his fleet to attack. The ensuing battle, which reached its greatest intensity by midmorning but lasted until late afternoon, was a confused melee fought in a haze of gun smoke.

Although 260 vessels were present in the Channel, only some 30 Spanish SHIPS and about 40 English ships were ever seriously engaged. Many Spanish vessels struggled to keep the unfavorable wind from driving them onto the Flanders coast, while the wind and the close quarters kept many English ships out of action. Howard did not get his squadron into the fight for some hours because he stopped to at-

The English fleet launches fireships against the Spanish Armada on the night before the Battle of Gravelines. *National Maritime Museum, London.*

tack and loot a damaged Spanish warship. Sir Francis DRAKE led the initial attack, taking the English ships to extremely close range before pouring shot into the Spanish rearguard, which had formed around Medina Sidonia's flagship. With smaller, quicker vessels, and more and better shot, the English inflicted serious damage on the Spanish while suffering surprisingly little themselves. Only two Spanish ships were sunk, but many others were shot full of holes and brought close to sinking. The Spanish also took heavy casualties—over 600 dead and more than 800 injured. English dead numbered well under 100.

Lack of shot and an afternoon squall ended the fighting; the English withdrew and the Spanish drifted, still pinned on shore by the wind. The English did not believe the fighting was ended, but the Spanish wanted no more. When the wind changed, Medina Sidonia sailed the Armada, which was still largely intact, into the North Sea, where storms completed the work begun by the English guns. Gravelines thus became the culmination of the Armada campaign. *See also* NAVY; SPAIN; WEAPONS.

Further Reading: Garrett Mattingly, *The Armada,* Boston: Houghton Mifflin, 1959; Colin Martin and Geoffrey Parker, *The Spanish Armada,* New York: Norton, 1988.

Greene, Robert (1558–1592)

Robert Greene was one of the most popular prose writers in Elizabethan England. Greene entered Cambridge (see UNIVERSITIES) in 1575 as a sizar, a student who waited tables in return for his EDUCATION. After 1578, he traveled several years in SPAIN and Italy before returning to Cambridge to complete a master's degree in 1583. He was granted another M.A. by Oxford in 1588 but was less interested in academic life than in the idle pleasures available in a university town. In the late 1580s, he abandoned his wife and child in Norwich and moved to LONDON to become a writer. Heavily influenced by John LYLY's *Euphues,* Greene started writing romantic tales that he called "love pamphlets"; among the best-known were *Menaphon* (1589) and *Pandosto* (1588), which may have inspired the plot used by William SHAKESPEARE in *The Winter's Tale.*

Greene also wrote romantic comedies for the stage, including *The Comical History of Alphonsus King of Aragon* (1588), which imitated the style of his friend Christopher MARLOWE. Greene also wrote *The Scottish History of James the Fourth, Slain at Flodden* (1590), which employed the kinds of fairy characters used later by Shakespeare in *A Midsummer Night's Dream.* Greene's most successful play, *The Honorable History of Friar Bacon and*

The title page from the 1592 edition of Robert Greene's *A Quip for an Upstart Courtier. By permission of the Folger Shakespeare Library.*

Friar Bungay (1591), was a comedy in prose and verse that was not performed until 1594, two years after his death. Greene attracted many wealthy patrons, including Robert DEVEREUX, Earl of Essex, but he squandered most of his income on dissolute living, being a regular drinking companion of fellow writers Thomas NASHE, Thomas KYD, Thomas LODGE, and Marlowe.

In about 1590, Greene began drawing on his own experiences to write a number of serious prose works on the theme of the prodigal son, such as *Never Too Late* (1590) and *A Quip for an Upstart Courtier* (1592). He also wrote a series of pamphlets describing the seamier side of London life, a topic for which his intimate acquaintance with the city's taverns and brothels proved invaluable. Modern social historians now rely on Greene for details about the seedier side of life in Elizabethan London. In 1592, Greene wrote an autobiographical piece entitled *A Groatsworth of Wit*, which criticized Shakespeare as an "upstart crow," perhaps for copying or rewriting some of Greene's work. According to Gabriel HARVEY, one of Greene's literary opponents, Greene died of a "fatal ban-quet of pickle herring" in September 1592. *See also* DRAMA.

Further Reading: Charles W. Crupi, *Robert Greene,* Boston: Twayne, 1986; John Clark Jordan, *Robert Greene,* New York: Octagon Books, 1965.

Greenwich Palace

The birthplace of Elizabeth I and of her father HENRY VIII, Greenwich Palace was a favorite residence of the Tudor monarchs. Acquired in the 1440s by Queen Margaret, wife of Henry VI (r. 1422–1461, 1470–1471), Greenwich Palace was a minor royal residence until the 1480s, when HENRY VII, Elizabeth's grandfather, enlarged and modernized the structure, making it one of the most important English PALACES. Situated in Kent on the south side of the Thames River east of LONDON, Greenwich was a short barge ride from the capital.

Faced in red brick, the palace was laid out around a courtyard 100 feet square. The royal apartments ran in two stories along the riverfront, connecting on the east with the royal chapel and on the west with the grand gatehouse that formed the main entrance to the palace from the river. Henry VIII, who was born at Greenwich in June 1491, was fond of the palace and spent considerable time and money upgrading its appearance and appointments. He constructed some of the finest gardens in Europe at Greenwich and engaged a host of foreign artists and craftsmen to decorate the palace in the Renaissance styles in vogue in Italy and elsewhere in Europe. The German painter Hans Holbein, who settled in England in 1532, worked on Greenwich.

Princess Elizabeth was born at Greenwich between 3:00 and 4:00 P.M. on Sunday, 7 September 1533. The queen, like her father, was partial to her birthplace and spent much time at Greenwich, but there, as elsewhere, she made few material changes to the palace. After the queen's death in 1603, Greenwich was used less frequently by JAMES I and his successors, and the building was severely damaged by parliamentary forces during the civil war in the 1640s. Charles II demolished most of the Elizabethan palace in the 1660s, but his attempts at rebuilding were stymied by lack of funds. In 1692, the Crown converted the partially renovated structure into the Royal Naval Hospital. *See also* ARCHITECTURE.

Further Reading: John Martin Robinson, *Royal Residences,* London: MacDonald and Company, 1982; Simon Thurley, *The Royal Palaces of Tudor England,* New Haven, CT: Yale University Press, 1993.

Gregory XIII (1502–1585)

Ugo Buoncompagni, who served as Pope Gregory XIII from 1572 to 1585, sought to regain England for Roman Catholicism by training and dispatching English Catholic missionaries (see CATHOLICISM, ENGLISH). Born in Bologna, where he taught law at the university from 1531 to 1539, Buoncompagni was ordained and made a bishop in 1558. Until 1563, he attended sessions of the reform Council of Trent (see COUNTER-REFORMATION) and in 1565 was named a cardinal.

In 1572, on the death of PIUS V—the pope who excommunicated Elizabeth (see *REGNANS IN EXCELSIS*)—Buoncompagni was elected pope as Gregory XIII. Although 70 years old, the new pope immediately implemented reforms decreed by the Council of Trent and initiated an aggressive missionary policy to regain Protestant Europe for Catholicism. He also attacked clerical abuses and established a list of forbidden books, the *Index Librorum Prohibitorum*. An ardent foe of PROTESTANTISM, Gregory ordered celebrations when he heard of the SAINT BARTHOLOMEW MASSACRE of HUGUENOTS in FRANCE in August 1572. To restore Catholicism in the British Isles, Gregory encouraged Irish rebels to resist the Elizabethan government of IRELAND, thereby fostering the growing identification of Catholicism with Irish resistance to English rule. Gregory also strongly endorsed the JESUIT MISSION to England begun by Edmund CAMPION and Robert PARSONS in 1580. To support this missionary effort, Gregory endowed an English College in Rome to train English priests for missionary work. He also encouraged PHILIP II of SPAIN to continue his military campaigns to restore Spanish, Catholic rule in the NETHERLANDS (see NETHERLANDS REVOLT), a policy that was of continuing concern to the English government and that led in 1585 to war between England and Spain.

Gregory is best known for his 1582 reform of the CALENDAR. The more accurate Gregorian calendar was quickly adopted by most of Catholic Europe, but it was not accepted by Protestant England until 1752. At his death in April 1585, Gregory had begun the successful restoration of Roman Catholicism to parts of Europe, but had made little progress in the British Isles.

Further Reading: J. N. D. Kelly, *The Oxford Dictionary of Popes,* New York: Oxford University Press, 1986.

Grenville, Sir Richard (1542–1591)

Sir Richard Grenville was one of the most colorful seamen of the Elizabethan age. Born into a Devon GENTRY family, Richard was the son of Roger Grenville, who died in 1545 when the ship *Mary Rose* capsized in Portsmouth harbor, one of the most famous naval disasters in Tudor history. Except for a brief stay at the INNS OF COURT after 1559, little is known about Grenville's EDUCATION. Restless and impulsive, Grenville was a pardoned in 1562 for killing a man during a LONDON street riot. He served in PARLIAMENT in 1563, but by 1566 he was in Hungary fighting Turks. Two years later, he took his growing family to IRELAND to participate in a plantation in the Munster region, but FITZMAURICE'S REBELLION

This portrait of the famous Elizabethan seaman Sir Richard Grenville was painted by an unknown artist about 1571. *By courtesy of the National Portrait Gallery, London.*

ended the scheme (see PLANTATIONS, IRISH). After helping to suppress the rebellion, Grenville returned to England and sat for Cornwall in the Parliament of 1571.

Grenville next proposed an expedition to the Pacific to search for the NORTHWEST PASSAGE and the continent of "Terra Austalis," which John DEE believed existed in the southern hemisphere. That project never materialized, but Grenville's plans were used by Sir Francis DRAKE for his voyage of circumnavigation in 1577 (see DRAKE'S CIRCUMNAVIGATION). In 1585, Grenville commanded the fleet his kinsman Walter RALEIGH had gathered to transport Ralph LANE and a group of colonists to Roanoke Island (see ROANOKE COLONY [1585]) on the Virginia coast. When he returned to Roanoke with supplies in 1586, the colonists were gone; they had, unbeknownst to Grenville, returned to England with Drake.

During the ARMADA crisis in 1588, Grenville served with Drake and later kept watch with Raleigh on the sea approaches to IRELAND. In 1591, Grenville was named second in command to Lord Thomas Howard of a squadron sent to the AZORES to intercept the Spanish treasure fleet from AMERICA (see AZORES EXPEDITION). Surprised by the main Spanish fleet, Howard withdrew, but Grenville in the *Revenge* was trapped and surrounded. For two days in September, the *Revenge* fought off Spanish attacks, inflicting damage on 15 galleons (see SHIPS). Severely wounded, Grenville ordered the ship destroyed, but his crew refused and surrendered. Grenville died shortly thereafter, and the *Revenge* sank during a hurricane. The fight of the *Revenge* was later described by Raleigh and celebrated in a poem by Alfred, Lord Tennyson.

Further Reading: A. L. Rowse, *Sir Richard Grenville of the Revenge,* London: Book Club Associates, 1977.

Gresham, Sir Thomas (c. 1518–1579)

Sir Thomas Gresham was the Crown's chief financial agent and the founder of London's ROYAL EXCHANGE. The son of a wealthy merchant and former mayor of LONDON, Gresham was educated at Cambridge (see UNIVERSITIES) and soon followed his father into trade and finance. In 1551, he was named the king's financial agent in Antwerp, the center of the European money market. In Antwerp, Gresham sought to alleviate the

Crown's worsening financial situation by negotiating loans at lower interest and working to improve the exchange rate. So successful and important was Gresham's work in Antwerp that he was retained in his post after EDWARD VI's death both by MARY I (even though he was a Protestant) and later by Elizabeth.

Besides his financial work, Gresham provided the government with valuable military and political intelligence, especially during his period as Elizabeth's ambassador to the NETHERLANDS from 1560 to 1563. He devised ingenious ways to evade the ban placed on the export of coin by the Netherlands government, smuggling it to England in consignments of pepper and armor. He strongly advised the Elizabethan government to reform the debased COINAGE of England, and Gresham himself had a large role in withdrawing the bad coin from the market and distributing the new minting. Indeed, the adage "bad coin drives out good"—that is, people will pass on debased coins and hoard coins of full value—is attributed to Gresham and is known as "Gresham's law." He also worked as a munitions agent for the Crown, securing WEAPONS, gunpowder, and armor in Europe and smuggling it to England. While improving the Crown's financial position, Gresham was also enriching himself, making sure that he obtained sizable commissions on most of the transactions he negotiated for the government.

When the death of his son in 1564 left him without an heir, Gresham used his fortune to build the Royal Exchange in London, a meeting place for merchants and bankers to conduct business. Modeled on the Bourse in Antwerp, the Exchange opened for business in 1567. In 1575, he also founded London's Gresham College as a place where free lectures could be delivered. Ill health caused Gresham to resign from the royal service in 1574. He died suddenly in London in November 1579.

Further Reading: S. T. Bindoff, *The Fame of Sir Thomas Gresham,* London: Cape, 1973; Perry E. Gresham with Carol Jose, *The Sign of the Golden Grasshopper: A Biography of Sir Thomas Gresham,* Ottawa, IL: Jameson Books, 1995.

Greville, Fulke, Lord Brooke (1554–1628)

Fulke Greville was a prominent Elizabethan poet and courtier and the biographer of Sir

Philip SIDNEY. Born into a Warwickshire GEN-TRY family, Greville was educated with Philip Sidney, whose lifelong friend he became. In 1568, Greville entered Jesus College, Cambridge (see UNIVERSITIES), but left before taking a degree to pursue a career at COURT. He became a member of the "Areopagus," a group of court poets and writers that included, among others, Sidney, Edmund SPENSER, and Gabriel HARVEY. The group sought through their works to elevate the level of English POETRY. Greville, who never married, wrote mainly love poetry, developing thereby a probably exaggerated reputation as a womanizer. Under the patronage of Philip Sidney's father, Sir Henry SIDNEY, Greville supported himself with income derived from a number of small offices attached to the Council for the Welsh Marches (i.e., borders), of which the elder Sidney was president.

In 1577, Greville accompanied Philip Sidney to Germany and in 1578 traveled to the NETHERLANDS with Sir Francis WALSING-HAM. In 1588, two years after Sidney's death, Greville served with the army at Tilbury (see TILBURY SPEECH) during the ARMADA crisis, and was shortly thereafter sent by the queen to Ostend to quell a mutiny among the English troops in the Netherlands. He served in all the Elizabethan parliaments after 1580 (see PARLIAMENT), mostly as member for Warwickshire, and was appointed treasurer of the NAVY in 1598.

JAMES I knighted Greville in 1603, but political disagreements with Sir Robert CECIL, the king's chief minister, forced Greville to retire from public office. He then started writing his biography of Sir Philip Sidney (published 1652), having already supervised the publication of Sidney's *Arcadia* in 1590. He resumed his political career after Cecil's death in 1612, becoming chancellor of the EXCHEQUER in 1614. He held various other official posts before resigning for ill health in 1621, the year the king created him Baron Brooke. Greville died in September 1628 of stab wounds inflicted by a servant who had attacked him for no apparent reason. *Caelica,* a collection of Greville's poetry, was published after his death.

Further Reading: Ronald A. Rebholz, *The Life of Fulke Greville, First Lord Brooke,* Oxford: Clarendon Press, 1971.

Grey, Jane (1537–1554)

For nine days in July 1553, Jane Grey was, much against her own will, queen of England. Jane was the eldest daughter of Henry Grey, Marquis of Dorset, and Frances Brandon, daughter of HENRY VIII's sister Mary. Under the terms of Henry VIII's will, Jane was heir to the throne after Henry's own three children, Edward (EDWARD VI), Mary (MARY I), and Elizabeth (see GREY CLAIM). Placed in the household of Queen Katherine PARR in 1546, Jane received a classical humanist EDUCATION (see HUMANISM) and developed Protestant opinions in religion. Because Jane was the same age as Edward VI and held her own claim to the throne, Protector Somerset (see SEYMOUR, EDWARD, DUKE OF SOMERSET) took her into his household in 1548 and planned to marry her to the king.

In 1551, Jane's father supported John DUDLEY, Duke of Northumberland, against Somerset for leadership of Edward's government. Somerset was overthrown in 1549 and eventually executed in 1552; for his support of the winning side, Henry Grey was rewarded with elevation to the title Duke of Suffolk. In 1553, when the death of Edward VI was imminent, Northumberland devised a scheme to exclude the Princesses Mary and Elizabeth from the throne and to replace them with Jane Grey (see NORTHUMBERLAND'S COUP). As part of the plan, Jane was married to Northumberland's son Guildford in May 1553.

Jane accepted her part in the scheme reluctantly, and fainted when she was told on 9 July that Edward was dead and she was queen. Her reign lasted only nine days; when Northumberland's fellow councilors realized that public opinion favored Mary, they deserted Jane and proclaimed Queen Mary in LONDON. Jane and her husband were lodged in the TOWER OF LONDON and condemned for TREASON with Northumberland. The sentence of death for Jane and Guildford was not carried out until February 1554 after the suppression of WYATT'S REBELLION, in which Jane's father was again involved. *See also DE-VISE;* GREY, KATHERINE; PROTESTANTISM; SUCCESSION, ACTS OF.

Further Reading: Mary M. Luke, *The Nine Days Queen: A Portrait of Lady Jane Grey,* New York: W. Morrow, 1986; Alison Plowden, *Lady Jane Grey and the House of Suffolk,* London: Sidgwick and Jackson, 1985.

Grey, Katherine (1540–1568)

As a descendant of the younger sister of HENRY VIII, Katherine Grey was a possible successor to her cousin Elizabeth. Katherine was the second daughter of Henry Grey, Duke of Suffolk, and his wife Frances Brandon, a niece of Henry VIII. In his will, Henry placed the Protestant Grey sisters next in line for the throne after his own children (see GREY CLAIM; STUART CLAIM). In May 1553, John DUDLEY, Duke of Northumberland, chief minister of the dying EDWARD VI, arranged a series of marriages with the Greys to strengthen his political position on the king's death. Katherine was married to Henry HERBERT, the heir of the Earl of Pembroke. After Edward's death on 6 July, when the PRIVY COUNCIL, led by Northumberland, proclaimed Katherine's older sister Jane GREY queen, Katherine stayed with Jane in the royal apartments at the TOWER OF LONDON (see *DEVISE;* NORTHUMBERLAND'S COUP). Jane's reign ended on 19 July with Northumberland's arrest and the proclamation of MARY I as rightful queen. Katherine was allowed to leave LONDON with Pembroke, her husband's father, who promptly repudiated his heir's marriage and turned Katherine out of his house.

In February 1554, Katherine's sister and father were executed as a result of the duke's participation in WYATT'S REBELLION. That summer, Katherine fell in love with Edward Seymour, Earl of Hertford, the son of Edward SEYMOUR, Duke of Somerset, the late lord protector to Edward VI. Because of her royal blood and her position in the succession, Katherine's MARRIAGE was a matter of state policy, not personal preference, and her relationship with Seymour had to be hidden. Nonetheless, the lovers married secretly in 1560, and by 1561 Katherine was pregnant. Terrified of Elizabeth's reaction to her condition, Katherine begged Robert DUDLEY, the queen's favorite, to intercede on her behalf (see FAVORITES). Elizabeth sent the lovers to the Tower and ordered their marriage invalidated, thereby illegitimizing their newborn son and removing him from the SUCCESSION.

Although sentenced to life in prison, Katherine and Hertford were allowed by sympathetic Tower jailers to sleep together occasionally. This kindness resulted in the birth of a second son in 1563. An infuriated Elizabeth sent husband and wife to separate places of confinement, and they never saw one another again. Katherine died of consumption in 1568. Her brief life had been made difficult by her nearness in blood to the throne, and by her scandalous behavior (for the times) of choosing her own husband rather than allowing the Crown to choose for her.

Further Reading: Hester W. Chapman, *Two Tudor Portraits: Henry Howard, Earl of Surrey and Lady Katherine Grey,* Boston: Little, Brown, 1963.

Grey claim (to the throne)

The Grey family's claim to the English Crown derived from the 1515 marriage of Mary Tudor, younger sister of HENRY VIII, to Charles Brandon, Duke of Suffolk. Although the couple married without his permission, Henry eventually forgave his best friend and favorite sister, and the match was allowed to stand. Born in 1517, Frances Brandon, the couple's eldest child, had three cousins standing before her in the succession—Henry's daughter Mary (see MARY I) and Margaret Tudor's two children, James V of Scotland (see STUART CLAIM) and Margaret DOUGLAS (see SUCCESSION, ACTS OF). In the 1530s, the births of Princess Elizabeth and Prince Edward (see EDWARD VI) pushed Frances Brandon further from the throne, while at the same time, Henry VIII's break with the Roman Catholic Church made Frances, a Protestant, a more acceptable royal heir than the Catholic children of Henry's elder sister Margaret.

When empowered by the 1544 Act of Succession to name in his will further heirs to the throne beyond his own children, Henry excluded Margaret's heirs from the succession and willed the Crown to pass, should his own children fail of heirs, to his Brandon niece and her heirs. By 1553, Frances Brandon, who had married Henry Grey, Duke of Suffolk, was mother to three daughters—Jane, Katherine, and Mary. To prevent the accession of his Catholic sister, Mary, the dying Edward VI conspired with his chief minister, John DUDLEY, Duke of Northumberland, to alter the succession as ordained by Henry VIII. They forced the royal judges to accept a document, the *DEVISE* for the succession, that excluded Edward's sisters, Mary and Elizabeth, and passed the Crown directly to Jane GREY.

After Edward's death on 6 July 1553, Jane was recognized as queen for nine days (see NORTHUMBERLAND'S COUP). The country, however, rallied to Mary, and by the end of July she was firmly on the throne and Jane was in the TOWER OF LONDON. Jane was executed in February 1554 after WYATT'S REBELLION. Jane's death passed the Grey claim to her sister Katherine. The marriage of Katherine GREY, the most prominent Protestant heir to Elizabeth, was an important matter of state policy. Thus, when Katherine secretly married Edward Seymour, Earl of Hertford, in 1560, a furious Elizabeth committed her to the Tower. Katherine died in prison in 1568, the Grey claim to the throne lingering on in her two sons. See the genealogical chart in Appendix 1: "Grey Claim to the English Throne."

Further Reading: Mary M. Luke, *The Nine Days Queen: A Portrait of Lady Jane Grey,* New York: W. Morrow, 1986; Alison Plowden, *Lady Jane Grey and the House of Suffolk,* London: Sidgwick and Jackson, 1985.

Grindal, Edmund (1519–1583)

Edmund Grindal was Elizabeth's second Archbishop of Canterbury. Born into a Cumberland peasant family, Grindal was educated at Cambridge (see UNIVERSITIES), where he was tutored by Nicholas Ridley, the future bishop of LONDON under EDWARD VI and a Protestant martyr under MARY I (see MARIAN MARTYRS). By 1549, Grindal was a Protestant, for in that year he argued vigorously and successfully against the Catholic doctrine of the real presence of Christ in the communion during a debate at Cambridge. He became Ridley's chaplain in 1551 and soon after became chaplain to Edward VI. In 1553, when Mary's accession ended his chances for a bishopric, Grindal fled to Germany and lived among the English exile community in Frankfurt until January 1559 (see MARIAN EXILES).

Under Elizabeth, Grindal became bishop of London, the most prestigious and difficult of English bishoprics. Grindal dealt harshly with Catholics, but leniently with PURITANS who refused to wear the required vestments (see CATHOLICISM, ENGLISH; VESTIARIAN CONTROVERSY). In 1566, Archbishop Matthew PARKER forced Grindal to dismiss 37 Puritan clergymen with whom Grindal strongly sympathized. In 1570, the queen, at Parker's recommendation, appointed Grindal Archbishop of York, an archdiocese where the main problem was Catholic recusancy, not Puritanism (see RECUSANTS).

On Parker's death in 1575, Elizabeth translated Grindal to Canterbury, but in 1576, within a few months of his appointment, Grindal fell into disfavor for his support of PROPHESYINGS, unauthorized conferences of Puritan ministers that Elizabeth wanted suppressed. When the queen commanded Grindal to halt the prophesyings, the archbishop wrote a firm but polite letter explaining his reasons for refusing to do so. When Elizabeth repeated her order, and Grindal repeated his refusal, the queen suspended him from office and ordered his deputies to suppress the meetings without his cooperation. Although his expulsion was discussed it was never carried out, and Grindal remained in office, but without the ability to exercise its powers, until his death in July 1583. *See also* PROTESTANTISM.

Further Reading: Patrick Collinson, *Archbishop Grindal,* Berkeley: University of California Press, 1979.

Guinea Company

The Guinea (or Africa) Company was a REGULATED COMPANY chartered by the queen in 1588 to conduct trade in the area between the Senegal and Gambia Rivers in West Africa. The English had been interested in African commerce since 1536, when William Hawkins had sailed to the area to trade for ivory and slaves. Interest became even more intense in the 1560s, when John HAWKINS, son of William, made West Africa the first stop in a profitable triangular trade that brought African slaves to SPANISH AMERICA and American gold, hides, and agricultural produce to England.

Elizabeth's 1588 charter gave certain merchants of LONDON and Exeter the exclusive right to trade in the area. The war with SPAIN limited English opportunities to enter the American slave trade in the 1580s and 1590s, but the Guinea Company made a reasonable profit by exchanging cloth and small trade goods with the local natives for gold and ivory. The company suffered from fierce opposition by the Portuguese, who had several factories (trading posts) on the West African coast and considered the area their exclusive preserve. English interlopers also frequently encroached on the company's monopoly (see MONOPOLIES).

The Guinea Company was rechartered in 1618 and 1630; after the restoration of the monarchy in 1660, the company was reconstituted as the Royal African Company. The company preserved its monopoly until 1752 when its African forts and trading posts were taken over by the Crown to become the beginning of a British colonial presence in West Africa.

Further Reading: G. D. Ramsay, *English Overseas Trade During the Centuries of Emergence,* London: Macmillan, 1957.

Guise, Marie de (1515–1560)

The daughter of a powerful French Catholic family (see GUISE FAMILY), Marie de Guise, the mother of Mary STUART, Queen of Scots, ensured that her daughter would be brought up as a Catholic in FRANCE. In 1538, Marie de Guise married James V of SCOTLAND, thus frustrating an attempt by HENRY VIII of England to marry Marie himself. In Scotland, the new queen had little political influence, especially after the deaths of her two infant sons in 1541. She won custody of her six-day-old daughter Mary at her husband's death in December 1542 but had little power until the English, under Edward SEYMOUR, Duke of Somerset, defeated the Scots at the Battle of Pinkie in September 1547. The defeat allowed Marie to assume leadership of the pro-French party and to foil attempts to send Mary to England to be the future wife of EDWARD VI.

In July 1548, Marie sent five-year-old Mary to France, where the princess was raised at the royal COURT as a Catholic. Marie spent a year with her daughter in France in 1550, returning to Scotland to become Mary's regent in April 1554. Believing her daughter's interests were best served by a Catholic Scotland closely allied with France, the new regent sought to strengthen the French connection and to suppress a growing Protestant movement. In 1558, Marie helped arrange her daughter's marriage to the dauphin (the heir to the French throne) and increased her pressure on Scottish Protestants.

In 1559, a rebellion led by the Protestant nobility of Scotland drove the regent from EDINBURGH and forced her to call for the assistance of French troops. Edinburgh was retaken, but in 1560 the reluctant intervention of Elizabeth of England on the side of the Protestant lords frustrated Marie's attempts to re-

gain control of the country. Marie de Guise died in Edinburgh Castle on 11 June 1560. Her death made possible the negotiations that led to the Treaty of Edinburgh, which removed all foreign troops from Scotland and gave the Catholic Queen of Scots a Protestant country to rule (see EDINBURGH, TREATY OF). Marie's body was transported to France, where her daughter saw it buried in March 1561, only months before returning to Scotland herself to take up her Crown. *See also* CATHOLICISM, ENGLISH.

Further Reading: Henry Dwight Sedgwick, *The House of Guise,* Indianapolis: Bobbs-Merrill, 1938; Jenny Wormald, *Mary, Queen of Scots,* London: Collins and Brown, 1991.

Guise family

On her mother's side, Mary STUART, Queen of Scots, was a member of the French aristocratic family of Guise, leaders of the Catholic party during the French civil wars of religion. Claude Guise, first Duke of Guise (1496–1550), Mary Stuart's grandfather, fought in Italy under FRANCIS I and served as regent of France during Francis's captivity in SPAIN (1525–1526). Marie de GUISE (1515–1560), daughter of the first duke, married James V of SCOTLAND in 1538. In December 1542, only days before her husband's death, Marie gave birth to Mary, the next monarch of Scotland. Sent to France in 1548, Mary came under the influence and protection of her uncles, Francis Guise, second Duke of Guise (1519–1563), and Cardinal Charles Guise (1525–1574). The second duke fought against HENRY VIII at Boulogne in 1545 and captured CALAIS from MARY I in 1558. Cardinal Guise introduced the inquisition into FRANCE and was a powerful force at the reforming Council of Trent, the body that initiated the Catholic COUNTER-REFORMATION.

Influential advisors of HENRI II, the Guise brothers ruled France during the brief reign (1559–1560) of Henri's son Francis II, to whom they had married their niece Mary Stuart in 1558. During the 1560s, the brothers sternly repressed the HUGUENOTS and worked to strengthen French influence and Catholicism in Scotland, where their sister had been regent until 1560 and their niece ruled in her own right after 1561. They encouraged Mary to press her claim to the throne of England against

Elizabeth, whom they considered a Protestant usurper. The second duke was assassinated by a Huguenot in 1563, and the ducal title passed to his son Henri Guise, the third duke (1550–1588).

Along with the French queen mother, Catherine de MEDICI, the third duke was a contriver of the SAINT BARTHOLOMEW MASSACRE of Huguenots in 1572. He led the CATHOLIC LEAGUE against the Protestants in the religious civil wars of the 1570s and 1580s and sought an alliance with PHILIP II of Spain to prevent Henri Bourbon (see HENRI IV), the Protestant heir to the throne, from assuming the Crown. His own ambition for the Crown aroused the suspicion of HENRI III, who had the duke assassinated in 1588, a year after his cousin Mary Stuart was executed in England.

Further Reading: Frederic J. Baumgartner, *France in the Sixteenth Century,* New York: St. Martin's Press, 1995; Henry Dwight Sedgwick, *The House of Guise,* Indianapolis: Bobbs-Merrill, 1938.

Guzman el Bueno, Alonso Perez de, Duke of Medina Sidonia (1550–1619)

Alonso Perez de Guzman el Bueno, the seventh Duke of Medina Sidonia, commanded the Spanish ARMADA against England in 1588. Born into an ancient aristocratic family of Castile, Medina Sidonia was one of the wealthiest and most influential noblemen in SPAIN. He served as hereditary captain-general of Andalusia, a nominally military position that usually required more administrative than military skill. He was unusual among the Spanish (or any other) aristocracy in being a peace-loving man who cared little for military life. A good administrator and a fair scholar, Medina Sidonia had served loyally during the Spanish conquest of Portugal in 1580.

In February 1588, upon the death of Alvaro de BÁZAN, Marquis of Santa Cruz, PHILIP II appointed Medina Sidonia admiral of the ocean sea and commander of the Armada. The duke strongly protested his fitness for the position, claiming that he was inexperienced in sea warfare, ignorant of Santa Cruz's plans, and even given to seasickness. Philip ignored the duke's protests, seeing the duke's piety as a necessary quality for the leader of a holy crusade against heretic England. Philip also believed the duke's ancient Castilan lineage would guarantee that ambitious ship captains would accept his right to command so exalted an enterprise. Although he believed the Armada was likely to fail, Medina Sidonia seems to have done his best to ensure success, following his detailed instructions as closely as possible and taking advice from his more experienced subordinates. However, the failure of Alessandro FARNESE, Duke of Parma, Philip's nephew and governor-general of the NETHERLANDS, to rendezvous with the Armada combined with the tenacity of the English fleet and the strength of North Sea gales to defeat the enterprise.

Although the duke was blamed for the failure of the Armada by many contemporaries in Spain and by later historians, Philip accepted that Medina Sidonia had done his best, and he relieved the duke of his post with thanks. Medina Sidonia returned to his vast estates in southern Spain where he lived quietly until his death in 1619. *See also* NAVY; SHIPS.

Further Reading: Garrett Mattingly, *The Armada,* Boston: Houghton Mifflin, 1959; Peter Pierson, *Commander of the Armada: The Seventh Duke of Medina Sidonia,* New Haven, CT: Yale University Press, 1989.

H

Habsburg family

In the sixteenth century, the Habsburg (or Hapsburg) family of Austria also ruled Germany, the NETHERLANDS, SPAIN and its American empire, much of Italy, and, for a time, England. In 1478, over a decade before his election as Holy Roman Emperor (i.e., ruler of Germany), Maximilian of Habsburg married Mary of Burgundy, only child of the last Duke of Burgundy. This union combined Mary's inheritance—the Netherlands—with the imperial Crown, the election to which had become virtually hereditary in the Habsburg family. In 1496, the couple's eldest son, Philip, married Joanna, daughter of Isabella and Ferdinand of Spain, thereby combining, on Isabella's death in 1504, his mother's Netherlands with his mother-in-law's Crown of Castile. On Philip's death in 1506, his eldest son, Charles Habsburg, was heir to the Crowns of Spain, Germany, and the Netherlands.

Succeeding his father immediately in the Netherlands, Charles had to wait until the death of his maternal grandfather (Ferdinand) in 1516 to become Charles I of Spain, and until the death of his paternal grandfather (Maximilian) in 1519 to become Emperor CHARLES V in Germany. Because he also controlled the growing Spanish empire in America and the Spanish possessions in Italy, Charles was a great threat to the French monarchy, and much of his reign was spent at war with FRANCE (see VALOIS FAMILY). Friendship with Charles was important to England because the emperor's maternal aunt, CATHERINE OF ARAGON, was married to HENRY VIII, and because Charles controlled the Netherlands,

England's important trading partner (see CLOTH INDUSTRY). When Henry sought to marry Elizabeth's mother, Anne BOLEYN, Charles's control of Italy prevented the pope from acting against the interests of Charles's aunt, which forced Henry to withdraw England from obedience to Rome to achieve annulment of his MARRIAGE. Charles continued a firm friend to his cousin, Mary (see MARY I), Catherine's daughter.

When Mary ascended the English throne in 1553, Charles arranged her marriage to his son Philip (see PHILIP II), who assumed the Spanish Crown in 1556. The marriage made Philip co-ruler of England, and any child of the union would have become future Habsburg ruler of both England and the Netherlands. But Mary died childless in 1558, and when Philip proposed marriage to his former sister-in-law Elizabeth, the new queen politely declined. Elizabeth's PROTESTANTISM, English PRIVATEERING in SPANISH AMERICA, and English assistance to Dutch rebels against Philip led to war between Spain and England in 1585. In 1588, Philip, hopeful of ending English interference in the Netherlands, sent the ARMADA to England to dethrone Elizabeth and restore CATHOLICISM. Although the Armada failed, war continued until 1604, when Philip's son, Philip III, and Elizabeth's successor, JAMES I, made peace. The Habsburgs continued to rule in Spain until 1700, in Germany until 1806, and in Austria until 1918. *See* the genealogical chart in Appendix 1: "Habsburg Dynasty in Spain and the Holy Roman Empire."

Further Reading: Karl Brandi, *The Emperor Charles V,* London: Jonathan Cape, 1970; H. G. Koenigsberger, *The Habsburgs and Europe, 1516–1660,* Ithaca, NY: Cornell University Press, 1971; Geoffrey Parker, *Philip II,* Boston: Little, Brown, 1978.

Hakluyt, Richard (c. 1552–1616)

Through his writings, Richard Hakluyt was instrumental in stimulating Elizabethan exploration of AMERICA. Born in LONDON, Hakluyt was educated at Oxford (see UNIVERSITIES), completing a master's degree in 1577 and eventually entering the ministry. He was raised from the age of five by a cousin, a London attorney who knew and introduced his ward to many prominent figures, including the mathematician John DEE and the cartographers (mapmakers) Gerardus Mercator and Abraham Ortelius.

Tremendously interested in geography, Hakluyt read widely on the subject in several languages and sought the acquaintance of such seafarers as Sir Humphrey GILBERT, Sir Francis DRAKE, and Sir Martin FROBISHER. Determined to promote English overseas expansion, Hakluyt gave a series of public lectures on geography at Oxford in the late 1570s, the first person ever to lecture on that subject at the university. In 1580, in *Discourse on the Strait of Magellan,* Hakluyt urged the fitting-out of an English expedition to find the NORTHWEST PASSAGE—a secure route to Asia that would allow England to trade wool for spices (see CLOTH INDUSTRY). Hakluyt also advocated the establishment of a permanent English colony in the East to facilitate Asian trade.

In his preface to an English account of Frenchman Jacques Cartier's American explorations, Hakluyt based English claims to North America on John Cabot's English-sponsored voyages in the 1490s. In 1582, Hakluyt published *Divers Voyages to America,* a collection of documents relating to various North American voyages of discovery. This popular work helped Hakluyt win a post as chaplain to the English ambassador in Paris, an appointment that allowed him to meet continental geographers and seafarers. In 1584, Hakluyt wrote *Discourse on Western Planting,* an argument for establishing English colonies that was shown to Elizabeth to support Sir Walter RALEIGH's colonization of Virginia.

In 1589, fired with patriotism born of the ARMADA victory, Hakluyt published the first edition of his monumental work, the *PRINCIPAL NAVIGATIONS, VOYAGES AND DISCOVERIES OF THE ENGLISH NATION,* a collection of documents covering all English voyages of exploration undertaken up to that time. Between 1598 and 1600, Hakluyt published a revised and enlarged three-volume edition of *Principal Navigations.* Although Hakluyt held various ecclesiastical appointments in his last years, his geographic interests continued—he made maps for the EAST INDIA COMPANY in 1600, helped organize the Virginia Company in 1606, and helped found the North-West Passage Company in 1612. Hakluyt died in November 1616.

Further Reading: Hakluyt Society, *Richard Hakluyt and His Successors,* London: Hakluyt Society, 1946; Samuel Eliot Morison, *The European Discovery of America: The Northern Voyages,* New York: Oxford University Press, 1971; George Bruner Parks, *Richard Hakluyt and the English Voyages,* New York: F. Ungar, 1961; A. L. Rowse, *The Elizabethans and America,* New York: Harper, 1959.

Hampton Court Palace

One of the largest royal PALACES in sixteenth-century Europe, Hampton Court was one of the favorite residences of Elizabeth's father, HENRY VIII. Hampton Court was begun by Henry's chief minister, Cardinal Thomas Wolsey, who constructed a large three-story residence along the Thames west of LONDON between 1515 and 1526. Wolsey's red brick palace consisted of a progression of courts built along a central axis and leading into one another through a series of ornate gatehouses. Already containing a suite of apartments built especially for use by the king, Hampton Court Palace came into Henry's possession in 1529 when he dismissed Wolsey from office.

Encouraged by Anne BOLEYN, Elizabeth's mother, Henry greatly enlarged and extended Hampton Court, building an entirely new set of lodgings for Anne. Henry also built new royal apartments for himself, a new kitchen, a tennis court, and a large great hall for the accommodation of the COURT. The king's apartments included the large Paradise Chamber, which was hung with jeweled tapestries and topped with a brilliantly painted and gilded ceiling. The palace also boasted a number of the ingenious mechanical devices that so fascinated the king, including the great as-

The great clock at Hampton Court Palace. *Courtesy of Donna Bronski.*

tronomical clock made by Nicholas Oursian in 1540. Set in a gatehouse of one of the inner courts, the clock still tells the hour, day, and month, as well as the number of days since the start of the year, the phases of the moon, and the time of high tide at old London Bridge.

Henry spent a great deal of time at Hampton Court Palace in his last years, as did Elizabeth as a princess. While at Hampton Court in October 1562, Elizabeth fell seriously ill with smallpox and almost died (see EPIDEMIC DISEASE). Although remaining one of her major residences, Hampton Court was thereafter one of Elizabeth's least favorite, the queen having come to believe that it was an unhealthful place. Although most of the royal apartments were demolished in the late seventeenth century by William III, who rebuilt the palace, much of the Tudor structure still exists, making Hampton Court one of the few Elizabethan palaces to survive into the twentieth century. Hampton Court is now open to the public. *See also* HAMPTON COURT, TREATY OF.

Further Reading: John Martin Robinson, *Royal Residences,* London: MacDonald and Company, 1982; Simon Thurley, *The Royal Palaces of Tudor England,* New Haven, CT: Yale University Press, 1993.

Hampton Court, Treaty of

The Treaty of Hampton Court (also known as the Treaty of Richmond) represented Elizabeth I's first formal commitment to the cause of European PROTESTANTISM and her first military involvement outside the British Isles. In 1562, representatives of the French HUGUENOTS requested Elizabeth's assistance in their fight against the extremist Catholic forces led by the GUISE FAMILY. Although disliking war, Elizabeth was driven to intervene by her fear that a united, Catholic FRANCE would invade England should the Guise forces win the civil war. She also believed that the war and the Huguenots' desperate need for her help offered England an excellent opportunity to regain CALAIS and perhaps to acquire several other French towns. Protestants in the English government—especially Sir William CECIL, the principal secretary; Robert DUDLEY, the royal favorite; and Sir Nicholas THROCKMORTON, the English ambassador in France—were also eager to assist their French co-religionists and to strike a blow against militant Catholicism.

Signed on 19 September 1562, the agreement reached at RICHMOND PALACE by Cecil and the Huguenot negotiators called for the queen to supply the French Protestants with 100,000 crowns (about £25,000) and 3,000 troops. In return for this aid, the Huguenots agreed to hand the port of Le Havre (known to the English as Newhaven) to the queen as a pledge for the future return of Calais. The English also agreed to assist the Huguenots in the defense of the towns of Rouen and Dieppe. If the Huguenots won the war with English help, Elizabeth hoped to take Calais as her reward; if the Huguenots lost, Elizabeth hoped at least to keep Le Havre, Dieppe, and Rouen to prevent them from becoming staging points for a Guise invasion of England.

Elizabeth's calculations went awry when Anthony of Navarre, the Huguenot leader, was killed and Francis, Duke of Guise, was assassinated. These deaths allowed the French queen mother, Catherine de MEDICI, to negotiate a settlement and unite all parties in an effort to drive out the English (see LE HAVRE EXPEDITION). As a result, Elizabeth got neither Calais nor Le Havre and lost most of her troops to disease during the long siege of Le Havre, an outcome that made Elizabeth unwilling to re-involve herself in continental conflicts or on behalf of continental Protestantism for over 20 years. Peace was eventually restored between the two countries by the 1564 Treaty of Troyes (see TROYES, TREATY OF). *See also* DUDLEY, AMBROSE, EARL OF WARWICK.

Further Reading: Frederic J. Baumgartner, *France in the Sixteenth Century,* New York: St. Martin's Press, 1995; P. S. Crowson, *Tudor Foreign Policy,* New York: St. Martin's Press, 1973.

Hapsburg family. *See* HABSBURG FAMILY.

Hardwick, Elizabeth, Countess of Shrewsbury (1520–1608)

Next to Queen Elizabeth herself, no woman in Elizabethan England exhibited the financial acumen and political sense of "Bess of Hardwick." Married four times, Elizabeth Hardwick outlived each husband, inheriting considerable wealth from each one in turn. In about 1532, at the age of 12, Hardwick married Robert Barlow, who died a year later. In 1549, she wed Sir William Cavendish, with whom she had six children. After Cavendish's death in 1557, Hardwick, who had a passion for building, completed construction of Chatsworth House, a large country mansion that she had begun in the early 1550s.

Elizabeth Hardwick shown later in life when she was Elizabeth Talbot, Countess of Shrewsbury, painted by an unknown artist. *By courtesy of the National Portrait Gallery, London.*

Hardwick's third husband was a wealthy Gloucestershire gentleman, Sir William St. Loe, whom she married in 1559. His death in the early 1560s made Hardwick one of the richest WOMEN in England. In 1567, she married George TALBOT, Earl of Shrewsbury, a wealthy and influential peer (see PEERAGE) who became custodian of Mary STUART, Queen of Scots, in 1569.

In the 1570s, Hardwick worked assiduously for the advancement of her Cavendish children, angering both the queen and her husband with her bold and ambitious schemes. By arranging a marriage between her daughter Elizabeth Cavendish and Charles Stuart, Earl of Lennox (brother of Henry STUART, Lord Darnley, the murdered husband of Mary of SCOTLAND), Hardwick incurred the wrath of the queen and earned a brief stay in the TOWER OF LONDON. Elizabeth objected to the match because Lennox (see STUART CLAIM) had a claim to the English throne. In the 1580s, Hardwick took advantage of that claim by trying unsuccessfully to persuade the queen to accept her granddaughter, Arabella STUART, child of the Lennox MARRIAGE, as heir to the Crown.

Hardwick's own marriage to Shrewsbury deteriorated in the 1580s, and she accused her husband of plotting to release Mary Stuart, a charge she was unable to substantiate and had to retract. The couple considered divorce, but Elizabeth effected a reconciliation. After Shrewsbury's death in 1590, Hardwick used her great wealth and freedom from spousal constraint to again engage in building. The construction of Hardwick Hall, the magnificent Tudor mansion that can still be seen in Derbyshire, took up the last two decades of Elizabeth Hardwick's life (see also ARCHITECTURE). She died there at the age of 87 in February 1608.

Further Reading: David N. Durant, *Bess of Hardwick,* New York: Atheneum, 1978.

Harington, Sir John (1561–1612)

From the letters of Sir John Harington, Elizabeth's much-indulged godson, come some of the most vivid descriptions our age has of the queen and her COURT. During the reign of MARY I, Harington's father, also named John Harington, won the undying affection of Eliza-

Sir John Harington, Queen Elizabeth's godson, was painted by Hieronimo Custodis. *By courtesy of the National Portrait Gallery, London.*

beth by smuggling letters from a friend to the princess while she and Harington were both imprisoned in the TOWER OF LONDON, an act of kindness that cost Harington a £1,000 fine. In gratitude, Queen Elizabeth stood godmother for Harington's son in 1561.

Young John Harington attended Eton and Cambridge (see UNIVERSITIES) but was an indifferent student. After his father's death in 1582, Harington was much at court, except for brief periods when his wit and gift for satire angered his godmother and earned him banishment from her sight. The first such escapade involved his circulation among the queen's maids of honor (see LADIES-IN-WAITING) of a decidedly improper tale that Harington had translated out of a long epic poem by the Italian poet Ludovico Ariosto. When the queen read his work, she banished Harington from the court until he had translated the entire poem, a task he completed by 1592 when he presented a magnificently bound copy to Elizabeth. Harington's second banishment came in 1596 over a treatise entitled *A New Discourse on a Stale Subject: The Metamorphosis of Ajax,* which Harington published under the pseudonym Misacmos. The work was a detailed description, with diagrams, of Harington's latest invention—the water closet.

(Ajax was a pun on "a jakes," an Elizabethan term for a privy or a toilet.) The treatise angered the queen not for its subject, but for its many unflattering asides on prominent courtiers, including the queen's late favorite, Robert DUDLEY, Earl of Leicester. Elizabeth ordered the "saucy poet" from the court until he learned better manners, which he apparently had by 1598 when the queen forgave him and had one of his water closets installed at RICHMOND PALACE.

In 1599, Elizabeth ordered Harington to accompany Robert DEVEREUX, Earl of Essex, to IRELAND, commanding her godson to keep a secret journal of the expedition as a check for her on the ambitious earl. Harington revealed his affection for the queen at her death, writing: "I can not blot from my memory's table the goodness of our sovereign Lady to me." Well favored by JAMES I, Harington continued at court until his death in November 1612.

Further Reading: Nona Fineberg, *Elizabeth, Her Poets, and the Creation of the Courtly Manner: A Study of Sir John Harington, Sir Philip Sydney, and John Lyly*, New York: Garland, 1988; Sir John Harington, *The Letters and Epigrams of Sir John Harington*, edited by Norman Egbert McClure, New York: Octagon Books, 1977.

Hariot, Thomas. *See* HARRIOT, THOMAS.

Harriot, Thomas (1560–1621)

Thomas Harriot (or Hariot) was an important Elizabethan mathematician and scholar and the first person to write an account of English settlement in what was to become the United States. Harriot was born and educated at Oxford (see UNIVERSITIES). He served as a cartographer and scientific advisor to Sir Walter RALEIGH, and he sailed with Sir Richard GRENVILLE on the first colonization voyage sent by Raleigh to Virginia in 1585 (see ROANOKE COLONY [1585]). The hardships of the North American wilderness overcame the colonists, and they convinced Sir Francis DRAKE to return them to England when he passed by their settlement on Roanoke Island (off what is now North Carolina) in June 1586.

Harriot turned his year on Roanoke into a descriptive account of the island entitled *BRIEF AND TRUE REPORT OF THE NEW FOUND LAND OF VIRGINIA,* which was published in 1588. A popular work, the *Report* was translated into French, German, and Latin within two years of its publication; it also contained reproductions of 23 drawings by fellow colonist John WHITE of the plant, animal, and human life native to Virginia (see illustration with entry for AMADAS-BARLOWE EXPEDITION). Upon his return, Harriot also prepared a navigation manual and various charts and maps of AMERICA for Raleigh. Harriot is also said to have been the first Englishman to have smoked tobacco, an American commodity Harriot thoroughly described in the *Report.*

From 1607 until his death, Harriot received a pension from Henry Percy, Earl of Northumberland, and was briefly imprisoned after the Catholic Gunpowder Plot of 1605 for casting JAMES I's horoscope at the request of his patron, who was suspected of involvement in the plot. Harriot spent his last years engaged in astronomical research and mathematical study. By 1610, he was using a telescope similar to Galileo's to study sunspots and observe other celestial phenomena. He also invented a number of aids to navigation and devised and perfected various algebraic theories. This research resulted in the publication of Harriot's *Artis Analyticae Praxis* in 1631, 10 years after his death.

Further Reading: Karen Ordahl Kupperman, *Roanoke: The Abandoned Colony,* New York: Barnes and Noble, 1993; J. W. Shirley, *Thomas Harriot,* New York: Clarendon Press, 1983.

Harrison, William (1534–1593)

A topographer, antiquary, and historian, William Harrison was the author of "THE DESCRIPTION OF ENGLAND," the most important surviving account of life in Elizabethan times (see ANTIQUARIANISM). Born in LONDON, Harrison was educated at St. Paul's School and Westminster School (see GRAMMAR SCHOOL), where his schoolmaster was Alexander NOWELL, the future dean of St. Paul's and author of the Anglican CATECHISM. Harrison also attended Cambridge and Oxford (see UNIVERSITIES), completing his studies at the latter in 1560. After his ordination in about 1556, Harrison served as chaplain to William Brooke, Lord Cobham, who, holding the ADVOWSON to the BENEFICE of Radwinter in Essex, gave the parish to Harrison in 1559. Although Harrison also held another Essex

benefice in the 1570s, he served Radwinter for the rest of his life.

Harrison was one of the team of writers, which also included Richard STANYHURST and Edmund CAMPION, who were assembled by Raphael HOLINSHED to compile his *Chronicles of England, Scotland, and Ireland,* now popularly known as HOLINSHED'S *CHRONICLES.* Harrison's contribution to the project was a treatise entitled "An Historical Description of the Island of Britain," which served as the introduction to the first edition of Holinshed in 1577. For the second edition, published by John HOOKER and another team of editors in 1587, Harrison reordered some of the sections of his work, retaining the original title for the first part of the treatise, but renaming the subsequent parts with the title "The Description of England." While the first part of the revised work concentrated on SCOTLAND and on the topography and history of the whole island of Britain, "The Description of England" focused on the social organization and physical resources of England and WALES. Harrison's detailed descriptions and lively writing style have today made "The Description of England" the most widely read and trusted source of information on Elizabethan social history.

Harrison also wrote two works that went unpublished in his lifetime. One is his great "Chronologie," which painstakingly lists the important events in history from the Creation until February 1593, two months before Harrison's death. The other is a treatise on weights and measures, which was written about 1587. Harrison died at Radwinter in April 1593.

Further Reading: William Harrison, *The Description of England,* edited by Georges Edelen, New York: Dover Publications, 1994; G. J. R. Parry, *A Protestant Vision: William Harrison and the Reformation of Elizabethan England,* Cambridge: Cambridge University Press, 1987.

Harvey, Gabriel (c. 1550–1630)

Gabriel Harvey was a prominent university lecturer and literary critic. Born in Essex, Harvey was educated at Cambridge (see UNIVERSITIES), where he was appointed professor of rhetoric in 1574. A quarrelsome man, Harvey embroiled himself in numerous academic controversies with his Cambridge colleagues. However, he also found a friend at Cambridge in Edmund SPENSER, who placed Harvey in his *The Shepheardes Calendar* as the character "Habbinol." Harvey's lectures, which argued that content was more important than form in the writing of verse, were published in 1577. Harvey's strongly held and expressed opinions on literature and individual poets and writers frequently caused him trouble and damaged his academic career. His election as master of Trinity Hall at Cambridge was blocked by the government in 1585 because of the offense given at COURT by his attack on the POETRY of Edward de VERE, Earl of Oxford.

In the 1590s, Harvey engaged in a long and acrimonious pamphlet debate with the poets Robert GREENE and Thomas NASHE. Harvey began the feud in 1592 by attacking Greene's work in the pamphlet *Four Letters.* Harvey and Nashe quarreled over both literary and religious issues. As a Puritan, Harvey attacked the work Nashe did for the government in answering the Puritan criticisms of the MARPRELATE TRACTS (see PURITANS). In 1599, as Harvey and Nashe grew increasingly vehement in their denunciations of each other, the government intervened, banning both men from publishing anything new and confiscating all previous works.

By the late 1590s, Harvey declared himself weary of Elizabethan literary fashions and advised young poets to take up a more practical occupation. After his debate with Nashe was suppressed, Harvey published almost nothing else, although he did write a favorable opinion of some of the works of William SHAKESPEARE in 1601. Failing to obtain any further academic preferment, Harvey spent the last 30 years of his life in retirement in Essex, where he devoted himself to medical and scientific studies. Harvey died at his Essex home in 1630.

Further Reading: Virginia F. Stern, *Gabriel Harvey,* Oxford: Clarendon Press, 1979.

Hastings, Henry, Earl of Huntingdon
(1536–1595)
Under Elizabeth, Henry Hastings, Earl of Huntingdon, was a leading Protestant claimant to the English throne. Through his mother, a daughter of Henry Pole, Lord Montague,

Hastings had a claim to the throne through the House of York (see YORKIST CLAIM). Hastings' great-grandmother was Margaret Pole, Countess of Salisbury and niece of Edward IV. HENRY VIII executed the countess in 1541, and her son Henry, Hastings' grandfather, in 1538—officially for TREASON, but in fact for their Yorkist blood. EDWARD VI, with whom Hastings was raised, knighted him in 1548, and, in May 1553, Hastings married a daughter of John DUDLEY, Duke of Northumberland.

Hastings succeeded to his father's earldom of Huntingdon in June 1560, and thereafter, often to the queen's annoyance, put himself forward as a better Protestant successor to Elizabeth than the surviving Grey sisters (see GREY, JANE; GREY, KATHERINE; GREY CLAIM). When Elizabeth almost died of smallpox in October 1562, political opinion in the country tended to support Huntingdon as the best successor. The earl was a zealous Puritan and a supporter of the Huguenot cause in France, even requesting in 1569 to be allowed to join the Huguenot armies (see HUGUENOTS; PURITANS). Both religion and his own dynastic interests made Huntingdon

Henry Hastings, Earl of Huntingdon, had a distant claim to the English throne. *By courtesy of the National Portrait Gallery, London.*

a strong opponent of the proposed marriage between Thomas HOWARD, Duke of Norfolk, and Mary STUART, Queen of Scots, the Catholic heir to Elizabeth's throne. When Norfolk's schemes led to the NORTHERN REBELLION in 1569, Elizabeth gave Huntingdon partial responsibility for Mary's safekeeping. Huntingdon was later a member of the commission appointed to view the CASKET LETTERS and other evidence of wrongdoing brought against Mary by her half brother, James STUART, Earl of Moray. In 1572, Huntingdon sat as a judge for Norfolk's treason trial and was thereafter lord president of the Council of the North, with responsibility for defending England's Scottish frontier.

A patron of Puritan preachers, Huntingdon was also a strong opponent of SPAIN, and he quickly took up arms in 1588 to defend the queen from possible Catholic plots during the ARMADA invasion. Huntingdon died childless in 1595. *See also* the genealogical chart in Appendix 1: "Yorkist Claimants to the English Throne in the Sixteenth Century."

Further Reading: Claire Cross, *The Puritan Earl: The Life of Henry Hastings, Third Earl of Huntingdon,* New York: St. Martin's Press, 1967.

Hatton, Sir Christopher (1540–1591)

Sir Christopher Hatton, although only the second son of a Northamptonshire GENTRY family, became one of the most prominent figures in the Elizabethan court and a special favorite of the queen (see FAVORITES). Hatton attended Oxford (see UNIVERSITIES) in the mid-1550s but took no degree, and he was admitted to the Inner Temple (see INNS OF COURT) in 1559, but he was not called to the bar—both common practices for a man seeking a career at COURT rather than in a profession. He was later criticized for having "danced his way" into royal favor, for Hatton seems to have first come to the queen's attention when he performed before her in a MASQUE given at the Inner Temple at CHRISTMAS 1561. By 1564, Hatton, having received several court appointments as well as grants of land and money, was in high favor and reputed to be the queen's lover.

Although looks, charm, and courtly prowess may have begun Hatton's career, the later positions of responsibility given him by Elizabeth indicated her recognition in him of higher abilities. In 1572, he became captain of the royal

guard, and in 1577 he received a knighthood and appointment to the PRIVY COUNCIL. He sat for Northamptonshire in several parliaments, becoming recognized as the queen's spokesman in the Commons. In the 1580s, he opposed the queen's proposed marriage to Francis VALOIS, Duke of Alençon, and fell out of favor briefly for his rivalry with Sir Walter RALEIGH and his support for the execution of Mary STUART, Queen of Scots. A moderate Anglican, he opposed extreme measures against both Catholics and PURITANS, and was suspected by the latter of being a secret Catholic (see CATHOLICISM, ENGLISH). In 1573, he was the target of an unsuccessful assassination attempt by a Puritan fanatic.

Hatton was a patron of several authors, including Edmund SPENSER and Thomas Churchyard, and he was one of the courtiers who invested in Sir Francis DRAKE'S CIRCUMNAVIGATION voyage in 1577. Drake renamed his flagship the *Golden Hind* after the markings on Hatton's coat of arms. In 1587, Hatton became lord chancellor, the most important legal position in the land, and in 1588 he followed Robert DUDLEY, Earl of Leicester, as chancellor of Oxford University and high steward of Cambridge. Hatton, who never married, died in London on 20 November 1591.

This portrait of Sir Christopher Hatton, who rose to become lord chancellor of England, was painted about 1589 by an unknown artist. *By courtesy of the National Portrait Gallery, London.*

Further Reading: Eric St. John Brooks, *Sir Christopher Hatton,* London: Jonathan Cape, 1947.

Hawkins, Sir John (1532–1595)

Sir John Hawkins was an English seaman who attempted in the 1560s to open the Spanish colonies in the Caribbean and on the American mainland to English trade. The Spanish government forbade its American colonies from trading with any foreign power, even though SPAIN could not supply all its colonies' needs, especially the need for slave labor. In 1562, Hawkins sailed to West Africa, took on a cargo of slaves, and then sailed to SPANISH AMERICA where he conducted a brisk trade with colonists willing to ignore Spanish trade law. His profits from the 1562 voyage stimulated interest in a second voyage, in which even the queen, Sir William CECIL, and Robert DUDLEY, Earl of Leicester, invested. This 1564 voyage was even more successful, paying huge dividends to its shareholders.

A third voyage, launched in 1567, ran into strong resistance from a Spanish colonial administration determined to stamp out the illegal trade. Hawkins lost all but two of his ships when ambushed by the Spanish at SAN JUAN D'ULLOA, the main port for Mexico City on

This portrait of the Elizabethan seaman Sir John Hawkins was painted by an unknown artist about 1581. *National Maritime Museum, London.*

Mexico's Caribbean coast; Hawkins and Sir Francis DRAKE, a relative who had accompanied Hawkins on the voyage, barely survived the passage back to England in 1569. The outcome of this ill-fated third voyage aggravated hostility between England and Spain and launched the anti-Spanish PRIVATEERING career of Drake.

In 1577, Hawkins became treasurer of the NAVY; in this office, and later as naval controller, he was instrumental in reorganizing the English fleet and in restructuring its procedures and tactics. As a rear admiral, he was third in command of the fleet in 1588 when it sailed against the Spanish ARMADA. Hawkins died in 1595 while with Drake on a raiding expedition to the Spanish West Indies. *See also* "TREASURE CRISIS" OF 1568.

Further Reading: James A. Williamson, *Hawkins of Plymouth,* 2nd ed., New York: Barnes and Noble, 1969.

Heminges, John (d. 1630)

John Heminges (or Heminge), a LONDON stage actor and colleague of William SHAKESPEARE, was a coeditor of the first edition of Shakespeare's plays, known as the FIRST FOLIO. Heminges probably started his acting career with the troupe known as the Queen's Men, but by 1594 was, with Shakespeare and Richard BURBAGE, a member of the CHAMBERLAIN'S MEN. In 1596, he became the official recipient of payment for the company's performances at COURT. Although listed in all the troupe's cast lists to 1629, Heminges probably ceased performing about 1611. He became trustee and overseer for the wills of company members, most of whom left him legacies. From Shakespeare's will, Heminges, along with fellow actors Henry CONDELL and Richard Burbage, received a small amount of money "to buy them rings." Heminges was also a trustee for some of Shakespeare's London property.

Along with Condell, Heminges edited and oversaw the printing of the First Folio of Shakespeare's plays in 1623. In their preface to the volume, which they entitled "To the Great Variety of Readers," Heminges and Condell stated their aim in undertaking the project to be "only to keep the memory of so worthy a friend and fellow alive." They were probably also interested in preventing others from laying claim to Shakespeare's works and in presenting a good printed text for each play. Besides the preface, the two editors provided a list of players, including themselves, who had performed the works of Shakespeare at the company's two main performance venues—the GLOBE THEATRE in Southwark and the Blackfriars Theatre in London. The editors also dedicated the First Folio to the earls of Pembroke and Montgomery, both noted patrons of the theatre. Heminges died a wealthy man in 1630, owning one quarter of the shares in both the Globe and the Blackfriars Theatres. *See also* SHAKESPEARE, WORKS OF.

Further Reading: Charles Connell, *They Gave Us Shakespeare: John Heminge and Henry Condell,* Boston: Oriel Press, 1982.

Heneage, Sir Thomas (c. 1534–1595)

Sir Thomas Heneage was a prominent Elizabethan courtier, as well as a privy councilor and a royal favorite. Born into a Lincolnshire GENTRY family, Heneage was educated at Queen's College, Cambridge (see UNIVERSITIES), which he entered in 1549. He came to COURT in the 1560s under the patronage of Sir William CECIL, who helped him secure seats in the Parliaments of 1563, 1571, and 1572 (see PARLIAMENTARY SESSIONS 1559–81). Cecil may have intended Heneage to act as a counterbalance to the court influence of Robert DUDLEY, Earl of Leicester, the queen's favorite and Cecil's frequent political rival (see FAVORITES). Heneage seems to have briefly eclipsed Leicester in the queen's favor in the mid-1560s, when perhaps the queen herself sought to tame Leicester's growing ambition by playing on his jealousy with Heneage.

Heneage was, for a time, much in the queen's company and received many rewards and favors, including a knighthood in 1577. He acquired enough wealth to build a new country home, Copt Hall in Essex, and to become a prominent figure in Essex politics and society. He also acquired the former LONDON residence of the abbots of St. Edmunds Bury, which he turned into a fine town house that allowed him to live in style in the capital. In the 1580s, he won political power as well as court position, becoming a member of the PRIVY COUNCIL. In 1587, being already treasurer of the royal chamber, he succeeded Sir

Christopher HATTON as vice-chamberlain, an important post in the royal household. In 1590, he was appointed chancellor of the Duchy of Lancaster, which made him chief legal officer of an important group of royal estates. He sat in PARLIAMENT for Essex between 1584 and 1593, serving as a spokesman for the Crown to the House of Commons. There is some evidence that the first performance of William SHAKESPEARE's *A Midsummer Night's Dream* took place at the celebration of Heneage's second marriage in May 1594. Heneage died shortly afterward in 1595.

Further Reading: Wallace T. MacCaffrey, *The Shaping of the Elizabethan Regime,* Princeton, NJ: Princeton University Press, 1968; J. E. Neale, *Elizabeth I and Her Parliaments 1584–1601,* New York: St. Martin's Press, 1958.

Henri II (1519–1559)

Henri II, who concluded the French monarchy's long war with the Habsburgs (see HABSBURG FAMILY), was king of FRANCE when Elizabeth came to the English throne in 1558. In 1526, Henri's father, FRANCIS I (see VALOIS FAMILY), won his release from captivity to SPAIN by agreeing to renounce claims to his Italian possessions. To ensure the French king's compliance with the agreement upon his release, CHARLES V demanded that Henri, then the seven-year-old Duke of Orleans, and his elder brother Francis be sent to Spain as hostages. When their father repudiated the agreement to return Italian lands, Charles angrily ordered that the boys be straitly confined and deprived of their French attendants. Finally released in 1529, Henri's experience left him with a deep hatred of Spain and its Habsburg rulers (see HABSBURG FAMILY).

In 1533, Henri married Catherine de MEDICI, with whom he eventually had 10 children. In 1536, he became dauphin (heir to the throne) on the death of his brother. Upon succeeding his father in 1547, he shifted France's diplomatic and military focus from Italy to the northwest, where he won back Boulogne from the government of EDWARD VI in 1550 and realized a lifelong ambition in 1558 by capturing CALAIS, the last English possession on the continent, from MARY I. He also intervened in SCOTLAND on behalf of the French regent Marie de GUISE, mother of his daughter-in-law, Mary STUART, Queen of Scots, who had been raised at the French COURT since 1548. Strongly influenced by his mistress, Diane de Poitiers, and by the Duke and Cardinal of Guise (see GUISE FAMILY), Henri continued the war with the Habsburgs, winning successes on his eastern frontier but suffering a shattering defeat at St. Quentin in 1557. Financial exhaustion led both Henri and PHILIP II of Spain to seek peace in 1559. Negotiations for the TREATY OF CATEAU-CAMBRÉSIS included Elizabeth, the new queen of England, who had inherited her sister's alliance with Spain and who unsuccessfully demanded the return of Calais.

Henri was beginning to turn his attention to the rapid spread of PROTESTANTISM in France when he died unexpectedly in July 1559 of injuries suffered at a tournament celebrating the peace. During a joust, a splinter from his opponent's shattered lance entered the king's eye and pierced his brain; he died several days later. He was succeeded by his son Francis II. *See also* the genealogical chart in Appendix 1: "Valois and Bourbon Dynasties of France."

Further Reading: Frederic J. Baumgartner, *Henry II, King of France 1547–1559,* Durham, NC: Duke University Press, 1988; R. J. Knecht, *French Renaissance Monarchy: Francis I and Henry II,* 2nd ed., London: Longman, 1996.

Henri III (1551–1589)

Marked by incessant civil war between Catholics and HUGUENOTS, the reign in FRANCE of Henri III, from 1574 to 1589, covered the middle years of Elizabeth's reign and saw a weakened France withdraw from any effective role in the NETHERLANDS, leaving the resolution of the NETHERLANDS REVOLT to England and SPAIN. The third son of HENRI II and Catherine de MEDICI, Henri, as Duke of Anjou, led the French royal armies to victory over the Huguenots at Jarnac and Moncouteur in 1569. In 1572, he, along with his mother and the Guises (see GUISE FAMILY), was an instigator of the SAINT BARTHOLOMEW MASSACRE of Huguenots.

At his mother's insistence, Henri sought election to the throne of Poland in 1573, but returned to Paris shortly after his coronation in 1574 to assume the Crown of France on the death of his brother, Charles IX (see VALOIS FAMILY). His Polish subjects deposed him in

1575. In France, his younger brother and heir, Francis VALOIS, Duke of Alençon, supported the Huguenots in the civil war, forcing Henri to back the CATHOLIC LEAGUE led by Henri, Duke of Guise. To remove his troublesome brother from France, Henri encouraged him to pay suit to Elizabeth, and the duke seemed close to winning the queen's hand on several occasions. After Alençon's death in 1584, the heir-presumptive to the French throne was a Huguenot, Henri Bourbon (see HENRI IV), cousin and brother-in-law of Henri III. With a Protestant heir, the king supported the Huguenots, but was forced to capitulate to Catholic rebels in 1585.

In the resulting War of the Three Henris, Henri III was caught in the increasing rivalry between the Protestant Henri Bourbon, the legal heir, and Henri Guise, who saw himself as the proper Catholic heir. In 1588, during the "Day of the Barricades," the king was besieged in Paris by the Catholic forces of Guise but managed to escape. In December 1588, the king arranged the assassination of Guise. In 1589, the year of his mother's death, Henri III was himself murdered by a fanatical Catholic friar. With the death of Henri III, the House of Valois, which had ruled France since 1328, came to an end, and the Crown passed to Henri IV, first king of the Bourbon dynasty. *See also* the genealogical chart in Appendix 1: "Valois and Bourbon Dynasties of France."

Further Reading: Frederic J. Baumgartner, *France in the Sixteenth Century,* New York: St. Martin's Press, 1995; A. Lynn Martin, *Henry III and the Jesuit Politicians,* Geneva: Droz, 1973.

Henri IV (1553–1610)

Henri IV, first king of the House of Bourbon, restored peace and political stability to FRANCE after almost 40 years of religious civil war. A cousin of the last Valois kings (see VALOIS FAMILY), Henri Bourbon (also known as Henri of Navarre) was raised as a Protestant. In 1572, after leading the HUGUENOT forces in the war of 1569–72, he married Margaret of Valois, sister of Charles IX, as part of the peace settlement. Because of his marriage, he was spared when other Huguenot leaders were killed during the SAINT BARTHOLOMEW MASSACRE in August 1572. Forced to declare himself a Catholic, Bourbon was held prisoner at the French COURT until 1576, when he escaped and repudiated his declaration of Catholicism.

In 1584, after the death of Francis VALOIS, Duke of Alençon, Bourbon became heir-presumptive to the childless HENRI III and leader of the Huguenots in the War of the Three Henris (1585–89), a power struggle between Bourbon and Henri, Duke of Guise (see GUISE FAMILY), leader of the CATHOLIC LEAGUE, for the succession to Henri III. Bourbon ascended the throne in 1589 after the assassination of Henri III, who had himself instigated the murder of Guise some months earlier. Unacceptable to his Catholic subjects, Henri IV appealed to Elizabeth for aid, and the queen, eager for a Protestant France and hoping to regain CALAIS as the price of her assistance, responded with troops and a loan of £20,000 (see BRITTANY EXPEDITIONS). In 1590, Alessandro FARNESE, Duke of Parma, governor-general of the NETHERLANDS, invaded France and compelled Henri to raise the siege of Paris. However, Parma's French campaign relieved pressure on Elizabeth's other allies, the Dutch rebels (see NETHERLANDS REVOLT), and with English assistance the Dutch began to advance against the Spanish-controlled southern provinces.

Despite English help, including a 1591 invasion of Normandy by Robert DEVEREUX, Earl of Essex, Henri IV was forced to accept Catholicism in July 1593 to end resistance to his rule and secure his Crown. In 1598, he promulgated the Edict of Nantes, guaranteeing the rights of the Huguenots, and made peace with PHILIP II of SPAIN, ending nine years of war. Over the next decade, Henri restored the French monarchy and the shattered French economy. He was assassinated in 1610 by a Catholic fanatic. *See also* the genealogical chart in Appendix 1: "Valois and Bourbon Dynasties of France."

Further Reading: Frederic J. Baumgartner, *France in the Sixteenth Century,* New York: St. Martin's Press, 1995; Mark Greengrass, *France in the Age of Henri IV,* New York: Longman, 1984; Desmond Seward, *The First Bourbon: Henri IV, King of France and Navarre,* Boston: Gambit, 1971.

Henry VII (1457–1509)

Henry VII was the founder of the Tudor dynasty and the grandfather of Elizabeth I. Born in WALES, Henry was the son of Edmund Tudor (a maternal half brother of Henry VI) and Margaret Beaufort, a wealthy heiress with a claim to the English throne (see BEAUFORT FAMILY; TUDOR FAMILY; see also genealogical charts in Appendix 1: "House of Tudor, 1485–1603"; "Houses of Lancaster, Beaufort, and Tudor"). Henry never knew his father, who died two months before his birth, and rarely saw his mother, who was only 13 when he was born.

Henry's youth coincided with the WARS OF THE ROSES, an intermittent dynastic conflict between the houses of Lancaster and York. Because the Beaufort claim derived from Lancaster, the Yorkist Edward IV gave Henry into the custody of a loyal Yorkist nobleman. With the temporary overthrow of Edward IV in 1470, Henry came into the custody of his paternal uncle, Jasper Tudor, Earl of Pembroke. In the fighting that restored the rule of Edward IV in 1471, Prince Edward of Lancaster was killed; the prince's death, followed two weeks later by the murder in the TOWER OF LONDON of his father, Henry VI, extinguished the male line of Lancaster and threw the family's claim onto Henry. To save his nephew from imprisonment or death, Pembroke, a staunch Lancastrian, fled the country with

This portrait of Elizabeth I's grandfather, Henry VII, was painted by an unknown artist about 1505. *By courtesy of National Portrait Gallery, London.*

Henry. From 1471 to 1483, Henry lived in exile in the French duchy of Brittany. He grew up to be a quiet young man, with little formal EDUCATION and French manners and preferences.

When Richard III, brother of Edward IV, usurped the throne from his nephew in 1483, the king's unpopularity offered Henry an opportunity to make good his claim to the Crown. In August 1485, Henry won the Battle of Bosworth, during which Richard III was slain. Hailed on the field as Henry VII, the new king was crowned in October and married in January 1486 to Elizabeth, daughter of Edward IV. The marriage insured that Henry's heirs would combine the blood of Lancaster and York. During his reign, Henry restored the strength and solvency of the monarchy, reduced the power of the nobility, and gave England peace, order, and stability. Like his granddaughter Elizabeth I—but unlike his son HENRY VIII— Henry VII was parsimonious, giving honors and rewards sparingly, and only for long and faithful service. By marrying his daughter into the Scottish royal family and his son into the Spanish royal house, Henry won recognition for his family from the other royal dynasties of Europe and unknowingly created the later STUART CLAIM to the English throne. Henry died on 21 April 1509 and was succeeded by his son, Henry VIII.

Further Reading: S. B. Chrimes, *Henry VII,* Berkeley: University of California Press, 1972.

Henry VIII (1491–1547)

Henry VIII was the father of Elizabeth I. The second son of HENRY VII and his wife Elizabeth of York, Prince Henry became heir to the throne on the death of his elder brother, Prince Arthur, in 1502 (see genealogical charts in Appendix 1: "House of Tudor, 1485–1603"; "Stuart Claim to the English Throne"; "Houses of Lancaster, Beaufort, and Tudor"; "Grey Claim to the English Throne"). Henry's accession to the throne in April 1509, two months short of his eighteenth birthday, was the first uncontested accession of an English monarch since 1422 (see WARS OF THE ROSES). Unlike his father, a reserved and parsimonious man who worked hard at the business of government, Henry VIII was outgoing, extravagant, and sensual, much like his

maternal grandfather, Edward IV (see BEAUFORT FAMILY; TUDOR FAMILY; YORKIST CLAIM). The young Henry—tall, handsome, and energetic—preferred the pursuit of pleasure to the drudgery of governing and left the management of affairs to his chief minister, Cardinal Thomas Wolsey. Fascinated by all things military, Henry plunged into European warfare, quickly spending his father's treasure.

In June 1509, he married CATHERINE OF ARAGON, a Spanish princess who had been briefly married to his late brother. Catherine gave birth to several children, but only one, Princess Mary (see MARY I), born in 1516, survived infancy. By the mid-1520s, when Catherine was past childbearing age, Henry became convinced that his lack of a legitimate male heir (see FITZROY, HENRY) was the result of God's curse on his improper union with his brother's widow. England had never been ruled by a woman, and Henry (like most Englishmen) feared for the future of the dynasty and the kingdom should Mary succeed. Henry's scruples coincided with his growing love for Anne BOLEYN, an English gentlewoman (see BOLEYN FAMILY). However, for

Hans Holbein painted this portrait of Henry VIII, Elizabeth I's father. *National Maritime Museum, London.*

political reasons (see CHARLES V; HABSBURG FAMILY), the pope denied Henry an annulment of his marriage to Catherine. Faced with this impediment, the king, dismissing Wolsey, turned to a new set of ministers, including Thomas CROMWELL, who encouraged him to break with the pope, establish, through PARLIAMENT, his headship of the English Church, and so obtain his own annulment without reference to Rome.

Henry married Anne in January 1533, and their daughter Elizabeth was born in September. Anne's failure to produce a son led to her execution for adultery in 1536 when Elizabeth was not yet three. Henry's next queen, Jane SEYMOUR, died in childbirth in October 1537 giving Henry the son he desired (see EDWARD VI). Although Henry married three more times (see ANNE OF CLEVES; HOWARD, KATHERINE; PARR, KATHERINE), he had no more children; at his death in January 1547, he left the Crown to his nine-year-old son, although declaring in his will that Mary and Elizabeth were next in line for the throne should their brother die without heirs.

Further Reading: Carolly Erickson, *Great Harry: The Extravagant Life of Henry VIII,* New York: Summit Books, 1980; Jasper Ridley, *Henry VIII: The Politics of Tyranny,* New York: Viking, 1985; J. J. Scarisbrick, *Henry VIII,* Berkeley: University of California Press, 1968; Lacey Baldwin Smith, *Henry VIII: The Mask of Royalty,* Chicago: Academy Chicago Publishers, 1982.

Henslowe, Philip (d. 1616)

Philip Henslowe was one of the most active and successful theatre managers in Elizabethan LONDON. Little is known of Henslowe's early life, although he apparently came to London from Sussex in about 1577. He settled in Southwark, across the Thames from London, and acquired property there through his MARRIAGE to a widow named Agnes Woodward. After a few years as a dyer of cloth, Henslowe became a real estate dealer, specializing in theatre properties. About 1588, he built the Rose Theatre on a site along the south bank of the Thames that he had acquired four years earlier. Under Henslowe's management after 1594, the Rose became the home of the Admiral's Men, led by the actor Edward ALLEYN, but also witnessed some performances by William SHAKESPEARE's company, the CHAMBERLAIN'S MEN.

Henslowe and Alleyn became business associates in 1592 when Alleyn married Henslowe's stepdaughter. The two men purchased an interest in the Bear Garden, a bearbaiting arena in Southwark, and, in 1600, built the Fortune, a new Southwark theatre modeled on the GLOBE THEATRE. Henslowe also managed another south bank theatre at Newington Butts. As theatre manager, Henslowe served as the acting company's banker, acquiring plays, purchasing costumes and props, and loaning money to the actors. Although respected as a theatre manager, Henslowe was also known as a tough businessman, especially in his real estate dealings.

After 1604, Henslowe left the running of the Fortune to Alleyn and concentrated on business opportunities provided by his new position as joint master (with Alleyn) of the "royal game of bears, bulls and mastiff dogs." Bear- and bullbaiting—the setting of dogs on chained bears or bulls—was a popular and, for Henslowe, profitable Elizabethan pastime (see ANIMAL SPORTS). Henslowe demolished the Bear Garden and built a new structure on the site called the Hope, which could be used both as a theatre and as a bear- and bullbaiting arena. Henslowe died in London in 1616. *See also* DRAMA.

Further Reading: Joseph W. Donohue Jr., ed., *The Theatrical Manager in England and America,* Princeton, NJ: Princeton University Press, 1971; G. B. Harrison, *Elizabethan Plays and Players*, Ann Arbor: University of Michigan Press, 1956.

Hepburn, James, Earl of Bothwell (1535–1578)

James Hepburn, Earl of Bothwell, the third and last husband of Mary STUART, Queen of Scots, was one of the chief instruments of Mary's fall from power. Bothwell, although a Protestant, supported the government of the Catholic regent, Marie de GUISE, Queen Mary's mother; for his support, the regent named him lord admiral and warden of the marches (borders with England) in 1556. In 1560, he met Mary Stuart, then queen of FRANCE, in Paris, and he was appointed by the queen to be her commissioner to SCOTLAND. He was named a privy councilor in 1561 when Mary returned to Scotland, but in 1562 he was exiled by the government of James STUART, Earl of Moray, the queen's half brother and chief councilor, who suspected Bothwell's ambition and taste for power. He escaped to England, where he was briefly imprisoned, and then fled to France before finally being recalled to Scotland by Mary in 1565 after her MARRIAGE to Henry STUART, Lord Darnley, and the exile of Moray.

Bothwell rapidly became one of the queen's strongest supporters, especially after the murder in March 1566 of David RIZZIO, the queen's Italian secretary. In February 1567, Bothwell was somehow involved in the mysterious death of Lord Darnley at Kirk o'Field outside EDINBURGH; although public opinion accepted his guilt, Bothwell was acquitted in the courts and received large gifts of land from the queen (see DARNLEY MURDER). In April, he took Mary captive, likely with her connivance, and divorced his Catholic wife to marry the queen according to Protestant rites. A rebellion of the Protestant Scottish lords overthrew the queen, and Bothwell escaped to Denmark, where he was imprisoned by the Danish king for abandoning his Danish wife in 1560 (see CARBERRY, BATTLE OF).

The CASKET LETTERS, a series of letters from Mary to Bothwell that seemed to prove the queen's involvement with the earl in a plot to murder Darnley, were later taken from Bothwell's servant by Moray and the Protestant lords and used to prevent Mary's release from English imprisonment. Bothwell, meanwhile, never saw Mary again; he fell into insanity and died in prison in 1578.

Further Reading: Robert Gore-Browne, *Lord Bothwell and Mary, Queen of Scots,* Garden City, NY: Doubleday, Doran, 1937; Antonia Fraser, *Mary, Queen of Scots,* New York: Delacorte Press, 1969; Jenny Wormald, *Mary, Queen of Scots,* London: Collins and Brown, 1991.

Herbert, Henry, Earl of Pembroke
(c. 1538–1601)

An important political figure in WALES, where his family had long been prominent, Henry Herbert, second Earl of Pembroke, was also the patron of an acting company that may have included William SHAKESPEARE. A nephew of Queen Katherine PARR, the last wife of HENRY VIII, Herbert was married to Katherine GREY in 1553 when his father supported NORTHUMBERLAND'S COUP, which attempted to place Jane GREY, Katherine's elder

sister, on the throne. With the failure of the coup, the earl repudiated his new daughter-in-law and had his son's politically dangerous marriage annulled.

Herbert succeeded his father to the earldom of Pembroke in 1570, and in 1577 he married Mary Sidney (see HERBERT, MARY), the daughter of Sir Henry SIDNEY. In 1586, Pembroke became lord president of Wales in succession to his father-in-law. Later in the same year, he took part in the trial of Mary STUART, Queen of Scots. In 1588, he took charge of the defense of Wales as the ARMADA approached England, offering to raise an army at his own cost. About 1592, he raised a company of actors known as Pembroke's Men. The year was an unfortunate one for the formation of an acting company, for a visitation of the PLAGUE had closed all the LONDON theatres, and the troupe was forced to go on tour in 1593. The tour was apparently unsuccessful, for the London theatre manager Philip HENSLOWE had to pawn the company's costumes for them.

Pembroke's Men are known to have performed several plays by Shakespeare, including *Henry VI* and *Titus Andronicus* (see SHAKESPEARE, WORKS OF), so it is possible that Shakespeare acted with the earl's company for a time. By 1597, Ben JONSON was a member of Pembroke's Men, but the performance of *Isle of Dogs,* the play Jonson co-wrote with Thomas NASHE, caused the company further difficulties. The government, considering the play seditious because of various critical references in it to foreign states with which England conducted trade, stopped the performances and briefly imprisoned Jonson. This episode and continuing ill health may have soured Pembroke on actors. The earl asked to be relieved of his Welsh duties in 1598, and little more is known of Pembroke's Men. The earl died in January 1601.

Further Reading: Sir Tresham Lever, *The Herberts of Wilton,* London: Murray, 1967.

Herbert, Mary, Countess of Pembroke (1561–1621)

Mary Herbert, Countess of Pembroke, was a celebrated patron of Elizabethan poets and writers. Born Mary Sidney, the daughter of Sir Henry SIDNEY, an Elizabethan lord deputy of IRELAND, the countess was also the sister of

Sir Philip SIDNEY and the niece of Robert DUDLEY, Earl of Leicester, the queen's favorite. In 1577, she married Henry HERBERT, Earl of Pembroke, who was an important political figure in WALES and the patron of an acting company known as Pembroke's Men.

The countess was well known for the support she gave to many struggling poets, some of whom found lodgings at Wilton House, the Pembroke country home near Salisbury. Besides encouraging and sheltering young poets, the countess's services to Elizabethan literature included inspiring her brother Philip Sidney to write his romance *Arcadia,* the second edition of which she brought to publication in 1593 after Sidney's death, and inspiring her son William Herbert, third Earl of Pembroke, to write POETRY and to support poets, including Ben JONSON. Her importance as a literary patron was recognized by Edmund SPENSER, who addressed one of the dedicatory sonnets of *The Faerie Queen* to her, and by the Devon poet William Browne, who coined for her the simple epitaph "Sidney's sister, Pembroke's mother" to commemorate what she had meant to Elizabethan literature.

The countess's own literary work included a translation of the Psalms and of *Antonius,* a French tragedy. She also wrote a dialogue entitled *Astraea,* which was intended as an ENTERTAINMENT for Elizabeth when she visited Wilton House during one of her summer progresses (see PROGRESSES, ROYAL). A questionable nineteenth-century tradition states that William SHAKESPEARE was a guest of the countess at Wilton House during a visit there by JAMES I in October 1603. Supposedly, the royal party was entertained by a performance of Shakespeare's *As You Like It.* The countess survived her husband by 20 years, dying in 1621.

Further Reading: Margaret P. Hannay, *Philip's Phoenix: Mary Sidney, Countess of Pembroke,* New York: Oxford University Press, 1990; Sir Tresham Lever, *The Herberts of Wilton,* London: Murray, 1967.

High Commission, Court of

The 1559 Act of Supremacy empowered Elizabeth, as supreme governor of the ANGLICAN CHURCH, to delegate her ecclesiastical authority to a special commission. The statute authorized such commissions to punish infractions of Church law, to settle disputes within the English Church, and to enforce uniformity of religious practice. The first commission established in 1559 included bishops, privy councilors (see PRIVY COUNCIL), and common lawyers, with the lay members outnumbering the clerical. Presided over by the archbishop, the commission could fine or imprison offenders, punishments not open to other CHURCH COURTS.

By about 1580, the more formally organized Court of High Commission evolved out of the series of special ecclesiastical commissions that had sat almost continuously beginning in 1559. Although originally established to deal with Catholic errors, heresies, and abuses still prevailing in the Anglican Church, High Commission came, by the 1590s (and especially under the chairmanship of Archbishop John WHITGIFT), to be an excellent instrument for repressing Puritan nonconformity (see PURITANS). Because its authority rested on the royal supremacy over the Church, not on the COMMON LAW, the Court of High Commission came to employ procedures that were of questionable legality in common law (see SUPREMACY, ROYAL). The most notorious of these was the *ex officio* oath, which required persons summoned before High Commission to swear an oath to answer all questions truthfully even though they had not been informed of the charges against them or the types of questions they were to be asked. Such a procedure could trap a Puritan who was conscientious about the taking of oaths into incriminating himself and his associates. A defendant could refuse the oath, as did the presbyterian activist Thomas CARTWRIGHT in 1591 (see PRESBYTERIAN MOVEMENT), but would then be subject to imprisonment for contempt.

Under Elizabeth's Stuart successors (see JAMES I; STUART CLAIM), the Court of High Commission became as hated in its ecclesiastical jurisdiction as Star Chamber was in its civil jurisdiction (see STAR CHAMBER, COURT OF). Like Star Chamber, High Commission was abolished by PARLIAMENT in 1641.

Further Reading: Patrick Collinson, *The Elizabethan Puritan Movement,* Oxford: Clarendon Press, 1990; Powel Mills Dowley, *John Whitgift and the English Reformation,* New York: Scribner, 1954.

Hilliard, Nicholas (c. 1547–1619)

Nicholas Hilliard was the most accomplished painter of miniatures in Elizabethan England. Born in Devon, the son of an Exeter goldsmith, Hilliard was apprenticed as a boy to a LONDON goldsmith. About 1560, Hilliard began experimenting with the art of miniature painting, which was known in Tudor England as LIMNING. Before the age of 20, he had done several portraits in miniature, including one of himself and one of Mary STUART, Queen of Scots. His style, which was heavily influenced by the work of Hans Holbein, court painter to HENRY VIII, attracted the attention of Elizabeth, who in 1572 appointed Hilliard to be the royal limner and goldsmith. Unlike the more realistic portrayals executed by his best pupil, Isaac OLIVER, Hilliard's numerous portraits of Elizabeth were more refined and idealized, and thus more to the aging queen's liking.

In the mid-1580s, Elizabeth granted Hilliard a monopoly on the painting of royal portraits in miniature (see MONOPOLIES). Although few of his works have survived, Hilliard painted the portraits of many prominent Elizabethan courtiers and was a friend of Sir Philip SIDNEY and Sir Christopher HATTON. In the late 1570s, Hilliard briefly

Portrait of Elizabeth I painted by miniaturist Nicholas Hilliard about 1575. *By courtesy of the National Portrait Gallery, London.*

entered the service of Francis VALOIS, Duke of Alençon, and spent two years at the French court where his work became extremely popular. Because his miniatures were designed as jewels, Hilliard continued to pursue his trade as a goldsmith and jeweler, making the pendants and lockets on which the miniatures could be worn and displayed. Hilliard is also known to have executed a number of large-scale paintings, but few of them can now be definitely identified as his work.

After the accession of JAMES I in 1603, Hilliard found himself in serious competition with Oliver, whose use of shadowing made Hilliard's more linear style of miniature painting seem outdated. Nonetheless, Hilliard won appointment as limner to the king, although Oliver was named official limner to James's wife, Queen Anne of Denmark. About 1600, Hilliard began writing his *Treatise on the Art of Limning,* but the work was unfinished at his death in January 1619. English limning reached its highest achievement under Hilliard, who also greatly influenced English portrait painting in the seventeenth century. *See also* ART and the illustrations for FAMILY and LIMNING.

Further Reading: Mary Edmond, *Hilliard and Oliver,* London: R. Hale, 1983.

holidays (holy days)

The modern word "holiday" derives from "holy days," the principal feast days of the medieval Church upon which work was to cease and celebrations or feasts were often held. With the exception of ACCESSION DAY, the anniversary of Elizabeth's coming to the throne on 17 November, all Elizabethan holidays had a religious origin. But, like their modern counterparts, the most important Elizabethan holidays, CHRISTMAS and EASTER, had also developed secular traditions and modes of celebration.

The Reformation had abolished many saints' days and other Catholic religious holidays, and the increasing influence of the PURITANS altered the manner and intensity of celebrations associated with many remaining holidays. The Puritans, for instance, objected to the feasting and secular celebration that surrounded Christmas, and, to some degree, to the holiday itself; its "-mas" ending, deriving from

"Christ's Mass," was a constant reminder of the despised Catholic MASS. By law, everyone was to attend church on holidays as well as on Sundays, and everyone was required to take communion at least three times a year, generally on Christmas, Easter, and Whitsunday (the Christian feast of Pentecost, which fell in May or June). The observance of religious holidays began on the evening before the day itself (Christmas Eve is a modern survival of this tradition), when fasts were to be observed. Fasts were also required on Fridays, during the six-week observance of Lent (prior to Easter), and during the four-week observance of Advent (prior to Christmas). Being traditional holdovers from the medieval Church, the fast requirements for Lent and Advent were not strictly enforced, and Friday fasts were maintained more as an economic measure for the encouragement of the fishing industry (see DIET) than as a religious observance.

In addition to the recognized holidays on the Anglican Church CALENDAR (see table below), many local holidays were observed. Despite Puritan objections to the drinking and sexual license they sometimes generated, parish Wake Days or Dedication Days, the feast day of the parish patron saint, were still widely celebrated. Also, many towns held annual fairs, which could be one day or longer, usually sometime between May and November. In general, the Elizabethan period was the beginning of the transition from medieval holy days of religious observance to modern secular holidays associated with a work break. *See also* ANGLICAN CHURCH.

Elizabethan Holidays

Holiday	Date	Religious Observance	Celebration
New Year's Day	1 January	Circumcision of Christ	Part of the 12-day Christmas celebration and the traditional day for gift giving
Twelfth Day	6 January	Epiphany (visit of Wise Men to the infant Jesus)	Culmination of the the Christmas celebration
Candlemas	2 February	Feast of the Purification of Mary	Until the Reformation, celebrated with a procession of candles
Shrovetide (Shrove Tuesday)	between 3 February and 9 March	Last day before Lent	The celebrations held on this day in parts of Europe were precursors of modern Mardi Gras
Ash Wednesday	between 4 February and 10 March	First day of Lent	Began 40 days of fasting before Easter
Lady Day	25 March	Annunciation of Mary	English year officially began on this day
Easter	between 22 March and 25 April	Resurrection of Christ	Observances extended from Palm Sunday, one week before, to two days after Easter
St. George's Day	23 April	Feast of St. George	St. George was the patron saint of England (not an official Elizabethan holiday)
May Day	1 May	Sts. Philip and Jacob	Celebrated as the first day of summer

Elizabethan Holidays, continued

Holiday	Date	Religious Observance	Celebration
Ascension Day	between 30 April and 3 June	Ascension of Christ	Summer festival
Whitsunday (observed from Sunday to Tuesday and called Whitsuntide)	between 10 May and 13 June	Pentecost (Holy Spirit descends on apostles)	Major summer festival celebrated with dancing, feasting, and plays
Trinity Sunday	between 17 May and 20 June	Feast day of Christian Trinity	Summer festival similar to Whitsunday
Midsummer Day	24 June	St. John the Baptist	Often a civic celebration with bonfires and parades of civic officials
Michaelmas	29 September	St. Michael the Archangel	Marked the completion of the harvest and the start of a new agricultural year
All Hallows (Hallowmas Hallowtide)	1 November	Feast of All Saints	All Saints (or All Hallows) Eve was 31 October, modern Halloween
Accession Day	17 November		Commemoration of Elizabeth's accession in 1558
St. Andrew's Day	30 November	Feast of St. Andrew	Advent observance leading to Christmas began on Sunday nearest St. Andrew's Day (27 November to 3 December)
Christmas	25 December	Birth of Christ	Christmas celebrations ran 12 days, to 6 January (Twelfth Day)

Note: Most of the listed holidays were officially recognized in the calendar of the Anglican Church. Many other saints' days and religious observances were celebrated in local communities and more conservative parishes.

Further Reading: David Cressy, *Bonfires and Bells: National Memory and the Protestant Calendar in Elizabethan and Stuart England*, London: Weidenfeld and Nicolson, 1989; Ronald Hutton, *The Rise and Fall of Merry England: The Ritual Year, 1400–1700*, New York: Oxford University Press, 1994; Ronald Hutton, *The Stations of the Sun: A History of the Ritual Year in Britain*, New York: Oxford University Press, 1996.

Holinshed, Raphael (c. 1498–1580)

Raphael Holinshed was the editor, compiler, and coauthor of a popular and influential history of England, SCOTLAND, and IRELAND. Although little is known of Holinshed's early life, he is believed to have come from Warwickshire and to have attended Christ's College, Cambridge (see UNIVERSITIES). He came to LONDON shortly after the accession of Elizabeth in 1558 and took a job as a translator in the printing shop of Reginald Wolfe, who was then at work on a voluminous chronicle of universal history based largely on the work of the early Tudor antiquary, John Leland (see ANTIQUARIANISM; PRINTING). When Wolfe died in 1573, Holinshed continued to work on an abridgement of Wolfe's chronicle that told the history of the British kingdoms.

The Chronicles of England, Scotland, and Ireland, now known popularly as HOLINSHED'S *CHRONICLES,* was published in two volumes in 1577 by John Harrison and George Bishop. Although Holinshed wrote or compiled much of the first volume, which covered English history, the publication was really the work of a syndicate of writers and compilers, including William HARRISON, Edmund CAMPION, and Richard STANYHURST. The *Chronicles* was immediately popular, although the queen ordered the deletion of certain offending passages in the section on Ireland.

After Holinshed's death in 1580, John HOOKER assumed editorship of a second edition of the *Chronicles,* which appeared in three volumes in 1587. The second edition, which carried the narrative to the year 1586, had a wide readership and assumed an important place in English literature when William SHAKESPEARE used it as source material for his history plays.

Further Reading: Annabel Patterson, *Reading Holinshed's Chronicles,* Chicago: University of Chicago Press, 1994.

Holinshed's *Chronicles*

The Chronicles of England, Scotland, and Ireland, now known popularly as Holinshed's *Chronicles* because it was written and compiled under the editorship of Raphael HOLINSHED, was one of the most popular Elizabethan histories of Britain and the source for William SHAKESPEARE's history plays. Collaborating with a team of writers and compilers that included William HARRISON, Richard STANYHURST, and Edmund CAMPION, Holinshed combined new material written by himself and his associates with material drawn from a wide variety of other chronicles and sources.

Working himself largely on the first volume covering the history of England, Holinshed reproduced almost verbatim large sections from the works of such sixteenth-century chroniclers as Edward Hall, Robert Fabyan, Polydore Vergil, Richard GRAFTON, and John STOW. He also included selections from writers like Sir Thomas More and from various medieval and classical chroniclers, such as Jean Froissart and Tacitus. The first edition

of Holinshed's *Chronicles,* published by John Harrison and George Bishop, appeared in two volumes in 1577. Although immediately popular with Elizabethan readers, the first edition angered the queen, who ordered the deletion of several passages on the recent political history of IRELAND that were not to her liking.

After Holinshed's death in 1580, John HOOKER, a writer and Exeter civic magistrate, collaborated with a team that included Abraham Fleming, Francis Thynne, and John Stow to produce a three-volume second edition that appeared in 1587. The new edition updated the *Chronicles* to 1586, with Hooker himself providing much of the new material for the Ireland section. The second edition provided source material for 13 of Shakespeare's plays—the 10 English history plays and *King Lear, Cymbeline,* and *Macbeth.* The queen also found fault with the second edition, ordering the removal of passages on the BABINGTON PLOT and the NETHERLANDS EXPEDITION of Robert DUDLEY, Earl of Leicester. *See also* SCOTLAND.

Further Reading: Richard Hosley, ed., *Shakespeare's Holinshed,* New York: Putnam Sons, 1968; Annabel Patterson, *Reading Holinshed's Chronicles,* Chicago: University of Chicago Press, 1994.

Hooker, John (1525–1601)

John Hooker was an editor of the 1587 edition of HOLINSHED'S *CHRONICLES* and the author of a treatise on the functioning of the Elizabethan PARLIAMENT. The son and grandson of former mayors of Exeter, Hooker was educated at a GRAMMAR SCHOOL in Cornwall and then tutored, during a stay in the German city of Strasburg, by the Protestant reformer Peter Martyr. About 1550, Hooker returned to England and took service with Miles Coverdale, the translator of the English Bible (see BIBLE, ENGLISH), who sent Hooker to study at Oxford (see UNIVERSITIES). In 1551, Hooker was made an Exeter freeman (i.e., a citizen with rights to vote and hold office), and in 1555 was appointed Exeter's first chamberlain and charged with keeping city records. By the time he resigned the chamberlainship in September 1601, Hooker had involved himself in virtually every aspect of municipal government, including the keeping of city accounts, the provision of WEAPONS for the civic armory, and the remodeling of the city council chamber.

Hooker's most important work was the organization and archiving of city records, which were in a highly disordered state when he took office. In the 1560s, Hooker helped pay for the education of his nephew, Richard HOOKER, who later used his learning to write the *LAWS OF ECCLESIASTICAL POLITY,* the great defense of the ANGLICAN CHURCH. Between 1568 and 1575, Hooker spent much time in IRELAND serving as agent and advisor to Sir Peter CAREW. Hooker's service in the Irish Parliament of 1569 and the English Parliament of 1571 resulted in three literary works—his journals of the two parliamentary sessions and his treatise entitled *THE ORDER AND USAGE OF THE KEEPING OF A PARLIAMENT IN ENGLAND* (1572). The three writings are among the most important surviving sources on the workings of Elizabethan Parliaments.

After 1575, Hooker wrote numerous works, including a biography of Carew, a *Description of the City of Exeter* (1919), and the "Synopsis Chorographical of Devonshire," a detailed study of the county (see ANTIQUARIANISM). His most important literary project was his co-editorship of a new edition of Holinshed's *Chronicles,* which appeared in 1586–87 and later served as a historical source for William SHAKESPEARE. Hooker's main contribution to the work was Book VI, which updated the history of Ireland to 1586. Hooker died in Exeter in November 1601.

Further Reading: Vernon F. Snow, *Parliament in Elizabethan England: John Hooker's Order and Usage,* New Haven, CT: Yale University Press, 1977; J. A. Wagner, *The Devon Gentleman: The Life of Sir Peter Carew,* Hull, England: University of Hull Press, 1998.

Hooker, Richard (c. 1554–1600)

Through his multivolume masterpiece, the *LAWS OF ECCLESIASTICAL POLITY,* theologian Richard Hooker defined the teachings and doctrines of the ANGLICAN CHURCH, which he also vigorously defended against the criticisms of both PURITANS and Catholics (see CATHOLICISM, ENGLISH). Born in Devon into a middle-class family of small means, Hooker's education at Exeter School (see GRAMMAR SCHOOL) was provided by his uncle John HOOKER, an Exeter magistrate who also brought his nephew to the attention of John JEWEL, Bishop of Salisbury. From 1568 until his death in 1571, Jewel paid for Hooker's education at Oxford (see UNIVERSITIES). After his patron's death, Hooker won a scholarship and so was able to complete his master's degree in 1577 and obtain a teaching position in Hebrew in 1579.

Ordained into the Anglican Church in 1581, Hooker began preaching at PAUL'S CROSS in LONDON a year later. He resigned his position at Oxford in 1584 and was given a BENEFICE in the country, but he never took up residence there. Instead, in 1585, Archbishop John WHITGIFT and other Anglican Church leaders, recognizing Hooker's ability as a writer and teacher, helped him win appointment to a London benefice that allowed him time to work on his *Laws of Ecclesiastical Polity,* a detailed exposition of Anglican doctrine. By strongly defending Anglican positions in his sermons, Hooker came into conflict with preachers of Puritan views and precipitated debates that helped him develop the ideas he later put forth in his writing.

In 1591, Hooker accepted a benefice in Wiltshire and there completed the first four books of the *Ecclesiastical Polity,* which were published in 1593. The fifth book appeared in 1597. Hooker's persuasive and articulate work was immensely important to the Anglican Church, giving it a powerful instrument with which to defend itself against the theological and political attacks of its Puritan and Catholic opponents. In 1595, the queen rewarded Hooker with a benefice near Canterbury, where Hooker died in November 1600, leaving the last three books of the *Ecclesiastical Polity* completed but unpublished. Because these volumes did not appear until 1648, doubts arose as to their authenticity, although most modern scholars are convinced they are Hooker's work. Hooker is often known today as "the judicious Hooker," from the inscription placed on his monument by contemporaries who considered his work a masterpiece of religious literature.

Further Reading: Stanley Archer, *Richard Hooker,* Boston: Twayne, 1983; Robert K. Faulkner, *Richard Hooker and the Politics of Christian England,* Berkeley: University of California Press, 1981.

Howard, Charles, Earl of Nottingham (1536–1624)

A cousin of Elizabeth (see HOWARD FAMILY), Charles Howard, Earl of Nottingham, was the

This portrait of Charles Howard, Earl of Nottingham, who was lord admiral of England during the Armada year, was painted by an unknown artist about 1602. *By courtesy of the National Portrait Gallery, London.*

commander of the English fleet against the ARMADA. A favorite of Elizabeth, Howard served at sea with his father in the 1550s and against the NORTHERN REBELLION in 1569. He succeeded his father as Lord Howard of Effingham in 1575. He was nearly 50 in 1585 when the queen named him lord admiral, a post that had been held by his father, great-grandfather, and two uncles. Although Sir Francis DRAKE was a more experienced seaman, he was unacceptable as fleet commander because he was not of gentle or noble birth, and his appointment would have caused jealousy and perhaps insubordination among ship captains of higher social rank.

Effingham sensibly listened to the advice of more experienced sailors and worked well with Drake, John HAWKINS, Martin FROBISHER, and other seasoned seamen. Although he supported Drake in his desire to

meet the Armada before it entered English waters, Effingham's tactics when it reached the Channel were conservative, preferring to harass the Spanish rather than attack at close quarters (see GRAVELINES, BATTLE OF). When the crisis passed and disease began ravaging the crews, Effingham stood by his men and vigorously protested the government's refusal to care for—or even to pay—its sailors. In 1590, Effingham joined with Hawkins and Drake in establishing what was called the Chest at Chatham, a charity for poor seamen. Effingham shared command of the CADIZ RAID (1596) with Robert DEVEREUX, Earl of Essex. Effingham's decision to return home without further action after the attack on Cadiz infuriated Essex, who thereafter became the admiral's bitter enemy.

From the late 1570s, Effingham was the patron of a company of actors known as Lord Howard's Men, and later as the Admiral's Men. With Edward ALLEYN as lead actor, the company was the first to perform most of the plays of Christopher MARLOWE. Elizabeth created Effingham the Earl of Nottingham in 1597, and her successor, JAMES I, continued to favor the earl, sending him to SPAIN in 1605 to negotiate peace. Nottingham held the post of admiral until 1619 when he retired with a large pension. Nottingham died in December 1624 at the age of 88. *See also* the genealogical chart in Appendix 1: "Howard Family in the Sixteenth Century—Elizabeth I's Maternal Relatives."

Further Reading: Robert W. Kenny, *Elizabeth's Admiral: The Political Career of Charles Howard, Earl of Nottingham,* Baltimore: The Johns Hopkins Press, 1970.

Howard, Katherine (c. 1521–1542)

Like her cousin Anne BOLEYN, Katherine Howard, the fifth wife of HENRY VIII, was executed for adultery. One of 10 children of Lord Edmund Howard, a younger brother of the third Duke of Norfolk (see HOWARD FAMILY), Katherine was raised in the household of her father's stepmother, Agnes, dowager Duchess of Norfolk. In 1536, Katherine engaged in an intimate relationship with her music instructor, Henry Manox. In 1537, she became sexually involved with a young gentleman (see GENTRY) named Francis Dereham. In 1539, her uncle, the Duke of Norfolk, had her appointed one of the LADIES-IN-WAITING to Queen ANNE OF CLEVES. Much dissatisfied with his new wife, Henry took an immediate liking to Katherine, whom he married in late July 1540, only weeks after the annulment of his marriage to Anne.

The new MARRIAGE signaled the rise to power at COURT of the Duke of Norfolk and the Catholic Howard faction, and the decline of the Protestant reform faction, which had supported the Cleves marriage. Bored with her aging husband, Katherine soon began a sexual relationship with Thomas Culpepper, a young courtier. Princess Elizabeth, then almost eight years old, spent some time with her cousin Katherine in the spring of 1541, receiving gifts of jewels from her stepmother. In August, Katherine appointed her former lover Dereham as her secretary. By November, Archbishop Thomas CRANMER, a reformist opponent of the Howards, informed the king of what he had discovered about Katherine's premarital liaisons with Manox and Dereham. Both men were arrested and forced to confess. Katherine confessed her relations with Manox and Dereham, but she blamed the Culpepper affair on Culpepper and on Lady Rochford, her chief lady-in waiting, who had arranged private meetings between the queen and her lover.

Devastated by the betrayal of his young wife, Henry imprisoned her in the TOWER OF LONDON and had PARLIAMENT condemn her by ATTAINDER rather than have her embarrassing story told in open court. Dereham and Culpepper were executed in December 1541, and Katherine and Lady Rochford, the widow of Elizabeth's uncle George Boleyn, died at the Tower in February 1542. Katherine's death, being so similar to that of her cousin, Anne Boleyn, may have given young Elizabeth her first understanding of what her father had done to her mother. *See also* the genealogical chart in Appendix 1: "Howard Family in the Sixteenth Century—Elizabeth I's Maternal Relatives."

Further Reading: Lacey Baldwin Smith, *A Tudor Tragedy: The Life and Times of Catherine Howard,* New York: Pantheon Books, 1961.

Howard, Thomas, Duke of Norfolk

(1536–1572)

A relative of the queen's and the only duke in Elizabethan England, Thomas Howard, Duke

of Norfolk, destroyed himself through his ambition to wed Mary STUART, Queen of Scots, and to share with her the Crown of England. Thomas, fourth Duke of Norfolk, was the son of the Earl of Surrey, whom HENRY VIII executed for treason in 1547, and grandson of Thomas, third Duke of Norfolk, who was saved from execution in 1547 by the death of Henry VIII. Although taught for a time by the Protestant writer and teacher John FOXE, who later wrote the "BOOK OF MARTYRS," the fourth duke grew up to be a vain and rather weak man with Catholic leanings. He was raised by his aunt Mary, the widow of Henry VIII's illegitimate son, Henry FITZROY, Duke of Richmond.

After being given his grandfather's ducal title in 1559, Norfolk served Elizabeth in SCOTLAND in 1560 and was a member of the PRIVY COUNCIL by 1562. He was the queen's commissioner for Scottish affairs in 1568. In 1569, feeling deprived by William CECIL, the queen's chief advisor, of the position at COURT that he believed was his due, Norfolk proposed himself as a suitable English husband for the imprisoned Mary Stuart. When Elizabeth refused to consider the proposal, the disgruntled duke left court uttering vague threats against

Elizabeth I's cousin, Thomas Howard, the fourth Duke of Norfolk, was executed for treason in 1572. *By courtesy of the National Portrait Gallery, London.*

Cecil and his supporters. When summoned back to court, Norfolk submitted and was imprisoned. He was also implicated in the 1570 uprising of the northern earls (see NORTHERN REBELLION), who had supported his MARRIAGE scheme.

The duke was eventually pardoned and released for his activities in 1569–70, but in 1571 he involved himself in the RIDOLFI PLOT to free Mary and dethrone Elizabeth. The plot also proposed a Spanish invasion, the restoration of CATHOLICISM, and the marriage of Norfolk to the Queen of Scots. For this new TREASON, Norfolk was tried, condemned, and executed in 1572. *See also* the genealogical chart in Appendix 1: "Howard Family in the Sixteenth Century—Elizabeth I's Maternal Relatives."

Further Reading: Neville Williams, *A Tudor Tragedy: Thomas Howard, Fourth Duke of Norfolk,* London: Barrie and Jenkins, 1964.

Howard family

Through her mother, Anne BOLEYN (whose own mother was a Howard), Queen Elizabeth was a member of the extensive Howard kinship, one of the most powerful noble families in Tudor England. The family rose to prominence in the fifteenth century when Sir John Howard supported Edward IV and the Yorkist cause during the WARS OF THE ROSES (see YORKIST CLAIM). Unlike many other Yorkists, Sir John did not abandon the dynasty when Richard III, Edward's brother, usurped his nephew's throne in 1483. For this loyalty, Richard created Sir John the first Howard Duke of Norfolk and his son Thomas the Earl of Surrey. When Henry Tudor (see HENRY VII) claimed the throne in 1485, Norfolk died fighting for Richard, and Surrey was imprisoned in the TOWER OF LONDON.

Released in 1489, Surrey gradually won back his lands and position by loyally serving the new Tudor dynasty (see TUDOR FAMILY). In 1514, HENRY VIII raised Surrey to his father's dukedom in gratitude for Surrey's brilliant victory over the Scots at Flodden in 1513. Thomas, second Duke of Norfolk, fathered numerous children, including, by his first wife, Thomas, third Duke of Norfolk; Elizabeth, mother of Anne Boleyn; and Edmund, father of Katherine HOWARD, fifth wife of Henry

VIII; and, by his second wife, William, Lord Howard of Effingham, father of Charles HOWARD, Earl of Nottingham, Elizabeth's lord admiral.

Thomas, third Duke of Norfolk, was a powerful political and military figure under Henry VIII; his daughter married the king's illegitimate son, Henry FITZROY, Duke of Richmond, and two nieces married the king himself. Nonetheless, the pride, ambition, and Catholicism of the duke and his eldest son aroused the suspicion of Henry VIII, who executed the son in January 1547 and would have executed the father had not his own death intervened. The duke lived until 1554, restored to his titles by MARY I; he was succeeded by his grandson, Thomas HOWARD, fourth Duke of Norfolk, who, like his father, destroyed himself through his ambition and Catholicism. Elizabeth reluctantly executed her Howard cousin in 1572 for plotting with Mary STUART, Queen of Scots, to seize the throne and restore Catholicism in England.

The Effingham branch of the Howards served Elizabeth loyally; Charles Howard, created Earl of Nottingham in 1597, led the English fleet against the ARMADA in 1588 and became one of Elizabeth's most favored advisors in the last years of her reign. *See also* the genealogical chart in Appendix 1: "Howard Family in the Sixteenth Century—Elizabeth I's Maternal Relatives."

Further Reading: David Head, *The Ebbs and Flows of Fortune: The Life of Thomas Howard, Third Duke of Norfolk,* Athens: University of Georgia Press, 1995; Neville Williams, *A Tudor Tragedy: Thomas Howard, Fourth Duke of Norfolk,* London: Barrie and Jenkins, 1964.

Huguenots

The term "Huguenots" refers to members of the Protestant communities that arose in sixteenth-century FRANCE. The first Huguenot community was founded at Meaux in 1546; it adopted the organization devised by the French reformer John CALVIN for the Protestant community at Strasbourg in Germany. In 1559, the Huguenot Church of Paris, which had been founded about 1555, called together representatives from 15 Protestant churches throughout France to create a Huguenot statement of faith. The resulting document was heavily influenced by the ideas of Calvin and thereby ensured that the French Protestant Church would be based on CALVINISM, like the reformed churches of England, SCOTLAND, and the NETHERLANDS.

By 1561, over 2,100 Huguenot churches existed in France. Because Protestantism spread through all social classes, including the nobility, the movement developed great political influence and aroused strong opposition. Huguenot leaders appealed to the Crown for liberty of conscience, but continued persecution led by the strongly Catholic GUISE FAMILY caused the Huguenots to take up arms and initiated a period of intermittent civil war in France that lasted from 1562 to the 1590s. The Huguenots also played a significant role in English history. In 1562, they negotiated the Treaty of Hampton Court with Elizabeth, who agreed to support the Huguenots with English troops in return for the port of Le Havre (see HAMPTON COURT, TREATY OF; LE HAVRE EXPEDITION). After 1570, the Elizabethan Church and economy were strengthened by a large influx of Huguenot refugees, especially to LONDON. Also, the French Crown's preoccupation with the Huguenots left France unable to intervene in the NETHERLANDS REVOLT, a situation that made England SPAIN's main opponent in Western Europe in the late sixteenth century.

In 1572, the SAINT BARTHOLOMEW MASSACRE destroyed the Huguenot leadership. In 1573, the Huguenots formed a political party dedicated to fighting for political and religious freedom. Under HENRI III (1574–1589), war continued between the Guise-led CATHOLIC LEAGUE and the Huguenots led by Henri of Navarre, who, after 1584, was heir to the throne. Henri III's assassination in 1589 made Navarre king as HENRI IV, but he could only end the war by becoming a Catholic, which he did in July 1593. The Huguenots' 40-year struggle for civil rights and freedom of worship ended in 1598, when Henri issued the Edict of Nantes granting both to his former coreligionists.

Further Reading: Frederic J. Baumgartner, *France in the Sixteenth Century,* New York: St. Martin's Press, 1995; R. J. Knecht, *The French Wars of Religion, 1559–1598,* 2nd ed., London: Longman, 1996; George A. Rothrock, *The Huguenots: A Biography of a Minority,* Chicago: Nelson-Hall, 1979.

humanism

The term "humanism" describes an educational program based on the moral and intellectual value of studying the literature of ancient Greece and Rome. Arising in Renaissance Italy in the fourteenth century, humanism spread northward and reached the English UNIVERSITIES of Oxford and Cambridge in the late fifteenth and early sixteenth centuries. A humanist program first sought to provide students with the ability to write and read classical Latin and Greek and then sought to imbue them with classical civic values—the belief that active involvement in public affairs was a worthwhile human activity and the idea that EDUCATION should prepare a student to render service to the state.

Early Christian humanists, such as the great Dutch scholar Erasmus and his English colleague Sir Thomas More, used their learning to better understand the Bible and to work for reform of abuses in the Catholic Church. Many later humanists left Catholicism for some form of PROTESTANTISM, but humanism was never strictly a Catholic or Protestant movement, and humanist studies were vigorously pursued by people in both religious camps. National monarchies used humanists as educators of royal children or as literate propagandists for royal policies. In England, HENRY VIII employed humanist writers in his efforts to persuade the pope and the rest of Europe of the rightness of his belief that his first MARRIAGE was invalid and should be dissolved.

Henry, who was the first English monarch to be given a humanist education, directed that all his children, including his illegitimate son, Henry FITZROY, Duke of Richmond, receive humanist training. Princess Mary (see MARY I), born in 1516 before the Reformation, imbibed a Catholic humanism and adhered to Rome, but Prince Edward (see EDWARD VI) and Princess Elizabeth, born in the 1530s during the English break with Rome, were trained by Protestant humanist scholars selected by their father. Both later adhered to Protestantism. However, all three shared a basic humanist grounding in classical languages and literature. For example, Elizabeth's humanist tutors, among them the well-known Roger ASCHAM, taught her to read and speak Latin, Greek, Italian, and French, the languages of scholarship and DIPLOMACY. *See also* CATHOLICISM, ENGLISH; REFORMATION, ENGLISH.

Further Reading: Fritz Caspari, *Humanism and the Social Order in Tudor England*, New York: Teachers College Press, 1968; Donald R. Kelley, *Renaissance Humanism,* Boston: Twayne Publishers, 1991; James Kelsey McConica, *English Humanists and Reformation Politics,* Oxford: Clarendon Press, 1965; J. B. Trapp, *Erasmus, Colet and More: The Early Tudor Humanists and Their Books,* London: British Library, 1991.

Hunsdon, First Lord. *See* CAREY, HENRY, LORD HUNSDON.

Hunsdon, Second Lord. *See* CAREY, GEORGE, LORD HUNSDON.

Huntingdon, Earl of. *See* HASTINGS, HENRY, EARL OF HUNTINGDON.

Hutton, Matthew (1529–1606)

Matthew Hutton was Elizabeth's last Archbishop of York. Born into a minor GENTRY family in Lancashire, Hutton entered Cambridge (see UNIVERSITIES) in 1546, achieving his bachelor of divinity degree by 1562. In 1561, he was elected Margaret Professor of Divinity, and in the following year became Regius Professor of Divinity. He thereafter held a number of church benefices, including at St. Paul's Cathedral in LONDON (see BENEFICE).

Hutton came to the notice of the queen in 1564 when he distinguished himself in a series of theological debates held in the royal presence at Cambridge. Rapidly acquiring a reputation as one of the best preachers and ablest scholars in the Church, Hutton in 1565 obtained both a doctorate in divinity and an important benefice at Westminster Abbey (see WESTMINSTER PALACE). In 1566, Hutton was permitted to preach at COURT and at PAUL'S CROSS in London. When Edmund GRINDAL was promoted to the archbishopric of York in 1570, Hutton was proposed as a possible successor to Grindal in the important bishopric of London, but his candidacy was opposed by Matthew PARKER, the Archbishop of Canterbury, who suspected Hutton of favoring PURITANS, and the plan was dropped. In the 1580s, when he was serving on the cathedral staff at York, Hutton's Puritan leanings led to an angry dispute with Edwin SANDYS, the Archbishop of York. Sandys brought 13 charges against Hutton in 1586. Although forced to submit to Sandys, Hutton ably defended himself and never admitted wrongdoing beyond the use of improper and disrespectful language.

Through the influence of William CECIL, Lord Burghley, Hutton was named Bishop of Durham in 1589 and president of the Council of the North in 1595. In February 1596, he became Archbishop of York. He founded a number of almshouses for the poor and GRAMMAR SCHOOLS in the York archdiocese and continued to support Puritans, even writing a letter in 1605 to Robert CECIL, chief minister of JAMES I, recommending that the prosecution of Puritans for nonconformity be relaxed. Hutton died in January 1606 and was buried in York Minster.

Further Reading: Patrick Collinson, *The Elizabethan Puritan Movement*, Oxford: Clarendon Press, 1990; Felicity Heal, *Of Princes and Prelates: A Study of the Economic and Social Position of the Tudor Episcopate*, Cambridge: Cambridge University Press, 1980.

Inns of Court

During the fourteenth century, several inns in LONDON became known as residences for apprentices learning the COMMON LAW (see Maps, "London"). Four of these—Gray's Inn, Lincoln's Inn, Inner Temple, and Middle Temple—were called the Inns of Court and acquired, during the 1450s, the power to license barristers, that is, pleaders at the bar. The licensing system led to the development at the Inns of an educational system for preparing young men for a legal career. This education consisted of an apprenticeship at law, not a course of formal legal training. The Inns also served a social function during the Tudor period by acting as finishing schools for sons of the GENTRY who had no intention of practicing law. For Elizabethan gentlemen, a period of residence at one of the Inns of Court was an experience that could form the social connections later required for the forging of fruitful political or economic alliances. *See also* EDUCATION; GRAMMAR SCHOOL; UNIVERSITIES.

Further Reading: C. W. Brooks, *Pettyfoggers and Vipers of the Commonwealth: The "Lower Branch" of the Legal Profession in Early Modern England,* Cambridge: Cambridge University Press, 1986; Wilfrid R. Prest, *The Inns of Court under Elizabeth I and the Early Stuarts, 1590–1640,* London: Longman, 1972.

Ireland

At the start of the sixteenth century, the English lordship of Ireland (the English monarch was titled lord of Ireland) was divided into two parts—the Englishry and the Irishry. The Englishry consisted of the largely independent ANGLO-IRISH lords, who held their lands from the English Crown and generally followed English law and custom, and the districts under direct English control—DUBLIN, the larger towns, and the PALE, the area of English administration surrounding Dublin (see Maps, "Tudor Ireland"). The Irishry consisted of numerous independent native Irish lordships ruled according to Irish law and custom.

Until the 1530s, when the Irish PARLIAMENT extended the English Reformation legislation to Ireland, the English Crown was content to preserve this division by ruling Ireland through an Anglo-Irish governor. In 1541, the Irish Parliament declared HENRY VIII to be king of Ireland, a change of title that also signaled a change in policy. Henceforth, the English Crown sought to create a unified Irish state ruled from Dublin and recognizing only English law and custom. Anglo-Irish governors were displaced by English lord deputies commanding English troops (see FITZWILLIAM, SIR WILLIAM; PERROT, SIR JOHN; RADCLIFFE, THOMAS, EARL OF SUSSEX; SIDNEY, SIR HENRY), English colonists were settled on Irish lands (see PLANTATIONS, IRISH), and English CALVINISM was imposed on the Irish Church (see REFORMATION, IRISH). However, under Elizabeth, this policy was only inconsistently applied because the queen refused to spend the money and commit the military resources required to effectively and permanently extend English rule into the Irish lordships.

With both the Anglo-Irish and the native Irish becoming increasingly disaffected, Elizabethan Ireland lapsed into a series of revolts (see FITZMAURICE'S REBELLION; DESMOND REBELLION) culminating in 1593 in the NINE

YEARS WAR, an insurrection that eventually led to Spanish intervention in Ireland (see KINSALE, BATTLE OF). The defeat, by 1603, of Hugh O'NEILL, Earl of Tyrone, leader of the Irish rebels during the Nine Years War, left JAMES I, Elizabeth's successor, an Irish kingdom that was economically ravaged but politically subordinated. The war also left the Irish and Anglo-Irish firmly committed to a Catholic Church that had become closely identified with resistance to Protestant English rule. *See also* CATHOLICISM, ENGLISH; PROTESTANTISM.

English Governors of Ireland

Thomas Radcliffe, Earl of Sussex (1559–1565)

Henry Sidney (1571–1575)

William Fitzwilliam (1575–1578)

Arthur, Lord Grey de Wilton (1580–1582)

John Perrot (1584–1588)

William Fitzwilliam (1588–1594)

William Russell (1594–1597)

Thomas, Lord Burgh (1597)

Robert Devereux, Earl of Essex (1599)

Charles Blount, Lord Mountjoy (1600–1603)

Note: Gaps in the sequence of Irish governors represent the brief tenures of temporary Lord Justices. Only the most important permanent appointments are listed above.

Further Reading: Steven G. Ellis, *Tudor Ireland,* London: Longman, 1985; Colm Lennon, *Sixteenth-Century Ireland: The Incomplete Conquest,* Dublin: Gill and Macmillan, 1994; Margaret MacCurtain, *Tudor and Stuart Ireland,* Dublin: Gill and Macmillan, 1972; David B. Quinn, *The Elizabethans and the Irish,* Ithaca, NY: Cornell University Press, 1966.

Islands Voyage

The Islands Voyage was an ambitious but unsuccessful English naval expedition launched against SPAIN in 1597. Conceived by Sir Walter RALEIGH and Robert DEVEREUX, Earl of Essex, the Islands Voyage had two purposes—to destroy the remnants of a Spanish fleet sheltering in the port of Ferrol and to intercept the treasure fleet coming from SPANISH AMERICA as it passed through the AZORES. Responding to the successful English attack on Cadiz (see CADIZ EXPEDITION [1596]), PHILIP II launched another armada against England, but, like the great ARMADA of 1588, the fleet of 1596 was dispersed by storms. The English commanders convinced a skeptical Elizabeth to give them SHIPS and men to destroy the Spanish fleet before it could reform.

Essex and Raleigh planned to join Lord Thomas Howard off Ferrol but storms delayed them at Plymouth, and Howard, who was too weak to attack Ferrol alone, had to return to England. Essex and Raleigh petitioned the queen to allow them to sail to AMERICA and intercept the treasure fleet there, but Elizabeth, who always put the defense of England first, flatly refused to allow her best admirals to go PRIVATEERING in American waters while the English coast was unprotected. She ordered the English fleet to attack the Spanish vessels at Ferrol with fireships. Unwilling to allow the vain and ambitious Essex to further enhance the reputation he had won at Cadiz, the queen ordered that someone else lead the attack on Ferrol.

Raleigh and Essex sailed in August 1597, but miscommunication and rivalry between the commanders dogged the expedition from the start. No attack was made on Ferrol, the treasure fleet was allowed to slip away in the Azores, and Raleigh and Essex quarreled bitterly with one another. The luckless English fleet turned for home in October, just as the refitted Spanish fleet left Ferrol to attempt another invasion of England. Both fleets were converging on England when autumn gales arose to scatter the English ships and send the Spanish vessels back to their home ports. Once again, storms, not the fleet, had protected England from invasion. The spectacular failure of the Islands Voyage allowed the war to continue and damaged the military reputation of Essex.

Further Reading: Robert Lacey, *Robert, Earl of Essex,* New York: Atheneum, 1971; Robert Lacey, *Sir Walter Ralegh,* New York: Atheneum, 1973.

James I (1566–1625)

James Stuart was the son of Mary STUART, Queen of Scots, and her second husband, Henry STUART, Lord Darnley. James was only a year old in 1567 when his mother's enforced abdication made him King James VI of Scotland. When the Tudor dynasty came to an end with the death of Elizabeth I in 1603, James became the first Stuart monarch of England as James I (see STUART CLAIM; TUDOR FAMILY). James's early years on the Scottish throne were marked by disorder and civil war. In 1582, James was seized by a group of presbyterian lords, who sought to offset Catholic influence at court by ruling Scotland themselves through a captive king. In 1583, the king escaped from his captors, and, at the age of 16, began his personal rule (see RUTHVEN RAID). James married Anne of Denmark in 1589 and fathered three children who reached adulthood—Henry, Charles (later Charles I), and Elizabeth.

In the 1590s, James gradually established his control over both the Scots nobility and the Church of Scotland. In the late 1590s, James published two books, *The True Law of Free Monarchies* and *Basilikon Doron,* which set forth his theory of "divine right" kingship. According to this theory, the king, being answerable only to God, could not be removed from his throne by the people. Such exalted notions of kingship were to get James's son, Charles I, into serious difficulties (Charles was executed by Parliament in 1649), but James himself advocated his divine right theory more than he practiced it.

Although Elizabeth I refused to name a successor during her lifetime, she gave James a large pension in 1586 and promised not to oppose his claims to the English Crown unless he provoked her by his activities in Scotland (see BERWICK, TREATY OF). These favors limited James's actions on his mother's execution in 1587 to mere protests, and ensured Scotland's neutrality in 1588 when the ARMADA sailed against England. Otherwise, James, to Elizabeth's intense annoyance, paid little attention to the stream of advice that flowed northward from the English COURT in the 1580s and 1590s.

This portrait of Elizabeth's successor, James I, was painted by John de Critz the elder. *National Maritime Museum, London.*

In the last years of Elizabeth's reign, Sir Robert CECIL; Robert DEVEREUX, Earl of Essex; and other important English courtiers conducted secret correspondence with James in the expectation that he would soon be king of England. English PURITANS looked hopefully to the accession of James for improvement in their condition, for James was reputed to be a strong Calvinist (see CALVINISM). Whether or not Elizabeth formally acknowledged him as her heir on her deathbed is in dispute, but he succeeded to the English throne in March 1603 without incident and with the support of the late queen's most important councilors. *See also* GOWRIE CONSPIRACY; the illustration for FAMILY; and the genealogical chart in Appendix 1: "Stuart Claim to the English Throne."

Further Reading: Antonia Fraser, *King James VI of Scotland and I of England,* London: Sphere Books Limited, 1977; S. J. Houston, *James I,* 2nd ed., London: Longman, 1995; D. Harris Willson, *King James VI and I,* New York: Henry Holt and Company, 1956.

James VI. *See* JAMES I.

Jenkinson, Anthony (c. 1530–1611)

Anthony Jenkinson was the foremost Elizabethan explorer of Asia and the Middle East. Little is known of Jenkinson's early life, except that between 1546 and 1553, in preparation for a career in trade, he traveled extensively in Europe, the Middle East, and North Africa. In 1557, the MUSCOVY COMPANY, a JOINT-STOCK COMPANY formed in 1553, sent Jenkinson to Russia to conduct trade and to explore the possibility of opening a land route to China. After spending several months establishing good relations with Czar Ivan the Terrible, Jenkinson left Moscow in April 1558 and traveled down the Volga to Astrakhan, where he became the first Englishman to navigate the landlocked Caspian Sea. Striking to the east, Jenkinson entered Bokhara, part of the modern Central Asian republic of Uzbekistan, but found the lawlessness of the region made a trade route to China impossible. Retracing his route to Moscow, Jenkinson returned to LONDON in the autumn of 1560 with the English explorer Stephen BOROUGH.

Although Bokhara and the Caspian region were not promising for trade, Jenkinson convinced the Muscovy Company to send a new expedition to Russia in 1561. He believed that if English merchants could establish a presence, from Russia, in the Persian kingdom south of the Caspian, they could draw off part of the Middle Eastern trade that normally flowed into Europe via the Mediterranean. Arriving in Moscow with Borough in May 1561, Jenkinson won valuable trade concessions from the czar by agreeing to purchase silks and jewels for him in the Persian markets. By November, Jenkinson was presenting letters from Queen Elizabeth to the shah of Persia and opening trade talks with Indian merchants. Despite being attacked by robbers and threatened with death by the shah, Jenkinson returned safely to Moscow in August 1563.

After spending the winter in Russia, Jenkinson returned to England in September 1564. In his later years, he tried unsuccessfully to convince the queen to fund further exploration for a Northeast Passage, and he undertook two other expeditions to Moscow, in 1566 and 1571. In the late 1570s, he interested himself in the American voyages of Sir Martin FROBISHER and sat on the commission that examined the ore Frobisher brought back in 1578. Jenkinson died at his home in Rutland in 1611.

Further Reading: F. R. Dulles, *Eastward Ho: The First English Adventurers to the Orient,* Freeport, NY: Books for Libraries Press, 1969; E. Delmar Morgan, *Early Voyages and Travels to Russia and Persia,* New York: B. Franklin, 1963.

Jesuit Mission

In 1580, three English Jesuits (members of the Society of Jesus, an order of Catholic priests founded by the Spaniard Ignatius Loyola in 1540) landed in England to begin the process of restoring the country to Roman Catholicism. In Europe, the Jesuits spearheaded the COUNTER-REFORMATION, working successfully to return large portions of the continent to Catholicism. Before 1580, the Jesuit order had 69 English members serving throughout the world, from FRANCE and Italy to Poland, Hungary, and even India. Jesuit interest in a mission to England itself developed slowly in the 1570s as English SEMINARY PRIESTS (Catholic priests not affiliated with any order) began to enter England in increasing numbers.

In 1579, when the Catholic exile William ALLEN founded the English College in Rome, the school's management was given to the Jesuits. The next year, the English Jesuits Edmund CAMPION and Robert PARSONS led the first Jesuit Mission to England. The Elizabethan government, well aware of the Jesuits' tendency to involve themselves in political plots, publicized the mission as an invasion. The Jesuits themselves promoted the mission as the beginning of a Catholic revival. The publicity increased government persecution of English Catholics and won the Jesuits the distrust of many seminary priests, who sought only to minister to their flocks and not to engage in political activities. After a year in England, Campion was captured and executed, and Parsons fled to France to escape a similar fate. The Jesuit Mission led in the 1580s to the passage of new PENAL LAWS against Catholics and to the stricter enforcement of existing laws.

In the last decades of Elizabeth's reign, the Jesuit Mission in England rarely numbered above 12 members. Three more Jesuits were executed after Campion, including Robert SOUTHWELL, a poet and writer who died at Tyburn (a LONDON execution site) in 1595 after being tortured repeatedly by the notorious Richard TOPCLIFFE. Another well-known English Jesuit, John GERARD, escaped from the TOWER OF LONDON in 1597 and left behind an autobiographical account of his missionary work in England. Although the Jesuit Mission made no progress in restoring England to Catholicism, its members did help preserve and strengthen a small English Catholic community (see CATHOLICISM, ENGLISH).

Further Reading: Bernard Basset, *The English Jesuits: From Campion to Martindale,* New York: Herder and Herder, 1968; Arnold Pritchard, *Catholic Loyalism in Elizabethan England,* Chapel Hill: University of North Carolina Press, 1979; E. E. Reynolds, *Campion and Parsons: The Jesuit Mission of 1580–1,* London: Sheed and Ward, 1980.

Jewel, John (1522–1571)

John Jewel, Bishop of Salisbury, was one of the most effective defenders of the ANGLICAN CHURCH, against both Catholics and PURITANS. Born in Devon, Jewel was educated at Barnstaple GRAMMAR SCHOOL and at Oxford (see UNIVERSITIES), where he earned his bachelor of divinity degree in 1552. In 1554, during the reign of MARY I, Jewel recanted his PROTESTANTISM and signed a series of Catholic articles. When the sincerity of his adherence to Catholicism was called into question, Jewel fled the country, joining the group of MARIAN EXILES resident at Frankfurt, Germany. In Frankfurt, Jewel issued a statement confessing his weakness in accepting Catholicism and retracting his repudiation of his true Protestant beliefs. In 1555, he was briefly involved in the doctrinal disputes that split the Frankfurt community, siding with the opponents of John KNOX. Jewel later traveled to Strasbourg and then to Zurich in Switzerland before touring Italy.

On Elizabeth's accession in 1558, Jewel returned to England. In 1560, Elizabeth appointed Jewel Bishop of Salisbury, and in 1565 he became a doctor of divinity at Oxford. Although Jewel agreed with many Puritan positions, he believed that debates over vestments (see VESTIARIAN CONTROVERSY) and the outward trappings of worship were less important than preaching the gospel. In 1559, Jewel preached a sermon at PAUL'S CROSS calling upon Catholics to prove the truth of their doctrines, a challenge that initiated a long pamphlet debate (see CHALLENGE SERMON). Jewel's most important contribution to the debate was his 1562 *Apologia Ecclesiae Anglicanae (Apology for the Church of England)*, the first systematic statement of Anglican doctrine. Translated into English in 1564 by Ann BACON, the mother of Francis BACON, the *Apologia* was placed in every English parish church by order of Archbishop Richard Bancroft in 1609.

Jewel spent his later years debating with Puritans; his last work, which appeared after his death, was an attack on the Puritan cleric Thomas CARTWRIGHT. At Salisbury, Jewel built a cathedral library and established a school for poor boys with academic promise. Among his pupils at Salisbury was Richard HOOKER, the future author of *LAWS OF ECCLESIASTICAL POLITY*, a work that greatly expanded the description of Anglican positions begun by Jewel in his *Apologia*. Jewel died in September 1571 and was buried in Salisbury Cathedral.

Further Reading: J. E. Booty, *John Jewel as Apologist of the Church of England,* London: S.P.C.K., 1963; Patrick Collinson, *The Elizabethan Puritan Movement,* Oxford: Clarendon Press, 1990.

Jews

Although small in number and forced to worship secretly, the Jewish community in Elizabethan LONDON grew with the expansion of English trade and the establishment of a Protestant English Church. Edward I had expelled all Jews from England in 1290, and no openly Jewish community had existed in the country since that time. However, by Elizabeth's reign, small clandestine communities of Sephardic (Spanish and Portuguese) Jews had settled in London and in the major ports of the south and east. London also had a community of Marranos (Christianized Spanish Jews) that numbered several hundred people. Having fled the persecuting Catholicism of SPAIN, the Marranos hoped for greater tolerance in Protestant England. Although open Jewish worship was not permitted, the Elizabethan government did not engage in active persecution, and the Marranos, though outwardly conforming Anglicans, tended to avoid Christian baptism and to conduct secret Jewish worship services in their homes.

Among the leaders of the Marrano community was Hector Nunez, a physician who enjoyed the confidence of both William CECIL, Lord Burghley, and Sir Francis WALSINGHAM. Nunez used his widespread business connections to help the government obtain important political and military intelligence. In 1588, Nunez was the first to inform Walsingham that the ARMADA was gathering at Lisbon. A Portuguese Marrano, Roderigo LOPEZ, became personal physician to Robert DUDLEY, Earl of Leicester, and then, in 1586, to the queen herself. Lopez used his influence to urge English support for Don Antonio, a claimant to the Portuguese throne, which PHILIP II had seized in 1580. Because Don Antonio was the son of a Marrano woman, Lopez hoped that he would be more tolerant of his Marrano subjects than was Philip.

When Sir Francis DRAKE's 1589 PORTUGAL EXPEDITION failed to put Don Antonio on the throne, Lopez became involved in a shadowy correspondence with Spain that his enemies at COURT used to destroy him (see LOPEZ PLOT). His trial and execution in 1594 began a brief anti-Semitic hysteria in London, which can still be seen in Christopher MARLOWE's *The Jew of Malta,* the most popular play in performance at the time, and William SHAKESPEARE's *The Merchant of Venice,* then being written. The Elizabethan Marrano community declined in size and influence after the Lopez episode, and Jews were not readmitted to England until 1656.

Further Reading: Cecil Roth, *A History of the Jews in England,* 3rd ed., Oxford: Clarendon Press, 1964.

John of Austria (1547–1578)

John of Austria (known as Don John), the half brother of PHILIP II of SPAIN, was one of the most famous military figures of sixteenth-century Europe. Known at birth simply as Jerónimo, Don John was the illegitimate son of CHARLES V and an obscure German woman. Unacknowledged by his father, Jerónimo was raised in Spain by friends of the emperor. Just before his death in 1558, Charles startled his only legitimate son, Philip, by instructing him to acknowledge and provide for a half brother whose existence had not previously been known to him. In 1559, Philip, then king of Spain, brought Jerónimo to the Spanish COURT and renamed him Don Juan (John) de Austria, after the Austrian house of HABSBURG, the Spanish royal family.

Handsome and popular, Don John was a notable contrast to his dour, secretive brother, who raised his newfound sibling high in the Spanish PEERAGE but allowed him no real authority. In 1567, Don John won Philip's confidence by informing the king of an assassination plot being hatched by his mentally unstable heir, Don Carlos. This service won for Don John the military commands that he desired. In 1567, he drove North African pirates from Gibraltar, and in 1569, he crushed a rebellion by Moriscos (Muslims who had been forced to convert to Christianity) in southern Spain. In 1571, Don John took command of a Christian fleet sent by Spain, Venice, the pope, and various Italian states to protect the Venetian outpost on Cyprus from an attacking Turkish fleet. On 7 October 1571, Don John led the allied fleet to victory in a huge naval battle at Lepanto. The triumph made Don John a hero across Europe, including England, where Elizabeth ordered services of thanksgiving in all churches.

By 1574, however, Don John was involved in plots to invade England, dethrone Elizabeth, and rule the country as the husband of Mary STUART, Queen of Scots. He had earlier been rumored to be plotting an invasion of IRELAND. Nothing came of these plans, for in 1576 Philip named his brother governor-general of the NETHERLANDS, with responsibility for ending the NETHERLANDS REVOLT. In this position, Don John achieved some successes, but Spanish authority in the Netherlands was still deteriorating when he died there of typhus at age 31 in October 1578.

Further Reading: Geoffrey Parker, *Philip II,* Boston: Little, Brown, 1978; Sir Charles Petrie, *Don John of Austria,* New York: Norton, 1967.

joint-stock company

A joint-stock company is a trading enterprise in which a number of people invest money and agree to share liability and profits in proportion to their investment. Unlike the members of a REGULATED COMPANY, investors in a joint-stock company did not trade in person; the company pooled the capital of the individual investors and traded as a corporate body through paid agents known as factors. As Elizabethan trade expanded into new regions, such as Russia, where Englishmen had not traded before, few individual merchants had the capital for the SHIPS and cargoes needed to open the new markets, let alone the wherewithal for warehousing, business permits, gifts to rulers and officials, and living expenses in foreign ports. Because it could provide a greater fund of capital, the joint-stock trading company became the preferred instrument for extending English trade to new markets. A number of joint-stock trading companies were founded during the Elizabethan period, the most famous being the EAST INDIA COMPANY, formed in 1600 to carry on trade with India and Asia (see also EASTLAND COMPANY; GUINEA COMPANY; LEVANT COMPANY; MERCHANT ADVENTURERS; MUSCOVY COMPANY).

Many Elizabethan naval and PRIVATEERING expeditions were organized on a joint-stock basis, with the queen, various nobles and gentlemen, and groups of merchants investing in an expedition and sharing in any profits of trade or piracy the expedition brought back. The queen; Robert DUDLEY, Earl of Leicester; and Sir William CECIL were, for instance, investors in John HAWKINS's sec-

ond trade voyage to SPANISH AMERICA in 1564; similarly, the queen and others invested in many of Sir Francis DRAKE's piratical raids on SPAIN and her colonies. Many of the naval expeditions launched against Spain after the start of war in 1585 were joint-stock ventures financed partly by the queen and partly by private individuals and groups. This type of funding meant that such expeditions could not be purely military—they also had to capture enemy ships and bring home booty to pay for themselves and to provide a dividend for the queen and the other investors. Since the Crown was too poor by itself to pay for large naval expeditions, such a method of funding was necessary, although not always conducive to sound military tactics or the defense needs of the realm. *See also* FOREIGN TRADE.

Further Reading: G. D. Ramsay, *English Overseas Trade during the Centuries of Emergence,* London: Macmillan, 1957.

Jonson, Ben (1572–1637)

Along with William SHAKESPEARE and Christopher MARLOWE, Ben Jonson was among the most talented of Elizabethan dramatists. Born in Westminster outside LONDON, Jonson was tutored at Westminster School (see GRAMMAR SCHOOL) by William CAMDEN. Apprenticed against his wishes into his stepfather's trade of bricklaying, Jonson turned instead to acting, at which he was not good, and then to writing plays, at which he was excellent. In 1597, while a member of Pembroke's Men, Jonson co-wrote *Isle of Dogs* with Thomas NASHE. The play was considered seditious, and Jonson was briefly imprisoned. In 1598, Jonson barely escaped execution for killing another actor during a quarrel. After his release, Jonson wrote a number of plays for Shakespeare's company, the CHAMBERLAIN'S MEN, to perform at the GLOBE THEATRE.

In 1603, Shakespeare and the Chamberlain's Men (by then, the King's Men) performed Jonson's *Sejanus;* because this tragedy was too political and because Jonson was known to be a Catholic, he was summoned before the PRIVY COUNCIL for questioning, but he again escaped without serious consequences. The King's Men also performed various other works by Jonson, including the tragedy *Catiline* (1611) and the comedies *Volpone*

(1606), *The Alchemist* (1610), *Bartholomew Fair* (1614), *The Devil Is an Ass* (1616), and *The Staple of News* (1625). In 1605, Jonson's Catholicism caused him to be questioned about the Gunpowder Plot (see CATHOLICISM, ENGLISH). Although his situation was for a time serious, he was eventually released, an escape that convinced him to abandon Catholicism.

Between 1605 and 1612, Jonson wrote most of the masques performed at COURT (see MASQUE). His works were particularly popular with Queen Anne and attracted many courtiers as participants; for instance, Penelope RICH, Sir Philip SIDNEY's "Stella," took part in the *Masque of Blackness* performed on Twelfth Night (see CHRISTMAS) in 1605. Jonson collaborated with set designer Inigo Jones on masques and other court ENTERTAINMENTs until 1631. In 1616, Jonson published a collected edition of his poems, plays, and masques, and was in the same year recognized as the unofficial poet laureate of the court. He was also responsible for the largest body of literary criticism produced by any Elizabethan writer. Although not uncritical of Shakespeare's writing, Jonson was a friend of Shakespeare's and wrote some dedicatory verses for the FIRST FOLIO in 1623. Jonson died in 1637 and was buried in Westminster Abbey. *See also* DRAMA; POETRY.

Further Reading: J. B. Bamborough, *Ben Jonson,* London: Hutchison, 1970; Rosalind Miles, *Ben Jonson: His Life and Work,* London: Routledge and Kegan Paul, 1986; David Riggs, *Ben Jonson,* Cambridge, MA: Harvard University Press, 1989.

justices of the peace

Justices of the peace (JPs) were the principal administrative and judicial officials of LOCAL GOVERNMENT in Elizabethan England. The office had originated in the thirteenth century when Edward I had appointed keepers of the peace to assist the sheriffs. Under the Tudors (see TUDOR FAMILY), the Crown and PARLIAMENT greatly expanded the powers and duties of the JPs, making them the chief county officials. By Elizabeth's death in 1603, over 300 statutes had been passed by Parliament (two-thirds under the Tudors) to extend or redefine the duties of JPs. Each year, the Crown selected JPs for each county by naming them to a county commission of the peace. The JPs were local gentlemen with an annual income of at least £20 and some measure of social and political influence in the county (see GENTRY).

JPs had the power to arrest, imprison, indict, and hear and determine felonies and trespasses; they were also charged with suppressing riots and disorders and tracking down criminals. In their counties, they collected the taxes voted to the Crown by Parliament (see TAXATION), ordered the sheriff to impanel juries (see COMMON LAW), and regulated vagabonds, alehouses, weights and measures, wage levels, and the production of certain metals. Under Elizabeth, JPs also acquired responsibility for enforcing religious laws, especially those against RECUSANTS (see PENAL LAWS). The county commissions of JPs met four times a year in quarter sessions, usually in the chief town of the county. The JPs supervised and administered local government, enforcing the proclamations of the Crown (see PROCLAMATION) and the acts of Parliament, to which many JPs were elected.

The commissions of the peace functioned under the general supervision of the PRIVY COUNCIL in LONDON. Members of the commission were not paid for their services, so local commissions could and did ignore, delay, or obstruct enforcement of Council orders or parliamentary statutes with which its members did not agree. However, London and the county commissions usually worked in harmony because dismissal from the commission was a serious blow to a gentleman's local social position, and the threat of dismissal could usually elicit cooperation. *See also* Maps, "Counties of England and Wales, 1603."

Further Reading: David Loades, *Tudor Government,* Oxford: Blackwell Publishers, 1997; John H. Gleason, *The Justices of the Peace in England, 1558–1640,* Oxford: Clarendon Press, 1969; A. G. R. Smith, *The Government of Elizabethan England,* New York: W. W. Norton, 1967.

K

Kempe, William (d. 1609)

William Kempe was the leading comic actor of Elizabethan England and a close colleague of William SHAKESPEARE. Kempe began his career as a member of Leicester's Men, a company of players under the patronage of Robert DUDLEY, Earl of Leicester. The troupe accompanied Leicester to the NETHERLANDS in 1585–86 (see NETHERLANDS EXPEDITION). Kempe then left the company to tour in Denmark, returning to England by 1590, by which time he was already acknowledged as the "most comical" actor in LONDON. By 1592, Kempe, along with Shakespeare, was a member of Lord Strange's Men, contributing "merriments," short passages of humorous repartee, to the company's comedic productions.

Kempe was also widely known for his "jigs," humorous song-and-dance sketches that were often obscene. Several of Kempe's jigs, such as *Kempe's New Jig betwixt a Soldier and a Miser and Sym the Clown* (1595), were entered in the STATIONERS' REGISTER. Kempe's jigs were so popular they even attracted the criticism of disapproving PURITANS. In 1594, Kempe and Shakespeare, both shareholders in the CHAMBERLAIN'S MEN, were summoned to COURT to appear before the queen. Kempe performed many comedic roles in Shakespeare's plays, including Peter in *Romeo and Juliet* and Dogberry in *Much Ado About Nothing*.

In 1599, he became one of the original shareholders in the new GLOBE THEATRE but sold his interest soon after to prepare for his most famous exploit, a month-long morris dance from London to Norwich (see DANCE). Although Kempe left London on 11 February 1600 and danced into Norwich on 11 March, only nine days were taken up with dancing, the rest being spent on recovery and promotion. An overseer accompanied Kempe to ensure that he actually danced every one of the roughly 100 miles. Bets and gifts, including an annuity from the mayor of Norwich, made the venture a profitable one for Kempe, who derived further income from the exploit through publication of a book entitled *Kempe's Nine Days Wonder*. Kempe is known to have later visited Germany and Italy and to have joined Worcester's Men about 1602. Although listed in the FIRST FOLIO (1623) as one of the principal actors in Shakespeare's plays, Kempe died in 1609.

Further Reading: G. B. Harrison, *Elizabethan Plays and Players*, Ann Arbor: University of Michigan Press, 1956; A. P. Rossiter, *English Drama from Early Times to the Elizabethans*, Folcroft, PA: Folcroft Library Editions, 1977.

kern

The ANGLO-IRISH term "kern," deriving from an Irish word for war band, describes both a group of Irish mercenaries and the individual members of the group. Unlike the GALLOW-GLASSES, who were heavily armed troops of Scottish descent living in IRELAND, and the REDSHANKS, who were mercenary troops from SCOTLAND hired only for summer campaigning, the kern were light-armed native Irish employed year-round by Irish chieftains and Anglo-Irish lords to maintain their authority against rebellious tenants and local rivals.

In medieval Ireland, the kern were unattached self-organized bands of mercenaries, numbering usually 20 to 30 men, that roamed the countryside seeking military employment with a local chief. Because the kern traditionally fought without armor or helmets and carried only swords and wooden throwing darts, they were ill-suited to pitched battles, especially against the armored forces of the English. However, this lack of expensive armor and weaponry made the kern an indispensable part of most Irish armies, for kern were highly mobile and relatively inexpensive to recruit and maintain (see WEAPONS).

The kern were useful in harrying a rival's tenants, burning his villages, and plundering his cattle and other property. Also, when employed with a core of heavily armed gallowglasses or redshanks, kern gave Irish armies of the Elizabethan period the numbers they required to meet the increasingly large forces put into the field by the DUBLIN government. As English authority spread over the island in the sixteenth and seventeenth centuries, the use of kern gradually declined.

Further Reading: Steven G. Ellis, *Tudor Ireland,* London: Longman, 1985; Colm Lennon, *Sixteenth-Century Ireland: The Incomplete Conquest,* Dublin: Gill and Macmillan, 1994; Margaret MacCurtain, *Tudor and Stuart Ireland,* Dublin: Gill and Macmillan, 1972; David B. Quinn, *The Elizabethans and the Irish,* Ithaca, NY: Cornell University Press, 1966.

Killigrew, Sir Henry (c. 1528–1603)

Sir Henry Killigrew was a leading Elizabethan ambassador and diplomat (see DIPLOMACY). Although Killigrew was born into a prominent GENTRY family in Cornwall, little is known about his early life. He served in EDWARD VI's Parliament in 1552, but his opposition to MARY I's marriage to Prince Philip of SPAIN (see PHILIP II) sent him into exile in FRANCE with Sir Peter CAREW in January 1554. Killigrew returned to England after the accession of Elizabeth in 1558.

In 1559, the new queen sent him on a diplomatic mission to Germany and as an assistant to Sir Nicholas THROCKMORTON in France. In 1566 and 1567, the last troubled years of Mary STUART's reign, Elizabeth sent Killigrew several times to SCOTLAND. Killigrew was dispatched to Germany in 1569 to serve as the queen's ambassador to the German Protestant princes and was sent back to France in 1571. He returned to Scotland in 1572 to participate in the ultimately abortive negotiations for the return of Mary to Scottish

custody. Killigrew eventually persuaded Elizabeth to send English troops into Scotland to assist in the capture of EDINBURGH Castle from Queen Mary's supporters (see MAITLAND, WILLIAM). He stayed in Scotland until 1575, when he returned to England and retired from diplomatic service.

The NETHERLANDS EXPEDITION of Robert DUDLEY, Earl of Leicester, caused Killigrew to come out of retirement in 1585. He spent the years 1585 to 1589 serving on the Dutch Council of State as an advisor to Leicester and other English commanders. By 1591, when the queen sent him to France as an advisor to Robert DEVEREUX, Earl of Essex, Killigrew was the Crown's oldest and most experienced diplomat. For his services during Essex's French campaign, which was designed to help HENRI IV secure his throne, Killigrew was knighted (see BRITTANY EXPEDITIONS). After the campaign ended, Killigrew took part in further negotiations in France and the NETHERLANDS, but was prevented by illness from serving as ambassador to France in 1595. Killigrew died in March 1603, only three weeks before the death of the queen.

Further Reading: Amos C. Miller, *Sir Henry Killigrew,* Leicester: University of Leicester Press, 1963.

King's (Queen's) Bench, Court of

The Court of King's Bench (or Court of Queen's Bench under a female monarch) was the most important COMMON LAW court dealing with criminal matters. King's Bench evolved out of the medieval practice of subjects bringing their disputes directly before the monarch, or before his or her council, for judgment. In the twelfth century, Henry II appointed five royal justices to hear disputes in King's Bench, and in the thirteenth century, the chief justice was made president of King's Bench. Like the other principal common law courts, Common Pleas and the EXCHEQUER, King's Bench was, since the thirteenth century, permanently situated at Westminster Hall in LONDON (see COMMON PLEAS, COURT OF; WESTMINSTER PALACE).

Initially, King's Bench heard only cases involving the rights of the Crown and disputes between subjects, but by the Elizabethan period, King's Bench acted as a court of appeal to retry cases that may have been mishandled or improperly decided in Common Pleas or in other courts. Under the Tudors, King's Bench also developed a civil competence, encroaching on the jurisdiction of Common Pleas by claiming actions that might have a criminal component, such as matters of debt and trespass. Nonetheless, although King's Bench and Common Pleas had developed roughly similar jurisdictions by the end of Elizabeth's reign in 1603, the volume of business coming before the latter was still more than three times that of the former. Like Common Pleas and the Exchequer, but unlike the newer prerogative courts of EQUITY (see CHANCERY, COURT OF; REQUESTS, COURT OF; STAR CHAMBER, COURT OF), King's Bench followed the often inflexible and expensive procedures of the common law, including conducting its proceedings in medieval French rather than in ENGLISH.

Further Reading: Marjorie Blatcher, *The Court of King's Bench, 1450–1550: A Study in Self-Help,* London: Athlone Press, 1978; C. W. Brooks, *Pettyfoggers and Vipers of the Commonwealth: The "Lower Branch" of the Legal Profession in Early Modern England,* Cambridge: Cambridge University Press, 1986; Wilfrid R. Prest, *The Inns of Court under Elizabeth I and the Early Stuarts, 1590–1640,* London: Longman, 1972.

King's Men. *See* CHAMBERLAIN'S MEN.

Kinsale, Battle of

The Battle of Kinsale was the decisive battle of the NINE YEARS WAR. On 21 September 1601, a Spanish force of 3,400 under Don Juan del Águila landed at the Munster town of Kinsale on the southern coast of IRELAND to support the rebellion against English rule being led by Hugh O'NEILL, Earl of Tyrone. Believing himself too weak to take the field, Águila fortified Kinsale and awaited reinforcements either from Tyrone or from SPAIN. The English lord deputy, Charles BLOUNT, Lord Mountjoy, fearing that the arrival of the Spaniards would precipitate a general insurrection in southern IRELAND, moved quickly to defeat Águila before Tyrone could join him. By mid-October, Mountjoy had laid siege to Kinsale with 7,000 men.

Because the experienced Spanish infantry offered Tyrone his first real chance to defeat the English in open battle (and so force Elizabeth to come to a favorable settlement), the earl risked a winter march across Ireland, from Ulster in the north to Munster in the south. Red Hugh O'DONNELL, Tyrone's son-in-law, left Ulster in early November and managed to elude a force under Sir George CAREW that Mountjoy had sent to stop him. Tyrone departed a week later and, after trying unsuccessfully to distract Mountjoy by raiding the PALE, joined O'Donnell in Munster in early December. Reinforced by a new landing of several hundred Spanish troops and by Munster Irishmen, Tyrone trapped Mountjoy's army between his forces and the Spanish in Kinsale. Exposed to the winter and low on supplies, Mountjoy's army was slowly reduced by disease and desertion.

On 24 December 1601, Tyrone abandoned his usual caution and agreed to a joint assault on Mountjoy by his forces and the Spaniards. However, Mountjoy's cavalry drove the Irish horsemen into the main body of Tyrone's army, and the resulting confusion allowed Mountjoy to scatter the Irish before Águila could even launch his attack. His allies defeated, Águila surrendered on 2 January 1602 and agreed to withdraw from Ireland. The Battle of Kinsale broke the Irish rebellion. Carew pacified Munster while Mountjoy reduced Ulster. Unable to offer resistance, Tyrone went into hiding and finally submitted in March 1603, thus ending the Nine Years War.

Further Reading: Steven G. Ellis, *Tudor Ireland,* London: Longman, 1985; John J. Silke, *Kinsale: The Spanish Intervention in Ireland at the End of the Elizabethan Wars,* New York: Fordham University Press, 1970.

Knollys, Sir Francis (c. 1514–1596)

Sir Francis Knollys was an outspoken and respected councilor of Elizabeth I. As a young man, Knollys served at the COURT of HENRY VIII, where his father, Robert Knollys, was a court official. A strong Protestant, Knollys became a favorite of EDWARD VI (see FAVORITES) and went into exile in Europe (see MARIAN EXILES) after the accession in 1553 of MARY I, Edward's Catholic half sister. In 1546, Knollys married Katherine Carey, who, through her mother Mary (Boleyn) Carey (see BOLEYN FAMILY), elder sister to Anne BOLEYN, was first cousin to Princess Elizabeth (see genealogical chart in Appendix 1: "Howard Family in the Sixteenth Century—Elizabeth I's Maternal Relatives"). This marriage connection won Knollys a position of influence at court after Elizabeth's accession in 1558.

The queen appointed Knollys a member of the PRIVY COUNCIL and named him vice-chamberlain of the household. From 1572 until his death, Knollys also served as treasurer of the royal household, a post that he passed on to his son William. By the 1560s, Knollys was a staunch Puritan and spoke frequently in favor of Puritan causes in various Elizabethan parliaments. In the 1580s and 1590s, Knollys's Puritanism brought him into frequent conflict with his fellow privy councilor Archbishop John WHITGIFT, who was engaged at the time in suppressing Puritan nonconformity (see CLASSICAL MOVEMENT; PRESBYTERIAN MOVEMENT; PROPHESYINGS; PURITANS). Knollys was given custody of Mary STUART, Queen of Scots, on her first arrival in England in 1568, but gave her into the keeping of George TALBOT, Earl of Shrewsbury, in 1569.

Knollys's daughter, Lettice KNOLLYS, a second cousin of Elizabeth, married Robert DUDLEY, Earl of Leicester, the queen's favorite, in 1578. Not trusting Leicester, Knollys demanded a second ceremony at which he himself could be present as witness. When Elizabeth learned of the marriage (which was a secret to no one but her), Knollys's position with the queen did not suffer, even though Leicester was briefly imprisoned and Lettice Knollys was forbidden the court. Sir Francis Knollys was made a Knight of the Garter in 1593 and died in 1596.

Further Reading: Alan Haynes, *The White Bear: The Elizabethan Earl of Leicester*, London: Peter Owen, 1987; J. E. Neale, *Elizabeth I and Her Parliaments 1584–1601*, New York: St. Martin's Press, 1958.

Knollys, Lettice (1540–1634)

Because she did what the queen could not—marry Robert DUDLEY, Earl of Leicester—Lettice (or Laetitia) Knollys earned Elizabeth's deep and abiding hatred. Born in Oxfordshire, the daughter of Sir Francis KNOLLYS, Lettice was the queen's cousin, her mother being the daughter of Mary Boleyn, Elizabeth's maternal aunt (see genealogical chart in Appendix 1: "Howard Family in the Sixteenth Century—Elizabeth I's Maternal Relatives"). Attractive, self-assured, and red-haired like the queen, Lettice began Elizabeth's reign as a much favored maid of honor (see LADIES-IN-WAITING). In the early 1560s, she married Walter DEVEREUX, later Earl of Essex. She had a brief relationship with Leicester in 1565 that was resumed with greater passion a decade later. So notorious was their affair that when Essex died suddenly of dysentery in September 1576, rumors flooded the COURT that Leicester had poisoned the earl to have his wife.

The couple was secretly married on 21 September 1578. Leicester hid the marriage until August 1579, when Jean de Simier, the French ambassador, revealed it to the queen in an effort to undermine Leicester's opposition to the proposed marriage of Elizabeth to Francis VALOIS, Duke of Alençon. Only with great difficulty was the furious queen dissuaded from sending Leicester to the TOWER OF LONDON. The queen then unsuccessfully badgered one of Leicester's cast-off lovers to confirm rumors that the earl had secretly married her; by this means, Elizabeth hoped to force Leicester to give up Lettice and live with a woman he did not love. The queen's affection for Leicester was such that she eventually forgave him and readmitted him to his old position at court, but Lettice she never forgave, and the new Countess of Leicester was barred from court for the rest of her husband's lifetime.

At the earl's death in 1588, Elizabeth demanded that his property be auctioned to meet the huge debt he owed to the Crown; this process nearly bankrupted the widowed countess, who soon thereafter married Sir Christopher BLOUNT. Through the influence of Robert DEVEREUX, Earl of Essex, Lettice's son by her first husband, the countess came to court and was presented to the queen in 1598. But Elizabeth's rancor soon revived and Lettice was again banished; the estranged cousins never met again. Their last link snapped tragically in February 1601, when Essex and Blount were executed for TREASON (see ESSEX'S REBELLION). Thereafter, the countess lived quietly in the country, dying at age 94 in 1634.

Further Reading: Alan Haynes, *The White Bear: The Elizabethan Earl of Leicester*, London: Peter Owen, 1987; Anne Somerset, *Ladies-in-Waiting*, New York: Alfred A. Knopf, 1984.

Knox, John (c. 1512–1572)

John Knox was a Scottish Protestant reformer whose preaching and writings strongly influenced the course of both the Scottish and English Reformations (see REFORMATION, ENGLISH; REFORMATION, SCOTTISH).

EDWARD VI licensed Knox to preach in the English towns of Berwick and Newcastle. In 1552, Knox, then a royal chaplain, preached a sermon before the king that complained of a direction in Archbishop Thomas CRANMER's *BOOK OF COMMON PRAYER* for communicants to assume a kneeling posture when receiving the wafer at communion. Knox believed that kneeling too strongly implied an endorsement of Catholic doctrines about the actual presence of Christ's body and blood in the Eucharist (see TRANSUBSTANTIATION). Knox's sermon led to the insertion in the Prayer Book, over Cranmer's objections, of the BLACK RUBRIC, a footnote that explained kneeling at communion as an act of piety, not of adoration.

Knox fled to John CALVIN's Geneva after the accession of MARY I, a Catholic, in 1553 (see MARIAN EXILES). He was a vigorous opponent of the Marian regime and published a fierce attack on the queen in a 1558 work entitled *First Blast of the Trumpet against the Monstrous Regiment of Women*. The pamphlet cited scripture and classical writers to prove that women had no right to rule over men. *First Blast* so offended Elizabeth that she refused to allow Knox to return to England in 1559. Knox went instead to SCOTLAND where he became a leader of the Scottish Reformation and a strong opponent of Mary STUART, Queen of Scots. By encouraging the Protestant lords of Scotland and rousing the Protestant majorities in EDINBURGH and other towns, Knox's preaching, although inspiring some desecration of Catholic churches, helped ensure the success of the Scottish Reformation.

Knox took the lead in organizing the reformed Church of Scotland on a presbyterian pattern (see PRESBYTERIAN MOVEMENT); he sought a Scottish Church based solely on scriptural principles and governed by a series of councils ranging from the national to the local levels. Knox was heartened by the fall of Mary Stuart in 1567, but the need of subsequent Scottish governments to stay on good terms with Mary's captor, Elizabeth of England, robbed Knox of any political voice, for Elizabeth would have nothing to do with the author of *First Blast*. Knox died in November 1572, much venerated but little heeded.

Further Reading: Andrew Lang, *John Knox and the Reformation,* Port Washington, NY: Kennikat Press, 1967;

Stewart Lamont, *The Swordbearer: John Knox and the European Reformation,* London: Hodder and Stoughton, 1991; Jasper Ridley, *John Knox,* Oxford: Oxford University Press, 1968.

Kyd, Thomas (1558–1594)

Thomas Kyd, a close friend of Christopher MARLOWE and an important member of the LONDON literary community in the 1590s, was one of the most popular tragic poets and playwrights of the Elizabethan era. Kyd was born in London, the son of a scrivener (a scribe or professional copyist). He attended the Merchant Taylors' School (see GRAMMAR SCHOOL), where he met the future poet Edmund SPENSER, but he does not seem to have attended a university (see UNIVERSITIES). He entered his father's profession, but abandoned it by the mid-1580s for a literary career.

Kyd made a name for himself as a playwright through the frequent production in the early 1590s of his play *The Spanish Tragedy*. This immensely popular drama was acted several times in London in 1592 by Lord Strange's Men, an acting company under the patronage of Ferdinando STANLEY, Lord Strange, into

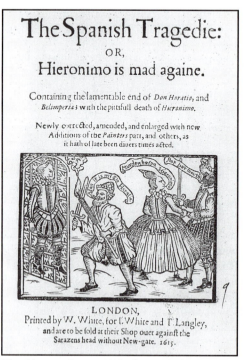

The title page from a 1615 edition of Thomas Kyd's play, *The Spanish Tragedy. By permission of the Folger Shakespeare Library.*

whose service Kyd had himself entered about 1590. *The Spanish Tragedy* was revived later in the decade by the CHAMBERLAIN'S MEN, a company of actors with which William SHAKESPEARE was associated. With this play, Kyd introduced the theme of revenge into Elizabethan drama. Apart from some translations of continental works and several pamphlets on contemporary London murders, no other publication can be definitely ascribed to Kyd, although he is thought to have written or collaborated on several anonymous plays of the period.

Kyd shared lodgings with Marlowe in the early 1590s and was part of a group of young writers, including Marlowe, Thomas NASHE, and Thomas LODGE, that regularly drank and caroused in London taverns. In early May 1593, the authorities arrested Kyd on suspicion of TREASON and heresy. They found documents in his lodging that denied the divinity of Christ, but Kyd convinced them that the papers belonged to Marlowe. Shortly after Marlowe's mysterious death in a tavern brawl on 30 May, Kyd was rearrested. He was tortured and forced to confess more about his late friend's atheistic views. Kyd was released soon after, but he died in poverty and debt in December 1594. *See also* DRAMA; POETRY.

Further Reading: Philip Edwards, *Thomas Kyd and Early Elizabethan Tragedy,* London: Longmans, 1966; Arthur Freeman, *Thomas Kyd, Facts and Problems,* Oxford: Clarendon Press, 1967.

L

ladies-in-waiting

At the Tudor court, access to the monarch was vital for furthering one's career and estate. For this reason, positions as personal attendants in the royal apartments and bedchamber were eagerly sought. With a queen on the throne, these positions went, of necessity, to women, who often came to serve as advocates, petitioners, and conduits of information for the men in their lives. Elizabeth's chamber staff consisted of four gentlewomen of the bedchamber, eight gentlewomen of the privy chamber, and six maids of honor. The first chief gentlewoman of the privy chamber was Katherine ASHLEY, who had been the queen's childhood governess. On Ashley's death in 1565, the post went to another longtime servant, Blanche PARRY. Many other chamber positions went to the queen's relatives, including her cousin Lettice KNOLLYS, who was a maid of honor.

Elizabeth's ladies served her meals, helped her dress, kept her informed and entertained, and generally functioned as her close family circle. The queen usually did not discuss matters of state with her ladies, but their usefulness in securing rewards and favors could be great, and they were often pestered by friends and relatives seeking to have a request or petition brought to the queen's attention. Besides being housed and fed at royal expense, the maids and ladies of the chamber had handsome salaries of some £30–£40 a year. The queen's ladies were expected to attend her daily, whether sick or well, and could not leave the COURT without permission, which was rarely granted since Elizabeth liked to have her regular servants about her and hated change in her domestic staff.

Elizabeth could be a difficult mistress, verbally and (on rare occasions) physically abusive when she was nervous, distressed, or ill. The queen could also be kindly and generous, especially in arranging suitable marriages for the young maids of honor. However, unauthorized dalliances brought severe consequences for both the maid and her lover. Walter RALEIGH and Edward de VERE, Earl of Oxford, both went to the TOWER OF LONDON for seducing one of the queen's ladies, and Elizabeth Vernon (see WRIOTHESLEY, ELIZABETH, COUNTESS OF SOUTHAMPTON) was roundly abused and threatened with prison when she was found to be pregnant by Henry WRIOTHESLEY, Earl of Southampton. For all the advantages that regular access to the monarch conferred, service in the queen's chamber was no sinecure. See also RALEIGH, ELIZABETH.

Further Reading: Anne Somerset, *Ladies-in-Waiting,* New York: Alfred A. Knopf, 1984.

Lambarde, William (1536–1601)

William Lambarde was the foremost Elizabethan antiquary (see ANTIQUARIANISM) and the author of the first English county history. The son of a merchant and sheriff of LONDON, Lambarde entered Lincoln's Inn (see INNS OF COURT) in 1556 and was called to the bar in 1567. The queen named him a justice of the peace for Kent in 1579 and later appointed him to several important recordkeeping offices, including, in 1601, keeper of records in the TOWER OF LONDON.

Lambarde devoted much time to scholarly legal pursuits; in 1568, he published *Archaionomia,* a collection of Anglo-Saxon

The Elizabethan antiquary William Lambarde, painted by an unknown artist. *By courtesy of the National Portrait Gallery, London.*

laws. His popular handbooks for JUSTICES OF THE PEACE and other public officials, *Eirenarcha* (1582) and *The Duties of Constables ... and Other Low and Lay Ministers of the Peace* (1583), were widely consulted and went through several editions. Although presented in manuscript to Sir Robert CECIL in 1591, Lambarde's *Archeion, or a Discourse upon the High Courts of Justice in England* was not published until 1635, and the diary of his work as a justice, *Ephemeris,* was not published until the twentieth century.

Although born in London, Lambarde lived in Kent, where he acquired property from his father and through each of his three marriages. In 1576, he published an immensely popular descriptive history of his adopted county, the *Perambulation of Kent,* which launched the genre of English county histories. He planned a similar history for the whole of England and WALES but abandoned the work when he learned that William CAMDEN was engaged in a project of the same kind (see *BRITANNIA*). In August 1601, only weeks before his death, he personally presented the queen with the manuscript of his *Pandecta Rotulorum,* a catalog of all documents housed in the Tower. Lambarde died at his manorhouse in Kent on 19 August 1601.

Further Reading: Retha M. Warnicke, *William Lambarde, Elizabethan Antiquary, 1536–1601,* London: Phillimore, 1973.

Lancaster, Sir James (1554–1618)

An early organizer of the EAST INDIA COMPANY, Sir James Lancaster was the first English trader and privateer to penetrate the Indian Ocean and the East Indies. Lancaster's father was a husbandman (see SOCIAL HIERARCHY) who apprenticed his son to a member of the Skinners' Company in 1571 (see LIVERIED COMPANY). Lancaster became a freeman of the company in 1579 and spent much of his early life plying his trade in Portugal. In 1588, Lancaster served against the ARMADA under Sir Francis DRAKE.

In 1591, he set sail as part of the first English expedition to the East Indies. Of the three ships that began the voyage, only Lancaster in the *Edward Bonaventure* reached the Indian Ocean, sickness and storms having turned back or destroyed the other vessels. Lancaster finally reached Penang on the Malay Peninsula, off which he captured several Portuguese vessels filled with pepper and other valuable cargoes from India. The return voyage was plagued by storms and lack of supplies. Lancaster sailed for SPANISH AMERICA, where part of his crew mutinied and left him marooned on an island until a French ship carried him to FRANCE. Lancaster finally reached England in May 1594. Within six months, Lancaster was at sea again, in command of a three-vessel fleet financed by LONDON merchants. Sailing to Pernambuco in Portuguese Brazil, he seized the port and loaded all the merchandise in the warehouses on his SHIPS, returning to England in July 1595 with a rich haul.

After helping to organize one of the PRIVATEERING expeditions of George CLIFFORD, Earl of Cumberland, Lancaster obtained command of the first East India Company expedition in 1601. Sickness again took a severe toll, although Lancaster's experiment of carrying along bottles of lime juice helped his crew better withstand the effects of scurvy. After reaching the East Indies, Lancaster captured a rich Portuguese vessel, opened trade relations with local rulers, and established the first English factory (trading post) in the region. He returned to England in September 1603 after a difficult voyage. JAMES I knighted

Lancaster, who devoted the rest of his life to building the East India Company and supporting efforts to discover the NORTHWEST PASSAGE. He died a wealthy man in June 1618.

Further Reading: F. R. Dulles, *The First English Adventurers to the Orient,* Freeport, NY: Books for Libraries Press, 1969; Sir William Foster, *The Voyages of Sir James Lancaster,* London: Hakluyt Society, 1940.

Lane, Sir Ralph (d. 1603)

Ralph Lane was the governor of Sir Walter RALEIGH's first Virginia colony (see ROANOKE COLONY [1585]). As a young man, Lane exhibited a desire for travel and adventure, unsuccessfully proposing various expeditions to William CECIL, Lord Burghley. In 1583, the government sent Lane to IRELAND to supervise the building of fortifications. In 1585, Lane joined the colonization expedition sent to Virginia by Walter Raleigh. The expedition was under the command of Sir Richard GRENVILLE, Raleigh's cousin, but the settlement to be established in North America was to be directed by Lane. Grenville and Lane quarreled bitterly, and when the former sailed for home to gather more supplies and colonists, Lane, anticipating Grenville's accusations against him, sent along a letter denouncing Grenville.

After the fleet's departure, Lane moved the colony of about 100 men from Wokokan Island to the north end of Roanoke Island (off present-day North Carolina; see illustration with AMADAS-BARLOWE EXPEDITION). Lane and his men explored the surrounding region for profitable commodities and quick sources of wealth, traveling as far north as Chesapeake Bay. Having arrived too late in the year to plant a crop, the colony soon found itself short of food and at odds with the local Indians, who grew increasing unwilling to trade with the Englishmen as their own food supplies dwindled. When a fleet under Sir Francis DRAKE stopped at Roanoke in June 1586, Lane and his colonists, then engaged in full-fledged hostilities with the Indians, eagerly boarded Drake's vessels and returned to England. When Lane and his men landed in July 1586, they likely brought ashore the first tobacco and potato plants seen in England.

During the ARMADA crisis of 1587–88, Lane was employed in raising troops and strengthening coastal defenses in Norfolk. In 1589, Lane served in the PORTUGAL EXPEDITION under Drake and Sir John NORRIS, and in 1590 he was part of a similar expedition under Sir John HAWKINS. Lane was posted to the army in Ireland in 1592 and was knighted for his services there in 1593. Although appointed keeper of Southsea Castle in Portsmouth, Lane exercised the office by deputy, for from 1595 until his death in October 1603, he resided in DUBLIN, where he continued to serve with the ARMY.

Further Reading: Karen Ordahl Kupperman, *Roanoke: The Abandoned Colony,* New York: Barnes and Noble, 1993; Samuel Eliot Morison, *The European Discovery of America: The Northern Voyages,* New York: Oxford University Press, 1971.

Langside, Battle of

The Battle of Langside ended any hope for Mary Stuart's restoration to the Scottish throne. After her confinement in Lochleven Castle in June 1567, Mary STUART, Queen of Scots, was forced to abdicate, and power passed to her half brother, James STUART, Earl of Moray, who ruled as regent for Mary's year-old son, James VI (see JAMES I). In the summer of 1567, the Confederate Lords, who had overthrown the queen, were united in their opposition to her continued rule, but by the end of the year, many of their number had second thoughts and began to speak for Mary's restoration. Mary's growing body of supporters attempted to blame her difficulties on her third husband, the exiled James HEPBURN, Earl of Bothwell.

To counter this rising pro-Mary sentiment, Moray used the meeting of PARLIAMENT in December 1567 to openly accuse the ex-queen of complicity in the murder of her second husband, Henry STUART, Lord Darnley (see DARNLEY MURDER). Although Moray hinted at the existence of the CASKET LETTERS, which would later seem to prove Mary's involvement in the murder, this first public accusation of the queen had little effect on Mary's supporters. Thus, when Mary escaped from Lochleven in May 1568, a large army quickly formed around her. Refusing offers to negotiate, Moray met the queen's army at Langside near Glasgow on 13 May. Mary's army was larger, perhaps by as many as 3,000 men, but at a critical point in the battle, Mary's commander, Archibald Campbell, Earl of Argyll, failed to lead the main body of the army forward. Argyll later claimed that he had fainted or suffered an epileptic fit, but it is more likely that he had again come to doubt Mary's fitness to rule, or had come to some treacherous agreement with Moray.

Watching from a nearby hill, Mary rode forward to encourage her troops, but many were already scattering and the battle was lost. The queen panicked; instead of regrouping to fight another day, she fled south, crossing into England two weeks later, against the advice of her supporters. Believing that Elizabeth would quickly restore her, Mary instead found herself placed into a confinement that ended only with her execution in 1587. *See also* SCOTLAND.

Further Reading: J. D. Mackie, *A History of Scotland,* 2nd ed., New York: Dorset Press, 1985; Jenny Wormald, *Mary, Queen of Scots,* London: Collins and Brown, 1991.

Laws of Ecclesiastical Polity

Richard HOOKER's eight-volume work, the *Laws of Ecclesiastical Polity,* is both a brilliant defense of the ANGLICAN CHURCH against Puritan criticisms (see PURITANS) and a systematic statement of Anglican philosophy. In the 1590s, Archbishop John WHITGIFT appointed Hooker to a pair of quiet country parishes where his clerical duties would not interfere with his writing. By Hooker's death in 1600, the first five volumes of the *Laws* had been published, and their arguments were being used by English Church leaders to influence debate in PARLIAMENT on various bills involving the treatment of Puritan nonconformists. The last three volumes, which were still undergoing revision when Hooker died, were not published until 1648 (sixth and eighth volumes) and 1662 (seventh volume). Because of this delay, questions were raised about the authenticity of these volumes, although most scholars today accept them as the work of Hooker.

In the *Laws,* Hooker refuted the Puritan claim that the presbyterian form of church government was mandated by scripture (see PRESBYTERIAN MOVEMENT). Hooker accepted the Bible as the guide for human spiritual life, but denied that it expressly prescribed any particular type of church government. He believed that the form church governance took was an indifferent matter that could be what-

ever human reason found to be convenient and appropriate. Hooker saw reason as the instrument by which humans could know and understand God's natural law, that is, the set of divine principles by which humans could order their lives and societies. Although a part of medieval philosophy, natural law was a concept still widely accepted in humanist (see HUMANISM) and Protestant thought, and it thus gave Hooker a firm basis on which to defend the practices and ceremonies of the Anglican Church.

Although Puritans had attacked the Anglican *BOOK OF COMMON PRAYER* as filled with unscriptural corruptions derived from Catholic practice, Hooker argued that ceremonies were also indifferent matters that could be ordered in any way Anglican Church officials thought proper. Hooker's acceptance of natural law also led him to defend both bishops and the royal supremacy, not as absolute necessities, but as acceptable forms of church government hallowed by tradition and reason (see SUPREMACY, ROYAL). Through the clarity, logic, and grace of Hooker's writing, the widely influential *Laws of Ecclesiastical Polity* gave the Anglican Church a set of philosophical principles by which it could distinguish itself from both Catholicism and Puritanism (see CATHOLICISM, ENGLISH).

Further Reading: Stanley Archer, *Richard Hooker,* Boston: Twayne, 1983; Robert K. Faulkner, *Richard Hooker and the Politics of Christian England,* Berkeley: University of California Press, 1981; Peter Lake, *Anglicans and Puritans,* Boston: Allen and Unwin, 1988.

Leaver, Thomas. *See* LEVER, THOMAS.

lectureships

Lectureships were salaried preaching appointments endowed by towns, parishes, or individuals that were instrumental in the development of Elizabethan Puritanism. The regular parish clergy were required by law to conduct worship services according to the *BOOK OF COMMON PRAYER,* a form of liturgy that many advanced Protestants, especially those MARIAN EXILES who had experienced the reformed churches of Europe, found to be entirely too conservative. By obtaining a lectureship, a Protestant reformer whose views were too extreme to acquire a regular Anglican BENEFICE could earn a livelihood and preach freely without interference from Church authorities. The lecturers did not conduct worship services but instead preached sermons after the regular Sunday service or in the morning or evening during the week.

By the early years of Elizabeth's reign, several LONDON parishes had already engaged lecturers who delivered sermons six mornings a week. In provincial towns, civic magistrates hired lecturers to preach weekday sermons; the town of Coventry engaged the reformer Thomas LEVER, and by the late 1570s, the town of Ipswich was employing two lecturers at the handsome stipend of £50 per year. Many reformers were also appointed to lectureships under the patronage of Protestant noblemen or gentlemen (see GENTRY); John FOXE preached for a time under the patronage of Thomas HOWARD, Duke of Norfolk. Robert DUDLEY, Earl of Leicester, and other prominent political figures of Puritan leanings employed preachers who had been expelled from their regular benefices for nonconformity (see PURITANS).

In the 1560s, many lecturers initiated local prophesyings, unauthorized conferences of Puritan preachers at which passages from the Bible were read and discussed (see PROPHESYINGS). Because parishioners were allowed to attend prophesyings, Puritan ideas were spread widely among local Anglican congregations. By allowing Puritan preachers opportunities to teach and deliver sermons—and so to circumvent the queen's and the official Church's opposition to radical preaching—lectureships did more than any other agency to establish and maintain Puritanism in Elizabethan England. *See also* ANGLICAN CHURCH.

Further Reading: Paul S. Seaver, *The Puritan Lectureships,* Stanford, CA: Stanford University Press, 1970.

Le Havre expedition

The Le Havre expedition (also known as the Newhaven expedition) was Elizabeth's first formal military involvement in a continental conflict. In September 1562, England and the French HUGUENOTS signed the Treaty of Hampton Court, which obligated Elizabeth to supply the Huguenots with a large subsidy and 3,000 troops for their war against the extremist Catholic forces led by the GUISE FAMILY (see HAMPTON COURT, TREATY OF). Pressured to aid the Huguenot cause by Protestants in her government—like William CECIL, Robert DUDLEY, and her ambassador in Paris, Sir Nicholas THROCKMORTON—Elizabeth accepted the agreement to prevent the Guises from winning the civil war and invading England. In return for her help, Elizabeth demanded that the Huguenots give her the port of Le Havre, which she hoped to exchange for CALAIS when the war was over.

On 1 October 1562, Elizabeth appointed Ambrose DUDLEY, Earl of Warwick (Robert Dudley's brother) to command the English forces. Warwick took control of Le Havre on 4 October, and English garrisons were sent to assist the Huguenots in defending Dieppe and Rouen. However, Rouen fell to the Catholics on 26 October and the English garrison in Dieppe had to be withdrawn. The PRIVY COUNCIL sent reinforcements to Warwick, and the queen reaffirmed her support for the Huguenot cause with more money. But the death in battle of Anthony of Navarre, the Huguenot leader, and the assassination, on 24 February, of the Catholic leader, Francis, Duke of Guise, allowed the queen mother, Catherine de MEDICI, to negotiate a settlement and unite all parties against the English.

Undaunted by the betrayal of the Huguenots, who had made peace without consulting her, Elizabeth decided to keep Le Havre. The combined French forces laid siege to the town, but Warwick held out until the PLAGUE struck his men in early June. In late July, the French captured the harbor, closing off the possibility of reinforcement by sea and dooming the English garrison. With the queen's permission, Warwick surrendered on 29 July, thus ending the Newhaven expedition in humiliation and failure. The French allowed Warwick and his survivors to return to England, but the costly fiasco left Elizabeth wary of any further foreign entanglements until the threat of Spanish invasion compelled her to intervene in the NETHERLANDS in the mid-1580s. *See also* WITTINGHAM, WILLIAM.

Further Reading: Frederic J. Baumgartner, *France in the Sixteenth Century,* New York: St. Martin's Press, 1995.

Leicester, Earl of. *See* DUDLEY, ROBERT, EARL OF LEICESTER.

Leicester's Netherlands expedition. *See* NETHERLANDS EXPEDITION.

Lennox, Countess of. *See* DOUGLAS, MARGARET, COUNTESS OF LENNOX.

Leslie, John (1527–1596)

John Leslie (or Lesley) was the most active and loyal supporter of Mary STUART, Queen of Scots, during her long imprisonment in England. Although the illegitimate son of a Scottish country priest, Leslie was educated at various Scottish and French UNIVERSITIES. He taught canon law (i.e., church law) at King's College, Aberdeen, in the early 1550s and was ordained a priest in 1558. In January 1561, he was among the Catholic clerics who debated religion with John KNOX and other reformers at EDINBURGH. A group of Catholic nobles sent him to FRANCE later in the year to persuade Mary to return to SCOTLAND. The queen took an immediate liking to him and brought him back to Scotland with her in August. He became the queen's chief ecclesiastical advisor in 1561, a privy councilor in 1565, and Bishop of Ross in 1566.

After Mary's abdication in 1567 and flight to England in 1568, Leslie defended her before the English commissioners convened in York to examine the charges brought against her by the government of her Protestant half brother, James STUART, Earl of Moray. Leslie then spent some months with Mary at Tutbury, her place of confinement, before coming to LONDON to represent her at the English COURT. In 1569, he used an assumed name to publish *A Defense of the Honor of the Right High, Mighty and Noble Princess Marie, Queen of Scotland . . .,* which was suppressed by the English government but later reprinted in Europe.

As the sole means of secure communication between Mary and her supporters, Leslie involved himself on Mary's behalf in the NORTHERN REBELLION of 1570 and the RIDOLFI PLOT of 1571. Imprisoned in the TOWER OF LONDON for the Ridolfi conspiracy, he was forced to give evidence against Thomas HOWARD, Duke of Norfolk, one of the principals of the plot. Leslie was released in 1573 but ordered to leave England; he im-

mediately began an unsuccessful search for support for Mary among the Catholic princes of Europe. In 1578, he published in Rome a Latin history of Scotland to the early fifteenth century. Leslie spent the last years of his life in France and the NETHERLANDS, dying near Brussels on 31 May 1596, nine years after Mary's execution in England.

Further Reading: Jenny Wormald, *Mary, Queen of Scots,* London: Collins and Brown, 1991.

Levant Company

The Levant (or Turkey) Company was an English JOINT-STOCK COMPANY chartered in 1581 to conduct trade with the Turkish-controlled eastern Mediterranean. The company had the exclusive right to trade with the empire of the Ottoman Turks, which in the late sixteenth century controlled not only Turkey, but Syria, Palestine, Egypt, and much of the Balkan Peninsula of Eastern Europe. The company shipped English linens and woolens to its factories (trading posts) at Smyrna (the modern town of Izmir) on the Aegean in western Turkey and to Aleppo on the Mediterranean in western Syria (see CLOTH INDUSTRY). In return, Levant company traders brought back to England spices, silks, carpets, fruits, currants, and other Eastern products.

In 1593, when the Levant Company merged with the Venice Company, the queen granted a new charter expanding the company's monopoly area to include the Venetian Republic in northern Italy and the overland trade route to India. In 1595, the Levant Company transformed itself into a REGULATED COMPANY. The Levant Company remained profitable into the seventeenth century, paying the salaries of the English ambassador in Turkey and of the English trade representatives in the Middle East. The company's annual trading fleets faced many difficulties, including Barbary pirates (from North Africa), Venetian rivals in the Middle East, French rivals in Turkey, and, after 1585, Spanish hostility in the western Mediterranean. Although the company's monopoly ended in 1753, it continued to pay the salaries of the ambassador and trade representatives until 1803. *See also* MONOPOLIES.

Further Reading: Mortimer Epstein, *The Early History of the Levant Company,* London: George Routledge and Sons, 1968; G. D. Ramsay, *English Overseas Trade during the Centuries of Emergence,* London: Macmillan, 1957; A. C. Wood, *A History of the Levant Company,* London: Frank Cass and Co., 1964.

Lever, Thomas (1521–1577)

Thomas Lever (or Leaver) was one of the leading Puritan preachers of Elizabethan England (see PURITANS). Born in Lancashire, Lever took his degrees at St. John's College, Cambridge (see UNIVERSITIES), becoming a college preacher in 1548. A friend of Roger ASCHAM, the Protestant tutor to Princess Elizabeth, Lever was also a member of a circle of extreme reformers at Cambridge. After his ordination in 1550, Lever was invited several times to preach at COURT before EDWARD VI. At the king's death in 1553, Lever supported the unsuccessful attempt to place Jane GREY, a Protestant, on the throne, and fled to Europe when Princess Mary (see MARY I), a Catholic, was proclaimed queen (see MARIAN EXILES; NORTHUMBERLAND'S COUP). In 1556, after spending time in Geneva and experiencing the church of John CALVIN, Lever became minister of an English exile community in Germany.

On his return to England in 1559, Lever won appointment to several benefices in the ANGLICAN CHURCH, including archdeacon of Coventry (1559) and prebendary at Durham Cathedral (1564) (see BENEFICE). By consistently refusing to wear the clerical dress prescribed by queen and PARLIAMENT, Lever was deprived of the latter position in 1568 (see VESTIARIAN CONTROVERSY). Because Lever continued to preach in Coventry and LONDON in the simple black gown preferred by Puritans, he was called before an ecclesiastical court in 1571 to answer for his nonconformity.

In the 1570s, Lever encouraged the holding of prophesyings throughout his archdeaconry (see PROPHESYINGS). These meetings of Puritan ministers and believers, which were occurring all over the country, angered the queen, and she ordered the bishops to suppress them. Because Lever received the unwelcome order to close all such gatherings in his archdeaconry in June 1577, only a month before his death, he was likely spared further difficulties with his ecclesiastical superiors.

Further Reading: Patrick Collinson, *The Elizabethan Puritan Movement,* Oxford: Clarendon Press, 1990.

limning

"Limning" was the Elizabethan term for the art of miniature painting, a highly popular art form among Elizabethan courtiers, nobles, GENTRY, and merchants, especially after 1570. HENRY VIII had commissioned miniature portraits of family members and of prospective spouses from miniature painters in Flanders, but the leading Elizabethan miniaturists were an Englishman, Nicholas HILLIARD, and a French émigré, Isaac OLIVER. Hilliard's work was technically stunning and highly popular. He was the greatest exponent of the art, writing his *Treatise on the Art of Limning* and refining his technique to the point of only painting in silk clothes to prevent any contamination of his work by dust.

During the course of the reign, miniatures evolved from small intimate portraits of friends and family members, or tokens of love and dalliance, to more elaborate romantic, theatrical, allegorical, and patriotic works of art worn as personal adornment. In the 1560s, miniatures were still precious objects meant mainly for royalty and nobility. In 1564, Elizabeth showed Sir James MELVILLE, the Scottish ambassador, her miniature portrait of Robert DUDLEY, Earl of Leicester, part of a collection of miniatures kept neatly wrapped in paper in the royal bedchamber. By the 1590s, Hilliard's studio was mass producing miniatures for a

A design for the Great Seal of Ireland by Nicholas Hilliard, the most famous Elizabethan limner, features Elizabeth I. © *The British Museum.*

much wider clientele. These later works glorified the state and the monarchy through allegorical and symbolical representations of the queen (see VIRGIN QUEEN).

Oliver fell into disfavor by painting the aging Elizabeth as he saw her in the 1590s, but Hilliard painted the so-called "Mask of Youth," an idealized image of the queen as a young woman. The much-praised and sought after painting both pleased the monarch and fit perfectly into the growing cult of Elizabeth as the embodiment of the state. Limning helped put the Renaissance fascination with personality at the service of the state by identifying the state with the personality of the monarch, and by glorifying the individual as a member of the state and a servant of the queen. *See also* ART.

Further Reading: Mary Edmond, *Hilliard and Oliver,* London: R. Hale, 1983.

liveried company

The liveried companies of LONDON were the Elizabethan successors to the medieval guilds, the civic associations of merchants and craftsmen that controlled the trade and industry of the city. Although Elizabethan London had almost 100 liveried companies, the 12 most powerful were the Mercers (dealers in textiles), Grocers (dealers in foodstuffs), Drapers (dealers in cloth, clothing, or dry goods), Fishmongers, Goldsmiths, Skinners, Merchant Taylors, Haberdashers (dealers in small wares and personal items), Salters, Ironmongers, Vintners (wine merchants), and Clothworkers. The Stationers' Company, the association of printers and booksellers, maintained the STATIONERS' REGISTER of published works, but, having been founded only in 1557, never acquired the power and prestige of the 12 great companies.

The companies regulated work conditions and practices within their trade, established rules of apprenticeship, administered benefactions, provided almshouses and other charities for the local poor, and encouraged the religious worship of their membership, usually at a specific company church. The liveried companies administered city courts, collected taxes, and organized civic celebrations; they also provided financial assistance to the widows and orphans of deceased members, as well as to members and their families during times of illness or other economic hardship.

Besides regulating the economic life of London, the liveried companies also dominated the city government by controlling access to the "freedom" of the city, in other words, to citizenship. Only by being a member of a company could a Londoner become a citizen, and only by being a citizen could a Londoner vote, start a business, and exercise other political and economic rights. The lord mayor of London was always chosen from among the senior leadership (known as the "livery") of the most important companies. While roughly 75 percent of Elizabethan London's male residents were freemen, or citizens, few of the city's female residents held citizenship.

Further Reading: Martin Holmes, *Elizabethan London,* New York: Frederick A. Praeger, 1969; Roy Porter, *London: A Social History,* Cambridge, MA: Harvard University Press, 1994.

local government

In Elizabeth's reign, England and WALES were divided into 53 shires (or counties), which served as the main units of local government (see Maps, "Counties of England and Wales, 1603"). Because the Crown had no professional and salaried bureaucracy, it relied on the social and political elite of each county (i.e., the local GENTRY) to administer the shires in the royal interest. Through a series of largely unpaid local offices, the gentry implemented government policy in the shires by enforcing royal proclamations and parliamentary statutes (see PARLIAMENT; PROCLAMATION).

In Elizabethan times, the most important local officials were the JUSTICES OF THE PEACE (JPs), who had both administrative and judicial functions. Each year the Crown appointed a commission of the peace for each county that included between 30 and 60 men selected on the basis of their social, political, and economic position within the shire. Most of the work of the commission was undertaken by the quorum, a specially nominated inner circle of JPs that was often centered on members with legal experience. The *custos rotulorum* was a member of the quorum appointed to keep the records of the commission. Another important county official was the sheriff, an ancient office that, by the Elizabethan period, conferred more prestige than power. The Elizabethan sheriff supervised local prisons, impaneled juries, and carried out criminal sentences imposed by the JPs.

Other shire officials included the coroner, who investigated suspicious deaths; the escheator, who enforced the Crown's feudal rights (see FISCAL FEUDALISM); the customer, who collected certain taxes (see TAXATION); and the constable, who kept peace within the hundred, an administrative subdivision of the shire. A more recent local office was that of lord lieutenant, a military official responsible for supervising the county MILITIA, storing and maintaining stocks of arms and ammunition, and organizing local defenses. Local noblemen were often named lord lieutenant for a group of counties, with deputy lieutenants under them responsible for one county each. Lord lieutenants were appointed on an ad hoc basis until the war with SPAIN in the 1580s demanded more regular arrangements for local defense; thereafter, lord lieutenants were appointed for life.

Working under the JPs in the shires were such parish officers as the constables, who kept the peace within a parish; watchmen, who assisted the constables; and surveyors of the highways and overseers of the poor, who maintained roads and supervised poor relief within each parish (see POOR LAWS).

Further Reading: David Loades, *Tudor Government,* Oxford: Blackwell Publishers, 1997; A. G. R. Smith, *The Government of Elizabethan England,* New York: W. W. Norton, 1967.

Lodge, Thomas (c. 1558–1625)

Thomas Lodge, whose writings supplied patterns for some of the works of William SHAKESPEARE, was among the most influential dramatists and romantic writers of Elizabethan England. The son of a former mayor of LONDON, Lodge was educated at the Merchant Taylors' School in London (see GRAMMAR SCHOOL) and at Trinity College, Oxford (see UNIVERSITIES). He entered Lincoln's Inn in 1578 (see INNS OF COURT) but soon left the law for a literary career. His first published work was the pamphlet *A Defense of Plays* (1580), which responded to an earlier attack on DRAMA by Stephen Gosson. When Gosson's reply attacked Lodge's character, Lodge published *An Alarm against Usurers* (1584), a denunciation of moneylenders who lured dissolute young gentlemen into debt.

Lodge, who in the 1590s was part of the riotous circle of young writers that included Thomas KYD and Christopher MARLOWE, probably based *An Alarm* on his own experience.

In the mid-1580s, Lodge published his first romance, *The Delectable History of Forbonius and Priscilla,* and a verse piece, *The Lamentable Complaint of Truth over England.* Lodge's *Scylla's Metamorphosis* (1589) was the first Elizabethan attempt at a romantic treatment in verse of a classical subject and became the inspiration for Shakespeare's later poem *Venus and Adonis.* In 1588, Lodge joined a PRIVATEERING expedition to the AZORES, and in 1591, he was part of a similar voyage to South America. On the Azores trip, Lodge wrote *Rosalynde,* his best-known romance and a likely source for Shakespeare's *As You Like It;* the South American voyage yielded another romance, *Margarite of America.*

In the 1590s, Lodge wrote a series of romances, including *Euphues Shadow* (1592), a collection of sonnets and lyric poems (1593), and several plays, including *The Wounds of the Civil War* (1594). He also wrote several pamphlets, including *Wit's Misery, and the World's Madness,* a denunciation of Elizabethan vices. In the late 1590s, Lodge embraced Catholicism, and in 1600 he began a new career as a physician, earning a degree at a French university. He practiced MEDICINE in London and in the NETHERLANDS, where he fled for a time after 1605 when the Gunpowder Plot made life in England difficult for Catholics (CATHOLICISM, ENGLISH). After 1600, he produced mostly medical works and translations. He died in London in October 1625. *See also* AMERICA; POETRY.

Further Reading: Wesley D. Rae, *Thomas Lodge,* New York: Twayne, 1967.

Lok, Michael (c. 1532–1615)

As the main financial backer for Sir Martin FROBISHER's voyages of American exploration, Michael Lok was instrumental in furthering the Elizabethan search for a NORTHWEST PASSAGE. Lok's father, a LONDON merchant, sent his son to FRANCE and the NETHERLANDS in about 1545 for training in languages and commerce. While engaged in trade in SPAIN and Portugal in the 1550s, Lok witnessed firsthand the lucrative Iberian trade with the

New World and conceived a desire to travel and see new lands himself.

Lok spent the next 20 years traveling around Europe and commanding numerous trade voyages to the Middle East. Having a facility for languages, Lok studied the history, culture, and trade potential of every land he visited, spending large sums on books and maps. In 1576, Lok's imagination was fired by Martin Frobisher's enthusiastic belief in the existence of a Northwest Passage around North America to Asia. At his own expense, Lok purchased most of the supplies for Frobisher's first voyage. When Frobisher returned with what seemed to be gold ore, Lok helped form (and became governor of) the Cathay Company, a JOINT-STOCK COMPANY created to finance Frobisher's next two voyages.

When the ore proved worthless and the 1577 and 1578 expeditions failed to find a Northwest Passage, Lok went bankrupt and was forced to beg the PRIVY COUNCIL for relief for his large family. Lok never recovered more than a small portion of the money he had invested, and he found himself financially embroiled with Cathay Company creditors and investors for the rest of his life. For a time, Lok was even imprisoned in the Fleet prison for failure to pay for one of the vessels used on Frobisher's third voyage. After his release in about 1587, Lok engaged for a time in trade in DUBLIN, and in 1592 he served as consul in Syria for the LEVANT COMPANY, a joint-stock enterprise trading in the Middle East. He died in 1615, still involved in legal actions arising from the unpaid debts of the long defunct Cathay Company.

Further Reading: Samuel Eliot Morison, *The European Discovery of America: The Northern Voyages,* New York: Oxford University Press, 1971.

London

Elizabethan London was the seat of English government and the largest and richest city in the British Isles (see Maps, "Elizabethan London"). In 1500, London was small by European standards, with a POPULATION of about 75,000. By the death of Elizabeth in 1603, London was one of the largest cities in Europe, with a population of about 200,000. It was far more populous than the second largest city in the realm, Norwich, which had about 15,000

people in 1603. Economic opportunity drew people from all over Britain to London; about one-eighth of the population of Elizabethan England lived in London at some time in their lives. Because its death rate was so high (see PLAGUE) and its birth rate so low, London relied on immigration to grow. Historical demographers estimate that over 3,000 immigrants entered Elizabethan London each year.

London was the political and legal capital of England; PARLIAMENT and the courts of COMMON LAW were situated only a mile outside the city at Westminster (see WESTMINSTER PALACE). London was also the nation's economic capital, its own political influence deriving from its great wealth. Over half the Crown's tax revenue from towns came from London, as did more than two-thirds of the Crown's CUSTOMS REVENUE and huge amounts of money from loans made to the Crown by city merchants (see BOROUGHS; TAXATION). Outside the university towns of Cambridge and Oxford, London was England's most important educational center, housing Gresham College (see GRESHAM, THOMAS), the INNS OF COURT, and the country's finest GRAMMAR SCHOOLS. Physically, London was a small town confined within its medieval walls; only about a half hour was required to walk from the TOWER OF LONDON on the east to St. Paul's Cathedral on the west.

The city was divided into 26 wards (including one for Southwark across the Thames), which were subdivided into 242 precincts. Each ward was administered by an alderman and each precinct by a common councilman. The courts of aldermen and of common council performed important legislative and judicial functions within the city government. London was also divided into 111 parishes and contained 100 LIVERIED COMPANIES. The companies regulated the city economy, collected taxes, and provided various social services. Only company members were citizens, or freemen, and only freemen could vote, establish businesses, or enjoy other civic and economic rights. By Elizabeth's reign, most adult male residents of London were freemen, while citizenship was rarely extended to WOMEN. *See also* illustrations for TOWER OF LONDON; WHITEHALL PALACE.

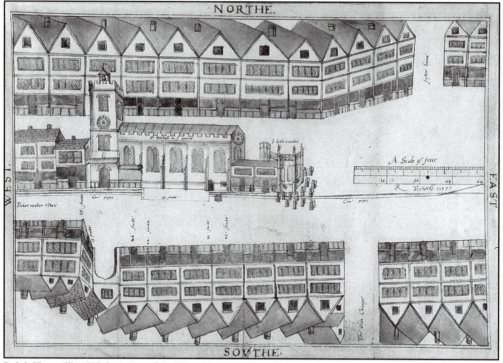

Ralph Treswell's 1585 depiction of the West-Cheap section of Elizabethan London. © *The British Museum.*

Further Reading: Ian Archer, *The Pursuit of Stability: Social Relations in Elizabethan London*, Cambridge: Cambridge University Press, 1991; A. L. Beier and Roger Finlay, eds., *London 1500–1700: The Making of the Metropolis*, London: Longman, 1986; Susan Brigden, *London and the Reformation*, Oxford: Clarendon Press, 1989; Frank F. Foster, *The Politics of Stability: A Portrait of the Rulers in Elizabethan London*, London: Royal Historical Society, 1977; Martin Holmes. *Elizabethan London*, New York: Frederick A. Praeger, 1969; Roy Porter, *London: A Social History*, Cambridge, MA: Harvard University Press, 1994; Francis Sheppard, *London: A History*, Oxford: Oxford University Press, 1998; Norman Lloyd Williams, *Tudor London Visited*, London: Cassell, 1991.

Lopez plot

The Lopez plot was an obscure and dubious Spanish conspiracy against Elizabeth that supposedly centered on the queen's physician, Roderigo LOPEZ, a Portuguese JEW. Uncovered and pursued furiously by Robert DEVEREUX, Earl of Essex, the queen's young favorite, the plot probably had more to do with political rivalries at COURT between Essex and the Cecils (see CECIL, ROBERT; CECIL, WILLIAM, LORD BURGHLEY) than with any actual treason by Lopez.

Essex hated Lopez, whose foreign and Jewish birth made him an easy target, because the physician had severely and publicly criticized Essex's policies and conduct. In 1594, sensing an opportunity for revenge, Essex ordered the arrest of a Spanish agent who had visited Lopez. Under interrogation, the agent revealed the existence of a Spanish conspiracy to kill Don Antonio, a claimant to the Portuguese throne (held by PHILIP II of SPAIN) then resident in England. Further investigation led to the capture of other Spanish agents, one of whom confessed that he had been sent to England to bribe Lopez to work for Spain. Essex and the Cecils arrested Lopez and subjected him to intense questioning. Lopez ably defended himself, and Robert Cecil reported to Elizabeth that Essex was persecuting her physician. The queen angrily rebuked Essex, an occurrence that likely did not improve the earl's opinion of Lopez.

Several days later, Essex announced that he had uncovered a plot by Lopez to poison the queen. The earl coerced the captive Spanish agents into backing up his story and sent his own agents out to stir up anti-Spanish and anti-Semitic feeling among the people—the popular earl was to prove himself dangerously adept at arousing public opinion in his favor.

Under further interrogation, Lopez broke and admitted guilt. Despite later recantations, Lopez was quickly tried and convicted of TREASON, but Elizabeth, doubtful of his guilt and suspicious of Essex, delayed signing the death warrant for three months. She finally gave in to pressure from Essex and public opinion, and Lopez was executed before jeering crowds at Tyburn in June 1594.

Further Reading: Robert Lacey, *Robert, Earl of Essex,* New York: Atheneum, 1971.

Lopez, Roderigo (d. 1594)

A Portuguese Jew living and practicing MEDICINE in England, Roderigo Lopez was destroyed by the vanity of Robert DEVEREUX, Earl of Essex, and immortalized by the genius of William SHAKESPEARE. Born into a Jewish family, Lopez fled his native Portugal in 1559 to escape the Catholic Inquisition. Trained as a doctor, he settled in LONDON and served until 1580 as house physician at St. Bartholomew's Hospital. His professional reputation grew rapidly in the 1580s and his patients soon included William CECIL, Lord Burghley, and Sir Francis WALSINGHAM. In 1586, he was appointed chief physician to the queen. His position at COURT and his growing wealth combined with his foreign Jewish birth to make him many enemies. By 1593, the chief among these was the Earl of Essex, the royal favorite, who hated Lopez because he had severely criticized the earl's policies and conduct toward Don Antonio, the claimant to the Portuguese throne (which PHILIP II of SPAIN had seized in 1580). Lopez may even have revealed to Don Antonio that Essex had contracted syphilis.

Lopez first became involved with court politics in 1589 when he helped persuade Elizabeth to back the PORTUGAL EXPEDITION, an ultimately unsuccessful naval enterprise that sought to put Don Antonio on the Portuguese throne. When Don Antonio came to England in 1590, Lopez, acting as interpreter between him and Essex, Antonio's chief political ally, became aware of the earl's attempts to use the Portuguese issue to further his own position at court. In 1594, Essex used rumors of Lopez's involvement in Spanish plots against Don Antonio and Elizabeth to press for the physician's arrest and trial for TREASON (see

LOPEZ PLOT). Although doubtful of Lopez's guilt and suspicious of the earl's motives, Elizabeth eventually consented to the physician's execution, which occurred at Tyburn on 7 June 1594. Lopez's declaration on the scaffold that he loved the queen "as well as he loved Jesus Christ" elicited much ridicule from the anti-Semitic crowd that witnessed his death; for although outwardly a practicing Christian, Lopez had long been suspected of being a practicing Jew in secret (see JEWS). Indeed, it is likely that Shakespeare used the well-known London physician as the model for the character of Shylock, the vengeful Jewish money-lender in *The Merchant of Venice. See also* SHAKESPEARE, WORKS OF.

Further Reading: Robert Lacey, *Robert, Earl of Essex,* New York: Atheneum, 1971.

Lord Chamberlain's Men. *See* CHAMBERLAIN'S MEN.

Lord Strange's Men. *See* STANLEY, FERDINANDO, LORD STRANGE.

"Lost Colony"

When John WHITE returned to England in 1590 without being able to ascertain the whereabouts of the settlers of the second English colony on Roanoke Island (see ROANOKE COLONY [1587]), the missing colonists passed into the English imagination as the "Lost Colony." Established on Roanoke Island (off present-day North Carolina) in 1587, Sir Walter RALEIGH's second Roanoke colony suffered immediately from the enmity the first colony (see ROANOKE COLONY [1585]) had created among the local Indians. Heavily dependent on Raleigh for supplies, the colonists sent White back to England to ensure regular shipments. Prevented by the ARMADA crisis from returning to Roanoke until 1590, White found no trace of the colony and was prevented by storms from investigating further. The Roanoke colonists were thus abandoned to their unknown fates.

When the first permanent English settlement was established at Jamestown (in what is now southern Virginia) in 1607, the settlers tried to find the lost colonists, who, if still alive, could greatly assist the survival of the new colony with their 20 years of experience in the region. Hope rose in 1608 when local Indians reported a fair-haired, light-skinned people living south of Jamestown; however, later reports said the Roanoke colonists were dead, having recently been massacred in an Indian war.

The story of the lost colonists as reported in 1612 in *History of Travel in Virginia Britannia* by William Strachey, former secretary of the Jamestown colony, was that the colonists had left Roanoke for the Chesapeake Bay, their original destination. There they had lived peacefully with the friendly Chesapeake Indians until about 1607, the year of Jamestown's founding, when Powhatan, the leader of the most powerful tribal confederation in the region, slaughtered the Chesapeakes and their English guests to forestall a prophecy that declared a rival to Powhatan's rule would arise from the Chesapeakes. Rumors said seven colonists—four men, two boys, and one girl—survived the massacre and fled south to live with friendly Indians to whom they taught the arts of building with stone and working copper. Although rumors of their existence persisted, no Roanoke colonists were ever found by the English. Today, the Lumbee tribe of central North Carolina, descendants of the Croatoan tribe that lived near Roanoke in the 1580s, claim that the colonists settled and eventually amalgamated with their people.

Further Reading: Karen Ordahl Kupperman, *Roanoke: The Abandoned Colony,* New York: Barnes and Noble, 1993.

Lumley, John, Lord Lumley
(c. 1534–1609)

John Lumley, Lord Lumley, was a wealthy and important patron of learning and the arts in Elizabethan England. Born in Yorkshire, Lumley was educated at Queen's College, Cambridge (see UNIVERSITIES). In 1549, he inherited the family title and wealth, which came largely from income derived from numerous coal pits (mines) scattered across the Lumley lands in the county of Durham in northern England (see Maps, "Counties of England and Wales, 1603"). In 1569, he was suspected of involvement in the RIDOLFI PLOT and briefly imprisoned. Thereafter, he avoided politics, although he came south each year to exercise his office as high steward of Oxford University, a post he held from 1559 until his

death, and to take part in meetings of the Society of Antiquaries, of which he was an active member along with such antiquarian scholars as William CAMDEN (see ANTIQUARIANISM).

Lumley enlarged and embellished his residence at Lumley Castle in Durham and refurbished NONSUCH PALACE, the former residence of HENRY VIII that Lumley inherited from his father-in-law, the Earl of Arundel. In 1592, Lumley, heeding Elizabeth's none-too-subtle hints, presented Nonsuch to the queen, who had long coveted it. For this wise generosity, Lumley received other lands from the queen.

In 1583, he established the Lumleian lectures at the College of Physicians (see MEDICINE), and in 1588 was one of the sponsors of the public lectures given by the mathematician Thomas Hood. The PRIVY COUNCIL endorsed Hood's lectures, hoping that seamen would attend them and thereby improve their mathematical and navigational skills. Lumley was also a collector of books and works of ART, amassing large holdings of both, including over 250 paintings. In 1603, Lumley entertained JAMES I at Lumley Castle as the new king made his way south to LONDON. Lumley subsequently became a tutor for James's eldest son, Prince Henry, who purchased Lumley's fine library of Latin books after Lumley's death in 1609.

Further Reading: Roy Strong, *Henry, Prince of Wales, and England's Lost Renaissance,* London: Thames and Hudson, 1986.

Lyly, John (c. 1554–1606)

John Lyly was the most popular English writer of the 1580s and was a strong influence on several prominent writers of the 1590s, including Robert GREENE and Thomas LODGE. Born in Kent and educated at both Oxford and Cambridge (see UNIVERSITIES), Lyly went in 1575 to LONDON, where he served for several years as secretary to Edward de VERE, Earl of Oxford. The publication in 1579 of *Euphues, the Anatomy of Wit,* the first part of his great romance novel, brought Lyly immediate acclaim. *Euphues and His England,* the second part of the work, was equally heralded on its publication in 1580. The distinct style of *Euphues,* which was elaborate, artificial, and marked by much alliteration and numerous historical, philosophical, and mythological allusions, heavily influenced various writers of the next decade, especially Thomas Lodge, who wrote several works in the "euphuic" style. *Euphues* also brought Lyly to the attention of William CECIL, Lord Burghley, who employed the writer in his household until 1582.

Lyly next turned to writing plays and became vice-master of Paul's Boys, a company of child actors that frequently performed at COURT. In the 1580s, Lyly wrote a series of plays for the company, including *The Woman in the Moon, Gallathea, Endimion, Love's Metamorphosis,* and *Mother Bombie*. Most of these plays were not published until the 1590s, and all except *Woman in the Moon* were prose works. When Paul's Boys disbanded in 1590, Lyly sought the court post of master of the revels, but the longevity of the incumbent, Edmund TILNEY, frustrated this ambition. In 1589, Lyly entered the MARPRELATE TRACTS controversy on the side of the bishops by publishing a tract entitled *Pappe with a Hatchet*.

In the 1590s, he served in PARLIAMENT for various constituencies. His popularity dwindled after 1590 as the court turned its attention to the new works of Christopher MARLOWE, Thomas KYD, and William SHAKESPEARE. Lyly spent his last years on the publication of his plays and in a largely unsuccessful search for court patronage. He died in London in November 1606. Edward Blount, the printer of Shakespeare's FIRST FOLIO, brought out an edition of Lyly's works in 1632. *See also* DRAMA.

Further Reading: Joseph W. Houppert, *John Lyly,* Boston: Twayne, 1975; G. K. Hunter, *John Lyly: The Humanist as Courtier,* Cambridge, MA: Harvard University Press, 1962.

M

Maitland, William (c. 1528–1573)

William Maitland of Lethington was secretary to Mary STUART, Queen of Scots, and SCOTLAND's most capable diplomat (see DIPLOMACY). In the late 1550s, Maitland served the Catholic regent of Scotland, Marie de GUISE, who sent him on diplomatic missions to England and FRANCE. He abandoned the regent and joined the Protestant Lords of the Congregation in 1559, having become alarmed at the growth of French power in Scotland. He negotiated the Treaty of Berwick with England in February 1560, and, in July 1560, helped negotiate the Treaty of Edinburgh (see BERWICK, TREATY OF; EDINBURGH, TREATY OF). Maitland was instrumental in persuading the Scots lords to support the EDINBURGH agreement, being convinced that an English alliance was of greater benefit to Scotland than a French one.

On Mary's return to Scotland in 1561, she named Maitland her secretary and gave him the management of Scottish relations with England. Not strongly attached to either PROTESTANTISM or Catholicism, Maitland endeavored to stabilize the Scottish monarchy by winning recognition from Elizabeth of Mary's right of inheritance to the English throne. Maitland hoped that a firm promise of the English Crown would prevent Mary from trying to restore Catholicism in Scotland. But Elizabeth's refusal to recognize Mary as her heir; the Scottish queen's MARRIAGE to Henry STUART, Lord Darnley; and Mary's increasing reliance on David RIZZIO, her Catholic secretary, reduced Maitland's influence with the queen by early 1566. Maitland probably knew of the plot to murder Rizzio, but he did not directly participate. He was also probably aware of the conspiracy, a year later, to murder Darnley, but again was not directly involved (see DARNLEY MURDER).

Although opposed to the queen's subsequent marriage to James HEPBURN, Earl of Bothwell, Maitland supported Mary until June 1567, when fear of Bothwell led him to join the Protestant opposition. When Bothwell fled after the Battle of Carberry, Maitland worked quietly for the imprisoned queen's restoration and continued to support her even after her flight to England in 1568 after the Battle of Langside (see CARBERRY, BATTLE OF; LANGSIDE, BATTLE OF). Maitland sought to effect the marriage of Mary to Thomas HOWARD, Duke of Norfolk, a scheme that led eventually to Norfolk's execution and Maitland's imprisonment by the Scottish regent, James STUART, Earl of Moray. Maitland was released after Moray's assassination in 1570, but in April 1571, during the civil war between supporters and opponents of Mary, he joined the pro-Mary forces holding Edinburgh Castle. Although suffering from increasingly bad health, Maitland stood siege in the castle until May 1573. He avoided execution only by dying in prison a few weeks later.

Further Reading: William Blake, *William Maitland of Lethington,* Lewiston, NY: E. Mellen Press, 1990.

Marian exiles

When MARY I came to the English throne in 1553, she began the process of restoring Catholicism as the religion of the realm (see CATHOLICISM, ENGLISH). One method her government used to limit opposition was to encourage prominent Protestants to leave the country. English Protestants were told to expect arrest but were given sufficient time and opportunity to escape. By 1554, almost 1,000 English men, women, and children had fled to Europe to save their lives and to protect their right to worship as they chose. These "Marian exiles" settled mainly in the Protestant cities of Germany and Switzerland, such as Strasbourg, Frankfurt, Emden, Wesel, Zurich, and Geneva.

Each community had its own social complexion. Frankfurt included many of EDWARD VI's bishops and councilors, and Zurich attracted many young reformers who would have careers in the Elizabethan Church. The wealthy Emden community contained many gentlemen (see GENTRY) and merchants, while the Wesel group comprised less wealthy craftsmen and artisans. Several exile communities experienced religious disputes that foreshadowed later conflicts within the ANGLICAN CHURCH. In Frankfurt, arguments between those who wished to worship as ordained by Edward VI's *BOOK OF COMMON PRAYER* clashed so severely with those who wished more radical reforms that the community split, with the reformist group moving to John CALVIN's Geneva in 1555.

The exiles were heavily involved in writing and distributing Protestant literature. They smuggled into England over 100 different works that explained Protestant beliefs and encouraged Protestants in England to hold to the faith, especially after Mary's government began burning individuals deemed heretics (see MARIAN MARTYRS). Among the works produced were John KNOX's *First Blast of the Trumpet against the Monstrous Regiment of Women,* the first edition of John FOXE's "BOOK OF MARTYRS," and the Geneva Bible (see BIBLE, ENGLISH).

Although some Marian exiles had left England for political reasons, such as Sir Peter CAREW, who fled for involvement in WYATT'S REBELLION, most were religious refugees who returned soon after Mary's death, determined to give England the reformed religion they had practiced in Europe. Many Marian exiles later served the Elizabethan church and state, such as Edmund GRINDAL, who became Arch-

bishop of Canterbury, and Francis WALSINGHAM, who became secretary of state. Others became the founders of the Puritan movement, which sought throughout Elizabeth's reign to institute a greater reform of the Anglican Church than the queen and PARLIAMENT had sanctioned in the ANGLICAN SETTLEMENT of 1559. *See also* CATHOLICISM, ENGLISH; PROTESTANTISM; PURITANS.

Further Reading: Christina Garrett, *The Marian Exiles,* Cambridge: Cambridge University Press, 1966.

Marian martyrs

By condemning Protestant opponents of her newly restored Catholic Church to death by burning, MARY I, Elizabeth's sister and predecessor, unwittingly created the Marian martyrs, whose faith and suffering lingered in the English national memory for hundreds of years, creating an undying hatred of the pope and Roman Catholicism (see CATHOLICISM, ENGLISH). When PARLIAMENT restored the English Church to papal allegiance in 1554, it also revived the government's authority to execute persons convicted of heresy in CHURCH COURTS. The statute granting this authority, *De Heretico Comburendo* ("Concerning the Burning of Heretics"), had been passed in 1401 but repealed under HENRY VIII (it was repealed again under Elizabeth). Determined to rid her realm of PROTESTANTISM, Mary sanctioned the opening of heresy trials in January 1555.

Because many upper-class Protestants had been encouraged to leave the country (see MARIAN EXILES), most of the men and women tried for heresy were of the lower classes—craftsmen and shopkeepers (see SOCIAL HIERARCHY), especially from LONDON and the towns of the southeast where Protestantism was strongest. A few leaders of EDWARD VI's Protestant Church were also brought to trial, the most notable being Archbishop Thomas CRANMER, author of the *BOOK OF COMMON PRAYER,* who found himself torn between his Protestant beliefs and his lifelong adherence to the royal supremacy and strict obedience to the monarch (see SUPREMACY, ROYAL). Cranmer at first recanted his Protestantism, but then recanted his recantation, dying in the flames in March 1556. Almost 300 people died for their Protestant faith in Mary's reign. This number was far fewer than the numbers being burned for heresy elsewhere in Catholic Europe, but it was unprecedented in English experience.

Instead of instilling a horror of heresy in the populace, as the government intended, the burnings only aroused sympathy for the victims and anger against the government. PHILIP II, Mary's husband, who was not averse to the principle of burning heretics, advised his wife to stop because of the damage the burnings were doing to her popularity. In Elizabeth's reign, when almost as many people died much less spectacularly for their Catholic faith, the memory of the Marian martyrs was immortalized by John FOXE's "BOOK OF MARTYRS," which transformed Protestant martyrs into English national heroes and turned Catholicism into the great enemy of both the English Church and state.

Further Reading: David Loades, *The Reign of Mary Tudor,* 2nd ed., London: Longman, 1991.

Marlowe, Christopher (1564–1593)

Except for William SHAKESPEARE, Christopher Marlowe is today considered the greatest Elizabethan dramatist. The son of a Canterbury shoemaker, Marlowe was educated at Cambridge (see UNIVERSITIES), where he earned a bachelor's degree in 1584. In 1587, university authorities delayed granting Marlowe his master's degree until they were assured by the PRIVY COUNCIL that his recent visit to William ALLEN's Catholic seminary at Rheims involved "matters touching the benefit of his country." Marlowe had been employed by Sir Francis WALSINGHAM, the secretary of state, to spy on Englishmen at Rheims for the government. Marlowe probably came to Walsingham's attention through the secretary's kinsman, Thomas Walsingham, who was Marlowe's literary patron.

Marlowe moved to LONDON about 1587, the year his play, *Tamburlaine the Great,* was first performed by the Admiral's Men. With its sweeping story, exotic Asian settings, and powerful blank verse, *Tamburlaine* was an immediate triumph, and Marlowe's plays were soon in demand by both theatre owners and well-known actors like Edward ALLEYN. Marlowe's other successes included *The Jew of Malta,* which later inspired Shakespeare's *The Merchant of Venice; Edward II; The Tragical History of Doctor Faustus;* and *The Tragedy of Dido, Queen of Carthage,* which was jointly written with Thomas NASHE. Left unfinished at Marlowe's death, the poem *Hero and Leander* was possibly written in competition with Shakespeare's *Venus and Adonis* for the patronage of Henry WRIOTHESLEY, Earl of Southampton. Marlowe is perhaps best known today for his poem "The Passionate Shepherd to His Love," which begins, "Come live with me, and be my love."

Given to drinking and frequenting taverns with his writer friends, Marlowe was often in trouble with the law; he spent two weeks in jail in 1589 for involvement in a brawl that left one man dead. In May 1593, his fellow playwright and roommate Thomas KYD was interrogated for certain atheistic writings found in his room. Under torture, Kyd incriminated Marlowe, who was summoned before the Council but otherwise not punished. On 30 May, Marlowe spent the day at a London tavern drinking and talking with three associates

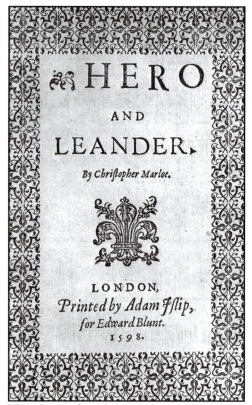

The title page from the 1598 edition of Christopher Marlowe's *Hero and Leander. By permission of the Folger Shakespeare Library.*

of Thomas Walsingham. After dinner, a quarrel erupted over the bill between Marlowe and one of the men. Marlowe drew a weapon and the man stabbed him in self-defense, killing the playwright instantly. Given Marlowe's intelligence work for the government and his recent interrogation by the Council, both contemporaries and modern historians have theorized that the quarrel was devised to hide the fact that Marlowe was, for unknown reasons, murdered. Many of Marlowe's literary contemporaries paid tribute to his talent; Shakespeare, whose own plays have been attributed to Marlowe by some in the twentieth century, remembered Marlowe in *As You Like It*.

Further Reading: Philip Henderson, *Christopher Marlowe,* 2nd ed., New York: Barnes and Noble Books, 1974; A. L. Rowse, *Christopher Marlowe: His Life and Work,* New York: Grosset and Dunlap, 1966; A. D. Wraight, *Christopher Marlowe and Edward Alleyn,* Chichester, England: Adam Hart, 1993.

Marprelate Tracts

Between 1587 and 1589, three men, Job Throckmorton, Robert Waldegrave, and John PENRY, secretly distributed a series of seven devastating printed attacks on the bishops of the ANGLICAN CHURCH throughout LONDON and England. The three published the tracts under the pseudonym Martin Marprelate (a wordplay based on "mar a prelate"). Throckmorton was probably the author of the tracts, Waldegrave was the printer, and Penry acted as business manager (see PRINTING). The Marprelate tracts aimed at thoroughly discrediting bishops and other ecclesiastical officials who were opposing Puritan reforms in the Anglican Church (see PURITANS).

The tracts attacked the bishops personally, ridiculing their learning, mocking their writing style, and taunting them with their inability to uncover the identity of Martin Marprelate. Because the tracts were written with power and conviction, they found a large audience in anticlerical circles (see ANTICLERICALISM). When the bishops launched an investigation into the source and authorship of the tracts, they uncovered much of the classical structure (see CLASSICAL MOVEMENT) that English Puritanism had been illegally and covertly developing within the sanctioned episcopal structure of the An-

glican Church in the 1580s. These discoveries caused alarm within the government and gave substance to the bishops' claims of the existence of a subversive Puritan threat to the stability and order of the English Church and state. When many of the leaders of the classical movement were discovered to be friends and associates of the Marprelate group, the bishops were able to arrest and prosecute the classis leaders and so root out the movement.

In 1589, the authorities discovered and destroyed the Marprelate press. Penry and Waldegrave fled to SCOTLAND, where the latter became printer to the Scottish king (see JAMES I). Penry returned to England and was executed in 1593 for being a separatist (see SEPARATISTS). Throckmorton was tried for being the author of the tracts, but he admitted nothing and was eventually freed after friends and relatives interceded on his behalf with Elizabeth.

Further Reading: Patrick Collinson, *The Elizabethan Puritan Movement,* Oxford: Clarendon Press, 1990; Donald J. McGinn, *John Penry and the Marprelate Controversy,* New Brunswick, NJ: Rutgers University Press, 1966.

marriage

Marriage was an important social milestone in Elizabethan England because it marked the official passage to adult independence. To be a householder, a man had to be married; few economically independent bachelors existed, even within the nobility and GENTRY. Because marriage required that a couple be able to support themselves, the average age of marriage in Elizabethan England was high—27 for men and 24 for women among the lower classes, and about three to four years younger among the upper classes and the citizens of LONDON (see SOCIAL HIERARCHY). Parental permission was required for anyone under 21 to marry, but many marriages, even of older children, were arranged by parents. Such arrangements were particularly common among the PEERAGE and gentry, where landed estates were involved, and where political alliances were as important as social and economic considerations.

The bride's parents were expected to provide her with a dowry, a settlement of money or property that came under her husband's control and that often determined her attractiveness as a prospective marriage partner (see WOMEN). Betrothal was a legally binding contract, and any breach of a promise to marry was prosecuted in the CHURCH COURTS. Prior to the wedding, marriage banns were called in the parish church on three successive Sundays. The banns were a type of marriage announcement designed to provide time and opportunity for uncovering impediments to the match. Such impediments might be the existence of a prior betrothal or marriage or the discovery that the couple was too closely related, a real possibility within the relatively small and highly intermarried landed classes.

The wedding itself was celebrated in the parish church with an exchange of rings. In the absence of a modern marriage certificate, legal recognition of the union was achieved by recording it in the parish register. Upon marriage, a woman took her husband's surname. Once married, a couple was legally required to live together, with separations permitted only by court order and then only for such extreme circumstances as cruelty and adultery. Divorce was rarely granted, although annulment (which ended HENRY VIII's first marriage) could be granted for good cause, such as discovery of a prior marriage.

Further Reading: Eric J. Carlson, *Marriage and the English Reformation*, Oxford: Blackwell, 1994; David Cressy, *Birth, Marriage and Death*, Oxford: Oxford University Press, 1997; Anthony Fletcher, *Gender, Sex and Subordination in England 1500–1800*, New Haven, CT: Yale University Press, 1995; Alan Macfarlane, *Marriage and Love in England 1300–1840*, Oxford: Blackwell, 1986; Lawrence Stone, *The Family, Sex and Marriage in England 1500–1800*, New York: Harper and Row, 1977.

marriage question

When Elizabeth came to the throne at age 25 in 1558, the necessity for her to marry quickly was almost universally acknowledged. This urgency arose from a practical need to secure the succession (see SUCCESSION, ACTS OF): Elizabeth required an undisputed heir. The heir apparent in 1558 was Mary STUART, Queen of Scots, a foreign and pro-French Catholic whose possible succession greatly troubled Protestants. Beyond the succession, the assumption of the age was that a woman could not rule a kingdom and required a husband to rule for her, a view accepted by MARY I, who quickly took PHILIP II of SPAIN as her

spouse. But Mary's loveless match, resulting in the loss of CALAIS during a war fought as Spain's reluctant ally, and the later disastrous marriage of Mary Stuart to Henry STUART, Lord Darnley (resulting in the DARNLEY MURDER and Mary's overthrow), taught Elizabeth the great dangers to queens of taking the wrong husband.

Complicated by the question of religion and the need for a useful alliance, foreign marriages could make England a mere pawn to another country's interests. Marriage to a subject deprived England of a valuable foreign alliance and threatened the creation of internal political factions. Even though Elizabeth's PRIVY COUNCIL urged her to marry in 1559, and the parliaments of 1559, 1563, 1566, and 1576 petitioned her to marry, both councilors and members of Parliament were seriously divided over which of the queen's many suitors would make the best husband. Thus, although there was strong agreement with the general principle that the queen must marry, there was much contradictory advice offered her as to whom, in particular, she should marry.

Many candidates were proposed, including Philip II, Archduke Charles of Austria, and Charles IX of France, all of whom were rejected for religion (all were Catholic) or age (Charles IX was 14). Eric XIV of Sweden was Protestant, but alliance with his small country brought no great political or military benefits. Elizabeth's two most serious marriage suits involved Robert DUDLEY, Earl of Leicester (see DUDLEY MARRIAGE SUIT), in the early 1560s, and Francis VALOIS, Duke of Alençon, in the late 1570s. For political and personal reasons, neither marriage occurred, and Elizabeth defied the expectations of her times and remained unmarried to her death. *See also* VIRGIN QUEEN.

Further Reading: Susan Doran, *Monarchy and Matrimony: The Courtships of Elizabeth I*, London: Routledge, 1996.

Mary I (1516–1558)

The daughter of HENRY VIII and CATHERINE OF ARAGON, Mary I was the half sister and predecessor of Elizabeth, and the first English queen regnant (i.e., reigning in her own right). Born in 1516, Mary, by age nine, had been betrothed by her father to both the French dau-

Mary I, daughter of Henry VIII and Catherine of Aragon, was Elizabeth's half sister and predecessor. *By courtesy of the National Portrait Gallery, London.*

phin (i.e., heir to the French throne) and to her maternal cousin CHARLES V of SPAIN. She was given a solid humanist education by the Spanish scholar Juan Luis Vives, who wrote *De Institutione Foeminae Christianae* (*On the Instruction of a Christian Woman*) for her guidance (see HUMANISM). From 1527 to 1533, during the long debate over the annulment of her parents' marriage, Mary gave her affection and loyalty to her mother and to her mother's nephew and protector, Charles V.

Her father's marriage to Anne BOLEYN and the birth of Elizabeth in 1533 led to the act of succession declaring Mary illegitimate and replacing her in the succession by her half sister (see SUCCESSION, ACTS OF). Her mother's death in 1536 and her father's constant pressure to accept her new status damaged Mary's health; frightened, sick, and alone, Mary capitulated when her exasperated father, who had just executed Anne Boleyn, began talking about executing her as well. Conscience-stricken and unshakably bound to her mother's church, Mary quietly lived out Henry's reign. Under her Protestant half brother, EDWARD VI, she became heir to the throne and the leading defender of conserva-

tive religion. At Edward's death in 1553, the country rallied around Mary's right to the throne and defeated the attempt of John DUDLEY, Duke of Northumberland, to exclude her from the throne in favor of Jane GREY, his Protestant daughter-in-law (see *DEVISE*; NORTHUMBERLAND'S COUP).

In 1554, Mary contracted marriage with Philip of Spain (see PHILIP II), son of Charles V; this unpopular match sparked WYATT'S REBELLION, an unsuccessful uprising that aimed to put Elizabeth on the throne. Mary sent Elizabeth to the TOWER OF LONDON, but could not prove the princess's involvement in the rebellion and had to release her. Mary used PARLIAMENT to return England to the Roman Catholic Church, but her age and poor health prevented children, and by 1557, Elizabeth's eventual succession was assured. Mary died in November 1558; her last years as queen were marred by the burning of heretics (see MARIAN MARTYRS), an action that earned her the name "Bloody Mary" and ingrained a deep fear of Catholicism in the English people, and by the loss to FRANCE of CALAIS, the last English possession on the continent. *See also* CATHOLICISM, ENGLISH; MARIAN EXILES; and the genealogical chart in Appendix 1: "House of Tudor, 1485–1603".

Further Reading: David Loades, *Mary Tudor,* Oxford: Basil Blackwell, 1989; David Loades, *The Reign of Mary Tudor,* 2nd ed., London: Longman, 1991.

Mary, Queen of Scots. *See* Stuart, Mary, Queen of Scots.

masque

A masque (or mask) was a type of court ENTERTAINMENT popular in Elizabethan and early Stuart England. Arriving in England from Italy and FRANCE in the early sixteenth century, the masque began as a group of costumed and masked individuals who appeared at COURT celebrations. Accompanied by torchbearers and often by songs and speeches, the masked figures mingled and danced with guests. HENRY VIII, particularly in his youth, was fond of participating in masques. By Elizabeth's reign, the masque had evolved into a more elaborately staged pageant with a mythological or allegorical theme. The masque participants performed a brief DRAMA and then joined their audience to DANCE and converse before being summoned back into the pageant by songs and verses.

As masques grew in length and grandeur, costumes became more fabulous, scenery more spectacular, and the machinery used for special effects—such as gods ascending or descending—more complex. Elizabethan masques often served the cult of the VIRGIN QUEEN, paying compliments to Elizabeth or symbolizing the glorious events of her reign. Some masques also took on political overtones. The spectacular entertainments staged in 1575 for Elizabeth at Kenilworth by Robert DUDLEY, Earl of Leicester, promoted Leicester's suit to marry the queen (see DUDLEY MARRIAGE SUIT). Masques were also a staple of the queen's summer progresses, as her hosts vied with one another in presenting Elizabeth with ever more gorgeous and elaborate entertainments (see PROGRESSES, ROYAL).

Under the influence of playwright Ben JONSON, court poet to JAMES I, the masque reached its height as a literary work and a social commentary. Working with Inigo Jones, who was famous for his fabulous scenery and ingenious machines, Jonson devised new types of masques, including the antimasque, a brief performance preceding the main pageant and emphasizing comical and grotesque elements in contrast to the elegance of the masque itself. Court masques, which were criticized by PURITANS as costly and frivolous, ceased in the 1640s with the start of the civil war. Although masques and other court entertainments returned with the restoration of the monarchy in 1660, they never reached the same level of popularity or dramatic quality achieved during the reigns of Elizabeth and James. The masque influenced the later development of other types of performing arts such as ballet, opera, and pantomime.

Further Reading: Sydney Anglo, *Spectacle, Pageantry, and Early Tudor Policy,* 2nd ed., Oxford: Oxford University Press, 1997; David Loades, *The Tudor Court,* London: Batsford, 1986; Stephen Orgel, *The Jonsonian Masque,* Cambridge, MA: Harvard University Press, 1965; Jean Wilson, *Entertainments for Elizabeth I,* Totowa, NJ: Rowman and Littlefield, 1980.

Mass

The communion service and central ritual of the Roman Catholic Church is known as the Mass. The name derived from the Latin formula of dismissal at the end of the service: *Ite,* *missa est* ("Go, it is ended"). According to Catholic teaching, the Mass is a sacramental re-enactment of the death and resurrection of Jesus. The Mass celebrant, who must be an ordained priest, is the agency whereby God transforms the bread and wine (without altering their physical appearance) into the body and blood of Christ, a doctrine known as TRANSUBSTANTIATION. Each Mass is seen by Catholics as a repetition of the sacrifice Christ made on the cross at Calvary.

Protestant reformers strongly objected to this sacrificial character and to the belief that the bread and wine became the actual body and blood of Christ. Although Protestant views of the nature of the communion elements varied, most reformers shared John CALVIN's belief that the bread and wine were merely commemorative of Christ's Last Supper (see CALVINISM). For this reason, many reformed churches distributed both bread and wine to congregants at communion, a departure from the Catholic tradition of distributing only the bread. The Protestant wine, being only wine, was more easily administered than the precious blood of Christ that was the Catholic wine. To encourage greater participation by the congregation, Protestants favored the use of the vernacular over the use of Latin; and to reduce the role of the priest, Protestants rejected the doctrine of transubstantiation.

In England, the ANGLICAN SETTLEMENT of 1559 repudiated the Mass and restored the 1552 *BOOK OF COMMON PRAYER* with its English communion service. The settlement specifically denied transubstantiation, but Elizabeth insisted on the addition of the following sentence (to be uttered at the distribution of the bread or wine) to make the communion service more acceptable to conservatives: "The body [or blood] of our Lord Jesus Christ which was given for thee, preserve thy body and soul unto everlasting life." Because this vague formulation could be read to imply belief in the actual presence of the body and blood of Christ in the bread and wine, PURITANS objected to the Prayer Book as being too close in spirit to the Mass and devoted much unsuccessful effort during Elizabeth's reign to obtaining revision of the service. *See also* CATHOLICISM, ENGLISH; PROTESTANTISM.

Further Reading: P. J. Fitzpatrick, *In Breaking of Bread: The Eucharist and Ritual,* Cambridge: Cambridge University Press, 1993; Norman L. Jones, *Faith by Statute,* London: Royal Historical Society, 1982.

master of the revels. *See* OFFICERS OF STATE.

Medici, Catherine de (1519–1589)

Catherine de Medici, daughter of a powerful Florentine merchant family and cousin to Pope Clement VII, became the wife of one French king, the mother of three others, and a powerful force in French politics during the reign of Elizabeth. Hoping, with the pope's aid, to extend French influence in Italy, FRANCIS I accepted Catherine as a bride for his second son in 1533. When the pope reneged on his promises, the French COURT dismissed Catherine as a low-born daughter of Italian shopkeepers, an unfit consort for a French prince. She became queen at HENRI II's accession in 1547 but had no influence with her husband, who was dominated by his mistress, Diane de Poitiers. After a decade of childlessness, Catherine gave birth to 10 children in rapid succession after 1544. In 1559, her husband's accidental death during a tournament initiated a period of civil and religious war in FRANCE.

In 1560, after the brief reign of her eldest son, Francis II (husband of Mary Stuart, Queen of Scots), Catherine became regent for her nine-year-old second son, Charles IX. She dominated him, but failed to impose either peace or order on a kingdom increasingly divided by religion. A decade of civil wars, in which even Elizabeth intervened on the Protestant side (see BLOIS, TREATY OF; HAMPTON COURT, TREATY OF; LE HAVRE EXPEDITION), culminated in 1572 in the SAINT BARTHOLOMEW MASSACRE, in which more than 10,000 HUGUENOTS perished. Catherine, fearing that the Huguenots meant to murder her and kidnap Charles IX in retaliation for an assassination attempt on their leader, instigated the bloodshed as a way to deprive the Protestants of their political and military leaders. Although celebrated in Catholic Europe, the massacre only turned the Huguenots against the monarchy and destroyed Catherine's credibility with Protestant rulers, especially Elizabeth.

After the 1574 accession of her third son, HENRI III, Catherine's political influence gradually waned. In the 1570s and early 1580s, she supported the ultimately unsuccessful suit of her youngest son, Francis VALOIS, Duke of Alençon, for the hand of Elizabeth, but her encouragement of the match rested mainly on a desire to remove the unruly duke from the kingdom and to obtain English financing for his political ambitions in the NETHERLANDS. After the duke's death in 1584, Henri of Navarre, a Protestant (see HENRI IV), became heir to the throne, and France sank deeper into religious war and civil turmoil. Catherine died in January 1589, only months before an assassin slew her remaining son and ended the VALOIS dynasty. *See also* genealogical chart in Appendix 1: "Valois and Bourbon Dynasties of France."

Further Reading: J. E. Neale, *The Age of Catherine de Medici,* New York: Barnes and Noble, 1959; R. J. Knecht, *Catherine de Medici,* London: Longman, 1998; Hugh Ross Williamson, *Catherine de Medici,* New York: Viking, 1973.

medicine

The practice of medicine in Elizabethan England involved specialists of three types—physicians, surgeons, and apothecaries—as well as a variety of healers and midwives. The highest ranking medical practitioner, both socially and professionally, was the physician, a university-trained specialist who was thoroughly grounded in the works of Galen and other doctors of the ancient world (see UNIVERSITIES). Physicians rarely saw patients personally, preferring to diagnose illness from a sample of the patient's urine.

Medical theory was based upon the ancient idea that the human body was composed of four humors of differing properties—blood (hot and moist), phlegm (cold and moist), yellow bile (hot and dry), and black bile (cold and dry). These humors corresponded to the four elements—air (blood), water (phlegm), fire (yellow bile), and earth (black bile)—and to four dispositions—sanguine (blood), phlegmatic (phlegm), choleric (yellow bile), and melancholic (black bile). Disease resulted from an imbalance of the humors, which physicians treated by prescribing medicines and foods that were thought to possess the opposite properties of the excessive humor. Thus, an overabundance of phlegm was treated with foods possessing the hot, dry qualities of yellow bile. Another way to restore balance was to bleed a patient, drawing off the excess or ill humors in the blood by having a surgeon apply leeches or make an incision in a vein.

Considered tradesmen, surgeons stood lower down the social scale than physicians (see SOCIAL HIERARCHY). Surgeons had little formal EDUCATION and learned their trade practically, by performing operations under the direction of physicians. Barbers also carried out simple surgical procedures, as well as dentistry. Although among the most privileged tradesmen in England, apothecaries had lower social status than physicians, whose prescriptions for medicines the apothecaries provided. WOMEN could not practice medicine as physicians, but many had some basic medical training and served as country healers and midwives. Because high fees put physicians' services beyond the reach of most commoners, many people turned to charlatans and sorcerers of both sexes for medical advice. To prevent quacks and folk healers (often women) from usurping the practice of medicine, the College of Physicians was founded in 1518. In the same year, the Surgeons and Barbers Companies merged to form a similar regulatory body for the practice of surgery. *See also* EPIDEMIC DISEASE; PLAGUE; WITCHCRAFT.

Further Reading: David F. Hoeniger, *Medicine and Shakespeare in the English Renaissance*, Newark: University of Delaware Press, 1992; J. A. Sharpe, *Early Modern England: A Social History 1550–1760*, 2nd ed., Oxford: Oxford University Press, 1997; Charles Webster, ed., *Health, Medicine, and Mortality in the Sixteenth Century*, Cambridge: Cambridge University Press, 1979.

Medina Sidonia, Duke of. *See* GUZMAN EL BUENO, ALONZO PEREZ DE, DUKE OF MEDINA SIDONIA.

Melville, Sir James (1535–1617)

Sir James Melville was a leading Scottish diplomat of the Elizabethan period, serving several times as Scottish ambassador to England. The third son of a Scottish GENTRY family, Melville went to the French court at age 14 to serve as a page to Mary STUART, Queen of Scots. By 1559, he had entered the service of HENRI II of FRANCE, who sent Melville to

SCOTLAND to ascertain whether Mary's half brother James STUART, future Earl of Moray, had any designs on his sister's Crown. In the early 1560s, Melville was engaged in DIPLOMACY in Germany, seeking unsuccessfully to arrange a MARRIAGE between Mary of Scotland and Archduke Charles of Austria and between Charles IX of France and a daughter of the Holy Roman emperor.

By 1564, Melville was in Scotland, where Mary made him a privy councilor and granted him a generous pension. To win Elizabeth's support for her marriage to Henry STUART, Lord Darnley, Mary sent Melville to England, where the Scottish ambassador ingratiated himself with the English queen. After his return to Scotland, Melville sought unsuccessfully to prevent the March 1566 murder of David RIZZIO. After the birth of Mary's son (see JAMES I) in June 1566, Melville carried the official tidings to Elizabeth but was back in EDINBURGH in December for the prince's baptism. After the murder of Darnley (see DARNLEY MURDER) in February 1567, Melville tried to dissuade the Scottish queen from marrying James HEPBURN, Earl of Bothwell, but succeeded only in winning the earl's enmity. Occurring in May 1567, the Bothwell marriage led within the year to Mary's abdication, flight from Scotland, and confinement in England.

Melville served as a diplomat for the various regency governments of James VI. When he came of age, James took his imprisoned mother's advice and asked Melville, then in retirement, to return to COURT as a royal advisor and ambassador. Melville served James loyally for the rest of the king's reign in Scotland but refused the king's requests to accompany him to England in 1603 when James succeeded Elizabeth. Melville retired to his estates to write his autobiography and to live quietly until his death in November 1617.

Further Reading: Antonia Fraser, *Mary, Queen of Scots,* New York: Delacorte Press, 1969; Sir James Melville, *Memoirs of Sir James Melville of Hahill,* edited by A. Francis Steuart. London: George Routledge and Sons, 1929; Jenny Wormald, *Mary, Queen of Scots,* London: Collins and Brown, 1991.

Merchant Adventurers

The London Company of Merchant Adventurers, incorporated as the Merchant Adventurers of England in 1564, was a REGULATED COMPANY that controlled the export of woolen cloth in Elizabethan England. Although the Merchant Adventurers also dealt in leather, tin, lead, and other commodities, woolen cloth, which by 1550 accounted for over 80 percent of English exports, comprised the vast majority of the company's business. In the early sixteenth century, the cloth merchants of London gained control of the NETHERLANDS cloth trade centered on Antwerp, squeezing out their main competitors. Because the London Adventurers provided the Crown with large loans and other vital financial services, the government allowed them to secure a monopoly on the English cloth trade. At the London Adventurers' insistence, the Crown designated English merchants operating from other ports as interlopers, thus excluding them from the cloth trade. Only by paying an entry fee to the London Adventurers, and by accepting an inferior status within the company as "redemptioners," could merchants from other English ports legally engage in the Antwerp cloth trade.

In 1560, Elizabeth removed another of the Adventurers' competitors by revoking the trade privileges that the Hanseatic League, an old and powerful trade association of German and Baltic towns, had enjoyed in England since 1474. By guaranteeing loans negotiated by Thomas GRESHAM, Elizabeth's financial agent in the Netherlands, the Adventurers won the Crown's support against the Hanseatic merchants. In the 1560s, political and religious unrest in the Netherlands (see NETHERLANDS REVOLT) led the company to move its continental headquarters from Antwerp; to prevent this move of operations from damaging its monopoly, the company petitioned Elizabeth for a royal charter of incorporation. Concerned about worsening relations with PHILIP II of SPAIN, the ruler of the Netherlands, the government issued the charter in 1564 and confirmed the company's monopoly. However, in an effort to encourage the growing domestic CLOTH INDUSTRY, the government also continued its licensing system to regulate the Merchant Adventurers' export of unfinished cloth.

The company transferred its operations to Hamburg in 1567, just in time to avoid the worst consequences of the trade embargo caused by the "TREASURE CRISIS" OF 1568.

At Hamburg, the Merchant Adventurers suffered from the hostility of the Hanseatic League and from the continued activity of English interlopers. By the end of Elizabeth's reign, the Merchant Adventurers' continental headquarters was at Middelburg in the independent United Provinces of the Netherlands.

The company was run by an elected governor and Court of Assistants, who arranged the annual trade marts at Antwerp or Hamburg, controlled the admission of new members, judged and corrected offending members and their apprentices, and detected and punished nonmember interlopers.

Further Reading: Douglas R. Bisson, *The Merchant Adventurers of England*, Newark: University of Delaware Press, 1993.

militia

In each county, all able-bodied men between the ages of 16 and 60 had an obligation to own arms and to defend the kingdom in time of invasion. Existing since Anglo-Saxon times, the English militia was administered by county officials—the lords lieutenant, sheriffs, and JUSTICES OF THE PEACE. Although use of the militia was regulated, responsibility for paying and supplying the troops was only vaguely defined. In theory, the royal government could not use militia units outside their home county unless the Crown agreed to assume the cost. In practice, monarchs used county militia wherever they wanted, in England and even overseas, ignoring both geographical restrictions and financial obligations. In 1558, PARLIAMENT passed an act requiring all laymen in the counties to equip themselves with WEAPONS and armor according to their wealth. The statute clearly described the military equipage required of each income category, and it placed responsibility for paying the militia squarely on the county, a requirement that aroused much local opposition. To monitor fulfillment of these obligations, a second act required local authorities to hold periodic musters of all men in the county subject to militia duty. At these musters, county militiamen reported for inspection of themselves and their horses and weapons, and for basic military training.

Under Elizabeth, the royal government began supplying the counties with more modern firearms. By the early 1570s, the PRIVY

COUNCIL had also initiated a program of giving the most promising 10 percent of the men in each county militia more extensive training in the use of guns and horses. Known as the trained bands, these specially prepared troops were the backbone of the county militia and often formed the core of royal armies sent overseas. Although this training was paid for by the counties, it was supervised by a royal official, the county muster-master, a professional soldier who not only trained and inspected the local militia, but also oversaw and maintained the county armory and helped select the members of the trained bands. By the 1580s, the Crown was also appointing county provost-martials who enforced martial law, especially on former (and traditionally disorderly) soldiers returning from foreign duty. Although appointment of muster-masters belonged to local officials by 1588, payment of muster-masters and provost-martials was also a county responsibility. *See also* ARMY; LOCAL GOVERNMENT.

Further Reading: Lindsay Boynton, *The Elizabethan Militia, 1558–1638,* London: Routledge and K. Paul, 1967; C. G. Cruickshank, *Elizabeth's Army,* 2nd ed., Oxford: Clarendon Press, 1966.

monopolies

The Crown had an undoubted PREROGATIVE right to regulate trade by granting to individuals certain monopolistic rights by letters patent. The recipients of such grants were licensed to import prohibited goods or were exempted from statutes that regulated the manufacture of important commodities. The Crown could also issue patents to foreign inventors or entrepreneurs to lure them into doing business in England. Although the Crown's right to dispense or suspend parliamentary statute was questionable, most of these types of grants proved economically beneficial to the country and aroused little opposition.

However, beginning in the 1580s, the Crown's extreme need for money to carry on the war with SPAIN led Elizabeth to grant monopolies as favors to courtiers, officials, and servants. Such monopolies acted as a cheap form of Crown patronage and as a ready source of revenue, for some monopolies were sold for cash to individuals or groups (see REVENUE, ROYAL). The grantees received a monopoly on the manufacture, sale, or import of a specified commodity or were empowered to license others to engage in such manufacture or sale. For instance, Sir Walter RALEIGH had a license on the production of playing cards, and Robert DEVEREUX, Earl of Essex, licensed the sale of sweet wines. By the 1590s, patents had been granted on such items as iron, steel, glass, vinegar, coal, salt, and soap. Because such monopolies usually led to higher prices for consumers, discontent over the grants was soon intense and widespread. Patentees also enjoyed wide search-and-seizure rights to protect their monopolies, and persons with grievances against monopolists had no remedy at law because the actions of monopolists arose from an exercise of the royal prerogative.

The PARLIAMENT of 1597 complained bitterly of monopolies, but the queen promised to reform the misuse of monopolistic patents, so Parliament took no action. When Parliament met again in 1601, the queen had still not acted, and an angry House of Commons sought to legislate on monopolies. Such legislation would have represented Parliament's first attempt to limit or modify a prerogative right; rather than risk such a fight, the queen agreed to review all monopolies and to cancel any that were harmful. All other monopolies were to be placed under the COMMON LAW. Elizabeth thanked the Commons for bringing the problem to her attention and issued a PROCLAMATION revoking certain monopolies, but she also affirmed the Crown's right to grant monopolies. In response to the parliamentary petition on monopolies, Elizabeth delivered her "GOLDEN SPEECH" to a Commons deputation in November 1601.

Further Reading: Harold G. Fox, *Monopolies and Patents,* Toronto: University of Toronto Press, 1947; Joan Thirsk, *Economic Policy and Projects: The Development of a Consumer Society in Early Modern England,* Oxford: Clarendon Press, 1978.

Moray, Earl of. *See* STUART, JAMES, EARL OF MORAY.

Morgan, William (1541–1604)

William Morgan was a Welsh Protestant reformer, bishop of the Welsh diocese of St. Asaph, and translator of the Bible into Welsh. Born in Caernarvonshire in WALES, Morgan was educated at St. John's College, Cambridge (see UNIVERSITIES), where he became proficient in both Hebrew and Greek. Between 1575 and 1588, Morgan held various church BEN-EFICES in Wales. With the encouragement and financial support of Archbishop John WHITGIFT and the assistance of his friend Archdeacon Edmund Prys, a gifted poet, Morgan undertook to translate the Bible into Welsh, a project he completed in 1588. At Whitgift's recommendation, the PRIVY COUNCIL ordered that a copy of Morgan's Bible be placed in every Welsh parish.

The high quality of Morgan's prose is credited not only with furthering PROTES-TANTISM in Wales (see REFORMATION, WELSH) but with standardizing the Welsh language and preventing it from falling into disuse. He became Bishop of Llandaff in 1595 and was named to the important Welsh bishopric of St. Asaph in 1601. Morgan was an excellent administrator and greatly raised the quality of pastoral care provided to the faithful of his diocese. He died in September 1604.

Further Reading: Glanmor Williams, *Renewal and Reformation: Wales c. 1415–1642,* Oxford: Oxford University Press, 1993.

Morris Dance. *See* DANCE.

Mountjoy, Lord. *See* BLOUNT, CHARLES, LORD MOUNTJOY.

Muscovy Company

Organized in 1553, the Muscovy (or Russia) Company was the first of the joint-stock trading companies (see JOINT-STOCK COMPANY). Known originally as the Merchant Adventurers for the Discovery of Lands, Countries, Isles, and Places Unknown, the company intended to open a new trade with Asia via a Northeast Passage. The company's first expedition, three ships under Sir Hugh Willoughby, sailed in 1553. Willoughby and the crews of two ships froze to death when they tried to winter off Lapland, but the crew of the third ship under Richard Chancellor entered the White Sea, landed at Archangel, and then journeyed overland to Moscow where they obtained permission from Czar Ivan the Terrible to begin trading. Upon Chancellor's return with this news in 1555, the company secured a charter from MARY I for the exclusive right to trade with Russia.

Over the next decade, the company sent out several other expeditions to Russia under Chancellor's navigator, Stephen BOROUGH, who with his brother, William BOROUGH, explored further for a Northeast Passage and maintained trade relations with the czar's government. In the 1560s and 1570s, the Muscovy Company sent seven expeditions into the Middle East and Central Asia to open trade relations with Turkey and Persia. Intending to reach China, company agent Anthony JENKINSON traveled from Moscow to the Caspian Sea and the region of Bokhara in Central Asia in the late 1550s. He found the area in political turmoil and realized that the company could conduct no stable trade via that route. On a second expedition in 1562, Jenkinson obtained permission from the shah of Persia to open trade with his kingdom; however, English trade with Persia collapsed a few years later when the Turks invaded Iran.

Although Russia became a good source of cordage for the English NAVY, the Muscovy Company was never profitable due to the high costs of trading with such a distant place and the difficulties of dealing with Ivan the Terrible. By 1600, Dutch merchants were cutting into the Russian market and the company's business began to dry up. In 1609, the joint-stock venture was wound up and the enterprise became a REGULATED COMPANY selling trade permits to merchants who wanted to enter its trade monopoly with Russia.

Further Reading: F. R. Dulles, *Eastward Ho: The First English Adventurers to the Orient,* Freeport, NY: Books for Libraries Press, 1969; G. D. Ramsay, *English Overseas Trade during the Centuries of Emergence,* London: Macmillan, 1957; Thomas Stuart Willan, *The Early History of the Russia Company, 1553–1603,* Manchester, England: Manchester University Press, 1956.

music

Elizabethan music, both religious and secular, was a product of several important influences—the Reformation, the rise of HUMANISM, the growth of English cultural and commercial contacts with Europe and the world, and the increasing acceptance of ENGLISH as a literary language. Most of the Tudors were musically inclined. HENRY VIII wrote songs, such as the rousing "Pastime with Good Company," and loved to sing, frequently engaging such courtiers as Sir Peter CAREW in the singing of "fremen songs," light, popular rounds for multiple voices.

Although not as gifted at musical composition as her father, Elizabeth wrote some instrumental pieces and played a keyboard instrument known as the virginal. In 1564, when seeking to impress Sir James MELVILLE, the ambassador of Mary STUART, Queen of Scots, Elizabeth contrived to have Melville brought secretly into her chamber so he could "accidentally" hear her playing and report its quality to the Scottish queen. Besides the virginal, the most popular instruments were the viol (a type of viola or cello), the lute (a stringed instrument), and various types of flutes and recorders. Musical ENTERTAINMENT among the lower classes was often accompanied by the bagpipe, the fiddle, or the pipe-and-tabor (a combination of drum and recorder).

The focus of the professional music establishment was the CHAPEL ROYAL, a choir and musical suite maintained by the Crown for the performance of sacred music in the royal chapels. Elizabeth also maintained a large company—more than 60 members—of singers and musicians to perform secular entertainments at COURT dances and masques. The most talented Elizabethan composers, such as William BYRD and Thomas TALLIS, were usually musicians of the Chapel Royal. The Elizabethans were particularly known for their keyboard compositions, the works of Byrd even influenced continental music, and for the development of the anthem, an English song form in which solo verses with instrumental accompaniment alternated with generally unaccompanied choral refrains.

The Elizabethan GENTRY and PEERAGE became important patrons of music during the reign, with many hiring musicians for their households, commissioning new compositions, and collecting instruments and printed music. Although the development of Elizabethan music did not match the brilliant flowering in Elizabethan literature (see DRAMA; POETRY), the period did see the rise of important new musical forms and themes, especially in secular compositions. *See also* DANCE; MASQUE; and Appendix 6: " Selected Sound Recordings of Tudor and Elizabethan Music."

Further Reading: David Wulstan, *Tudor Music,* Iowa City: University of Iowa Press, 1986.

N

Nashe, Thomas (1567–1601)

Thomas Nashe was one of the best-known dramatists, satirists, and pamphleteers in Elizabethan LONDON. The son of a Suffolk clergyman, Nashe was educated at Cambridge (see UNIVERSITIES). His first published work was a preface to Robert GREENE's *Menaphon,* which appeared in 1589. The preface criticized certain well-known actors and playwrights, including Thomas KYD (see also DRAMA). Because writing was his livelihood, Nashe produced works for various noble and ecclesiastical patrons, including George CAREY, Lord Hunsdon, and Archbishop John WHITGIFT, who employed Nashe to answer the MARPRELATE TRACTS. In producing these religious pamphlets, Nashe worked with the novelist and dramatist John LYLY and was soon embroiled in a pamphlet war, over issues of both literature and religion, with the Puritan literary critic Gabriel HARVEY (see PURITANS). The dispute with Harvey grew so acrimonious that in 1599 the PRIVY COUNCIL banned the men from publishing further against each other and confiscated the previous pamphlets of both.

Among Nashe's most important works were the satire *Pierce Penniless* (1592); a pamphlet answering Harvey's charges of plagiarism, *Have with You to Saffron Walden* (1596); and one of the first adventure novels in English, *The Unfortunate Traveller* (1594). His only surviving dramatic works are a comedy entitled *Summer's Last Will and Testament* (1592) and whatever share he had in revising Christopher MARLOWE's *The Tragedy of Dido, Queen of Carthage* (1593). Nashe's most controversial play was the satirical comedy *Isle of Dogs,* which he co-wrote with Ben JONSON in 1597. Although now lost, *Isle of Dogs* contained references the government found to be seditious, for the play was closed, Jonson was arrested and briefly imprisoned, and Nashe had to flee London for the Norfolk port of Great Yarmouth. Nashe's last known work before his death in 1601 was *Lenten Style* (1599), a comedic tribute to the red herring, the basis of many livelihoods in Great Yarmouth.

Further Reading: Charles Nicholl, *A Cup of News: The Life of Thomas Nashe,* London: Routledge and Kegan Paul, 1984.

navy

The English navy was built by the Tudors, for the medieval kings of England owned few SHIPS (see TUDOR FAMILY). When an English king wished to transport an ARMY to FRANCE, he collected a navy from port towns that owed him ships as part of their feudal service and from merchants who leased him their trade vessels. HENRY VII, Elizabeth's grandfather, created the nucleus of the royal navy by constructing warships, building the first drydock in northern Europe at Portsmouth, and encouraging the expansion of the English merchant fleet. HENRY VIII, Elizabeth's father, created a standing navy by building almost 50 new vessels during his reign and by keeping part of his fleet at sea every summer to suppress pirates. Henry also experimented with new ship designs and new types of guns and gun placements.

Naval innovation continued under Elizabeth, whose reign saw English ships change

Depiction of an encounter between the English fleet and the Spanish Armada in 1588. *National Maritime Museum, London.*

from platforms for land forces engaged in combat on the seas to platforms for large guns capable of disabling or sinking enemy vessels. Elizabeth maintained the Council of Marine her father had established to administer the navy and established her main naval bases at Woolwich and Portsmouth. The size of the Elizabethan navy was set at 24 vessels, and the annual naval budget was maintained at about £10,000 to keep the fleet in repair. Unlike Henry VIII's navy, which never ventured far from English shores, the Elizabethan fleet sailed around the world as the queen pursued a policy of loaning royal ships to private trading and PRIVATEERING expeditions. The queen's goals were profit and the expansion of overseas trade and exploration, policies that destroyed the old idea that the navy was merely for the defense of England.

When Sir John HAWKINS became treasurer of the navy in 1577, he initiated a naval building program, constructing almost 20 new ships. His use of progressive ship designs and innovative ideas on naval gunnery made the English fleet of the 1580s more maneuverable and better armed than any other navy of the time. Although assisted by the weather and the errors of the Spanish command, the English navy performed with distinction in the Channel battles with the ARMADA in 1588. *See also* AZORES EXPEDITION; DRAKE, SIR FRANCIS; GRAVELINES, BATTLE OF; HOWARD, CHARLES, EARL OF NOTTINGHAM; ISLANDS VOYAGE; PORTUGAL EXPEDITION; WINTER, SIR WILLIAM.

Further Reading: D. M. Loades, *The Tudor Navy,* Brookfield, VT: Ashgate Publishers, 1992; N. A. M. Rodger, *The Safeguard of the Sea: A Naval History of Britain,* New York: W. W. Norton, 1998.

Netherlands

The Netherlands, also known as the Low Countries, were of vital political and economic importance to Elizabethan England (see Maps, "Netherlands, 1590s"). In 1555–56, CHARLES V resigned the rule of the Netherlands and the Crown of SPAIN to his son PHILIP II. Wedged into the northwest corner of Europe between

FRANCE and the German Holy Roman Empire, the 17 provinces of the Netherlands were bound together only by the HABSBURG FAMILY dynasty. The provinces had different histories, political institutions, languages, and economies. The southern provinces, such as Flanders, Brabant, Artois, and Hainault, spoke French dialects and contained large and prosperous towns, such as Bruges, Antwerp, and Ghent. Brussels, the center of the Habsburg administration, was also located in Brabant. The northern provinces, such as Holland, Zeeland, and Friesland, spoke Dutch or German dialects and, while also containing such growing towns as Amsterdam, Leiden, and Utrecht, were more rural and less populous than the south. The north was also more heavily influenced by reformist religious ideas; by 1560, a growing minority of the northern population had accepted the ideas of John CALVIN, despite the efforts of the Catholic Habsburgs to use the inquisition to stamp out heresy in the provinces.

The political state of the Netherlands was of vital concern to England because whoever ruled the Netherlands controlled the opposite shore of the English Channel, the most direct route for invasion. Habsburg rule in the Netherlands meant the coast opposite Protestant England was controlled by Catholic Spain, the greatest power in Europe. The economic state of the Netherlands was also of great importance to England because the economies of the two countries were bound together by the CLOTH INDUSTRY. English wool growers and cloth manufacturers sold their products to textile makers in the Netherlands, who employed many workers, especially in the southern provinces, to process and finish English wool and cloth for resale throughout Europe. As the trade war of 1563–65 and the trade embargo following the "TREASURE CRISIS" OF 1568 proved, any disruption of trade hurt both states.

In 1563, when the Netherlands banned the importation of certain English goods to protest English commercial policies, the resulting shutdown of trade bankrupted English merchants and left Flemish textile workers unemployed. The clamor of both sides forced the two governments to resume normal trade relations in 1565. The 1568 crisis also caused economic disruption, especially in the Netherlands, and

had to be resolved by the Treaty of Nymegen in 1573 and the Treaty of Bristol in 1574 (see NYMEGEN, TREATY OF; BRISTOL, TREATY OF). By causing rebellion and political upheaval in the Netherlands, Catholic Habsburg rule threatened not only the English state and church, but also the English economy. *See also* NETHERLANDS EXPEDITION; NETHERLANDS REVOLT.

Further Reading: Edward Grierson, *The Fatal Inheritance: Philip II and the Spanish Netherlands*, Garden City, NY: Doubleday, 1969; Jonathan I. Israel, *The Dutch Republic: Its Rise, Greatness, and Fall 1477–1806*, Oxford: Clarendon Press, 1998; Geoffrey Parker, *Spain and the Netherlands, 1559–1659*, Short Hills, NJ: Enslow Publishers, 1979; James D. Tracy, *Holland under Habsburg Rule, 1506–1566: The Formation of a Body Politic*, Berkeley: University of California Press, 1990.

Netherlands expedition

The Treaty of Nonsuch, signed in August 1585, created the first formal military and political link between England and the United Provinces of the NETHERLANDS, then in revolt against PHILIP II of Spain (see NETHERLANDS REVOLT; NONSUCH, TREATY OF). The treaty committed Elizabeth to sending the Dutch 5,000 foot soldiers and 1,000 horsemen, along with garrison troops for the CAUTIONARY TOWNS of Flushing and Brill. To command the English forces, Elizabeth agreed to appoint a "gentleman of quality," who was understood by the Dutch to be Robert DUDLEY, Earl of Leicester, a long-time supporter of Dutch independence. Receiving his official appointment in October, Leicester landed on 10 December at Flushing, where he was greeted by enthusiastic crowds and by his nephew Sir Philip SIDNEY, commander of the Flushing garrison.

After lengthy discussions with the earl, the Dutch offered him the positions of governor and captain-general of the United Provinces, thus greatly increasing his military and political responsibilities beyond the bounds set by the queen. Despite her acceptance of the Nonsuch agreement, Elizabeth was anxious to limit both her involvement with rebels and her financial obligations; the Dutch, on the other hand, were eager to firmly commit the queen and her financial and military resources to their cause. Leicester's acceptance of the new titles enraged the queen, who rebuked the earl and threatened the STATES-GENERAL with abrogation of the treaty. Although the threat was never carried out, Leicester's standing with the Dutch was seriously damaged.

Plagued by quarrels with Dutch politicians and a lack of supplies from England, Leicester achieved little during the campaign of 1586. Alessandro FARNESE, Duke of Parma, the Spanish governor-general, captured several towns and defeated Leicester at Zutphen, where Philip Sidney was mortally wounded in September. Depressed by failure and financially burdened by the need to supply his men out of his own purse, Leicester received permission to come to England at the end of the year. He returned to the Netherlands in July 1587 with 4,500 additional troops and £30,000, but he accomplished no more than in the previous year. By the fall, military failure and disputes with Dutch leaders had ended the earl's effectiveness as English commander, and Elizabeth recalled him. Leicester resigned his command to Peregrine BERTIE, Lord Willoughby, and left the Netherlands forever.

Further Reading: Alan Haynes, *The White Bear: The Elizabethan Earl of Leicester,* London: Peter Owen, 1987; F. G. Oosterhoff, *Leicester and the Netherlands, 1586–1587,* Utrecht: HES, 1988.

Netherlands Revolt

The revolt of the NETHERLANDS against HABSBURG rule was the chief cause of war between Elizabethan England and Habsburg SPAIN. In 1559, PHILIP II of Spain, ruler of the Netherlands, left the provinces never to return. Henceforth, he ruled the Netherlands from Spain through a series of governor-generals, the first of whom was his half sister Margaret of Parma. Attempts by Philip to reorganize the church in the Netherlands and to strengthen and centralize the administration at Brussels led to a revolt in 1566 of the landowning nobility and gentry. The success of the revolt encouraged the provinces' Protestant minority, which erupted in a series of iconoclastic riots (i.e., disorders in which religious art and images were destroyed) that left Catholic churches severely damaged.

In 1567, Philip sent Fernandez ALVAREZ DE TOLEDO, Duke of Alva, to restore order. As governor-general, Alva used his matchless Spanish troops and the Council of Troubles (or Council of Blood), a ruthless judicial tribunal, to root out and punish rebellion. Leadership

of the rebellion fell upon WILLIAM, PRINCE OF ORANGE, a wealthy Dutch nobleman. Alva's military successes caused concern in England, where the government feared the presence across the Channel of a Spanish army and a strong Catholic state under Spanish control. By 1572, rebels from the Dutch provinces took to the sea to attack Spanish shipping. Known as SEA BEGGARS, these seaborne raiders began committing indiscriminate acts of piracy in the Channel, forcing Elizabeth to expel them from all English ports on 1 March 1572. A month later, the sea beggars fell upon the undefended Dutch ports of Brill and Flushing (see CAUTIONARY TOWNS), seizing them as permanent bases for the rebellion. By the fall, most of the northern provinces had expelled the Spaniards, many of the southern towns were in revolt, and the States (i.e., legislature) of Holland named William of Orange stadtholder (i.e., governor and command-in-chief) of the province.

In 1573, Don Luis de Requesens replaced Alva as governor-general; to impede his campaign of reconquest, the rebels of the increasingly Protestant northern provinces opened the dikes and flooded the low-lying provinces of Holland and Zeeland. In 1576, after de Requesens's death, the leaderless and long unpaid Spanish troops mutinied and sacked the wealthy city of Antwerp; over 8,000 citizens died during the three days of the "Spanish Fury." This brutal act led to the Pacification of Ghent, a treaty of peace and alliance between the Protestant north and the Catholic south against the Spanish administration. The next Spanish governor-generals, JOHN OF AUSTRIA (Philip's half brother) and Alessandro FARNESE, Duke of Parma (Philip's nephew), sought to break the union. After Don John's death in 1578, Parma restored Spanish authority in the south, but in the north in 1579, Holland, Zeeland, and the provinces of the northeast signed the Union of Utrecht, seeking some form of self-government under their STATES-GENERAL, a legislative body composed of representatives from the various provincial legislatures (States).

In 1580, the States-General accepted Francis VALOIS, Duke of Alençon, heir to the French throne, as ruler and military leader of the Netherlands, and in July 1581 the States-

General passed the Act of Abjuration formally renouncing allegiance to Philip II. In 1584, the death of Alençon and the assassination of Orange, along with further Spanish successes in the south, convinced Elizabeth to intervene militarily on behalf of the United Provinces of the north, even though the union, whose rule she had declined, was by then a republic governed by the States-General. The Anglo-Dutch Treaty of Nonsuch of 1585 brought English troops to the Netherlands under Robert DUDLEY, Earl of Leicester, and led to war between England and Spain (see NETHERLANDS EXPEDITION; NONSUCH, TREATY OF). The treaty convinced Philip that the Netherlands would never be pacified until the Protestant regime of Elizabeth had been overthrown in England.

In 1588, Philip sent the ARMADA against England, hoping to use the fleet to ferry Parma's troops across the Channel to depose Elizabeth and restore Catholicism. After the failure of the Armada, the Anglo-Spanish naval war dragged on until 1604. In the Netherlands after 1590, the United Provinces of the Dutch Republic, with English assistance, regained the initiative that ensured their independence. In 1609, Spain and the United Provinces acknowledged military stalemate and agreed to a 12-year truce that partitioned the original Netherlands into the independent and largely Protestant United Provinces of the north (roughly, modern Holland) and the largely Catholic Spanish Netherlands to the south (roughly, modern Belgium). *See also* PROTESTANTISM.

Further Reading: Pieter Geyl, *The Revolt of the Netherlands, 1555–1609*, London: Cassell, 1988; Jonathan I. Israel, *The Dutch Republic: Its Rise, Greatness, and Fall 1477–1806*, Oxford: Clarendon Press, 1998; Geoffrey Parker, *The Dutch Revolt*, Ithaca, NY: Cornell University Press, 1977; G. D. Ramsay, *The Queen's Merchants and the Revolt of the Netherlands*, Manchester, England: Manchester University Press, 1986; C. H. Wilson, *Queen Elizabeth and the Revolt of the Netherlands*, Berkeley: University of California Press, 1970.

Newfoundland fishery

The Newfoundland cod fishery enhanced the DIET of poor Elizabethans, strengthened the national economy, provided the country with experienced seamen, and stimulated English interest in North AMERICA. From the beginning of the sixteenth century, Spanish, French, Portuguese, and English fishermen left their countries' western ports in the early spring to cross the Atlantic and fish the waters off eastern Canada. English fishermen left Bristol and other ports in March or April to reach the fishing grounds by early May. Part of the crew set out in small boats called shallops to catch cod, while the rest of the crew worked onshore at St. John's or other Newfoundland harbors to clean, salt, and cure the fish. Although the crews worked until August or September, vessels called "sack ships" came out from England in midsummer to load and begin selling the early season catch.

With some 160 fast days in the Catholic CALENDAR, fish were much in demand in Catholic Europe, and cod, the favorite European food fish, were large and plentiful in the Grand Banks and other rich fishing areas off Newfoundland and Labrador. When England's break with Roman Catholicism lessened the number of church-mandated fast days, the Elizabethan government intervened by passing through the Parliament of 1563 an act declaring both Wednesday and Saturday to be fish days. By stimulating internal demand for fish, the government hoped to protect and strengthen an industry it considered vital for both the country's economy and its defense.

By Elizabeth's reign, civil war in FRANCE and Spanish warfare in the NETHERLANDS and the Mediterranean had damaged the French and Spanish fishing industries and allowed the English to dominate the Newfoundland fishery and the European trade in cod. When Sir Humphrey GILBERT explored Newfoundland in 1583, he found that the English fishermen controlled the best sites both for landing and curing their catch. As relations with SPAIN deteriorated, the Elizabethan government's desire to maintain this economic dominance was overshadowed by its need for large numbers of experienced seamen for the NAVY. Because the Newfoundland cod fishery was the great training ground for English sailors, protecting the fishery meant ensuring a supply of seamen who could be called upon quickly, as they were during the ARMADA crisis of 1588, to defend England from seaborne invasion.

Further Reading: R. G. Lounsbury, *The British Fishery at Newfoundland,* Hamden, CT: Archon Books, 1969;

Samuel Eliot Morison, *The European Discovery of America: The Northern Voyages,* New York: Oxford University Press, 1971.

Newhaven expedition. *See* LE HAVRE EXPEDITION.

Nine Years War

The Nine Years War, also known as Tyrone's Rebellion, was the longest and costliest Irish uprising of Elizabeth's reign. The war was sparked by Lord Deputy Sir William FITZWILLIAM's high-handed division of the lordship of Monaghan in the northern Irish province of Ulster, an action that threatened other Irish lords with a similar reduction of their power and territory. Led by Hugh O'NEILL, Earl of Tyrone, and his son-in-law Red Hugh O'DONNELL, the chief Irish lords of Ulster bound themselves by oath in a secret alliance against the English government in DUBLIN. The war began in April 1593, as Tyrone deceived the government by pretending to assist it against Irish rebels who were actually acting under his direction. The ruse was an attempt to buy time while Tyrone's agents negotiated with PHILIP II for Spanish assistance.

In February 1595, Tyrone revealed his true intentions by destroying the English garrison on the River Blackwater. Declared a traitor in June, Tyrone surprised the government by supplementing traditional Irish guerrilla tactics with a well-trained infantry force comprising not only Irishmen and REDSHANKS, but also seasoned Spanish and English veterans armed with guns purchased from Scottish and ANGLO-IRISH merchants. Better led and disciplined than most Irish armies in the Elizabethan period, and facing a series of bickering and incompetent English commanders, Tyrone's troops won major victories at Clontibret (1595) and Yellow Ford (1598) (see YELLOW FORD, BATTLE OF). These successes spread the war throughout most of IRELAND by 1598. When Robert DEVEREUX, Earl of Essex, arrived in Ireland with an army of 16,000 men in 1599, Tyrone refused him battle and played on his political ambition to draw him into an unauthorized truce that left Essex free to return to England and Tyrone free to dominate Ireland.

Unable through lack of artillery to capture the towns, Tyrone sought the support of the Anglo-Irish by appealing to their Catholicism. In late 1599, Tyrone sent Elizabeth a series of demands that, if accepted, would have made Ireland an autonomous Catholic state governed by the great Irish and Anglo-Irish lords. The English government responded by sending a capable lord deputy in Charles BLOUNT, Lord Mountjoy, and by adopting a strategy of placing small, mutually supporting garrisons across the countryside to disrupt the Irish economy. In 1601, when Spanish troops landed at Kinsale to support the Irish, Tyrone risked a pitched battle and suffered a severe defeat (see KINSALE, BATTLE OF). Sir George CAREW then crushed the rebellion in the south and Mountjoy's garrisons brought famine to the north, forcing most of Tyrone's allies to submit by the end of 1602. Tyrone went into hiding, finally surrendering in March 1603. The war cost the English government nearly £2 million, more than any previous Irish conflict, but it left England in complete control of Ireland for the first time in 400 years.

Further Reading: Steven G. Ellis, *Tudor Ireland,* London: Longman, 1985; Hiram Morgan, *Tyrone's Rebellion: The Outbreak of the Nine Years War in Tudor Ireland,* Rochester, NY: Boydell Press, 1993; Sean O'Faolain, *The Great O'Neill,* New York: Duell, Sloan and Pearce, 1942, reprint ed., Dufour Editions, 1977).

Nobility. *See* PEERAGE.

Noel, Alexander. *See* NOWELL, ALEXANDER.

Nonsuch Palace

Built by HENRY VIII after 1538 to rival the king of France's (see FRANCIS I) new palace at Chambord, Nonsuch Palace was one of the most fanciful Tudor residences and a favorite of Elizabeth I. Located about 12 miles southwest of LONDON in Surrey, Nonsuch was one of the few Tudor PALACES built on a previously undeveloped site, with no earlier structure to serve as the core of the new residence. Compared with such great palaces as WHITEHALL PALACE and HAMPTON COURT PALACE, which could house and feed the whole COURT (numbering up to 1,500 people), Nonsuch was a small house meant only for the monarch and his or her personal servants, along with a small portion of the court, consisting perhaps of the

PRIVY COUNCIL, royal FAVORITES, and selected guests.

Nonsuch, which covered merely two acres (in contrast to Whitehall's 23 acres), had no great hall for feeding the court and no audience chambers for the reception of ambassadors or the staging of court ENTERTAINMENTs. Set in a 1,700-acre deer park, Nonsuch comprised a pair of two-story quadrangles with two large octagonal towers at the ends. The inner court was entered through an ornate gatehouse crowned with a great clock and containing a marble fountain and a large statue of Henry VIII. The walls of the building were covered with elaborately decorated stucco panels or a surfacing of engraved slate. Decoration of the palace was directed by Nicholas Bellin, an Italian artist stolen from the service of the French king. The palace was also surrounded by a series of formal gardens.

In the 1550s, MARY I granted Nonsuch to the Earl of Arundel, who completed some of the construction left unfinished at the death of Henry VIII in 1547. Arundel left the palace to his son-in-law, John LUMLEY, Lord Lumley, who tactfully presented it to Elizabeth in 1592. The queen, who had made no secret of her desire to reacquire Nonsuch, thanked Lumley for having "garnished and replenished" the palace, and granted him other property elsewhere. Nonsuch, like so many Tudor palaces, was heavily damaged during the civil war of the 1640s. In 1665, Charles II gave the palace to his mistress, Barbara Villiers, Duchess of Cleveland, who had it demolished.

Further Reading: John Martin Robinson, *Royal Residences,* London: MacDonald and Company, 1982; Simon Thurley, *The Royal Palaces of Tudor England,* New Haven, CT: Yale University Press, 1993.

Nonsuch, Treaty of

The Treaty of Nonsuch created a formal political and military alliance between Elizabethan England and the NETHERLANDS provinces in revolt against PHILIP II of SPAIN (see NETHERLANDS REVOLT). Several events in 1584 caused Elizabeth to reconsider her longstanding refusal to formally support foreign subjects in rebellion against their lawful monarch. The death of Francis VALOIS, Duke of Alençon, in June, and the assassination of WILLIAM, PRINCE OF ORANGE, in July, left the Protestant rebels in the Netherlands without a leader or a constitutional head of state, a situation that threatened to tip the military balance in favor of the able Spanish governor-general, Alessandro FARNESE, Duke of Parma. When HENRI III of France refused the rule of the rebellious provinces, fear of what a Spanish victory in the Netherlands would mean for the security of Protestant England led William CECIL, Lord Burghley, to abandon his opposition to English involvement in the provinces and to begin working with Dutch politicians to open talks between the queen and the Dutch STATES-GENERAL.

Dutch representatives arrived in LONDON in March 1585, while William DAVISON, the English ambassador in the Netherlands, met with rebel leaders in Holland. Davison proposed that the towns of Flushing and Brill (see CAUTIONARY TOWNS) be surrendered to English control as pledges of good faith. Accepting this suggestion, the States-General sent a delegation to England to negotiate a formal treaty. Hurried along by the deteriorating military situation, the talks finally concluded in August 1585 with the signing of the Treaty of Nonsuch. Elizabeth agreed to supply the Dutch with 5,000 foot soldiers and 1,000 horsemen, along with garrison troops for Flushing and Brill, the towns that were handed over to the English as security. Elizabeth was also to appoint a "gentleman of quality" to command the English troops and to sit on the Dutch Council of State.

Because of the need for haste, the treaty was vague on many points, including who was to pay for the English troops and what, if any, political role the English commander—who turned out to be Robert DUDLEY, Earl of Leicester—should play (see NETHERLANDS EXPEDITION). Although the treaty led to many misunderstandings between the new allies, it committed Elizabeth to the Dutch cause and threw England into war with Spain.

Further Reading: Pieter Geyl, *The Revolt of the Netherlands, 1555–1609,* London: Cassell, 1988; Jonathan I. Israel, *The Dutch Republic: Its Rise, Greatness, and Fall 1477–1806,* Oxford: Clarendon Press, 1998; Geoffrey Parker, *The Dutch Revolt,* Ithaca, NY: Cornell University Press, 1977; G. D. Ramsay, *The Queen's Merchants and the Revolt of the Netherlands,* Manchester, England: Manchester University Press, 1986; C. H. Wilson, *Queen Elizabeth and the Revolt of the Netherlands,* Berkeley: University of California Press, 1970.

Norden, John (1548–1625)

Writer and cartographer John Norden was the first Englishman to design and undertake a complete series of histories of the counties of England (see ANTIQUARIANISM). Born probably in Middlesex into a minor GENTRY family, Norden in January 1593 won authorization from the PRIVY COUNCIL "to travel through England and Wales to make more perfect descriptions, charts, and maps" of each county (see Maps, "Counties of England and Wales"). Norden titled his survey of the counties the *Speculum Britanniae,* and he completed the first volume in the series, covering Middlesex, in 1593. Lack of funds slowed Norden's work, although he was much encouraged in his plans by William CECIL, Lord Burghley. Norden managed to complete full surveys only for Hertfordshire (1598), Northampton (1610), and Cornwall (1610), with partial work done for Essex and Norfolk, and perhaps for Kent and Surrey (the manuscripts have been lost).

Norden's surveys contained not only written descriptions of the counties, but finely detailed maps showing roads and pictorial details. Norden's maps were well known and widely used; John SPEED used the Norden maps of Cornwall, Essex, Middlesex, Surrey, and Sussex in several of his publications. Norden's "A Description of the Honor of Windsor" (1607), which was dedicated to JAMES I, contains an excellent "Plan or Bird's-Eye View" of WINDSOR CASTLE and maps depicting the various surrounding forests and parks. Norden also prepared the best surviving maps of Elizabethan LONDON and WESTMINSTER PALACE and is said to have produced a map in 16 sheets showing all the sites of battles fought in Britain between the Norman Conquest of 1066 and the reign of Elizabeth.

Norden also held several surveying positions, including the surveyorship of the duchy of Cornwall and the surveyorship of Crown lands in Berkshire, Devon, Surrey, and other counties. In 1607, he published a manual of surveying, *The Surveyor's Dialogue.* He also published *An Intended Guide for English Travellers* in 1625 and a book of simple Protestant devotions entitled *The Pensive Man's Practice,* which was so popular it went through 40 printings before Norden's death.

Further Reading: A. L. Rowse, *The England of Elizabeth,* Madison: University of Wisconsin Press, 1978.

Norfolk, Duke of. *See* HOWARD, THOMAS, DUKE OF NORFOLK.

Norris, Sir John (c. 1547–1597)

Sir John Norris was an important Elizabethan military leader and a commander of English troops in IRELAND and the NETHERLANDS. Born in Oxfordshire, Norris attended Oxford (see UNIVERSITIES) but left in 1571 to serve as a soldier with the Huguenot forces in FRANCE and against rebels in Ireland (see HUGUENOTS). He spent much of the early 1580s in the Netherlands (see NETHERLANDS REVOLT) fighting with the Dutch rebels against SPAIN. In 1584–85, he returned to Ireland, where he served the English government as lord president of Munster, a region of southern Ireland.

By the spring of 1585, he was back in the Netherlands, where he became a subordinate of Robert DUDLEY, Earl of Leicester, who came to the Netherlands in late 1585 as commander of the military forces that Elizabeth had promised the Dutch through the Treaty of Nonsuch (see NETHERLANDS EXPEDITION; NONSUCH, TREATY OF). Although believing his long experience in the Netherlands made him better qualified than Leicester to command the English forces, Norris nonetheless served Leicester well, winning the Battle of Grave in 1586 and subsequently accepting knighthood from the earl. In 1588, during the ARMADA crisis, Norris was Leicester's deputy in the main English camp at Tilbury (see TILBURY SPEECH) and was given responsibility for defending the shores of Kent against a Spanish landing.

In April 1589, Norris shared command with Sir Francis DRAKE of the PORTUGAL EXPEDITION, an enterprise aimed at disrupting Spanish shipping and, if possible, overthrowing the rule of PHILIP II in Portugal. Raids on Corunna and Lisbon failed, and the fleet returned to England having done more damage to its commanders' reputations than to Spain. From 1591 to 1593, Norris fought with the English forces supporting HENRI IV of France (see BRITTANY EXPEDITIONS); he and Sir Martin FROBISHER successfully defended the Breton fort of Crozon from Spanish attack in 1593. In 1595, Norris returned to Munster to help suppress the rebellion of Hugh O'NEILL, Earl of Tyrone (see NINE YEARS WAR). Exasperated by the continuing political unrest that plagued Ireland, Norris died in Munster in 1597.

Further Reading: John S. Nolan, *Sir John Norrys and the Elizabethan Military World,* Exeter: University of Exeter Press, 1997.

Northern Rebellion

In 1568, Thomas HOWARD, Duke of Norfolk, enlisted the aid of Thomas Percy, Earl of Northumberland, and Charles Neville, Earl of Westmorland, the heads of the two greatest noble families in the north of England, in furthering his bid to wed Mary STUART, Queen of Scots, and to have Mary recognized as heir to the English throne. By supporting Norfolk, the earls were not so much interested in enhancing the duke's position as in preserving their own. The control and influence their families had once exerted over northern England had been declining under the Tudors, and they were especially threatened by the centralizing policies of Elizabeth and her chief advisor, William CECIL. Many northern Catholics disliked the queen's Protestant Church, and the earls hoped to use this religious discontent to serve their own political ends.

When Elizabeth refused to countenance the duke's plans to marry the Queen of Scots, Norfolk left COURT uttering vague threats against Cecil and his supporters. As the only duke in England and a distant relative of the queen's, Norfolk felt denied his proper position at court by the influence of Cecil. When Elizabeth summoned the duke back to LONDON, he submitted almost immediately. Fearful that they might be summoned next, the northern earls rose in rebellion, calling out their tenants and any disgruntled Catholics. The rebels seized Durham and restored Catholic worship in the cathedral. The earls demanded the restoration of Catholicism throughout the kingdom, the release of Mary Stuart, and the dismissal of Cecil (see CATHOLICISM, ENGLISH). They also received money from the pope through Roberto Ridolfi, an Italian banker and secret papal agent living in England.

The arrival of a royal army under Thomas RADCLIFFE, Earl of Sussex, dispersed the rebel force, and the two earls fled into SCOTLAND. The execution of several hundred rebels in early 1570 restored quiet to the North, which came more fully under the control of the queen's Council of the North. Westmorland fled to the NETHERLANDS, where he lived on a pension from PHILIP II of SPAIN. Northumberland, after being ransomed by Elizabeth from the Scots for £2,000, was executed at York in 1572. Norfolk survived his association with the rebel earls, only to die in June 1572 for his involvement in the RIDOLFI PLOT.

Further Reading: Neville Williams, *A Tudor Tragedy: Thomas Howard, Fourth Duke of Norfolk,* London: Barrie and Jenkins, 1964.

Northumberland, Duke of. *See* DUDLEY, JOHN, DUKE OF NORTHUMBERLAND.

Northumberland's coup

The coup orchestrated in 1553 by John DUDLEY, Duke of Northumberland, sought to remove Princess Mary (see MARY I) and, somewhat surprisingly, Princess Elizabeth from the succession. The coup grew out of the fears of EDWARD VI that Mary, his Catholic half sister and heir, would, upon her accession, overthrow the Protestant Church that had been created during his reign. The coup also arose out of Northumberland's fears that the accession of Mary would mean the end of his political power and perhaps even of his freedom or his life. As his health deteriorated in the spring of 1553, Edward drew up a *DEVISE* to alter the succession as laid down in the 1544 Act of Succession (see SUCCESSION, ACTS OF) and in the will of HENRY VIII. Because only PARLIAMENT could amend its own acts, the *Devise* was technically illegal, and the king and Northumberland had to bully councilors and judges into accepting it.

The *Devise* passed the Crown directly to the heirs of Edward's Protestant cousin, Frances Grey (see GREY CLAIM), a niece of Henry VIII and the wife of Henry Grey, Duke of Suffolk. Because the Greys had no sons, the Crown was to pass to their strongly Protestant eldest daughter, 15-year-old Jane GREY. In May 1553, Northumberland married his son Guildford to Jane to ensure that her future son and heir would be his grandson, which is why the duke also moved to exclude Elizabeth from the throne. When Edward died on 6 July, the PRIVY COUNCIL kept the death secret for three days. Jane, who had never been a willing participant in the scheme, promptly fainted when informed of her accession on 9 July.

Either through oversight or the unexpected rapidity of the king's death, Northumberland had neglected to gain control of Mary's person. The princess fled from her country house in Norfolk into Suffolk, and a growing band of supporters began to form around her. When Northumberland left LONDON on 14 July to arrest Mary, the princess was being proclaimed queen all across the country. On 18 July, the Privy Council in LONDON abandoned Northumberland and proclaimed Mary; the reign of Queen Jane, only nine days old, was over. Although Northumberland declared himself a Catholic, he was arrested and executed on 22 August. Jane Grey and her husband remained in the TOWER OF LONDON until February 1554, when her father's involvement in WYATT'S REBELLION led to the execution of all three.

Further Reading: Barrett L. Beer, *Northumberland,* Kent, OH: Kent State University Press, 1973; W. R. Jordan, *Edward VI: The Threshold of Power,* Cambridge, MA: Harvard University Press, 1970; David Loades, *John Dudley, Duke of Northumberland,* Oxford: Clarendon Press, 1996.

Northwest Passage

Like the other nations of Europe, Elizabethan England wanted a practical trade route to Asia, the source of silks, spices, and other valuable commodities. In the late fifteenth century, Portuguese mariners pioneered a southeastern route to Asia around Africa's Cape of Good Hope. In 1519, Ferdinand Magellan opened for SPAIN a southwestern route to Asia by sailing through the straits at the southern tip of South America that now bear his name. The English had sought a northern route to Asia since the 1490s, when HENRY VII sent John Cabot to find a northwestern passage around North America. When Cabot failed to return from his second voyage, the English search for a Northwest Passage ceased.

HENRY VIII, who came to the throne in 1509, was more interested in European war than in American exploration, but by Elizabeth's reign, increasing rivalry with Spain revived interest in finding a Northwest Passage. Certain that the route existed, and determined to compete with Spain for the spice trade, various prominent Elizabethans, such as Sir Humphrey GILBERT, called for voyages of exploration to find the passage (see Maps, "American Voyages of Elizabethan Exploration"). Between 1576 and 1578, Martin FROBISHER led three expeditions around Greenland and into the network of islands and waterways off northeastern North America. His belief that he had discovered gold shifted the focus of his last two voyages from a search for the passage to a search for wealth. In 1578, Francis DRAKE, having sailed through the Straits of Magellan, explored the west coast of North America hoping to find a passage from the other side; he sailed as far north as the site of modern Vancouver before turning west across the Pacific (see DRAKE'S CIRCUMNAVIGATION).

Between 1585 and 1587, John DAVIS led three voyages that explored well to the north in the wide strait (later named Davis Strait) between Greenland and Baffin Island. Davis found no practical, ice-free route to Asia, but he did find the openings of various promising waterways. In 1610–11, Henry Hudson followed one of Davis's leads into the great bay of northern Canada that was later named after him. He did not find a passage into the Pacific, but he did establish England's claim to northern Canada. A successful Northwest Passage by water from Greenland to Alaska was not made until 1905, when the Norwegian explorer Roald Amundsen finally accomplished it.

Further Reading: John Davis, *The Voyages and Works of John Davis, the Navigator,* New York: S. Franklin, 1970; Samuel Eliot Morison, *The European Discovery of America: The Northern Voyages,* New York: Oxford University Press, 1971; Leslie H. Neatby, *In Quest of the North West Passage,* New York: Crowell, 1958; George M. Thomson, *The Search for the North-West Passage,* New York: Macmillan, 1975.

Norton, Thomas (1532–1584)

Thomas Norton was a poet, a playwright, and a Puritan activist in PARLIAMENT (see PURITANS). Norton was born in LONDON, the son of a wealthy grocer. He was educated at Cambridge (see UNIVERSITIES) and, like his father, became a member of the Grocers' Company (see LIVERIED COMPANIES). While still in his teens, he entered the service of Edward SEYMOUR, Duke of Somerset, uncle and lord protector of EDWARD VI. In 1555, he began legal training at the INNS OF COURT, where he befriended a fellow student named Thomas SACKVILLE. While studying the law, Norton married a daughter of Thomas CRANMER, the late Archbishop of Canterbury.

Since 1550, Norton had engaged in various literary pursuits, writing POETRY and publishing an English translation of a Latin letter from the reformer Peter Martyr to Somerset. In 1561, he published his English translation of John CALVIN's *Institutes of the Christian Religion,* a project encouraged by his wife's stepfather, a Calvinist printer (see CALVINISM; PRINTING). Norton also collaborated with Sackville on the writing of a play entitled *Gorboduc,* which was performed at the Inner Temple on Twelfth Night in 1561 (see CHRISTMAS). Written in blank verse and patterned after the works of the Roman playwright Seneca, *Gorboduc* was the first English tragedy. The play borrowed a tale from an English legend, telling of the evils that befell King Gorboduc when he tried to divide his kingdom between his two sons.

Norton served in the Parliaments of 1559 and 1563 and was a member for London in the Parliaments of 1571, 1572, and 1581. An increasingly committed Puritan, Norton was a strong advocate in Parliament for harsher measures against Catholics (see PENAL LAWS). In 1581, Norton was appointed the queen's censor, a position that allowed him to conduct examinations of Catholics suspected of TREASON. He performed his office so zealously, and he sent so many Catholics to torture, that he became known as the "rackmaster." Norton was himself briefly imprisoned in 1584 for his strident advocacy of Puritan positions in Parliament. His imprisonment damaged his health and he died at his house in London in March 1584. *See also* CATHOLICISM, ENGLISH; DRAMA; PARLIAMENTARY SESSIONS (1559–1581); PROTESTANTISM.

Further Reading: Michael A. R. Graves, *Thomas Norton: The Parliament Man,* Oxford: Blackwell, 1994.

Nottingham, Earl of. *See* HOWARD, CHARLES, EARL OF NOTTINGHAM.

Nowell, Alexander (c. 1507–1602)

Alexander Nowell (or Noel) was dean of St. Paul's Cathedral in LONDON and the author of the Anglican CATECHISM. Born in Lancashire, Nowell was educated at Brasenose College, Oxford (see UNIVERSITIES), eventually becoming an instructor of logic. In 1551, after his ordination to the ministry, he became a member of the clerical staff at Westminster Abbey and master of Westminster School (see GRAMMAR SCHOOL; WESTMINSTER PALACE). During the reign of EDWARD VI, Nowell acquired a great reputation as a preacher, delivering sermons at COURT, PAUL'S CROSS, and other notable venues.

After the accession of MARY I in 1553, Nowell was elected to PARLIAMENT, but he was not allowed to serve because he was also a member of CONVOCATION. A convinced Protestant, Nowell then fled abroad, joining Marian exile communities in Europe (see MARIAN EXILES). He returned to England on Elizabeth's accession in 1558 and was appointed dean (i.e., the head of the chapter or clerical staff of a cathedral) of St. Paul's Cathedral in 1560, a position he held for 42 years. Nowell had a stormy relationship with the queen. He lost a chance to be provost of the school at Eton when he took a wife, the queen preferring her higher clergy to be celibate. In 1562, he earned a royal rebuke for giving the queen a richly ornamented copy of the *BOOK OF COMMON PRAYER,* which Elizabeth found too Catholic for her tastes. In 1564, the queen interrupted Nowell's sermon to scold him for attacking the use of crucifixes, which he opposed and she did not. He also got into trouble for publicly criticizing the queen's failure to marry and bear children. "If your parents had been of the same mind," he asked in Elizabeth's hearing, "where had you been then?"

Nowell is best known as the author of three catechisms. His so-called "Large Catechism" was approved by Convocation in 1563 and was printed in 1572. The "Middle Catechism" was an abridgment of the "Large Catechism," and the "Small Catechism" of 1572 was based on the catechism in the Prayer Book of 1549. Nowell also wrote part of the Anglican Catechism that was authorized for use in

1604, two years after his death. *See also* AN-GLICAN CHURCH and the illustration for GRAMMAR SCHOOL.

Further Reading: Patrick Collinson, *The Elizabethan Puritan Movement,* Oxford: Clarendon Press, 1990.

Nymegen, Treaty of

Signed in April 1573 by Elizabeth I and Fernandez ALVAREZ DE TOLEDO, Duke of Alva, the Spanish governor-general of the NETHERLANDS, the Treaty of Nymegen lifted the trade embargo that had existed between England and the Netherlands since the "TREASURE CRISIS" OF 1568. The agreement represented a preliminary adjustment of Anglo-Spanish relations that was extended and regularized in the 1574 Treaty of Bristol (see BRISTOL, TREATY OF).

In December 1568, Huguenot pirates chased Spanish ships carrying gold and silver coin for the payment of Spanish troops in the Netherlands into English Channel ports (see HUGUENOTS). Learning that PHILIP II had borrowed the money from Italian bankers and that it did not officially become his property until it reached its destination, Elizabeth had the coin impounded, negotiated new terms with the bankers, and borrowed the money herself. The Spanish ambassador in England, Gerau de Spes, vigorously protested this action, portraying it in such an unfavorable light to Alva that the Spanish governor took de Spes's advice and seized all English men and goods in the Netherlands in January 1569. Word of these seizures arrived in England at about the same time as word of the Spanish attack on John HAWKINS's fleet in the Mexican port of SAN JUAN D'ULLOA the previous September. The English government responded by confiscating all Spanish goods in English ports, thus initiating the trade embargo that was finally ended four years later by the Treaty of Nymegen.

Negotiations to restore trade began in 1570, but continued unrest in the Netherlands and English concern over the RIDOLFI PLOT prevented any agreement. Alva finally reopened talks on his own initiative in early 1573 because he was concerned that Elizabeth might increase her financial aid to WILLIAM, PRINCE OF ORANGE, the Dutch rebel leader, who had recently sent representatives to LONDON. With political and economic conditions finally favoring settlement, the negotiations were quickly concluded. Both parties agreed to end the embargo and to support one another against mutual enemies for two years. Alva ensured the success of the talks by accepting an English formula for the restoration of property that had been confiscated in 1569. With the subsequent Treaty of Bristol, the Nymegen agreement normalized Anglo-Spanish relations until the outbreak of war between the two countries in 1585.

Further Reading: P. S. Crowson, *Tudor Foreign Policy,* New York: St. Martin's Press, 1973.

O

Oatlands Palace

Built by her father, Oatlands Palace was one of Elizabeth's principal royal residences in the Thames Valley near LONDON. Just as HENRY VIII built ST. JAMES'S PALACE as a smaller London retreat from nearby WHITEHALL PALACE, so Oatlands was constructed near HAMPTON COURT PALACE to provide the king with greater opportunities to hunt. Oatlands was located on the south bank of the Thames about five miles southwest of Hampton Court near Weybridge. In 1539 and 1540, PARLIAMENT set aside a large tract of the south bank of the Thames west of Hampton Court as a new royal hunting ground, an action taken to accommodate an increasingly ill and corpulent monarch who still enjoyed the hunt. Anxious "to have his game and pleasure ready at hand," Henry planned a new residence near to his hunting and to Hampton Court, having acquired the Oatlands site through an exchange of property with the Rede family in 1538.

Built in the early 1540s, Oatlands was a rambling structure covering 10 acres (Hampton Court covered 6 acres and Whitehall 23 acres). Like St. James's, Oatlands was built of brick. Though covering a sizable area, it had no great hall and so could not accommodate the full COURT. According to surviving drawings of the palace, Oatlands was built around a large, square central court with the royal apartments forming a triangular cluster of buildings that lay beyond. Elizabeth somewhat extended the large outer court of the palace by building a complex of kitchens and court offices.

Entrance to the central court from the south was through a tall gatehouse with oriel windows and octagonal turrets, matched by a somewhat smaller gatehouse on the north end of the court that led to the royal apartments. The most notable feature of the royal apartments was the prospect tower, which was similar in appearance to some of the towers at NONSUCH PALACE. Like so many Tudor royal residences, Oatlands was demolished during the civil war in the mid-seventeenth century, and little else is known of its design and appearance. *See also* ARCHITECTURE; PALACES.

Further Reading: John Martin Robinson, *Royal Residences,* London: MacDonald and Company, 1982; Simon Thurley, *The Royal Palaces of Tudor England,* New Haven, CT: Yale University Press, 1993.

O'Donnell, Hugh (1572–1602)

Hugh O'Donnell, known as "Red Hugh," was the head of the Ulster lordship of Tirconnell and a leader of the Irish insurgents during the NINE YEARS WAR. O'Donnell saw his first military action in 1584 when he was only 12. In 1587, Lord Deputy Sir John PERROT, fearing the possible consequences of O'Donnell's proposed marriage to a daughter of Hugh O'NEILL, Earl of Tyrone (the chief Irish nobleman in Ulster), lured O'Donnell aboard an English vessel and had him arrested as he sat drinking. O'Donnell languished in Dublin Castle until 1591, when he escaped with the assistance of Tyrone. The following year, O'Donnell's mother, who had ruled Tirconnell during O'Donnell's captivity, engineered her senile husband's deposition and saw her son installed as lord.

On the outbreak of the Nine Years War in 1593, O'Donnell acted as an able second in command to Tyrone, achieving the capture by treachery of Sligo Castle and organizing an

Irish appeal for assistance to PHILIP II of SPAIN. O'Donnell fought alongside his father-in-law at the victories of Clontibret in 1595 and Yellow Ford in 1598 (see YELLOW FORD, BATTLE OF) and raided across western and northern IRELAND, disrupting the authority of the DUBLIN government and greatly extending his own.

On the landing of Spanish forces at Kinsale in southern Ireland in September 1601 (see KINSALE, BATTLE OF), O'Donnell marched a portion of the Irish ARMY across the island to link up with the Spaniards. Although winter was approaching and Sir George CAREW had stationed himself at Cashel with 2,500 men to intercept the Irish, O'Donnell executed a brilliant flanking march that evaded Carew and brought his forces safely to Kinsale, where he was joined a week later by Tyrone and the rest of the army. After the disastrous Irish defeat at Kinsale on 24 December 1601, O'Donnell sailed to Spain to seek further assistance for the Irish cause. He died in Spain at Simancas in 1602 amid rumors (probably untrue) that he had been poisoned. Although the biography published shortly after his death, the *Life of Red Hugh O'Donnell*, gives O'Donnell a paramount position among the Irish war leadership, evidence indicates that he generally acted as Tyrone's subordinate.

Further Reading: Steven G. Ellis, *Tudor Ireland*, London: Longman, 1985; Hiram Morgan, *Tyrone's Rebellion: The Outbreak of the Nine Years War in Tudor Ireland*, Rochester, NY: Boydell Press, 1993; Sean O'Faolain, *The Great O'Neill*, New York: Duell, Sloan and Pearce, 1942, reprint ed., Dufour Editions, 1997; Micheline Kerney Walsh. *Hugh O'Neill: An Exile of Ireland, Prince of Ulster*. Dublin: Four Courts Press, 1996.

officers of state

Although English medieval government operated through the seals used to authenticate official documents, with the great officers of state being those who controlled the Great Seal, the Privy Seal, and the Signet, Elizabethan government functioned through ministers of state who implemented the decisions of the queen, the PRIVY COUNCIL, and PARLIAMENT. This change in method was signaled by the decline in importance of the *lord chancellor,* the keeper of the Great Seal. Twice during Elizabeth's reign, from 1558 to 1579, and again from 1592 to 1596, the chancellorship was vacant. During the first period, the Great Seal was held by

Lord Keeper Sir Nicholas BACON, and from 1587 to 1591, the chancellor, the Crown's most important legal officer, was Sir Christopher HATTON, a man of limited legal training. The *lord privy seal*, the keeper of the Privy Seal, supervised a staff of clerks who received royal orders and grants initiated under the Signet and prepared documents for authentication by the Great Seal. The lord privy seal also oversaw the Court of Requests (see REQUESTS, COURT OF).

The two Elizabethan *secretaryships of state* developed from the principal secretaryship, the monarch's private secretary and keeper of the Signet (the monarch's personal seal). During the sixteenth century, the importance of the office tended to reflect the man who held it. In the 1530s, Thomas CROMWELL based his great authority on the secretaryship, and, from 1558 to 1572, Sir William CECIL acted as Elizabeth's chief minister while holding the secretaryship. Under Cecil, the *principal secretary* acted as a link between the Crown, the Privy Council, and Parliament, setting the Council's agenda and managing Parliament's deliberations. Under Sir Francis WALSINGHAM from 1573 to 1590, one of the secretaries began to specialize in foreign affairs, supervising, as Walsingham did, the Crown's diplomatic service and assuming responsibility for state security and an extensive foreign and domestic intelligence network (see DIPLOMACY).

The office of *lord treasurer,* the post held by Cecil after 1572, was responsible for financial affairs and for the collection of CUSTOMS REVENUE; the treasurer presided, either directly or through the *chancellor of the Exchequer,* over the financial court of the EXCHEQUER, one of the courts of COMMON LAW. The *lord chamberlain* supervised the daily routine of the COURT, including ceremonies, travel arrangements, and ENTERTAINMENT, although much responsibility for organizing the latter was assigned to the *master of the revels.*

The *lord admiral* was responsible for the organization, supply, and personnel of the NAVY, and was, during war, commander of the fleet. Charles HOWARD, Lord Howard of Effingham, lord chamberlain from 1573, became lord admiral in 1585, serving in that key post during the ARMADA invasion of 1588. *See also* illustrations for BACON, SIR NICHOLAS; CECIL, WILLIAM.

Chief Officers of the Crown

Office	Duties	Elizabethan Officeholders
Lord Admiral	The Lord Admiral was the chief naval officer of England, responsible for naval administration and, if he was of proper age and fitness, commander of the English fleet at sea.	Edward Fiennes de Clinton, Lord Clinton, Earl of Lincoln, 1558–1585 Charles Howard, Lord Howard of Effingham, Earl of Nottingham, 1585–1619
Lord Chancellor	From medieval times, the Chancellor was the keeper of the Great Seal, and, by Elizabethan times, was the chief legal officer of the Crown, presiding over the Court of Chancery and the House of Lords. Twice during the reign, Elizabeth left the chancellorship vacant and appointed instead a Lord Keeper of the Great Seal.	Vacant 1558–1579 [Sir Nicholas Bacon (Lord Keeper)] Sir Thomas Bromley, 1579–1587 Sir Christopher Hatton, 1587–1591 Vacant 1592–1596 [Sir John Puckering (Lord Keeper)] Sir Thomas Egerton, 1596–1603
Lord Chamberlain	The Chamberlain, the chief officer of the royal household, supervised an extensive staff of grooms, pages, carvers, cupbearers, physicians, chaplains, and yeoman of the guard, among others. Twice Elizabeth gave the position to sons of former chamberlains, thus giving the office a quasi-hereditary nature. The Master of the Revels was subordinate to the Chamberlain.	William Howard, Lord Howard of Effingham, 1558–1572 Thomas Radcliffe, Earl of Sussex, 1572–1583 Charles Howard, Lord Howard of Effingham, Earl of Nottingham, 1584–1585 Henry Carey, Lord Hunsdon, 1585–1596 William Brooke, Lord Cobham, 1596–1597 George Carey, Lord Hunsdon, 1597–1603
Lord Privy Seal	The Lord Privy Seal was the head of the eight-man Privy Seal Office and keeper of the Privy Seal, which the monarch used to authenticate answers to petitions and special money transactions. The Lord Privy Seal also directed the Court of Requests.	Sir William Cecil, 1559–1572 William Howard, Lord Howard of Effingham, Earl of Nottingham, 1572–1573 Sir Thomas Smith, 1573–1576 Sir Francis Walsingham, 1576–1590 William Cecil, Lord Burghley, 1590–1598 Sir Robert Cecil, 1598–1603
Lord Treasurer	The Lord Treasurer oversaw royal financial affairs and presided over the Exchequer. Under the Tudors, the office had great prestige and was usually given to a peer. The Chancellor of the Exchequer was subordinate to the Treasurer.	William Paulet, Marquis of Winchester, 1558–1572 William Cecil, Lord Burghley, 1572–1598 Thomas Sackville, Lord Buckhurst, Earl of Dorset, 1598–1608
Secretary of State	Prior to 1540, the Secretary of State was the monarch's personal secretary and the keeper of the Signet, the monarch's personal seal. After 1540, a second secretary was often appointed to assist the Principal Secretary. Under Elizabeth, the Principal Secretaries managed the agenda of the Privy Council, represented the Crown in Parliament, and headed the diplomatic service.	Sir William Cecil, 1558–1572 Sir Thomas Smith, 1572–1576 Sir Francis Walsingham, 1573–1590 Thomas Wilson, 1577–1581 William Davison, 1586–1587 Sir Robert Cecil, 1596–1603 John Herbert, 1600

Seals of Government

Seal	Function
Great Seal	Originating in the twelfth century, the Great Seal, a circular, double-sided seal placed in the keeping of the Lord Chancellor, was—and still is—the main seal for authenticating royal grants. By Elizabethan times, formal procedure called for royal grants and orders originated by warrants authenticated under the Privy Seal or the Signet to then be sent to the Chancellor for validation with the Great Seal.
Privy Seal	A small seal bearing the royal coat of arms, the Privy Seal was used to validate the monarch's answer to various petitions and to authorize special money transactions. The Lord Privy Seal oversaw a small staff of clerks who received documents sealed with the royal Signet and prepared documents for authentication with the Great Seal.
Signet	The Signet, a small, single-sided seal developed in the fourteenth century as the monarch's private seal, was kept by the king's secretary. Because the Great Seal and the Privy Seal remained at Westminster in the keeping of the Chancellor and the Lord Privy Seal, respectively, monarchs wanted a personal seal that traveled with them and allowed them to authenticate royal grants and orders wherever they were in the kingdom. Such documents were then taken to Westminster for validation by the Privy and Great Seals.

Further Reading: John Guy, *The Tudor Monarchy*, Oxford: Oxford University Press, 1997; David Loades, *Tudor Government*, Oxford: Blackwell Publishers, 1997; A. G. R. Smith, *The Government of Elizabethan England*, New York: W. W. Norton, 1967.

Oliver, Isaac (c. 1556–1617)

Isaac Oliver was one of the most prominent and sought-after miniature painters (see LIMNING) in Elizabethan England. Born in Rouen in FRANCE, Oliver came to LONDON with his family in about 1562. Although his father was a goldsmith, Oliver became a student of the famed miniaturist Nicholas HILLIARD, who, as royal limner, painted miniature portraits of the queen and many well-known courtiers. Oliver eventually developed a style that was more realistic than Hilliard's and made greater use of shadowing. Although the queen preferred the more idealized portraiture of Hilliard, Oliver won great acclaim for his work both at COURT and among the GENTRY and the London merchant community.

After 1588, Oliver spent several years in Venice and elsewhere in Italy studying Italian ART. He may also have studied art in the NETHERLANDS, for in 1602 he married the daughter of the well-known Dutch painter Marcus Gheeraerts the Elder. In 1604, JAMES I appointed Oliver limner to his wife, Queen Anne. Oliver painted the king and his entire family, as well as many prominent members of James I's court. Oliver died in London in October 1617 and left his painting equipment and portraits, finished and unfinished, to his son Peter, who also became a miniaturist.

Further Reading: Mary Edmond, *Hilliard and Oliver*, London: R. Hale, 1983.

O'Neill, Hugh, Earl of Tyrone (c. 1550–1616)

Hugh O'Neill, second Earl of Tyrone and chief of the O'Neill clan in Ulster, led the Irish forces during the NINE YEARS WAR. Hugh was the son of Matthew O'Neill, who was murdered about 1558 at the instigation of his half brother Shane O'NEILL. When his older brother was also murdered, Hugh O'Neill was taken under the protection of the English government and raised in the PALE, perhaps even going for a time to England. Elizabeth hoped that Hugh would prove a more tractable leader of the O'Neills than his cousin Turlough Luineach O'NEILL, who had succeed Shane as clan chief in 1567.

By the 1580s, the Crown had re-established Hugh O'Neill in Ulster and recognized him as Earl of Tyrone. By the early 1590s, Tyrone, with the help of his son-in-law, Red

Hugh O'DONNELL, had defeated Turlough Luineach and supplanted him as leader of the Ulster O'Neills. By 1593, Tyrone began to plot rebellion with other Ulster chiefs, even going so far as to make contact with SPAIN. In 1593, at the start of the Nine Years War, Tyrone maintained outwardly friendly relations with the English government while covertly supporting the uprisings of other Ulster chiefs. In 1595, Tyrone seized the fort on the Blackwater and was proclaimed a traitor. His victory over the English at Yellow Ford in 1598 (see YELLOW FORD, BATTLE OF) extended his authority into central IRELAND and threw DUBLIN into momentary panic.

Elizabeth sent Robert DEVEREUX, Earl of Essex, into Ireland in 1599, but Tyrone refused to meet Essex in open battle. The two earls then concluded a six-month truce that allowed Essex to pursue his political ambitions in England and gave Tyrone time to await the arrival of help from PHILIP II of Spain. Spanish troops landed at Kinsale in southern Ireland in 1601 (see KINSALE, BATTLE OF), but when Tyrone marched south to meet them, he was heavily defeated by Charles BLOUNT, Lord Mountjoy, the lord deputy. Tyrone submitted to the government in 1603, but in 1607 he fled to Rome, where he lived on a papal pension until his death in 1616. JAMES I confiscated his lands, using them for the Ulster plantation of Protestant English and Scottish settlers whose descendants still live in modern Northern Ireland (see PLANTATIONS, IRISH).

Further Reading: Steven G. Ellis, *Tudor Ireland*, London: Longman, 1985; Hiram Morgan, *Tyrone's Rebellion: The Outbreak of the Nine Years War in Tudor Ireland*, Rochester, NY: Boydell Press, 1993; Sean O'Faolain, *The Great O'Neill, a Biography of Hugh O'Neill, Earl of Tyrone, 1550–1616*, New York: Duell, Sloan and Pearce, 1942, reprint ed., Dufour Editions, 1997; Micheline Kerney Walsh, *Hugh O'Neill: An Exile of Ireland, Prince of Ulster*, Dublin: Four Courts Press, 1996.

O'Neill, Shane (c. 1530–1567)

Shane O'Neill was the paramount Irish chieftain in Ulster in the 1560s and was one of Elizabeth's most formidable Irish opponents. The eldest son of Con O'Neill, first Earl of Tyrone, Shane O'Neill succeeded his father as chief of the O'Neills in 1559 after defeating an attempt by his illegitimate half brother, Matthew O'Neill, to claim their father's position.

To seal his victory, Shane incited his supporters to murder Matthew, an action that led Elizabeth to refuse confirmation of either Shane's chieftainship or his earldom of Tyrone.

For leadership of the O'Neills, the most powerful family in the northern Irish province of Ulster, the queen favored Shane's nephew, Hugh O'NEILL, the second son of Matthew. To make him pro-English and to protect him from his uncle, Elizabeth had Hugh educated in the PALE and perhaps, for a time, in England, where he remained until 1568. Elizabeth's support for Hugh drove Shane O'Neill into rebellion and threw Ulster into turmoil until 1562, when Shane agreed to go to England and submit himself to the queen. In return, Elizabeth acknowledged Shane as captain of Ulster, but upon his return to IRELAND, Shane O'Neill reopened hostilities with the government and Ulster suffered another four years of continuous warfare. In 1565, after defeating the Scots settled in Antrim, O'Neill virtually extinguished English authority in Ulster. To maintain his position against English counterattacks, O'Neill appealed for aid to the pope, the king of FRANCE, and Mary STUART, Queen of Scots—all of whom had an interest in weakening Elizabeth.

The lord deputy of Ireland, Sir Henry SIDNEY, led an English army into Ulster to suppress the rebellion, but by the time Sidney's forces reached the north, O'Neill had been defeated and put to flight by his Irish enemies, the O'Donnells. O'Neill took refuge with the MacDonnells, former opponents who at first welcomed him, but then, on 2 June 1567, brutally murdered him, sending his head as a gift to Sidney in DUBLIN. O'Neill's career illustrated both the weakness of English control in northern Ireland and the growing connection between Catholicism and Irish opposition to English rule (see CATHOLICISM, ENGLISH).

Further Reading: Steven G. Ellis, *Tudor Ireland*, London: Longman, 1985; Colm Lennon, *Sixteenth-Century Ireland: The Incomplete Conquest*, Dublin: Gill and Macmillan, 1994; Margaret MacCurtain, *Tudor and Stuart Ireland*, Dublin: Gill and Macmillan, 1972; David B. Quinn, *The Elizabethans and the Irish*, Ithaca, NY: Cornell University Press, 1966.

O'Neill, Turlough Luineach (c. 1531–1595)

From 1567 to 1593, Turlough Luineach O'Neill was leader of the O'Neill clan, the most powerful family in the Ulster region of northern IRELAND. In 1562, when Shane O'NEILL traveled to LONDON to submit to the queen, Turlough O'Neill sought to supplant his cousin as leader of the clan. The loyalty of Shane's followers, and the subsequent return of Shane himself with Elizabeth's acknowledgment of his position, ended Turlough's bid for the chieftainship. However, upon Shane's death in June 1567, Turlough O'Neill was duly installed as leader of the clan. The DUBLIN government also accepted O'Neill's leadership in Ulster, especially since he made no move to assist FITZMAURICE'S REBELLION in southern Ireland in 1569–70.

Turlough O'Neill's 1569 marriage to the half sister of the Scottish Earl of Argyll alarmed the government because it assured O'Neill of a steady supply of REDSHANKS mercenaries from SCOTLAND, although O'Neill's wife was later credited with strongly influencing her husband to live at peace with the Dublin administration. In the mid-1570s, Sir Thomas SMITH and Walter DEVEREUX, Earl of Essex, attempted, with the queen's consent, to colonize parts of Ulster (see PLANTATIONS, IRISH; ULSTER ENTERPRISE [ESSEX]; ULSTER ENTERPRISE [SMITH]). O'Neill declined to assist either plantation scheme and openly opposed the larger Essex enterprise. Accordingly, Essex invaded O'Neill's territory in September 1574, causing much damage but making little progress in winning control of the area. Realizing that the reduction of Ulster would be a long and costly process, Elizabeth withdrew her support from Essex and his colonization scheme collapsed.

In 1575, the government made peace with O'Neill and Elizabeth created him Earl of Clanconnell. When the DESMOND REBELLION erupted in southern Ireland in 1579, O'Neill used the government's weakness to extend his control throughout Ulster and to extract major concessions for his continued good behavior. Fearing that O'Neill was in contact with the pope, the government made peace on O'Neill's terms. However, throughout the 1580s, O'Neill's position gradually weakened as the government supported his English-educated kinsman, Hugh O'NEILL, Earl of Tyrone. By 1592, most of the Ulster O'Neills backed Tyrone, and Turlough resigned his chieftain-

ship in Tyrone's favor in May 1593. Turlough O'Neill died on the run from his enemies in September 1595.

Further Reading: Steven G. Ellis, *Tudor Ireland,* London: Longman, 1985; Colm Lennon, *Sixteenth-Century Ireland: The Incomplete Conquest,* Dublin: Gill and Macmillan, 1994; Margaret MacCurtain, *Tudor and Stuart Ireland,* Dublin: Gill and Macmillan, 1972; David B. Quinn, *The Elizabethans and the Irish,* Ithaca, NY: Cornell University Press, 1966.

Orange, Prince of. *See* WILLIAM, PRINCE OF ORANGE.

The Order and Usage of the Keeping of a Parliament in England

Written by John HOOKER, chamberlain of the city of Exeter, the *Order and Usage* is the most detailed surviving description of the form and functioning of an Elizabethan PARLIAMENT. While in IRELAND serving as agent for Sir Peter CAREW, Hooker sat in the stormy Irish Parliament of 1569. The session witnessed much fruitless argument and personal attack, and was characterized by Hooker as "more like to a bear-baiting of loose persons than an assembly of wise and grave men in parliament." Responding to a petition from several members for a general reform of parliamentary procedures and conduct, Hooker offered to produce, for the guidance of future Irish Parliaments, a manual that described how Parliament was conducted in England. The result of this offer was the *Order and Usage,* which was based on Hooker's experiences as member for Exeter in the English Parliament of 1571.

Published in about 1572, the *Order and Usage* describes the purpose, composition, structure, membership, and mode of operation of an Elizabethan Parliament. Hooker began by listing the reasons why the monarch should call a Parliament—ordering religion, finalizing royal marriages, determining the succession (see SUCCESSION, ACTS OF), declaring war, suppressing rebellion, levying taxes (see TAXATION), framing necessary laws, and repealing outdated statutes. Hooker next explained the composition of Parliament—monarch, Lords (bishops and PEERAGE), Commons (knights of the shires and representatives of the BOROUGHS), and clergy (meeting separately in CONVOCATION). He then described in detail the roles played by each of these components and the interaction among them during a session. The *Order and Usage* also contains sections describing the election and privileges of members, the code of behavior for debate, the procedures for passing bills into law, and the manner of opening and closing sessions.

By focusing more heavily on the Commons than on Convocation or the Lords, the *Order and Usage* reflects the growing belief of the GENTRY and urban middle classes (see SOCIAL HIERARCHY) that lawmaking was a corporate activity shared among all the politically aware classes in the realm, and not simply restricted to the Crown and the nobility. Accurate and detailed, Hooker's descriptive analysis of Elizabethan Parliaments is among the most valuable political works produced during the period.

Further Reading: Vernon F. Snow, *Parliament in Elizabethan England: John Hooker's "Order and Usage,"* New Haven, CT: Yale University Press, 1977; J. A. Wagner, *The Devon Gentleman: The Life of Sir Peter Carew,* Hull, England: University of Hull Press, 1998.

Ormond, Earl of. *See* BUTLER, THOMAS, EARL OF ORMOND.

Oxenham, John (c. 1535–1580)

John Oxenham is a prime example of the daring and courage with which Elizabethan seamen and adventurers assailed the Spanish Empire. Other than a strong likelihood that he was born in Devonshire, Oxenham's early life is almost completely unknown. In 1572, he sailed with Sir Francis DRAKE on an expedition that attacked Nombre de Dios on the isthmus of Panama (see Maps, "Spanish America in the Sixteenth Century"). When the English raiders captured a mule train carrying silver up the isthmus from Peru, both Oxenham and Drake realized the advantages of gaining access to the Pacific. Because Spanish treasure ships in the Pacific felt safe from

attack, they were virtually unarmed. Drake eventually devised a plan for a voyage of circumnavigation to raid the west coast of South America (see DRAKE'S CIRCUMNAVIGATION). Oxenham came to believe that a permanent English presence in Panama would allow privateers (see PRIVATEERING) to intercept treasure as it came up from Peru (see SPANISH AMERICA). Once seized, the treasure could be transported across the narrow isthmus for quick shipment to England. He began making preparations for an expedition to seize Panama, convincing Drake, John HAWKINS, and others to invest in the venture.

Oxenham left Plymouth in 1576 with a company of about 50 men. Having established good relations with the local Cimaroons (Africans who had escaped from Spanish slavery and banded together against their former masters) during the 1572 expedition, Oxenham was depending on their assistance to capture the isthmus. The Cimaroons did not disappoint him, and the English raiders were able to hold Panama for most of 1577. However, while Oxenham and his men were crossing the isthmus in search of Peruvian treasure, the Spanish found and destroyed the English SHIPS and supplies that had been hidden on the Caribbean coast. Cut off, the Englishmen were soon surrounded and captured. Although most of his men were hanged or sent to the galleys, Oxenham and his officers were imprisoned in Lima (Peru), where they were executed in 1580.

Further Reading: John Cummins, *Francis Drake,* New York: St. Martin's Press, 1995; Harry Kelsey, *Sir Francis Drake: The Queen's Pirate,* New Haven, CT: Yale University Press, 1998; Christopher Lloyd, *Sir Francis Drake,* Boston: Faber and Faber, 1979; John Sugden, *Sir Francis Drake,* New York: Simon and Schuster, 1990.

Oxford, Earl of. *See* VERE, EDWARD DE, EARL OF OXFORD.

Oxford University. *See* UNIVERSITIES.

palaces

At her accession in 1558, Elizabeth I inherited almost 50 royal residences, many of which had been acquired, built, or enlarged by her father, HENRY VIII. Unlike her more free-spending father, who had once owned almost 70 royal houses, Elizabeth engaged in little construction, and the number of houses owned and occupied by the monarch declined during her reign. Because Elizabeth and her COURT (which could number 1,500 persons, depending on the time of year) moved frequently from house to house, most of the queen's residences were in southeastern England, especially in the Thames Valley, where travel by barge facilitated the transfer of such large groups of people and their baggage.

Elizabeth's principal residences were WHITEHALL PALACE, GREENWICH PALACE, HAMPTON COURT PALACE, RICHMOND PALACE, Eltham, Woodstock, Hatfield, ST. JAMES'S PALACE, and OATLANDS PALACE. NONSUCH PALACE, which her father had built but her sister, MARY I, had given away, became royal property again in 1592 (see LUMLEY, JOHN, LORD LUMLEY). Only a few royal residences had both sufficient lodgings for the full court and a great hall in which the members of the court could be fed in shifts; the chief of these large houses were Whitehall, Greenwich, Hampton Court, Richmond, Eltham, and Woodstock, although the last, being further from LONDON, was used less frequently. The monarch's official residence, and the only structure in Elizabethan England to be designated a "palace," was WESTMINSTER PALACE, which lay along the Thames west of London.

Although the administrative center of England and the seat of the COMMON LAW courts, Westminster was not actually used as a royal residence after a fire partially damaged the structure during Henry VIII's reign.

The TOWER OF LONDON, situated along the Thames east of the capital, was used mainly as a prison and an armory, but it could serve also as a royal residence. The queen's mother, Anne BOLEYN, lodged in the royal apartments at the Tower before her coronation in 1533. Although less used by Elizabeth and unable to accommodate the full court, WINDSOR CASTLE (from which the present British royal family takes its name), on the Thames west of London, had been a royal residence since the eleventh century.

Further Reading: John Martin Robinson, *Royal Residences,* London: MacDonald and Company, 1982; Simon Thurley, *The Royal Palaces of Tudor England,* New Haven, CT: Yale University Press, 1993.

Pale

The term "Pale" described a region of IRELAND comprising DUBLIN and four surrounding counties in which the authority of the English government of Ireland was most fully exercised. From the late fourteenth to the early sixteenth centuries, English government policy in Ireland was mainly defensive, attempting to check the further advance of the native Irish and to fortify the areas remaining under the control of the Dublin administration. By the reign of Elizabeth, the Pale encompassed the town of Dublin and the lowland counties of Meath, Louth, Dublin, and Kildare. Besides greater obedience to the English government, these counties were also characterized by greater use of, and respect for, English language, culture, law, and social structures (see COMMON LAW; ENGLISH; SOCIAL HIERARCHY).

The first use of the term Pale to describe the region around Dublin occurred in 1495, when a statute of the Irish PARLIAMENT called for the construction of ditches around the "Inglishe pale." The defensive perimeter established to protect CALAIS, England's last possession on the continent of Europe in the sixteenth century, was also called a pale, and the term may have been borrowed from Calais to describe the similarly defensive character of the Dublin region.

Further Reading: Steven G. Ellis, *Tudor Ireland,* London: Longman, 1985; Colm Lennon, *Sixteenth-Century Ireland: The Incomplete Conquest,* Dublin: Gill and Macmillan, 1994; Margaret MacCurtain, *Tudor and Stuart Ireland,* Dublin: Gill and Macmillan, 1972; David B. Quinn, *The Elizabethans and the Irish,* Ithaca, NY: Cornell University Press, 1966.

Parker, Matthew (1504–1575)

Matthew Parker, the first Elizabethan Archbishop of Canterbury, was educated at Cambridge (see UNIVERSITIES), where he associated with a well-known group of religious reformers who were active in the 1520s. Ordained a priest in 1527, Parker became Anne BOLEYN's chaplain in 1535 and HENRY VIII's in 1538. As a moderate Protestant, he prospered in his career during the reign of EDWARD VI, being appointed vice-chancellor of Cambridge (1549) and dean of Lincoln (1552). He preached frequently at COURT before the young king, and, in 1547, he married—something no cleric could do openly under Henry VIII.

In 1554, because Parker had supported Jane GREY's unsuccessful usurpation of the throne, MARY I, a devout Catholic, stripped him of his ecclesiastical positions (see NORTHUMBERLAND'S COUP). Unlike many other Protestants who fled the realm for Europe during Mary's reign, Parker lived in hiding with his family in Norfolk. He reluctantly accepted Elizabeth's appointment of him as Archbishop of Canterbury in 1559, claiming that he did so only to keep a promise to Anne Boleyn that he would always look after her daughter's spiritual welfare. His moderate PROTESTANTISM, untainted with the radicalism many MARIAN EXILES brought back from Europe, mixed with his experience and his connection to her mother to make Parker a congenial choice for the queen.

Parker spent much of his primacy attempting to impose conformity in doctrine and practice on the growing Puritan minority among the clergy (see PURITANS; VESTIARIAN CONTROVERSY). Neither adept at politics nor a member of the PRIVY COUNCIL, Parker had great difficulty carrying out his program. He got little support from the queen and was actively hindered by the more Protestant members of the Council, such as Robert DUDLEY, Earl of Leicester, who awarded ecclesiastical positions in their gift to clergymen Parker had deprived of their BENEFICEs for nonconformity (see LECTURESHIPS). Despite his troubles with Puritan clergy and councilors, he worked hard to maintain the ANGLICAN SETTLEMENT of 1559 and to give the English Church a better-educated preaching clergy.

Further Reading: Victor J. K. Brook, *A Life of Archbishop Parker,* Oxford: Clarendon Press, 1962.

Parliament

Parliament is the supreme legislature of England, comprising the monarch, the House of Lords, and the House of Commons. Parliament developed in the thirteenth century out of the Great Council, a formal meeting of the king and his barons (landholding nobles) called three times a year to discuss and settle matters of great importance to the realm. In the fourteenth and fifteenth centuries, the royal need for money to conduct foreign wars and quell internal rebellions won for Parliament the right to consent to any extraordinary TAXATION. The Reformation in the 1530s extended the legislative competence of Parliament into new areas, including property rights and religious issues (see REFORMATION, ENGLISH).

The Elizabethan House of Lords consisted of 70 to 80 members—2 archbishops, 26 bishops, and the rest titled lay peers summoned to each session by special writ (see PEERAGE). By 1603, the House of Commons numbered 462—90 representatives from the counties of England and WALES and 372 from the 191 parliamentary BOROUGHS (towns), with LONDON sending four representatives. In the counties, only male residents holding lands

An engraving published in 1608 of Queen Elizabeth enthroned before Parliament. *By permission of the Folger Shakespeare Library.*

worth at least 40 shillings per year could vote, a qualification that essentially restricted the franchise to the GENTRY. In the boroughs, voting qualifications were much more idiosyncratic, depending upon how each town's charter defined a burgess (i.e., a voter). In many boroughs, the vote was restricted to a small number of people. According to law, borough representatives were to be residents of the town, but, with the exception of London, which always elected citizens, most borough representatives in the Elizabethan period were county gentry, among whom competition for parliamentary seats was fierce.

Summoned and dismissed by the monarch, the Elizabethan Parliament was an irregular, occasional, and brief part of government—Elizabeth called only 10 Parliaments in 44 years. Parliament provided legislative remedies for public matters brought before it by the PRIVY COUNCIL (e.g., the ANGLICAN SETTLEMENT of religion was debated and approved by Parliament, not simply imposed by the Crown) and for private matters brought before it by petition. Parliamentary statute, passed by the Lords and Commons and approved by the monarch, was the highest law of the realm, controlling and modifying even the COMMON LAW. The Commons, which met in St. Stephen's Chapel at WESTMINSTER PALACE, had the right to initiate all tax bills (see SUBSIDY). Debate in the Commons was directed by the speaker, a Crown nominee elected by the House at the start of each session. Besides choosing the speaker, the Crown also used its influence to ensure the election of privy councilors to move bills in the government's interest through the large and unwieldy Commons.

To become statute, a bill passed through three readings: the first reading informed members of the bill's content; the second initiated debate; and the third, after revision and transfer of the paper bill to parchment, refined the wording of the measure. Upon receiving the assent of the monarch, a bill passed after third reading became statute. The debates and decisions of the Lords and Commons were recorded by the clerk of each House, who kept journals of all parliamentary activities. See also PARLIAMENTARY SESSIONS (1559–1581) and (1584–1601).

Further Reading: G. R. Elton, *The Parliament of England 1559–1581,* Cambridge: Cambridge University Press, 1986; M. A. R. Graves, *Elizabethan Parliaments, 1559–1601,* 2nd ed., London: Longman, 1996; T. E. Hartley, *Elizabeth's Parliaments: Queen, Lords and Commons 1559–1601,* New York: St. Martin's Press, 1992; J. E. Neale, *Elizabeth I and Her Parliaments 1559–1581,* New York: St. Martin's Press, 1958; J. E. Neale, *Elizabeth I and Her Parliaments 1584–1601,* New York: St. Martin's Press, 1958; J. E. Neale, *The Elizabethan House of Commons,* rev. ed., Harmondsworth, England: Penguin Books, 1963.

parliamentary sessions (1559–1581)

Elizabeth I summoned four parliaments in the first two decades of her reign. The First Parliament met for three and a half months in the spring of 1559 and concerned itself primarily with the ANGLICAN SETTLEMENT of religion. It abolished papal authority in England, declared Elizabeth supreme governor of the Church, and passed an Act of Uniformity making a modified version of the 1552 *BOOK OF COMMON PRAYER* the required liturgy for the English Church.

The Second Parliament lasted four years but actually met for only two three-month sessions. In the 1563 session, Parliament passed the STATUTE OF ARTIFICERS and petitioned the queen to marry and settle the succession (see SUCCESSION, ACTS OF). Unwilling to do either, Elizabeth returned an evasive answer and prorogued the Parliament (i.e., adjourned its meeting until later). In the 1566–67 session, the queen evaded further attempts to settle the succession by again giving vague promises and by remitting one-third of the SUBSIDY granted her by the House of Commons. Elizabeth also defeated Puritan efforts to modify the 1559 religious settlement (see PURITANS).

The Third Parliament, which ran for one two-month session in 1571, reacted to the NORTHERN REBELLION and to Elizabeth's excommunication by the papal bull *REGNANS IN EXCELSIS* (1570). To protect the queen, Parliament declared it TREASON to possess a papal bull, to deny the royal supremacy, or to accuse the queen of heresy (see SUPREMACY, ROYAL). To discourage young Catholics from becoming SEMINARY PRIESTS, Parliament ordered all subjects who had gone overseas without license to return within six months or suffer forfeiture of their possessions.

The Fourth Parliament was the longest of the reign, lasting 11 years, although it met for

Sessions of Elizabethan Parliaments, 1559–1581	
Parliament	**Dates in Session**
First Parliament	23 January 1559–8 May 1559
Second Parliament	11 January 1563– 2 January 1567
First Session	11 January 1563–10 April 1563
Second Session	30 September 1566–2 January 1567
Third Parliament	2 April 1571–29 May 1571
Fourth Parliament	8 May 1572–19 April 1583
First Session	8 May 1572–30 June 1572
Second Session	8 February 1576–15 March 1576
Third Session	16 January 1581–18 March 1581

Sessions of Elizabethan Parliaments, 1584–1601	
Parliament	**Dates in Session**
Fifth Parliament	23 November 1584–14 September 1585
Session	23 November 1584–29 March 1585
Sixth Parliament	15 October 1586–23 March 1587
Seventh Parliament	4 February 1589–29 March 1589
Eighth Parliament	19 February 1593–10 April 1593
Ninth Parliament	24 October 1597–9 February 1598
Tenth Parliament	27 October 1601–19 December 1601

only three brief sessions. The 1572 session reacted to the RIDOLFI PLOT by pressuring the queen to execute Mary STUART, Queen of Scots, and Thomas HOWARD, Duke of Norfolk. Elizabeth refused to proceed against Mary, but Norfolk was put to death in June. The 1576 session witnessed Peter WENTWORTH's unprecedented attack on the queen and further unsuccessful attempts by Puritans to alter religion. The 1581 session added to the PENAL LAWS against Catholics by imposing heavier fines and imprisonment on RECUSANTS and those attending Catholic services. The Parliament elected in 1572 was then dissolved in 1583 without meeting again.

Further Reading: J. E. Neale, *Elizabeth I and Her Parliaments 1559–1581,* New York: St. Martin's Press, 1958.

parliamentary sessions (1584–1601)

In the last two decades of her reign, Elizabeth summoned six parliaments. The queen had made only sparing requests for TAXATION in her early years, but after the start of war with SPAIN in 1585, the government's demands for subsidies became heavier and more frequent (see SUBSIDY). Although remaining in existence until September 1585, Elizabeth's Fifth Parliament met in only one four-month session ending in March 1585. For Elizabeth's protection, this Parliament embodied the BOND OF ASSOCIATION in the QUEEN'S SAFETY ACT and extended the PENAL LAWS by declaring it TREASON for a Catholic priest to be in England.

The Sixth Parliament, meeting in 1586 after discovery of the BABINGTON PLOT, pressed Elizabeth to execute the intended beneficiary of that conspiracy, Mary STUART, Queen of Scots. Mary was executed in February 1587, several weeks before the session ended. This Parliament also witnessed an unsuccessful attempt by PURITANS to make significant revisions to the *BOOK OF COMMON PRAYER.*

The Seventh Parliament, meeting for two months in the spring of 1589, was assembled primarily to follow up the ARMADA victory of 1588 by voting new taxation to support the English war effort.

Meeting in the spring of 1593, the Eighth Parliament saw more agitation by Peter WENTWORTH (see PARLIAMENTARY SESSIONS 1559–1581) and faced new demands for money to fight the war. This Parliament also passed laws to control the activities of both Puritan nonconformists and Catholic RECUSANTS.

The Ninth Parliament, which met during the winter of 1597–98, expressed its weariness with war taxation by petitioning the queen to redress abuses that had arisen from her practice of granting MONOPOLIES. The session also saw passage of a new POOR LAW and economic legislation for the regulation of the CLOTH INDUSTRY.

The Tenth and last Parliament of the reign met at the end of 1601. The session heard angry complaints about the queen's failure to deliver on her promises of the previous session to correct the abuse of monopolies. Realizing her error, Elizabeth issued a PROCLAMATION of reform and agreed to meet a deputation from the Commons to express her thanks for their concern. This meeting resulted in the delivery by the queen of her famous "GOLDEN SPEECH," a virtual summary of her reign that came, in time, to seem a farewell address to her subjects.

Further Reading: J. E. Neale, *Elizabeth I and Her Parliaments 1584–1601,* New York: St. Martin's Press, 1958.

Parma, Duke of. *See* FARNESE, ALESSANDRO, DUKE OF PARMA.

Parr, Katherine (1512–1548)

Katherine Parr, the sixth and last wife of HENRY VIII, was the daughter of Sir Thomas Parr, the master of the king's household. She married the king, her third husband, on 12 July 1543. Katherine was a convinced Protestant who conducted her own religious scholarship and wrote her own prayers and devotions, including *The Lamentation or Complaint of a Sinner.* She was not, however, an extremist, and she exhibited a high degree of religious toleration, something that helped her win and hold the affection and respect of her still essentially Catholic husband. Katherine also earned the affection of Henry's children, Mary (see MARY I), Elizabeth, and Edward (see EDWARD VI), who had been isolated from their father by his position and personality, and from one another by the political and personal circumstances of their births and their mothers' marriages. Katherine tried to be mother to all three and to form them into a close FAMILY.

In 1544, the king named Katherine regent during his absence on campaign in FRANCE. In 1546, the conservative faction at COURT sought to destroy the rival reformist faction by discrediting the queen with charges of heresy. By attempting to argue theology with the king, a topic he, and most men of that time, believed women were unfit to discuss, Katherine angered Henry, which encouraged her enemies to move against her. She saved herself by begging the king's forgiveness and explaining her theological debates as attempts merely to distract the aging king from his many pains and ailments. Henry immediately rescinded the warrant for her arrest and declared them as "perfect friends as ever at any time before."

In April 1547, three months after Henry's death, Katherine married Thomas SEYMOUR, who had courted her before her MARRIAGE to Henry. Katherine took 13-year-old Princess Elizabeth into her household, but soon had her removed to her own house when the princess began receiving, and not entirely discouraging, improper advances from Seymour (see

ASHLEY, KATHERINE). Katherine died in childbed in September 1548.

Further Reading: Anthony K. Martienssen, *Queen Katherine Parr,* London: Secker and Warburg, 1973.

Parry, Blanche (1508–1590)

As the longest serving of Elizabeth's household servants, Blanche Parry held a place of special favor with the queen. Born in Herefordshire, Blanche Parry was distantly related to the Cecil family (see CECIL, WILLIAM, LORD BURGHLEY). In 1536, shortly after executing Anne BOLEYN, Elizabeth's mother, HENRY VIII appointed Parry to be an attendant to the princess, then about three years old. Parry may have been part of the princess's household even earlier, for she later claimed to have seen Elizabeth rocked in her cradle. Upon Elizabeth's accession in November 1558, Parry became the queen's second lady of the bedchamber after Katherine ASHLEY, Elizabeth's former governess. After Ashley's death in 1565, Parry became first lady of the bedchamber, a position she held until her death. In 1562, the queen granted Parry considerable estates in her native Herefordshire.

Parry's close and constant contact with Elizabeth made her an excellent messenger and advocate, and she was frequently approached by disgraced courtiers wanting her to speak favorably of them to the queen, or by those seeking to gain access or to pass private letters to the queen. In 1587, increasing blindness forced Parry to curtail many of her other duties, although she retained her official position in the bedchamber. Like her mistress, Parry never married, which further endeared her to Elizabeth, who hated the disruption her ladies' marriages caused within her household (see LADIES-IN-WAITING; MARRIAGE). On Parry's death in 1590, the queen paid for her servant to be buried in Westminster Abbey with the honors due a baroness.

Further Reading: Carolly Erickson, *The First Elizabeth,* New York: Summit Books, 1983.

Parry, Sir Thomas (d. 1560)

Like other longtime members of Elizabeth's household, Thomas Parry held claims to the queen's trust and affection that few others ever achieved. Parry joined the household of Princess Elizabeth in the 1530s, serving the princess as cofferer, or financial comptroller of the household, a position to which he was never suited. A mark of Elizabeth's affection for Parry was that she retained him in her household even though she later took to checking his untrustworthy accounts herself, initialing each page as her grandfather, HENRY VII, had done.

In 1549, during the reign of EDWARD VI, Thomas Parry and Katherine ASHLEY were arrested and interrogated in the TOWER OF LONDON concerning their mistress's relationship with Thomas SEYMOUR, Lord Sudeley. Sudeley—after the death of his wife Katherine PARR, the former queen—had secretly proposed MARRIAGE to the princess, using both Parry and Ashley as intermediaries on his behalf. Recognizing the danger of such a treasonous match, Elizabeth refused Sudeley and then saved herself and her politically naive servants by confessing to nothing more than the improper advances by Sudeley described in Parry's and Ashley's depositions. Parry was released and remained in Elizabeth's service until 1554, when the princess was sent to the Tower for suspected complicity in WYATT'S REBELLION. He returned to Elizabeth's household as steward when the princess was sent into exile from COURT at Hatfield in 1555.

At her accession in 1558, Elizabeth knighted Parry, named him to the PRIVY COUNCIL, and gave him the lucrative post of master of the Court of Wards. In 1559–60, Parry promoted Robert DUDLEY as a husband for the queen. Although his seeming lack of understanding of the political consequences of such a match put him in conflict with some of his fellow councilors, his position on the marriage may simply have reflected his sense of his longtime mistress's own wishes. Parry died in December 1560 and was buried with honor in Westminster Abbey.

Further Reading: Carolly Erickson, *The First Elizabeth,* New York: Summit Books, 1983; Paul Johnson, *Elizabeth I,* New York: Holt, Rinehart and Winston, 1974.

Parsons, Robert (1546–1610)

Robert Parsons (or Persons) was a Jesuit priest and the most uncompromising leader of the English Catholic community in exile (see CATHOLICISM, ENGLISH). The son of a Somerset blacksmith, Parsons was educated at Oxford (see UNIVERSITIES). In 1575, his Catholic views caused him to leave the university and the country, and led him eventually to Rome, where he was ordained as a Jesuit priest in 1578. Working with William ALLEN, Parsons helped organize the English JESUIT MISSION and was, himself, one of the Jesuits who landed in England in June 1580. Parsons and fellow missionary Edmund CAMPION stayed in LONDON until July, when they decided to split up for reasons of safety. Concealing himself in the houses of Catholic gentlemen (see GENTRY; PRIEST HOLES), Parsons toured the western counties, saying MASS, administering sacraments, and preaching. Returning to London in October, Parsons helped set up a secret PRINTING press, which produced his *A Brief Discourse Containing Certain Reasons Why Catholics Refuse to Go to Church* and Campion's controversial *Decem Rationes* [*Ten Reasons*].

Shortly after Campion's capture in July 1581, Parsons left England for good. In 1582, he traveled to SPAIN to urge the invasion of England, believing that military intervention by the Catholic rulers of Europe was the best means to restore Catholicism in England. Parsons spent the 1580s shuttling between Spain and Rome, working with Allen to convince both PHILIP II and the pope to undertake an invasion of England. In 1584, he was in the NETHERLANDS advising Alessandro FARNESE, Duke of Parma, on the numbers and capabilities of the English exiles. Parsons assumed full direction of the Jesuit Mission in England in 1585 and became rector of the English College in Rome in 1587.

The failure of the ARMADA in 1588 drew Parsons to Spain, where he spent several years establishing English seminaries and urging Philip to launch another invasion. A prolific writer, Parsons strongly advocated the right of the English Catholic community to depose the heretic English queen. But many English Catholics repudiated Parsons when PARLIAMENT declared it TREASON even to possess a copy of his *Conference about the Next Succession* (1594), a pamphlet arguing for the right of deposition. He further angered English Catholics in 1598 when he appointed George BLACKWELL as archpriest (see ARCHPRIEST CONTROVERSY). Parsons died in Rome in April 1610.

Further Reading: Michael L. Carrafiello, *Robert Parsons and English Catholicism, 1580–1610*, London: Associated University Presses, 1998; Francis Edwards, *Robert Parsons: The Biography of an Elizabethan Jesuit, 1546–1610*, St. Louis: Institute of Jesuit Sources, 1995; E. E. Reynolds, *Campion and Parsons: The Jesuit Mission of 1580–1*, London: Sheed and Ward, 1980.

Paulet, Sir Amias (c. 1536–1588)

Sir Amias Paulet was the last official custodian of Elizabeth's longtime prisoner, Mary STUART, Queen of Scots. In 1571, Paulet succeeded his father in the post of governor of Jersey, an island in the English Channel. In 1576, Elizabeth appointed him the English ambassador to the French court, a post he held until 1579. As a convinced Puritan, Paulet was deeply sympathetic to the cause of the HUGUENOTS and had little taste for the proposed MARRIAGE between the queen and Francis VALOIS, Duke of Alençon (see PURITANS). Paulet's manner was too stern and reserved for the liking of the queen's favorite, Robert DUDLEY, Earl of Leicester, but it won him the confidence of the queen's Puritan secretary of state, Sir Francis WALSINGHAM.

In 1585, Walsingham proposed Paulet as the new keeper of the imprisoned Queen of Scots. Ordered to keep his charge more closely

Sir Amias Paulet, the last custodian of Mary Stuart, Queen of Scots, as painted in the nineteenth century by George Perfect Harding. *By courtesy of the National Portrait Gallery, London.*

and strictly confined, Paulet inspected all her correspondence, restricted her spending and almsgiving, limited her contact with others, and disregarded her desire to maintain the rules of COURT etiquette in her household. Paulet was courteous to his prisoner, but firmly required fulfillment of all the government's instructions for her keeping. Repelled by his Puritanism, Mary unsuccessfully demanded that the queen replace Paulet with a less severe jailer. Paulet suffered from the queen's parsimony, being required occasionally to pay household expenses out of his own pocket. In 1587, Paulet worked with Walsingham to uncover the BABINGTON PLOT through strict surveillance of Mary's correspondence and a careful search of her papers. These activities uncovered the evidence that led to Mary's trial and condemnation in October 1586.

Although Paulet had once assured the government of his willingness to kill Mary rather than allow her to fall into the hands of rescuers, he returned a horrified refusal when Elizabeth hinted to him that he should privately murder the Scottish queen to relieve Elizabeth of the responsibility of signing the death warrant. After Mary's execution on 8 February 1587, Paulet served Elizabeth in various capacities, including as commissioner to the government of the NETHERLANDS. Paulet died in LONDON in September 1588.

Further Reading: Antonia Fraser, *Mary, Queen of Scots,* New York: Delacorte Press, 1969; Jenny Wormald, *Mary, Queen of Scots,* London: Collins and Brown, 1991.

Paulet, William, Marquis of Winchester (c. 1485–1572)

William Paulet, Marquis of Winchester, served as Queen Elizabeth's first lord treasurer. Born into a Hampshire GENTRY family, Paulet was sheriff of his county in 1512, knighted in 1525, and a member of the PRIVY COUNCIL by 1526. HENRY VIII appointed Paulet comptroller of the royal household in 1532. A highly capable financial officer who refrained from political involvement and supported the king's religious changes, Paulet rose rapidly in the royal administration. He was named treasurer of the household in 1537; chamberlain and great master of the household in 1543 and 1545, respectively; and lord president of the Privy

Council in 1546. Henry raised Paulet to the PEERAGE as Baron St. John of Basing in 1539.

Paulet was a member of EDWARD VI's regency Council and initially supported Lord Protector Edward SEYMOUR, Duke of Somerset, but in 1549 shifted his allegiance to John DUDLEY, the future Duke of Northumberland, who supplanted Somerset as the head of the royal government. In 1550, Paulet was rewarded for this switch with the important office of lord treasurer and the earldom of Winchester. Following Somerset's execution in 1552, Paulet became Marquis of Winchester. In 1553, Winchester opposed NORTHUMBERLAND'S COUP, which unsuccessfully sought to prevent MARY I from taking the throne. The queen rewarded Winchester by retaining him as lord treasurer. Although unhappy with the queen's MARRIAGE to PHILIP II of SPAIN, Winchester accepted Mary's decision and supported her religious policies as loyally as he had supported those of her father.

On her accession in 1558, Elizabeth reappointed Winchester as lord treasurer, even though he was almost 70 years old. At first, Winchester worked closely with the queen's principal secretary, Sir William CECIL, but by the late 1560s, Winchester, ever the moderate, found the pro-Protestant activism of Cecil's foreign policy too extreme for his tastes, and he conspired with Robert DUDLEY, Earl of Leicester, and other Cecil rivals to curb the secretary's influence with the queen. Winchester died, still in office, in March 1572. Ironically, the treasurership passed to Cecil. Asked how he retained high office through four reigns, Winchester replied, "By being a willow, not an oak."

Further Reading: Wallace MacCaffrey, *Elizabeth I*, London: Edward Arnold, 1993.

Paul's Cross

Paul's Cross was an open-air pulpit that stood near the cross in the churchyard of St. Paul's Cathedral in LONDON. Public sermons had been delivered there since the fourteenth century, and regular preaching under the supervision of the Bishop of London had taken place at the site since the late fifteenth century, when an endowment to support preaching was cre-

ated by Bishop Thomas Kempe. Until the English Reformation, when the selection of preachers and the content of sermons came under close government control, the Bishop of London and his chaplains selected the speakers (see REFORMATION, ENGLISH). Through the numerous religious upheavals that England underwent between the 1530s and the 1560s, Paul's Cross became a national barometer for religious change.

By Elizabethan times, the site had become so important and frequented by such crowds that galleries had been built to accommodate royal and noble listeners and to seat foreign dignitaries, who came to the sermons to gauge shifts in royal religious policy. For commoners, benches were available at a cost of one pence per sermon. The choice of preachers for Paul's Cross became particularly important during the first months of Elizabeth's reign, when no one was certain how or even if the new queen intended to alter the English Catholic Church that she inherited from her half sister, MARY I. The selection of Dr. William Bill, a noted reformer, to deliver the first sermon of the reign at Paul's Cross in late November 1558 heartened Protestants and gave alarm to Catholics. As the government and PARLIAMENT slowly crafted the ANGLICAN SETTLEMENT of religion in the spring of 1559, the preachers who were selected to speak at Paul's Cross, and the topics on which they were allowed to preach, told the English people and foreign governments how far and in what direction Elizabeth and her ministers intended to modify the doctrine and practice of the English Church.

Later in the reign, Paul's Cross speakers indicated the government's stand on numerous religious controversies involving both Catholic and Puritan issues (see ANGLICAN CHURCH; PURITANS). The Paul's Cross pulpit remained the most important site for public sermons until its destruction in 1643, ironically, by sermon-loving but antigovernment Puritans.

Further Reading: Walter Robert Matthews and W. M. Atkins, eds., *A History of St. Paul's Cathedral*, London: Phoenix House, 1957; Walter Thornbury, *Old London: Cheapside and St. Paul's*, London: Alderman Press, 1986.

Peele, George (c. 1558–1596)

George Peele was one of the most creative and versatile dramatists in Elizabethan England. Born in LONDON and educated at Oxford (see UNIVERSITIES), Peele completed his bachelor's degree in 1577 and his master's degree in 1579. At Oxford, he was noted for his POETRY and his translation of Euripides and was notorious for his wild living. After Peele's return to London, his dissolute lifestyle continued, being interrupted neither by expulsion from his father's house in 1579 nor MARRIAGE in 1583. To earn money, Peele wrote verse dedicated to and in praise of various potential patrons, including the queen, for whom the play *The Arraignment of Paris* was meant as a piece of flattery. Printed in 1584, *The Arraignment of Paris* was novel in that it was written in a variety of meters.

Between sessions of drinking and brawling with such fellow writers as Thomas NASHE, Thomas KYD, Christopher MARLOWE, Thomas LODGE, and Robert GREENE, Peele performed as an actor in the troupe known as the Admiral's Men and later in the Queen's Men, and he wrote and produced a series of successful pageants for the city of London. The only surviving examples of the ENTERTAINMENT Peele devised for the city are *Device of the Pageant Borne before Woolstone Dixi* (1585) and *Descensus Astraeae* (1591).

Known as a prolific writer who liked to experiment with styles and formats, Peele's plays include *Edward I* (1593); *The Battle of Alcazar* (1594), based on the life of Sir Thomas STUKELEY; *The Old Wives' Tale* (1595); and *The Love of King David and Fair Bethsabe* (1599). His poems include *The Tale of Troy* (1589); the *Eclogue Gratulatory* (1589), dedicated to Robert DEVEREUX, Earl of Essex; *Polyhymnia* (1590); and *Honor of the Garter* (1593), dedicated to the Earl of Northumberland. In the last two years before his death in 1596, Peele suffered from illness and increasing financial problems brought on by his extravagant lifestyle. On Peele's death, his work was much praised by his literary colleagues.

Further Reading: G. K. Hunter, *Lyly and Peele*, Harlow, England: Published for the British Council and the National Book League by Longmans, 1968; Werner Senn, *Studies in the Dramatic Construction of Robert Greene and George Peele*, Bern, Switzerland: Francke, 1973.

peerage

The lay members of the peerage of England and Wales were landholders characterized by their hereditary titles of nobility, their hereditary right to be summoned personally to PARLIAMENT by the monarch, and their right to be tried before other peers. The right of personal summons to the House of Lords, the upper chamber of Parliament, was formalized in the fifteenth century. The spiritual peers in the House of Lords were the archbishops, bishops, and, until the dissolution of the monasteries in the 1530s, the abbots of the largest monastic houses. They held lands by virtue of their Church offices.

The lay peers or the lords temporal were the holders of one of the five titles of nobility granted by the monarch: duke, marquis, earl, viscount, or baron. Titles of nobility were acquired either by inheritance or by creation by the monarch. The lay peers were a small fraction of the English population, never numbering much more than 60 men during the course of Elizabeth's reign.

The Elizabethan Lay Peerage

Lay Titles of Nobility (Wife's Title)	Number of Men Holding Such Rank Under Elizabeth I
Duke (Duchess)	1; none after 1572
Marquis or Marquess (Marchioness)	2–3
Earl (Countess)	about 20
Viscount (Viscountess)	2–3
Baron or Lord (Baroness or Lady)	about 35–40

The title of duke, the highest rank in the peerage, was created in 1337 by Edward III, who conferred it exclusively on royal princes. Richard II extended its use outside the royal family in the late fourteenth century, but the title was rarely granted to anyone until after Elizabeth's death. After the execution of Thomas HOWARD, fourth Duke of Norfolk in 1572, Elizabethan England had no dukes. Richard II created the title of marquis (or marquess) in the late fourteenth century. The title of earl went back to the eleventh and twelfth centuries when the Norman kings conferred earldoms on hereditary noblemen in return for military and administrative service in the counties. Henry VI created the title of viscount in 1440. The title of baron, the lowest rank in the hereditary peerage, originally referred to landholders who gave military service to the king, and then to the hereditary landholders whom the king summoned to Parliament. The title became a formal rank in the peerage in the late fourteenth century.

Elizabeth was sparing in her creation of new titles, far more so than her father and brother. William CECIL, raised to the peerage as Lord Burghley in 1570, was one of the few men ennobled by the queen for political services, and even he attained only the rank of baron. Robert DUDLEY's creation as Earl of Leicester in 1564 was one of the few titles granted by Elizabeth purely for favor and not, as was the queen's usual practice, for long service. *See also* SOCIAL HIERARCHY.

Further Reading: M. L. Bush, *The English Aristocracy,* Manchester, England: Manchester University Press, 1984.

Pembroke, Countess of. *See* HERBERT, MARY, COUNTESS OF PEMBROKE.

Pembroke, Earl of. *See* HERBERT, HENRY, EARL OF PEMBROKE.

penal laws

The Elizabethan penal laws placed restrictions on the civil and political rights of English Roman Catholics (see CATHOLICISM, ENGLISH). In 1559, Elizabeth's first PARLIAMENT made celebration of the Catholic MASS illegal and required all subjects to attend Anglican services on Sundays and holy days (see HOLIDAYS). Recusancy (refusal to attend) incurred a fine of 12 pence for each absence (see RECUSANTS). The Parliament of 1563 made upholding the authority of the pope punishable by death for a second offense. Parliament also required clergymen and many laypersons to take the oath of supremacy, something most Catholics would not do because it meant denying the authority of the pope (see SUPREMACY, ROYAL).

In the 1560s, little active persecution of Catholics occurred in England; fines for non-attendance went uncollected and oath-taking was easily evaded. The situation changed in the early 1570s with the imprisonment in England of Mary STUART, Queen of Scots; the increasing rivalry with Catholic SPAIN; and the discovery of the RIDOLFI PLOT. Outright repression of English Catholics flowed from the papal bull *REGNANS IN EXCELSIS,* which excommunicated Elizabeth and declared her subjects absolved of their allegiance to her, and from the political intrigues with foreign Catholic princes conducted by English Jesuits working secretly in England (see JESUIT MISSION) and English Catholic exiles working openly abroad (see ALLEN, WILLIAM; PARSONS, ROBERT).

While the laws against recusancy also operated against radical PURITANS and Protestant SEPARATISTS who refused to participate in Anglican services, much of the penal legislation of the 1580s and 1590s was aimed squarely at Catholics, especially priests. Publishing or implementing a papal bull in England became TREASON in 1571. In 1581, Parliament raised recusancy fines to a ruinous £20 per month and declared it treason to reconcile anyone to Catholicism, to become reconciled oneself, or to persuade anyone to withdraw his or her allegiance from the queen or the ANGLICAN CHURCH. In 1585, it became treason for a Catholic priest simply to be in England, and a crime to send money overseas to support Jesuits or SEMINARY PRIESTS. In 1593, Catholic recusants were forbidden to travel more than five miles from home without a special license. Even more severe disabilities were placed on English Catholics under JAMES I. Most of these restrictions remained in force until the nineteenth century. *See also* ANGLICAN SETTLEMENT.

Further Reading: Peter Holmes, *Resistance and Compromise: The Political Thought of the Elizabethan Catholics,* Cambridge: Cambridge University Press, 1982; David Lunn, *The Catholic Elizabethans*, Bath: Downside Abbey, 1998; Arnold Pritchard, *Catholic Loyalism in Elizabethan England*, Chapel Hill: University of North Carolina Press, 1979; Alexandra Walsham, *Church Papists: Catholicism, Conformity and Confessional Polemic in Early Modern England*, Rochester, NY: Boydell Press, 1993.

Penry, John (1563–1593)

John Penry was one of the printers and distributors, if not the author, of the MARPRELATE

TRACTS, a notorious series of Puritan pamphlets that attacked the Anglican bishops. Born into a wealthy GENTRY family in WALES, Penry entered Cambridge (see UNIVERSITIES) in 1580. In 1586, he transferred to Oxford and joined that university's growing Puritan movement (see PURITANS). Appalled by the backwardness of the Church in his native Wales (see REFORMATION, WELSH), Penry began to preach his increasingly radical and separatist ideas to conservative Welsh congregations (see SEPARATISTS). Penry also began writing religious pamphlets in which he vigorously attacked abuses within the Welsh Church, as well as everyone he believed responsible for promoting or maintaining such evils. Writing in a blunt and ridiculing style, with no regard for the possible consequences of his words, Penry was briefly imprisoned for his pamphlet *Aequity,* which called for more Puritan preaching in Wales.

Between 1587 and 1589, Penry issued from the secret press of Robert Waldegrave a series of abusive attacks upon the Anglican bishops, and even upon Queen Elizabeth herself. Along with Waldegrave and Job Throckmorton, Penry printed and distributed the first two Marprelate Tracts in the fall of 1588. In August 1589, the government, after an extensive search, discovered the Marprelate press in Manchester and destroyed the eighth tract, which was then in preparation. Penry and Waldegrave fled to SCOTLAND, where Waldegrave remained to become printer to the Scottish king (see JAMES I) while Penry returned to England to reinvolve himself in the growing English separatist movement.

Penry's separatist activities led to his arrest and trial for TREASON in 1593; he was convicted and condemned to death largely on the testimony of witnesses who had been racked. Although accused of writing the Marprelate Tracts, Penry denied authorship, and the identity of "Martin Marprelate" remains uncertain to this day. Penry was hanged on 29 May 1593. *See also* ANGLICAN CHURCH; PRINTING.

Further Reading: Patrick Collinson, *The Elizabethan Puritan Movement,* Oxford: Clarendon Press, 1990; Donald J. McGinn, *John Penry and the Marprelate Controversy,* New Brunswick, NJ: Rutgers University Press, 1966.

Perrot, Sir John (c. 1527–1592)

Sir John Perrot served as lord president of the southern Irish province of Munster and as lord deputy of IRELAND. Because of his close resemblance to the late king, Perrot was rumored to be an illegitimate son of HENRY VIII and thus a half brother of Elizabeth. After serving for a time in the household of William PAULET, Marquis of Winchester, Perrot became a favorite of EDWARD VI (see FAVORITES). During the reign of MARY I, Perrot, a Protestant, was briefly imprisoned for allegedly plotting against the government and for sheltering fugitive heretics on his Welsh estates. On her accession in 1558, Elizabeth appointed Perrot vice-admiral of South WALES.

In 1570, Perrot reluctantly accepted the lord presidency of Munster, a region of southern Ireland then in the grip of FITZMAURICE'S REBELLION. A physically powerful man with an impulsive nature and an abrasive manner, Perrot spent three years ruthlessly crushing the uprising. In 1573, after the surrender of James Fitzmaurice FITZGERALD, the leader of the rebellion, Perrot asked to be relieved and rashly returned to England without license when his request was not answered. In 1584, Perrot returned to Ireland as lord deputy, his previous experience in Munster making him appear the best man to supervise the recently initiated Munster plantation (see PLANTATIONS, IRISH). However, his impetuosity and harsh manner soon alienated him from his leading English councilors and from the more important ANGLO-IRISH lords. His failure to control the Irish PARLIAMENT, where he lost an important bill seeking to replace CESS with a regular tax, and his frequent and costly campaigns against Turlough Luineach O'NEILL and other Irish rebels in Ulster, angered the queen and led to his recall in 1588.

In 1591, Perrot was sent to the TOWER OF LONDON, charged with speaking contemptuously of the queen, with encouraging rebellion in Ireland, and with treasonously corresponding with PHILIP II of SPAIN. Real evidence existed only for the first charge, but Perrot had made many enemies (such as Sir Christopher HATTON, whose daughter Perrot had seduced) who pushed successfully for a trial. Convicted of treason in April 1592, Perrot was condemned to death, although rumor suggested that the queen might pardon her "brother." However, Perrot foiled both the queen and the executioner by dying in the Tower on 26 June.

Further Reading: Steven G. Ellis, *Tudor Ireland,* London: Longman, 1985; Colm Lennon, *Sixteenth-Century Ireland: The Incomplete Conquest,* Dublin: Gill and Macmillan, 1994; Margaret MacCurtain, *Tudor and Stuart Ireland,* Dublin: Gill and Macmillan, 1972; David B. Quinn, *The Elizabethans and the Irish,* Ithaca, NY: Cornell University Press, 1966.

Persons, Robert. *See* PARSONS, ROBERT.

Philip II (1527–1598)

Philip II was the son of the Holy Roman Emperor CHARLES V and heir to the HABSBURG FAMILY dominions in SPAIN, the NETHERLANDS, Italy, and AMERICA (see genealogical chart in Appendix 1: "Habsburg Dynasty in Spain and the Holy Roman Empire"). Philip married his first wife, a Portuguese princess, in 1543, the same year his father named him regent of Spain, a position Philip exercised thereafter whenever Charles was abroad.

Philip II of Spain, Elizabeth I's brother-in-law—and later, a suitor—became her great adversary. *National Maritime Museum, London.*

In 1553, Philip was a widower with a child when his father proposed him as a possible husband for MARY I, the new Catholic queen of England and daughter of Philip's great-aunt, CATHERINE OF ARAGON. Philip was cool toward the match, but he obeyed his father's wishes and married the queen of England in July 1554. He spent only brief periods in England, returning to the Netherlands in 1555, and to Spain to assume the Crown in 1557. While in England, he advised Mary to pardon her half sister, the Princess Elizabeth, for any part she may have played in WYATT'S REBELLION, and to cease or at least limit the burnings of Protestants (see MARIAN MARTYRS). In 1557, Philip convinced his wife and her reluctant advisors to bring England into war against FRANCE as Spain's ally. Although Philip won a victory at St. Quentin with the aid of English troops, the French, much to Mary's sorrow, captured CALAIS, England's last continental possession, in January 1558. After Mary's death in November 1558, Philip made unsuccessful overtures for the hand of Queen Elizabeth, who ended her sister's Anglo-Spanish alliance but was careful not to openly antagonize Philip.

Over the next two decades, relations between Spain and England worsened as the English abandoned Catholicism (see CATHOLICISM, ENGLISH), attempted to break Spain's trade monopoly with her American colonies (see SPANISH AMERICA), and sent financial and military aid to Dutch Protestants in revolt against Philip in the Netherlands (see NETHERLANDS EXPEDITION; NETHERLANDS REVOLT). War broke out between the two countries in 1585, and Philip sent the ARMADA against England in 1588 in an attempt to overthrow Elizabeth and restore Catholicism. The failure of the Armada did not end the war, which continued beyond the reigns of both Philip and Elizabeth. In his later years, the king, who had outlived four wives, became a virtual recluse in his brooding palace, El Escorial. Philip died there in September 1598, succeeded by his one surviving son, Philip III.

Further Reading: Henry Kamen, *Philip of Spain,* New Haven, CT: Yale University Press, 1997; Geoffrey Parker, *Philip II,* 3rd ed., Chicago: Open Court, 1995.

Piers, John (c. 1523–1594)

John Piers (or Peirse) was Elizabeth's fourth Archbishop of York. Born in the village of South Hinksey near Oxford, Piers attended Magdalen College School (see GRAMMAR SCHOOL) before entering Magdalen College, Oxford (see UNIVERSITIES), in 1542. He became a fellow of Magdalen College in 1546, teaching at the college until 1558, when he took holy orders and was sent to serve as minister in a small rural parish in Buckinghamshire. Because his new assignment lacked the intellectual stimulation to which he was accustomed at the university, Piers fell into the habit of frequent drinking at the local alehouse. Upbraided for this by a ministerial colleague, Piers adopted strict abstinence and never took alcohol again.

In 1567, a year after obtaining his doctor of divinity degree from Oxford, Piers was reassigned to a larger parish in Essex, and thereafter held a series of increasingly important benefices (see BENEFICE), including Dean of Salisbury Cathedral, where he thoroughly purged all remaining Catholic practices and ceremonies. In April 1576, Piers became Bishop of Rochester, but was transferred to the wealthier and more important bishopric of Salisbury in November 1577. Favored and trusted by the queen, Piers was given the delicate task of persuading Edmund GRINDAL, the disgraced and suspended Archbishop of Canterbury, to resign, a task that ended with Grindal's death in 1583.

In 1585, Elizabeth, who rarely involved bishops in political issues, asked Piers's advice on whether England should intervene in the NETHERLANDS, the bishop replying that England should. Piers was also active in suppressing the PRESBYTERIAN MOVEMENT at Oxford in the late 1580s. After the defeat of the ARMADA, the queen honored Piers by appointing him to preach the sermon at the thanksgiving service held at St. Paul's Cathedral in LONDON on 24 November 1588. On the death of Archbishop Edwin SANDYS in 1589, Elizabeth named Piers Archbishop of York, a post he held until his death in September 1594.

Further Reading: Patrick Collinson, *The Elizabethan Puritan Movement,* Oxford: Clarendon Press, 1990.

Pius V (1504–1572)

In 1570, Michele Ghislieri, Pope Pius V, issued the bull (i.e., papal edict), *REGNANS IN EXCELSIS*, that excommunicated Elizabeth I from the Roman Catholic Church. Born near Alessandria, Italy, Ghislieri became a Dominican friar noted for his asceticism. He was appointed a bishop in 1556 and a cardinal of the Church in 1557. As inquisitor-general for the Lombardy region of northern Italy, he vigorously suppressed the teaching of reformist doctrines. Elected pope as Pius V in 1566, he worked to reform the papal COURT by rooting out corruption and immorality and by reducing court expenditure. Through promulgation of the bull *In Coena Domini* in 1568, he sought to strengthen papal authority and Church discipline throughout Catholic Europe.

For political reasons, the papacy had waited patiently for over a decade after her accession for Elizabeth to return herself and her country to the Roman Catholic fold. The NORTHERN REBELLION of 1569, during which the rebels restored Catholic worship to parts of northern England, convinced Pius to take action against the heretical queen in an effort to give heart to the northern rebels and to all English Catholics. Without consulting any Catholic ruler, Pius issued *Regnans in Excelsis,* excommunicating Elizabeth and absolving her subjects from their allegiance to her. Because it put English Catholics in a difficult position, and also because it put pressure on Catholic monarchs, such as PHILIP II of SPAIN, to take action against Elizabeth, *Regnans in Excelsis* was unpopular both in England and in the Catholic courts of Europe. Other than stimulate the passage by PARLIAMENT of PENAL LAWS against English Catholics, the bull had little immediate effect.

Pius was more successful in his other great initiative—the organization, with Spain and Venice, of a naval expedition against the Turks in the eastern Mediterranean. In 1571, the effort resulted in the great naval victory won at Lepanto by JOHN OF AUSTRIA, the half brother of Philip of Spain. Pius died in 1572 and was canonized as a saint of the Catholic Church in 1712. *See also* CATHOLICISM, ENGLISH.

Further Reading: J. N. D. Kelly, *The Oxford Dictionary of Popes,* New York: Oxford University Press, 1986.

plague

The deadliest and most persistent form of EPIDEMIC DISEASE in Elizabethan England was the bubonic plague, the terrible Black Death that had swept across Europe from Asia in the late 1340s. Historical demographers believe that the 1348–50 and 1367 visitations of the Black Death helped cause the POPULATION of fourteenth-century England to decline from about 5.5 million to around 3 million. Although far less virulent and more localized, Elizabethan outbreaks of the plague still caused high mortality rates in certain towns or regions.

The bubonic plague is carried by a type of flea *(Xenopsylla cheopis)* that usually lives on rats. When rat populations increased, the fleas could initiate an outbreak of the disease by transferring to human hosts. Poor sanitation, ignorance of the cause of plague, ineffective medical treatments (see MEDICINE), and the government's inability to control the movement of infected persons helped spread the disease once an outbreak started. The mortality rate of plague was usually about 50 percent, but could climb to near 100 percent if the pneumonic plague was present. The deadliest form of the disease, the pneumonic plague attacked the pulmonary system and could be transmitted directly from person to person.

Elizabethan eruptions of the plague struck mainly during the hot summer months and most severely in the largest towns, where overcrowding and poor sanitation helped the disease flourish (see BOROUGHS). Although isolated outbreaks could occur, the plague often followed merchants and travelers from the NETHERLANDS to LONDON, which was particularly hard hit during the reign, and then radiated outward to other English towns along the routes of domestic trade. The most widespread and serious eruptions of plague in Elizabethan England occurred in 1563, 1578–79, 1582, 1592–93, and 1603. The 1578–79 outbreak carried off almost 30 percent of the population of Norwich. The 1592–93 visitation caused the closure of London theatres, and the more deadly 1563 and 1603 outbreaks are estimated to have killed nearly a quarter of London's population. Children, the poor, and the elderly were particularly vulnerable. The last great English outbreak of the plague occurred in 1665–66, after which improved sanitation and more effective public health measures helped curb the disease.

Further Reading: Paul Slack, *The Impact of Plague in Tudor and Stuart England,* Oxford: Clarendon Press, 1985.

plantations, Irish

By installing Protestant settlers on lands taken from Catholic Irish, the Irish plantation policy of the Elizabethan government helped create the religious conflict that still plagues IRELAND today. Plantations were attempts to establish colonies of new settlers on territories seized from—and cleared of—their original occupants. The POPULATION of Elizabethan Ireland was divided between people of Irish (Gaelic) descent and people of English descent, known as the ANGLO-IRISH, whose forbears had settled in Ireland in the Middle Ages. Prior to the 1520s, the English Crown had sought to rule Ireland either by cooperating with the Anglo-Irish nobility and pacifying the Irish chieftains, or by attempting to extend a centralized English administration across the island from DUBLIN.

In the sixteenth century, as both England and SCOTLAND adopted PROTESTANTISM, Irish resistance to English rule in Ireland began to identify itself more closely with Catholicism, thus adding a religious component to the ongoing political struggle for control of Ireland. Under the Tudors and Stuarts, a policy evolved of dispersing and dispossessing the Catholic Gaelic population by establishing plantations of Protestant English and Scottish settlers on land formerly held by Gaelic clans. These English plantation schemes sought to populate the island with settlers who used English law, followed English customs, and supported the Crown. The first colonization efforts were undertaken by the Catholic government of MARY I, which stripped certain Irish landholders of two-thirds of their property and gave it to settlers from England or to persons of English descent living in Ireland. Under Elizabeth, the English plantation settlers became almost exclusively Protestant and became known as "New English," to distinguish them from the largely Catholic Anglo-Irish, who were called "Old English."

The Elizabethan plantation schemes, such as those proposed by Sir Peter CAREW and attempted by Walter DEVEREUX, Earl of Essex, provoked fierce Irish resistance, which culminated in the rebellions in Ulster led by Hugh O'NEILL, Earl of Tyrone, in the 1590s (see NINE YEARS WAR; ULSTER ENTERPRISE [ESSEX]; ULSTER ENTERPRISE [SMITH]).

The rebels destroyed many English plantations, but Tyrone's eventual defeat convinced the government of JAMES I that the core of Irish resistance in Ulster could be crushed only by planting Ulster with reliable Protestant settlers, a policy that was launched in 1609. Cleared of Catholic Irish, Ulster received thousands of Protestant settlers in the seventeenth century, thus planting the seeds of the Protestant-Catholic conflict that still haunts Northern Ireland in the twentieth century.

Further Reading: Steven G. Ellis, *Tudor Ireland,* London: Longman, 1985; Colm Lennon, *Sixteenth-Century Ireland: The Incomplete Conquest,* Dublin: Gill and Macmillan, 1994; Margaret MacCurtain, *Tudor and Stuart Ireland,* Dublin: Gill and Macmillan, 1972; David B. Quinn, *The Elizabethans and the Irish,* Ithaca, NY: Cornell University Press, 1966.

poetry

The late Elizabethan period, from the 1570s to the 1600s, was one of the most creative and prolific periods in the history of English poetry. This poetic flowering began in the quarter century between 1550 and 1575, when humanist scholars and Protestant reformers used ENGLISH, long considered inferior to Latin and Greek as a literary language, to teach and to preach (see HUMANISM; PROTESTANTISM; REFORMATION, ENGLISH). Prose works of scholarship like Roger ASCHAM's *Schoolmaster* (1570), and religious works like John FOXE's "BOOK OF MARTYRS," Thomas CRANMER's *BOOK OF COMMON PRAYER* (1549, 1552), and William WHITTINGHAM's Geneva Bible (1560) (see BIBLE, ENGLISH), illustrated the strength and flexibility of Elizabethan English.

Poetry, the pastime of courtiers in earlier decades, reached a wider audience in the 1560s with the publication of Richard Tottel's anthology, *Songs and Sonnets* (1557), a work generally known as "Tottel's Miscellany." By popularizing the COURT poetry of HENRY VIII's time and the work of unknown contemporary poets, such as George GASCOIGNE, Tottel inspired a host of similar poetry collections that helped build demand for English verse. This growing interest in poetry was illustrated by the popularity of *A Mirror for Magistrates,* a collection of poetic laments supposedly spoken by participants in the WARS OF THE ROSES. Compiled by various editors and containing the

efforts of such contemporary poets as Thomas SACKVILLE and Thomas Churchyard, the *Mirror* went through four editions between 1559 and 1587.

The plainer, simpler poetry published by Tottel and the *Mirror* in the 1560s was superseded in the next two decades by the more ornate and innovative lyric poetry (i.e., verse expressing intense personal emotion) written by Edmund SPENSER and Sir Philip SIDNEY. Spenser was the first English poet to use print to deliberately disseminate his work to a wider public (see PRINTING). His *The Faerie Queen* (1590–1609) was a lyric epic of Protestant nationalism, casting Elizabeth as the Faerie Queen herself. Sidney's work was also fused with Protestant fervor and tied to the cult of the VIRGIN QUEEN. While Spenser inspired every English poet of the 1590s to try lyric poetry, Sidney, through his *Astrophil and Stella* (1591) cycle, initiated a great flood of sonnet sequences, including a cycle by William SHAKESPEARE (see SONNET, SHAKESPEAREAN). By 1590, English poetry was being enriched by many talented poets innovating new forms and exploring new topics. *See also* illustration for SPENSER, EDMUND.

Further Reading: Fred Inglis, *The Elizabethan Poets: The Making of English Poetry from Wyatt to Ben Jonson,* London: Evans Brothers, 1969; Emrys Jones, ed., *Sixteenth Century Verse,* Oxford: Oxford University Press, 1992.

Pole conspiracy

Although of little danger to the queen, the Pole conspiracy was the first Catholic plot of Elizabeth's reign to aim at replacing her with Mary STUART, Queen of Scots, and the first evidence of the development of a potentially dangerous English Catholicism (see CATHOLICISM, ENGLISH). The ANGLICAN SETTLEMENT of 1559 dashed the hopes of English Catholics that Elizabeth would favor their Church, and it led many to dismiss her as a heretical usurper and to recognize Mary, Queen of Scots, as the rightful ruler of England.

In the autumn of 1562, Arthur Pole and his brothers, nephews to Cardinal Reginald Pole, who had been Archbishop of Canterbury under MARY I, sought unsuccessfully to convince Mary Stuart's powerful French relatives, the GUISE FAMILY, to provide military support for a coup to dethrone Elizabeth and to proclaim Mary. As grandchildren of Edward IV's niece, Margaret Pole, Countess of Salisbury, whom HENRY VIII had executed in 1541, the Poles were among the last holders of the YORKIST CLAIM to the throne (see genealogical chart in Appendix 1: "Yorkist Claimants to the English Throne in the Sixteenth Century"). Arthur Pole used his Yorkist blood and his connections with former Catholic councilors of Queen Mary, such as Lord Hastings of Loughborough and Sir Edward Waldegrave, to contact the French and Spanish ambassadors in LONDON, who made vague promises but gave little real support or credence to the conspiracy. The involvement of the ambassadors aroused the suspicion of Sir William CECIL, who had long believed that the Spanish ambassador was protecting and encouraging gatherings of disaffected English Catholics.

Pole and his associates were arrested in October 1562 and lodged in the TOWER OF LONDON, the government deciding to proceed against them by act of ATTAINDER. Cecil used the conspiracy to convince PARLIAMENT and his fellow councilors of the growing threat from Catholics to the queen's security, and as an excuse to raid the French and Spanish embassies in February 1563 to flush out English Catholics and to discredit the Spanish ambassador. Far from putting a Catholic queen on the throne, the Pole conspiracy led to the first anti-Catholic statutes of the reign (see PENAL LAWS). The Parliament of 1563 made anyone who refused twice to take the oath upholding the royal supremacy over the English Church guilty of TREASON, and it forbade Catholics from serving in the House of Commons (see SUPREMACY, ROYAL).

Further Reading: Wallace T. MacCaffrey, *The Shaping of the Elizabethan Regime*, Princeton, NJ: Princeton University Press, 1968.

poor laws

Concerned that growing numbers of poor and homeless people constituted a threat to the political and social order, sixteenth-century English Parliaments passed a series of statutes designed to create a national, parish-based system for helping and controlling the poor (see PARLIAMENT). Several factors increased poverty during the Tudor period. POPULATION growth increased the labor supply and led to unemployment, which, by forcing people to move about the country seeking work, caused the problem of vagabondage. Inflation deepened poverty by causing prices to rise twice as fast as wages. The Reformation aggravated the problem by leading to the dissolution of the monasteries and other medieval religious institutions that had traditionally handled poor relief.

The first Tudor poor law, the statute of 1536, dealt with begging and vagabonds by forbidding the former and dividing the latter into two classes—the sturdy and the impotent. Sturdy beggars were to be put to work and charged with felony if they refused to work. Care of the impotent poor was placed on parishes, which were to take up a voluntary collection from parishioners for poor relief and to distribute the sums collected among the local needy. Under Elizabeth, poor laws were passed in 1563, 1572, and 1576, but the poor law of 1598, as modified in 1601, repealed all previous acts and established a national system of poor relief that lasted into the nineteenth century.

The 1598 act made parish collections for the poor compulsory. Each parish had to appoint overseers of the poor who could confiscate the goods of any parishioner refusing to contribute to the poor rates (i.e., the parish assessments for poor relief). The law defined vagrants as "masterless men," that is, those not rooted in a community and under the authority of their social superiors, and men in so-called "dangerous" professions, such as minstrels and peddlers, or men refusing to work for the wages set by statute (see SOCIAL HIERARCHY). Vagabonds could be whipped and returned to their home parishes. Disabled poor were to be given employment funded by the poor rates. Although the poor laws alleviated some poverty, their real accomplishment was to reinforce the social status quo by encouraging deference to authority and by discouraging vagabondage and disorder.

Further Reading: Paul Slack, *The English Poor Law, 1531–1782*, Cambridge: Cambridge University Press, 1995.

population

Although absolute population figures for Elizabethan England are difficult to calculate, studies clearly show that the trend in population from 1520 to 1620 was a gradual and almost continuous increase. England's population had decreased sharply in the century between 1350 and 1450, with PLAGUE and climatic changes accounting for much of the decline. By 1520, better harvests and fewer outbreaks of disease allowed the population of England and WALES to reach about 2.3 million, an increase over 1450 but still significantly lower than the country's population in the early fourteenth century (see EPIDEMIC DISEASE). This upward trend briefly reversed in the 1550s, when bad harvests, plague outbreaks, and political and economic upheaval caused a slight decrease.

The start of Elizabeth's reign coincided with better economic times and with a lessening of the plague, although serious outbreaks did occur several times during her reign. By 1580, the population had increased to about 3.5 million and the average life expectancy had risen to about 40 years. At Elizabeth's death in 1603, the population stood at just over 4 million. Although the towns were growing, Elizabethan England was still predominantly rural, with only about 10 percent of the population in 1603 living in towns of 4,000 or more. LONDON, by far the largest city in England, grew from about 120,000 people in 1558 to over 200,000 by 1603. London benefited in part from foreign immigration; Elizabethan England drew Protestant refugees from religious conflicts in FRANCE, the NETHERLANDS, and Germany. Norwich, Bristol, and York, with 1603 populations somewhere between 10,000 and 15,000, were the country's next largest cities.

The southern and eastern counties had the highest population densities. The general trend of movement was from the north and west to the south and east, with London being the great population magnet. Poor soil and continuing border warfare with SCOTLAND made parts of the north relatively uninhabited. Because the economy was unable to keep up with the rise in population, increased demand for food, clothing, and industrial products drove up both prices and rates of unemployment. Wages also declined as the availability of laborers increased. After Elizabeth's accession, the accuracy of demographic information improved because the government began supplying parishes with parchment on which to record local population statistics.

Further Reading: E. A. Wrigley and R. S. Schofield, *The Population History of England, 1541–1871,* Cambridge: Cambridge University Press, 1981.

portraits of Elizabeth I. *See* ELIZABETH I, PORTRAITS OF.

Portugal expedition

The Portugal expedition of 1589 (also known as the Don Antonio Expedition) was an English attempt to destroy the remnants of the Spanish ARMADA and to wrest the Crown of Portugal from PHILIP II. In August 1588, as the surviving ships of the great Armada struggled back to SPAIN, William CECIL, Lord Burghley, suggested a retaliatory strike at Lisbon. Seeking to replenish her exhausted treasury, Elizabeth expanded the project by suggesting an attack on the American treasure fleet in the AZORES. When a shortage of SHIPS and supplies delayed the venture until the spring of 1589, the PRIVY COUNCIL decided to send along a land force capable of capturing Lisbon and restoring Don Antonio to the Portuguese throne, which the Spanish had taken from him in 1580.

A large English fleet, organized on a joint-stock basis (see JOINT-STOCK COMPANY) with contributions from the queen and numerous English merchants and courtiers, departed England in April under the command of Sir Francis DRAKE and Sir John NORRIS. The fleet sailed first to the Spanish port of Corunna, where an attack captured part of the town. However, the raid did little damage to Spanish shipping and diverted English attention from more than 50 Armada vessels lying defenseless in nearby ports. The raid also cost the English more than 2,000 soldiers, who departed for England with the spoils of Corunna. The fleet then sailed to Lisbon, but the land-sea attack launched on the Portuguese capital was poorly planned and executed, and the expected uprising in Don Antonio's favor never occurred. Although the English army captured some outlying districts of Lisbon, heat, disease, and lack of supplies reduced the army's strength and forced the English command to abort the attack and retreat to their ships.

Further raids were made on the Spanish coast, but neither time nor strength remained to seek treasure ships in the Azores, and the fleet returned to England. Although the expedition brought back £30,000 of plunder and 150 captured cannon, the failure to destroy the remaining Armada ships, the lack of support for Don Antonio, and the inability to seize the treasure ships disappointed the queen, led Drake to retire from active service, and discouraged investment in future joint-stock enterprises.

Further Reading: R. B. Wernham, *After the Armada: Elizabethan England and the Struggle for Western Europe, 1588–1595,* Oxford: Clarendon Press, 1984; R. B. Wernham, ed., *The Expedition of Sir John Norris and Sir Frances Drake to Spain and Portugal, 1589,* Aldershot, England: Gower, 1988.

predestination. *See* CALVINISM.

prerogative

The royal prerogative consisted of all the powers and privileges that English law reserved for the Crown to enable it to conduct the business of state and govern the realm efficiently. For instance, only the monarch could summon or dissolve PARLIAMENT, and only the monarch could grant pardons or issue proclamations (see PROCLAMATION). In the Elizabethan period, the scope of the prerogative was vague, thus allowing the Crown considerable flexibility in administering the government and ensuring justice. Under the prerogative, the Crown had wide latitude in conducting foreign policy, setting Church policy, and maintaining law and order in the kingdom.

The Crown had the prerogative right to appoint and dismiss ministers of state and judges, which allowed the development in the fifteenth and sixteenth centuries of prerogative courts, such as Star Chamber, Requests, and Chancery (see STAR CHAMBER, COURT OF; REQUESTS, COURT OF; CHANCERY, COURT OF). The authority of these courts rested on the Crown's prerogative right to dispense justice, not on the COMMON LAW. However, English legal theory placed the Crown firmly under the law; the queen, for instance, could not issue proclamations inconsistent with the common law or repeal or suspend a statute of Parliament merely by prerogative.

All members of the Elizabethan political classes, including the queen herself, accepted that the highest authority in the realm was not the Crown, but the Crown in Parliament, supported by the PRIVY COUNCIL and the judiciary. Thus, the queen could not simply impose taxes over and above her regular revenues from land and customs duties—she was required to obtain the consent of Parliament for the collection of any extraordinary taxes (see CUSTOMS REVENUE; REVENUE, ROYAL; TAXATION). This financial limitation placed bounds on other aspects of the royal prerogative; for instance, the queen, although invested by the prerogative with the conduct of foreign policy, could not make or continue war without the financial acquiescence of Parliament.

The use and extent of the royal prerogative became a major issue between Crown and Parliament in the seventeenth century, but it engendered little debate in the sixteenth century because Elizabeth and her Tudor predecessors (see TUDOR FAMILY), including HENRY VIII when he overthrew papal authority in England, almost always sought the sanction of law through Parliament for their actions.

Further Reading: G. R. Elton, *The Parliament of England 1559–1581,* Cambridge: Cambridge University Press, 1986; John Neville Figgis, *The Divine Right of Kings,* New York: Harper and Row, 1965.

presbyterian movement

A presbyterian form of church government replaces bishops with an oligarchic system of church assemblies, or presbyteries, composed of ministers and representative elders. A national assembly governs the church through regional diocesan synods or councils and local parish presbyteries. The system was adopted by the Scottish Church in 1560 and began to develop informally and illegally in the English Church in the 1570s, along with PROPHESYINGS. Prophesyings were public conferences of local Puritan ministers that were designed to improve preaching and understanding of the Bible; the queen ordered their suppression because prophesyings were solely Puritan initiatives lacking any royal or parliamentary sanction (see PARLIAMENT; PURITANS).

In the 1580s, the presbyterian movement reformed around the classes (see CLASSICAL MOVEMENT), a series of church courts comprising local Puritan ministers and elders of their congregations. The classes sought to maintain Puritan notions of worship and morality among the clergy and laity of participating congregations. Whether such local courts ever developed into an interconnected national system is unlikely, for the queen ordered their suppression in the 1590s in the wake of the MARPRELATE TRACTS controversy.

Under Archbishop John WHITGIFT, Anglican bishops detected and rooted out all illegal presbyterian assemblies, and advocates of a presbyterian system, such as Thomas CARTWRIGHT, were persecuted and imprisoned or forced to flee the realm. Both Elizabeth and her successor, JAMES I, realized that the abolition of bishops and the institution of a presbyterian system would ultimately mean the end of royal control over the Church (see SUPREMACY, ROYAL).

Further Reading: Patrick Collinson, *The Elizabethan Puritan Movement,* Oxford: Clarendon Press, 1990.

priest holes

Priest holes were secret hiding places, often ingeniously contrived, built into the country homes of Catholic GENTRY for the concealment from the authorities of Catholic clergymen. In 1580, PARLIAMENT responded to the arrival of the first Jesuits in England (see JESUIT MISSION) by enacting statutes (see PENAL LAWS) that made it TREASON to convert an English subject to Catholicism and that outlawed the harboring of Catholic priests. A second statute in 1585 made it treason merely for a Catholic priest to be in England. By giving greedy, unscrupulous, or devoutly anti-Catholic Englishmen a license to hunt priests, these statutes initiated the construction of small, secure places of concealment in the gentry homes where priests headquartered.

The most skillful designer of priest holes was Nicholas Owen, whose two brothers were priests and who acted as a servant for the Jesuits Edmund CAMPION and Henry GARNET. While engaged on a mundane construction or remodeling project, Owen would work at night to construct priest holes that could foil even long and careful searches. Owen often devised hiding places within hiding places and usually contrived some sort of escape route and some means (e.g., a tube) whereby the occupant of the hole could be fed during prolonged searches. Owen helped John GERARD escape from the TOWER OF LONDON in 1597 and was

himself captured in 1605 when he came out of a hiding place to avoid starvation and to draw searchers away from Garnet, who lay concealed in another priest hole in the same house.

Not all priest holes were as clever or elaborate as Owen's constructions; many were merely makeshift hiding places in attics, over ceilings, or behind walls. Many were dark, cramped, and airless; when a noted priest hunter named George Eliot invaded their house of refuge in July 1581, Campion and two other priests found themselves hustled into a dark, stifling hiding hole barely big enough for the three men to lay side by side. In a period without canned food and modern plumbing, extended stays in even the most cleverly designed priest holes were difficult propositions. Nonetheless, such hiding places, some of which were only rediscovered in the twentieth century, made possible the work of Catholic priests in Elizabethan England.

Further Reading: John Bossy, *The English Catholic Community 1570–1850,* New York: Oxford University Press, 1976; David Lunn, *The Catholic Elizabethans,* Bath: Downside Abbey, 1998; Patrick McGrath, *Papists and Puritans under Elizabeth I,* New York: Walker and Company, 1967.

The Principal Navigations, Voyages and Discoveries of the English Nation

As a history of past English explorations and an inspiration for future exploration, trade, and colonization efforts, Richard HAKLUYT's *The Principal Navigations, Voyages and Discoveries of the English Nation* was one of the most influential publications in Elizabethan England. Hakluyt published his first edition of *Navigations* in 1589, the year after the English victory over the Spanish ARMADA. The volume was an anthology, a collection of eyewitness travel and exploration accounts and related documents. The scope of the 700,000-word book was explained in its lengthy subtitle: *Made by Sea or over Land, to the Remote and Farthest Distant Quarters of the Earth at Any Time within the Compass of These 1,500 Years.*

Most of the book consisted of eyewitness accounts of English explorations of the previous century; only about one-tenth covered medieval and pre-Columbian voyages. Hakluyt's revised and expanded edition of *Navigations* (1598–1600) added accounts of sixteenth-century exploits, such as the voyages of Sir Francis

DRAKE and the colonization efforts of Sir Humphrey GILBERT and Sir Walter RALEIGH. When accounts were available only in a foreign language, Hakluyt printed the original along with his own ENGLISH translation. If several accounts existed for a voyage, Hakluyt printed them all to provide as much information as possible. Except in his introduction to the collection, Hakluyt made no comment on the materials, allowing his readers to evaluate each account according to their own needs. The documents collected included government and business letters, commissions, naval instructions, private records of merchant companies, reports from government and business agents abroad, logs of ship captains, all manner of correspondence, and pro-colonization propaganda tracts.

Hakluyt's intended audience was the merchants, seafarers, geographers, and government officials who had been using these same documents piecemeal to plan new voyages of trade and discovery. Such men needed to know all they could about the parts of the world they planned to visit—climate, sailing conditions, trading opportunities, political arrangements, and everything else that previous English visitors had discovered. While Hakluyt's purposes were highly practical, the thrill of adventure, the descriptions of exotic places, and the sense of English history and achievement that his book provided helped prepare literate English people to countenance and support English colonization efforts in North AMERICA in the next century.

Further Reading: Irwin R. Blacker, ed., *The Portable Hakluyt's Voyages,* New York: Viking Press, 1965; George Bruner Parks, *Richard Hakluyt and the English Voyages,* 2nd ed., New York: F. Ungar, 1961.

principal secretary. *See* OFFICERS OF STATE.

printing

The first English printing press was established at Westminster in the 1470s by William Caxton, who produced the first books printed in ENGLISH. By the start of the English Reformation in the 1530s, an increasing number of printers were flourishing in England, particu-

This engraving from the drawings of Flemish artist Jan van Straet shows the interior of a sixteenth-century printer's shop. Published in the 1580s, the engraving shows two presses, with printers, compositors, and proofreaders hard at work. *By permission of the Folger Shakespeare Library.*

larly in LONDON. Because the printing press was an ideal way to quickly and cheaply disseminate new religious ideas, HENRY VIII sought to control what was printed in his kingdom, both to promote his own religious views and to suppress ideas he found unacceptable. A PROCLAMATION of 1538 required all English books to be licensed by the PRIVY COUNCIL before printing and distribution. In 1557, MARY I extended government censorship of printing by granting the London Stationers' Company the exclusive right to print most English materials (see LIVERIED COMPANY). Given powers of search and seizure to maintain its monopoly against interlopers (see MONOPOLIES), the company further protected its members' rights by requiring that all licensed titles be entered in the STATIONERS' REGISTER.

Elizabeth confirmed the Stationers' charter and extended responsibility for licensing printed materials to officials of the ANGLICAN CHURCH. However, illegal Catholic and Puritan presses continued to distribute unlicensed religious works throughout the kingdom (see CATHOLICISM, ENGLISH; PURITANS). The Catholic printer William Carter was executed for his activities in 1582, and the illicit printing of the MARPRELATE TRACTS in the late 1580s started an extensive search for hidden Puritan presses. In 1586, a Star Chamber decree (see STAR CHAMBER, COURT OF) empowered government authorities to limit the number of presses and printers and to forbid all printing outside London (where it could be more easily regulated), except for the licensed printers at the UNIVERSITIES in Oxford and Cambridge.

Previously, the Crown had designated one man as official royal printer—Richard GRAFTON held the post under EDWARD VI—but Elizabeth quickly recognized the political and economic benefits of granting monopolies to print specific kinds of materials among numerous printers. Thus, Richard Tottel held the monopoly on law books, William Seres printed all prayer books, and John Day printed catechisms. By shutting other printers out of certain markets, the printing patents, like all Elizabethan monopolies, caused much anger. Many unlicensed editions were creatively printed and distributed, and one-third of all editions published in the late Elizabethan period never appeared in the Stationers' Register. *See also* illustrations for BIBLE, ENGLISH; FIRST FOLIO; GRAMMAR SCHOOL; GREENE, ROBERT; MARLOWE, CHRISTOPHER; SPENSER, EDMUND.

Further Reading: Colin Clair, *A History of Printing in Britain,* London: Cassell, 1965.

privateering

Privateers were owners or captains of SHIPS who were privately commissioned by the English government to attack enemy vessels. Privateers were licensed by letters of marque, royal commissions authorizing private individuals to outfit and arm ships in time of war. Without such a license, a privateer was simply a pirate. Such well-known English seafarers as Francis DRAKE and John HAWKINS engaged in privateering against SPAIN. After 1589, as the Crown's military commitments in Europe began to absorb most of its resources, conduct of the naval war against Spain fell largely into the hands of privateers. An average of about 150 privateering expeditions set sail from England each year after the start of war in 1585.

In the early years, most privateering ventures were outfitted in the West Country (the extreme southwestern counties of Devon and Cornwall), but by the 1590s, most privateering enterprises originated in LONDON, financed by the city's great merchants. London's merchants replaced profits from trade (which were disrupted by war) with profits from the sale of privateer booty. The annual value of prizes—captured ships and cargoes—brought back to England by privateers was often over £200,000, the yearly income of the Crown in the early years of Elizabeth's reign. The expeditions of the most famous English captains were often joint-stock ventures with the government, out of which the queen expected financial return as much as military success (see JOINT-STOCK COMPANY). Few of these better-known voyages realized the profits enjoyed by the smaller privateering enterprises of the merchant community, but these public-private expeditions did register the occasional spectacular success, such as the capture in 1592 of the immensely rich East Indies vessel, the *Madre de Dios.* The plundered treasures of the *Madre de Dios* brought the queen and her fellow investors a handsome return and stimulated further privateering efforts with hopes of similar success.

Further Reading: K. R. Andrews, *Elizabethan Privateering,* Cambridge: Cambridge University Press, 1964; Neville Williams, *The Sea Dogs: Privateers, Plunder and Piracy in the Elizabethan Age,* New York: Macmillan, 1975.

Privy Council

The Privy Council was a select body of royal councilors that served as the chief instrument of Elizabethan government. The Tudor Privy Council was more flexible in scope and more wide-ranging in duties than any other royal board in Europe. English privy councilors exercised three basic functions: they advised the monarch on matters of policy, handled day-to-day administration, and acted as judicial boards for cases of various types (see REQUESTS, COURT OF; STAR CHAMBER, COURT OF). Privy councilors oversaw the defense of the realm; regulated trade, industry, prices, and wages; managed royal and national finance; enforced religious statutes, including those against RECUSANTS; supervised royal officials, including judges and JUSTICES OF THE PEACE; managed PARLIAMENT for the Crown; and occasionally inquired into matters of public morality.

Elizabeth's Privy Council was far smaller and more exclusive in membership than earlier royal councils. The Council of MARY I, Elizabeth's sister and immediate predecessor, had grown to more than 50 members, but the Elizabethan Council never numbered more than 19, and it stood at only 13 at the queen's death in 1603. Unlike Mary, Elizabeth appointed almost no clerical councilors, John WHITGIFT, Archbishop of Canterbury, being her only ecclesiastical appointee. Most Council meetings were attended by from 6 to 12 members, the queen herself appearing rarely, and most day-to-day business was conducted by an inner group of 5 or 6 trusted councilors who also held some great office of state. For most of the reign this inner working group consisted of such men as William CECIL, Lord Burghley, who was also lord treasurer; Sir Francis WALSINGHAM, who was secretary of state; Thomas RADCLIFFE, Earl of SUSSEX; Charles Howard, Lord Howard of Effingham; and the queen's favorite, Robert DUDLEY, Earl of Leicester (see FAVORITES).

On matters of policy, Council members met to discuss an issue, formulate a consensus, and then offer their best advice to the queen, who then set the policy for the Council to implement. Elizabeth, however, was notorious for her indecision and procrastination, and councilors often had to manipulate her into making a decision, as when Walsingham maneuvered Mary STUART, Queen of Scots, into endorsing the BABINGTON PLOT as a way to force Elizabeth to consent to Mary's trial and execution.

Further Reading: Michael Pulman, *The Elizabethan Privy Council in the Fifteen-Seventies,* Berkeley: University of California Press, 1971.

proclamation

A proclamation was a legislative order, administrative regulation, or formal policy announcement issued by the Crown under the royal PREROGATIVE. Proclamations were issued by the Crown alone, without the consent of either the PRIVY COUNCIL (which advised on proclamations) or PARLIAMENT. Proclamations were inferior to parliamentary statutes, which could be neither altered nor contradicted by royal proclamations. A proclamation expired at the death of the monarch who issued it. The Crown used proclamations to announce war or peace, quell rebellion, control trade and industry, announce important policy changes, issue instructions for implementing a parliamentary statute or Council order, or implement religious policies.

Proclamations could not create felonies or treasons, touch property rights protected by the COMMON LAW, or deprive anyone of life or limb. Proclamations were useful for dealing with emergency situations or for handling problems when Parliament was not sitting. Elizabeth issued 382 proclamations during her reign, almost 200 more than her sister and brother (see EDWARD VI; MARY I) combined. Proclamations were delivered to local officials (see LOCAL GOVERNMENT) through a county's sheriff and would be read aloud before being posted in customary and prominent places throughout the county, such as at the fronts of churches and guildhalls or at town gates and market crosses.

Elizabethan proclamations began with the heading "By the Queen" and ended with the location from which they were issued and the invocation "God Save the Queen." The right of Elizabeth and her Tudor (see TUDOR FAM-

ILY) predecessors to use proclamations was rarely questioned, although the exact scope and authority of proclamations, like the scope and authority of the royal prerogative itself, was vague.

Further Reading: Frederic A. Youngs Jr., *The Proclamations of the Tudor Queens,* Cambridge: Cambridge University Press, 1976.

prodigy houses

During the reign of Elizabeth, the rise of a political cult identifying the queen as the embodiment of the state combined with the queen's annual habit of going on formal summer tours known as progresses (see PROGRESSES, ROYAL) to promote the development of an exclusively Elizabethan architectural phenomenon known as prodigy houses. Designed to reflect the grandeur of the queen and the glory of her COURT, prodigy houses were large and expensive aristocratic country residences built specifically to attract a stay from the queen and her court as they moved on slow summer progress through the towns and countryside of southern and southeastern England.

The term "prodigy" derived from the Latin word meaning "portent," and came to describe an extraordinary structure out of proportion with its surroundings. Prodigy houses used every known architectural device to portray splendor and lavish display, and their design sought to approximate the needs and layout of the court as imposed upon an ordinary country household. William CECIL, Lord Burghley, for example, entertained the queen at the enormous houses he built at Burghley in Northamptonshire and at Theobalds in Hertfordshire. In 1591, the Earl of Hertford, preparing for a three-day visit by the queen, engaged over 300 workmen to enlarge his house at Elvetham, to erect a series of outbuildings to lodge the court, and to dig a pond with three large islands as a setting for an elaborate outdoor ENTERTAINMENT.

By the 1580s, the architect Robert SMYTHSON had become closely identified with the design and building of the kind of lavish country houses associated with the prodigy house trend; his best-known projects were Longleat House in Wiltshire and Hardwick Hall in Derbyshire. *See also* ARCHITECTURE; VIRGIN QUEEN.

Further Reading: Mark Girouard, *Robert Smythson and the Architecture of the Elizabethan Era,* South Brunswick, NJ: Barnes, 1967.

progresses, royal

No English monarch made better or more extensive political use of royal progresses than Elizabeth I. Progresses were formal summer tours of the kingdom conducted by the queen and a portion of the COURT, usually between the months of August and October when the weather was generally good and the harvest was being gathered. For Elizabeth, royal progresses were, first and foremost, an opportunity to see—and be seen by—her subjects. Following an itinerary published well in advance, a progress would carry the queen to various of the more distant royal residences (see PALACES), to the country homes of the local nobility or GENTRY, or to lodgings provided by a town or one of the UNIVERSITIES.

Having spent the winter moving haphazardly between the larger royal residences in London and the Thames Valley, such as WHITEHALL PALACE, GREENWICH PALACE, RICHMOND PALACE, and HAMPTON COURT PALACE, Elizabeth gladly left those houses to the intensive summer cleaning their primitive domestic sewage systems demanded. Traveling on horseback or in an open litter, the queen stopped frequently to talk to the people who crowded the roadside to watch her pass. If Elizabeth enjoyed progresses, her household officials did not, being responsible for loading and transporting hundreds of carts stuffed with the queen's household goods and those of her attendants. Providing accommodations for the queen's followers could also be an overwhelming task, both for those seeking lodging and for those expected to supply it.

While a great honor, entertaining the queen on progress in one's home or town was also a crushing expense, and a source of much anxiety lest the quality of accommodations or ENTERTAINMENT fall short of court expectations. Elizabeth, wrote William HARRISON, considered that "every nobleman's house is her palace," and the queen on progress stopped for short periods at almost any suitable lodging along her route. William CECIL, Lord

Burghley, spent the huge sum of £1,000 to host the queen for 10 days in 1591, and Robert DUDLEY, Earl of Leicester, spent a fortune to entertain the queen at Kenilworth in 1575. Competition to host the queen led to an Elizabethan architectural phenomenon known as PRODIGY HOUSES—large and splendid aristocratic country homes built specifically to attract a royal progress. The architect Robert SMYTHSON was particularly known for the design and building of such homes. *See also* ARCHITECTURE; PALACES.

Further Reading: Zillah Dovey, *An Elizabethan Progress,* Herndon, VA: Sutton Publishers, 1996; Jane Osborne, *Entertaining Elizabeth: The Progresses and Great Houses of Her Time,* London: Bishopsgate Press, 1998.

prophesyings

To improve the faith and training of parish clergy, Puritan ministers in the 1570s began holding a series of public conferences at which several sermons would be preached on the same Biblical text, the text would be discussed by the ministers present, and the proceedings would be summarized for the attending public by a moderator. Thus, though ostensibly for the education of clergy and divinity students, the prophesyings also exposed the laity to Puritan teachings (see PURITANS) and to criticisms of the bishops and the ANGLICAN CHURCH.

Reaching their height in the mid-1570s, prophesyings aroused the hostility of Elizabeth because most such gatherings were convened and conducted by the ministers themselves, not by royal or parliamentary authority (see PARLIAMENT). In 1577, the queen ordered Edmund GRINDAL, Archbishop of Canterbury, to suppress all prophesyings. But Grindal, like several other bishops who were in sympathy with Puritan aims, had been quietly encouraging prophesyings as a means to improve preaching and to increase clerical and lay knowledge of the Bible, both important Puritan objectives. When the archbishop declined to obey the queen's order, Elizabeth suspended him from office and commanded his deputies to put an end to prophesyings. The resulting crackdown halted the movement, although some more militant Puritans continued to meet illegally.

Prophesyings were the first step in the formation of an informal and illegal system of presbyterian church government (see PRESBYTERIAN MOVEMENT), which aimed to replace bishops with a hierarchy of assemblies comprising ministers and church elders. Because laypeople attended and observed prophesyings, the gatherings were important not only for improving preaching among ministers but for spreading Puritan ideas among the people and thereby creating new adherents to the Puritan movement.

Further Reading: Patrick Collinson, *The Elizabethan Puritan Movement,* Oxford: Clarendon Press, 1990.

Protestantism

Protestantism refers to the basic set of beliefs shared by the Christian Churches that arose in sixteenth-century Europe as a result of the Reformation. The term derives from the formal "Protestation" a minority of pro-Lutheran German princes made against the decisions of the Catholic majority at the imperial diet (i.e., council) called by the Holy Roman Emperor CHARLES V at Speyer in 1529.

The basic tenets of Protestant belief tended to reject any doctrine that stressed the role of the clergy or of church institutions and ceremonies in achieving salvation. Thus, Protestants accepted the Bible as the supreme source of divine revelation. Whereas the Catholic Church opposed vernacular Bibles and insisted that the clergy interpret scripture to the laity, Protestants demanded that believers be able to read and study the Bible for themselves. Following an idea that Martin Luther derived from the writings of St. Paul, Protestants also accepted the doctrine of justification by faith, meaning that Christians are saved only by faith in Jesus Christ and not by any of their own works or efforts. By rejecting the Catholic doctrine of salvation through faith *and* good works, Protestants undermined the role of the church hierarchy and of ritual in the salvation of believers.

From the principle of justification by faith, John CALVIN evolved the doctrine of predestination, which declared that God had foreordained all people for either salvation or damnation (see CALVINISM). Although good works were useless in earning salvation, righteous living could be a sign of one's membership in the godly Elect, those people predestined for heaven. Presdestination, with all its implications for political and economic life, was a central tenet of the Calvinistic Churches of SCOTLAND, FRANCE, and the NETHERLANDS, and of the PURITANS in England and AMERICA.

Protestants also accepted the priesthood of all believers, a notion that considered the true church to be a worshipping body of Christians, and not the clergy or an institutional ritual. This principle rejected Catholic ceremonial and sacramentalism, as well as a privileged church hierarchy. It also overthrew the Catholic doctrine of TRANSUBSTANTIATION, the central core of which was the power of the priest to initiate the miracle of the MASS in changing bread and wine into the body and blood of Christ. Although Protestant churches differed over whether Christ's body and blood were ever actually present during communion, all reformed denominations rejected the Mass and denied transubstantiation. *See also* CATHOLICISM, ENGLISH; REFORMATION, ENGLISH; REFORMATION, IRISH; REFORMATION, SCOTTISH; REFORMATION, WELSH.

Further Reading: Patrick Collinson, *The Elizabethan Puritan Movement,* Oxford: Clarendon Press, 1990.

Puritans

The word "puritan" was first used in the mid-1560s by conforming Anglicans as a term of contempt or ridicule for those members of the English Church who demanded further Protestant reform or purification of worship, more and better preaching, and stricter adherence to the dictates of scripture. The term covered a wide variety of doctrines, attitudes, and positions; Puritans were united only in their demand that the ANGLICAN CHURCH be purged of any ideas, doctrines, rituals, or other elements that they regarded as Roman Catholic, superstitious, or unscriptural.

While Puritans viewed their religious life in terms of a duty to do only what God had specifically commanded in the Bible, Anglicans accepted a greater freedom to do whatever the Bible did not specifically prohibit. More moderate Puritans were willing to work within the English Church and through PARLIAMENT to achieve reform. More radical Puritans opposed episcopacy (i.e., the hierarchy of bishops) and advocated a presbyterian form of church gov-

ernment (see PRESBYTERIAN MOVEMENT) or even the independence of local congregations. In the 1590s, a few Puritan groups began to separate themselves from the Anglican Church (see CONGREGATIONALISTS; SEPARATISTS), believing they would never be able to worship as they chose under a church controlled by the Crown and bishops. Elizabeth's determination to rigidly uphold the 1559 ANGLICAN SETTLEMENT of religion and to strictly enforce royal supremacy over the Church led to clashes with Puritans over vestments (see SUPREMACY, ROYAL; VESTIARIAN CONTROVERSY), preaching (see LECTURESHIPS), and the nature of Church government.

By the 1590s, Puritans were demanding stricter observance of the Sabbath and stronger measures to root out immorality, positions that often provoked a strong reaction from non-Puritans because they included attempts to close down theatres and restrict other forms of ENTERTAINMENT (see HOLIDAYS). In the seventeenth century, Puritanism became the heart of resistance to the Crown and was instrumental in the coming of the civil war and the eventual destruction of the monarchy. Under Elizabeth I, the Puritans tried unsuccessfully to alter the Church, both through Parliament and through such illegal means as the presbyterian movement, the PROPHESYINGS of the 1570s, and the CLASSICAL MOVEMENT of the 1580s. Always fearful of SPAIN and Catholic Europe, most Puritans remained loyal to their Protestant queen, even though they disagreed with her on matters of church ritual and doctrine.

Further Reading: R. J. Acheson, *Radical Puritans in England, 1550–1660,* London: Longman, 1990; John Adair, *Puritans: Religion and Politics in Seventeenth-Century England and America,* Gloucester, England: Sutton Publishing, 1998; Patrick Collinson, *The Elizabethan Puritan Movement,* Oxford: Clarendon Press, 1990; Peter Lake, *Moderate Puritans and the Elizabethan Church,* Cambridge: Cambridge University Press, 1982; Patrick McGrath, *Papists and Puritans under Elizabeth I,* New York: Walker and Company, 1967.

purveyance

Purveyance, a royal privilege dating from the Middle Ages, allowed royal officials to compel vendors to sell goods and commodities to the government at predetermined prices, usually below market rates. Any Crown purchase, whether to feed the COURT, equip the ARMY, or maintain the NAVY, could be subject to purveyance. In theory, the prices paid were to reflect the rates prevailing in the nearest market, but the system had great potential for abuse and corruption, and the prices paid often varied widely from actual market rates.

Purveyance generated bitter complaint against the government and was frequently attacked in PARLIAMENT. Many schemes for reform were suggested and various bills were proposed in the House of Commons, but little changed because purveyance remained the best way to supply Crown needs. In 1581, the government revived a plan first proposed under Edward SEYMOUR, Duke of Somerset, lord protector for EDWARD VI; the plan called for transforming purveyance into a general tax for the support of the COURT. Nothing came of this proposal, which reappeared under JAMES I with the same lack of success.

Elizabeth's government negotiated fixed tax payments with many counties. Local JUSTICES OF THE PEACE collected these payments in lieu of the goods and services due to the Crown from the county under purveyance (see LOCAL GOVERNMENT). By 1600, purveyance was worth almost £40,000 in savings to the Crown each year. *See also* REVENUE, ROYAL; TAXATION.

Further Reading: D. C. Coleman, *The Economy of England, 1450–1750,* Oxford: Oxford University Press, 1977.

Q

Queen of Scots. *See* STUART, MARY, QUEEN OF SCOTS.

Queen's Bench, Court of. *See* KING'S (QUEEN'S) BENCH, COURT OF.

Queen's Safety Act

The Act for the Queen's Safety, passed by PARLIAMENT in 1585, extended throughout the kingdom the protections erected around the queen by the BOND OF ASSOCIATION. One of the most pressing concerns of the Parliament of 1584–85 was for the queen's safety, especially in light of the recent assassination of WILLIAM, PRINCE OF ORANGE, by a Catholic agent, and the continuing plotting of the Catholic supporters of Mary STUART, Queen of Scots.

Patterned after the Bond of Association, the act declared that anyone supporting a claimant to the throne who sought to advance his or her claim by assassination of the queen was guilty of TREASON. The act also authorized loyal subjects to pursue and kill both those who had attempted the murder and the claimant on whose behalf they had acted. The act differed from the Bond in that it did not empower subjects to also seek out and kill the claimant's heirs. Although it mentioned no one by name, the act, like the Bond, was clearly aimed at Mary Stuart. Elizabeth intervened in December 1584 while the bill was being debated to object to the provision allowing for destruction of heirs, which was an attempt to include Mary's Protestant son, James VI (see JAMES I) OF SCOTLAND, in the consequences of any Catholic plot on his mother's behalf.

In March 1585, a new bill, devised in consultation with the queen herself, was introduced into Parliament. This bill excluded heirs from the vengeance of loyal subjects unless the heirs' involvement in the assassination plot could be conclusively proven. Thus, under the Queen's Safety Act, should the queen be assassinated by the Queen of Scots' supporters, Mary Stuart would die for it, but her son James would be unharmed unless proven to be part of the conspiracy. The act also created a mechanism for determining who was involved in any assassination attempt, and who was thus subject to the penalty of treason as meted out by Elizabeth's subjects. Should any rebellion, invasion, or murder plot be undertaken against the queen, a commission would be created to investigate the deed and determine the guilty parties. Upon passage of the act, the Bond of Association was amended to conform to it. The Queen's Safety Act remained in force until repealed during Victoria's reign in the nineteenth century.

Further Reading: John Neale, *Elizabeth I and Her Parliaments 1584–1601,* New York: St. Martin's Press, 1958.

R

Radcliffe, Thomas, Earl of Sussex
(c. 1526–1583)

Thomas Radcliffe, third Earl of Sussex, was one of the most effective Elizabethan governors of IRELAND. Like the queen herself, Radcliffe was part of the powerful and extensive HOWARD FAMILY, his mother being a daughter of the second Duke of Norfolk. Educated at Cambridge (see UNIVERSITIES), Radcliffe was admitted to Gray's Inn (see INNS OF COURT) in 1561. Knighted by HENRY VIII in 1544 for his service in the king's French campaign, Radcliffe also served under Lord Protector Edward SEYMOUR, Duke of Somerset, at the battle of Pinkie in SCOTLAND in 1547.

At her accession in 1553, MARY I elevated Radcliffe to the PEERAGE as Lord Fitzwalter. In 1554, Radcliffe helped suppress WYATT'S REBELLION and participated in the negotiations for the queen's marriage to Philip (see PHILIP II) of SPAIN. Mary appointed Radcliffe lord deputy of Ireland in 1556, a year before he succeeded his father as Earl of Sussex. Because Sussex had proved himself an effective administrator and capable military leader, Elizabeth continued him in office on her accession in 1558 and raised him to the higher dignity of lord lieutenant of Ireland in 1560. Although his long campaign in Ulster against the rebel chief Shane O'NEILL brought only a partial and temporary peace to northern Ireland, Sussex was more successful against rebels in central Ireland and was able to carry out the queen's orders to establish English settlements in the region (see PLANTATIONS, IRISH). Poor health and continuing unrest in Ulster led Sussex to request his recall in 1564.

In 1569, Elizabeth appointed Sussex lord lieutenant of the north of England, a position that gave him chief responsibility for stamping out the NORTHERN REBELLION of 1569–70. Success in the north won Sussex appointment to the PRIVY COUNCIL in 1570. Associating himself with the political opposition to the royal favorite, Robert DUDLEY, Earl of Leicester, Sussex supported a series of ultimately unsuccessful efforts to arrange a MARRIAGE for the queen, especially the various proposals put forth by Francis VALOIS, Duke of Alençon, in the late 1570s and early 1580s. Despite earn-

This portrait of Thomas Radcliffe, Earl of Sussex, an Elizabethan lord deputy of Ireland, was painted by an unknown artist about 1565. *By courtesy of the National Portrait Gallery, London.*

ing the political enmity of Leicester, Sussex remained in favor and an important member of the Council until his death in June 1583.

Further Reading: Steven G. Ellis, *Tudor Ireland,* London: Longman, 1985; Wallace T. MacCaffrey, *The Shaping of the Elizabethan Regime,* Princeton, NJ: Princeton University Press, 1968; Wallace T. MacCaffrey, *Queen Elizabeth and the Making of Policy,* Princeton, NJ: Princeton University Press, 1981.

Raleigh, Elizabeth (1565–1647)

Elizabeth Throckmorton, the future wife of the courtier and explorer Sir Walter RALEIGH, was a maid of honor to Queen Elizabeth. The youngest child and only daughter of the Elizabethan diplomat Sir Nicholas THROCKMORTON, Elizabeth Throckmorton was only 6 when her father died. She lived with her mother until 1584, when she came to COURT and was taken into royal service as one of the queen's LADIES-IN-WAITING. Although not wealthy, she attracted the attention of Raleigh, a rising royal favorite, in 1590 (see FAVORITES). The couple were secretly married in November 1591 after Throckmorton discovered that she was pregnant.

The new Lady Raleigh kept her secret from the queen by withdrawing to her brother's LONDON house, where she gave birth to a son in March 1592. However, the queen soon learned of the child and, infuriated by what she saw as the treachery of her maid and her favorite, threw both Lady Raleigh and her husband into the TOWER OF LONDON. Although both were released in December 1592, Sir Walter Raleigh was forbidden the queen's presence for over a year, and Lady Elizabeth Raleigh was never forgiven; an attempt to reinstate her at court failed in 1601. Although she came occasionally to London after 1592, Lady Raleigh lived mostly at Sherborne, Raleigh's country home in Dorset. A second son, named Walter, was born at Sherborne in 1593. Lady Raleigh spent much of the late 1590s separated from her husband, who led an expedition to the Orinoco basin in South America in 1595 and was one of the leaders of the CADIZ RAID in 1596.

After the accession of JAMES I in 1603, Sir Walter Raleigh's enemies at court convinced the king that Raleigh had plotted against him. Convicted of TREASON, Raleigh was imprisoned in the Tower, where Lady Raleigh lived

with him until 1610, when the king ordered her to live elsewhere. She gave birth to a third son, named Carew, in or near the Tower in 1605. In 1609, the king confiscated Sherborne, giving Lady Raleigh a small pension in its place. Although Elizabeth Raleigh was a persistent suitor on her husband's behalf, he was executed on 29 October 1618. Lady Raleigh was allowed to keep her husband's head, which she had embalmed and kept with her until her death in 1647.

Further Reading: Jack H. Adamson and H. F. Follard, *The Shepherd of the Ocean: An Account of Sir Walter Ralegh and His Times,* Boston: Gambit, 1969; Stephen Coote, *A Play of Passion: The Life of Sir Walter Raleigh,* London: Macmillan, 1993; Robert Lacey, *Sir Walter Ralegh,* New York: Atheneum, 1973; A. L. Rowse, *Sir Walter Ralegh: His Family and Private Life,* New York: Harper, 1962; Norman Lloyd Williams, *Sir Walter Raleigh,* Baltimore: Penguin, 1965; Hugh Ross Williamson, *Sir Walter Raleigh,* Westport, CT: Greenwood Press, 1978; John Winton, *Sir Walter Ralegh,* New York: Coward, McCann and Geoghegan, 1975.

Raleigh, Sir Walter (c. 1552–1618)

A poet, courtier, soldier, and historian, Sir Walter Raleigh did more than any other Elizabethan to promote English exploration and colonization of North America. Born into a Devonshire GENTRY family, Raleigh (he favored the spelling Ralegh) was educated at Oxford (see UNIVERSITIES). He spent the early 1570s in FRANCE fighting with the HUGUENOTS as part of a contingent of Devonshire volunteers. In the late 1570s, he helped his half brother Sir Humphrey GILBERT fight rebels in IRELAND and outfit PRIVATEERING expeditions against Spanish shipping. After 1581, he was mostly at COURT, where he was much favored by the queen, who knighted him in 1584 and appointed him captain of her guards in 1587.

Between 1583 and 1589, Raleigh invested over £40,000 in six colonizing expeditions to North America, having received a grant from Elizabeth to plant colonies along the eastern coast of the continent, which area Raleigh named Virginia, in honor of the VIRGIN QUEEN. Although responsible for introducing potatoes and tobacco to England and Ireland, Raleigh's ventures (see "LOST COLONY"; ROANOKE COLONY [1585] and [1587]) were unsuccessful in establishing a permanent English colony in AMERICA. Raleigh was briefly imprisoned in 1592 for his unauthorized marriage to Elizabeth Throckmorton, one of the queen's LADIES-IN-WAITING (see RALEIGH, ELIZABETH). He was forbidden the queen's presence for a time, but was back in favor by 1595 when he set off on a fruitless search for the legendary Eldorado, supposedly to be found in Guyana. He was part of the successful English attack on Cadiz in 1596 (see CADIZ RAID) and the unsuccessful ISLANDS VOYAGE of 1597. He quarreled with the royal favorite Robert DEVEREUX, Earl of Essex, in 1597, and thereafter was a consistent opponent of the earl's and was much blamed for his downfall.

In 1603, JAMES I, persuaded by Raleigh's many enemies that the Devon gentleman was a dangerous conspirator, had Raleigh arrested and tried for TREASON. From 1603 to 1616, Raleigh lay in the TOWER OF LONDON, where he composed POETRY and wrote his *History of the World*. Released to search for gold along the Orinoco in South America, Raleigh found none, but he burned a Spanish settlement and was re-arrested upon his return on the insistence of the Spanish king, with whom James was attempting to negotiate a marriage for his son. Raleigh was executed on 29 October 1618. *See also* AMADAS-BARLOWE EXPEDITION.

This portrait of the soldier, poet, and courtier Sir Walter Raleigh was painted about 1588. *By courtesy of the National Portrait Gallery, London.*

Further Reading: Jack H. Adamson and H. F. Follard, *The Shepherd of the Ocean: An Account of Sir Walter Ralegh and His Times*, Boston: Gambit, 1969; Stephen Coote, *A Play of Passion: The Life of Sir Walter Raleigh*, London: Macmillan, 1993; Stephen Jay Greenblatt, *Sir Walter Ralegh: The Renaissance Man and His Roles*, New Haven, CT: Yale University Press, 1973; Robert Lacey, *Sir Walter Ralegh*, New York: Atheneum, 1973; David B. Quinn, *Raleigh and the British Empire*, New York: Collier Books, 1962; A. L. Rowse, *Sir Walter Ralegh: His Family and Private Life*, New York: Harper, 1962; Norman Lloyd Williams, *Sir Walter Ralegh*, Baltimore: Penguin, 1965; Hugh Ross Williamson, *Sir Walter Raleigh*, Westport, CT: Greenwood Press, 1978; John Winton, *Sir Walter Ralegh*, New York: Coward, McCann and Geoghegan, 1975.

recusants

Anyone in Elizabethan England who refused to attend Anglican services was a recusant. The term referred mainly to Catholics, but it could also be applied to Protestants, such as radical PURITANS (see also SEPARATISTS) who found the ANGLICAN CHURCH too Catholic in its rituals for their tastes. The Act of Uniformity of 1559 assessed a fine of one shilling a week on all recusants. An act of 1581 increased the recusancy fine to the ruinously high sum of £20 per month. Catholics tried to avoid the fines by attending services but refusing to take communion, even though they were enjoined to do so at least three times per year; such occasional conformity was outlawed by the PENAL LAWS, a series of parliamentary statutes passed in the second half of Elizabeth's reign to respond to Catholic plots on behalf of Mary STUART, Queen of Scots, and to the activities of SEMINARY PRIESTS.

The penal laws imposed stiff fines and serious disabilities on English Catholics. The act of 1581 made it TREASON (and thus punishable by death) to persuade someone, or to be persuaded by someone, to join the Catholic faith with the intention of withdrawing one's obedience from the queen. The 1593 Act Against Popish (i.e., Catholic) Recusants restricted the movement of recusants, confining them to within five miles of their homes unless they obtained a license to travel from a bishop or justice of the peace (JP). The penal laws were intended to destroy the Catholic minority community that began to develop in England after 1570, the year of the papal bull (proclamation) declaring Elizabeth a heretic and absolving her Catholic subjects from their allegiance to her (see PIUS V; *REGNANS IN EXCELSIS*).

Recusancy fines were more strictly collected after such incidents as the RIDOLFI PLOT had frightened the government into believing Catholic invasions or uprisings were imminent. Recusancy fines, which were collected by the local JPs, tended to be more loosely enforced in such Catholic areas as Lancashire, where many of the local gentlemen were themselves Catholic. *See also* CATHOLICISM, ENGLISH; JUSTICES OF THE PEACE.

Further Reading: John Bossy, *The English Catholic Community 1570–1850*, New York: Oxford University Press, 1976; Peter Holmes, *Resistance and Compromise: The Political Thought of the Elizabethan Catholics*, Cambridge: Cambridge University Press, 1982; David Lunn, *The Catholic Elizabethans*, Bath: Downside Abbey, 1998; Arnold Pritchard, *Catholic Loyalism in Elizabethan England*, Chapel Hill: University of North Carolina Press, 1979; Alexandra Walsham, *Church Papists: Catholicism, Conformity and Confessional Polemic in Early Modern England*, Rochester, NY: Boydell Press, 1993.

redshanks

The redshanks were Scottish mercenaries who played an important role in the wars of Elizabethan IRELAND. Light infantrymen from the Highlands and western isles of SCOTLAND, the redshanks usually hired themselves out to an Irish lord for the summer months. Their name came from their habit of going into battle bare-legged and in kilts. Poverty and overpopulation in their homelands, combined with the increasing demand for their services in Ireland, drove many Scotsmen to contract out as mercenaries. Because the redshanks were such an important component of Irish armies, especially in the Connacht and Ulster regions of northern Ireland, Irish chieftains were careful to maintain good relations with the most important redshank clans, such as the MacDonalds, Campbells, and MacLeans, and with the chief noblemen of Highland Scotland, such as the earls of Argyll.

To ensure a steady supply of mercenaries, Irish leaders in Ulster regularly married Scottish wives. Turlough Luineach O'NEILL's MacDonald wife brought him a handsome dowry of 1,200 redshanks. In the 1590s, the English government began taking steps to curb the flow of mercenaries from Scotland to Ireland. Besides making it worth the Earl of Argyll's time to discourage mercenary recruitment in his territories, the English distributed subsidies in the western islands to keep men at home and sent naval forces into the North Channel between Scotland and Ireland to intercept mercenary shipping. *See also* GALLOWGLASSES; KERN.

Further Reading: Steven G. Ellis, *Tudor Ireland*, London: Longman, 1985; Colm Lennon, *Sixteenth-Century Ireland: The Incomplete Conquest*, Dublin: Gill and Macmillan, 1994; Margaret MacCurtain, *Tudor and Stuart Ireland*, Dublin: Gill and Macmillan, 1972; David B. Quinn, *The Elizabethans and the Irish*, Ithaca, NY: Cornell University Press, 1966.

Reformation, English

The Reformation in England began in the 1530s as a political act of the Crown rather than as a popular movement of the people. Unable to obtain an annulment of his MARRIAGE from the pope, HENRY VIII worked through PARLIAMENT to end papal authority in England and make himself head of the English Church (see SUPREMACY, ROYAL). Besides permitting Henry to repudiate CATHERINE OF ARAGON and marry Anne BOLEYN, the break with the Church of Rome allowed him to abolish the English monasteries and seize their landed wealth for himself and his supporters. However, beyond altering the governance and economic position of the Church, Henry made few changes; at the king's death in 1547, the English Church was essentially a Catholic Church without the pope. Under Henry VIII, a papal Catholic could be executed for TREASON while a Protestant could be burned for heresy.

Powerful as the king seemed, he could never have broken with Rome without the acquiescence of Parliament and the political elite of the realm. Although Protestants were still a small minority in the 1540s, support for the pope was slight, ANTICLERICALISM was strong, and resistance to the royal policies was negligible. A truly Protestant Church appeared during the reign of EDWARD VI (1547–1553), when Parliament abolished the MASS, permitted the marriage of clergy, and seized chalices and other valuable Church paraphernalia associated with the Mass. Worship services were conducted in English according to the *BOOK OF COMMON PRAYER*, the 1552 version of which was based squarely on the doctrines of

CALVINISM. The rapidity of these changes, and the seeming greed of Edward's ministers for Church lands and goods, led to a backlash that supported the restoration of papal Catholicism under MARY I, Catherine of Aragon's daughter (see CATHOLICISM, ENGLISH). However, Mary was also determined to eradicate heresy, and her burning of Protestants generated much ill will for her English Catholic Church (see MARIAN EXILES; MARIAN MARTYRS).

Although a majority of the English POPULATION at Elizabeth's accession in 1558 may have tended toward Catholicism, few opposed the new queen's decision to restore PROTESTANTISM. As the daughter of Anne Boleyn, Elizabeth was the symbol of her father's break with Rome, and so virtually obligated to institute a Protestant Church. Thus, the ANGLICAN SETTLEMENT of 1559 made Elizabeth supreme governor of the church, restored the Prayer Book, and based ANGLICAN CHURCH doctrine on Calvinist principles. Despite increasing opposition from PURITANS, those within the Church seeking more radical reform, and from a minority who continued to adhere to papal Catholicism, Elizabeth stoutly maintained her Anglican Church as established in 1559, and by her death in 1603, it claimed the allegiance of the great majority of English men and women. *See also* REFORMATION, IRISH; REFORMATION, SCOTTISH; REFORMATION, WELSH; SEPARATISTS.

Further Reading: A. G. Dickens, *The English Reformation,* 2nd ed., University Park: Pennsylvania State University Press, 1989.

Reformation, Irish

Unlike England, where the break with the Roman Catholic Church initiated by the Crown in the 1530s led, by 1600, to a Protestant nation, IRELAND by 1600 had passed through similar experiences only to come to a renewed commitment to CATHOLICISM. In 1536, the Irish PARLIAMENT followed the example of its English counterpart and declared HENRY VIII head of the Irish Church. Suppression of the monasteries in the English PALE followed in 1539–40, with monastic lands going eventually to ANGLO-IRISH landowners, government leaders in DUBLIN, and about 20 Englishmen. Outside the Pale, where the authority of the Dublin government was slight or nonexistent, most monasteries continued to function.

Significant resistance to English religious policies did not appear until the reign of EDWARD VI, when the government abolished the MASS and appointed Protestants to Irish bishoprics. By restoring Catholic practice, MARY I stifled this opposition after 1553. However, Elizabeth's accession in 1558 restored PROTESTANTISM to the Irish Church. Like the English Parliament in 1559 (see ANGLICAN SETTLEMENT), the Irish Parliament of 1560 passed an Act of Supremacy declaring Elizabeth supreme governor of the Church, and an Act of Uniformity mandating use of the *BOOK OF COMMON PRAYER* for all worship services (see SUPREMACY, ROYAL). All citizens were required to attend church on Sunday or be fined 12 pence for their recusancy (see RECUSANTS).

Up to this point, the Irish and English Reformation experiences had been similar (see REFORMATION, ENGLISH), but after 1560 they diverged, with Protestantism taking strong root in England and fading away in Ireland. The reasons for Protestantism's failure in Ireland were several. The Dublin government controlled only part of the island and was never able to consistently enforce religious uniformity. Also, the Irish Church had few Protestant clergymen; most had to be brought from England, a circumstance that strengthened the perception that Protestantism was a foreign imposition and not an Irish movement. Finally, the weakness of the Protestant Church of Ireland gave Catholicism time to regroup and allowed priests from Catholic Europe to revive Irish Catholicism (see COUNTER-REFORMATION). The Catholic Church won the allegiance of the Anglo-Irish and the native Irish by identifying itself with resistance to English political and cultural conquest. By Elizabeth's death in 1603, England had won political control of Ireland, but Catholicism had won religious dominance in the island. *See also* REFORMATION, SCOTTISH; REFORMATION, WELSH.

Further Reading: Steven G. Ellis, *Tudor Ireland*, London: Longman, 1985; Alan Ford, *The Protestant Reformation in Ireland, 1590–1641*, Portland: Four Courts Press, 1997; Samantha A. Meigs, *The Reformations in Ireland: Tradition and Confessionalism, 1400–1690*, New York: St. Martin's Press, 1997.

Reformation, Scottish

Reformation in SCOTLAND was not initiated by the Crown, as occurred in England, but in opposition to the Crown and as a nationalistic reaction to the perception that a foreign power was imposing Catholicism. This perception was the reverse of the contemporaneous situation in IRELAND, where PROTESTANTISM suffered from its identification with the English government in DUBLIN (see REFORMATION, ENGLISH; REFORMATION, IRISH). The death of James V in 1542 left Scotland to be governed by a series of regents for James's infant daughter, Mary STUART, Queen of Scots. The weakness of the government allowed the spread of CALVINIST ideas, especially in EDINBURGH and the towns of the southern lowlands. By the late 1550s, Mary was in FRANCE and the regency was held by her French mother, Marie de GUISE, whose government was supported by French troops.

By 1559, when the regent tried to suppress John KNOX and the influential Protestant preachers, Protestantism came to be identified with friendship for England, while Catholicism meant alliance with France. To protect the Protestant preachers, the powerful Lords of the Congregation, a confederation of Protestant landholders, took arms against the Catholic regent and her French troops. Elizabeth I broke the ensuing military stalemate in 1560 by sending English troops into Scotland to support the Lords. The death of Marie de Guise and the conclusion of the Treaty of Edinburgh in the summer of 1560 led to the withdrawal of all foreign troops and left the Lords of the Congregation in control (see EDINBURGH, TREATY OF).

In August 1560, the Scottish PARLIAMENT abolished papal authority, banned the MASS, and established a presbyterian church based on Calvinist doctrines and independent of the Crown (see CALVINISM; PRESBYTERIAN MOVEMENT). When Mary, Queen of Scots, returned to Scotland in 1561, she promoted tolerance for fellow Catholics but reluctantly accepted the Protestant national church. After Mary's deposition in 1567, the various regency governments of young James VI (see JAMES I) were unquestionably Protestant, but sought to impose a greater measure of royal control on the Scottish Church. In 1572, the government restored bishops as a means of re-establishing this control. Between 1578 and 1610, the authority of the bishops waxed or waned depending on the political position of the king. By James's death in 1625, the Scottish Church was still an unusual hybrid, a presbyterian church with bishops. *See also* REFORMATION, WELSH.

Further Reading: Ian B. Cowan, *The Scottish Reformation,* New York: St. Martin's Press, 1982; Gordon Donaldson, *The Scottish Reformation,* Cambridge: Cambridge University Press, 1960.

Reformation, Welsh

The Reformation in WALES was imposed from above by the English Crown in the same manner and at the same time as Reformation was undertaken in England (see REFORMATION, ENGLISH). PROTESTANTISM was not nearly as strong in Wales in the 1530s and 1540s as it was in England during those decades. Wales exhibited much less ANTICLERICALISM than did England, and, being on the western coast of Britain, lacked the close and regular contacts with Europe that had brought reformist ideas and writings into LONDON and southeastern England. Although Wales did not send representatives to PARLIAMENT until 1542, all the Reformation statutes enacted by Parliament in the 1530s applied to Wales, as well as to England.

HENRY VIII's chief advantage in his successful effort to alter religion in Wales was the strong bond of loyalty and affection the Welsh people felt for the Welsh Tudor dynasty (see TUDOR FAMILY). Also, most of the important noble and GENTRY families of Wales quickly conformed to the Crown's religious dictates, thus reinforcing a habit of conformity among the common people of Wales. By Elizabeth's reign, Welsh reformers and antiquaries (see ANTIQUARIANISM) supplemented loyalty to the dynasty with arguments that presented the ANGLICAN CHURCH as a restoration of the early Celtic Church of Wales stripped of the impurities with which it had been polluted over the centuries by the Church of Rome.

In 1563, Parliament authorized a Welsh translation of the Bible, which was undertaken by a small group of Welsh reformers, largely at their own expense. Richard DAVIES, bishop of the Welsh diocese of St. David's, and reformer William SALESBURY, who had published an ENGLISH-Welsh dictionary in 1547, published

Welsh translations of the New Testament and the *BOOK OF COMMON PRAYER* in 1567. Although Salesbury did most of the translating, the two men shared the cost of the project. A Welsh translation of the entire Bible, completed by William MORGAN, bishop of the Welsh diocese of St. Asaph, appeared in 1588. These translations combined with Elizabeth's appointment of native Welshmen to Welsh bishoprics to firmly establish Protestantism and the Anglican Church in Wales by the queen's death in 1603.

Further Reading: J. Gwynfor Jones, *Wales and the Tudor State: Government, Religious Change and the Social Order, 1534–1603,* Cardiff: University of Wales Press, 1989; Glanmor Williams, *Renewal and Reformation: Wales c. 1415–1642,* Oxford: Oxford University Press, 1993; Glanmor Williams, *Wales and the Reformation,* Cardiff: University of Wales Press, 1997.

Regnans in Excelsis

Promulgated by Pope PIUS V in February 1570, the bull (i.e., papal edict) *Regnans in Excelsis* excommunicated Elizabeth I, deprived her of her title to the Crown of England, and absolved her subjects from their allegiance to her. A papal court tried Elizabeth *in absentia* and found her to have unjustly seized control of the kingdom of England and the English Church, over which the pope was declared to have true headship. Elizabeth was also found guilty of appointing heretical ministers, abolishing Catholic worship, persecuting Catholic worshippers, and compelling her subjects to forsake the pope and embrace heresy.

Besides cutting Elizabeth off from the Roman Catholic Church, the bull also excommunicated any English subjects who continued to obey her and recognize her authority. After waiting for a decade after Elizabeth's accession for her return to Roman Catholicism, the pope issued *Regnans in Excelsis* in 1570 to encourage the northern rebels of the previous year (see NORTHERN REBELLION) by assuring them that their actions in forcibly restoring Catholic worship in the areas under their control were lawful and justified. Pius issued the bull without consulting any Catholic ruler, and both PHILIP II of Spain and the Holy Roman Emperor Maximilian II strongly disapproved of the pope's action.

Pius made no attempt to persuade any Catholic power to take military action against England to put the bull into effect. In England, the bull put Catholics into a difficult position. It gave the government grounds to view all English Catholics as potential traitors, and severe PENAL LAWS were passed against Catholics in the PARLIAMENT of 1571 and in subsequent Parliaments. In the next decades, especially with the coming of the Spanish ARMADA in 1588, English Catholics had to choose between their faith and their country. Although most Catholics chose their country by denying or ignoring the pope's power to deprive the queen of her title, the continual plots of the supporters of Mary STUART, Queen of Scots (see BABINGTON PLOT; RIDOLFI PLOT), and of the Jesuits active in England (see JESUIT MISSION), made life difficult for both the English government and English Catholics throughout the reign. *See also* CATHOLICISM, ENGLISH; RECUSANTS.

Further Reading: John Bossy, *The English Catholic Community 1570–1850,* New York: Oxford University Press, 1976; Peter Holmes, *Resistance and Compromise: The Political Thought of the Elizabethan Catholics,* Cambridge: Cambridge University Press, 1982; David Lunn, *The Catholic Elizabethans,* Bath: Downside Abbey, 1998; Arnold Pritchard, *Catholic Loyalism in Elizabethan England,* Chapel Hill: University of North Carolina Press, 1979; Alexandra Walsham, *Church Papists: Catholicism, Conformity and Confessional Polemic in Early Modern England,* Rochester, NY: Boydell Press, 1993.

regulated company

The merchant members of a regulated trading company, unlike the investors in a JOINT-STOCK COMPANY, traded with their own capital and at their own risk and profit. Members paid an entrance fee and followed the general guidelines and restrictions laid down by the company, but otherwise conducted their own business largely in their own way. Regulated companies were an older form of trading enterprise than the joint-stock company, and they tended to be the preferred method of conducting trade in established markets, such as the cloth markets of Western Europe, where English merchants had done business for hundreds of years (see CLOTH INDUSTRY).

Because they did not personally conduct trade, the investors in a joint-stock trading company did not need to be merchants themselves, simply individuals with capital to invest. The members of a regulated trading company were always merchants because they conducted all trade on their own for themselves, not on behalf of the company. The largest regulated company in Tudor England was the MERCHANT ADVENTURERS, an association of wool and cloth merchants, whose trade centered on the NETHERLANDS and Western Europe. Other regulated companies formed during the Elizabethan period included the EASTLAND COMPANY, the GUINEA COMPANY, and the short-lived Morocco Company. *See also* EAST INDIA COMPANY; LEVANT COMPANY; MUSCOVY COMPANY.

Further Reading: Douglas R. Bisson, *The Merchant Adventurers of England*, Newark: University of Delaware Press, 1993; G. D. Ramsay, *English Overseas Trade during the Centuries of Emergence*, London: Macmillan, 1957; G. D. Ramsay, *The English Woollen Industry, 1500–1750*, London: Macmillan, 1982.

Requests, Court of

The Court of Requests, known also as the Court of Poor Men's Causes, was a PREROGATIVE court of EQUITY that developed out of the royal Council in the fifteenth century as a way to provide speedy, efficient redress for subjects too poor to avail themselves of the costly and complicated procedures of the courts of COMMON LAW. Fifteenth-century monarchs appointed certain royal councilors to hear poor people's requests, especially concerning matters of trade, property, contracts, FAMILY law, and fraud.

Requests developed from a function of the Council into a separate court of law under the early Tudors (see TUDOR FAMILY). The court began to keep records in 1493, was permanently established at WHITEHALL PALACE in LONDON in 1516, and became officially known as the Court of Requests after 1529. By 1550, Requests was no longer run by members of the PRIVY COUNCIL but by two permanent professional judges known as masters of requests, who formalized the simple rules under which the court functioned. Unlike the common law courts, Requests did not meet in set terms but sat throughout the year. A case began when a subject presented a petition to the queen. The defendant was required to answer the petition, and evidence was gathered by questions put to witnesses who were compelled to appear before the court.

Requests was more popular than the common law Court of Common Pleas (see COMMON PLEAS, COURT OF), whose jurisdiction in civil cases it paralleled, because its procedures were simpler, speedier, and less costly. By the 1590s, Common Pleas began to interfere in the hearing of cases by Requests, claiming that Requests lacked proper authority to hear suits because its existence was not based on royal grant, ancient custom, or parliamentary statute. Requests continued to function until the start of the civil war in 1642. Although not specifically abolished by statute like Star Chamber (see STAR CHAMBER, COURT OF), the Court of Requests was not re-established after the monarchy was restored in 1660. *See also* PARLIAMENT.

Further Reading: W. J. Jones, *The Elizabethan Court of Chancery*, Oxford: Clarendon Press, 1967.

revenue, royal

The ordinary revenues with which the Crown supported itself and conducted the business of government came from a variety of sources. As opposed to extraordinary revenue—TAXATION that could only be granted by vote of PARLIAMENT—the Crown's ordinary revenues belonged to the monarch by right and could be spent without approval from Parliament. Royal estates generated the largest portion of Crown revenues. This revenue also included income generated by lands forfeited to the Crown through TREASON and by the monastic properties confiscated by HENRY VIII when he broke with the Church of Rome. Although most of the monastic lands had been sold or granted away by Elizabeth's reign, the queen's annual revenues from land varied between £50,000 and £100,000.

The queen also received revenue from the profits of justice—the fines, fees, and assessments of the royal courts—and from the income deriving from the Crown's ancient feudal rights (see FISCAL FEUDALISM). The most important feudal assessments were livery, a small tax paid by heirs upon inheriting land legally held of the Crown, and wardship, the monarch's right to hold the lands and dispose of the marriages of minors (see MARRIAGE). Elizabeth received almost £15,000 per year from wardship. The queen derived another £15,000 each year from two taxes on the clergy—first fruits, a one-time payment representing a portion of the first year's income of any church BENEFICE, and tenths, a fixed annual payment representing a percentage of the yearly income of a benefice (see also TITHES). Before the Reformation, these payments had gone to the pope.

The CUSTOMS, taxes on imports and exports, were another important revenue component, averaging £75,000 per year under Elizabeth. The Crown also relied on loans, both from LONDON merchants and from foreign lenders; Elizabeth attempted to limit the amount of her borrowing, but the Spanish war required her government to be more active in international money markets at the end of the reign. The Crown also obtained indirect financial benefit from the right of PURVEYANCE, by which it could set the price it would pay for needed commodities. At the start of her reign, Elizabeth's annual income from all sources, including parliamentary taxation, was over £250,000; by the end of the reign, increased war taxation had raised Elizabeth's yearly income to over £600,000.

Further Reading: F. C. Dietz, *English Public Finance 1485–1641,* 2nd ed., London: F. Cass, 1964; John Guy, *The Tudor Monarchy,* Oxford: Oxford University Press, 1997.

Riccio, David. *See* RIZZO, DAVID.

Rich, Penelope, Lady Rich (1563–1607)

The inspiration for "Stella" in Sir Philip SIDNEY's cycle of love sonnets, Penelope Rich, Lady Rich, may also have been the mysterious "dark lady" to whom William SHAKESPEARE alluded in some of his sonnets (see SONNET, SHAKESPEAREAN). She was born Penelope Devereux, daughter of Walter DEVEREUX, first Earl of Essex, and brother of the second earl, Robert DEVEREUX, Elizabeth's favorite in the 1590s (see FAVORITES).

Penelope was proposed as a bride for Philip Sidney in 1576, but her father died before the match could be arranged and she was instead married in 1581 to the unattractive but wealthy Robert Rich, Lord Rich, by her guardian, Henry HASTINGS, Earl of Huntingdon. Sidney, however, fell deeply in love with Penelope, his almost bride. How much Lady Rich encouraged Sidney's attentions is uncertain, for she had fallen in love with Charles BLOUNT, Lord Mountjoy, whose mistress she

became after Sidney's death in 1586. Sidney poured his passion for Lady Rich into the *Astrophil and Stella* sonnets, which are addressed to Lady Rich as "Stella."

In the 1590s, Lady Rich and her lover Mountjoy were strong supporters of her brother, Robert Devereux, Earl of Essex. When Essex fell into disgrace in 1599 after his questionable undertakings as lord deputy of IRELAND, Mountjoy was sent to DUBLIN in his place. Lady Rich also fell into disfavor for writing an impertinent letter to the queen in her brother's behalf. Although implicated in her brother's conspiracy in 1601 (see ESSEX'S REBELLION), Lady Rich suffered only a brief spell of house arrest. She lived in retirement until Elizabeth's death in 1603, when she was welcomed back to COURT by JAMES I and made a lady of the bedchamber (see LADIES-IN-WAITING) to Queen Anne.

In 1605, Lord Rich divorced her and she secretly married Mountjoy (by then, Earl of Devonshire), by whom she had given birth to five children (she had six by Lord Rich). She died in 1607. The theory that Lady Rich was Shakespeare's "dark lady" (not blonde, as preferred by Elizabethan notions of beauty) was proposed in the nineteenth century. The sonnets describe a woman who was sensual, desirable, and promiscuous (she apparently seduced the poet's friend), qualities that could describe Lady Rich, who was known as a great beauty. However, most modern Shakespeare scholars either reject the theory or consider it unprovable.

Further Reading: Katherine Duncan-Jones, *Sir Philip Sidney,* New Haven, CT: Yale University Press, 1991; Sylvia Freedman, *Poor Penelope: Lady Penelope Rich, An Elizabethan Woman,* Abbotsbrook, England: Kensal Press, 1983.

Richmond, Duke of. *See* FITZROY, HENRY, DUKE OF RICHMOND AND SOMERSET.

Richmond, Treaty of. *See* HAMPTON COURT, TREATY OF.

Richmond Palace

Of all the PALACES Elizabeth inherited from her father (see HENRY VIII), Richmond in Surrey was her favorite. When the old royal palace of Sheen burned down in 1497, Elizabeth's grandfather, HENRY VII, immediately replaced

A view from the Thames River of Richmond Palace, Elizabeth I's favorite residence. © *The British Museum.*

it with a large new structure that he called Richmond, the title of his former earldom. Located along the Thames southwest of LONDON, Richmond became a symbol of the power and glory of the new Tudor dynasty (see TUDOR FAMILY).

Laid out around a series of large courts, the palace covered 10 acres and was surrounded by gardens, fruit orchards, and elm-lined walks. Of the three main courts, the outer Wardrobe Court was formed by two-story brick buildings that contained lodgings for members of the COURT. The Middle Court was flanked by the great hall and the royal chapel, which were each 100 feet long and 40 feet across. The great windows in the hall were separated by paintings of England's great warrior kings, including Henry VII as victor of the Battle of Bosworth. The windows of the richly decorated chapel were interspersed with paintings of England's most saintly kings, including Edward the Confessor and St. Edmund. The last of the main courts, the higher and more ornate Inner Court, housed the royal apartments and was ringed by 14 towers topped with onion domes that were themselves crowned with painted weather vanes that sang in the wind. Each of the main courts gave way to three or four subsidiary courts that housed offices,

stables, and storerooms. The palace also boasted 18 kitchens, the noise and bustle of which impressed the Spaniards who stayed at Richmond with Prince Philip (see PHILIP II) during MARY I's reign.

Elizabeth loved Richmond not only because it was built by her grandfather, whose memory she honored, but also for more practical reasons. The palace had an ingenious custom-built plumbing system that gave it an excellent supply of fresh water drawn from two nearby springs. And even more important in the cold, damp English climate, Richmond's chambers and state rooms were free of drafts, leading Elizabeth to call the palace "a warm nest for my old age." The queen spent her last weeks at Richmond, dying in the palace on 24 March 1603.

Further Reading: John Martin Robinson, *Royal Residences,* London: MacDonald and Company, 1982; Simon Thurley, *The Royal Palaces of Tudor England,* New Haven, CT: Yale University Press, 1993.

Ridolfi plot

The Ridolfi plot was a Catholic conspiracy against Elizabeth coordinated by Roberto Ridolfi, an Italian banker living in England. Ridolfi was a secret papal agent who had brought *REGNANS IN EXCELSIS,* the papal bull excommunicating Elizabeth, into England in

1570. In 1571, Ridolfi concocted a plot with the Spanish ambassador, and others, that called for 6,000 Spanish troops from the NETHERLANDS to invade England and to bring money and arms to support the English Catholics who would join the invasion. Thomas HOWARD, fourth Duke of Norfolk, whom Ridolfi had persuaded to join the conspiracy, would raise a revolt in conjunction with the invasion and either rescue Mary STUART, Queen of Scots (then confined in England), or seize Queen Elizabeth. Catholicism would be restored in England, and Mary and Norfolk would jointly rule both SCOTLAND and England (see CATHOLICISM, ENGLISH).

The plotters later decided that Elizabeth would be assassinated, an action to which both PHILIP II of SPAIN and the pope agreed. Ridolfi left England to meet with the Spanish authorities in the NETHERLANDS in March 1571; the plot began to unravel when one of Ridolfi's messengers to his fellow conspirators in England was captured and confessed all he knew. Norfolk was arrested and condemned for TREASON, and PARLIAMENT called for his and Mary's execution. The government expelled the Spanish ambassador, and Elizabeth allowed, for the first time, the publication of the CASKET LETTERS, which seemed to prove Mary's complicity in the murder of her husband, Henry STUART, Lord Darnley (see DARNLEY MURDER). Elizabeth was hesitant to execute either Mary or Norfolk, but finally consented to the duke's execution, which took place on 2 June 1572. The queen spared Mary despite the outcry against her. Ridolfi returned to Italy where he lived until 1612.

Further Reading: Francis Edwards, *The Marvellous Chance: Thomas Howard, Fourth Duke of Norfolk, and the Ridolfi Plot, 1570–1572,* London: Hart-Davis, 1968.

Rizzio, David (c. 1533–1566)

David Rizzio (or Riccio) was a key figure in Scottish politics during the personal rule of Mary STUART, Queen of Scots. An accomplished musician and singer, Rizzio began his career in his native Italy, performing at the court of the Duke of Savoy. In 1561, he accompanied the duke's ambassador to SCOTLAND, where he won a position as a singer in the Scottish queen's private suite of performers. By 1564, Rizzio had advanced sufficiently in the queen's confidence to be appointed her French

secretary. When Henry STUART, Lord Darnley, arrived in Scotland in 1565, Rizzio befriended him and promoted his MARRIAGE to the queen, a position that did not endear Rizzio to the queen's Protestant ministers, who were suspicious of Darnley's ambition and Rizzio's foreign birth and Catholicism; nevertheless, Mary and Lord Darnley married that year.

When the queen became pregnant in late 1565, rumors began to circulate that Rizzio, not Darnley, was the father. Such gossip, and the queen's increasing reliance on Rizzio for advice, soon alienated the weak and unstable Darnley, who conspired with James STUART, Earl of Moray, then in exile in England, and other Protestant lords to rid the country of the queen's enemies, especially one "stranger [i.e., foreigner] Italian called David." On 9 March 1566, Darnley admitted an armed party led by Patrick, Lord Ruthven (see RUTHVEN RAID), into the palace at Holyrood, where they invaded the queen's chambers and seized Rizzio as he sat at supper with Mary. Dragging Rizzio out of the pregnant queen's sight, but not her hearing, the murderers stabbed the secretary over 50 times, leaving Darnley's dagger in the corpse as a sign of his complicity in the act.

As he had turned on Rizzio, Darnley now betrayed his confederates, denying all knowledge of the conspiracy. To bolster her political position, Mary accepted Darnley's protestations of innocence, but she never forgave him for his part in Rizzio's murder. Within a year, Darnley was himself murdered, likely with the passive connivance, if not the active support, of his wife (see DARNLEY MURDER). The career and death of David Rizzio revealed the deep and violent tensions that existed in Scotland between the francophile Catholic queen and her increasingly Protestant subjects.

Further Reading: Antonia Fraser, *Mary, Queen of Scots,* New York: Delacorte Press, 1969; Jenny Wormald, *Mary, Queen of Scots,* London: Collins and Brown, 1991.

Roanoke Colony (1585)

In 1584, Walter RALEIGH obtained a six-year grant from Queen Elizabeth to establish an English colony in North America. Raleigh immediately sent out the AMADAS-BARLOWE EXPEDITION to explore the east coast of the continent and locate a likely settlement site. After exploring Roanoke and Hatteras

(Hatarask) Islands and claiming the region for England (see Maps, "Roanoke Area in the 1580s"), the expedition returned with a glowing description of the area and two Indians named Manteo and Wanchese. Hoping to secure the queen's financial backing for his colonization efforts, Raleigh named the newly explored region "Virginia," after the VIRGIN QUEEN. When this ploy failed, Raleigh attracted private backers by claiming that Virginia could supply England with commodities then only available from the Spanish-controlled Mediterranean.

In April 1585, six vessels carrying 600 men left Plymouth under the command of Sir Richard GRENVILLE, Raleigh's cousin. By July, the colonization expedition had, with the aid of Manteo and Wanchese, established friendly relations with the Roanoke chief Wingina, who allowed the Englishmen to settle on the northern end of Roanoke Island. Because much of the colony's food supply had been lost when one of the ships ran aground, Grenville decided in August to leave a settlement of only about 100 men under Ralph LANE and to return to England with the rest of the colonists.

Seeking sources of immediate wealth, Lane began to explore the surrounding region and in the fall discovered Chesapeake Bay. In the spring, Lane decided to move the colony

At Secoton village, members of the first Roanoke colony were "well entertained there of the Savages." The drawing is by John White. © *The British Museum.*

to Chesapeake when he heard reports from the Indians that pearls and metals that sounded like gold and copper could be found in the area. The coming of spring brought hostilities with the Indians. Having arrived too late to plant crops, the colonists bartered for food with the Indians, whose willingness to trade lessened as their own food supplies declined.

In June, having learned through Manteo of Indian plans to attack the settlement, Lane launched a preemptive raid on the Roanoke village that left Wingina dead. One week later, a relief expedition of 29 vessels under Sir Francis DRAKE reached Roanoke after a successful raid on the Spanish West Indies. Given the precarious state of the colony's food supply and its relations with its Roanoke neighbors, Lane and the surviving colonists left for England with Drake on 18 June 1586. *See also* AMERICA; *BRIEF AND TRUE REPORT OF THE NEW FOUND LAND OF VIRGINIA;* HARRIOT, THOMAS; ROANOKE COLONY (1587); SPANISH AMERICA; WHITE, JOHN; and illustration for AMADAS-BARLOWE EXPEDITION.

Further Reading: David N. Durant, *Raleigh's Lost Colony*, New York: Atheneum, 1981; Karen Ordahl Kupperman, *Roanoke: The Abandoned Colony*, New York: Barnes and Noble, 1993; David B. Quinn, *Set Fair for Roanoke: Voyages and Colonies, 1584–1606*, Chapel Hill, University of North Carolina Press, 1984.

Roanoke Colony (1587)

After the voluntary return of the first Roanoke colonists (see ROANOKE COLONY [1585]) in 1586, Sir Walter RALEIGH sent out a second colonization expedition in 1587. Unlike the all-male first colony, the new venture, under the governorship of John WHITE, a member of the first colony, included whole families. Three vessels carrying 89 men, 17 women, and 11 children departed Plymouth on 8 May 1587. Although intending to settle on Chesapeake Bay, the settlers were forced on 22 July to take up the first colony's site on Roanoke Island (off present-day North Carolina) when the ships' crews, eager to raid in the Spanish West Indies, refused to sail up the Chesapeake (see Maps, "Roanoke Area in the 1580s").

The ill will the previous colonists had left among the Roanoke Indians led quickly to tragedy. On 28 July, George Howe, who had gone alone to catch crabs, was found murdered, perhaps an act of revenge for the previous colony's killing of the Roanoke chief Wingina. Attempts to re-establish relations with the Indians through Manteo, one of the Indians who had gone to England with the AMADAS-BARLOWE EXPEDITION in 1584, failed. On 18 August, White's daughter Eleanor, the wife of Ananias Dare, gave birth to a daughter. The first English child born in North America, the baby was christened Virginia Dare by her grandfa-

ther. Poor relations with the Indians meant the colony was totally dependent on England for supplies, and the colonists decided that White was best suited to ensuring that Raleigh sent regular provisions and that the English public remained aware of, and interested in, the colony. Accordingly, White set sail on 27 August and reached England on 16 October.

In April 1588, White set out with two relief ships, but he had to turn back when the crews' taste for piracy led to an unfortunate encounter with a Spanish vessel. The ARMADA crisis of 1588 tied up all shipping and prevented White from returning to Virginia until 1590. On 16 August, he landed on Roanoke but found no trace of the colony, only the word "Croatoan" carved on a tree. This seemed to indicate the colony had moved to nearby Croatoan Island, but storms prevented investigation and White returned to England without ever knowing what became of his family and the "LOST COLONY" of Roanoke. *See also* AMERICA; *BRIEF AND TRUE REPORT OF THE NEW FOUND LAND OF VIRGINIA;* HARRIOT, THOMAS; SPANISH AMERICA.

Further Reading: David N. Durant, *Raleigh's Lost Colony*, New York: Atheneum, 1981; Karen Ordahl Kupperman, *Roanoke: The Abandoned Colony*, New York: Barnes and Noble, 1993; David B. Quinn, *Set Fair for Roanoke: Voyages and Colonies, 1584–1606*, Chapel Hill: University of North Carolina Press, 1984.

Robsart, Amy. *See* DUDLEY, AMY.

Royal Exchange

The Royal Exchange, the LONDON stock market built as a meeting place for bankers and merchants to conduct business, was constructed by Sir Thomas GRESHAM in 1566–67. In 1565, Gresham, the Crown's financial agent in Antwerp and an extremely wealthy man, offered to build an exchange if the city of London would provide a site. Upon completion of the building, Gresham promised to transfer ownership to the city and to his guild, the Mercers' Company (see LIVERIED COMPANIES).

Gresham ceremonially laid the first brick in June 1566, and the building was completed by the next year. Modeled on the Antwerp Bourse, the structure had a square, paved central court surrounded by a covered walkway. Statues, including one of the queen, were placed in a series of columned arches surrounding the square. Above the walkway, the building housed 100 shops of various kinds, including milliners, armorers, booksellers, goldsmiths, and apothecaries (see MEDICINE). Fruit sellers and other small merchants set up shop around the gates. The main entrances were on the north and south, with a large clocktower, its bell summoning merchants at 6:00 A.M., rising just to the east of the south entrance. A grasshopper, the symbol of the Gresham family, stood at each of the corners of the building.

In January 1572, Elizabeth visited the structure and declared it the Royal Exchange. Gresham's promise to turn the Exchange over to the city and the Mercers was not fulfilled until 1596 when his wife died. She had enjoyed the income from the Exchange since Gresham's death in 1579, and after her death the income became an endowment for Gresham College, which Sir Thomas Gresham had founded in London in 1575. The Exchange burned to the ground in the Great Fire of 1666. A rebuilt Exchange opened three years later and stood until it was demolished in 1838.

Further Reading: Perry E. Gresham with Carol Jose, *The Sign of the Golden Grasshopper: A Biography of Sir Thomas Gresham,* Ottawa, IL: Jameson Books, 1995.

Russell, Elizabeth, Lady Russell
(1529–1609)

Elizabeth Russell was the wife of Lord John Russell (son of Francis RUSSELL, Earl of Bedford) and the third daughter of Sir Anthony COOKE, the tutor to EDWARD VI. The Cooke sisters were known as the most learned women in England, thanks to the excellent education given to them by their father (see BACON, ANN; CECIL, MILDRED). Elizabeth Cooke married Sir Thomas Hoby in 1558; Hoby died in 1566 in Paris where he was serving as English ambassador. Pregnant with the couple's second child, Elizabeth Hoby hurried back to England to give birth there to a son named Thomas Posthumous Hoby.

Although in her mid-forties when she married Lord John Russell in 1574, Lady Russell bore her new husband two daughters—Elizabeth, for whom the queen stood godmother, and Anne. Lord Russell predeceased his father in 1584, and Lady Russell had her husband buried in Westminster Abbey in a tomb decorated with Latin and Greek inscriptions devised by Lady Russell herself. In 1592,

the queen stopped while on progress (see PROGRESSES, ROYAL) at Lady Russell's house in Berkshire and was entertained by a MASQUE written by John LYLY. In 1596, Lady Russell, who owned a town house in LONDON's Blackfriars district, led a successful effort among her Blackfriars neighbors to prevent James BURBAGE from opening a public theatre in the area.

As an old woman, Lady Russell intervened frequently and usually unwelcomely in the lives of her children and her Bacon and Cecil nieces and nephews. She nagged Anthony Bacon about his lifestyle and his Catholic friends—Lady Russell was, like all Cookes, a strong Protestant—and bombarded Sir Robert CECIL, the secretary of state, with political advice and demands for support in her many lawsuits. She became involved in a particularly long and bitter legal fight in Star Chamber with Lord Admiral Charles HOWARD, Earl of Nottingham, over custody of Donnington Castle (see STAR CHAMBER, COURT OF). Even in old age, Lady Russell engaged in scholarly pursuits, completing an ENGLISH translation of a French religious treatise in 1605. She died, having composed her own epitaphs, in 1609. *See also* BACON, FRANCIS.

Further Reading: B. W. Beckingsale, *Burghley: Tudor Statesman,* New York: St. Martin's Press, 1967; Georgiana Blakiston, *Woburn and the Russells,* London: Constable, 1980.

Russell, Francis, Earl of Bedford
(c. 1527–1585)

A firm Protestant, Francis Russell, second Earl of Bedford, was an Elizabethan privy councilor and diplomat (see DIPLOMACY). The son of John Russell, a prominent courtier under HENRY VIII, Francis Russell was educated at Cambridge (see UNIVERSITIES). During the reign of EDWARD VI, Russell served in PARLIAMENT for Bedfordshire and as sheriff of the county. In 1549, he helped his father quell the Prayer Book Rebellion, an uprising against the First *BOOK OF COMMON PRAYER* in Devon and Cornwall. Russell supported NORTHUMBERLAND'S COUP in 1553, and, as a consequence, spent some time in prison after MARY I won the throne. Opposed to Mary's Catholic regime, Russell secretly supported WYATT'S REBELLION in 1554, carrying letters from Wyatt to Princess Elizabeth.

After succeeding to the earldom of Bedford in 1555, he fled to the English Protestant community in Geneva and spent time in Venice (see MARIAN EXILES) before returning to England in 1557. In the last year of Mary's reign, to win his way into the queen's good graces, Bedford served in the Anglo-Spanish ARMY in FRANCE and was appointed lord lieutenant of several western counties. Upon her accession in 1558, Elizabeth appointed Bedford to the PRIVY COUNCIL and sent him on embassies to the French king and to Mary STUART, Queen of Scots. The earl involved himself in the ANGLICAN SETTLEMENT of religion, helping to devise the new liturgy and serving on the commission charged with administering the oath of supremacy (see SUPREMACY, ROYAL).

In 1564, Bedford was appointed warden of the Scottish marches (i.e., borders) and governor of the border town of Berwick. He also served on various diplomatic missions to SCOTLAND, including acting as Elizabeth's representative at the baptism of Prince James (see JAMES I). In 1572, he was a commissioner at the trial of Thomas HOWARD, Duke of Norfolk, and later in the year had the expensive honor of entertaining the queen, who visited his house at Woburn while on progress (see PROGRESSES, ROYAL). He served as lord president of WALES in 1576, and in 1581 he was named one of the commissioners charged with negotiating the queen's MARRIAGE to Francis VALOIS, Duke of Alençon. Despite declining health, Bedford in his later years diligently attended meetings of the Privy Council and took a leading role in the administration of the West Country, where he was the ranking peer (see PEERAGE), even standing godfather to Francis DRAKE. He died in LONDON in July 1585. *See also* RUSSELL, ELIZABETH, LADY RUSSELL.

Further Reading: Georgiana Blakiston, *Woburn and the Russells,* London: Constable, 1980.

Russia Company. *See* MUSCOVY COMPANY.

Ruthven raid

The Ruthven raid was an attempt by Scottish Protestant noblemen to prevent James VI (see JAMES I) from embracing Catholicism. In 1582, 16-year-old James VI fell under the influence of his French Catholic cousin, Esmé Stuart, Seigneur d'Aubigny, whom James had raised

to the Scottish PEERAGE as Duke of Lennox. Lennox had succeeded in overthrowing the pro-English regent, James Douglas, Earl of Morton, in 1578 and in engineering his execution in 1581. The rising power of Lennox caused Scottish presbyterians and the English government to worry that James would adopt Catholicism and return SCOTLAND to an alliance with France. In early 1581, James sought to calm these fears by signing, and causing Lennox to sign, the "King's Covenant," a document repudiating Catholicism. The Covenant, however, failed of its purpose, for a group of Protestant nobles led by John Erskine, Earl of Mar, and William Ruthven, Earl of Gowrie, seized the king in August 1582 and carried him captive to Ruthven Castle.

Supported by English funds, the Ruthven raiders took control of the Scottish government and forced Lennox to flee to FRANCE. The General Assembly of the Scottish Presbyterian Church, much relieved at its deliverance from Catholicism, gathered in EDINBURGH to sing the 124th Psalm: "We have escaped as a bird from the snare of the fowlers." In June 1583, James, then 17, escaped from Ruthven Castle and, with a single servant, rode to St. Andrews where he proclaimed himself of full age and able to rule without a regent. Although no Catholic, James emerged from captivity a convinced opponent of presbyterianism and determined to control the Scottish Church.

In early 1584, the king arrested and executed his chief captor, the Earl of Gowrie. In May, the Scottish PARLIAMENT passed the "Black Acts," which declared the king head of the church, forbade the General Assembly from meeting without royal consent, made bishops Crown appointees, and prohibited ministers from preaching politics. The English government, meanwhile, gave the remaining Ruthven raiders sanctuary in England and allowed them to cross the border in 1585 when James was ready to pardon them. The Ruthven raid demonstrated the volatility of Scottish politics and the need of the English government to work with whatever group or faction provided the best hope of keeping Scotland Protestant and pro-English. *See also* GOWRIE CONSPIRACY.

Further Reading: J. D. Mackie, *A History of Scotland,* 2nd ed., New York: Dorset Press, 1985; D. Harris Willson, *James VI and I,* New York: Henry Holt and Company, 1956.

Sackville, Thomas, Earl of Dorset

(1536–1608)

Thomas Sackville was lord treasurer of England, as well as a playwright and poet. Because the Sackvilles were cousins to the BOLEYN FAMILY, Thomas Sackville was a distant relative of Queen Elizabeth. His father was a financial official of the Crown through four reigns, from 1538 to 1566. Sackville was educated at both Oxford and Cambridge (see UNIVERSITIES), and in 1554 began his legal training at the INNS OF COURT in LONDON. In the early 1560s, while still a student, Sackville began writing plays and POETRY. With fellow student Thomas NORTON, Sackville wrote the play *Gorboduc,* the first English tragedy. Written in blank verse, *Gorboduc* was performed at the Inner Temple on Twelfth Night in 1561 (see CHRISTMAS). Drawn from English legend, but written in the style of the Roman playwright Seneca, the play describes the sorrows that befall King Gorboduc when he divides his kingdom between his sons Ferrex and Porrex. Sackville also contributed two pieces to the 1563 edition of *A Mirror for Magistrates,* a collection of verse accounts of the downfall of famous figures.

His mounting debts in England forced Sackville to travel for a time in Europe, where he was briefly imprisoned in Rome on suspicion of being a spy. He returned to England upon his father's death in 1566 to take up a huge landed inheritance that restored his financial position. In 1567, the queen elevated Sackville to the PEERAGE as Lord Buckhurst; she also granted him a house at Knole in Kent, which he rebuilt on a magnificent scale.

Buckhurst undertook various administrative and diplomatic duties, including serving as the queen's envoy in the NETHERLANDS (see DIPLOMACY). In 1586, he was given the difficult task of informing Mary STUART, Queen of Scots, that she had been condemned to death. He was made a Knight of the Garter in 1589 and succeeded William CECIL, Lord Burghley, as lord treasurer in 1598. JAMES I retained him as treasurer and created him Earl of Dorset. In 1608, as the king's extravagance brought the country near to bankruptcy, Dorset was accused of taking bribes. The earl collapsed and died while appearing before the PRIVY COUNCIL to answer the charges.

Further Reading: Norman Berlin, *Thomas Sackville,* New York: Twayne Publishers, 1974; J. Swart, *Thomas Sackville: A Study in Sixteenth-Century Poetry,* Groningen, Netherlands: J. B. Wolthers, 1949.

Saint Bartholomew Massacre

On 24 August 1572, the feast of Saint Bartholomew, thousands of French Protestants, known as HUGUENOTS, were murdered at the instigation of the French queen mother, Catherine de MEDICI. In the 1560s, FRANCE suffered from a series of civil wars between Catholics and Huguenots. In August 1570, the peace of Saint Germain had ended the latest conflict by granting liberty of conscience and freedom of worship to Huguenots everywhere except in heavily Catholic Paris. The agreement also allowed Protestants to hold public office and gave them possession of four cities— La Rochelle, Montauban, Cognac, and La Charité. The peace also led in 1572 to the signing of the Treaty of Blois, a defensive alliance against SPAIN with Elizabethan England (see

BLOIS, TREATY OF), and plans for a MARRIAGE between the sister of Charles IX and Henri of Navarre (see HENRI IV), a prince of royal blood and titular leader of the Huguenots.

In June 1572, Catherine called Admiral Gaspard de Coligny, the most prominent of the Protestant leaders, to court to arrange the marriage. When Catherine realized that Coligny's influence over the young king was beginning to rival her own, she grew alarmed and plotted with the ultra-Catholic GUISE FAMILY to murder the admiral. An unsuccessful attempt on Coligny's life occurred on 22 August, when Paris was full of Huguenots awaiting the wedding. News of the assassination attempt caused Protestants to loudly demand revenge. Fearing the Huguenots might carry out their threats, Catherine conspired with the Guises to murder the Huguenot leadership while it was so conveniently assembled in Paris; only Navarre and the other Protestant princes of royal blood were to be spared. The king agreed to the plan only after lengthy argument with his mother.

In the early morning of 24 August, tolling bells signaled the start of bloodshed; Catholic Paris exploded in anti-Huguenot violence as Catherine's plan to kill the Protestant leadership became the mass murder of all Huguenots who could be caught. Coligny and some 4,000 Protestants died in Paris by various means—shooting, hanging, drowning, stabbing, or defenestration (being thrown out a window or pushed off a roof). In all, over 10,000 died throughout France. Catholic Europe applauded the massacre; PHILIP II called it "one of the greatest joys of my life." In Protestant England, Elizabeth dressed her COURT in mourning and listened in stern silence to the French ambassador's attempt to explain the deed. The Huguenot party, shorn of its aristocratic leadership, turned on the monarchy and became strongly republican. The French wars of religion resumed, removing France from involvement in the coming Anglo-Spanish conflict over the NETHERLANDS REVOLT. *See also* CATHOLIC LEAGUE.

Further Reading: Robert McCune Kingdon, *Myths about the St. Bartholomew's Day Massacres, 1572–1576*, Cambridge, MA: Harvard University Press, 1988; Henri Nogueres, *The Massacre of Saint Bartholomew*, translated by Claire Elaine Engel, New York, Macmillan, 1962; N. M. Sutherland, *The Massacre of St.*

Bartholomew and the European Conflict, 1559–1572, London: Macmillan, 1973.

St. James's Palace

St. James's Palace was one of Elizabeth's principal LONDON residences. HENRY VIII built St. James's concurrently with WHITEHALL PALACE in the 1530s. Henry wanted a smaller residence near London where he could occasionally escape from cares of state and formal COURT life. To this end, he constructed St. James's about a half mile west of Whitehall across St. James's Park. Just as for Whitehall, Henry had to demolish numerous existing structures to build St. James's, including an old hospital for lepers.

Although much smaller than Whitehall, St. James's was also built around a series of courts—the Colour Court, the Ambassador's Court, the Friary Court, and the unnamed western court. Built of red brick, with bricks of a darker shade used to create running patterns, St. James's most remarkable feature was the four-story gatehouse on its north side. The gatehouse had two crenelated octagonal turrets at its corners and a central span with a large clock. The gatehouse was decorated with a crown, a Tudor rose, and the initials "H.A." for Henry VIII and Anne BOLEYN, Elizabeth's mother and Henry's wife at the time St. James's was constructed. The chapel at St. James's measured 70 feet long and 23 feet wide and was spanned by a magnificent ceiling decorated with geometric shapes, chivalric devices and mottoes, the initials "HR" (Latin for *Henricus Rex,* "King Henry"), and the date 1540.

Being uninterested in the expensive habits of building and remodeling, Elizabeth made few changes to St. James's. However, under the Stuarts, and especially in the eighteenth century, St. James's underwent extensive renovation, leaving the gatehouse, the chapel, and one or two other rooms, such as the Guard Chamber, as the only parts of the Elizabethan palace that remain today. Although one of Elizabeth's smaller palaces, St. James's was the principal royal residence of the kings of Great Britain in the early eighteenth century, and foreign ambassadors to Great Britain are still formally accredited to the "Court of St. James." The palace was heavily damaged by fire in 1809.

Rebuilt by George IV in the 1820s, St. James's was soon supplanted as the monarch's main London residence by Buckingham Palace, located just to the southeast on St. James's Park.

Further Reading: John Martin Robinson, *Royal Residences,* London: MacDonald and Company, 1982; Simon Thurley, *The Royal Palaces of Tudor England,* New Haven, CT: Yale University Press, 1993.

St. Paul's Cross. *See* PAUL'S CROSS.

Salesbury, William (c. 1517–c. 1584)

William Salesbury was an important Welsh reformer and a collaborator with Richard DAVIES on the first translations into Welsh of the New Testament and the *BOOK OF COMMON PRAYER.* Born into a distinguished Welsh GENTRY family, Salesbury was educated at Oxford (see UNIVERSITIES) and at the INNS OF COURT in LONDON. Both a strong Protestant and an advocate for the preservation of the Welsh language, Salesbury had, by 1547, published a collection of proverbs and a Welsh-ENGLISH dictionary, possibly the two earliest works to be published in Welsh. Salesbury also produced many other religious works supporting the Reformation (see REFORMATION, WELSH).

In 1563, Salesbury joined with Richard Davies, Bishop of St. David's, to promote a private bill in PARLIAMENT authorizing the translation of the Bible and the Prayer Book into Welsh, a task the two men considered vital to the success of the Reformation in Wales (see BIBLE, ENGLISH). The bill passed, but Parliament made no provision for funding to support the work. Salesbury and Davies thus collaborated both on producing the translations and on paying for the project.

Salesbury did most of the work on the Welsh New Testament, which was published in 1567. His work was criticized for its odd spelling scheme and its difficult constructions, but it provided the basis for the later and widely used Welsh translation of the entire Bible prepared by William MORGAN. Although something of an eccentric—he is said to have worked in a secret room that could only be reached by climbing up a chimney—Salesbury was a leading figure in the reform of the Welsh Church.

Further Reading: Glanmor Williams, *Renewal and Reformation: Wales c. 1415–1642,* Oxford: Oxford University Press, 1993; Glanmor Williams, *Wales and the Reformation,* Cardiff: University of Wales Press, 1997.

San Juan d'Ulloa

Located on the eastern coast of Mexico, San Juan d'Ulloa was the main port for Mexico City. In the late summer of 1568, the English seaman John HAWKINS was in SPANISH AMERICA conducting illegal trade in slaves with Spanish colonists. Hawkins left the port of Cartagena on the Spanish Main (the South American coast of Spanish America) in late August, but contrary winds prevented his six-vessel fleet from sailing east, forcing him to enter San Juan d'Ulloa on 15 September to make repairs and collect supplies.

Because the Spanish garrison was expecting a treasure fleet, they did not identify Hawkins as an Englishman until after he had seized control of a series of strategic shore batteries. By assuring the Spanish authorities that his intentions were peaceful, Hawkins extracted a promise of food and time to effect repairs from the captain of the port. However, the silver fleet bearing the new viceroy of the Indies to Mexico City arrived on 17 September, much earlier than expected. Hawkins permitted the Spanish ships to enter the port after the viceroy agreed to allow the English to retain control of the batteries until their repairs were completed, at which time they were to depart unmolested. To seal this agreement, the two sides exchanged hostages. But the viceroy, considering the English heretics and enemies of SPAIN, launched a surprise attack on the morning of 23 September.

Although the shore batteries were quickly recaptured by the Spanish, a naval battle raged for most of the day (see NAVY; SHIPS). One English ship escaped, but two more were captured and two others sank, leaving Hawkins and his second in command, Francis DRAKE, to escape with two ships and what little they could salvage of their cargo. News of the battle at San Juan d'Ulloa, when it reached England at the end of the year, considerably aggravated the ongoing "TREASURE CRISIS" OF 1568 and began the souring of Anglo-Spanish relations that led eventually to war with Spain. By instilling an intense hatred of Spaniards in Hawkins, Drake, and other English seafarers who heard of their experience, the viceroy's treachery also helped start an unofficial war on Spanish shipping by English pirates and privateers (see PRIVATEERING).

Further Reading: James A. Williamson, *Hawkins of Plymouth,* 2nd ed., New York: Barnes and Noble, 1969.

Sandys, Edwin (c. 1516–1588)

Edwin Sandys was Elizabeth's third Archbishop of York. Born into a Lancashire GENTRY family, Sandys was educated at Furness Abbey and then at St. John's College, Cambridge (see UNIVERSITIES). From the early 1540s, he served in a number of increasingly important church benefices (see BENEFICE). A zealous Protestant who had risen rapidly in the English Church under EDWARD VI, Sandys supported NORTHUMBERLAND'S COUP in 1553, even preaching at Cambridge in favor of Jane GREY's cause (see DUDLEY, JOHN, DUKE OF NORTHUMBERLAND). He was briefly imprisoned in the TOWER OF LONDON by the Catholic regime of MARY I but was released and fled to Antwerp in 1554. He then moved among the various English exile communities in Germany before returning to England after Elizabeth's accession in 1558.

Sandys involved himself in framing the new Anglican liturgy and was allowed to preach at St. Paul's Cathedral in LONDON and at COURT. Like other MARIAN EXILES, Sandys thought the ANGLICAN SETTLEMENT of 1559 was too conservative, and he particularly opposed the vestments ministers were required to wear (see VESTIARIAN CONTROVERSY). In December 1559, he became Bishop of Worcester, initiating an immediate visitation for the reform of his diocese (see CHURCH COURTS). Sandys was one of the translators of the Bishops' Bible (see BIBLE, ENGLISH) in the 1560s, and in 1570 he succeeded Edmund GRINDAL as Bishop of London. A Puritan at heart (see PURITANS), Sandys fell into temporary disfavor with the queen for supporting PROPHESYINGS in his diocese.

Sandys became Archbishop of York in March 1576, again in succession to Grindal. In this new position, Sandys, a stern and quarrelsome man, was soon involved in various disputes with his subordinates and with lay leaseholders of church lands. He argued with William WHITTINGHAM, one of the translators of the Geneva Bible, over the validity of Whittingham's ordination, and with John AYLMER, his successor as Bishop of London, over the revenues of the London bishopric. A learned man, Sandys founded a GRAMMAR SCHOOL in his archdiocese at Hawkshead and engaged Richard HOOKER, the future author of the *LAWS OF ECCLESIASTICAL POLITY,* to tutor his son. Sandys died in July 1588.

Further Reading: Patrick Collinson, *The Elizabethan Puritan Movement,* Oxford: Clarendon Press, 1990.

Santa Cruz, Marquis of. *See* BAZÁN, ALVARO DE, MARQUIS OF SANTA CRUZ.

Scotland

During the course of Elizabeth's reign, Scotland (see Maps, "Sixteenth-Century Scotland") went from being a Catholic kingdom allied with FRANCE to a Protestant kingdom allied with England. The most important factor in Anglo-Scottish relations under Elizabeth was the fact that Mary STUART, the Catholic Queen of Scotland, was next heir to the English throne (see STUART CLAIM). Since the late thirteenth century, when Edward I had sought to impose English overlordship on Scotland, the northern kingdom had maintained an alliance with France, England's long-standing enemy. In 1559, only months after Elizabeth's accession, this alliance became particularly close when Mary Stuart also became Queen of France, thus placing the power of France behind her claim to the English Crown. However, the 1560 Scottish Reformation, by giving England and Scotland a shared religion on which to base a political alliance, led to the Treaty of Edinburgh, whereby Scotland was freed of French troops and influence (see EDINBURGH, TREATY OF; REFORMATION, SCOTTISH).

In 1561, Mary Stuart, recently widowed, returned from France to Scotland, where her spectacular misrule was marked by the murder of her secretary, David RIZZIO; the murder of her second husband, Henry STUART, Lord Darnley (see DARNLEY MURDER); and her mysterious third marriage to Darnley's likely killer, James HEPBURN, Earl of Bothwell. Deposed in favor of her infant son James VI (see JAMES I) in 1567, Mary tried and failed to regain her Crown in 1568 (see CARBERRY, BATTLE OF; LANGSIDE, BATTLE OF). Driven into England where she expected the assistance of her cousin Elizabeth, Mary found herself confined in a series of English country houses for the next 19 years. Elizabeth could neither give Mary her freedom nor bring herself to order Mary's death.

Raised a Protestant, Scotland's James VI was more highly motivated by the promise of eventual succession to the English throne than by affection for a mother he never knew (see SUCCESSION, ACTS OF). By concluding the Treaty of Berwick with Elizabeth in 1586, James signaled his willingness to sacrifice the latter to have the former (see BERWICK, TREATY OF). In 1587, when Mary was finally executed for plotting against Elizabeth (see BABINGTON PLOT; RIDOLFI PLOT), James did no more than protest. On Elizabeth's death in 1603, the Crowns of Scotland and England were peacefully united in the person of Mary's Protestant son, and the process that led to the eventual political union of Scotland and England in 1707 was begun.

Further Reading: Caroline Bingham, *The Stewart Kingdom of Scotland 1371–1603*, New York: St. Martin's Press, 1974; Ian B. Cowan, *The Scottish Reformation: Church and Society in Sixteenth-Century Scotland*, New York: St. Martin's Press, 1982; Gordon Donaldson, *All the Queen's Men: Power and Politics in Mary Stewart's Scotland*, London: Batsford Academic and Educational, 1983; Gordon Donaldson, *Scotland: James V to James VII.* New York: Praeger, 1965; J. D. Mackie, *A History of Scotland*, 2nd ed., New York: Dorset Press, 1985; Fitzroy Maclean, *A Concise History of Scotland,* New York: Beekman House, 1970; Rosalind Mitchison, *A History of Scotland*, 2nd ed., London: Routledge, 1982; Jenny Wormald, *Court, Kirk, and Community: Scotland, 1470–1625*, Toronto: University of Toronto Press, 1981.

sea beggars

The sea beggars were an informal and irregular Dutch naval force created in 1568 to support the Dutch rebellion against SPAIN (see NETHERLANDS REVOLT). The beggars were welcomed into English ports and soon became a thorn in the side of Fernandez ALVÁREZ DE TOLEDO, Duke of Alva, the Spanish commander trying to subdue the rebellion in the NETHERLANDS. The beggars quickly became a menace to shipping in the English Channel, where they indiscriminately attacked neutral vessels. The complaints of victimized merchants compelled Elizabeth to expel the beggars from English ports on 1 March 1572. Deprived of any secure land base, the beggars descended on the Dutch ports of Flushing and Brill (see CAUTIONARY TOWNS), which were but lightly defended by the Spanish. The capture of these ports revitalized the Dutch war

effort, not only giving the rebel fleet secure bases, but providing a beachhead for rebel land forces. The continued activities of the sea beggars were instrumental in ensuring the eventual triumph of the rebellion in the northern provinces of the Spanish Netherlands and in drawing England further into conflict with Spain. *See also* WILLIAM, PRINCE OF ORANGE.

Further Reading: Geoffrey Parker, *The Dutch Revolt,* Ithaca, NY: Cornell University Press, 1977.

secretary of state. *See* OFFICERS OF STATE.

seminary priests

During the reign of Elizabeth, over 800 Englishmen were trained as Roman Catholic priests in continental seminaries, and many of them returned to England to preach the faith and administer the sacraments to English Catholics. The two principal English seminaries were at Douai in the NETHERLANDS and at Rome. The Douai seminary was founded by Cardinal William ALLEN in 1568. The first seminary priests returned to England in 1574. They scattered about the country ministering secretly to English Catholics and receiving the support and protection of Catholic GENTRY families. These first missionaries were secular priests (i.e., they were not members of any religious order like the Society of Jesus, or Jesuits) and were usually not interested in political activity. The first seminary priest was executed in 1577 for breaking the law that forbade anyone from bringing a papal bull into England.

In 1580, the first English Jesuits entered the country; many of the Jesuits were interested in plotting against Elizabeth and bringing about the political restoration of Catholicism (see CATHOLICISM, ENGLISH; JESUIT MISSION). The two best known Jesuits active in England were Edmund CAMPION, who was executed in 1581, and Robert PARSONS, who saved his life by fleeing abroad. In 1581, PARLIAMENT made it TREASON to reconcile anyone to the Catholic faith with the intent of convincing them to withdraw their allegiance from the queen. In 1584, simply being a Catholic priest in England became treason (see PENAL LAWS).

Seminary priests were shadowed by spies and stalked by informers; they traveled about in disguise but always carried the incriminating articles of their office—the MASS books and vestments. They were heavily dependent on the Catholic gentry and their household servants for shelter and sustenance. Many Catholic homes contained a PRIEST HOLE, a small hiding space in a chimney, ceiling, floor, or false wall where a priest could hide during searches or at times of heightened watchfulness. The Elizabethan government executed 123 Catholic priests, four of them Jesuits. The seminary priests did not re-convert England, but they did prevent the remaining body of English Catholics from leaving the faith, and they stabilized and strengthened the English Catholic community to survive the persecution of Elizabethan and Stuart times.

Further Reading: John Bossy, *The English Catholic Community 1570–1850,* New York: Oxford University Press, 1976; John Gerard, *The Autobiography of a Hunted Priest,* translated by Philip Caraman, New York: Pellegrini and Cudahy, 1952; Arnold Pritchard, *Catholic Loyalism in Elizabethan England,* Chapel Hill: University of North Carolina Press, 1979.

separatists

Separatists were radical PURITANS who rejected the ANGLICAN CHURCH as established by PARLIAMENT in 1559 (see ANGLICAN SETTLEMENT). They believed that the established Church had to be abandoned; that they had to "separate" themselves from it and establish a new more scriptural church in its place. Separatists rejected a national church subject to the authority of the queen, Parliament, and bishops, and sought instead a church of self-governing congregations adhering strictly to the injunctions of scripture. They found the doctrine, ritual, and governance of the Anglican Church, as defined by Parliament and the opinions of the queen, to be too Catholic, non-scriptural, and anti-Christian to be tolerated.

Separatist congregations began to spring up, especially in LONDON, in the 1580s and 1590s. An important separatist group known as the Brownists, for their leader Robert BROWNE, arose in Norfolk in the 1580s. The Brownists moved to Middelburg in the NETHERLANDS to escape persecution, but soon disbanded because of poverty and personal quarrels. However, the Brownist separatist tradition remained alive in eastern England through the writings and teaching of

Browne's follower, Henry BARROW, whose followers, known as Barrowists, advocated a church of independent congregations. The Elizabethan government persecuted many of these congregations and imprisoned the leaders; other congregations were forced into exile.

One London separatist group fled to the Netherlands in 1593 after its leaders were executed; the descendants of this group sailed to the New World in the *Mayflower* in 1620 to find a place to worship as they chose. The separatist idea of independent congregations thus took root among the Puritan colonists of New England, and Browne and Barrow are today seen as founders of modern Congregationalism (see CONGREGATIONALISTS).

Further Reading: Edward H. Bloomfield, *The Opposition to the English Separatists, 1570–1625,* Washington, DC: University Press of America, 1981; Stephen Brachlow, *The Communion of Saints,* New York: Oxford University Press, 1988; B. R. White, *The English Separatist Tradition,* London: Oxford University Press, 1971.

serjeants-at-law. See COMMON LAW.

Seymour, Edward, Duke of Somerset
(c. 1500–1552)

Edward Seymour, elder brother of Queen Jane SEYMOUR, was lord protector for his nephew EDWARD VI. After studying at both Oxford and Cambridge (see UNIVERSITIES), Seymour began a career as a soldier and courtier. He was knighted for his service in the French campaign of 1523, and by 1530 was a household servant of HENRY VIII and a royal favorite to whom the king gave money and other rewards (see FAVORITES). His sister's marriage to Henry in 1536 led to Seymour's elevation to the PEERAGE and his appointment to the PRIVY COUNCIL. The birth of his nephew in October 1537 brought Seymour the earldom of Hertford and large grants of land. His sister's death a few weeks later stopped neither the rewards nor the king's favor.

In the 1540s, Seymour served ably in military campaigns in FRANCE and SCOTLAND. As the prince's eldest uncle and a moderate Protestant in religion, Seymour won appointment through Henry VIII's will to Edward's regency council. On Henry's death in January 1547, Seymour circumvented the will by having the young king create him Duke of

Somerset and declare him lord protector of the realm and governor of the king's person. Somerset thus ruled as de facto king on behalf of his nine-year-old nephew. He sought a union with Scotland and invaded the northern kingdom in 1547 when his offer was rejected. He won the battle of Pinkie, but his costly policy of garrisoning Scotland bankrupted the government and led to dissatisfaction with his regime. His issuance of the First *BOOK OF COMMON PRAYER* alienated Catholics, and his economic policies angered many regardless of religion. His furious temper, refusal to listen to criticism, and inability to delegate authority alienated his fellow councilors.

In 1549, the trial and execution of his unstable brother, Thomas SEYMOUR, Lord Seymour of Sudeley, whose treasons involved attempting MARRIAGE with Princess Elizabeth, combined with a series of rebellions against Somerset's religious and economic policies to bring down the government. In October 1549, John DUDLEY, later Duke of Northumberland, led the Privy Council in overthrowing Somerset. Although eventually released from the TOWER OF LONDON, Somerset remained a serious threat to the new regime and Dudley engineered his execution for TREASON in January 1552.

Further Reading: W. K. Jordan, *Edward VI: The Young King: The Protectorship of the Duke of Somerset,* Cambridge, MA: Harvard University Press, 1968.

Seymour, Jane (1509–1537)

Jane Seymour was the third wife of HENRY VIII and the mother of EDWARD VI. The eldest daughter of Sir John Seymour, a Wiltshire gentleman, Jane inherited royal blood from her mother and was thus a distant cousin of Henry VIII. She attracted the king's attention in 1535, when she was at COURT as one of the LADIES-IN-WAITING to Queen Anne BOLEYN, the mother of Princess Elizabeth. Growing weary of his high-strung, outspoken queen, Henry found the quiet, demure Jane a refreshing alternative. Jane's brothers, Edward and Thomas SEYMOUR, who were already well-favored royal servants, encouraged their sister to display these qualities and win the king's love.

When Anne Boleyn miscarried of a son in January 1536, Henry began to seriously question his MARRIAGE and to intensify his courtship of Jane. Anne was arrested, tried, and ex-

ecuted for adultery in May 1536; her marriage to the king was pronounced invalid and Princess Elizabeth was declared illegitimate by PARLIAMENT and removed from the SUCCESSION. Henry married Jane on 30 June, having received a dispensation to wed his cousin from Archbishop Thomas CRANMER on the day of Anne's execution. The new queen chose as her motto, "Bound to obey and serve," a distinct change in tone from the previous queen.

Jane's marriage greatly increased her brothers' influence and standing at court. As queen, Jane reconciled Henry with his eldest daughter, Princess Mary (see MARY I), who had been estranged from her father since her late mother's banishment from court in 1531 (see CATHERINE OF ARAGON). On 12 October 1537, Jane gave birth to the long-awaited male heir, the future Edward VI. However, the queen died of puerperal fever 12 days later and was buried in St. George's Chapel at WINDSOR CASTLE. As he lay dying in January 1547, Henry called out for Jane and ordered that he be buried next to her at Windsor.

Further Reading: William Seymour, *Ordeal by Ambition: An English Family in the Shadow of the Tudors,* London: Sidgwick and Jackson, 1972.

Seymour, Thomas, Lord Seymour of Sudeley (c. 1508–1549)

Thomas Seymour, the younger of Queen Jane SEYMOUR's two brothers, served HENRY VIII in various diplomatic and military capacities in the 1530s and 1540s (see DIPLOMACY). When his elder brother, Edward SEYMOUR, became lord protector and Duke of Somerset at the accession of EDWARD VI in 1547, Thomas, as the king's next uncle, claimed the governorship of the royal person, thereby causing much tension between himself and his brother. The protector compromised with Thomas by naming him to the PRIVY COUNCIL, securing him a PEERAGE, and appointing him lord admiral.

Thomas Seymour then undertook a number of reckless and provocative actions, including secretly marrying the former queen, Katherine PARR; seeking the hand of Princess Elizabeth after Katherine's death; and attempting to win the confidence of the young king by slipping him pocket money. His inappropriate sexual advances to Princess Elizabeth while she was resident in Katherine Parr's household in

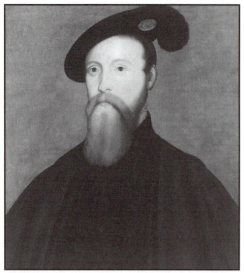

This portrait of Thomas Seymour, Lord Seymour of Sudeley, was painted by Nicholas Denizot. *National Maritime Museum, London.*

1547–48 brought the princess and her servants (see ASHLEY, KATHERINE ; PARRY, THOMAS) under suspicion when the admiral was arrested for TREASON in January 1549. Princess Elizabeth, in her teens at the time, was flattered by Seymour's attention and attracted by his looks and charm, but never seriously swayed by his treasonous proposals of MARRIAGE. Through her steadfast refusal to admit to any wrongdoing, the princess saved herself and her household from anything worse than embarrassment.

Seymour's dangerous schemes and unstable personality put him beyond salvation, even by his brother, the lord protector. Upon hearing of Seymour's execution on 20 March 1549, Elizabeth is reported to have remarked, "This day died a man with much wit and very little judgment."

Further Reading: Paul Johnson, *Elizabeth I,* New York: Holt, Rinehart and Winston, 1974; J. E. Neale, *Queen Elizabeth I,* Chicago: Academy Chicago Publishers, 1992; William Seymour, *Ordeal by Ambition: An English Family in the Shadow of the Tudors,* London: Sidgwick and Jackson, 1972.

Shakespeare, William (1564–1616)

William Shakespeare is considered by many to be the greatest poet and playwright in the English language. He was born in April 1564 in Stratford-on-Avon, the son of John Shakespeare, a glove maker and dealer in timber and grain. As far as is known, Shakespeare's only formal education was acquired at the GRAMMAR SCHOOL in Stratford. In 1582, he married Anne Hathaway, with whom he had three children—Susanna, born in 1583, and Hamnet and Judith, twins born in 1585. Little else is known about Shakespeare's life before his appearance on the LONDON theatrical scene about 1592.

By 1594, Shakespeare was part of the CHAMBERLAIN'S MEN acting company (later known as the King's Men). He was successful enough by 1597 to help pay his father's many debts and to buy a house, New Place, and other property in and around Stratford. Two years later, he became a shareholder in Richard BURBAGE's new London theatre, the GLOBE THEATRE, where he also served as playwright and actor. He returned to Stratford about 1610, dying there on 23 April 1616. Because Hamnet, his only son, died in 1596 and his daughters' children died childless, he left no direct descendants (see SHAKESPEARE FAMILY). Because we know so little about large parts of Shakespeare's life, and because his EDUCATION seems to have been brief, many other Elizabethan figures have been proposed as the true author of Shakespeare's plays, the most popular candidates being Francis BACON, Christopher MARLOWE, and Edward de VERE, Earl of Oxford. Opponents of Shakespeare's authorship argue that the son of a provincial glove maker lacked the education and experience to write brilliant plays that spoke of their author's familiarity with the COURT, the military camp, the legal world, and other specific realms of experience.

A severe lack of documentary evidence only adds to the mystery—no manuscript survives for any of Shakespeare's 37 plays (see SHAKESPEARE, WORKS OF; SONNET, SHAKESPEAREAN), and only six signatures can be definitely attributed to him. Most Shakespeare scholars, however, dismiss the arguments for alternative authorship as unconvincing; they maintain that Shakespeare was well-known in the London theatre community and had already gained a reputation as a talented playwright by the end of the 1590s. In the preface to the FIRST FOLIO (first collected edition) of Shakespeare's plays, published in 1623 by John HEMINGES and Henry CONDELL, the

Although no fully authenticated portrait of William Shakespeare exists, this painting, known as the Chandos portrait, was owned in the seventeenth century by a London actor. *By courtesy of the National Portrait Gallery, London.*

Possible Dating of Shakespeare's Works	
Comedies	
All's Well That Ends Well	1602–03
As You Like It	1599
The Comedy of Errors	1592–94
Love's Labor's Lost	1594–95
Measure for Measure	1604
The Merchant of Venice	1596–97
Merry Wives of Windsor	1597
A Midsummer Night's Dream	1595–96
Much Ado about Nothing	1598–99
The Taming of the Shrew	1593–94
Troilus and Cressida	1601–02
Twelfth Night	1601–02
The Two Gentlemen of Verona	1594
Romances	
Cymbeline	1609–10
Pericles, Prince of Tyre	1607–08
The Tempest	1611
The Winter's Tale	1610–11
Poems	
The Phoenix and Turtle	1601
The Rape of Lucrece	1593–94
Sonnets	1593–99
Venus and Adonis	1592–93
Histories	
Henry IV, Part 1	1596–97
Henry IV, Part 2	1598
Henry V	1599
Henry VI, Part 1	1589–90
Henry VI, Part 2	1590–91
Henry VI, Part 3	1590–91
Henry VIII	1612–13
King John	1594–96
Richard II	1595
Richard III	1592–93
Tragedies	
Antony and Cleopatra	1606–07
Coriolanus	1607–08
Hamlet	1600–01
Julius Caesar	1599
King Lear	1605
Macbeth	1606
Othello	1604
Romeo and Juliet	1595–96
Timon of Athens	1607–08
Titus Andronicus	1593–94

Note: Adapted from *The Riverside Shakespeare,* Boston: Houghton Mifflin, 1974, 48–56.

playwright Ben JONSON first attested to the greatness of Shakespeare, saying, he was "not of an age, but for all time." *See also* DRAMA; POETRY; and illustration for FIRST FOLIO.

Further Reading: Dennis Kay, *Shakespeare: His Life, Work, and Era,* New York: William Morrow, 1992; Peter Levi, *The Life and Times of William Shakespeare,* New York: Henry Holt and Company, 1988; A. L. Rowse, *William Shakespeare,* New York: Harper and Row, 1963; S. Schoenbaum, *Shakespeare's Lives,* Oxford: Clarendon Press, 1991.

Shakespeare, works of

William SHAKESPEARE wrote, or has had attributed to him, 37 plays (see FIRST FOLIO). Although the complete lack of any manuscripts makes the dating of the plays highly conjectural, most are thought to have been written in LONDON between about 1592 and Elizabeth's death in 1603. Dates are assigned by a careful reading of both internal evidence (e.g., allusions to datable events; nature and type of rhyme, imagery, or vocabulary) and external evidence (e.g., actual date of publication; the date the work was entered in the STATIONERS' REGISTER). Several of the classic tragedies, such as *Othello, King Lear,* and

Macbeth, were written in the first years of JAMES I, and the last few works, including *The Tempest* and *Henry VIII,* were probably written in Stratford.

The plays can be divided into four categories: the history plays, such as *Henry V* and *Richard III,* which draw on English history for their themes; the comedies, such as *The Two Gentlemen of Verona* and *The Taming of the Shrew,* which employ extensive rhyme and wordplay and borrow heavily from Roman and other comic traditions; the tragedies, such as *Hamlet, Macbeth,* and *King Lear,* which in their powerful explorations of human conflict are often considered the greatest dramas ever written; and the romances or tragicomedies, such as *Cymbeline* and *The Winter's Tale,* which were written late in the playwright's career and explore themes of reconciliation rather than conflict.

Shakespeare was also known for his POETRY; he published the love poems *Venus and Adonis* and *The Rape of Lucrece* in the early 1590s, and a collection of 154 sonnets, entitled simply *Shakespeare's Sonnets,* in May 1609 (see SONNET, SHAKESPEAREAN). The two love poems were dedicated to Henry WRIOTHESLEY, Earl of Southampton, a young courtier whose wealth made him much sought after by writers as a literary patron. Written probably in the 1590s, the sonnets are also believed to have been in some way associated with Southampton, who was prominent at COURT during this period as a friend of the royal favorite, Robert DEVEREUX, Earl of Essex. Scholars have searched the sonnets for biographical information on Shakespeare himself, looking intently but so far unsuccessfully for the identities of "Mr. W. H.," to whom the poems are dedicated, and the "dark lady," who is mentioned in a number of sonnets.

Shakespeare's elegy (i.e., a poem of mourning, reflection, or melancholy), *The Phoenix and Turtle,* appeared in 1601. The 1609 edition of the sonnets also contained a poem entitled *A Lover's Complaint,* which it attributed to Shakespeare; however, modern scholars dispute this attribution. In 1599, a collection of poetry entitled *The Passionate Pilgrim* printed the words "by W. Shakespeare" on its title page, but only five of the poems (two sonnets and three verses from the play *Love's Labor's Lost*) are known to be Shakespearean;

a few are known to be by other poets, and the Shakespearean authorship of the rest is doubtful. *See also* DRAMA; GLOBE THEATRE.

Further Reading: Dennis Kay, *Shakespeare: His Life, Work, and Era,* New York: William Morrow, 1992; Peter Levi, *The Life and Times of William Shakespeare,* New York: Henry Holt and Company, 1988; A. L. Rowse, *William Shakespeare,* New York: Harper and Row, 1963; S. Schoenbaum, *Shakespeare's Lives,* Oxford: Clarendon Press, 1991.

Shakespeare family

Although considered by many to be the greatest writer in the English language, William SHAKESPEARE's family origins are obscure and known only from occasional mentions in civic and legal records. Shakespeare's father, John Shakespeare (c. 1530–1601), was born in Warwickshire, the son of Richard Shakespeare, a yeoman farmer (i.e., not of the GENTRY class). John became a glove maker in Stratford, where he married Mary Arden (c. 1540–1608) about 1557. The couple had eight children, of whom the following five are known: William (1564–1616), Gilbert (1566–1612), Joan (1569–1646), Richard (1574–1613), and Edmund (1580–1607).

John Shakespeare became an alderman of Stratford in 1565, town bailiff in 1568, and chief alderman (head of the town council) in 1571. By 1575, John owned several houses in Stratford, but his financial fortunes declined in the following years, and he was dropped from the council in 1586. John mortgaged and lost much of his property, including his wife's inheritance, and was frequently suing or being sued for debt. In 1592, he was listed as a recusant (see RECUSANTS), but his nonattendance at church may have been out of fear of being arrested there for debt rather than for Catholicism. His son William, to whom he left his remaining property in Stratford, helped him obtain a coat of arms in 1596, thus allowing John to die a gentlemen in 1601 (see COLLEGE OF ARMS).

Mary Shakespeare lived on in Stratford with her daughter Joan and her son-in-law William Hart, a hat maker, until 1608. Although Shakespeare's brother Gilbert was a haberdasher in LONDON in the late 1590s, he was, by 1602, back in Stratford, where he acted as William's agent in land transactions. He died, unmarried, in February 1612. The next brother, Richard, apparently never left

Stratford; other than occasional minor brushes with the law, little is known of his life. Youngest brother Edmund Shakespeare became an actor in London, but nothing is known of his career; he died in December 1607.

William Shakespeare married Anne Hathaway (c. 1556–1623) in 1582, only six months before the birth of the couple's first daughter, Susanna (1583–1649). Beyond giving birth to twins in 1585—Hamnet (1585–1596) and Judith (1585–1662)—and receiving her husband's "second-best" bed in his will, little else is known of Anne Shakespeare's life. Hamnet Shakespeare died at age 11 in August 1596. The other twin, Judith, married Thomas Quiney in 1616 and bore two sons—Richard in 1618 and Thomas in 1620—but both of these grandsons of William Shakespeare died unmarried in 1639. Susanna Shakespeare married John Hall, a Puritan physician, in 1607, and gave birth to her only child, Elizabeth, in February 1608. The Halls inherited most of William Shakespeare's property, including New Place in Stratford. Elizabeth Hall, Shakespeare's only granddaughter, died childless in 1670, leaving her grandfather without any direct descendants.

Further Reading: C. Martin Mitchell, *The Shakespeare Circle: A Life of Dr. John Hall, Shakespeare's Son-in-Law,* Birmingham, England: Cornish Brothers, 1947; A. L. Rowse, *William Shakespeare,* New York: Harper and Row, 1963; S. Schoenbaum, *Shakespeare's Lives,* Oxford: Clarendon Press, 1991.

ships

The changes in sixteenth-century ship design that created the Elizabethan fleet were the result of a major shift in the tactics of naval warfare. The fleets of HENRY VIII, like all contemporary European fleets, fought naval battles by carrying a complement of soldiers to board an enemy vessel and engage in hand-to-hand combat. Ships were platforms allowing land forces to fight land battles at sea. When the Elizabethan NAVY engaged the ARMADA in 1588, ships had become gun platforms that could destroy enemy vessels from a distance by firing powerful broadside volleys. Speed, maneuverability, and firepower, not number of soldiers carried, were the important features of late sixteenth-century warships. This change in tactics was stimulated by the mid-century development of heavily armed galleys, small, single-deck vessels rowed by oarsmen.

Appearing almost simultaneously in the Spanish, French, and Portuguese fleets, galleys were more maneuverable than larger, higher sailing ships; they could row close to a larger vessel, do extensive damage with their heavy guns, and then slip away unscathed. Although they could not navigate the open seas like vessels under sail, galleys were ideal for warfare in coastal waters or inland seas like the Mediterranean, where the Spanish made excellent use of them. To counter galleys, European ship designers created the galleon, a more maneuverable multi-deck sailing ship. Galleons incorporated features of galley design to allow them to carry more and heavier guns, thus making possible the delivery of broadside fire against an enemy vessel.

The special needs and capabilities of the English fleet inspired English naval designers to modify the galleon designs of other European navies. Lacking an overseas empire, fearful of foreign invasion, and engaged in raiding foreign ships and colonies, England did not need vessels with large cargo capacities, like the Spanish and Portuguese, but quick, maneuverable ships suitable for home defense and PRIVATEERING. Thus, Elizabethan galleons were designed almost purely for war. They were smaller, quicker, and more heavily armed, using the iron shot—English iron was plentiful—that caused more damage from a greater distance than Spanish bronze shot (see GRAVELINES, BATTLE OF). Although the Elizabethans built on the work of others, their own naval innovations gave them among the best warships afloat in the late sixteenth century. *See also* WINTER, SIR WILLIAM and illustrations for AMADAS-BARLOWE EXPEDITION; GOWER, GEORGE; GRAVELINES, BATTLE OF; NAVY; TOWER OF LONDON.

Further Reading: D. M. Loades, *The Tudor Navy,* Brookfield, VT: Ashgate Publishers, 1992; N. A. M. Rodger, *The Safeguard of the Sea: A Naval History of Britain,* New York: W. W. Norton, 1998.

Shrewsbury, Countess of. *See* HARDWICK, ELIZABETH, COUNTESS OF SHREWSBURY.

Shrewsbury, Earl of. *See* TALBOT, GEORGE, EARL OF SHREWSBURY.

Sidney, Sir Henry (1529–1586)

As lord deputy, Sir Henry Sidney was instrumental in maintaining English rule in IRELAND. Because his father, Sir William Sidney, was an official in the household of Prince Edward, Henry Sidney was selected to be one of the prince's childhood companions. When the prince came to the throne as EDWARD VI in 1547, he showed Sidney great favor, knighting him in 1550. Although Sidney married a daughter of John DUDLEY, Duke of Northumberland, he took no part in NORTHUMBERLAND'S COUP in July 1553, and was soon in favor with Edward's successor, MARY I, who appointed him vice-treasurer of Ireland in 1556. In Ireland, Sidney served under his brother-in-law, Lord Deputy Thomas RADCLIFFE, the future Earl of Sussex.

By the time Sidney returned to England in 1559, Elizabeth was queen, and she appointed him president of the Council of Wales, a post he held until his death. In 1565, Elizabeth sent Sidney back to Ireland as lord deputy. He crushed the rebellion of Shane O'NEILL in Ulster, persuaded other Irish chieftains to submit to the queen's authority, and calmed Irish religious fears by delaying or laxly enforcing much anti-Catholic legislation. Seeking to

This portrait of Sir Henry Sidney, an Elizabethan lord deputy of Ireland, was painted by Arnold van Brounckhorst about 1573. *By courtesy of the National Portrait Gallery, London.*

pacify southern Ireland, Sidney imprisoned the troublesome Gerald FITZGERALD, Earl of Desmond, and set up English presidencies to administer Irish provinces. Combined with various schemes to plant English settlers on Irish lands, the presidencies, by seeming to prove the DUBLIN government's desire to impose English law and religion on the Irish, caused a massive rebellion in southern Ireland in 1569–70 (see FITZMAURICE'S REBELLION; PLANTATIONS, IRISH).

Sidney resigned his post in 1571 but was reappointed lord deputy in 1575. Attempting to put the Irish government on a sounder financial footing, Sidney imposed an unpopular tax on landholders, but he fell afoul of the queen's Irish favorite, Thomas BUTLER, Earl of Ormond, when he refused to exempt Ormond from the tax (see FAVORITES). The earl then accused Sidney of corruption, and, despite a brilliant defense of his actions written by his son Philip SIDNEY, Sir Henry was recalled in 1578. Swayed by Ormond's charges, Elizabeth refused Sidney further employment, and he spent his last years on his estates or at his post in WALES, where he died in May 1586.

Further Reading: Katherine Duncan-Jones, *Sir Philip Sidney,* New Haven, CT: Yale University Press, 1991; Steven G. Ellis, *Tudor Ireland,* London: Longman, 1985.

Sidney, Sir Philip (1554–1586)

Handsome and talented, Sir Philip Sidney was accepted in his time as the archetypal Elizabethan courtier-poet. The son of Sir Henry SIDNEY, lord deputy of IRELAND, and the nephew of Robert DUDLEY, Elizabeth's favorite, with PHILIP II of SPAIN standing as his godfather, Philip Sidney was born into a wealthy and highly favored courtier family. Sidney was educated at Shrewsbury School (see GRAMMAR SCHOOL), where he met his lifelong friend, Fulke GREVILLE, and at Oxford (see UNIVERSITIES), where he befriended such future figures of prominence as William CAMDEN, Richard HAKLUYT, Walter RALEIGH, and Edmund CAMPION.

In 1572, Sidney witnessed the SAINT BARTHOLOMEW MASSACRE in Paris while on a tour of Europe to further his EDUCATION (see GRAND TOUR). In 1577, at age 22, he was sent on a diplomatic mission to Germany. A strong Protestant, he fell into disfavor in 1579 when

Sir Philip Sidney, a prominent Elizabethan courtier and poet, was the nephew of Elizabeth I's favorite, Robert Dudley, Earl of Leicester. *By courtesy of the National Portrait Gallery, London.*

he advised the queen to forego her proposed marriage to Francis VALOIS, the Catholic Duke of Alençon. Temporarily deprived of an official post, Sidney turned to literature. He had already defended his father's Irish policies in *Discourse on Irish Affairs* (1577) and had written a play, *The Lady of May,* which was presented to Elizabeth in 1578. In the early 1580s, he began writing a prose romance entitled *Arcadia,* which influenced many later writers, including William SHAKESPEARE, and the first English sonnet cycle, *Astrophil and Stella,* which expressed his passion for Penelope ("Stella"), daughter of Walter DEVEREUX, Earl of Essex (see RICH, PENELOPE, LADY RICH). Wishing to make English literature as vigorous as continental writing, Sidney became the head of a circle of poets and writers that included Greville, Gabriel HARVEY, and Edmund SPENSER, who dedicated his *Shepheardes Calendar* (1579) to Sidney. In his *Defense of Poesie* (1595), Sidney set standards for the new English literature he envisioned.

Sidney also became interested in American exploration through his friendship with John DEE. He invested in the voyages of Sir

Martin FROBISHER and was about to set sail with Sir Francis DRAKE in 1585 when Elizabeth named him governor of Flushing, one of the Dutch CAUTIONARY TOWNS. In September 1586, he was mortally wounded leading a charge against the Spanish during Leicester's NETHERLANDS EXPEDITION. Matching the tenor of his life, the heroic manner of his death caused great sorrow and elicited written tributes from nearly every poet in England. *See also* DRAMA; POETRY.

Further Reading: Katherine Duncan-Jones, *Sir Philip Sidney,* New Haven, CT: Yale University Press, 1991; Fulke Greville, Baron Brooke, *Sir Fulke Greville's Life of Sir Philip Sidney,* Folcroft, PA: Folcroft Press, 1971; A. C. Hamilton, *Sir Philip Sidney: A Study of His Life and Works,* Cambridge: Cambridge University Press, 1977; Roger Howell, *Sir Philip Sidney: The Shepherd Knight,* Boston: Little, Brown, 1968.

skimmington ride

The skimmington ride was a highly symbolical procession of ritual shaming carried out in English towns and villages in the sixteenth and seventeenth centuries to humiliate and condemn a wife for usurping or disputing her husband's authority over her (see MARRIAGE). Early modern English society regarded WOMEN as subordinate to, and dependent on, the men from whom they drew their public identity—whether as daughter, wife, or widow. Thus, any woman who refused to accept such subordination was disrupting the accepted social order and deserved criticism and correction.

To conduct a skimmington, the neighbors of the couple would choose two of their number—both men—to dress up as the offenders. The man chosen to play the wife wore women's clothes, thus symbolizing the errant wife's unnatural attempts to assume a man's proper authority. The procession often began with a re-enactment of the incident that had given offense. The actors representing the couple were then paraded about the community on a staff or a horse in the midst of a derisive crowd that ended the ritual by seizing the "wife" and throwing her in a pond or dung heap. Through this ridicule and humiliation, the community hoped to reinforce its values concerning gender and to deter inappropriate behavior by wives.

Although skimmingtons were more common in some parts of the country (e.g., the southwestern counties) than others, they occurred frequently enough to be depicted in woodcuts of the period. In most cases, these illustrations showed the husband with horns, the sign of cuckoldry, for men who allowed their wives to dominate them were thought to be at great risk of becoming cuckolds.

Further Reading: Anthony Fletcher, *Gender, Sex and Subordination in England 1500–1800,* New Haven, CT: Yale University Press, 1995; Alan Harper, *Sex in Elizabethan England,* Stroud, England: Sutton, 1997.

Smerwick, Siege of

The siege at Smerwick in southern IRELAND in November 1580 ended the first attempt by the pope to intervene militarily in Ireland in behalf of Irish rebels against the Elizabethan government. The DESMOND REBELLION began in Ireland in July 1579 when James Fitzmaurice FITZGERALD (see FITZMAURICE'S REBELLION) landed with a force of 600 Spanish and Italian troops provided by Pope GREGORY XIII. The papal force built a fort on Smerwick Bay in southwestern Ireland and called upon all Irishmen to rise in defense of the Catholic religion (see REFORMATION, IRISH). Although Fitzmaurice was killed in August, the presence of the papal force threw southern Ireland into rebellion under the younger brothers of Gerald FITZGERALD, 14th Earl of Desmond, who eventually assumed leadership of the uprising.

In 1580, Elizabeth appointed Lord Grey de Wilton, a zealous Protestant, lord deputy of Ireland, with instructions to quell the Desmond rebellion and end the threat from the papal force at Smerwick. This threat increased in September 1580 when 700 additional papal troops landed at Smerwick, an event that further encouraged the Desmond rebels. In November, Grey joined forces with Thomas BUTLER, Earl of Ormond, a staunch royalist and an enemy of Desmond, to lay siege to the Smerwick fort. Unable to hold out, the papal garrison surrendered on 10 November 1580.

Fearing any strengthening of Catholicism in Ireland and wishing to deter future Irish rebels and papal invaders, Grey massacred the entire garrison and its Irish allies, except for 15 leaders who were held for ransom. Although approved by Elizabeth, this harsh action failed to prevent the Spanish from landing troops at Kinsale in 1601 to support Hugh O'NEILL,

Earl of Tyrone, leader of the Irish forces during the NINE YEARS WAR. The massacre at Smerwick illustrated how fearful the Elizabethans were of the possibility of having a Catholic and pro-Spanish Ireland just off their western shore. *See also* KINSALE, BATTLE OF.

Further Reading: Nicholas P. Canny, *The Elizabethan Conquest of Ireland: A Pattern Established 1565–76,* New York: Barnes and Noble Books, 1976; Steven G. Ellis, *Tudor Ireland,* London: Longman, 1985; Cyril Falls, *Elizabeth's Irish Wars,* London: Methuen, 1950; Colm Lennon, *Sixteenth-Century Ireland: The Incomplete Conquest,* Dublin: Gill and Macmillan, 1994; Margaret MacCurtain, *Tudor and Stuart Ireland,* Dublin: Gill and Macmillan, 1972; David B. Quinn, *The Elizabethans and the Irish,* Ithaca, NY: Cornell University Press, 1966.

Smith, Sir Thomas (1513–1577)

Sir Thomas Smith was a classical scholar, an experienced civil servant, and secretary of state (see OFFICERS OF STATE). Born in Essex, Smith was educated at the local GRAMMAR SCHOOL and at Cambridge (see UNIVERSITIES), where he completed a master's degree in 1533. In 1542, after several years of study in Paris and at Padua in Italy, Smith returned to Cambridge, where he joined John Cheke, future tutor to EDWARD VI, in campaigning to reform the pronunciation of Greek. In 1544, Smith became Regius Professor of Civil Law at Cambridge and vice-chancellor of the university. A strong Protestant and a loyal supporter of the regency government of Edward SEYMOUR, Duke of Somerset, Smith was knighted, appointed to the PRIVY COUNCIL, and named secretary of state in 1548.

In October 1549, when Somerset was overthrown, Smith was deprived of his offices and his professorship and was imprisoned in the TOWER OF LONDON. He was released in 1550 but took no further part in government during Edward VI's reign or during the reign of MARY I. Upon Elizabeth's accession in 1558, Smith returned to public office, being appointed ambassador to FRANCE in 1562 (see DIPLOMACY). Although Smith quarreled bitterly with Sir Nicholas THROCKMORTON, his ambassadorial colleague in France, the two men were able to resolve the issues arising from the LE HAVRE EXPEDITION and conclude the Treaty of Troyes in April 1564 (see TROYES, TREATY OF).

In the early 1570s, Smith won the queen's permission to establish a plantation on the Ards

Peninsula in the Ulster province of northern IRELAND (see PLANTATIONS, IRISH; ULSTER ENTERPRISE [SMITH]). However, the venture, which experienced difficulties from the start, came to ruin in October 1573 when Smith's only child, his illegitimate son Thomas, was murdered by his Irish servants. Although Smith was readmitted to the Privy Council and reappointed secretary of state in 1574, ill health and the shock of his son's death limited his service after the spring of 1576.

During his career, Smith wrote many scholarly works, including tracts advocating MARRIAGE for the queen and scholarly tracts on Roman coinage. His most important work was *De Republica Anglorum* (1584), a detailed description of the functioning of Elizabethan government that is of enormous importance to modern historians. Smith died at his home in Essex in August 1577. *See also* ANTIQUARIANISM; ULSTER ENTERPRISE (ESSEX).

Further Reading: Mary Dewar, *Sir Thomas Smith,* London: University of London, Athlone Press, 1964.

Smythson, Robert (1535–1614)

Robert Smythson was the foremost architect of Elizabethan England. Born into a family of mason-builders, Smythson was the first of his family to engage also in building design. Although a relatively new profession in sixteenth-century England, the practice of ARCHITECTURE developed rapidly in the Elizabethan and Jacobean (i.e., time of JAMES I) periods to accommodate the increasing demands of a status-conscious GENTRY and nobility for large and impressive country houses (see PRODIGY HOUSES).

In the 1570s, Smythson worked on two large projects in Wiltshire—the building of Sir John Thynne's Longleat House and the renovation of Wardour Castle. Smythson began work on Wollaton Hall in Nottinghamshire in 1580; it was the first Elizabethan country mansion to be designed and built by one person. When completed, Wollaton became a classic example of Elizabethan Renaissance architecture; unlike most great houses of the time, it was not built around a courtyard but gave the appearance of being a castle, with high, rounded turrets at the corners. But Wollaton was not like the defensive piles of the Middle Ages, it was designed for gracious country living, the façade being highly decorated and pierced by many large windows to let in the light.

After Wollaton, Smythson designed Worksop Manor for George TALBOT, Earl of Shrewsbury. His work for the earl so impressed the Countess of Shrewsbury (see HARDWICK, ELIZABETH) that she employed Smythson on her own project after the earl's death in 1590—the reconstruction of Hardwick Hall, her home in Derbyshire. Before his death in 1614, Smythson completed or collaborated on the design and building of many other great country mansions of the period.

Further Reading: Mark Girouard, *Robert Smythson and the Architecture of the Elizabethan Era,* South Brunswick, NJ: Barnes, 1967.

social hierarchy

The Elizabethan social hierarchy was characterized by a high degree of stratification, with individuals divided into a number of clearly delineated classes and ranks. Arising out of the medieval system of feudalism, whereby the king granted land (and the peasants who worked the land) to a lord in return for military service, Elizabethan social distinctions were based primarily on the holding of land. Although feudal institutions no longer accurately reflected the realities of Elizabethan society, England was still heavily rural, with almost 90 percent of the POPULATION living on isolated farmsteads or in villages or towns under 2,000 people. Political and economic power was concentrated in the 3–4 percent of the population that constituted the landholding elite—the royal family, the titled PEERAGE, and the GENTRY (see LOCAL GOVERNMENT).

Under Elizabeth, who had no spouse, children, or living siblings, the royal family consisted largely of the queen herself, although she had many distant cousins among the nobility and gentry. The peers, who possessed titles of nobility and the right to be summoned to the House of Lords in PARLIAMENT, numbered about 60 during Elizabeth's reign. The number of Elizabethans entitled—through landed wealth, lifestyle, and degree of local influence—to claim the status of gentleman numbered about 16,000 in 1603. Both the peerage and the gentry were subdivided by title and degree of wealth.

Over 80 percent of the population consisted of rural residents lacking the land and lifestyle to qualify as gentry; these rural commons were divided into yeomen, husbandmen, cottagers, and landless laborers. A yeoman farmed at least 50 acres of freehold land, that is, land not rented or leased from someone else (usually a nobleman or gentleman) and capable of being inherited by the yeoman's heirs. A yeoman also had an annual income of at least 40 shillings, the income level required for a man to vote in the county elections for Parliament. Husbandmen rented between 5 and 50 acres of land from larger landholders. Cottagers worked a few acres of land attached to their cottages, and so had to supplement their income by working for others. Landless laborers had no land at all and depended entirely on wage work. Husbandmen, cottagers, and landless laborers made up the great majority of the English rural population.

The remaining 10–15 percent of the Elizabethan population comprised a growing body of town dwellers—professionals (e.g., lawyers, physicians, university professors), merchants, craftsmen, and civil and military officers of the Crown. Along with the wealthier yeoman, these groups were called the "middling sort," and they constituted the most upwardly mobile portion of society. As their wealth grew, they began to acquire the land and adopt the lifestyle that would mark them as gentlemen, a status often given them unofficially by local society if not officially by the COLLEGE OF ARMS.

Finally, the clergy represented English society in miniature, with the archbishops and bishops recognized as a sort of ecclesiastical peerage, and some of the vicars and chaplains of the poorer villages sharing the low social status of the cottagers and laborers in their parishes. Despite its rigid formal distinctions of class, Elizabethan society was becoming increasingly fluid, as wealthy merchants and lawyers rose into the gentry and poorer gentlemen sank to yeoman status.

Elizabethan Social Hierarchy

Peerage	Gentry	Rural Commons	Clergy	Townsmen	"Middling Sort"
Duke			Archbishop		
Marquis					
Earl			Bishop	Mayor of London	
Viscount					
Baron					
	Knight		Archdeacon	Alderman	
	Esquire		Beneficed Priest	Merchant	Professionals (e.g., lawyers, physicians, royal civil servants)
	Gentleman				
		Yeoman	Deacon	Craftsman, Tradesman	Yeoman
		Husbandman	Vicar	Journeyman	
		Cottager		Apprentice	
		Landless Laborer	Chaplain	Servant	

Further Reading: Mary, Abbott, *Life Cycles in England, 1560–1720: Cradle to Grave*, London: Routledge, 1996; Peter Clark, *English Provincial Society from the Reformation to the Revolution: Religion, Politics and Society in Kent, 1500–1640*, Sussex, England: Harvester Press, 1977; William Harrison, *The Description of England: The Classic Contemporary Account of Tudor Social Life*, edited by Georges Edelen, Washington, DC: Folger Shakespeare Library, 1994; Ronald Hutton, *The Rise and Fall of Merry England: The Ritual Year, 1400–1700*, Oxford: Oxford University Press, 1996; Kate Mertes, *The English Noble Household: 1250 to 1600: Good Governance and Politic Rule*, Oxford: Blackwell, 1988; Muriel St. Clare Byrne, *Elizabethan Life in Town and Country*, 7th ed., Gloucester: A. Sutton, 1987; J. A. Sharpe, *Early Modern England: A Social History, 1550–1760*, London: Edward Arnold, 1987; Keith Wrightson, *English Society 1580–1680*, New Brunswick, NJ: Rutgers University Press, 1982.

Society of Antiquaries. *See* ANTIQUARIANISM.

Somerset, Duke of. *See* SEYMOUR, EDWARD, DUKE OF SOMERSET.

sonnet, Shakespearean

The English sonnet, a sixteenth-century English variation on a popular Italian verse form, is one of the most common poetic forms in English and American poetry. Because the English form is associated so closely with its most famous practitioner, William SHAKESPEARE, it has become widely known as the Shakespearean sonnet. The Italian poets Dante and Petrarch first developed the sonnet verse form in the thirteenth and fourteenth centuries. The Italian sonnet had 14 lines, an eight-line octave rhyming *abbaabba,* and a six-line sestet usually rhyming *cdecde,* although variations were possible. The octave usually defined a problem or described an experience that was reacted to in the sestet.

Sir Thomas Wyatt, who wrote poetry for Anne BOLEYN, and Henry Howard, Earl of Surrey, a cousin of Princess Elizabeth (see HOWARD FAMILY), imported the sonnet into England in the 1530s and 1540s. They modified the sonnet by ending the sestet with a rhyming two-line couplet (e.g., *cddcee*), a common device in English POETRY, and by using pentameter, the most common English rhythm scheme. Elizabethan poets, including Shakespeare, further altered the rhyme scheme to produce the standard Shakespearean form: *ababcdcdefefgg*. However, the sonnet form was

flexible, and variations in rhyme and meter were frequently employed.

Themes varied greatly as well. Early English sonnets explored courtly love and other amorous themes, but Elizabethan poets reacted against this trend by writing anti-love sonnets that complained of courtly pretense and the fickleness of lovers (see COURT). In his collection of 154 sonnets, Shakespeare wrote on both themes. Shakespeare's Sonnet 138, reproduced below, uses the standard English rhyme scheme to express a decidedly anti-love theme.

> When my love swears that she is made of truth,
> I do believe her though I know she lies,
> That she might think me some untutored youth,
> Unlearnèd in the world's false subtleties.
> Thus vainly thinking that she thinks me young,
> Although she knows my days are past the best,
> Simply I credit her false-speaking tongue:
> On both sides thus is simple truth suppressed,
> But wherefore says she not she is unjust?
> And wherefore say not I that I am old?
> O love's best habit is in seeming trust,
> And age in love loves not to have years told.
> Therefore I lie with her, and she with me,
> And in our faults by lies we flattered be.

Further Reading: Emrys Jones, ed., *The New Oxford Book of Sixteenth Century Verse,* Oxford: Oxford University Press, 1992; J. W. Lever, *The Elizabethan Love Sonnet,* London: Methuen, 1978; William Shakespeare, *Love Poems and Sonnets of William Shakespeare,* New York: Doubleday, 1957.

Southampton, Countess of. *See* WRIOTHESLEY, ELIZABETH, COUNTESS OF SOUTHAMPTON.

Southampton, Earl of. *See* WRIOTHESLEY, HENRY, EARL OF SOUTHAMPTON.

Southwell, Robert (1561–1595)

Robert Southwell was a leading member of the English JESUIT MISSION and a noted Catholic poet. Born near Norwich into a GENTRY family related to the Cecils (see CECIL, WILLIAM), Southwell entered William ALLEN's English Catholic College at Douai in the NETHERLANDS in 1577 when he was 16. In 1578, he traveled to Rome, and two years later he was ordained a priest in the Jesuit order. He became prefect of studies at the English College in Rome, but was determined to return to England as a missionary, an increasingly dangerous ambition given the severe anti-Jesuit statutes (see PENAL LAWS) being passed by Elizabethan Parliaments (see CATHOLICISM, ENGLISH; PARLIAMENTARY SESSIONS [1559–1581], [1584–1601]).

In July 1586, he landed secretly in England with fellow Jesuit Henry GARNET. Traveling under the name Cotton, Southwell began ministering to longtime Catholics and seeking new converts. After 1589, he found sanctuary in the LONDON home of Anne Howard, Countess of Arundell, whom he served as chaplain. He wrote a series of encouraging letters and tracts that were surreptitiously circulated in manuscript form among the persecuted Catholic community. His *An Epistle of Comfort,* written about 1591, was printed in Europe and secretly distributed in England.

Through its network of spies, the English government knew of Southwell's activities almost from the start. The authorities finally arrested Southwell on 20 June 1592 as he was celebrating MASS. During the following three years of imprisonment, Southwell wrote a great body of POETRY, much of it, like the well-known poem "The Burning Babe," on themes of hope, encouragement, and spiritual love. He also completed *St. Peter's Complaint,* an account of the last days of Christ narrated by Saint Peter. A collection of his poems entitled *Maeconiae* was published in 1595, and his *Fourfold Meditation of the Four Last Things* appeared posthumously in 1606. After undergoing several periods of torture conducted during his years of confinement by the notorious Richard TOPCLIFFE, Southwell was brought to trial and condemned to death in February 1595. He was hanged at Tyburn on 21 February. *See also* CATHOLICISM, ENGLISH.

Further Reading: Christopher Devlin, *The Life of Robert Southwell: Poet and Martyr,* New York: Greenwood Press, 1969.

Spain

Spain during the Elizabethan period was the heart of a world empire that included Italy, the NETHERLANDS, Mexico, Peru, the West Indies, large portions of North and South America, and, after 1580, Portugal and its possessions in Africa and Asia. From 1556 to 1598, this Spanish empire was ruled by PHILIP II,

Elizabeth's former brother-in-law. Although his father, CHARLES V (see HABSBURG FAMILY), had been raised in the Netherlands, Philip grew up in Castile, one of the constituent parts of the united Spanish monarchy. Thus, despite the international character of his dominions, Philip always had a Spanish point of view and relied almost exclusively on Spanish, especially Castilian, advisors.

An intelligent but traditional-minded man, Philip made all important political decisions in Madrid, using his excellent postal service to communicate orders to his viceroys. As his reign progressed, Philip became more rigidly dedicated to his Catholic faith, seeing himself and Spain as the implacable foes of heresy. Prior to 1560, England and Spain had usually been on friendly terms and had often been allies. Elizabeth's rejection of Philip's MARRIAGE proposal and her decision to return the English Church to PROTESTANTISM strained relations, and subsequent events brought the two countries into increasing conflict. After 1568, English attempts to break Spain's trade monopoly in SPANISH AMERICA led to an undeclared war on the high seas and to increasingly daring English PRIVATEERING raids on Spanish shipping and colonies. The NETHERLANDS REVOLT against Philip's rule, being in part motivated by Protestantism, reluctantly drew Elizabeth into supporting her coreligionists against Spain. Philip, meanwhile, plotted, somewhat half-heartedly, with English Catholic exiles and the supporters of Mary STUART, Queen of Scots, to overthrow Elizabeth.

By the mid-1580s, Philip decided that he could never reconquer the Netherlands until he had crushed Protestantism in England. The war that broke out between the two countries in 1585 led to the descent of the ARMADA on England in 1588 and to various English attacks on Spain (see AZORES EXPEDITION; CADIZ RAID [1587]; CADIZ RAID [1596]; ISLANDS VOYAGE; PORTUGAL EXPEDITION). The war outlasted both Philip and Elizabeth, being finally concluded by their successors in 1604. By then, Spain, although still the greatest power in Europe, had failed to hold the Netherlands, crush England, or restore European Catholicism.

Further Reading: J. H. Elliott, *Imperial Spain, 1469–1716,* New York: St. Martin's Press, 1967; A. W. Lovett, *Early*

Habsburg Spain 1517–1598, Oxford: Oxford University Press, 1986; John Lynch, *Spain, 1516–1598: From Nation State to World Empire,* Oxford: Blackwell, 1992.

Spanish America

In 1493, Pope Alexander VI, a Spaniard, tried to settle the rival claims of SPAIN and Portugal to new discoveries in the Atlantic by drawing a north-south line on the map 100 leagues west of the AZORES (located about 800 miles west of Portugal). All lands west of the line (i.e., the New World) belonged to Spain, and all lands east of the line (i.e., Africa and India) to Portugal. In 1494, the two countries revised the papal division in the Treaty of Tordesilles, which moved the line further west. The new division granted Spain dominion in most of the New World, but guaranteed Portugal its Atlantic sea-lanes and inadvertently gave it a claim to Brazil.

In Spanish America, which slowly expanded by Elizabethan times to include the Caribbean islands and the mainland territories surrounding the Caribbean—from Florida through Mexico and Central America to northern South America and Peru—Spain maintained a rigid trade monopoly, denying other European powers access to its colonial markets (see Maps, "Spanish America in the Sixteenth Century"). Anxious to exploit the American resources that Spain controlled, Protestant England refused to accept the papal division of the world into Spanish and Portuguese spheres.

In 1562, the English trader John HAWKINS tested those monopolies by sailing to Portuguese West Africa to acquire slaves to sell in Spanish America. Although Hawkins's venture was a breach of Spanish trade regulations, the inability of Spain to fully supply the needs of her colonists gave Hawkins a ready welcome in the Caribbean, where he traded his human cargo for gold, silver, hides, and sugar. The success of Hawkins's venture whetted English appetites for Spanish American trade, and Hawkins launched new voyages in 1564 and 1567 with the financial backing of the queen and numerous important courtiers.

By Hawkins's third voyage, the Spanish government had tightened enforcement of its colonial trade monopoly, and the English could find no one in Spanish America willing to trade with them. Eager for profits, the English trad-

ers turned pirate, convincing the citizens of Rio de la Hacha to trade by burning part of the town. However, at SAN JUAN D'ULLOA on the Mexican coast, the Spanish viceroy, after agreeing to terms with Hawkins, treacherously attacked the English, destroying four ships and killing or capturing over 120 men.

After 1568, the action at San Juan d'Ulloa and the unwavering refusal of PHILIP II to open Spanish America to English trade created a virtual state of war between England and Spain in American waters, even though the two countries remained at peace in Europe. The subsequent PRIVATEERING raids on Spanish America by Sir Francis DRAKE, who had been with Hawkins at San Juan, and other Englishmen aggravated the friction generated by religious differences and the NETHERLANDS REVOLT to bring England and Spain to open war in 1585. *See also* AMERICA.

Further Reading: Charles Gibson, *Spain in America,* New York: Harper and Row, 1967; Carl Ortwen Sauer, *The Early Spanish Main,* Berkeley: University of California Press, 1969.

Spanish Armada. *See* ARMADA.

Speed, John (c. 1552–1629)

John Speed was among the foremost cartographers and historians of Elizabethan England. Born in Cheshire, Speed, like his father, was a tailor, being admitted to membership in the Merchant Taylors' Company in LONDON in 1580. Interested in geography and history, Speed began drawing maps for recreation. Through the poet and courtier Sir Fulke GREVILLE, who shared his enthusiasm for history and genealogy, Speed joined the Society of Antiquaries, where he met the historian William CAMDEN and the antiquary Sir Robert COTTON (see ANTIQUARIANISM).

Encouraged by his fellow members of the Society, Speed began to devote more time to making maps and writing history. In 1598, he presented some of his maps to the queen, and in 1600 he gave others to the Merchant Taylors' Company (see LIVERIED COMPANY). His first published map appeared in Camden's sixth edition of *BRITANNIA* in 1607. Between 1608 and 1610, Speed published a series of 54 maps of the counties of England and WALES. In 1611, these maps appeared with descriptive text in

Speed's *Theatre of the Empire of Great Britain* and *History of Great Britain*.

Speed followed these two popular volumes of geography and history with two works on religion, *Genealogies Recorded in Sacred Scripture* (1611) and *A Cloud of Witnesses . . . Confirming . . . God's Most Holy Word* (1616). Speed's histories were widely read by contemporaries, and his maps are still of tremendous value to modern historians. Many of Speed's original maps can be found in the British Museum in London. Speed died at the age of 77 in July 1629.

Further Reading: John Speed, *The Counties of Britain: A Tudor Atlas,* introduction by Nigel Nicolson, county commentaries by Alasdair Hawkyard, New York: Thames and Hudson, 1989.

Spenser, Edmund (c. 1552–1599)

Considered by contemporaries to be the foremost poet of his age, Edmund Spenser was born in LONDON, attended the Merchant Taylors' School (see GRAMMAR SCHOOL), and earned two degrees at Cambridge (see UNIVERSITIES). In 1579, he published *The Shepheardes*

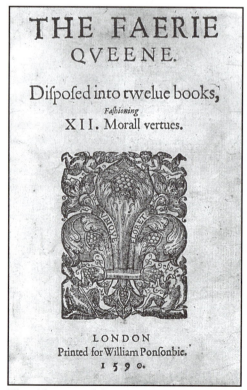

THE FAERIE QVEENE.

Difpofed into twelue books,

Fafhioning

XII. Morall vertues.

LONDON
Printed for William Ponfonbie.
1 5 9 0.

The title page of the 1590 edition of Edmund Spenser's *The Faerie Queene. By permission of the Folger Shakespeare Library.*

Calendar, an enthusiastically received poem dedicated to Sir Philip SIDNEY. With its arrangement as a calendar of 12 eclogues (i.e., poems cast in the form of dialogues between shepherds), and its inclusion of extended fables in some of the eclogues*, The Shepheardes Calendar* was highly innovative.

The poem's success brought Spenser to the notice of the COURT and led, in 1580, to his appointment as secretary to the new lord deputy of IRELAND. In Ireland, Spenser became an undertaker of Munster (a region of southern Ireland), meaning he acquired property tax- and rent-free as part of a colonization scheme that took land from native Irish and gave it to English settlers (see PLANTATIONS, IRISH). Spenser held an official post as clerk of Munster but spent much time working on his great epic, *The Faerie Queen,* and exchanging verses with his neighbor, Sir Walter RALEIGH. *The Faerie Queen* was to comprise 12 books, each depicting an adventure of one of the knights of the great queen Gloriana (i.e., Elizabeth). Spenser accompanied Raleigh to London in 1589 to present the first three books to the queen. Dedicated to Elizabeth and containing sonnets addressed to important courtiers, Books I–III earned Spenser a £50 annuity for life.

In the 1590s, Spenser published a series of other important works, including his three-volume collection of verse entitled *Complaints* (1591); his sonnet cycle *Amoretti* and the ode *Epithalamion* (both 1595), which together commemorate the wooing and wedding of his second wife; the allegorical poem *Colin Clouts Come Home Again* (1595), which uses his hero from *The Shepheardes Calendar* to describe his visit to London; and *Astrophil* (1595), a lament on the death of Sir Philip Sidney.

Books IV–VI of *The Faerie Queen* appeared in 1596, and *A View of the Present State of Ireland,* which denigrated the Irish and supported English conquest of the island, was published posthumously in 1633. In October 1598, Spenser fled Ireland when rebels burned his house. He spent his last months in London in financial distress. He died in January 1599 and was buried in Westminster Abbey at the expense of Robert DEVEREUX, Earl of Essex. *See also* POETRY.

Further Reading: Gary F. Waller, *Edmund Spenser: A Literary Life,* London: Macmillan, 1994.

Stanley, Ferdinando, Lord Strange
(1559–1594)

Ferdinando Stanley, Lord Strange, was the patron and namesake of a theatrical company that included some of the leading actors in Elizabethan LONDON, including, for a time, William SHAKESPEARE. The son of Henry Stanley, fourth Earl of Derby, Lord Strange entered Oxford in 1572 at about age 12. By the late 1570s, Strange, who was himself a poet, had become a noted literary patron. His company of players, Lord Strange's Men, began about 1576 as a troupe of acrobats led by the famous tumbler John Symons. The company performed throughout England and even appeared at COURT in the early 1580s.

In about 1589, the company began performing plays, and by 1592, the noted comic actor William KEMPE and a little-known performer and playwright named William Shakespeare had joined the troupe. Led by the famous actor Edward ALLEYN, Lord Strange's Men appeared at Philip HENSLOWE's Rose Theatre and at The Theatre, James BURBAGE's playhouse in London, as well as at court. Working sometimes in partnership with another company, the Admiral's Men, Strange's troupe put on some of the first productions of plays by Shakespeare, including performances of *Titus Andronicus* and *Henry VI, Part 2* (see SHAKESPEARE, WORKS OF).

The company shut down in 1592 when an outbreak of PLAGUE caused the London authorities to close all theatres. Strange succeeded his father, who had supported his own company of provincial players, as fifth Earl of Derby in 1593. When a Roman Catholic exile suggested to the new earl that he claim the throne by right of his mother, who was a great-niece of HENRY VIII, Derby denounced the plot. His death shortly thereafter in 1594 was rumored to be the result of poison administered by vengeful Catholic agents, although that seems unlikely. After the earl's death, Lord Strange's Men were reconstituted under the patronage of Henry CAREY, Lord Hunsdon, the lord chamberlain of England, and became known until 1603 as the CHAMBERLAIN'S MEN. *See also* DRAMA; GLOBE THEATRE.

Further Reading: Roslyn Lander Knutson, *The Repertory of Shakespeare's Company, 1594–1613*, Fayetteville: University of Arkansas Press, 1991; Peter Thomson, *Shakespeare's Theatre*, 2nd ed., London: Routledge, 1992.

Stanyhurst, Richard (1547–1618)

Richard Stanyhurst was one of the team of writers who helped prepare the first edition of HOLINSHED'S *CHRONICLES*. Stanyhurst was born into a prominent ANGLO-IRISH family in DUBLIN, his grandfather having served as lord mayor of the city. Educated at a GRAMMAR SCHOOL in Waterford, Stanyhurst came to England in 1563 to enter University College, Oxford (see UNIVERSITIES), where he completed his degree in 1568. After studying law at the INNS OF COURT, Stanyhurst returned to IRELAND and immersed himself in the study of Irish history and geography.

At Oxford, Stanyhurst had befriended Edmund CAMPION, who persuaded Stanyhurst to join him in contributing to *The Chronicles of England, Scotland, and Ireland* being prepared by an editorial team under the direction of Raphael HOLINSHED. With Campion's help, Stanyhurst wrote a treatise entitled the "Description of Ireland," which was similar to "THE DESCRIPTION OF ENGLAND" being written for the project by William HARRISON. Stanyhurst's "Description," dedicated to Sir Henry SIDNEY, lord deputy of Ireland and a friend of Stanyhurst's father, introduced the Irish section of the first edition of Holinshed's *Chronicles* (1577).

In about 1580, Stanyhurst moved to the NETHERLANDS, where his ENGLISH translation of Virgil's *Aeneid* was published in 1582. Although Stanyhurst was a noted Latin scholar, his translation was almost universally condemned by English critics as unreadable. Thereafter, Stanyhurst confined himself to writing in Latin, producing a history of medieval Ireland in 1584 and a life of St. Patrick in 1587. Because Stanyhurst never returned to Ireland and wrote about the island from an English point of view, he has been attacked by later Irish critics for not knowing or understanding the island and its people.

Under the influence of Campion, Stanyhurst converted to Catholicism in the Netherlands and became involved in various Catholic plots against the Elizabethan government, thereby earning the frequent attention of English spies. He visited SPAIN in the 1590s and had an audience with PHILIP II, whom he found to be kind and affable. After the death of his wife in 1602, Stanyhurst entered the Catholic priesthood and became chaplain to Philip's daughter and to the English Benedictine convent in Brussels. Stanyhurst died in Brussels in 1618.

Further Reading: Colm Lennon, *Richard Stanihurst the Dubliner, 1547–1618,* Dublin: Irish Academic Press, 1981.

Star Chamber, Court of

The Court of Star Chamber was the formal court of EQUITY that evolved under the Tudors from informal meetings of earlier royal Councils to hear petitions brought to the king by his subjects. In the fifteenth century, the Council began to gather in the Star Chamber at Westminster (so named because of the stars painted on its walls and ceiling) to conduct its judicial business. In 1487, an act of PARLIA-MENT authorized the Council sitting in Star Chamber to "punish divers misdemeanours."

HENRY VII, Elizabeth's grandfather, used Star Chamber to curb disorder and judge cases involving the rights of the Crown. HENRY VIII's chief ministers, Thomas Wolsey and Thomas CROMWELL, expanded the work of the court, which by 1540 had separated from the PRIVY COUNCIL to become a separate court of equity operating under the royal PREROGATIVE. Petitioners who felt themselves unable to obtain fair judgment in the courts of the COMMON LAW, or whose matters did not come under the jurisdiction of the common law, could bring their cases before the monarch's councilors in Star Chamber. Prior to Elizabeth's reign, Star Chamber dealt mainly in civil cases involving disputed titles to land, such as cases of fraud, forgery, trespass, and forcible entry and dispossession.

Under Elizabeth, Star Chamber's focus narrowed to misdemeanor criminal matters, such as assaults, riots, unlawful assemblies, extortion, subornation of juries, perjury, corruption, and seditious libel. Star Chamber had no jurisdiction over felonies, and it could not impose the death penalty, nor hear cases that might involve the death penalty. Star Chamber punishments included fines, imprisonment, flogging, the pillory, and mutilation of the ears and nose.

In the early Tudor period, Star Chamber was popular as a fair, efficient court for settling suits between subjects. The shift in focus to criminal matters under Elizabeth wore away some of this popularity, although the volume of business coming before the court continued to increase. The use of Star Chamber by Elizabeth's Stuart successors (see JAMES I) to uphold royal authority by suppressing criticism of Crown policies caused the court to be hated as an instrument of royal oppression. As part of its effort to reform what it saw as abuses perpetrated by the Crown, Parliament abolished Star Chamber in 1641.

Further Reading: G. R. Elton, *Star Chamber Stories,* London: Methuen, 1958; John Guy, *The Court of Star Chamber and Its Records to the Reign of Elizabeth I,* London: H.M.S.O., 1985; Michael Stuckey, *The High Court of Star Chamber,* Holmes Beach, FL: Gaunt, 1998.

States-General

The States-General was the national assembly of the United Provinces of the Netherlands, the independent republic that developed in the northern provinces of the NETHERLANDS during the course of the provinces' long revolt (1568–1609) against SPAIN. The States-General was instituted in the Netherlands in the fifteenth century by the ruling dukes of Burgundy, and was continued in the sixteenth century by the succeeding HABSBURG FAMILY, as a means to facilitate the assessment and collection of provincial taxes. Rather than negotiate for taxes with each of the 17 provincial States (legislatures), the Habsburgs found it more efficient to convene one States-General composed of delegates from the various provincial assemblies.

In 1576, in the midst of a Netherlands-wide rebellion (see NETHERLANDS REVOLT) against PHILIP II of Spain, this assembly—originally intended for the promotion of Habsburg rule—met without Habsburg sanction and took for itself sovereign powers that had previously been reserved for the ruler of the Netherlands. In 1579, with the creation of the Union of Utrecht, a pact between the northern provinces that remained in rebellion after the southern provinces returned to their Habsburg allegiance, the States-General became the central assembly of the new independent union. However, unlike the later American Congress, which exercised certain sovereign powers over the individual states of the United States, sovereignty in the Dutch Republic remained vested solely in the provincial States of the seven provinces of the union. The States-General, which comprised the delegates of each of the provincial States, could make no important national decisions without the unanimous consent of the provincial assemblies.

The main functions of the States-General were the administration and TAXATION of the Generality Lands, those areas of the Dutch Republic that lay outside the seven provinces and that had been freed from Spanish control, and the general oversight of military and foreign affairs. Thus, once the provincial States had unanimously agreed to seek an alliance with England, delegates from the States-General arrived in LONDON in 1585 to conduct the negotiations that led to the Treaty of Nonsuch, whereby Elizabeth agreed to supply the Dutch with financial and military assistance (see NONSUCH, TREATY OF). The States-General remained in existence until the collapse of the Dutch Republic in 1795. The name was revived in 1814 for the bicameral parliament of the newly created Kingdom of The Netherlands.

Further Reading: Edward Grierson, *The Fatal Inheritance: Philip II and the Spanish Netherlands,* Garden City, NY: Doubleday, 1969; Jonathan I. Israel, *The Dutch Republic: Its Rise, Greatness, and Fall 1477–1806,* Oxford: Clarendon Press, 1998; Geoffrey Parker, *Spain and the Netherlands, 1559–1659,* Short Hills, NJ: Enslow Publishers, 1979; James D. Tracy, *Holland under Habsburg Rule, 1506–1566: The Formation of a Body Politic,* Berkeley: University of California Press, 1990.

Stationers' Company. *See* STATIONERS' REGISTER.

Stationers' Register

Every book printed in Elizabethan England, except for those printed on the presses of the UNIVERSITIES at Oxford and Cambridge, had to be registered with the Stationers' Company, a corporate body to which all professional printers and booksellers belonged (see LIVERIED COMPANY). By entering books or plays in the Stationers' Register, authors established copyright to their works and forestalled the production of unauthorized editions.

Today, when used in conjunction with other kinds of internal and external evidence, the date of registration can help set the chronology for the works of important Elizabethan poets and playwrights, especially William SHAKESPEARE. For instance, Shakespeare's love poem *Venus and Adonis* was registered on 18 April 1593, indicating that this poem was one of his earlier works. *Hamlet,* although published in various editions in 1603–04, was registered on 26 July 1602, and this earlier date, along with allusions in the play to Julius Caesar, suggest that Shakespeare began *Hamlet* about 1599, when he was finishing the play *Julius Caesar.*

MARY I issued the Stationers' Company charter in 1557 and Elizabeth confirmed it in 1559. Besides establishing copyright, the Stationers' Company and its register allowed the government to restrict publishing it considered subversive or inflammatory in either politics or religion, and to create lucrative publishing MONOPOLIES. For instance, the queen sold Richard Tottel a monopoly on the printing of law books and William Seres a patent on the printing of psalters and prayer books; because these kinds of monopolies left many smaller printers virtually without work, the Company was called upon to root out the inevitable proliferation of unauthorized editions that followed the granting of a publishing monopoly.

In 1586, the PRIVY COUNCIL, seeking to suppress the activities of unlicensed Catholic and PURITAN presses, also empowered the Stationers' Company to inspect all PRINTING sites and to confiscate all illegal publications and equipment. The fact that almost one-third of the surviving works for the Elizabethan period were never entered in the Stationers' Register suggests the difficulty, if not the futility, of the Company's efforts in this regard.

Further Reading: Cyprion Blagden, *The Stationers' Company: A History,* Cambridge, MA: Harvard University Press, 1960; John Feather, *A History of British Publishing,* New York: Croom Helm, 1988.

Statute of Apprentices. *See* STATUTE OF ARTIFICERS.

Statute of Artificers

The 1563 Statute of Artificers (also known as the Statute of Apprentices) was a sweeping labor code that attempted to solve the problems of vagabondage and unemployment by limiting wages and the mobility of workers. PARLIAMENT also hoped the statute would improve the quality of English manufactured goods by improving the training of craftsmen. The statute made the guild apprenticeship system national by requiring a seven-year apprenticeship in all urban crafts and agricultural trades. Sons of the laboring poor were effectively barred from apprenticeships by strict property qualifications, thus keeping most rural agricultural workers in the fields. Masters in each craft were prevented from making excessive use of cheap labor by limits placed on the number of apprentices and journeymen each master could employ.

The statute also fixed maximum, but not minimum, wages, and it ordered JUSTICES OF THE PEACE to meet during their Easter term to set local wage rates in line with current prices. Other provisions of the act regulated the length of the workday, required employers to engage workers for at least one year, prohibited workers from leaving before the end of their term of service, and required unmarried women between the ages of 12 and 40 to enter service. The statute aimed at ensuring enough cheap labor for agricultural purposes by preventing poor laborers from leaving the countryside and going into the towns, especially LONDON, to take up new, more lucrative crafts. The Statute of Artificers, which was to remain in force for over 200 years, did somewhat stabilize the supply of labor on the land, but it utterly failed to compel most workers to remain in the locality and with the trade into which they were born. *See also* AGRICULTURE; POPULATION; SOCIAL HIERARCHY.

Further Reading: Margaret G. Davies, *The Enforcement of English Apprenticeship, 1563–1642,* Cambridge, MA: Harvard University Press, 1956.

Stewart, Arabella. *See* STUART, ARABELLA.

Stewart claim (to the throne). *See* STUART CLAIM (TO THE THRONE).

Stewart, Henry, Lord Darnley. *See* STUART, HENRY, LORD DARNLEY.

Stewart, James, Earl of Moray. *See* STUART, JAMES, EARL OF MORAY.

Stewart, Mary, Queen of Scots. *See* STUART, MARY, QUEEN OF SCOTTS.

Stow, John (c. 1525–1605)

John Stow was one of the most important and most accurate Elizabethan chroniclers of English history. Born in LONDON, Stow was a tailor by trade, being admitted to membership in the Merchant Taylors' Company (see LIVERIED COMPANY) in 1547. Stow's business flourished, and by 1560 he was able to begin devoting much of his time and money to his study of English history and antiquities (see ANTIQUARIANISM). His first project, published in 1561, was the editing of a new edition of *The Works of Geoffrey Chaucer.* His first original work, *Summary of English Chronicles* (1565), although criticized by rival chronicler Richard GRAFTON, was popular enough to run into several fully revised and updated editions.

Although Stow was examined several times by the PRIVY COUNCIL in the late 1560s for possessing Catholic books and pamphlets, he was never punished and continued to work with Archbishop Matthew PARKER on the editing of various medieval English chronicles, including editions of Matthew of Westminster's *Flores Historiarum* (1567) and Matthew Paris's *Chronicle* (1571). Stow's most important work, *The Chronicles of England,* was first published in 1580 and was reissued in 1592 (and in later editions) as *The Annals of England Faithfully Collected out of the Most Authentical Authors, Records and Other Monuments of Antiquity, from the First Inhabitation until This Present Year.* Popularly known as the *Annals,* Stow's work borrowed extensively, without acknowledgment, from the *Chronicles* of Raphael HOLINSHED. With John HOOKER and other editors, Stow was part of the team that published a revised edition of HOLINSHED'S *CHRONICLES* in 1587.

Stow devoted the 1590s to researching and compiling his *Survey of London* (1598), a valuable study of the origins, development, and customs of the city. Stow compiled information by collecting and studying documents and by exploring and observing every part of London. In his last years, Stow's studies and publishing projects ate up his fortune and left him dependent on the charity of the Merchant Taylors' Company. He died in London in April 1605.

Further Reading: John Stow, *A Survey of London Written in the Year 1598,* London: J. M. Dent and Sons, 1997.

Strange, Lord. *See* STANLEY, FERDINANDO, LORD STRANGE.

Stuart, Arabella (1575–1615)
Arabella Stuart, daughter of Charles Stuart, Earl of Lennox, and Elizabeth Cavendish, stood too near to the throne to escape a life of sorrow and frustration. Her paternal uncle, Henry STUART, Lord Darnley, was the second husband of Mary STUART, Queen of Scots, and her cousin was thus Mary and Darnley's son, James VI of SCOTLAND (see JAMES I). In the last years of Elizabeth's reign, Arabella was next in line for the English Crown after James VI and was therefore a focus of intrigue for those who opposed the accession of the King of Scots to the English throne.

Because her parents died young, Arabella was raised from the age of seven by her maternal grandmother, Elizabeth HARDWICK, who had by the 1580s become the wife of George TALBOT, Earl of Shrewsbury. As a young woman, Arabella became a friend and companion of her imprisoned aunt, the Queen of Scots, who was for many years entrusted to Shrewsbury's keeping. Elizabeth, ever suspicious of any possible successors to her throne, frustrated all plans for the girl's marriage. Arabella's position was also hurt by the intrigues of her grandmother, the Countess of Shrewsbury, who persistently but unsuccessfully sought to have her granddaughter named as Elizabeth's successor. After 1590, the countess kept her granddaughter a virtual prisoner at Hardwick Hall, the countess's family home in Derbyshire.

After his accession in 1603, James I, who by then had two sons, welcomed Arabella to COURT, but, like Elizabeth, forbade her to marry. In 1610, she defied the king by secretly marrying William Seymour, who had his own distant claim to the throne thanks to the secret MARRIAGE of his grandparents, Edward Seymour and Katherine GREY. For this new unauthorized marriage, the king imprisoned Arabella at Lambeth Palace and sent Seymour to the TOWER OF LONDON. Husband and wife both escaped their prisons in 1611, but Arabella was recaptured and sent to the Tower, where anxiety and despair eventually robbed her of both life and sanity. Arabella died in September 1615 and was buried in Westminster Abbey in the new tomb of the Queen of Scots. *See also* STUART CLAIM and the genealogical chart in Appendix 1: "Stuart Claim to the English Throne."

Further Reading: David N. Durant, *Arabella Stuart: A Rival to the Queen,* London: Weidenfield and Nicolson, 1978; P. M. Handover, *Arabella Stuart,* London: Eyre and Spottiswoode, 1957; Ian McInnes, *Arabella,* London: W. H. Allen, 1968.

Stuart claim (to the throne)
The claim of the Scottish royal family of Stuart to the English throne derived from the 1503 marriage of James IV of SCOTLAND to Margaret Tudor (1489–1541), eldest daughter of HENRY VII. The son born of this marriage in 1512 became James V of Scotland at his father's death in 1513 and heir to his then childless uncle, HENRY VIII of England. In 1515, Margaret Tudor, then in her second marriage, to Archibald Douglas, Earl of Angus, gave birth to Margaret DOUGLAS, whose claim at birth to the English throne was inferior only to that of her elder half brother. Although both of Margaret Tudor's children were eventually superseded in the succession by Henry VIII's own children—Mary (see MARY I), Elizabeth, and Edward (see EDWARD VI)—the Scottish claims were revived in the 1530s when Henry VIII severed the English Church from Rome (see REFORMATION, ENGLISH).

Because James V and Margaret Douglas were orthodox Catholics, both were unacceptable to Henry VIII (see SUCCESSION, ACTS OF) but acceptable to English conservatives seeking a Catholic heir. James V died in December 1542, four years before Henry. He left his Scottish throne and his claim to the English throne to an infant daughter, Mary (see STUART, MARY, QUEEN OF SCOTS), born six days before his death. In 1544, Margaret Douglas married Matthew Stuart, Earl of Lennox, a member of a junior branch of the Scottish royal line. After the deaths without heirs of Henry VIII's children Edward VI and Mary I,

Margaret Douglas's two sons, Henry STUART, Lord Darnley, and Charles Stuart, Earl of Lennox, stood third and fourth in line for the English throne after their second cousin Elizabeth and their first cousin Mary, Queen of Scots. The marriage in 1565 of the two cousins, Mary and Darnley, combined the two Scottish claims in the person of their son, James VI of Scotland (see JAMES I).

Raised a Protestant after his mother was driven from Scotland to exile and imprisonment in England, James became a far more acceptable heir to England than his Catholic mother ever was. He finally made good the Stuart claim to the English throne when the childless Elizabeth died in March 1603. A remnant of his family's claim continued to haunt him in the person of his cousin, Arabella STUART, the daughter of his uncle, the Earl of Lennox. Persecuted and denied marriage, Arabella and her claim to the Crown died in the TOWER OF LONDON in 1615. *See also* the genealogical chart in Appendix 1: "Stuart Claim to the English Throne."

Further Reading: Maurice Ashley, *The House of Stuart: Its Rise and Fall,* London: J. M. Dent, 1980; Mortimer Levine, *The Early Elizabethan Succession Question,* Stanford, CA: Stanford University Press, 1966; Mortimer Levine, *Tudor Dynastic Problems, 1460–1571,* New York: Barnes and Noble, 1973; Rosalind Mitchison, *A History of Scotland,* 2nd ed., London: Routledge, 1982.

Stuart, Henry, Lord Darnley

(1546–1567)

Henry Stuart, Lord Darnley, was the son of Matthew Stuart, Earl of Lennox, and Margaret DOUGLAS, daughter of Margaret TUDOR. As a grandnephew of HENRY VIII, Darnley was a distant cousin of Elizabeth I and had a claim to the throne of England second only to that of Mary STUART, Queen of Scots. Darnley was born in Yorkshire and raised in England. With Elizabeth's permission, Darnley visited his cousin Mary in SCOTLAND in 1565. Mary was attracted to the young man, and she was encouraged in her affections for him by her trusted Italian advisor, David RIZZIO. Although the match was highly unpopular with the Scots nobles, the two were married in July 1565.

Darnley's crude and arrogant behavior soon alienated almost everyone at the Scottish court, including the queen. By early 1566, the

This posthumous portrait by Renold Elstracke of Henry Stuart, Lord Darnley, and his wife Mary, Queen of Scots, was probably made in about 1603, the year Darnley's son ascended to the English throne as James I. *By permission of the Folger Shakespeare Library.*

pregnant queen refused Darnley all access to herself and to power. Jealous of the influence Rizzio had with the queen, Darnley joined a conspiracy of Scots nobles against the royal favorite. In March 1566, he admitted a party of armed men into Holyrood Palace and led them to Rizzio, who was murdered within the queen's hearing. Despite Darnley's participation in the murder, the queen reconciled with him to win his support against the other murderers. She did not, however, forgive or forget, and she continued to deny him all real power.

Darnley tried to flee the country but was prevented from doing so by the onset of syphilis. Mary, now influenced by James HEPBURN, Earl of Bothwell, persuaded Darnley to convalesce at a house at Kirk o'Field outside EDINBURGH. Darnley was murdered there in February 1567, likely through the agency of Bothwell and possibly with the connivance of the queen (see DARNLEY MURDER). The son of Mary and Darnley, born in June 1566, eventually became James VI of Scotland and JAMES I of England. *See also* STUART CLAIM and the genealogical chart in Appendix 1: "Stuart Claim to the English Throne."

Further Reading: Caroline Bingham, *Darnley: A Life of Henry Stuart, Lord Darnley,* London: Constable, 1995; Jenny Wormald, *Mary, Queen of Scots,* London: Collins and Brown, 1991.

Stuart, James, Earl of Moray

(1531–1570)

An illegitimate son of James V, James Stuart, Earl of Moray, was a leading figure in the government of his half sister, Mary STUART, Queen of Scots, and the first regent for her son James VI (see JAMES I). James V acknowledged James Stuart as his son and provided for his education at St. Andrews University, where the reformer John KNOX converted him to PROTESTANTISM. After James V's death in 1542, Stuart supported the Catholic regent, Marie de GUISE, mother of the queen, but by 1560 he joined the Lords of the Congregation, a group of Protestant nobles in rebellion against her. By 1561, the death of Marie de Guise and the conclusion of the Treaty of Edinburgh ended the civil war between Protestants and Catholics and made possible the return of Mary, then a widow, to SCOTLAND (see EDINBURGH, TREATY OF).

Mary came to an understanding with her Protestant half brother, whom she created Earl of Moray and leader of her council. The new regime made no attempt to impose uniformity of religion on Scotland; the queen accepted the primacy of the Protestant Church of Scotland, and Moray tolerated the Catholicism of the queen and a minority of her subjects. This arrangement collapsed in 1565 when the queen married Henry STUART, Lord Darnley, whose influence threatened Moray's position. In August, before fleeing to England, Moray led an ineffective rebellion known as the CHASE-ABOUT RAID. Mary pardoned him for his rebellion in March 1566, shortly after the assassination of her secretary, David RIZZIO, an act with which Moray agreed. The earl was probably also a passive participant in the murder of Lord Darnley in February 1567 (see DARNLEY MURDER). Upon learning of Mary's intention to wed James HEPBURN, Earl of Bothwell, Moray fled to FRANCE, but he returned after the queen's forced abdication in July 1567 to become regent for the infant James VI.

When Mary escaped from confinement in May 1568, Moray defeated her forces at the Battle of Langside (see LANGSIDE, BATTLE OF), then cooperated with William CECIL and other Protestants in the English government to convince Elizabeth to keep Mary a prisoner in England, where she had fled after Langside.

As part of this effort, Moray produced the CASKET LETTERS, which seemed to prove Mary's involvement in the murder of Darnley. Moray was assassinated in January 1570 by Hamilton of Bothwellhaugh, whose family supported Mary Stuart. *See also* STUART CLAIM and the genealogical chart in Appendix 1: "Stuart Claim to the English Throne."

Further Reading: Maurice Lee, *James Stewart, Earl of Moray,* New York: Columbia University Press, 1953.

Stuart, Mary, Queen of Scots

(1542–1587)

Mary Stuart was the only surviving child of James V of SCOTLAND and his French wife, Marie de GUISE. The sudden death of her father made Mary queen of Scotland within days of her birth. Mary was sent to FRANCE in 1548 to frustrate English attempts to bring her to England as the future wife of EDWARD VI. She was raised in France as a Catholic by her Guise relatives (see GUISE FAMILY) who arranged her MARRIAGE to the dauphin (the heir to the French throne) in 1558. Mary became queen of France at her husband's accession as Francis II in 1559, but she returned to Scotland in 1561 after Francis's death.

Although a Catholic, Mary accepted the Protestant reformation that had swept Scotland in 1560 (see REFORMATION, SCOTTISH) and ruled with the advice of her Protestant half brother, James STUART, Earl of Moray, an ille-

Mary Stuart, Queen of Scots, painted by an unknown artist about 1578. *By courtesy of the National Portrait Gallery, London.*

gitimate son of James V. As a granddaughter of Margaret Tudor, Queen Elizabeth's aunt, Mary had a strong claim to the English Crown, and she pressed her cousin Elizabeth to recognize her as heir to the throne. When Elizabeth declined to do so, Mary refused to confirm the 1560 Treaty of Edinburgh (see EDINBURGH, TREATY OF). In 1565, the Scottish queen married Henry STUART, Lord Darnley, another cousin with a claim to the English throne. Darnley proved weak, devious, and arrogant, and he soon alienated Mary, who denied him any part in the government. Although Darnley connived at the murder of her Italian favorite, David RIZZIO, Mary enlisted his support against the Protestant nobles who committed the murder and was able to regain control of the government. In June 1566, Mary gave birth to a son she named James.

As Darnley's position in Scotland grew increasing untenable, he sought to flee the country but was prevented from doing so by the onset of syphilis. Mary convinced him to recuperate at Kirk o'Field, a house outside EDINBURGH. Darnley was murdered there in February 1567 (see DARNLEY MURDER). Mary gave substance to charges that she had plotted the murder with James HEPBURN, Earl of Bothwell, when she married Bothwell after he carried her off to his castle. A confederation of Protestant nobles defeated the forces of Mary and Bothwell at Carberry in June 1567 and forced the queen to abdicate in the following month in favor of her year-old son (see CARBERRY, BATTLE OF). In May 1568, she escaped from Lochleven Castle, but defeat at the Battle of Langside forced her to flee to England, where she was held in confinement for 19 years by order of Queen Elizabeth (see LANGSIDE, BATTLE OF).

Mary's frequent plotting with English and foreign Catholics (see RIDOLFI PLOT; BABINGTON PLOT) to win her freedom and to dethrone Elizabeth in favor of herself led, at last, to her trial for TREASON in 1586 and her execution in February 1587. Her son, James VI of Scotland, strongly protested her execution, but took no action, being unwilling to jeopardize his own claim to the English succession. Raised a Protestant, Mary's son followed Elizabeth on the English throne in 1603 as JAMES I. See also STUART CLAIM; illustra-

tion for STUART, HENRY, LORD DARNLEY; and the genealogical charts in Appendix 1: "Stuart Claim to the English Throne;" "House of Tudor, 1485–1603."

Further Reading: Gordon Donaldson, *Mary, Queen of Scots*, London: English Universities Press, 1974; Antonia Fraser, *Mary, Queen of Scots*, New York: Delacorte Press, 1969; Rosalind K. Marshall, *Queen of Scots*, Edinburgh: HMSO, 1986; Jenny Wormald, *Mary, Queen of Scots*, London: Collins and Brown, 1991.

Stucley, Sir Thomas. *See* STUKELEY, SIR THOMAS.

Stukeley, Sir Thomas (c. 1525–1578)

Sir Thomas Stukeley (or Stucley) was a flamboyant and treacherous adventurer and pirate. Although born into a West Country family, Stukeley's strong resemblance to HENRY VIII led to rumors that he was the king's illegitimate son. Little is known of Stukeley's early life. A servant of Edward SEYMOUR, Duke of Somerset, Stukeley fled to FRANCE when Somerset fell from power in 1549. In 1552, Stukeley returned to England and informed the government that HENRI II planned to attack CALAIS and had sent him to England to learn about the town's defenses. The astounded PRIVY COUNCIL was unsure whether Stukeley was telling the truth or simply attempting to win a handsome reward. Aware of Stukeley's connections to Somerset, John DUDLEY, Duke of Northumberland, the chief minister of EDWARD VI, refused to believe Stukeley's tales and imprisoned him in the TOWER OF LONDON. Released shortly thereafter, Stukeley fled again to the continent and entered the service of the Duke of Savoy.

In the 1560s, Stukeley came to the COURT of Elizabeth with a scheme for founding an English colony in Florida. Although he was able to persuade the queen to provide a ship, the colonization plan was nothing more than a ruse to put together a fleet with which to conduct acts of piracy. The queen arrested Stukeley in 1565 when outraged foreign governments demanded that action be taken against him for his attacks on their shipping. Stukeley was pardoned in 1566 and allowed to go to IRELAND, where he expressed a willingness to aid Shane O'NEILL in Ulster and attempted to ingratiate himself with Sir Peter CAREW. However, by June 1569 he was imprisoned in DUBLIN

Castle for engaging in suspicious correspondence with PHILIP II of SPAIN.

Released for lack of evidence, Stukeley fled to Spain and began plotting TREASON in earnest. He won the favor of Philip by fighting bravely at the Battle of Lepanto in 1571, and soon began advocating a Catholic invasion of Ireland. He persuaded Pope GREGORY XIII to support the effort but then betrayed the pope by diverting the papal troops intended for Ireland to the King of Portugal's invasion of Morocco. This betrayal was his last, for Stukeley was killed in Morocco at the Battle of Alcazar in August 1578.

Further Reading: John Izon, *Sir Thomas Stucley,* London: Andrew Melrose, 1956.

subscription crisis

The subscription crisis was provoked by Archbishop John WHITGIFT's attempt to remove Puritan nonconformists from benefices within the ANGLICAN CHURCH (see BENEFICE). In October 1583, Whitgift required all Anglican clergy to accept three articles. The first article stated that the queen had supreme authority on earth in all matters spiritual—a statement designed to uncover Catholics, who ascribed such authority to the pope, and presbyterians, who vested such power in church councils (see PRESBYTERIAN MOVEMENT). The second article declared that the *BOOK OF COMMON PRAYER* contained nothing contrary to scripture, a statement many PURITANS were unwilling to accept because they believed the Prayer Book allowed many Catholic usages (see VESTIARIAN CONTROVERSY). The third declaration required acceptance of the THIRTY-NINE ARTICLES, the basic statement of Anglican faith passed by CONVOCATION and issued by the queen in 1563. Puritans also quibbled with many of the doctrines set forth in this statement.

Whitgift's articles (especially the second one) caused an uproar; some 350 clergymen refused to subscribe (i.e., sign) and stood to lose their livelihoods. Lay supporters of these clergymen, ranging from county JUSTICES OF THE PEACE to such Puritan sympathizers on the PRIVY COUNCIL as William CECIL, Lord Burghley; Sir Francis WALSINGHAM; and Sir Francis KNOLLYS, protested the archbishop's actions. When the Council summoned

Whitgift to explain himself, he declared that the English Church was his charge and that he required freedom of action to properly administer it. In 1584, he lessened the demand for article two by asking only for a promise to use the Prayer Book. This compromise prevented most Puritans from losing their benefices.

However, Whitgift continued to employ the Court of High Commission to punish the most radical Puritan nonconformists, a practice that led to the convening of the Lambeth Conference in 1584 (see HIGH COMMISSION, COURT OF). Meeting under the presidency of Robert DUDLEY, Earl of Leicester, the conference brought Whitgift and his supporters together with leading Puritans but accomplished little else. The Puritans then turned to PARLIAMENT to curb Whitgift. This tactic failed when Elizabeth backed the archbishop and the ANGLICAN SETTLEMENT of 1559. Even though the subscription crisis brought the Anglican Church leadership into conflict with the Protestant GENTRY, the people upon whom the Crown relied to govern the counties (see LOCAL GOVERNMENT), Elizabeth's support settled the matter in Whitgift's favor.

Further Reading: Patrick Collinson, *The Elizabethan Puritan Movement,* Oxford: Clarendon Press, 1990.

subsidy

Under the Tudors (see TUDOR FAMILY), the subsidy was a parliamentary tax on lands, goods, and wages that was to be carefully and realistically assessed on each individual each time the tax was voted. The subsidy began as a supplement to the fixed amounts raised by the older types of parliamentary taxation, the tenth and fifteenth, the assessments of which, being based on medieval tradition, had ceased to be realistic reflections of national wealth in the sixteenth century. The rate of subsidy assessment varied, but, with realistic current valuations, a tax rate of 10 percent might raise as much as £100,000 per year for the government, making subsidies attractive to the Crown.

Early in her reign, Elizabeth, who was by nature parsimonious, limited how much TAXATION she asked of PARLIAMENT, but the long and expensive war with SPAIN after 1585 forced the Crown to ask for more and bigger subsidies from later Parliaments. Because the task of assessing and collecting parliamentary taxes fell on the unpaid local JUSTICES OF THE PEACE, Elizabethan assessments for subsidies had already begun the process of hardening into fixed amounts, as had happened with the tenth and fifteenth in earlier centuries. Elizabethan assessments were thus already less in line with real land and property values than subsidy assessments made earlier in the century, and later Parliaments often had to be asked for several subsidies at a time to help fund the Spanish war.

Further Reading: F. C. Dietz, *English Public Finance, 1485–1641,* 2nd ed., London: F. Cass, 1964; G. R. Elton, *England under the Tudors,* 3rd ed., London: Routledge, 1991.

Succession, Acts of

In an age of personal monarchy, an uncontested succession to the throne was of vital importance to the political and economic stability of the realm. In the fifteenth century, the WARS OF THE ROSES (see also YORKIST CLAIM) showed how damaging contending claims to the Crown could be. The fear of renewed dynastic war haunted HENRY VIII in the 1520s because he had no male heir. Henry had a daughter, Mary (see MARY I), but England had never known a reigning queen, and a woman ruler seemed unnatural to most men, who considered governing an exclusively male occupation. In 1533, Henry's fears for the succession led him to divorce his wife, CATHERINE OF ARAGON, to marry Anne BOLEYN, who also bore him a daughter, Elizabeth.

In March 1534, PARLIAMENT passed the Act of Succession, the first English statute to define the future succession to the Crown. The act declared the Aragon marriage invalid and the Boleyn marriage "true, sincere, and perfect." Mary, by implication illegitimate, was removed from the succession and the Crown was settled on Henry's children by Anne. In June 1536, after the execution of Anne Boleyn, a second Succession Act repealed the first statute, declared the first two marriages invalid, pronounced both Mary and Elizabeth illegitimate, and settled the succession on Henry's heirs by his new wife, Jane SEYMOUR, who finally produced the long-awaited son, Edward (see EDWARD VI), in October 1537.

But the king's matrimonial adventures, and the religious upheaval that accompanied them, left the succession after Edward in confusion. If the sickly prince died without heirs, who would follow him—his two bastardized sisters, his Catholic Stuart cousins in SCOTLAND, or his Protestant Grey cousins? In 1544, the third Succession Act declared the proper succession to be Edward and his heirs, Mary and her heirs, and then Elizabeth and her heirs. Empowered by this act to name further heirs in his will, Henry altogether excluded the Scottish Stuart line (see STUART CLAIM), which descended from his elder sister Margaret, and placed the Grey line (see GREY CLAIM), which descended from his younger sister Mary, next after Elizabeth. Ironically, because the holders of the Stuart and Grey claims in the next generation were Mary STUART, Queen of Scots, and Jane GREY, all serious claimants to the throne after Edward's death in 1553 were WOMEN, thus ensuring that the female rule Henry tried so hard to avoid would come to pass.

Under Elizabeth, the succession was complicated by the question of religion and by the queen's aversion to having a recognized successor who could serve as a focus for discontent, as she herself had unwillingly become during the reign of her sister, Mary I. Thus, the queen dealt harshly with Katherine Grey and Arabella Stuart, two women who had claims to the throne. Elizabeth invalidated Katherine Grey's secret marriage to taint her sons with illegitimacy and so bar them from the succession, and she denied Arabella Stuart any marriage at all. Both women died in confinement, victims of their too-close proximity to the Crown.

Further Reading: Mortimer Levine, *The Early Elizabethan Succession Question,* Stanford, CA: Stanford University Press, 1966; Mortimer Levine, *Tudor Dynastic Problems, 1460–1571,* New York: Barnes and Noble, 1973.

sumptuary laws

Although laws regulating DIET and dress were enacted throughout Europe from Roman times to the nineteenth century, Tudor sumptuary statutes mainly concerned restricting the wearing of certain types, qualities, and colors of apparel to certain social classes (see GENTRY; PEERAGE; SOCIAL HIERARCHY). Although social mobility was increasing, Tudor society was highly class conscious, and sumptuary laws attempted to maintain class distinctions in an increasingly fluid social environment. Sumptuary laws also arose out of religious concerns, intensified by the Reformation and the rise of Puritanism (see PURITANS; REFORMATION, ENGLISH), that widespread extravagance in dress and diet had harmful effects on public morals. Economic concerns also prompted sumptuary legislation, as the government tried to encourage domestic industries, especially the CLOTH INDUSTRY, and to discourage overconsumption of foreign goods.

PARLIAMENT passed the most extensive and detailed Tudor sumptuary statute in 1510, early in the reign of HENRY VIII. Later sumptuary laws amended and reaffirmed the directives of the 1510 enactment. Adopted in 1559, the major Elizabethan sumptuary statute reiterated the importance of previous legislation and detailed all existing restrictions on apparel. For instance, the statute restricted the wearing of cloth of gold to earls and above, the wearing of woolen cloth made outside the realm to peers and their families, and the wearing of fur trim made from fur obtained outside England to men whose annual income exceeded £100. Servants could wear no fur at all unless they were the servants of peers or gentlemen (i.e., no merchant could dress his servants in fur), and husbandmen and common laborers could wear no hose worth more than 10 pence a yard.

The restricted colors were purple, which was confined to the royal family alone, and scarlet, which was reserved for the monarch and the highest nobility. Punishment for violations of the statute ranged from confiscation of the offending article to fines running from a few shillings to £10. Regular re-enactment of sumptuary legislation was necessary because the laws were rarely enforced and frequently ignored. In 1597, Elizabeth had to issue a PROCLAMATION calling again for adherence to sumptuary legislation and expanding and elaborating the existing restrictions (see FASHION, MEN; FASHION, WOMEN). *See also* REFORMATION, ENGLISH.

Further Reading: Alan Hunt, *Governance of the Consuming Passions: A History of Sumptuary Law,* New York: St. Martin's Press, 1996; Aileen Ribeiro, *Dress and Morality,* New York: Holmes and Meier, 1986.

supremacy, royal

The royal supremacy refers to the right of the English monarch to control the English Church. Prior to the 1530s, control over the English Church was shared between the English Crown and the papacy. The unwillingness of the pope, for political reasons, to grant HENRY VIII an annulment of his marriage led Henry to embrace a theory that claimed the king had been given the rule of England by God, had no superior on earth in England, and thus had the rule of the English Church, as well as of the English state. Henry forced the English Church to accept him as its supreme head, and he had the Archbishop of Canterbury pronounce his divorce and marry him to Anne BOLEYN, Elizabeth's mother.

Because the king's headship over the Church came from God, not PARLIAMENT, the 1534 Act of Supremacy only acknowledged the royal right to control the Church and gave the king authority to punish anyone who denied that right. Henry did not claim the sacramental functions of a priest; he could not, for instance, administer the sacraments. He did, however, claim the right to appoint bishops, discipline and tax clergy, declare doctrine, determine ritual, and conduct Church administration. Although most of these functions were exercised through Parliament, the king's authority in these matters was understood to exist independent of Parliament.

In 1559, when Elizabeth I sought to re-establish the royal supremacy, which her sister MARY I had abolished, she faced difficulties imposed by her gender and by the growth of English PROTESTANTISM. That a woman should govern the state, let alone the Church, was a difficult proposition for most Englishmen. That any layperson, male or female, should hold absolute sway over ecclesiastical matters was a proposition increasingly questioned not only by Catholics, but also by radical Protestants, especially the MARIAN EXILES who had observed the continental churches of Germany and Switzerland. To meet these objections, the Elizabethan Act of Supremacy (see ANGLICAN SETTLEMENT) gave the queen the title of supreme governor, rather than her father's more exalted title of supreme head. Also, by stating that the right to govern the Church was given to the Crown by Parliament, the act associated Parliament with the queen in the leadership of the Church and gave Parliament greater authority over Church doctrine and administration. *See also* ANGLICAN CHURCH.

Further Reading: Claire Cross, *The Royal Supremacy in the Elizabethan Church,* New York: Barnes and Noble, 1969; Norman L. Jones, *Faith by Statute,* London: Royal Historical Society, 1982.

Survey of Cornwall

Published in 1602, Richard CAREW's *Survey of Cornwall* is one of the most readable surviving examples of the Tudor county history, a historical genre developed by Elizabethan antiquaries (see ANTIQUARIANISM). A distant cousin of Sir Peter CAREW and of George CAREW, Earl of Totnes, and a member of a long-standing Cornish GENTRY family, Richard Carew was a member of the Antiquarian Society and a colleague of such well-known Elizabethan antiquaries as William CAMDEN and Sir Robert COTTON. Carew began writing the *Survey* more than a decade before its publication; he abandoned the project for a time before revising and completing the work in 1602.

The *Survey* is divided into two books, the first being a general history and topographical survey of the county of Cornwall and the second being a series of detailed descriptions of the nine individual hundreds (an ancient administrative division of an English shire) that comprise the county. Book 1 begins with descriptions of the location, climate, and inhabitants of Cornwall. Carew spent much time on Cornish minerals, especially the history and customs of the tin mining industry. He also discussed the county's chief agricultural commodities, its birds and wildlife, and its fish and waterways. Turning to the inhabitants of Cornwall, Carew explained types of land tenure; houses, roads, and bridges; and the history of the Cornish language (a form of ancient Celtic). Carew then estimated the size and distribution of the Cornish POPULATION and listed the county's important figures, including many of Carew's own ancestors and relatives. The book concludes with sections on social class (see SOCIAL HIERARCHY), civil and religious government (see LOCAL GOVERNMENT), and Cornish recreations.

Book 2 lists important persons, places, and events in each of the hundreds, as well as providing topographical and historical surveys of each hundred. Unlike other Elizabethan antiquaries, Carew was less interested in the natural beauty of his county than in the improvements made to it by humans. The *Survey* therefore gives more attention to towns, villages, fields, mines, and gardens than to coastlines and wild moors. This attention to human detail, as well as Carew's focus on his own and neighboring families, makes the *Survey of Cornwall* a valuable resource for social historians of the Elizabethan period.

Further Reading: F. E. Halliday, ed., *Richard Carew of Antony: The Survey of Cornwall,* London: Andrew Melrose, 1953.

Sussex, Earl of. *See* RADCLIFFE, THOMAS, EARL OF SUSSEX.

T

Talbot, Elizabeth, Countess of Shrewsbury. *See* HARDWICK, ELIZABETH, COUNTESS OF SHREWSBURY.

Talbot, George, Earl of Shrewsbury
(c. 1528–1590)

George Talbot, sixth Earl of Shrewsbury, was the longtime custodian of Mary STUART, Queen of Scots. A soldier in his early life, Talbot took part in the 1547 Scottish campaign led by Edward SEYMOUR, Duke of Somerset. Talbot succeed his father in the wealthy earldom of Shrewsbury in September 1560. In February 1568, two years after the death of his first wife, Shrewsbury became the fourth husband of Elizabeth HARDWICK, thus initiating what was to be a stormy marriage.

In 1569, Queen Elizabeth placed her unwelcome prisoner, Mary Stuart, in the earl's keeping. Shrewsbury kept Mary honorably confined in his houses at Tutbury, Chatsworth, and Sheffield Castle, treating her as a queen and allowing her to maintain the semblance of COURT etiquette. For this costly and difficult service, the earl suffered Mary's complaints about the harshness of her treatment and the PRIVY COUNCIL's suspicions about the leniency of her treatment. When the relationship between the earl and his wife deteriorated, the countess denounced her husband to the Council for plotting with Mary, but she had to withdraw the charges when she could produce no proof. Shrewsbury sought permission for a divorce, but the queen forced husband and wife to reconcile.

Despite the earl's marital problems and the suspicions of her ministers, Elizabeth trusted Shrewsbury completely, appointing him high steward of England and naming him a judge at the 1572 trial of Thomas HOWARD, Duke of Norfolk, whom Shrewsbury succeeded as earl marshal of England. Mary was removed from Shrewsbury's keeping in September 1584 and placed in the more strictly exercised custody of Sir Amias PAULET. Shrewsbury attended Mary's trial in October 1586 and her execution in February 1587. He died on 18 November 1590.

Further Reading: David N. Durant, *Bess of Hardwick: Portrait of an Elizabethan Dynast,* New York: Atheneum Publishers, 1978; Antonia Fraser, *Mary, Queen of Scots,* New York: Delacorte Press, 1969.

Tallis, Thomas (c. 1505–1585)

A friend, mentor, and collaborator of the Elizabethan composer William BYRD, Thomas Tallis was one of the most important figures in Tudor MUSIC. Tallis began his career as an organist at the Abbey of the Holy Cross in Waltham, Essex. At the dissolution of the abbey in 1540, Tallis moved first to Canterbury, where he served as a clerk at the cathedral, and then to LONDON, where he was appointed a gentleman of the CHAPEL ROYAL by HENRY VIII. By 1572, he was organist at the Chapel Royal, a position he shared with his former pupil William Byrd.

In January 1575, Elizabeth granted Tallis and Byrd a monopoly on the printing, publishing, and sale of music and music paper (see MONOPOLIES). The partners' first publication was a collection of their own motets (i.e., choral works on a sacred theme) entitled *Cantiones Sacrae.* Dedicated to the queen, *Cantiones*

Sacrae, which contained 16 pieces by Tallis and 18 by Byrd, was the only work Tallis published during his lifetime save for five pieces that appeared in a collection of anthems printed by John Day in 1563. Unlike Byrd, who became a Catholic, Tallis was a conforming Anglican and wrote many hymns and musical accompaniments that were to become traditional elements of Anglican worship.

Tallis was the first composer to write music to the ENGLISH words used in the Anglican service, and the first to adapt medieval compositions and formats to Anglican worship. Much of his church music, including his *Venite* for four voices and his much-loved *Litany,* were first published in 1641 in John Barnard's *First Book of Selected Church Music.* Through the popularity of his church music, such as the 40-part motet, *Spem in Alium,* and his many hymns, Tallis gave the ANGLICAN CHURCH a rich musical heritage, and through his collaboration with Byrd, Tallis had a strong influence on later English composers. Tallis, who had served in the Chapel Royal through four reigns and several shifts in religion, died at his house at Greenwich on 23 November 1585.

Further Reading: Paul Doe, *Tallis,* 2nd ed., London: Oxford University Press, 1976; David Wulstan, *Tudor Music,* Iowa City: University of Iowa Press, 1986.

Tarlton, Richard (d. 1588)

Richard Tarlton was the most popular jester and comic actor in Elizabethan England. Little is known about Tarlton's early life; accounts written after his death variously place his birth in Shropshire, Essex, or LONDON. In 1583, when he was already a well-known performer, Tarlton became a founding member of the Queen's Men acting company. He frequently performed at COURT for the queen, who found him amusing until she judged some of his jokes at the expense of royal FAVORITES Robert DUDLEY, Earl of Leicester, and Sir Walter RALEIGH to have gone too far.

Tarlton also performed frequently at The Theatre, James BURBAGE's popular London playhouse. He was also a writer of comedies, although many of his works, such as *Tarlton's Toys* (1576), *Tarlton's Tragical Treaties* (1578), and *Tarlton's Devise upon This Unlooked for Great Snow* (1579), are now lost and known only from their listing in the STATIONERS'

REGISTER. His *Seven Deadly Sins,* written for the Queen's Men in 1585, was among his most popular and widely performed works.

So popular was he that long after his death in 1588, his well-known image—a small, flat-nosed man dressed in a russet coat with large breeches and carrying a long stick—appeared on pubs, inns, and other establishments throughout London and southeastern England. Many pamphlets, poems, and ballads supposedly by or clearly about Tarlton also appeared after his death. Certain references to Yorick in William SHAKESPEARE's play *Hamlet* are thought to be about Tarlton. *Tarlton's Jests,* which was published in 1611, contains a version of his career and records various episodes from his life, including a story (later told also of Raleigh) about how his friend shouted "fire!" and doused Tarlton with a bucket of water the first time he saw him smoking.

Further Reading: G. B. Harrison, *Elizabethan Plays and Players,* Ann Arbor: University of Michigan Press, 1956.

taxation

To meet budgetary shortfalls or to fight wars, the English monarch had to ask PARLIAMENT for grants of extraordinary taxation to supplement the Crown's ordinary revenues (see REVENUE, ROYAL). The medieval view was that subjects had a duty to support the government with taxes in times of emergency. Deciding when emergencies existed had always been left to the Crown. Nonetheless, the expectation was that monarchs would fund the ordinary workings of government out of their own revenues, such as the income from royal lands, and not trouble Parliament for taxation.

By the sixteenth century, the costs of government, of maintaining the monarch and the royal COURT, and, especially, of waging war, had risen dramatically, while the Crown's ordinary revenues had risen only slightly or declined. Although Elizabeth was a frugal monarch who had no FAMILY to support, she had to turn increasingly to Parliament to meet expenses, particularly after the start of war with SPAIN in 1585. Since the late fifteenth century, the first Parliament of a reign had granted the monarch the right to collect customs duties for life, as the Parliament of 1559 did for Elizabeth (see CUSTOMS REVENUE). However, the usual parliamentary grant was the tenth and fifteenth, a tax assessed on moveable property. By Elizabethan times, this tax no longer reflected the actual value of property but was set at a fixed amount, with one tenth and fifteenth raising about £30,000 from the laity and about one-third that amount from the clergy. If the government required more money, it asked for several tens and fifteenths and often spread collection (which was handled in the counties by the JUSTICES OF THE PEACE) over several years (see LOCAL GOVERNMENT).

From HENRY VIII's reign, the government began asking for subsidies, a tax in varying percentages on land, goods, fees, and wages that was to be reassessed each time it was granted to reflect the true value of the taxable items. Depending on the rate asked for, a SUBSIDY could raise over £100,000. However, by Elizabeth's reign, the subsidy, like the tenth and fifteenth, had begun to harden into a lesser fixed amount, and Elizabeth had to ask for several subsidies at one time.

Further Reading: F. C. Dietz, *English Public Finance 1485–1641,* 2nd ed., London: F. Cass, 1964.

tenth and fifteenth. *See* TAXATION.

Thirty-nine Articles
The Thirty-nine Articles constituted the formal statement of doctrine for the ANGLICAN CHURCH. Although promulgated as part of the ANGLICAN SETTLEMENT of religion in 1559, the articles, in their Latin form, were not formally approved by CONVOCATION until 1563. They were further revised and reissued in ENGLISH in 1571. The Elizabethan articles of religion were a revision of the Forty-two Articles, a Protestant statement of faith issued by the government of EDWARD VI in 1553 (see DUDLEY, JOHN, DUKE OF NORTHUMBERLAND). Those articles became irrelevant only a few months after their issuance when MARY I came to the throne and returned the English Church to papal rule and Roman Catholic doctrine.

The Elizabethan revision of Edward's statement of faith tended to be conservative—a compromise between competing forms of PROTESTANTISM that was designed to include as many people as possible within the new English Church. To this end, the Elizabethan articles denied the Catholic doctrine of TRAN-SUBSTANTIATION and based Anglican doctrine squarely on the authority of the Bible (see BIBLE, ENGLISH), but also used more moderate language than the earlier set of articles and allowed for the possibility of receiving Christ's body in a spiritual sense during communion, something that smacked too much of Catholicism for later PURITANS. The articles also softened the full-blown Calvinist doctrine of predestination and recognized that some ceremonies and practices were things indifferent to salvation and thus could vary in their form and usage without harming faith. The articles also recognized the monarch as head of the Church, but denied to her or him the power to administer sacraments or preach the word of God.

In 1559, many returning MARIAN EXILES, anxious to establish in England the more extreme forms of CALVINISM they had experienced in Europe, found the Thirty-nine Articles to be too conservative and expected that they would be altered or replaced within a short time. However, Elizabeth was satisfied with the tone and content of the articles and, much to the displeasure of Puritans, refused to make anything more than minor alterations to them during her reign. The Thirty-nine Articles are still the basis of Anglican doctrine today.

Further Reading: William P. Haugaard, *Elizabeth and the English Reformation,* Cambridge: Cambridge University Press, 1968; Oliver O'Donovan, *On the Thirty-Nine Articles: A Conversation with Tudor Christianity,* Exeter: Paternoster Press, 1986.

Throckmorton, Elizabeth. *See* RALEIGH, ELIZABETH.

Throckmorton, Sir Nicholas
(1515–1571)
Sir Nicholas Throckmorton was one of Elizabeth's ablest diplomats (see DIPLOMACY). When his distant relative, Katherine PARR, became queen in 1543, Throckmorton was appointed a member of her household, where he came into contact with Princess Elizabeth, who lived with Parr in 1547–48. At COURT after 1547, Throckmorton became a Protestant and a favorite of EDWARD VI (see FAVORITES), who knighted him. In 1554, Throckmorton went to the TOWER OF LONDON for involvement with Sir Peter CAREW and others in WYATT'S REBELLION. At his trial, Throckmorton so ably defended

Elizabethan diplomat Sir Nicholas Throckmorton was painted by an unknown artist about 1562. *By courtesy of the National Portrait Gallery, London.*

himself that he won an acquittal from the jury, whose members were themselves imprisoned for their verdict. Released in 1555, Throckmorton fled to Europe and stayed there until Elizabeth's accession to the throne in 1558 (see MARIAN EXILES).

In 1559, Elizabeth sent Throckmorton to FRANCE with instructions to work for the return of CALAIS and to learn of French intentions in SCOTLAND. He established good relations with Mary STUART, Queen of Scots, and kept Elizabeth's government informed of the plans of her powerful Guise uncles (see GUISE FAMILY). In the early 1560s, Throckmorton worked closely with the HUGUENOTS, and urged the queen to back them as a way to regain Calais. He argued strongly for the 1562 Treaty of Hampton Court, whereby the queen sent English troops to support the Huguenots (see HAMPTON COURT, TREATY OF; LE HAVRE EXPEDITION). Throckmorton was in Le Havre in February 1563, just before the PLAGUE-struck English garrison surrendered to the French. Sent to Rouen to conclude a peace treaty, Throckmorton was arrested by Catherine de MEDICI, who considered him responsible for the English intervention; he was not released until April 1564.

In 1565, Elizabeth sent Throckmorton to Scotland in an unsuccessful attempt to inter-est Mary in a marriage to Robert DUDLEY, Earl of Leicester. In 1567, Throckmorton returned to Scotland to learn of the Scottish lords' intentions toward their recently deposed queen. Always an adherent of Leicester and an opponent of William CECIL, Throckmorton, hoping to overthrow Cecil and settle the succession, became involved with Leicester in the secret plans of Thomas HOWARD, Duke of Norfolk, to wed Mary Stuart. When the plot collapsed, Throckmorton was imprisoned in the Tower. He was soon released, but his diplomatic career was finished. Throckmorton died shortly thereafter in February 1571; his daughter, Elizabeth Throckmorton, later married Sir Walter RALEIGH.

Further Reading: A. L. Rowse, *Ralegh and the Throckmortons,* London: Macmillan, 1962.

Throckmorton plot

The Throckmorton plot, an English Catholic conspiracy to murder Elizabeth and place Mary, Queen of Scots, on the English throne, seriously disrupted diplomatic relations between England and SPAIN and led to the creation of the BOND OF ASSOCIATION to protect Elizabeth. The plot was led by two young Catholic gentlemen, Francis Throckmorton and his brother Thomas, nephews of the Elizabethan diplomat Sir Nicholas THROCKMORTON (see DIPLOMACY).

After studying at Oxford, the brothers toured Europe (see GRAND TOUR), where they became involved with English Catholic exiles who were plotting with Spanish and papal agents to restore Catholicism in England (see CATHOLICISM, ENGLISH). In Paris, Francis Throckmorton met Mary's agent, Thomas Morgan, who put the young Englishman in contact with the Spanish ambassador in LONDON, Bernadino de Mendoza. In 1583, Throckmorton returned to London, where he began direct correspondence with Mary and coordinated communications between her, Morgan, and Mendoza. Sir Francis WALSINGHAM, Elizabeth's secretary of state, soon intercepted these communications. In November 1583, after being watched by Walsingham's spies for six months, Francis Throckmorton was arrested. Before he was taken, Throckmorton managed to destroy or send to Mendoza various damaging documents. Even so, a search of the house revealed a list of Catholic nobles and gentlemen willing to support a Spanish invasion.

Thomas Throckmorton fled the country after his brother's arrest, but other conspirators were taken and lodged in the TOWER OF LONDON with Francis, who confessed everything after being sent twice to the rack. Throckmorton was executed in July 1584. Mendoza, whose participation in the plot was too great to be overlooked, was ordered to leave the country in January 1584. He was the last Spanish ambassador to be resident in England during Elizabeth's reign. To explain Mendoza's expulsion, the English government published a pamphlet describing the Throckmorton conspiracy and the ambassador's role in it. The plot so alarmed the PRIVY COUNCIL that it issued the Bond of Association, whereby loyal Protestants pledged themselves to defend the queen and to destroy those who sought to harm her.

Further Reading: A. L. Rowse, *Ralegh and the Throckmortons,* London: Macmillan, 1962.

Tilbury Speech

On 8 August 1588, with the outcome of the previous week's naval encounters between the English fleet and the Spanish ARMADA still uncertain, Queen Elizabeth visited her troops at Tilbury. Arriving by state barge, the queen was met by Robert DUDLEY, Earl of Leicester, the army's commander. The queen and Leicester inspected the troops before Tilbury Fort and then participated in a prayer service. The queen wore a white velvet dress and rode a white horse; a silver cuirass (an armored breastplate) crossed her chest, and a page carried her silver helmet before her. Elizabeth passed slowly among her troops calling out "The Lord bless you all."

After spending the night in a nearby house, Elizabeth returned next day, 9 August, to address the army. Rumors were circulating in the camp that the Armada was returning and that Spanish troops in the NETHERLANDS were already embarking for England. Mounted again on her white gelding, Elizabeth delivered the following address to her army:

My loving people, we have been persuaded by some that are careful of our safety to take heed how we commit ourselves to armed multitudes, for fear of treachery. But I assure you, I do not desire to live in distrust of my faithful and loving people. Let tyrants fear! I have always so behaved myself that, under God, I have placed my chiefest strength and safeguard in the loyal hearts and goodwill of my subjects; and therefore am come amongst you, as you see, at this time, not for my recreation and disport, but being resolved, in the midst and heat of battle, to live or die amongst you all, and to lay down for God, for my kingdom, and for my people, my honor and my blood, even in the dust. I know I have the body of a weak and feeble woman, but I have the heart and stomach of a king, and of a king of England too; and I think foul scorn that Parma [Spanish commander in the Netherlands] or Spain, or any prince of Europe, should dare to invade the borders of my realm; to which, rather that any dishonor should grow by me, I myself will take up arms, I myself will be your general, judge, and rewarder of every one of your virtues in the field. I know already for your forwardness you deserve rewards and crowns; and we do assure you, on the word of a prince, they shall be duly paid to you. In the meantime, my Lieutenant-General [Leicester] shall be in my stead, than whom never prince commanded a more noble or more worthy subject; not doubting but that by your obedience to my general, by your concord in the camp, and by your valor in the field, we shall shortly have a famous victory over these enemies of God, my kingdom, and my people.

The Tilbury speech, joyously received, was recorded by Lionel Sharp, one of the queen's chaplains, and was later read to anyone who had been unable to hear the queen deliver it. The speech was a defining moment of the reign, the queen using the supposed disadvantage of her sex to explain for her people what she understood to be the nature of her special relationship with them. *See also* GRAVELINES, BATTLE OF.

Further Reading: Paul Johnson, *Elizabeth I,* New York: Holt, Rinehart and Winston, 1974; Garrett Mattingly, *The Armada,* Boston: Houghton Mifflin, 1959.

Tilney, Edmund (d. 1610)

As master of the revels for the last half of Elizabeth's reign, Edmund Tilney was responsible for expanding the authority of the office over LONDON theatres and acting companies. Born into a Suffolk GENTRY family, Tilney was distantly related to the HOWARD FAMILY and served as MP (member of PARLIAMENT) for the Surrey town of Gatton, a seat controlled by the Howard family. In 1568, Tilney wrote a tract on MARRIAGE entitled *The Flower of Friendship;* although Elizabeth had only recently fended off the unwelcome urgings of Parliament for her to marry, Tilney dedicated the work to her. If this indiscretion had any ill effects on Tilney's career, they had passed by 1579 when the queen appointed Tilney master of the revels, a position he held until his death.

The master of the revels headed the Office of Revels and organized all court ENTERTAINMENT. The mastership gave Tilney an allowance of £20 per year for lodgings and £15 per year for wardrobe and the expenses of running the Revels Office. In 1583, Tilney carried out royal orders by organizing a troupe of actors under royal patronage to be known as the Queen's Men. Throughout the 1580s, Tilney gradually extended the scope of his office to include the oversight of all acting companies, whose appearances at COURT he arranged, and all London theatres. By the 1590s, acting under the authority of the lord chamberlain, the chief officer of the royal household, Tilney was exercising increasing control over what was or was not performed. In 1589, for instance, he advised the mayor of London to close the theatres because of the suspected involvement of certain playwrights in the MARPRELATE TRACT controversy. As master, he also licensed all performances and censored plays the government found objectionable, such as *Sir Thomas More,* which is believed to have been at least partially written by William SHAKESPEARE.

After the accession of JAMES I in 1603, Tilney increasingly turned the work of his office over to his deputy, Sir George Buck, although Tilney continued to keep the office accounts and to collect the lucrative fees due to the master. Buck succeeded Tilney as master of the revels when the latter died at his house in Surrey in 1610. *See also* DRAMA; LYLY, JOHN.

Further Reading: Sydney Anglo, *Spectacle, Pageantry, and Early Tudor Policy,* 2nd ed., Oxford: Oxford University Press, 1997.

tithes

In medieval England, parish priests and holders of church benefices were entitled, for their support, to one-tenth of the produce and a portion of the labor of the peasants who worked the land pertaining to the parish or other BENEFICE. These payments in kind were known as tithes. The "great tithes" consisted of one-tenth of the wheat, oats, or other major grain crop of the parish, while the "small tithes" involved payments of lambs, fish, poultry, eggs, and similar products.

After the Reformation, when the ADVOWSON, or right to appoint a priest to the benefice, fell to laymen, particularly to gentlemen (see GENTRY; REFORMATION, ENGLISH) who acquired many former monastic properties, the laymen often kept the great tithes for themselves, leaving their clerical appointees to subsist on the small tithes.

By the Elizabethan period, many tithe payments in kind had been transformed into fixed annual monetary payments, and, in some cases, the payment of tithes in any form had ceased altogether. Unable to make a proper living, many parish ministers initiated suits in the CHURCH COURTS against the holder of the advowson or against the members of the parish for reinstatement of the ancient tithe payments. Disputes over tithes greatly contributed to the chronic poor relations that existed between the English clergy and laity, and exacerbated lay ANTICLERICALISM.

Further Reading: A. G. Dickens, *The English Reformation,* 2nd ed., University Park: Pennsylvania State University Press, 1989.

tonnage and poundage. *See* CUSTOMS REVENUE.

Topcliffe, Richard (1532–1604)

Richard Topcliffe was notorious in Elizabethan England as the master persecutor and torturer of Catholics, especially of captured Catholic priests. Born into a GENTRY family in Lincolnshire, Topcliffe was elected to PARLIAMENT for the town of Beverley in 1572, and was returned for the constituency of Old Sarum for every Parliament from 1586 until his death. Topcliffe entered the service of William CECIL, Lord Burghley, in 1573, becoming expert at extracting information under torture from Catholic priests and suspected Catholic plotters. Because the nature and extent of his activities at the TOWER OF LONDON soon began to arouse unfavorable comment even among Protestants, Topcliffe was given authority to interrogate prisoners in his own house, where, he boasted, he had a machine of his own invention that "compared with which the ordinary rack was mere child's play."

Topcliffe was so enthusiastic about his work that Burghley once had him briefly imprisoned for exceeding his instructions in the interrogation of certain prisoners. Topcliffe conducted the torture of some of the Babington conspirators (see BABINGTON PLOT) in 1586 and racked the Jesuit Robert SOUTHWELL 13 times during the three years of Southwell's imprisonment between 1592 and 1595. In the latter year, Topcliffe again found himself in prison for the savage excess with which he racked another Catholic, Thomas Fitzherbert.

Topcliffe was also a zealous hunter of Catholics, and in 1597 he led a briefly successful campaign to close down theatres in LONDON after Thomas NASHE's play, *Isle of Dogs,* was found to be critical of the government. As a result of Topcliffe's efforts, Nashe had to flee the city and playwright Ben JONSON was arrested. Aware of Topcliffe's activities, Elizabeth found them extremely distasteful but accepted the need for them when torture seemed the only way to acquire information about dangerous plots and treasons. In about 1602, the queen granted Topcliffe the Fitzherbert estates in Derbyshire, where he died in retirement in 1604.

Further Reading: James Heath, *Torture and English Law,* Westport, CT: Greenwood Press, 1982; Paul Johnson, *Elizabeth I,* New York: Holt, Rinehart and Winston, 1974; Leonard A. Parry, *The History of Torture in England,* Montclair, NJ: Patterson Smith, 1975.

Totnes, Earl of. *See* CAREW, GEORGE, EARL OF TOTNES.

Tower of London

Although originally a fortress and royal residence, the Tower of London was, by the sixteenth century, the most important English state prison. About 1077, William the Conqueror began building a large stone castle along the Thames at the southeast corner of the old Roman wall surrounding LONDON. Completed about 1097, the central keep of William's construction still remains; it is known as the White Tower because it was originally whitewashed. Various medieval kings surrounded the White Tower with new constructions, including the massive defensive enclosures built in the thirteenth century by Henry III and Edward I. In the twelfth century, during a period of civil war, King Stephen took up residence in the fortress, thereby initiating a tradition that new monarchs stay a few days at the Tower before moving in procession through London to their coronation at Westminster Abbey (see WESTMINSTER PALACE). Although this tradition ended in the sixteenth century, the Tower was used intermittently as a royal residence until the mid-seventeenth century.

By Tudor times, the Tower complex served as the royal mint, armory, and zoo, but it was used mainly as a state prison and the site of state executions. During the WARS OF THE ROSES in the fifteenth century, various important people mysteriously met their deaths or disappeared inside the Tower, including the deposed Henry VI, who was murdered there in 1471, and the two sons of Edward IV, who disappeared after being sent there by their uncle, Richard III, in 1483. Under HENRY VIII, the Tower witnessed the imprisonment and executions of two queens, including Elizabeth's mother, Anne BOLEYN, and of such other important and famous figures as Sir Thomas More and Thomas CROMWELL. Elizabeth was herself imprisoned in the Tower for a time in 1554 when she was suspected of supporting WYATT'S REBELLION and of plotting to depose her Catholic sister, MARY I. During Elizabeth's reign, the Tower continued to lodge numerous state prisoners, including Thomas HOWARD, Duke of Norfolk; Robert DEVEREUX, Earl of Essex; and many of the Catholic priests and missionaries who were executed for TREASON during the reign.

Conditions of imprisonment in the Tower often depended on a prisoner's social class and the nature of his or her crime. High-ranking prisoners, such as the Duke of Norfolk, were courteously treated and allowed visitors, books, playing cards, and occasional exercise in the

An early seventeenth-century view of the Tower of London (with the White Tower in the center) by Wenceslaus Hollar. © *The British Museum.*

Tower yard or on its walls. Catholic priests and plotters were often denied such privileges and sometimes subjected to torture if they refused to reveal required information. The lieutenant of the Tower had an annual budget for feeding and maintaining poorer and long-held prisoners, while wealthier prisoners whose confinement was of shorter duration were often expected to contribute to the cost of their upkeep and were required to pay for special foods or services permitted them by the queen. By the end of Elizabeth's reign, the royal apartments in the Tower had fallen into disrepair and the fortress was seen more as a prison and storehouse than as a royal residence.

Further Reading: Derek Wilson, *The Tower,* New York: Charles Scribner's Sons, 1978.

transubstantiation

Transubstantiation, the Catholic doctrine of the Eucharist, holds that during the sacrifice of the MASS (the Roman Catholic worship service), the bread and wine of communion are changed by God, on the elevation of the priest, into the actual body and blood of Christ. Except in appearance, the bread and wine have ceased to exist. Protestants denied the need to repeat the sacrifice of Calvary in the Mass and rejected the role of the priest as God's instrument in achieving the miracle. Most Protestants came to see the taking of bread and wine as merely commemorative of the Last Supper and denied the presence of the actual body and blood of Christ in the service.

By the Elizabethan period, rejection of transubstantiation had become an important component of Protestant belief, just as acceptance of the doctrine had become a defining element of Catholic belief. The ANGLICAN SETTLEMENT of religion denied the validity of transubstantiation and gave the new Anglican Church a Protestant view of the Eucharist. *See also* ANGLICAN CHURCH; CATHOLICISM, ENGLISH; PROTESTANTISM.

Further Reading: P. J. Fitzpatrick, *In Breaking of Bread: The Eucharist and Ritual,* Cambridge: Cambridge University Press, 1993.

travel

Although England and WALES are roughly the size of Wisconsin, travel through Elizabethan Britain was difficult. No national road system existed, the maintenance of highways being left to local parishes (see LOCAL GOVERNMENT). Some of the best roads in the country were those following the excellent system of highways built by the Romans before A.D. 410 for the rapid passage of their legions from one part of the island to another. Scarcely anything better was built in either England or Wales before the eighteenth century. City and town streets were little better than rural roads, often becoming impassable quagmires during spring rains.

Rivers could be serious obstacles to travel, for bridges solid enough to withstand floods were expensive and rare. Many smaller rivers and streams had to be forded on foot or horseback, with the latter being the most common mode of Elizabethan transportation. Although passenger carriages had appeared in England in the 1550s, they were used primarily by the wealthy and mainly in LONDON. Elizabeth I often traveled by carriage when on progress, but most other English travelers went by horse or foot (see PROGRESSES, ROYAL). Even for the queen, a long ride in a carriage lacking modern suspension must have been a bone-jarring experience on rough Elizabethan roadways. With a good horse, an Elizabethan traveler could traverse the kingdom fairly rapidly; the 170-mile journey from London to Exeter in the West Country usually took about three days. Thanks to an excellent system of royal couriers, who changed horses at regular intervals, the government could quickly send and receive news, with messages taking about two days to travel from the ports of the West Country to London, and less than one day to reach the capital from Dover on the Channel.

Travel by water was somewhat easier, with ferrymen plying a regular trade on the Thames between London and the more important royal PALACES, such as GREENWICH PALACE, RICHMOND PALACE, and HAMPTON COURT PALACE. However, outside the southeast, and especially in northern England and the mountains of central Wales, travel was difficult and infrequent. Although the GENTRY and nobility often moved between London and their home counties—and increasingly, overseas (see GRAND TOUR)—travel was limited by modern standards, with even the queen never journeying outside the southeastern corner of the kingdom during her lifetime.

Further Reading: Thomas Burke, *Travel in England from Pilgrim and Pack-Horse to Light Car and Plane,* London: B.T. Batsford, 1942; Penry Williams, *Life in Tudor England,* New York: G. P. Putnam's Sons, 1964.

treason

Because of the constant fear of Catholic plots and invasion, Elizabethan Parliaments passed much legislation expanding the definition of treason to include the activities of Catholic priests and sympathizers (see PARLIAMENTARY SESSIONS [1559–1581], [1584–1601]; PENAL LAWS). Unlike MARY I, who burned her religious opponents as heretics against the Catholic Church, Elizabeth executed her religious opponents as traitors against the English state. The basic English treason statute of 1352 made it treason to seek the death of the king or queen, to levy war against the king in England, or to support his enemies. Because treason involved a betrayal of the allegiance subjects owed their sovereign, a particularly heinous crime in a feudal society built on mutual trust between lord and vassal, the penalty for treason was death and confiscation of goods and property.

Commoners convicted of treason were hung, drawn, and quartered—i.e., dragged (drawn) to the execution site, hung but cut down before death, disemboweled, beheaded, and then cut into quarters. Traitors of noble birth were usually spared the horrors of this process and simply beheaded. In the 1530s, HENRY VIII expanded the scope of treason to include denying the royal supremacy (see SUPREMACY, ROYAL) or speaking against his marriages to Anne BOLEYN and Jane SEYMOUR. The religious nature of Elizabethan treason laws appeared in Elizabeth's first Parliament, which declared it treason to defend by word or deed the ecclesiastical jurisdiction of a foreign ruler or cleric (i.e., to support papal authority in England). The Parliament of 1563 declared refusing the oath to uphold the queen's supremacy over the English Church to be treason.

Elizabeth's excommunication by the papal bull *REGNANS IN EXCELSIS* led, in 1571, to acts making it treason to receive a papal bull in England, to deny that Elizabeth was queen or had the right to name a successor, to declare her a heretic, or to claim a place in the succession (see SUCCESSION, ACTS OF). In 1581, it became treason to reconcile others to Catholicism or to be reconciled oneself, or to draw any subject away from his or her allegiance to the queen or the ANGLICAN CHURCH. By 1585, simply being in England was treason for any Englishman ordained into the Catholic priesthood, and giving aid and comfort to a Catholic priest also became a capital offense.

Further Reading: John G. Bellamy, *The Tudor Law of Treason,* London: Routledge and K. Paul, 1979.

"treasure crisis" of 1568

The "treasure crisis" of 1568 caused the first serious breach in diplomatic relations between SPAIN and Elizabethan England (see DIPLOMACY). In November 1568, five small Spanish vessels sailed into the harbors of Plymouth and Southampton seeking shelter from storms and Huguenot pirates (see HUGUENOTS). The ships turned out to be carrying the huge sum £85,000 in gold and silver coin bound for the NETHERLANDS as payment for the troops of

Fernandez ALVAREZ DE TOLEDO, Duke of Alva. The treasure was brought ashore, whether by order of the English government or by request of the Spanish is unclear, and documents were discovered proving that the money, borrowed from Genoese bankers, would not belong to PHILIP II of Spain until it reached Alva. At this same point in time, on 3 December, Sir William CECIL received word of the Spanish attack on John HAWKINS and Francis DRAKE in the Spanish-American port of SAN JUAN D'ULLOA in September.

Learning of the Hawkins disaster and assured that the money was not yet the property of Spain, Elizabeth asked what terms the bankers would give her. Considering Elizabeth a much safer risk than Philip, the bankers agreed to loan her the money. The Spanish ambassador in England, Gerau de Spes, angrily protested this decision and advised Alva to seize all English ships and goods in the Netherlands, which Alva did on 29 December. The English retaliated by seizing Spanish ships and goods in English ports and placing de Spes under house arrest. Alva also instituted an embargo on English trade with the Netherlands that lasted almost five years.

Although the embargo harmed the economy of the Netherlands more than the economy of England, which found new trade outlets in Germany, the disruption of relations with Spain presented Elizabethan England with its first real threat of invasion. The English government, anxious about Spanish successes in the Netherlands and the possibility of internal plots on behalf of Mary STUART, Queen of Scots, feared that Philip might use the incident to retaliate militarily against England. Although neither country was ready for open war in the 1560s, the process whereby Anglo-Spanish relations deteriorated to that point began with the "treasure crisis." *See also* BRISTOL, TREATY OF; NYMEGEN, TREATY OF.

Further Reading: Wallace T. MacCaffrey, *The Shaping of the Elizabethan Regime,* Princeton, NJ: Princeton University Press, 1968.

treasurer. *See* OFFICERS OF STATE.

Treaty of Berwick (1560). *See* BERWICK, TREATY OF (1560).

Treaty of Berwick (1586). *See* BERWICK, TREATY OF (1586).

Treaty of Blois. *See* BLOIS, TREATY OF.

Treaty of Bristol. *See* BRISTOL, TREATY OF.

Treaty of Cateau-Cambrésis. *See* CATEAU-CAMBRÉSIS, TREATY OF.

Treaty of Edinburgh. *See* EDINBURGH, TREATY OF.

Treaty of Hampton Court. *See* HAMPTON COURT, TREATY OF.

Treaty of Nonsuch. *See* NONSUCH, TREATY OF.

Treaty of Nymegen. *See* NYMEGEN, TREATY OF.

Treaty of Richmond. *See* HAMPTON COURT, TREATY OF.

Treaty of Troyes. *See* TROYES, TREATY OF.

Troyes, Treaty of

The Treaty of Troyes between England and FRANCE ended the hostilities arising from Elizabeth's decision in 1562 to intervene in the French civil war on the side of the HUGUENOTS. Under the terms of the Treaty of Hampton Court, an agreement concluded with the Huguenot leadership by Sir William CECIL, Elizabeth sent an English garrison to hold the French town of Le Havre in pledge for the return of CALAIS to England when the Huguenots won the war (see HAMPTON COURT, TREATY OF). However, the Le Havre garrison under Ambrose DUDLEY, Earl of Warwick, suffered severely from the PLAGUE and then found itself surrounded when the Huguenots concluded a separate peace and joined the French royal army in besieging Le Havre. When the garrison was forced to surrender on 29 July 1563, Elizabeth opened negotiations with the French government that led, in April 1564, to the signing of the Treaty of Troyes.

Despite deep personal animosity between them, Elizabeth's two ambassadors in France, Sir Nicholas THROCKMORTON and Sir Thomas SMITH, were able to bring the negotiations to a successful conclusion. Besides ending the conflict, the Treaty of Troyes obligated France to reimburse Elizabeth for the cost of the expedition. The French also reaffirmed the acknowledgment of England's right to Calais that had been included in the 1559 Treaty of Cateau-Cambrésis, although both parties understood implicitly that the French payment of Elizabeth's expenses eliminated any real possibility of Calais being returned to England (see CATEAU-CAMBRÉSIS, TREATY OF).

The Treaty of Troyes significantly improved relations between England and France and led, in 1572, to the Treaty of Blois, an agreement that recognized the growing threat to both countries from SPAIN (see BLOIS, TREATY OF). After the disastrous outcome of the LE HAVRE EXPEDITION and the successful conclusion of the Treaty of Troyes, Elizabeth avoided further foreign entanglements and refused, despite pressure from her Protestant councilors, to give further aid to the Huguenots in their continuing struggle against the French Crown and the CATHOLIC LEAGUE.

Further Reading: Frederic J. Baumgartner, *France in the Sixteenth Century,* New York: St. Martin's Press, 1995; P. S. Crowson, *Tudor Foreign Policy,* New York: St. Martin's Press, 1973.

Tudor family

The Tudor family, of which Elizabeth I was the last member to wear the Crown, was the ruling dynasty of England for 118 years, from 1485 to 1603. The family originated in northwest WALES, tracing its ancestry to Ednyfed Fychan (d. 1246), steward to the Welsh prince Llywelyn the Great. In the 1420s, Owain ap Maredudd (Owain "son of Maredudd"), a descendant of Ednyfed Fychan, came to England, where he anglicized his name to Owen Tudor (from Tudur, his grandfather's name), perhaps to escape the civil disabilities placed on the Welsh by English law. Owen Tudor obtained a position in the household of Catherine of Valois, the widowed queen of Henry V (r. 1413–1422) and mother of Henry VI (r. 1422–1461, 1470–1471), kings of the royal house of Lancaster. Catherine fell in love with Owen, and the two were married secretly because the Council that governed for young Henry VI would never have sanctioned the MARRIAGE of the queen mother to an obscure Welshman.

The marriage produced two sons—Edmund and Jasper Tudor. Although the children had French royal blood through their mother, they had no English royal blood and no place in the English succession. In 1452, Henry VI brought his half brothers to COURT, gave them lands, and raised them to the English PEERAGE as Earl of Richmond (Edmund) and Earl of Pembroke (Jasper). In 1456, Edmund married Margaret Beaufort (see BEAUFORT FAMILY), a wealthy heiress and cousin to Henry VI. In January 1457, three months after Edmund's death, Margaret gave birth to a son, Henry Tudor, who inherited his mother's distant claim to the English throne.

The political upheaval of the WARS OF THE ROSES led to the extinction of the male line of Lancaster and to a break in the rival line of York, when Richard III usurped his nephew's throne in 1483. Henry Tudor invaded England from France in 1485 to make good his claim to the Crown. He won the throne (becoming HENRY VII) at the Battle of Bosworth, where Richard III was killed. Thus by a series of improbable circumstances, the obscure Welsh family of Tudor mounted the English throne. Henry VII (r. 1485–1509) was followed on the throne by his son HENRY VIII (r. 1509–1547), and three grandchildren—EDWARD VI (r. 1547–1553), MARY I (r. 1553–1558), and Elizabeth I (r. 1558–1603). *See also* genealogical charts in Appendix 1: "House of Tudor, 1485–1603."

Further Reading: Ralph A. Griffiths and Roger S. Thomas, *The Making of the Tudor Dynasty,* New York: St. Martin's Press, 1985.

Turkey Company. *See* LEVANT COMPANY.

Twelfth Night/Twelfth Day. *See* CHRISTMAS.

Tyrone, Earl of. *See* O'NEILL, HUGH, EARL OF TYRONE.

Tyrone's Rebellion. *See* NINE YEARS WAR.

U

Ulster enterprise (Essex)

In 1573, the year Sir Thomas SMITH's Ulster plantation (see PLANTATIONS, IRISH; ULSTER ENTERPRISE [SMITH]) came to ruin, Walter DEVEREUX, Earl of Essex, proposed a much more elaborate colonization scheme for northern IRELAND. Unlike Smith's joint-stock venture, Essex financed his expedition by mortgaging his English estates to the queen for £10,000 (see JOINT-STOCK COMPANY). Although Elizabeth agreed to share the costs of raising a force of 1,200 men, the expedition was a private effort; the earl had no government commission or salary. For conquering and colonizing the Antrim area of Ulster, Essex was to receive extensive rights and privileges in the region, including freedom from CESS and control of trade and the administration of justice. Part of the land to be conquered was to be reserved for the queen and part for the group of adventurers, like Sir Peter CAREW, and courtiers, like the sons of Henry CAREY, Lord Hunsdon, who accompanied the expedition.

Arriving in Ulster in the summer of 1573, Essex soon found himself facing a coalition of Irish chiefs, including Turlough Luineach O'NEILL, leader of the powerful O'Neill clan. The Irish leaders argued that because Essex held no government position, their opposition to his venture constituted no TREASON to the queen. As supplies dwindled and the weather deteriorated, many of the 400 adventurers who had accompanied Essex abandoned the venture, and the earl made little headway against the united Irish with his force of ill-armed recruits. In 1574, to meet the Irish leaders' arguments, the queen made Essex governor of Ulster and sent him reinforcements. Most of the Irish leaders then either withdrew their forces or submitted, but supply remained a problem and Lord Deputy William FITZWILLIAM in DUBLIN was uncooperative, seeing Essex's position in Ulster as a threat to his own authority.

Growing desperate, Essex invited his chief opponent, Sir Brian O'Neill, to a feast in November 1574. The earl then treacherously murdered O'Neill's company and sent the chief himself to Dublin for execution. In 1575, Essex sent a force under Francis DRAKE to attack the Scots on Rathlin Island, which was part of the earl's grant. On the island, the English troops found and massacred 600 men, women, and children. In May 1575, Elizabeth ended the project, recalled Essex, and negotiated a peace with Turlough O'Neill. The venture had been a costly failure both in money and lives.

Further Reading: Steven G. Ellis, *Tudor Ireland,* London: Longman, 1985; Colm Lennon, *Sixteenth-Century Ireland: The Incomplete Conquest,* Dublin: Gill and Macmillan, 1994; Margaret MacCurtain, *Tudor and Stuart Ireland,* Dublin: Gill and Macmillan, 1972; David B. Quinn, *The Elizabethans and the Irish,* Ithaca, NY: Cornell University Press, 1966.

Ulster enterprise (Smith)

The first attempt to establish an English plantation in northern IRELAND was undertaken by the queen's principal secretary (see OFFICERS OF STATE), Sir Thomas SMITH, and his son Thomas (see PLANTATIONS, IRISH). The Smiths received approval to colonize the Ards Peninsula of Ulster in 1572. To cover transportation and supply costs, they organized the venture as a joint-stock enterprise and stimulated investment by distributing pamphlets promoting the scheme (see JOINT-STOCK COMPANY). Investors were to receive land according to the amount of their investment. The Smiths first planned to clear the land of the "wicked, barbarous and uncivil people" who inhabited it, and then parcel out to the new English owners groups of poor Irish peasants to work the land for them. The Irish laborers were to be "gently entertained," but would also be denied most political and civil rights. Under these terms, the Smiths gathered a group of some 700 adventurers in Liverpool by May 1572.

After obtaining some of the Smiths' promotional literature, the local Irish chiefs protested their loyalty to the Crown and began to make preparations to resist the enterprise. In DUBLIN, the lord deputy warned that the venture would only cause rebellion. The queen, always concerned by the expense and political disruption associated with suppressing Irish rebellions, withdrew her approval of the expedition. While Sir Thomas Smith tried to convince the queen to reverse her decision, most of the adventurers abandoned the enterprise to join the band of volunteers Sir Humphrey GILBERT was raising for the NETHERLANDS.

The younger Smith finally landed in Ulster in late August with a force of only about 100 men. He was quickly attacked by one of the local chiefs and driven into Carrickfergus, where he appealed in vain for help from Lord Deputy William FITZWILLIAM in Dublin. Smith's group eventually reformed and took up some of the land in their grant, but in the fall of 1573, Thomas Smith the younger was killed by some of his Irish laborers, who then boiled his body and fed it to their dogs. The distraught elder Smith launched two new expeditions in 1574 and 1575, but enthusiasm and support for the project had evaporated with the news of his son's terrible end, and the Smiths' Ulster enterprise quickly faded out. *See also* ULSTER ENTERPRISE (ESSEX).

Further Reading: Steven G. Ellis, *Tudor Ireland,* London: Longman, 1985; Colm Lennon, *Sixteenth-Century Ireland: The Incomplete Conquest,* Dublin: Gill and Macmillan, 1994; Margaret MacCurtain, *Tudor and Stuart Ireland,* Dublin: Gill and Macmillan, 1972; David B. Quinn, *The Elizabethans and the Irish,* Ithaca, NY: Cornell University Press, 1966.

Uniformity, Acts of. *See* BOOK OF COMMON PRAYER.

Unitarianism. *See* ANABAPTISTS.

universities

The two English universities, Oxford and Cambridge, arose in the twelfth century when groups of male students gathered around the learned monks and teachers living in each town. By the thirteenth century, each university comprised a group of residential colleges. The colleges were corporations of students and instructors (masters) that had their own statutes, buildings, customs, and landed endowments. These medieval universities educated lower-class boys for careers in the English Church. Students attended lectures and participated in academic debates. The curriculum centered on the seven liberal arts (grammar, rhetoric, logic, arithmetic, geometry, astronomy, and music), the three philosophies (moral philosophy, natural philosophy, and metaphysics), and legal studies, the universities being the only training grounds in England for the civil and canon law used in medieval CHURCH COURTS.

By Elizabeth's reign, the Reformation had brought the universities, like the English Church itself, under royal control (see REFORMATION, ENGLISH; SUPREMACY, ROYAL). With the teaching of canon law prohibited after 1535, most of the universities' original purpose disappeared, and attendance declined sharply in the 1530s and 1540s. But in the 1550s, the universities revived as training centers for the wellborn sons of the GENTRY. By 1603, most JUSTICES OF THE PEACE, members of PARLIAMENT, and royal officials (see OFFICERS OF STATE) had received some university training. In the 1590s, the yearly number of incoming freshmen at Oxford was about 360, almost three and a half times the number of the 1510s. Many incoming students did not complete the full four-year course of study for a degree, leaving after two or three years to tour Europe (see GRAND TOUR) or to begin legal studies in the COMMON LAW at the INNS OF COURT.

The Elizabethan curriculum still focused on the seven liberal arts and the three philosophies, but it had been sufficiently influenced by HUMANISM to place heavier emphasis on the study of Greek and Latin. The expansion of Elizabethan trade and exploration also created a demand for more courses in geography and history and a call from men such as Francis BACON and Sir Humphrey GILBERT for more training in such practical skills as navigation. Although many Elizabethan clergymen took advanced degrees in divinity, and Cambridge, in particular, acquired a reputation as a Puritan school, the English universities by 1603 were increasingly secular institutions providing education for the sons of gentlemen. *See also* EDUCATION; GRAMMAR SCHOOL.

Further Reading: Hugh F. Kearney, *Scholars and Gentlemen: Universities and Society in Pre-Industrial Britain,* Ithaca, NY: Cornell University Press, 1970.

V

Valois family

Four members of the Valois dynasty occupied the French throne during Elizabeth's reign, and one member of the family almost married Queen Elizabeth. Having ruled FRANCE since 1328, the Valois family was one of the longest established royal dynasties in Europe when the Tudors first came to the English throne in 1485. Francis I (r. 1515–1547), a contemporary of HENRY VIII, was a Renaissance prince of taste and distinction; his constant battle for dominance in Italy with CHARLES V (see HABSBURG FAMILY), ruler of SPAIN, Germany, and the NETHERLANDS, threw Western Europe into political and economic disorder.

HENRI II, son of Francis I, continued the war until the financial exhaustion of both countries led him to make peace with PHILIP II of Spain, son of Charles V, in 1559, the first year of Elizabeth's reign. Henri II died in July 1559 of injuries received at a tournament celebrating the peace of Cateau-Cambrésis (see CATEAU-CAMBRÉSIS, TREATY OF). The French Crown passed to Henri's son Francis II (r. 1559–1560), the husband of Mary STUART, Queen of Scots, the Catholic claimant to the English throne. Only in his teens and sickly, Francis II was dominated by his wife's maternal uncles, the duke and cardinal of Guise (see GUISE, MARIE DE; GUISE FAMILY) who, as staunch Catholics, aimed to destroy PROTESTANTISM in France and restore Catholicism in England (see CATHOLICISM, ENGLISH). Francis II's death in December 1560 made his younger brother king as Charles IX and handed political power to his mother, Catherine de MEDICI. She sent Mary, Queen of Scots, back to Scotland and sought to balance the power of the Guises and the Catholic party with the growing strength of the Protestant HUGUENOTS. Civil war between the two religious factions culminated in the SAINT BARTHOLOMEW MASSACRE of 1572, when a frightened queen mother ordered the murder of Huguenot leaders who had gathered in Paris for a royal wedding.

When Charles IX died in 1574, the Crown passed to another brother, HENRI III (r. 1574–1589), who in the late 1570s promoted the MARRIAGE of his only remaining brother and heir, Francis VALOIS, Duke of Alençon, to the much older Queen Elizabeth. After much indecision, Elizabeth finally rejected the duke, who, after intervening disastrously in the Netherlands, died in 1584. The duke's death left the childless Henri III without a Catholic successor; the next heir was Henri Bourbon, the king's cousin and a Huguenot. In 1589, after further civil war, both Catherine de Medici and her son died; Henri Bourbon succeeded as HENRI IV (r. 1589–1610) but was not able, even with the help of Elizabeth (see BRITTANY EXPEDITIONS), to establish himself and the new Bourbon dynasty until he converted to Catholicism in 1593. *See also* the genealogical chart in Appendix 1: "Valois and Bourbon Dynasties of France."

Further Reading: Frederic Baumgartner, *France in the Sixteenth Century,* New York: St. Martin's Press, 1995; Milton Waldman, *Biography of a Family: Catherine de Medici and Her Children,* Boston: Houghton Mifflin, 1936.

Valois, Francis (Hercules), Duke of Alençon (1554–1584)

Francis Valois, Duke of Alençon, was Elizabeth I's most persistent and most seriously considered foreign MARRIAGE suitor. Alençon, the youngest son of HENRI II of FRANCE and Catherine de MEDICI, was christened Hercules but renamed Francis in 1560 after the death of his elder brother, Francis II. He became heir to the French throne in 1574 at the accession of his brother HENRI III, against whom he had openly conspired. He also inherited his brother's title, Duke of Anjou, but he is best known in Elizabethan history as the Duke of Alençon. He first paid suit to Elizabeth in 1572, when he was 18 and she 39. Negotiations for the match dragged on until 1576, while the duke plotted with HUGUENOTS against his mother and brother and generally made a nuisance of himself. To be rid of his unstable sibling, Henri III urged Alençon to win the leadership of the Dutch rebels, who were seeking a ruler to direct their war against SPAIN and were having difficulty interesting Elizabeth in the position.

By October 1578, Alençon had concluded an agreement with the Dutch legislature, the STATES-GENERAL, making him Protector of the Netherlands in return for military assistance against Spain. In August 1579, Elizabeth reopened marriage talks by allowing Alençon to visit her in person. Although the duke was ugly, short, and pockmarked, Elizabeth was delighted with him, calling him "my frog" and flirting with him before the COURT. Horrified by the idea of a French, Catholic consort, and fearful of their 46-year-old queen dying in childbed to leave the duke ruling over them, English Protestants vigorously opposed the match, as did Robert DUDLEY, Earl of Leicester, and other members of the PRIVY COUNCIL. Advised by the Council to reject the duke, Elizabeth did so reluctantly, sending him away with a large gift of money.

In 1581, Elizabeth revived the courtship in an attempt to gain France as an ally in the NETHERLANDS. In November, the queen slipped a ring on the duke's finger and announced their engagement, but within days she again changed her mind. Frustrated in his marriage suit, Alençon proved equally unsuccessful in war. His campaign in the Netherlands in 1583 ended in quarrels with the Dutch and defeat by the Spaniards. In June 1584, before he could resume campaigning, Alençon died in France at age 30, leaving the Dutch without a ruler and the French king without a Catholic heir. *See* genealogical chart in Appendix 1: "Valois and Bourbon Dynasties of France."

Further Reading: Susan Doran, *Monarchy and Matrimony: The Courtships of Elizabeth I,* London: Routledge, 1996; Wallace T. MacCaffrey, *Queen Elizabeth and the Making of Policy, 1572–1588,* Princeton, NJ: Princeton University Press, 1981.

Vere, Edward de, Earl of Oxford (1550–1604)

A noted Elizabethan courtier and poet, Edward de Vere, 17th Earl of Oxford, has in the twentieth century become a leading candidate for authorship of the plays traditionally attributed to William SHAKESPEARE. On his father's death in 1562, the 12-year-old earl became a ward of William CECIL, whose daughter Anne he married in December 1571 (see also CECIL, MILDRED). Educated at Cambridge and Oxford (see UNIVERSITIES), the earl showed an early aptitude for MUSIC, POETRY, and DANCE, but also displayed a violent and unstable personality. In 1567, Cecil hushed up the earl's involvement in the death of one of Cecil's servants, the coroner's jury having to be convinced that the "accidental" death was caused by the servant carelessly running onto Oxford's sword.

In 1571, after serving against the NORTHERN REBELLION, Oxford came to COURT, where his skill at dancing and verse made him a favorite of Elizabeth. He fled England in 1572, possibly after an attempt to rescue his imprisoned cousin, Thomas HOWARD, Duke of Norfolk. After being restored to favor in England, Oxford returned to Europe with permission in 1574, traveling for the next two years in Italy. His extravagant lifestyle and conversion to Catholicism estranged Oxford from his wife and father-in-law, but the queen continued to favor him despite his growing debts and involvement in a violent quarrel with Sir Philip SIDNEY at WHITEHALL PALACE in 1579. Elizabeth finally sent Oxford to the TOWER

OF LONDON in 1581 when he impregnated Anne Vavasour, one of her LADIES-IN-WAITING. Oxford won his release by promising to return to his wife, who died in 1588. In 1582, Oxford fought a duel with Vavasour's cousin, an incident that resulted in the deaths of several servants. In 1585, the earl served under John NORRIS in the NETHERLANDS.

Oxford is known to have written plays for a juvenile acting company known as Oxford's Boys and to have financially supported an adult company. Although none of his plays have survived, the earl's interest in and patronage of Elizabethan DRAMA led to the proposal in 1920 that Oxford, an accomplished courtier, may have been the true author of the plays attributed to the ill-educated countryman William Shakespeare. Although dismissed by most Shakespeare scholars, not least because Oxford was dead by 1604, well before the later plays are thought to have been written, the theory is still upheld by many "Oxfordians."

Further Reading: Eleanor Brewster, *Oxford: Courtier to the Queen*, New York: Pageant Press, 1964; Charlton Ogburn, *The Mysterious William Shakespeare*, 2nd ed., McLean, VA: EPM Publications, 1992; Peter Sammartino, *The Man Who Was William Shakespeare*, New York: Cornwall Books, 1990; Edward de Vere, *The Poems of Edward de Vere*, Chapel Hill: University of North Carolina Press, 1981.

Vere, Sir Francis (1560–1609)

Sir Francis Vere was one of England's most talented and experienced military commanders. A distant cousin of Edward de VERE, Earl of Oxford, Vere was born in Essex and decided early in life to pursue a military career. In 1585, Vere volunteered to serve in the NETHERLANDS EXPEDITION led by Robert DUDLEY, Earl of Leicester. Joining the cavalry under Peregrine BERTIE, Lord Willoughby, Vere soon received command of 150 men in the Bergen-op-Zoom garrison. In 1587, after distinguishing himself in numerous engagements, Vere was knighted by Willoughby, who had succeeded Leicester as English commander in the NETHERLANDS. After a brief visit to England, Vere returned to the Netherlands in 1589 to succeed Willoughby as commander.

Over the next five years, Vere proved himself a brilliant military strategist and an excellent leader. He captured several important

Dutch towns from the Spanish, including Breda in 1589, Nymegen in 1591, and Groningen in 1594. By 1593, Vere was being paid by the Dutch STATES-GENERAL, an arrangement that had Elizabeth's approval. In 1596, Vere and 1,000 of his Netherlands veterans joined the CADIZ RAID on SPAIN itself. During the expedition, Vere quarreled with Sir Walter RALEIGH, and the two finally agreed that Raleigh would command at sea and Vere on land. In the attack on Cadiz, Vere's experience helped steady the impetuous leadership of Robert DEVEREUX, Earl of Essex, and Vere shared in the popular acclaim that greeted the leaders of the expedition in England. Vere also participated in the unsuccessful ISLANDS VOYAGE of 1597, finding himself caught between Essex and Raleigh, the expedition's quarreling commanders.

On Vere's return to the Netherlands in 1598, the queen appointed him to negotiate a new treaty with the States-General and to be governor of Brill (see CAUTIONARY TOWNS). On the accession of JAMES I in 1603, Vere retained his governorship, but he retired from active service when England made peace with Spain and withdrew from the war in 1604. In his last years, Vere wrote accounts of his military campaigns and contributed to the support of the new library at Oxford (see UNIVERSITIES) founded by his friend Sir Thomas BODLEY. Vere died in August 1609, only four months after Spain recognized Dutch independence.

Further Reading: Geoffrey Parker, *The Dutch Revolt*, Ithaca, NY: Cornell University Press, 1977.

Vernon, Elizabeth. *See* WRIOTHESLEY, ELIZABETH.

vestiarian controversy

The vestiarian controversy, a dispute between Anglican bishops and radical Protestants over proper clerical dress, was a significant event in the emergence of the PURITANS as a distinct movement within the ANGLICAN CHURCH. Because Elizabeth liked ceremony and ritual in worship services, the ANGLICAN SETTLEMENT in 1559 required ministers to wear certain vestments (the ceremonial attire worn by clergymen when conducting rites and services).

However, more radical Protestants were critical of the queen's tastes, believing such vestments to be unnecessary remnants of the Catholic past. The MARIAN EXILES, those English Protestants who had fled to Europe to avoid the Catholic regime of MARY I, were especially unwilling to accept the vestments, for they had experienced firsthand the plain dress and austere churches of the reformed Protestant communities of Germany and Switzerland.

In the 1560s, many Anglican clergy ignored the vestments prescribed by law, preferring instead to wear the simple black gowns favored by continental Protestants. In 1566, when Archbishop Matthew PARKER of Canterbury ordered strict enforcement of the law, 37 LONDON clergymen refused to comply and were deprived of their benefices (see BENEFICE); unrest over the issue also arose in other parts of the country. The bishops themselves were divided on the issue; many agreed with the deprived clergymen. Elizabeth continued to insist on the vestments mandated by PARLIAMENT through the *BOOK OF COMMON PRAYER,* but the divisions among the bishops meant that no consistent policy was pursued on the issue, and the vestments question continued to vex church authorities throughout the Elizabethan period. The vestiarian dispute was the first major point of contention between the Anglican authorities and the Church's more radical members, who soon became a distinct faction known as Puritans, because they sought in many ways and on many issues to "purify" the English Church of its Catholic vestiges. *See also* CATHOLICISM, ENGLISH; PROTESTANTISM.

Further Reading: Patrick Collinson, *The Elizabethan Puritan Movement,* Oxford: Clarendon Press, 1990; John Henry Primus, *The Vestments Controversy,* Kampen, Netherlands: J. H. Kok, 1960.

Virgin Queen

On Elizabeth's accession in 1558, her gender was thought to be her greatest liability as a monarch. Ruling a kingdom was considered a man's job, and everyone accepted that the queen needed a husband (see MARRIAGE QUESTION), both to help her govern and to maintain order among her male advisors. The great achievement of Elizabeth's reign was her success in turning the supposed weakness of being a woman into an instrument for controlling, disciplining, and directing the strong and proud men who formed her COURT, her PRIVY COUNCIL, and her military command.

Elizabeth accomplished this transformation by remaining unmarried and by making herself the center of a secular, political cult of devotion that in some ways replaced the medieval religious cult of the Virgin Mary, which the Reformation had destroyed (see REFORMATION, ENGLISH). Where the knightly ideal of chivalry had dedicated itself to the Virgin, and to devotion to and protection of chaste femininity, Elizabethan courtiers dedicated themselves to the service and protection of a ruler who was not only a woman, but a virgin as well. The cult of the Virgin Queen allowed Elizabeth to equate herself with the state and to channel the often touchy pride and ready violence of her courtiers away from disorder and into controlled competition for her favor. And that favor, whether in the form of titles, lands,

By remaining unmarried and by making herself the center of a secular, political cult, Elizabeth I successfully ruled a male-dominated society. This miniature oil painting from the seventeenth century reinforces the Virgin Queen cult by giving Elizabeth the face of a young maiden. *By permission of the Folger Shakespeare Library.*

offices, or mere royal recognition, had to be earned by loyal service.

Beginning with an element of romance, as when the younger Elizabeth balanced her favors to Robert DUDLEY, Earl of Leicester, with those shown to Sir Christopher HATTON and other courtiers, the cult of the Virgin Queen became, by Elizabeth's later years, almost a form of worship, with the name and idea of Elizabeth inspiring men to fight, write, paint (see ELIZABETH I, PORTRAITS OF), and colonize. Courtiers could also use the idea of the Virgin Queen to seek to manipulate Elizabeth. Thus, when his 1584 expedition to the New World claimed part of the east coast of North America for England (see AMADAS-BARLOWE EXPEDITION), Walter RALEIGH sought to win the queen's support for his plan to establish an English settlement there by naming the region Virginia, in honor of the Virgin Queen. By using her gender and chastity as a focus of devotion and service, Elizabeth I became one of the strongest and most effective rulers in English history.

Further Reading: Roy Strong, *The Cult of Elizabeth: Elizabethan Portraiture and Pageantry,* London: Thames and Hudson, 1977; Neville Williams, *All the Queen's Men: Elizabeth I and Her Courtiers,* New York: Macmillan, 1972.

W

Wales

Because of their Welsh name and descent, the Tudor monarchs had a greater claim on the loyalty of the Welsh people than had any previous English ruling dynasty. HENRY VII, Elizabeth's grandfather, promoted this special relationship with carefully calculated acts of generosity toward the Welsh, although the organization and government of Wales under Henry differed little from the arrangements made by his predecessors. The country was divided into the Principality of Wales and the marcher (i.e., border) lordships; the Prince of Wales was first Henry VII himself, and then his sons Prince Arthur (whose very name was an attempt to cultivate the Welsh) and Prince Henry (see HENRY VIII).

Between 1536 and 1543, a series of statutes abolished the private marcher lordships and divided the principality and the former marcher jurisdictions into shire ground, either as part of five new shires (i.e., counties) or as annexations to existing English shires. PARLIAMENT also replaced Welsh customs and law with the English COMMON LAW and introduced JUSTICES OF THE PEACE on the English model to administer the new shires. Parliament also extended the Reformation into Wales, which was less anticlerical (see ANTICLERICALISM) than England, and allowed the Welsh to send representatives to Parliament, the first Welsh MPs (members of Parliament) being elected in 1542. These statutes erased the political border between the two countries and tied Wales more fully into the English system of law and LOCAL GOVERNMENT.

Under Elizabeth, the Reformation came slowly to Wales, but English law and customs largely displaced Welsh practices (see REFORMATION, WELSH). In 1588, Bishop William MORGAN translated the Bible into Welsh, and the government ordered a copy placed in every Welsh church to facilitate the reading of Scripture and the spread of the reformed religion (see BIBLE, ENGLISH). However, each church was also required to have a copy of the English Bible to facilitate the adoption of the ENGLISH language, Welsh parishioners being able to learn English by comparing the two translations. By Elizabeth's death in 1603, loyalty to the queen and the dynasty had led a majority of the Welsh population to accept PROTESTANTISM.

Further Reading: John Davies, *A History of Wales,* London: Penguin Press, 1993; J. Gwynfor Jones, *Early Modern Wales, 1525–1640,* New York: St. Martin's Press, 1994; W. S.K. Thomas, *Tudor Wales, 1485–1603,* Llandsul, Wales: Gomer Press, 1983.

Walsingham, Sir Francis (1532–1590)

Although a staunch Puritan, and therefore not personally influential with the queen (see PURITANS), Sir Francis Walsingham was a key figure in Elizabethan DIPLOMACY and intelligence gathering. Born into a GENTRY family of Kent, Walsingham entered Cambridge (see UNIVERSITIES) but soon left to travel in Europe (see GRAND TOUR) and attend Gray's Inn (see INNS OF COURT). A convinced Protestant fluent in French and Italian, Walsingham spent the reign of MARY I on the continent, mainly studying law at the University of Padua in Italy (see MARIAN EXILES).

Sir Francis Walsingham, painted by John de Critz the elder. *By courtesy of the National Portrait Gallery, London.*

After Elizabeth's accession in 1558, he came to COURT under the patronage of Sir William CECIL, who found him a place in PARLIAMENT and used him for diplomatic missions. From 1571 to 1573, he was the English ambassador at Paris, where he helped shelter Protestants during the SAINT BARTHOLOMEW MASSACRE in August 1572. In 1573, the queen named Walsingham secretary of state and a member of the PRIVY COUNCIL, and, in 1577, she granted him a knighthood. His experiences at the French court led him to advocate a strong Protestant foreign policy based on alliance with the French HUGUENOTS and on English aid to the Dutch Protestant rebels who were fighting SPAIN. Ever alert for Catholic conspiracies against Queen Elizabeth, he organized a large and effective intelligence service that made use of English merchants overseas and undercover agents working both in England and abroad. By means of this spy network, Walsingham tracked the activities of Jesuits (see JESUIT MISSION) and SEMINARY PRIESTS in England, received advance warning from Spain of plans to launch the ARMADA, and unraveled the plots against Elizabeth that formed around Mary STUART, Queen of Scots, including the BABINGTON PLOT in 1586.

Walsingham repeatedly urged the execution of Mary but was overruled by the queen until he was able, as part of the Babington investigation, to draw Mary into condoning, in writing, the murder of Elizabeth. Walsingham also invested regularly in voyages of exploration, including those of Sir Francis DRAKE and Sir Martin FROBISHER, and was a literary patron of writers who advocated exploration and colonization, such as Richard HAKLUYT. Although the queen disliked Walsingham's gloomy, pessimistic demeanor, she found his diplomatic and security work invaluable, and she continued to employ him until his death in 1590.

Further Reading: Wallace T. MacCaffrey, *Queen Elizabeth and the Making of Policy, 1572–1588,* Princeton, NJ: Princeton University Press, 1981; Wallace T. MacCaffrey, *Elizabeth I: War and Politics 1588–1603,* Princeton, NJ: Princeton University Press, 1992; Conyers Read, *Mr. Secretary Walsingham and the Policy of Queen Elizabeth,* Hamden, CT: Archon Books, 1967.

Wars of the Roses

The "Wars of the Roses" is a nineteenth-century term for a series of intermittent dynastic conflicts for the English Crown in the fifteenth century. These struggles, which lasted for 30 years, from 1455 to 1485, ended with the establishment of the Tudor dynasty (see TUDOR FAMILY). The deposition of Richard II (r. 1377–1399) in 1399 broke the direct line of succession to the English throne and led to a contest for the Crown between the Lancastrian and Yorkist branches of the House of Plantagenet, which both claimed descent from Edward III (r. 1327–1377). (The allusion to "roses" comes from a scene in William SHAKESPEARE's *Henry VI,* in which the partisans of York pluck white roses and the supporters of Lancaster pick red roses.)

The incompetence and mental instability of Henry VI of Lancaster (r. 1422–1461, 1470–1471) allowed the development of powerful baronial factions backed by groups of armed retainers, and caused respect for the Crown to decline. This breakdown of royal authority led to increasing disorder in the counties, where local officials attached themselves to, or were dominated by, powerful and wealthy local lords.

The Crown began to recover its power and authority after Edward IV of York (r. 1461–1470, 1471–1483) regained the throne in 1471. Conflict returned briefly in the mid-1480s when Richard III (r. 1483–1485) removed his nephew Edward V (r. 1483) from the throne. This act of usurpation allowed Henry Tudor (see HENRY VII), heir to the Lancastrian claim, and grandfather to Queen Elizabeth, to invade the kingdom and win the Crown by force at Bosworth Field on 22 August 1485. Bosworth thus began the rule of the Tudor dynasty, which continued until Elizabeth's death in 1603. *See also* BEAUFORT FAMILY; SUCCESSION, ACTS OF.

Further Reading: Christine Carpenter, *The Wars of the Roses*, Cambridge: Cambridge University Press, 1997; John Gillingham, *The Wars of the Roses*, Baton Rouge: Louisiana State University Press, 1981; Anthony Goodman, *The Wars of the Roses*, New York: Dorset Press, 1990; J. R. Lander, *The Wars of the Roses*, New York: Capricorn Books, 1967; Robin Neillands, *The Wars of the Roses*, London: Cassell, 1992; Charles Ross, *The Wars of the Roses*, London: Thames and Hudson, 1987; Desmond Seward, *The Wars of the Roses*, New York: Viking, 1995.

Warwick, Earl of. *See* DUDLEY, AMBROSE, EARL OF WARWICK.

weapons

The most important development in weaponry during Elizabeth's reign was the gun's displacement of the longbow as the preeminent weapon of English armies (see ARMY; MILITIA). Six feet long and made of the finest yew wood, the longbow had a glorious history, having enabled the armies of medieval England to win brilliant victories at Crecy (1346),

This gentleman soldier of the late 1590s wears his sword and carries a halberd, a combination spear and axe. *By permission of the Folger Shakespeare Library.*

Poitiers (1356), and Agincourt (1415). The longbow was still in common use at Elizabeth's accession in 1558, but it had largely disappeared from English armies (and European warfare) by the queen's death in 1603. As guns became more powerful and more accurate, they clearly exhibited their superiority not only as a weapon of war, but as an instrument for keeping families supplied with game during times of peace.

The most common types of small arms were the arquebus, a heavy gun fired from a rest; the caliver, a smaller, lighter handgun; and the musket, a large-caliber shoulder gun. Loading one of these firearms was a time-consuming process and obliged the musketeer to carry much ancillary equipment, including a flask of powder, a bag of bullets, several yards of cloth match to light the powder, paper for wadding, a ramrod, and a flint or steel to light the match. Loading the gun required pouring the right amount of powder into the barrel (too little and the shot fell short, too much and the barrel exploded), ramming the bullet and paper wadding into the barrel (wadding prevented the bullet from rolling out), and touching the lighted match to the powder.

Sieges and naval warfare required heavier guns (see NAVY), which ranged in size from the robinet (firing a one-inch ball) to the cannon (firing an eight-inch ball). Other types of heavy artillery included the falconet, the falcon, the minion, the demi-culverin, the culverin, and the demi-cannon, each of which had a different range and caliber. Although the English made use of iron shot, in Europe, the smaller guns usually fired heavy bronze shot, while the larger weapons usually fired stone shot, which, being lighter, required less powder and reduced the chances of the gun exploding. Other common Elizabethan weapons included the pike, an 18-foot-long ash pole with an iron tip; the bill, a simple spear; the halberd, a combination spear and axe; and a three-foot-long sword and short dagger. *See also* illustrations for "BOOK OF MARTYRS."

Further Reading: C. G. Cruickshank, *Elizabeth's Army,* 2nd ed., Oxford: Clarendon Press, 1966; Charles John Ffoulkes, *Sword Lance and Bayonet: A Record of the Arms of the British Army and Navy,* 2nd ed., New York: Arco, 1967; A. Vesey Norman, *A History of War and Weapons, 449 to 1660: English Warfare from the Anglo-Saxons to Cromwell,* New York: Crowell, 1966.

Wentworth, Paul (1533–1593)

Like his elder brother Peter WENTWORTH, Paul Wentworth was an outspoken advocate for parliamentary freedom of speech. Wentworth, the son of a Buckinghamshire gentleman (see GENTRY), acquired a large block of former monastic properties through MARRIAGE (see WOMEN). A zealous Puritan (see PURITANS), Wentworth sat for Buckingham in the Parliaments of 1563 and 1566 (see PARLIAMENTARY SESSIONS [1559–1581]). In the latter session, Wentworth was active in promoting a Commons petition requesting the queen to marry and name a successor. Elizabeth returned an evasive reply to the petition, and when Wentworth and his colleagues continued to press the issue, the queen instructed the Commons through Sir Francis KNOLLYS to proceed no further with the matter.

At Parliament's next sitting on 11 November 1566, Wentworth made a motion asking whether the queen's command contravened the liberties and privileges of the House of Commons. This motion started a debate that raged all day (i.e., from about 9 A.M. to adjournment at 2 P.M.), preventing the discussion of any other business. During the debate, Wentworth questioned the extent of royal authority and insisted that the queen was required to name an heir. Next day, Elizabeth ordered discussion on Wentworth's motion to stop. A compromise was reached in late November, whereby the queen withdrew her two orders halting debate, and the Commons agreed to discuss the matter no further.

Wentworth was again prominent in Parliament in 1581, when he moved that the Commons declare a public fast and attend preaching each morning before the start of each day's session. Although opposed by Knollys and other government officials in the Commons, the motion passed on division. The queen sent a message indicating her disapproval of Wentworth's motion, but she excused the offense as proceeding from religious zeal and from her own leniency toward Wentworth's brother Peter, who in the previous parliamentary session had been briefly imprisoned for delivering a speech critical of the queen. The Commons responded by rescinding Wentworth's motion. Wentworth died at his home at Burnham in 1593. Although less fiery in his opposition to the Crown than his brother, Paul Wentworth was a notable defender of the rights and privileges of the Commons.

Further Reading: J. E. Neale, *Elizabeth I and Her Parliaments*, 2 vols., New York: St. Martin's Press, 1958.

Wentworth, Peter (c. 1524–1596)

Peter Wentworth was a parliamentary critic of the royal PREROGATIVE and a strong advocate for wider freedom of speech in PARLIAMENT. Elected to the Parliament of 1571, Wentworth rose in the Commons to attack Sir Humphrey GILBERT for the "disposition to flatter or fawn on the Prince" that Gilbert had exhibited in a speech defending the royal prerogative. In the Parliament of 1572, the Commons voted a resolution of thanks to Elizabeth for consenting to meet a parliamentary committee sent to request the execution of Mary STUART, Queen of Scots, for her involvement in the RIDOLFI PLOT. However, because Elizabeth refused to proceed against Mary, Wentworth believed she deserved no thanks and opposed the resolution.

On 8 February 1576, during the next parliamentary session, Wentworth moved a resolution on freedom of speech. He attacked the queen for the "great faults" she had committed in the previous Parliament by not settling the succession and by limiting discussion of the matter in the Commons (see SUCCESSION, ACTS OF). A horrified House, utterly unaccustomed to such frank criticism of the queen, stopped him in mid-speech and placed him in custody. After a month in the TOWER OF LONDON, Wentworth was released by the queen and forced to make humble submission on his knees at the bar of the House before being allowed to resume his seat.

Wentworth landed in the Tower again during the parliamentary session of 1586–87, when the queen's refusal to allow the Commons to discuss measures for presbyterian reform of the Church led him to again demand wider freedom of speech for members, and to begin organizing meetings outside the House with other Puritan MPs to discuss ways to advance the presbyterian program (see PRESBYTERIAN MOVEMENT; PURITANS). Such opposition measures were unacceptable to the political culture of the age, and no one protested Wentworth's confinement.

After his release, Wentworth wrote *A Pithy Exhortation to Her Majesty for Establishing Her Successor to the Crown,* a tract urging Elizabeth to name an heir. Unimpressed by Wentworth's arguments, Elizabeth imprisoned him again in 1591. He entered the Tower for good in 1593 when the government learned of his plans to launch a concerted campaign in the next parliamentary session to persuade the queen to settle the succession. An unrepentant Wentworth died in the Tower in 1596. *See also* WENTWORTH, PAUL.

Further Reading: J. E. Neale, *Elizabeth I and Her Parliaments,* 2 vols., New York: St. Martin's Press, 1958.

Westminster Abbey. *See* WESTMINSTER PALACE.

Westminster Hall. *See* WESTMINSTER PALACE.

Westminster Palace

Once the monarch's official residence, Westminster Palace was, by the reign of Elizabeth I, the home of the courts of COMMON LAW, the meeting place of PARLIAMENT, and the administrative headquarters of the English government. Westminster Palace is located just west of LONDON along a bend on the Thames; Edward the Confessor substantially rebuilt the royal church on the site, Westminster Abbey, in the 1050s, and William II built a great royal hall adjacent to the abbey in the 1090s. As Westminster Abbey became the center of royal ceremony, being the coronation site of every monarch since 1066 and the burial place of most monarchs down to the Tudors, Westminster Hall became the nucleus of the principal royal residence in the country.

In the Middle Ages, Westminster also developed as the headquarters of various government departments, the first structure in Western Europe to serve such a function. In the thirteenth century, the chief courts of the common law (see KING'S [QUEEN'S] BENCH, COURT OF; COMMON PLEAS, COURT OF) were permanently sited at Westminster, and by the sixteenth century, the House of Commons met in St. Stephen's Chapel, part of Westminster Palace. As the only royal residence to also serve as a seat of government, Westminster was the only royal site in England

to be referred to officially as a "palace." In the 1520s, HENRY VIII built a new London residence called Whitehall (see WHITEHALL PALACE), and Westminster, which had been damaged by a recent fire and which the king considered too old and shabby to continue as a residence, was handed over entirely to the law courts and the royal bureaucracy. Thus, Elizabeth I never lived at Westminster, but it remained the center of Elizabethan law and government and was the site of various important events of the reign, such as the trial of Thomas HOWARD, Duke of Norfolk, which took place in Westminster Hall.

Westminster suffered later from the fire of 1698, which destroyed much of nearby Whitehall, and the fire of 1834, which spared Westminster Hall but destroyed St. Stephen's Chapel and most of the rest of Westminster Palace. After 1835, the current Houses of Parliament were rebuilt around Westminster Hall on the site of the old palace. Today, when speaking informally of Parliament or the central administration of the British government, one still refers to "Westminster." *See also* illustrations for COMMON LAW; PARLIAMENT.

Further Reading: John Martin Robinson, *Royal Residences,* London: MacDonald and Company, 1982; Simon Thurley, *The Royal Palaces of Tudor England,* New Haven, CT: Yale University Press, 1993.

White, John (d. 1593)

The maps and drawings of the Elizabethan painter and cartographer John White are the most vivid depictions we have of Native American life in sixteenth-century Virginia. As a member of Sir Walter RALEIGH's first attempt to establish an English colony in Virginia, White and his fellow settlers left Plymouth, England, with Sir Richard GRENVILLE in April 1585. Grenville landed the colonists on Roanoke Island (off what is now North Carolina), where they established a settlement under the governorship of Sir Ralph LANE (see ROANOKE COLONY [1585]). In June 1586, the colonists asked Sir Francis DRAKE, then passing by on his return from the Spanish West Indies, to take them back to England. White's year in Virginia resulted in the execution of a series of paintings of Indian life and of the native flora and fauna, as well as the drafting of a series of maps of the North American coast. In 1588, 23 of White's drawings were reproduced

John White's drawing of an American Indian warrior in body paint. © *The British Museum.*

in the *BRIEF AND TRUE REPORT OF THE NEW FOUND LAND OF VIRGINIA,* which was published in LONDON by fellow colonist Thomas HARRIOT.

Raleigh named White governor of his second colonization expedition, which left England with 117 settlers in July 1587 (see ROANOKE COLONY [1587]). In August, shortly after their arrival at Roanoke, the colonists asked White to return to England to press their considerable need for supplies on Raleigh. Although reluctant to leave his family, White embarked for England on 27 August 1587, only nine days after the birth of his granddaughter, Virginia Dare, the first English child born in North America. Accompanied by an Indian, White reached England in October.

In April 1588, White set out for Roanoke with two relief ships, but, the crews being more interested in piracy than in Virginia, White had to turn back when his ships had the worse of an encounter with a Spanish vessel. The AR-MADA crisis of 1588 tied up all shipping and prevented White from returning to Virginia until 1590. On 16 August, White finally landed on Roanoke, but he found no trace of the colony (see "LOST COLONY"). In February 1593, shortly before his death, White described his last voyage to AMERICA in a letter to Richard HAKLUYT, who later printed it in his *PRINCIPAL NAVIGATIONS. See also* illustrations for AMADAS-BARLOWE EXPEDITION; DAVIS, JOHN; FROBISHER, SIR MARTIN; ROANOKE COLONY (1585).

Further Reading: David N. Durant, *Raleigh's Lost Colony,* New York: Atheneum, 1981; Karen Ordahl Kupperman, *Roanoke: The Abandoned Colony,* New York: Barnes and Noble, 1993; David B. Quinn, *Set Fair for Roanoke: Voyages and Colonies, 1584–1606,* Chapel Hill: University of North Carolina Press, 1984.

Whitehall Palace

Whitehall Palace was Queen Elizabeth's main LONDON residence. In 1529, immediately upon dismissing Thomas Wolsey, Archbishop of York, from office as his chief minister, HENRY VIII seized York Place, the official London residence of the Archbishops of York. Because the king's own London residence, ancient WESTMINSTER PALACE, seemed old fashioned and run-down, Henry planned to use the site of Wolsey's palace for his new London home. Retaining the core of York Place, Henry demolished hundreds of houses, many of which were the London residences of important courtiers, and built what became the largest palace in Europe at the time. Whitehall Palace covered 23 acres on a site along the Thames north of Westminster. The new palace had no regular layout but extended west from the river in a series of buildings, gardens, and courts connected by an innovative network of long galleries. King Street, a public thoroughfare, ran through the middle of the palace, which culminated, on its western end, in St. James's Park, on the other side of which Henry built smaller ST. JAMES'S PALACE as his private retreat from the cares of state.

The most striking of Whitehall Palace's galleries, the Privy Gallery, ran across the "Holbein Gate," the ornate gatehouse on the northern end of King Street. The great hall, in which the COURT could be fed, had been part of York Place, but the royal apartments on the east side of the palace along the river were new

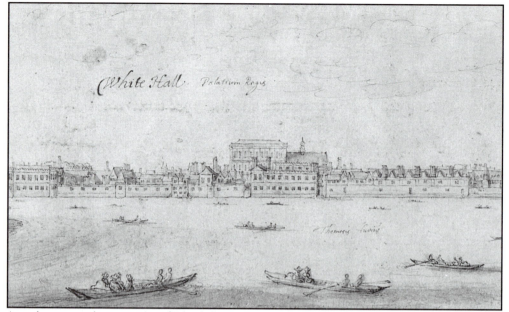

An early seventeenth-century view of Whitehall Palace from the Thames: a detail from a drawing by Wenceslaus Hollar. © *The British Museum.*

constructions. Elizabeth's mother, Anne BOLEYN, was the first occupant of the queen's apartments. Elizabeth, as reigning queen (not wife of the king), lived in what had been her father's state rooms, which included a great Presence Chamber for audiences and a large Privy Chamber containing a portrait of the Tudor dynasty painted for Henry VIII by Hans Holbein (see TUDOR FAMILY).

In Elizabeth's reign, the privy garden of the palace contained an open-air pulpit topped by a great sounding board that allowed preachers to easily address a large audience packed onto the walks of the surrounding garden. Whitehall burned in 1698 and thereafter ceased to be a royal residence. Nothing remains of it today but the seventeenth-century banqueting house, the site of Charles I's execution in 1649. Because the site of the palace was later occupied by government offices, the term "Whitehall" came by the nineteenth century to refer generally to the great departments of state. *See also* PALACES.

Further Reading: John Martin Robinson, *Royal Residences,* London: MacDonald and Company, 1982; Simon Thurley, *The Royal Palaces of Tudor England,* New Haven, CT: Yale University Press, 1993.

Whitgift, John (c. 1530–1604)

John Whitgift was Elizabeth's last and most successful Archbishop of Canterbury. The son of a wealthy merchant, Whitgift was educated at St. Anthony's School (see GRAMMAR SCHOOL) in LONDON and at Cambridge (see UNIVERSITIES), where he held several important university positions, including, by 1567, the vice-chancellorship and the prestigious Regius Chair in Divinity. Ordained in 1560, Whitgift became chaplain to the queen in 1567. In 1571, Whitgift obtained a special dispensation to hold several benefices at once (see BENEFICE). He was named prolocutor (i.e., presiding officer and spokesman) for the lower house of CONVOCATION in 1572, and in the same year published the *Answer to a Certain Libel Instituted, an Admonition to the Parliament,* which defended the Anglican Church against the parliamentary and clerical supporters of the PRESBYTERIAN MOVEMENT (see ADMONITION CONTROVERSY).

In 1577, Elizabeth appointed Whitgift to an ecclesiastical position—the bishopric of Worcester—and a political position—the vice presidency of the Council for Wales. Seeking an archbishop who would defend the ANGLICAN CHURCH against the attacks of Presbyterians and PURITANS, Elizabeth appointed Whitgift Archbishop of Canterbury in 1583. Unlike his two Elizabethan predecessors—Matthew PARKER and Edmund GRINDAL—Whitgift, the only cleric Elizabeth

John Whitgift was Elizabeth's last Archbishop of Canterbury. *By courtesy of the National Portrait Gallery, London.*

appointed to the PRIVY COUNCIL, had the full confidence of both the queen and William CECIL, Lord Burghley. Whitgift strictly enforced conformity to Anglican doctrine and practice, rooting out secret Presbyterians and nonconforming Puritans and SEPARATISTS. In 1588–89, he led the effort to uncover the authors of the MARPRELATE TRACTS. However, Whitgift was always careful to avoid creating Puritan martyrs, as illustrated by his treatment of Thomas CARTWRIGHT, who was allowed to withdraw to the Channel Islands after several years of imprisonment. Whitgift used the Court of High Commission to punish deviations from orthodoxy (see HIGH COMMISSION, COURT OF), but exhibited leniency whenever a measure of compliance was shown, and he never proceeded to extremes.

As she lay dying at RICHMOND PALACE in March 1603, the queen summoned Whitgift to her side to give comfort. In January 1604, Whitgift took part in the Hampton Court Conference, where he backed JAMES I in his refusal to allow Puritan changes to Anglican doctrine. The archbishop did support the Puritan request for a new English translation of the Bible (see BIBLE, ENGLISH). Whitgift died on 29 February 1604.

Further Reading: Powel Mills Dawley, *John Whitgift and the English Reformation,* New York: Scribner, 1954.

Whittingham, William (c. 1524–1579)

William Whittingham was a translator of the Geneva Bible, the most widely read ENGLISH translation in Elizabethan England (see BIBLE, ENGLISH). Whittingham was born at Chester and educated at Oxford (see UNIVERSITIES). Between 1550 and 1553, he traveled the continent, visiting FRANCE, Germany, and the NETHERLANDS, acquiring both a proficiency in French and a Protestant wife. His own extreme Protestant views forced him to flee England shortly after the accession of MARY I in July 1553 (see MARIAN EXILES). A member of the English exile community in Frankfurt, Whittingham joined John KNOX in demanding a thorough reform of the *BOOK OF COMMON PRAYER.* Knox moved to John CALVIN's Geneva after supporters of the Prayer Book expelled him from the Frankfurt community; Whittingham joined Knox in Geneva and eventually succeeded him as minister of the English congregation. Whittingham is usually considered the author of *A Brief Discourse of the Troubles at Frankfurt,* an account of the theological disputes that split the Frankfurt exile community.

In 1557, Whittingham produced English translations of the New Testament and the Psalms, then worked with other exiles to publish a new English edition of the complete Bible. Known as the Geneva Bible, it immediately became popular. Whittingham stayed in Switzerland until the Geneva Bible was published in 1560 and then returned to England to enter the service of Robert DUDLEY and his brother, Ambrose DUDLEY, Earl of Warwick. In 1562, Whittingham served as Warwick's chaplain during the LE HAVRE EXPEDITION to support the HUGUENOTS. For this service, Whittingham was named Dean of Durham.

Utterly opposed to the ANGLICAN SETTLEMENT of 1559, which he felt did not go nearly far enough in purging the English Church of Catholic elements, Whittingham was frequently at odds with Church authorities, on one occasion even locking the Bishop of Durham out of Durham Cathedral. He also removed images from churches without permission and attempted to institute unauthorized Genevan forms of worship. In 1578, he was accused of being improperly ordained; the charge proved true, for Whittingham's status as a clergyman rested not on Anglican ordination but on his calling by the Geneva congregation in the 1550s. Whittingham died in June 1579 before any action could be taken against him.

Further Reading: Patrick Collinson, *The Elizabethan Puritan Movement,* Oxford: Clarendon Press, 1990; Christina Garrett, *The Marian Exiles,* Cambridge: Cambridge University Press, 1966.

William, Prince of Orange (1533–1584)

William of Orange was the principal leader of the NETHERLANDS REVOLT against SPAIN and one of the founders of the independent United Provinces of the Netherlands. William was born into a Lutheran family that controlled the German principality of Orange and vast estates in the Spanish-ruled Netherlands. CHARLES V took a liking to the boy and ordered that he be raised Catholic. In 1558, after succeeding his father (Charles V) as ruler of the NETHERLANDS and Spain, PHILIP II appointed Orange to the Netherlands Council of State, and in 1559, Philip made Orange stadtholder (i.e., governor and command-in-chief) of the Dutch provinces of Holland and Zeeland. From these positions of influence, the prince gradually assumed the leadership of a group of nobles who believed the Spanish regency government was denying them their rightful part in running the country. Orange assumed a wider leadership role when the political complaints of the nobility merged with popular protests against Philip's attempts to impose a rigid Catholic orthodoxy throughout the country.

In 1566, after continuing government persecution of heretics caused Protestant mobs to attack and desecrate Catholic churches, Philip sent Spanish troops to restore order. When Orange fled to his German estates and refused to appear before a Spanish tribunal, Philip confiscated his holdings in the Netherlands. Realizing he had little future in a Catholic, Spanish Netherlands, Orange reverted to his childhood PROTESTANTISM and took up arms against Spain. Throughout the 1570s, the prince both led the rebellion and sought foreign financial and military aid, especially from England. Philip outlawed Orange in 1580 and

offered a reward for his assassination. The prince survived one attempt on his life in 1582 but was shot to death by a Spanish agent in Delft on 10 July 1584.

In England, Orange's death raised fears of similar Catholic attempts on the life of Elizabeth, and it spurred the heretofore reluctant queen to think seriously about intervening militarily on behalf of the Dutch (see BOND OF ASSOCIATION). During his lifetime, Orange acquired the nickname "William the Silent," not for his reticence, but through an accident of translation. An opponent in the regency government called him *schluwe,* meaning "sly," but this Dutch word was mistranslated into Latin as *taciturnus* ("quiet") and so came into English as "silent."

Further Reading: C. V. Wedgwood, *William the Silent,* rev. ed., New Haven, CT: Yale University Press, 1960.

Williams, Sir Roger (c. 1540–1595)

Having fought in almost all the major Elizabethan military campaigns in Europe, Sir Roger Williams was among the most experienced Elizabethan soldiers and military leaders. Born into a Welsh GENTRY family, Williams entered Brasenose College, Oxford (see UNIVERSITIES), in 1552. Little else is known of his early life, but by 1570 he was serving as a mercenary with the Spanish forces in the NETHERLANDS under Fernandez ALVAREZ DE TOLEDO, Duke of Alva. Although he became a colonel in the Spanish army, Williams had switched sides and joined the Dutch rebels by 1572.

In the late 1570s, he served under another English soldier fighting in the Netherlands, Sir John NORRIS. In July 1584, Williams was in Delft with WILLIAM, PRINCE OF ORANGE, when Orange was assassinated by a Spanish agent. In 1585, Williams joined the English NETHERLANDS EXPEDITION led by Robert DUDLEY, Earl of Leicester. Williams returned to England in 1588 to serve in the ARMY gathered at Tilbury (see TILBURY SPEECH) to resist any ARMADA landing. He next offered his services to HENRI IV of FRANCE. When the queen sent Robert DEVEREUX, Earl of Essex, to France with an army to support Henri against the CATHOLIC LEAGUE, Williams fought with Essex at Dieppe (see BRITTANY EXPEDITIONS). After Essex's departure in

1592, Williams commanded the English forces in France, spending the last years of his life campaigning for Henri and acting as the king's unofficial envoy to Elizabeth.

Having attached himself to Essex's interest, Williams, on his death in LONDON in 1595, left all his property to the earl, who arranged for Williams to have a proper soldier's burial at St. Paul's Cathedral. Williams was the author of two works on the NETHERLANDS REVOLT—*The Actions of the Low Countries* (1618) and *A Brief Discourse of War* (1590). In these two books, Williams analyzed the war in the Netherlands, described the aims of Spanish policy, discussed techniques of fortification, and argued the merits of firearms over the English longbow (see WEAPONS). Williams has been suggested as a possible model for the character of Fluellen in William SHAKESPEARE's *Henry V* (see SHAKESPEARE, WORKS OF).

Further Reading: John X. Evans, ed., *The Works of Sir Roger Williams*, Oxford: Clarendon Press, 1972; Geoffrey Parker, *The Dutch Revolt*, Ithaca, NY: Cornell University Press, 1977.

Willoughby de Eresby, Lord. *See* BERTIE, PEREGRINE, LORD WILLOUGHBY DE ERESBY.

Winchester, Marquis of. *See* PAULET, WILLIAM, MARQUIS OF WINCHESTER.

Windsor Castle

Windsor Castle was much favored by Elizabeth I, who spent more money on renovating it than on any other royal residence. Today, it is the oldest surviving English royal residence. Although now not far outside the LONDON metropolitan area, in Elizabethan times, Windsor was about 25 miles west of London. Standing at a strategic site at the west end of the Thames Valley, the first stone castle at Windsor, replacing an earlier Anglo-Saxon structure, was built shortly after the Norman Conquest in 1066. In the thirteenth century, Henry III built the first great stone keep and greatly extended the castle's walls. In the fourteenth century, Edward III built the Round Tower, which still survives today; in the fifteenth century, Edward IV and HENRY VII, Elizabeth's great-grandfather and grandfather, respectively, built St. George's Chapel. A bril-

liant example of English gothic ARCHITECTURE, St. George's is the chapel of the Order of the Garter, an English chivalric order, and a royal mausoleum, in which are buried Henry VI, Edward IV, HENRY VIII and Jane SEYMOUR, Charles I, and George VI, among others.

At Windsor, Elizabeth constructed a new gallery, a new private chapel, and a new banqueting house. Because the castle occupies a low hill surrounded by the town of Windsor, Elizabeth had part of the surrounding park raised so that townspeople could not see into her private walking area. Although Elizabeth spent less time at Windsor than in some of the newer PALACES built by her father, she often retreated there to escape PLAGUE in London, as she did during the autumn and winter of 1563 when the soldiers returning from the LE HAVRE EXPEDITION brought sickness back with them from FRANCE.

On St. George's Day, 23 April, the queen usually attended Garter ceremonies at Windsor. Tradition says that William SHAKESPEARE wrote *The Merry Wives of Windsor*, which contains much Windsor lore, at the request of the queen, who wanted to see Shakespeare's character Falstaff fall in love (see SHAKESPEARE, WORKS OF). Although partially open to the public, Windsor is still a royal residence today. During World War I, the present British royal family discarded its German surname (Saxe-Coburg) and adopted the name Windsor.

Further Reading: Mark Girouard, *Windsor, the Most Romantic Castle,* London: Hodder and Stoughton, 1993; A. L. Rowse, *Windsor Castle in the History of England,* New York: G. P. Putnam's Sons, 1974.

Winter, Sir William (d. 1589)

Sir William Winter (or Wynter) was an experienced Elizabethan naval commander who is often credited with instituting the improvements in ship design and armament that helped the English fleet overcome the Spanish ARMADA. The son of a Bristol merchant and sea captain, Winter went to sea at an early age as a member of his father's trading expeditions to SPAIN and the eastern Mediterranean. He entered the royal naval service about 1544 when his father was appointed treasurer of the NAVY. Between 1544 and 1547, Winter was part of three royal naval campaigns, two against SCOTLAND in 1544 and 1547 and one against FRANCE in 1545. In July 1549, Winter was appointed surveyor of the navy, and, in November 1557, master of ordnance, two posts that he retained until his death. He sailed to the Middle East in 1553 and saw action against the French at Conquet in 1558.

In 1559, Winter conducted a blockade of the Firth of Forth that prevented French reinforcements from landing in Scotland and thereby facilitated the negotiation of the Treaty of Edinburgh in 1560 (see EDINBURGH, TREATY OF). In 1563, he was with the English fleet that supported the LE HAVRE EXPEDITION. The queen knighted Winter in August 1573 and held him in high favor at COURT. Winter invested in numerous voyages of trade and exploration, including those of John HAWKINS and Francis DRAKE (see also PRIVATEERING). Two of his sons served with Drake, and a nephew was part of DRAKE'S CIRCUMNAVIGATION voyage.

After 1577, when Hawkins was named treasurer of the navy, an office Winter believed he deserved, the two men often clashed, with Winter eventually accusing Hawkins of corruption and inefficiency. Nonetheless, Winter's work as a naval administrator was vital in strengthening the fighting capability of the English fleet. In the engagements with the Armada in 1588, Winter commanded the *Vanguard* in the main fleet under Lord Admiral Charles HOWARD. Winter first proposed the idea of attacking the Armada with fireships, and he and his sons (one of whom was killed) fought brilliantly in the Battle of Gravelines. Winter died in 1589. *See also* GRAVELINES, BATTLE OF; SHIPS.

Further Reading: D. M. Loades, *The Tudor Navy,* Brookfield, VT: Ashgate Publications, 1992.

witchcraft

Although popular fear of witches in Britain and AMERICA is most closely associated with the seventeenth century, the majority of executions for witchcraft in England probably occurred during the Elizabethan period. In the late fifteenth century, European society began to view sorcery and heresy as two sides of the same crime. To obtain magical powers, the witch was believed to make an explicit pact with the devil.

Because this association with Satan threatened all of Christian society, Pope Innocent VIII, in a papal bull issued in December 1484, declared the Church ready to work for the eradication of witchcraft throughout Europe.

In 1486, Heinrich Kramer and Jacob Sprenger, two members of the Dominican order of friars, published an encyclopedia of witchcraft and demonology known as the *Malleus Maleficarum.* This work described how Satan planned to destroy the world through witchcraft, and it laid down guidelines for conducting a witch trial. The *Malleus* was also extremely misogynistic (i.e., anti-woman), seeing WOMEN as the devil's chosen agents in his plot against humanity. Over the next two centuries, the vast majority of people tried for witchcraft, both in Europe and in England, were women.

The first English law against witchcraft was passed by PARLIAMENT in 1542. However, few prosecutions occurred until after the passage in 1563 of the Elizabethan witchcraft statute, which set the legal requirements for convicting someone of being a witch. The statute required the submission of definite evidence that the accused had committed harmful acts through the use of witchcraft. Even though this standard was much higher than that required by the 1604 statute of JAMES I, which needed no overt act for conviction, many people were hanged for witchcraft under Elizabeth. One theory for the rise in witchcraft prosecutions at the start of Elizabeth's reign is that fear of witches was brought back to England by the returning MARIAN EXILES, who had spent several years living in areas of Europe where witch hysteria was already in full force in the 1550s. Fear of witches intensified in England under James I, who considered himself an expert on the subject, having published a book on witches (entitled *Daemonology*) in 1597. In the seventeenth century, belief in witchcraft traveled to America with the Puritan colonists and led to the Salem witch hysteria that erupted in Massachusetts in 1692 (see PURITANS).

Further Reading: A. D. J. Macfarlane, *Witchcraft in Tudor and Stuart England*, New York: Harper and Row, 1970; J. A. Sharpe, *Instruments of Darkness: Witchcraft in England 1550–1750*, New York: Penguin, 1996; Keith Thomas, *Religion and the Decline of Magic: Studies in Popular Beliefs in Sixteenth and Seventeenth Century England*, Oxford: Oxford University Press, 1997.

Deborah Willis, *Malevolent Nurture: Witch-Hunting and Maternal Power in Early Modern England*, Ithaca, NY: Cornell University Press, 1995.

women

The rights of women in medieval England were severely restricted by the feudal system of landholding, whereby the king granted land to his closest followers in return for military service. Because an estate had to support a knight, it descended intact to the eldest son. Organized for war, feudal society was a masculine society in which women had little part. Because the COMMON LAW developed in this feudal environment, it carried feudal strictures on the rights of women into the Elizabethan period, long after feudalism itself had broken down. Under the common law, married women could not inherit or administer land, make wills, sign contracts, sue or be sued, or make trusts or bonds. The legal term for the status of married women was "coverture," which meant literally that a woman's legal identity was "hidden" or "covered" by her husband's.

As a minor, a girl was under the guardianship of her father, who arranged her MARRIAGE (see FAMILY). As a wife, a woman passed to the guardianship of her husband, who controlled any land she brought to the marriage. The husband could not sell or lease his wife's land, and one-third of his estate (known as the widow's dower) passed to her upon his death. The rest of the estate could be sold, leased, or disposed of in any manner the husband saw fit. If the couple had adult children, the eldest son inherited the entire estate (except for the widow's dower) on the father's death.

The feudal-common law tradition of female subservience also touched princesses. When Elizabeth inherited the greatest property right in law, the Crown, she was expected to marry and thus have her right to rule limited by, if not subsumed into, her husband (see MARRIAGE QUESTION; VIRGIN QUEEN). However, Elizabethan women did have certain rights under other types of law. Even under the common law, widows and unmarried adult women could inherit land, make wills, sign contracts, and exercise other legal and property rights denied to married women. Under EQUITY law, married women had a legal identity and could sue or be sued. Equity courts also recognized contracts that common law courts did not, such as premarital agreements giving the wife her own income or the right to administer her own property (see STAR CHAMBER, COURT OF; REQUESTS, COURT OF; CHANCERY, COURT OF). Canon (or Church) law also allowed married women to make bonds to protect their rights to property or the rights of children by a former marriage. CHURCH COURTS also handled the probate of wills and so dealt frequently with widows who were executors of their husband's wills or administrators of the estate if the husband died intestate. *See also* FASHION, WOMEN.

Further Reading: Carroll Camden, *The Elizabethan Woman*, rev. ed., Mamaroneck, NY: P. P. Appel, 1975; Maria L. Cioni, *Women and Law in Elizabethan England*, New York: Garland, 1985; Kathy Lynn Emerson, *Wives and Daughters: The Women of Sixteenth Century England*, Troy, NY: Whitston Publishing Co., 1984; Pearl Hogrefe, *Tudor Women*, Ames: Iowa State University Press, 1975; Lisa Jardine, *Still Harping on Daughters: Women and Drama in the Age of Shakespeare*, Totowa, NJ: Barnes and Noble, 1983; Mary Prior, ed. *Women in English Society, 1500–1800*, New York: Methuen, 1985; Retha M. Warnicke, *Women of the English Renaissance and Reformation*, Westport, CT: Greenwood Press, 1983.

Wriothesley, Elizabeth, Countess of Southampton (1573–1655)

While serving at COURT, Elizabeth Vernon, the future Countess of Southampton, incurred the wrath of Queen Elizabeth by becoming pregnant by her lover, Henry WRIOTHESLEY, Earl of Southampton. Elizabeth Vernon was born into a Shropshire GENTRY family, the first cousin of Robert DEVEREUX, Earl of Essex, the queen's favorite in the 1590s (see FAVORITES). She was introduced at court by Essex and taken into the queen's service as a maid of honor (see LADIES-IN-WAITING). In 1595, she attracted the attention of Southampton, a literary patron of William SHAKESPEARE and a friend and confidant of Essex. When she became pregnant by Southampton in 1598, the couple married secretly for fear of the queen, who always reacted furiously to any court dalliance on the part of her maids and ladies. When the new countess's condition became apparent, Elizabeth imprisoned Southampton and so roundly abused his wife that she fled to the home of Essex's sister Penelope RICH, Lady Rich. The countess gave birth to a daughter, Penelope, in November 1598.

Released in 1599, Southampton accompanied Essex to IRELAND, while the countess and her daughter remained with Lady Rich. The earl and countess of Southampton were separated again in 1601, when the earl was imprisoned in the TOWER OF LONDON for his involvement in ESSEX'S REBELLION. Although spared the fate of the executed Essex, in part because of his wife and young child, Southampton was not allowed to see his wife for almost a year. On the accession of JAMES I in 1603, the earl and countess of Southampton were again received at court, and the king stood as godfather for the couple's first son, James, in 1605. The countess outlived her husband, who died in 1624, by more than 30 years, dying in 1655. During the civil war, the aged countess sheltered Charles I in her home at Titchfield when he fled to the Isle of Wight.

Further Reading: G. P. V. Akrigg, *Shakespeare and the Earl of Southampton,* Cambridge, MA: Harvard University Press, 1968; A. L. Rowse, *Shakespeare's Southampton: Patron of Virginia,* New York: Harper and Row, 1965.

Shown in this Daniel Mytens portrait as he was later in life, Henry Wriothesley, Earl of Southampton, was, as a young man, a patron of William Shakespeare and a friend of Robert Devereux, Earl of Essex. *By courtesy of the National Portrait Gallery, London.*

Wriothesley, Henry, Earl of Southampton (1573–1624)

Born into a wealthy family with Catholic sympathies, Henry Wriothesley, third Earl of Southampton, became a prominent patron of Elizabethan literature, and the only known patron of William SHAKESPEARE. On his father's death in 1581, the young earl became a ward of William CECIL, Lord Burghley. While a student at Cambridge (see UNIVERSITIES) in the 1580s, Southampton developed a strong interest in the theatre. In 1588, admission to the INNS OF COURT in LONDON allowed the earl to frequent the city's playhouses, a popular pastime of young gentlemen. Presented at COURT in the early 1590s, Southampton became a close friend and associate of Robert DEVEREUX, Earl of Essex.

Anticipating that Southampton would come into a handsome fortune upon attaining his majority in 1594, various Elizabethan literary figures sought the earl's patronage by dedicating works to him. The first to do so was Shakespeare, who in 1593 and 1594 dedicated the poems *Venus and Adonis* and *The Rape of Lucrece* to Southampton (see SHAKESPEARE, WORKS OF). Successful in attracting the earl's support, Shakespeare may also have addressed many of his sonnets to Southampton. Although a favorite at court (see FAVORITES), Southampton was refused permission to accompany Essex on the CADIZ RAID in 1596. He did participate in the ISLANDS VOYAGE of 1597 and won favorable notice for his capture of a Spanish frigate. In 1598, Southampton spent several weeks in prison for impregnating and secretly marrying Elizabeth Vernon (see WRIOTHESLEY, ELIZABETH), one of the queen's maids of honor (see LADIES-IN-WAITING). About the time of his MARRIAGE, Southampton abandoned his family's Catholicism and joined the ANGLICAN CHURCH.

In 1599, Southampton accompanied Essex to IRELAND and by 1600 was deeply involved in planning ESSEX'S REBELLION. To incite Londoners to support the uprising, Southampton persuaded the players at the GLOBE THEATRE to perform Shakespeare's *Richard II,* which contained a scene depicting the deposition of a king. Arrested with Essex after the failure of the uprising, Southampton was condemned to death but had his sentence commuted to life imprisonment in the TOWER OF LONDON on the intervention of Sir Robert CECIL. At his accession in 1603, JAMES I pardoned the earl, who remained in high favor for most of the reign. After his release, Southampton was again in demand as a literary patron. The earl died in the NETHERLANDS in November 1624. *See also* DRAMA; POETRY.

Further Reading: G. P. V. Akrigg, *Shakespeare and the Earl of Southampton,* Cambridge, MA: Harvard University Press, 1968; A. L. Rowse, *Shakespeare's Southampton: Patron of Virginia,* New York: Harper and Row, 1965.

Wyatt, Sir Thomas. *See* WYATT'S REBELLION.

Wyatt's Rebellion

Wyatt's Rebellion, an uprising of English gentlemen (see GENTRY) against MARY I's decision to wed Prince Philip of SPAIN (see PHILIP II), cost Princess Elizabeth her freedom—and nearly her life. In July 1553, the accession of Mary I as reigning queen—an unprecedented event in English history—raised the problem of the royal MARRIAGE. All men agreed that the queen had to marry, and that her husband should have some share in the government, but few wanted a foreign husband (especially a Spaniard or Frenchman) who might make England subservient to the interests and policies of his own country.

In late 1553, after Mary irrevocably committed herself to the Spanish match, a group of gentlemen opposed to any foreign marriage met secretly to plan an uprising to remove Mary from the throne and replace her with her half sister Elizabeth. The leaders of the group included Sir Nicholas THROCKMORTON, Sir Peter CAREW, and other future Elizabethan figures. The conspirators planned a four-fold rising to take place in Kent, Devon, and two other counties on Palm Sunday, 18 March 1554. The government learned of plans for the uprising in January, and the conspirators were forced to act before they were ready. As a result, only the Kentish phase, organized by Sir Thomas Wyatt, was able to take the field.

Wyatt led 4,000 men from Kent to LONDON in early February, causing much fear and confusion in the capital and the government. The queen refused to flee as she was urged, and the government was able to hold the capital and defeat Wyatt, who surrendered on 7 February. Wyatt was executed for TREASON on 11 April. Because her father, the Duke of Suffolk, had joined the Wyatt conspirators, Jane GREY, still in the TOWER OF LONDON for her part in the July 1553 coup attempt against Mary (see NORTHUMBERLAND'S COUP), was executed in February along with her husband, Guildford Dudley. The Spanish ambassador urged the execution of Elizabeth as well, and for a time this seemed likely, but the government could not prove her involvement in the conspiracy and the princess was eventually released from the Tower. *See also* BEDINGFIELD, SIR HENRY.

Further Reading: D. M. Loades, *Two Tudor Conspiracies,* Cambridge: Cambridge University Press, 1965.

Wynter, Sir William. *See* WINTER, SIR WILLIAM.

Y

Yellow Ford, Battle of

The Battle of Yellow Ford was the worst single defeat suffered by English forces in IRELAND in the sixteenth century. Occurring on 14 August 1598, in the midst of the NINE YEARS WAR, the Battle of Yellow Ford was fought in northern Ireland about nine miles north of the south-central Ulster town of Armagh. Hugh O'NEILL, Earl of Tyrone, the leader of rebel forces in northern Ireland, ambushed an English ARMY under Henry Bagenal that was carrying supplies to the beleaguered garrison in the fort on the River Blackwater. Bagenal's army of 4,200 contained over 1,800 untrained and ill-disciplined recruits who straggled well behind the vanguard as the army struggled through the rough terrain north of Armagh.

Attacked suddenly by a force of over 5,000 men under Tyrone and his son-in-law Red Hugh O'DONNELL, the English vanguard was routed, with over 800 men, including Bagenal, killed. Over 300 of the Irish soldiers in Bagenal's army deserted to Tyrone, and some 2,000 survivors fled into Armagh, having lost most of their WEAPONS and supplies. The defeat forced the abandonment of the Blackwater and Armagh garrisons, and the whole of Ulster fell under Tyrone's control. DUBLIN and the PALE lay unprotected, and the government feared Tyrone was about to descend on the capital.

Fears of an English landing in his rear prevented Tyrone from menacing Dublin, but O'Donnell invaded northwestern Ireland, overthrowing all government authority there, and Tyrone sent a force of 700 into central and southern Ireland to destroy the English plan-

tations in Leix-Offaly and Munster (see PLANTATIONS, IRISH). The victory at Yellow Ford was the high point of Irish military fortunes during the Nine Years War and served to awaken the LONDON and Dublin governments to the serious threat Tyrone and his allies presented to continued English rule in Ireland.

Further Reading: Steven G. Ellis, *Tudor Ireland*, London: Longman, 1985; Hiram Morgan, *Tyrone's Rebellion: The Outbreak of the Nine Years War in Tudor Ireland*, Rochester, NY: Boydell Press, 1993; Sean O'Faolain, *The Great O'Neill*, New York: Duell, Sloan and Pearce, 1942, reprint ed., Dufour Editions, 1997; Micheline Kerney Walsh, *Hugh O'Neill: An Exile of Ireland, Prince of Ulster*, Dublin: Four Courts Press, 1996.

Yonge, Thomas. *See* YOUNG, THOMAS.

Yorkist claim (to the throne)

The Yorkist claim to the English throne derived from Richard, Duke of York (1411–1460), who descended through his mother from the second son of Edward III (r. 1327–1377). His right to the throne was thus technically superior to that of his Lancastrian cousins, who descended from the third son of Edward III. In 1460, after years of mental illness had rendered the Lancastrian King Henry VI (r. 1422–1461, 1470–1471) unfit to rule, the Duke of York laid his claim before PARLIAMENT. The Lords forced a compromise whereby Henry VI continued to rule, but York replaced Henry's son as heir to the throne. This agreement intensified the dynastic struggle between the York and Lancaster families known as the WARS OF THE ROSES, and led to York's death in battle in December 1460 and his eldest son's seizure of the throne as Edward IV in March 1461.

After a brief restoration, the Lancastrians were finally overthrown in 1471 when Henry VI was murdered in the TOWER OF LONDON only weeks after his son's death in battle. These deaths left Henry Tudor (see TUDOR FAMILY), the last male descendent of Henry VI's Beaufort cousins (see BEAUFORT FAMILY), as the remaining Lancastrian claimant to the Crown. Tudor had little chance to make good his claim until Richard III, Edward IV's brother, usurped his nephew's throne in 1483. The unpopularity of this act won Tudor the support he needed to invade the kingdom and win the Crown (see HENRY VII) at the Battle of Bosworth in August 1485. Although Richard III had died childless at Bosworth, and Edward IV's two sons had presumably been murdered in the Tower by their uncle, numerous Yorkists remained to threaten the security of the Tudor dynasty.

The sons of Edward IV's sister Elizabeth, John, Edmund, and Richard de la Pole, either died in battle or were executed. Other Yorkists who died for their royal blood were Edward, Earl of Warwick, Edward IV's nephew, executed in 1499, and Warwick's sister Margaret, Countess of Salisbury, executed in 1541. In 1538, HENRY VIII destroyed Margaret's son Henry Pole, Lord Montegue, and Edward IV's grandson, Henry Courtenay, Marquis of Exeter. Henry sent Exeter's son Edward COURTENAY, Earl of Devon, to the Tower, where he languished until released by MARY I in 1553. Thanks to her father, Elizabeth I had few living Yorkists to contend with when she came to the throne in 1558. *See also* HASTINGS, HENRY, EARL OF HUNTINGDON. *See* the genealogical chart in Appendix 1: "Yorkist Claimants to the English Throne in the Sixteenth Century."

Further Reading: Mortimer Levine, *The Early Elizabethan Succession Question*, Stanford, CA: Stanford University Press, 1966; Mortimer Levine, *Tudor Dynastic Problems, 1460–1571*, New York: Barnes and Noble, 1973.

Young, Thomas (1507–1568)

Thomas Young (or Yonge) served as Elizabeth's first Archbishop of York. Born in Pembrokeshire in WALES, he was educated at Oxford (see UNIVERSITIES), earning his bachelor's degree in 1529 and his master's in 1533. Beginning in the early 1540s, Young held a series of church positions in Wales, including precentor (choir leader) at St. David's Cathedral. On the accession of MARY I in 1553, Young was one of a half dozen clerics who stood up in CONVOCATION to resign their offices and affirm their adherence to Protestant principles. Young then fled to Europe, spending the rest of Mary's reign in exile in Germany (see MARIAN EXILES). He returned to England on Elizabeth's accession and was restored to his former offices in 1559.

On the removal of the Marian incumbent in December 1559, Young became the first Elizabethan Bishop of St. David's in Wales. Supported by Robert DUDLEY, the royal favorite, and recommended by Matthew PARKER, the Archbishop of Canterbury, Young became Archbishop of York early in 1561. He worked to bring the archdiocese into conformity with the ANGLICAN SETTLEMENT of 1559 and also undertook the political pacification of his province as president of the Council of the North, the Crown's chief administrative organ in the north of England.

In the early 1560s, the queen placed Charles Stuart, the younger son of Elizabeth's cousin Margaret DOUGLAS, Countess of Lennox, in Young's custody. Because Stuart and his elder brother, Henry STUART, Lord Darnley (the second husband of Mary STUART, Queen of Scots), had a claim to the English throne, Young's charge was to overturn the Catholic tendencies instilled in Stuart by his mother. Young was a strong foe of political corruption and was even known to have rebuked the queen for some of her actions. Young died in June 1568 and was buried in York Minster.

Further Reading: Patrick Collinson, *The Elizabethan Puritan Movement,* Oxford: Clarendon Press, 1990.

APPENDIX 1

Genealogies

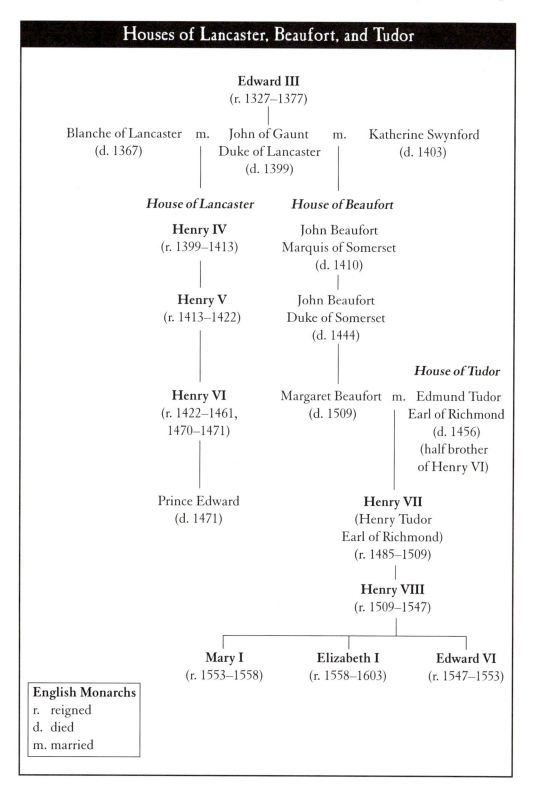

Houses of Lancaster, Beaufort, and Tudor

Edward III
(r. 1327–1377)

Blanche of Lancaster m. John of Gaunt m. Katherine Swynford
(d. 1367) Duke of Lancaster (d. 1403)
(d. 1399)

House of Lancaster *House of Beaufort*

Henry IV John Beaufort
(r. 1399–1413) Marquis of Somerset
(d. 1410)

Henry V John Beaufort
(r. 1413–1422) Duke of Somerset
(d. 1444)

House of Tudor

Henry VI Margaret Beaufort m. Edmund Tudor
(r. 1422–1461, (d. 1509) Earl of Richmond
1470–1471) (d. 1456)
(half brother
of Henry VI)

Prince Edward **Henry VII**
(d. 1471) (Henry Tudor
Earl of Richmond)
(r. 1485–1509)

Henry VIII
(r. 1509–1547)

Mary I **Elizabeth I** **Edward VI**
(r. 1553–1558) (r. 1558–1603) (r. 1547–1553)

English Monarchs
r. reigned
d. died
m. married

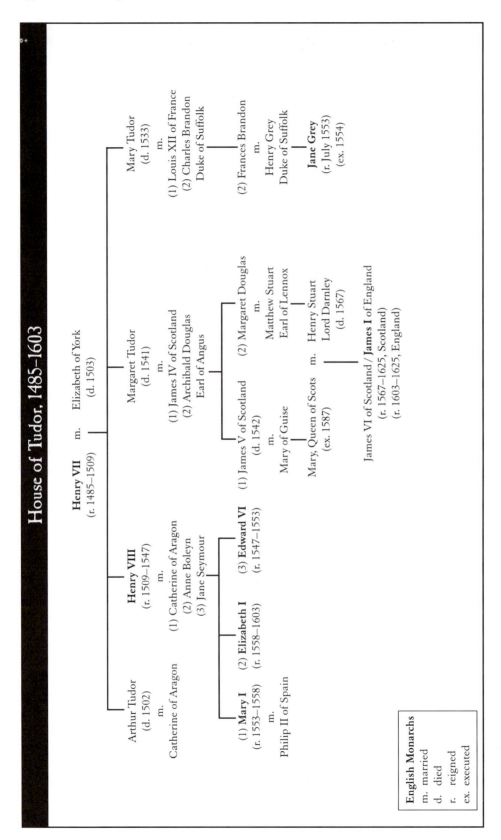

House of Tudor, 1485–1603

Henry VII (r. 1485–1509) m. Elizabeth of York (d. 1503)

Arthur Tudor (d. 1502) m. Catherine of Aragon

Henry VIII (r. 1509–1547) m. (1) Catherine of Aragon (2) Anne Boleyn (3) Jane Seymour

(1) **Mary I** (r. 1553–1558) m. Philip II of Spain

(2) **Elizabeth I** (r. 1558–1603)

(3) **Edward VI** (r. 1547–1553)

Margaret Tudor (d. 1541) m. (1) James IV of Scotland (2) Archibald Douglas Earl of Angus

(1) James V of Scotland (d. 1542) m. Mary of Guise

Mary, Queen of Scots (ex. 1587) m.

(2) Margaret Douglas m. Matthew Stuart Earl of Lennox

Henry Stuart Lord Darnley (d. 1567)

James VI of Scotland / **James I** of England (r. 1567–1625, Scotland) (r. 1603–1625, England)

Mary Tudor (d. 1533) m. (1) Louis XII of France (2) Charles Brandon Duke of Suffolk

(2) Frances Brandon m. Henry Grey Duke of Suffolk

Jane Grey (r. July 1553) (ex. 1554)

English Monarchs
m. married
d. died
r. reigned
ex. executed

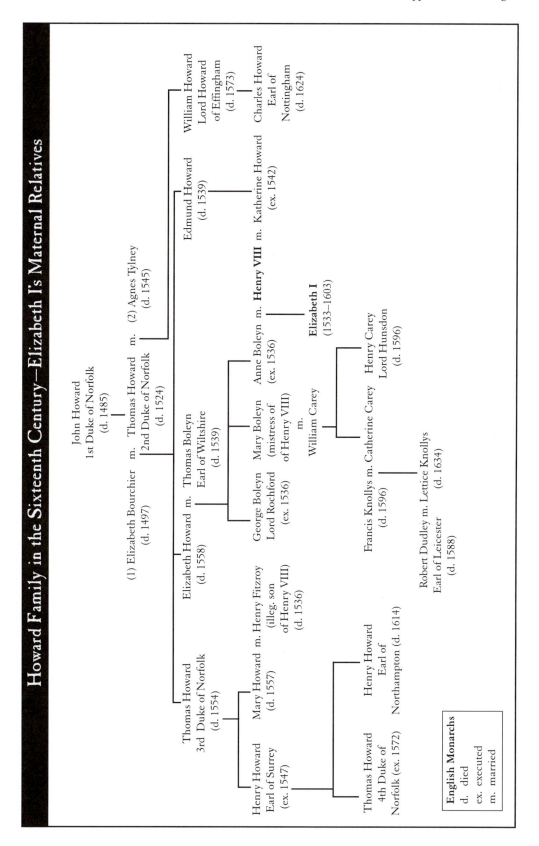

Howard Family in the Sixteenth Century—Elizabeth I's Maternal Relatives

John Howard
1st Duke of Norfolk
(d. 1485)

(1) Elizabeth Bourchier   m.   Thomas Howard   m.   (2) Agnes Tylney
(d. 1497)   2nd Duke of Norfolk   (d. 1545)
                                   (d. 1524)

Elizabeth Howard   m.   Thomas Boleyn
(d. 1558)   Earl of Wiltshire
                          (d. 1539)

Edmund Howard
(d. 1539)

William Howard
Lord Howard
of Effingham
(d. 1573)

George Boleyn
Lord Rochford
(ex. 1536)

Mary Boleyn
(mistress of
of Henry VIII)
m.
William Carey

Anne Boleyn   m.   Henry VIII
(ex. 1536)

Katherine Howard
(ex. 1542)

Charles Howard
Earl of
Nottingham
(d. 1624)

Elizabeth I
(1533–1603)

Thomas Howard
3rd Duke of Norfolk
(d. 1554)

Mary Howard   m.   Henry Fitzroy
(d. 1557)   (illeg. son
                      of Henry VIII)
                      (d. 1536)

Francis Knollys   m.   Catherine Carey
(d. 1596)

Henry Carey
Lord Hunsdon
(d. 1596)

Robert Dudley   m.   Lettice Knollys
Earl of Leicester   (d. 1634)
(d. 1588)

Henry Howard
Earl of Surrey
(ex. 1547)

Henry Howard
Earl of
Northampton (d. 1614)

Thomas Howard
4th Duke of
Norfolk (ex. 1572)

English Monarchs

d.   died
ex. executed
m. married

Yorkist Claimants to the English Throne in the Sixteenth Century

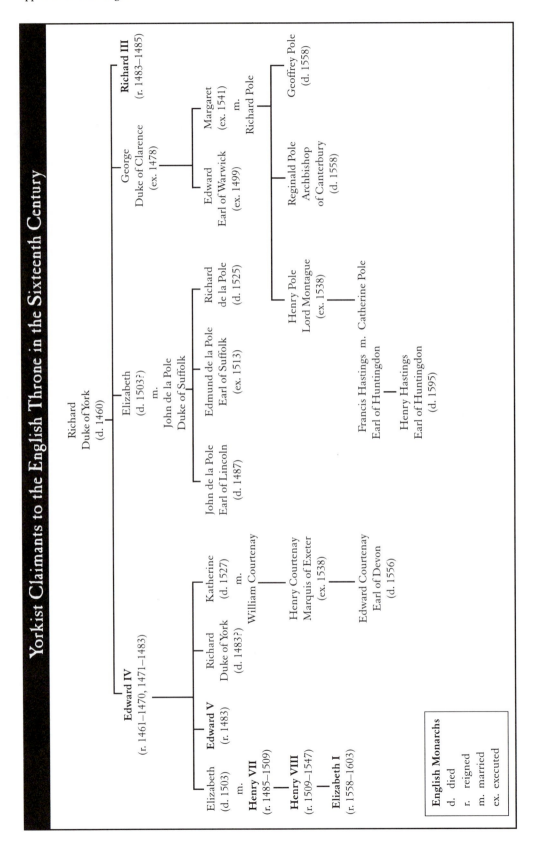

Richard
Duke of York
(d. 1460)

Edward IV
(r. 1461–1470, 1471–1483)

Elizabeth
(d. 1503?)
m.
John de la Pole
Duke of Suffolk

George
Duke of Clarence
(ex. 1478)

Richard III
(r. 1483–1485)

Elizabeth
(d. 1503)
m.
Henry VII
(r. 1485–1509)

Edward V
(r. 1483)

Richard
Duke of York
(d. 1483?)

Katherine
(d. 1527)
m.
William Courtenay

John de la Pole
Earl of Lincoln
(d. 1487)

Edmund de la Pole
Earl of Suffolk
(ex. 1513)

Richard
de la Pole
(d. 1525)

Edward
Earl of Warwick
(ex. 1499)

Margaret
(ex. 1541)
m.
Richard Pole

Reginald Pole
Archbishop
of Canterbury
(d. 1558)

Geoffrey Pole
(d. 1558)

Henry Pole
Lord Montague
(ex. 1538)

Henry VIII
(r. 1509–1547)

Henry Courtenay
Marquis of Exeter
(ex. 1538)

Francis Hastings m. Catherine Pole
Earl of Huntingdon

Elizabeth I
(r. 1558–1603)

Edward Courtenay
Earl of Devon
(d. 1556)

Henry Hastings
Earl of Huntingdon
(d. 1595)

English Monarchs

d.   died
r.   reigned
m.   married
ex.   executed

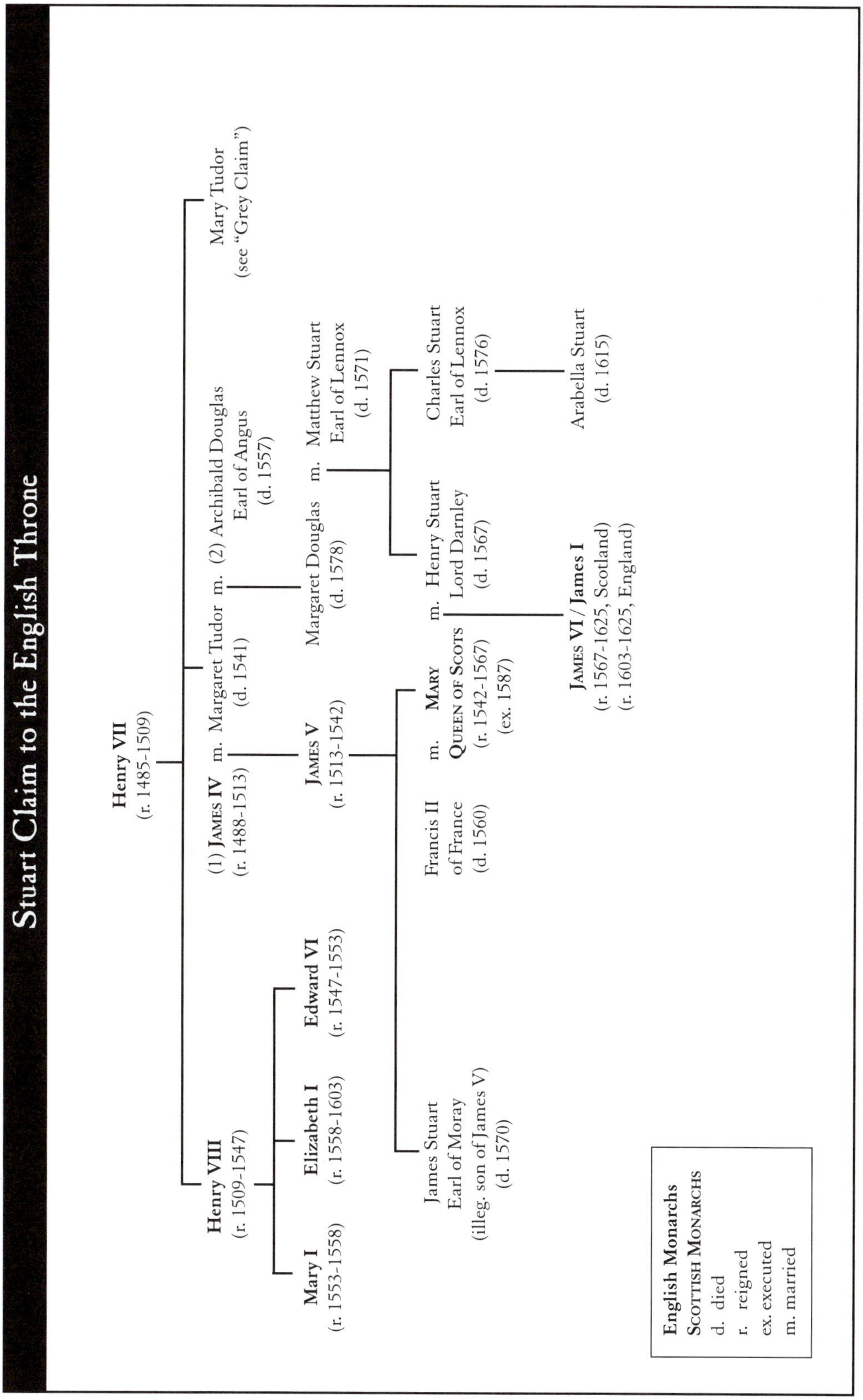

Stuart Claim to the English Throne

Henry VII
(r. 1485–1509)

Henry VIII
(r. 1509–1547)

Mary I
(r. 1553–1558)

Elizabeth I
(r. 1558–1603)

Edward VI
(r. 1547–1553)

(1) **James IV** m. Margaret Tudor m. (2) Archibald Douglas
(r. 1488–1513)   (d. 1541)   Earl of Angus
(d. 1557)

James V
(r. 1513–1542)

Margaret Douglas   m. Matthew Stuart
(d. 1578)   Earl of Lennox
(d. 1571)

Mary Tudor
(see "Grey Claim")

James Stuart
Earl of Moray
(illeg. son of James V)
(d. 1570)

Francis II   m. **Mary**   m. Henry Stuart
of France   **Queen of Scots**   Lord Darnley
(d. 1560)   (r. 1542–1567)   (d. 1567)
(ex. 1587)

Charles Stuart
Earl of Lennox
(d. 1576)

James VI / James I
(r. 1567–1625, Scotland)
(r. 1603–1625, England)

Arabella Stuart
(d. 1615)

English Monarchs
Scottish Monarchs
d. died
r. reigned
ex. executed
m. married

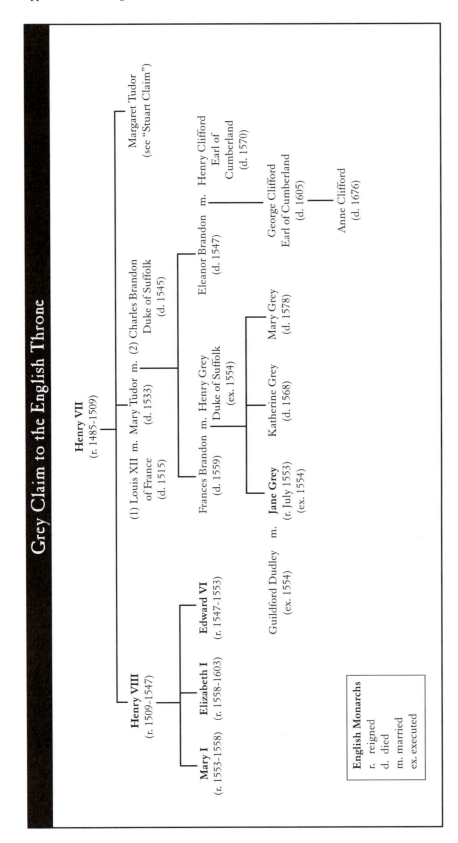

Grey Claim to the English Throne

Henry VII
(r. 1485–1509)

Margaret Tudor
(see "Stuart Claim")

(1) Louis XII m. Mary Tudor m. (2) Charles Brandon
of France   (d. 1533)   Duke of Suffolk
(d. 1515)   (d. 1545)

Eleanor Brandon m. Henry Clifford
(d. 1547)   Earl of
                 Cumberland
                 (d. 1570)

George Clifford
Earl of Cumberland
(d. 1605)

Anne Clifford
(d. 1676)

Frances Brandon m. Henry Grey
(d. 1559)   Duke of Suffolk
                 (ex. 1554)

Mary Grey
(d. 1578)

Katherine Grey
(d. 1568)

Jane Grey
(r. July 1553)
(ex. 1554)

Guildford Dudley m.
(ex. 1554)

Henry VIII
(r. 1509–1547)

Edward VI
(r. 1547–1553)

Elizabeth I
(r. 1558–1603)

Mary I
(r. 1553–1558)

English Monarchs
r. reigned
d. died
m. married
ex. executed

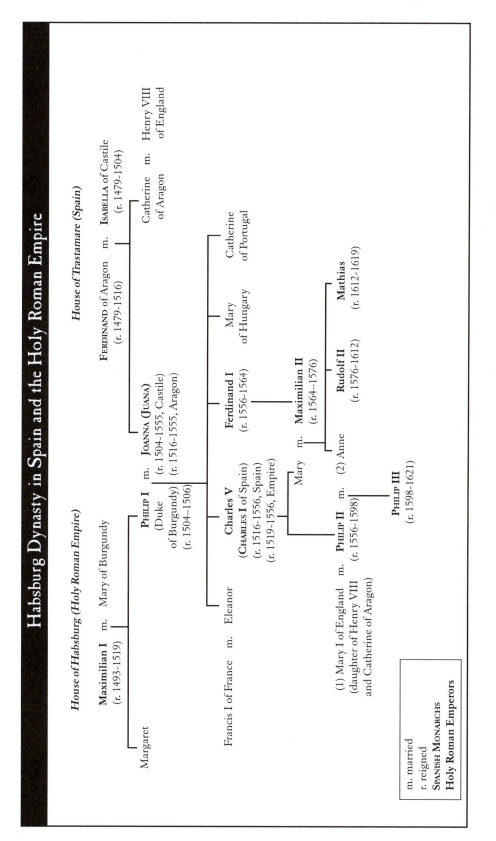

Habsburg Dynasty in Spain and the Holy Roman Empire

House of Habsburg (Holy Roman Empire)

House of Trastamare (Spain)

Maximilian I m. Mary of Burgundy
(r. 1493-1519)

FERDINAND of Aragon m. **ISABELLA** of Castile
(r. 1479-1516)   (r. 1479-1504)

Margaret

Catherine m. Henry VIII
of Aragon   of England

PHILIP I m. **JOANNA (JUANA)**
(Duke   (r. 1504-1555, Castile)
of Burgundy)   (r. 1516-1555, Aragon)
(r. 1504-1506)

Francis I of France m. Eleanor

Catherine
of Portugal

Charles V **Ferdinand I** Mary
(**CHARLES I** of Spain) (r. 1556-1564) of Hungary
(r. 1516-1556, Spain)
(r. 1519-1556, Empire)

Mary m. **Maximilian II** Rudolf II Mathias
(r. 1564-1576) (r. 1576-1612) (r. 1612-1619)

Mary m. **PHILIP II** (2) Anne
(r. 1556-1598)

(1) Mary I of England m.
(daughter of Henry VIII
and Catherine of Aragon)

PHILIP III
(r. 1598-1621)

m. married
r. reigned
SPANISH MONARCHS
Holy Roman Emperors

343

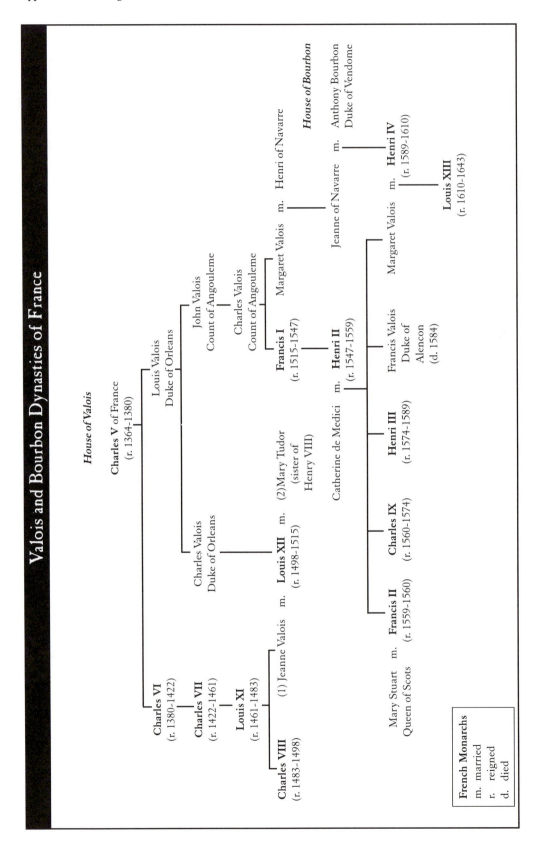

Valois and Bourbon Dynasties of France

House of Valois

Charles V of France
(r. 1364-1380)

Louis Valois
Duke of Orleans

John Valois
Count of Angouleme

Charles Valois
Count of Angouleme

Margaret Valois   m.   Henri of Navarre

House of Bourbon

Anthony Bourbon
Duke of Vendome

Jeanne of Navarre   m.

Henri IV
(r. 1589-1610)

Louis XIII
(r. 1610-1643)

Charles VI
(r. 1380-1422)

Charles VII
(r. 1422-1461)

Louis XI
(r. 1461-1483)

Charles VIII
(r. 1483-1498)

(1) Jeanne Valois   m.   **Louis XII**
(r. 1498-1515)

Charles Valois
Duke of Orleans

(2) Mary Tudor
(sister of
Henry VIII)

Francis I
(r. 1515-1547)

Henri II
(r. 1547-1559)

Catherine de Medici   m.

Francis Valois
Duke of
Alencon
(d. 1584)

Margaret Valois   m.

Francis II
(r. 1559-1560)

Charles IX
(r. 1560-1574)

Henri III
(r. 1574-1589)

Mary Stuart   m.
Queen of Scots

French Monarchs
m. married
r. reigned
d. died

344

APPENDIX 2

Elizabethan Archbishops of Canterbury and York and Roman Catholic Popes

Archbishops of Canterbury	Archbishops of York	Roman Catholic Popes
Matthew Parker (1559–1575)	Thomas Young (1561–1568)	Pius IV *(Gian-Angelo de Medici)* (1559–1565)
Edmund Grindal (1576–1583)	Edmund Grindal (1570–1576)	Pius V *(Michele Ghislieri)* (1565–1572)
John Whitgift (1583–1604)	Edwin Sandys (1577–1588)	Gregory XIII *(Ugo Buoncompagni)* (1572–1585)
	John Piers (1589–1594)	Sixtus V *(Felix Peretti)* (1586–1590)
	Matthew Hutton (1595–1606)	Urban VIII *(Giambattista Castagna)* (1590)
		Gregory XIV *(Niccolo Sfondrato)* (1590–1591)
		Innocent IX *(Gian-Antonio Fachinetto)* (1591)
		Clement VIII *(Ippolito Aldobrandini)* (1592–1605)

APPENDIX 3

European Monarchs in the Sixteenth Century

English Monarchs

House of Tudor

Henry VII
(1485–1509)

Henry VIII
(1509–1547)

Edward VI
(1547–1553)

Mary I
(1553–1558)

Elizabeth I
(1558–1603)

House of Stuart

James I
(1603–1625)
(James VI of Scotland
from 1567)

French Monarchs

House of Valois

Louis XII
(1498–1515)

Francis I
(1515–1547)

Henri II
(1547–1559)

Francis II
(1559–1560)

Charles IX
(1560–1574)

Henri III
(1574–1589)

House of Bourbon

Henri IV
(1589–1610)

Louis XIII
(1610–1643)

Scottish Monarchs

House of Stuart

James IV
(1488–1513)

James V
(1513–1542)

Mary, Queen of Scots
(1542–1567)

James VI
(1567–1625)
(James I of England
from 1603)

Spanish Monarchs

House of Trastamare

Ferdinand of Aragon/
Isabella of Castile
(joint monarchs of
Spain)
(1479–1504)

Ferdinand of Aragon/
Joanna of Castile*/
Philip I (Habsburg)
of Castile (joint
monarchs of Spain)
(1504–1506)

Ferdinand of Aragon/
Joanna of Castile (joint
monarchs of Spain)
(1506–1516)

House of Habsburg

Charles I (also Holy
Roman Emperor as
Charles V after 1519)
(1516–1556)

Philip II
(1556–1598)

Philip III
(1598–1621)

*Although Joanna of Castile, daughter of Ferdinand and Isabella and mother of Charles I, succeeded her mother as queen of Castile in 1504 and remained queen until her death in 1555, mental instability prevented her from ever ruling. Spain was thus effectively ruled only by her father King Ferdinand between 1504 and 1516, and only by her son Charles I between 1516 and 1556.

APPENDIX 4

Selected Historical Fiction
with Tudor and Elizabethan Characters and Settings

Two excellent sources of information on works of historical fiction for the Elizabethan period, and for many other periods of history as well, are Lynda G. Adamson, *World Historical Fiction: An Annotated Guide to Novels for Adults and Young Adults*, Phoenix: Oryx Press, 1999, and Donald K. Hartman and Gregg Sapp, *Historical Figures in Fiction*, Phoenix: Oryx Press, 1994.

America

Fletcher, Inglis. *Roanoke Hundred*. Indianapolis: Bobbs-Merrill, 1954.

Hunt, Angela Elwell. *Roanoke*. Wheaton, IL: Tyndale House, 1996.

Plaidy, Jean. *Daughter of Satan*. New York: Putnam, 1973.

Anne Boleyn

Anthony, Evelyn. *Anne Boleyn*. New York: Crowell, 1957.

Barnes, Margaret Ayer. *Brief Gaudy Hour: A Novel of Anne Boleyn*. Philadelphia: Macrae-Smith, 1949.

Beck, L. Adams. *Anne Boleyn*. Garden City, NY: Doubleday, 1934.

Fenton, Edward. *Anne of the Thousand Days*. New York: New American Library, 1970.

Hardwick, Mollie. *Blood Royal*. New York: St. Martin's Press, 1989.

Lofts, Norah. *The Concubine*. Garden City, NY: Doubleday, 1963.

Maxwell, Robin. *The Secret Diary of Anne Boleyn*. New York: Arcade, 1997.

Plaidy, Jean. *Murder Most Royal*. New York: Putnam, 1972.

Catherine of Aragon

Lofts, Norah. *The King's Pleasure*. Garden City, NY: Doubleday, 1969.

Plaidy, Jean. *The King's Secret Matter*. New York: Putnam, 1995.

John Dee

Ackroyd, Peter. *The House of Doctor Dee*. London: Hamilton, 1993.

Robert Devereux, Earl of Essex

Eckerson, Olive. *My Lord Essex*. New York: Holt, 1955.

Margaret Douglas, Countess of Lennox

Hill, Pamela. *The Green Salamander*. New York: St. Martin's Press, 1977.

Sir Francis Drake

Fredman, John. *Does the Queen Still Live?* London: Allen, 1979.

Mason, F. Van Wyck. *Golden Admiral*. Garden City, NY: Doubleday, 1953.

Robert Dudley, Earl of Leicester

Letton, Jennette and Letton, Francis. *The Robsart Affair*. New York: Harper, 1956.

Plaidy, Jean. *Gay Lord Robert*. New York: Putnam, 1971.

Scott, Walter. *Kenilworth*. New York: Columbia, 1993.

Edward VI

Twain, Mark. *The Prince and the Pauper*. New York: Harper and Brothers, 1881.

Elizabeth I, As Main Character

Anthony, Evelyn. *All the Queen's Men*. New York: Crowell, 1960.

Bennetts, Pamela. *My Dear Lover England*. New York: St. Martin's Press, 1975.

Birkhead, Margaret. *Trust and Treason*. New York: St. Martin's Press, 1991.

Buckley, Fiona. *The Doublet Affair*. New York: Scribner's, 1998.

———. *To Shield a Queen*. New York: Scribner's, 1997.

Dessau, Joanna. *Absolute Elizabeth*. New York: St. Martin's Press, 1979. (Sequel to *The Red-Haired Brat*)

———. *The Red-Haired Brat*. New York: St. Martin's Press, 1979.

Ellis, Amanda. *Elizabeth, the Woman*. New York: Dutton, 1951.

Elsna, Hebe. *Prelude for Two Queens*. London: Collins, 1972.

———. *The Queen's Ward*. New York: Beagle, 1971.

Garrett, George P. *The Succession*. Garden City, NY: Doubleday, 1983.

Harper, Karen. *The Poyson Garden*. New York: Delacorte, 1999.

Heaven, Constance. *The Queen and the Gypsy*. New York: Coward-McCann, 1977.

Irwin, Margaret. *Elizabeth and the Prince of Spain*. New York: Harcourt, Brace, 1953. (Sequel to *Elizabeth, Captive Princess*)

———. *Elizabeth, Captive Princess*. New York: Harcourt, 1948. (Sequel to *Young Bess*)

———. *Young Bess*. New York: Harcourt, 1945.

Kay, Susan. *Legacy*. New York: Crown, 1986.

Kenyon, Frank Wilson. *Shadow in the Sun*. New York: Crowell, 1958.

Letton, Jennette and Letton, Francis. *The Young Elizabeth*. New York: Harper and Brothers, 1953.

Miles, Rosalind. *I, Elizabeth*. New York: Doubleday, 1994.

Osborne, Maggie. *Chase the Heart*. New York: Morrow, 1987.

Plaidy, Jean. *Queen of This Realm*. New York: Putnam, 1985.

Thane, Elswyth. *The Tudor Wench*. New York: Harcourt, 1932.

Thorpe, Helen. *Elizabeth, Queen and Woman*. New York: Roy, 1972.

Wilson, Derek A. *Her Majesty's Captain*. Boston: Little, Brown, 1978.

Elizabeth I, Set in Reign of

Bennetts, Pamela. *Envoy from Elizabeth*. New York: St. Martin's Press, 1973.

Bryher, Winifred. *The Player's Boy*. New York: Pantheon, 1953.

Burd, Elizabeth. *Immortal Queen*. New York: Ballantine, 1956.

Carr, Philippa. *The Lion Triumphant*. New York: Putnam, 1973. (Sequel to *The Miracle at St. Bruno's*)

———. *The Witch from the Sea*. New York: Putnam, 1975. (Sequel to *The Lion Triumphant*)

Chisholm, P. F. *A Famine of Horses*. New York: Walker, 1995.

———. *A Season of Knives*. New York: Walker, 1996.

———. *A Surfeit of Guns*. New York: Walker, 1997.

Domning, Denise. *Lady in Waiting*. New York: New American Library, 1998.

Emerson, Kathy Lynn. *Face Down in the Marrow-Bone Pit*. New York: St. Martin's Press, 1997.

———. *Face Down upon an Herbal*. New York: St. Martin's Press, 1998.

Finney, Patricia. *Firedrake's Eye*. New York: St. Martin's Press, 1992.

———. *Unicorn's Blood*. New York: St. Martin's Press, 1998.

Goldstein, Lisa. *Strange Devices of the Sun and the Moon*. New York: St. Martin's Press, 1993.

Hardwick, Mollie. *The Merrymaid*. New York: St. Martin's Press, 1984.

Heyer, Georgette. *Beauvallet*. New York: Dutton, 1968.

Kingsley, Charles. *Westward Ho!*. New York: Buccaneer, 1985.

Macleod, Alison. *The Muscovite*. Boston: Houghton Mifflin, 1971.

———. *Prisoner of the Queen*. Boston: Houghton Mifflin, 1973.

Malpass, Eric. *A House of Women*. New York: St. Martin's, 1975.

Morgan, Cynthia. *Court of Shadows*. New York: Ballantine, 1992.

Tourney, Leonard D. *Familiar Spirits*. New York: St. Martin's Press, 1984.

———. *Frobisher's Savage*. New York: St. Martin's Press, 1994.

———. *Knaves Templar*. New York: St. Martin's Press, 1991.

———. *Low Treason*. New York: Dutton, 1982.

———. *Old Saxon Blood*. New York: St. Martin's Press, 1988.

Wiat, Philippa. *Lion without Claws*. New York: St. Martin's Press, 1977.

Wiggs, Susan. *Vows Made in Wine*. New York: HarperCollins, 1995.

York, Robert. *My Lord the Fox*. New York: Vanguard, 1986.

Simon Forman

Dhondy, Farrukh. *Black Swan*. Boston: Houghton Mifflin, 1993.

Lady Jane Grey

Mullally, Margaret. *A Crown in Darkness*. New York: St. Martin's Press, 1975.

Elizabeth Hardwick

Westcott, Jan V. *The Tower and the Dream*. New York: Putnam, 1974.

Henry VIII

Barnes, Margaret Campbell. *King's Fool*. Philadelphia: Macrae-Smith, 1959.

———. *My Lady of Cleves*. Philadelphia: Macrae-Smith, 1946.

Beahn, John E. *A Man Born Again: Saint Thomas More*. New York: Bruce, 1954.

Carr, Philippa. *The Miracle at St. Bruno's*. New York: Putnam, 1972

George, Margaret. *The Autobiography of Henry VIII: With Notes by His Fool, Will Somers*. New York: St. Martin's Press, 1986.

Lide, Mary. *Command of the King*. New York: St. Martin's Press, 1991.

Peters, Maureen. *Henry VIII and His Six Wives*. New York: St. Martin's Press, 1972.

Plaidy, Jean. *St. Thomas's Eve*. New York: Putnam, 1970.

Prescott, H. F. M. *The Man on a Donkey*. New York: Macmillan, 1952.

Riley, Judith Merkle. *The Serpent Garden*. New York: Viking, 1996.

Katherine Howard

Ford, Ford Madox. *The Fifth Queen Crowned*. New York: Vanguard, 1963.

Plaidy, Jane. *The Rose without a Thorn*. New York: Putnam, 1994.

Ireland

Bell, Sam Hanna. *Across the Narrow Sea*. Wolfboro, NH: Blackstaff, 1987.

Chambers, Anne. *The Geraldine Conspiracy*. Dublin: Marino, 1995.

Hannon, Edward G. *Man Alive-Man Dead*. London: Mitre, 1975.

Joyce, Brenda. *The Game*. New York: Avon, 1994.

L'Amour, Louis. *Fair Blows the Wind*. New York: Dutton, 1978.

Llywelyn, Morgan. *Grania*. New York: Crown, 1986.

———. *The Last Prince of Ireland*. New York: Morrow, 1992.

Wiggs, Susan. *Dancing on Air*. New York: HarperCollins, 1996.

Lettice Knollys

Holt, Victoria. *My Enemy the Queen*. Garden City, NY: Doubleday, 1978.

Christopher Marlowe

Burgess, Anthony. *A Dead Man in Deptford*. New York: Carroll and Graf, 1995.

Cook, Judith. *The Slicing Edge of Death*. New York: St. Martin's Press, 1993.

Cowell, Stephanie. *Nicholas Cooke*. New York: Norton, 1993.

DeMaria, Robert. *To Be a King*. Indianapolis: Bobbs-Merrill, 1976.

Garrett, George P. *Entered from the Sun*. Garden City, NY: Doubleday, 1990.

Maguire, Liam. *Icarus Flying*. Morden Park, England: Ormond, 1993.

Mary I

Dukthas, Ann. *In the Time of the Poisoned Queen*. New York: St. Martin's Press, 1998.

Lewis, Hilda Winifred. *I Am Mary Tudor*. New York: McKay, 1972.

Plaidy, Jean. *In the Shadow of the Crown*. New York: Putnam, 1988.

Katherine Parr

Eady, Carol Maxwell. *Her Royal Destiny*. New York: Harmony, 1985.

Luke, Mary M. *The Ivy Crown*. Garden City, NY: Doubleday, 1984.

Plaidy, Jean. *The Sixth Wife*. New York: Putnam, 1969.

Sir Walter Raleigh

Garrett, George P. *Death of the Fox*. San Diego: Harcourt, 1971.

Graham, Winston. *The Grove of Eagles*. Garden City, NY: Doubleday, 1964.

Nye, Robert. *The Voyage of the Destiny*. New York: Putnam, 1982.

Rose, Mark. *Golding's Tale*. New York: Walker, 1972.

Schoonover, Lawrence. *To Love a Queen*. Boston: Little, Brown, 1973.

Sutcliff, Rosemary. *Lady in Waiting*. New York: Coward-McCann, 1957.

Turner, Judy. *Ralegh's Fair Bess*. New York: St. Martin's Press, 1974.

Scotland

Blair, Anna. *A Tree in the West*. London: Collins, 1976.

Hunter, Mollie. *The Spanish Letters*. New York: Funk and Wagnalls, 1967.

Johansen, Iris. *The Magnificent Rogue*. New York: Bantam, 1993.

Kerr, Robert. *The Stuart Legacy*. New York: Stein and Day, 1973.

Lennox-Smith, Judith. *Till the Day Goes Down*. New York: St. Martin's Press, 1992.

Lindsey, Johanna. *A Gentle Feuding*. New York: Avon, 1984.

Thomas Seymour, Lord Seymour

Lane, Jane. *Heirs of Squire Harry*. London: Davies, 1974.

William Shakespeare

Alexander, Louis C. *The Autobiography of Shakespeare*. Port Washington, NY: Kennikat Press, 1970.

Burgess, Anthony. *Nothing Like the Sun*. New York: Norton, 1996.

Burton, Philip. *You, My Brother*. New York: Random House, 1973.

Cowell, Stephanie. *The Players*. New York: Norton, 1997.

Fisher, Edward. *The Best House in Stratford*. New York: Abelard-Schuman, 1965.

———. *Love's Labour's Lost: A Novel about Shakespeare's Lost Years*. New York: Abelard-Schuman, 1963.

———. *Shakespeare and Son*. New York: Abelard-Schuman, 1962.

Friedlander, Mark P. *The Shakespeare Transcripts*. Woodbridge, CT: Ox Bow, 1993.

Hays, Tony. *Murder on the Twelfth Night*. Bell Buckle, TN: Iris, 1993.

Jowett, Margaret. *A Cry of Players*. New York: Roy, 1963.

Kellerman, Faye. *The Quality of Mercy*. New York: Morrow, 1989.

MacInnes, Colin. *Three Years to Play*. New York: Farrar, Straus and Giroux, 1970.

Malpass, Eric Lawson. *The Cleopatra Boy*. New York: St. Martin's Press, 1974.

———. *Sweet Will*. New York: St. Martin's Press, 1974.

Mortimer, John Clifford. *Will Shakespeare*. New York: Dell, 1977.

Rooke, Leon. *Shakespeare's Dog*. New York: Knopf, 1983.

Tourney, Leonard D. *The Player's Boy Is Dead*. New York: Harper and Row, 1980.

Arabella Stuart

Haycraft, Molly Costain. *Too Near the Throne*. Philadelphia: Lippincott, 1962.

Leslie, Doris. *Wreath for Arabella*. New York: Pocket Books, 1969.

Mary Stuart, Queen of Scots

Balin, Beverly. *King in Hell*. New York: Coward-McCann, 1971.

Bowen, Marjorie. *Double Dallilay*. London: Cassell, 1933.

Byrd, Elizabeth. *Maid of Honour: A Novel Set in the Court of Mary Queen of Scots*. New York: St. Martin's Press, 1979.

Dukthas, Ann. *A Time for the Death of a King*. New York: St. Martin's Press, 1994.

Dunnett, Dorothy. *The Game of Kings*. New York: Putnam, 1961.

———. *Queen's Play*. New York: Vintage Books, 1997.

Fallon, Frederic. *The White Queen*. Garden City, NY: Doubleday, 1972.

George, Margaret. *Mary Queen of Scotland and the Isles*. New York: St. Martin's Press, 1992.

Harwood, Alice. *Seats of the Mighty*. Indianapolis: Bobbs-Merrill, 1956.

Lane, Jane. *Parcel of Rogues*. New York: Rinehart, 1948.

Plaidy, Jean. *The Captive Queen of Scots*. New York: Putnam, 1970.

———. *Royal Road to Fotheringay*. New York: Putnam, 1968.

APPENDIX 5

Selected Motion Pictures
with Tudor and Elizabethan Characters and Settings

Elizabeth, *1998*
Starring Cate Blanchett, Joseph Fiennes, Geoffrey Rush, Christopher Eccleston, and Fanny Ardent. Directed by Shekhar Kapur. Color. Available from <http://www.amazon.com>.

Nominated for the Academy Award for best film of 1998, *Elizabeth* is a wonderfully entertaining costume drama but absolutely wretched history. The heart of the film is the increasingly violent power struggle between Catholic and Protestant factions at the English court. As a Protestant, Elizabeth (Blanchett) is the target of Catholic intrigues, both before and after she ascends the throne. The young queen gains confidence in herself as she survives several rather dramatically contrived attempts on her life by the Catholic Duke of Norfolk (Eccleston), and several plots hatched by her own disloyal councilors, including her lover Robert Dudley (Fiennes). She also wisely sidesteps a marriage proposal from a hilariously manic Duke of Alençon, who ruins his chances for the queen's hand by displaying a fondness for wearing the queen's clothes.

The one man the queen can trust is the sinister Francis Walsingham (Rush), a master spy willing to do whatever is necessary to secure Elizabeth on her throne. All these characters were actual Elizabethan figures, but none of them behaved in this way—the depiction of Walsingham (a stern and moralistic Puritan) as the cold-blooded seducer and murderer of the Queen Regent of Scotland (Ardent) is particularly outrageous. Most of the events portrayed in the film (except the more far-fetched attempts on Elizabeth's life) happened, but they are drawn from throughout Elizabeth's 44 years on the

throne and telescoped into the first 5 years of the reign. Blanchett gives a strong performance, and the film is a good, if somewhat dark, evocation of life at the Elizabethan court, but if you want something approaching accurate Elizabethan history, view *Elizabeth R* instead.

Elizabeth R, *1972*
Starring Glenda Jackson, Robert Hardy, Ronald Hines, Robin Ellis, and Vivian Pickles. Directed by Roderick Graham, Richard Martin, Claude Whatham, Donald Whatham, and Herbert Wise. 540 minutes (six 90-minute cassettes); VHS; color. Available from CBS/Fox Video, P.O. Box 900, Beverly Hills, CA 90213, 800-800-2369.

This series is a well-acted and generally accurate retelling of the life of Elizabeth I from the death of her father in 1547, when she was 13, to her own death in 1603 at age 69. Jackson is outstanding as Elizabeth, a role the actress first played in the 1971 film *Mary, Queen of Scots*. The six episodes of this series, which was first broadcast in the U.S. on PBS, focus on the following events of the queen's life: Elizabeth's trials during the reigns of her half brother and half sister; her romantic relationship with Robert Dudley, Earl of Leicester (Hardy), and political partnership with Sir William Cecil (Hines); her marriage flirtation with the French Duke of Alençon; her relationship with Mary, Queen of Scots (Pickles); the Armada crisis; and the career of Robert Devereux, Earl of Essex (Ellis).

Elizabeth, the Queen, *1968*
Starring Judith Anderson and Charlton Heston. Directed by George Schaefer. 76 min-

utes; VHS, Beta; color. Available from Films for the Humanities and Sciences, P.O. Box 2053, Princeton, NJ 08543, 800-257-5126.

Although not as entertaining as *The Private Lives of Elizabeth and Essex* from 1939, this depiction of the complex relationship between Elizabeth (Anderson) and her last and much younger favorite, Robert Devereux, Earl of Essex (Heston), is more historically accurate. Heston is a somewhat overly heroic Essex, but the film does a good job of interpreting a relationship—monarch and favorite—that was familiar to the sixteenth century but is foreign to the twentieth.

Fire over England, *1937*

Starring Flora Robson, Raymond Massey, Laurence Olivier, and Vivien Leigh. Directed by William K. Howard. 81 minutes; VHS, Beta; black and white. Available from Nostalgia Family Video, P.O. Box 606, Baker City, OR 97814, 800-784-8362; Moore Video, P.O. Box 5703, Richmond, VA 23220, 804-745-9785; Video Yesteryear, Box C, Sandy Hook, CT 06482, 800-243-0987.

This retelling of the Armada crisis of 1588 made some history of its own by being the first film to pair Olivier and Leigh. Olivier plays a fictional character, a dashing young English gentleman and naval officer who (of course) arouses the romantic interest of the queen (Robson) and one of the ladies of the court (Leigh). He volunteers to go to Spain, posing as an English Catholic opposed to the Elizabethan regime, to discover King Philip's (Massey) invasion plans and learn the names of the pro-Spanish traitors among the English gentry and nobility. His adventures in Spain and with the English fleet are all very exciting and romantic, and all very fictional. The film's strengths are Robson's powerful portrayal of Elizabeth and its realistic depiction of the growing anxiety that the looming crisis with Spain created throughout England in the years before the Armada.

Henry V, *1944*

Starring Laurence Olivier, Robert Newton, Leslie Banks, Esmond Knight, and Renee Asherson. Directed by Laurence Olivier. 136 minutes; VHS, Beta; color. Available from Paramount Home Video, Bluhdorn Building, 5555 Melrose Avenue, Los Angeles, CA 90038, 213-956-3952; Home Vision Cinema, 5547 N. Ravenswood Avenue, Chicago, IL 60640, 800-826-3456.

Although the history behind this film adaptation of Shakespeare's play is early fifteenth century, the first act and part of the second act are presented here as if they were a sixteenth-century performance for an Elizabethan audience at the Globe Theatre. The stage performance eventually transforms into realistic historical settings. The film is thus an excellent evocation of the Elizabethan stage and a glimpse of how the Elizabethans viewed the turbulent history of their country in the previous century.

Mary, Queen of Scots, *1971*

Starring Vanessa Redgrave, Glenda Jackson, Patrick McGoohan, Timothy Dalton, and Nigel Davenport. Directed by Charles Jarrott. 110 minutes; color. Available from Universal Studios Home Video, 100 Universal City Plaza, Universal City, CA 91608, 818-777-1000.

Although generally accurate, this portrayal of the life of Mary of Scotland (Redgrave) could not resist staging several dramatic—though fictional—meetings between Mary and Elizabeth (Jackson). In real life, so far as we know, the two cousins never met. The film is highly sympathetic to Mary, whose unfortunate personal and political choices are made to seem sensible by the way the men in her life are portrayed—her Guise uncles are calculating; her half brother Moray (McGoohan) is stern and cold; her second husband Darnley (Dalton) is treacherous, cruel, and dissolute; and her last husband, Bothwell (Davenport), is strong, brave, and loyal. Mary's complicity with Bothwell in the murder of Darnley is left ambiguous, and the queen's brief, disastrous marriage to Bothwell is portrayed as tragic romance. However, both Jackson and Redgrave give powerful and realistic performances.

The Private Lives of Elizabeth and Essex, *1939*

Starring Bette Davis, Errol Flynn, Vincent Price, Olivia de Havilland, and Nanette Fabray. Directed by Michael Curtiz. 106 minutes; VHS, Beta; color. Available from CBS/Fox Video, P.O. Box 900, Beverly Hills, CA 90213, 800-800-2369.

This retelling of the story of Elizabeth (Davis) and the young favorite of her later years, Robert Devereux, Earl of Essex (Flynn), is well-acted and lavishly costumed, but almost completely fictional in its depiction of the central relationship. Hollywood has always been fascinated by the Virgin Queen, never quite believing the "virgin" part; here the queen and Essex are clearly lovers, which the real Elizabeth and Essex probably were not. Flynn and Davis appear much too close in age to convincingly portray the nearly 30-year difference in age that existed between the real Elizabeth and Essex. Davis's portrayal of Elizabeth as a politically sensible woman who chooses her kingdom over her lover is more realistic than Flynn's swashbuckling portrayal of a surprisingly naive Essex. The film is entertaining, but its look and feel are strictly 1930s Hollywood, not sixteenth-century England.

Shakespeare in Love, 1998

Starring Joseph Fiennes, Gwyneth Paltrow, Geoffrey Rush, Colin Firth, Ben Affleck, and Judi Dench. Directed by John Madden. Color.

This wonderful film, which won the 1998 Best Picture Oscar, far surpasses *William Shakespeare: His Life and Times* in devising creative and entertaining ways to explain the mysteries surrounding Shakepeare's life and career. In 1590s London, young playwright William Shakespeare (Fiennes) is struggling through a severe case of writer's block, trying to write a comedy tentatively titled *Romeo and Ethel, the Pirate's Daughter*. This dubious comedy is transformed into the great tragedy *Romeo and Juliet* through the power of Shakespeare's passionate relationship with Viola de Lesseps (Paltrow), a noblewoman who disguises herself as a young man to act the part of Romeo (women being prevented from appearing on the stage even in women's roles).

Filled with mistaken identities, misunderstood motives, and an impossible romance, the film is itself a Shakespearean play. The story of how the playwright juggles the financial concerns of theatre owner Philip Henslowe (Rush), the ego of actors like Edward Alleyn (Affleck), and the ire of the Duke of Wessex (Firth), Viola's noble husband-to-be, is told with humor, wit, and energy. Filled with actual Elizabethan figures (except for Wessex), the film fills the gaps in our knowledge about their lives with fun and believable explanations that are true to the spirit of the period. Fiennes and Paltrow (who won the Best Actress Oscar) give strong performances, and Dench (who won the Best Supporting Actress Oscar) is outstanding in her few brief appearances as Queen Elizabeth. The scenes of rehearsal and performance are excellent depictions of the look and feel of the Elizabethan theatre.

The Six Wives of Henry VIII, 1971

Starring Keith Michell, Annette Crosbie, Dorothy Tutin, Anne Stallybrass, Elvi Hale, Angela Pleasence, and Rosalie Crutchley. Directed by John Glenister and Naomi Capon. 540 minutes (six 90-minute cassettes); VHS; color. Available from Facets Multimedia, Inc., 1517 W. Fullerton Avenue, Chicago, IL 60614, 800-331-6197; Video Collectibles, 1500 Clinton Street, Buffalo, NY 14206, 800-268-3891; The Video Catalog, 7000 Westgate Drive, St. Paul, MN 55114, 800-733-6656.

Whereas Bette Davis and Glenda Jackson defined the role of Elizabeth I in various films, Michell became the definitive Henry VIII in this six-part series first broadcast on PBS. Each episode focuses on one of Henry's six wives. The series offers a high degree of historical accuracy and provides well-rounded portraits of each queen—Catherine of Aragon (Crosbie), Anne Boleyn (Tutin), Jane Seymour (Stallybrass), Anne of Cleves (Hale), Katherine Howard (Pleasence), and Katherine Parr (Crutchley). Michell takes Henry from handsome sheltered prince to gross aging monarch in a portrayal that leaves no doubt that the king was always absolute master of his ministers, wives, and kingdom.

The Virgin Queen, 1955

Starring Bette Davis, Richard Todd, and Joan Collins. Directed by Henry Koster. 92 minutes; VHS; color. Available from CBS/Fox Video, P.O. Box 900, Beverly Hills, CA 90213, 800-800-2369.

Davis, who played Queen Elizabeth opposite Errol Flynn in the 1939 film *The Private Lives of Elizabeth and Essex*, reprises the role here in this highly imaginative retelling of the romance between Sir Walter Raleigh (Todd) and Elizabeth Throckmorton (Collins), a lady-in-waiting to the queen. In 1592, Elizabeth briefly imprisoned Raleigh in the Tower for his affair and secret marriage with Throckmorton; although soon released, Raleigh was forbidden the queen's presence for some time thereafter. As depicted here, the relationship between Raleigh and the queen is largely fiction, but Davis's portrayal of the queen is a powerful and accurate interpretation of what we know of the personality of Elizabeth I.

William Shakespeare: His Life and Times, 1977

Starring Tim Curry, Nicholas Clay, Ian McShane, Paul Freeman, Ron Cook, Janet Spencer-Turner, and Patience Collier. Directed by Peter Wood, Mark Cullingham, Robert Knights. 320 minutes (6 cassettes); VHS; color. Available from Bonneville Worldwide Entertainment, Broadcast House, 55 North 300 West, Suite 315, Salt Lake City, UT 84110-1160, 801-575-3680.

Adapted from the television program *Life of Shakespeare*, this six-part series traces the life of William Shakespeare from 1590 to 1603, the last years of Elizabeth. The episodes are interesting, if occasionally muddled, attempts to explain some of the great mysteries of Shakespeare's life and career: What was his relationship with his patron the Earl of Southampton? Who was the "dark lady"? Why are no Shakespeare manuscripts in existence today? How could a man with a grammar school education from a provincial English town write so accurately of the court and other worlds seemingly beyond his experience? The series' answers to these questions are educated and usually entertaining fiction. Shakespeare as played by Tim Curry (yes, Dr. Frank N. Furter from the *Rocky Horror Picture Show*) is passionate, talented, and slightly disreputable. The series is strongest when it portrays the Chamberlain's Men performing Shakespeare's plays at the Globe and at court—an excellent visualization of the London theatre scene in the 1590s.

Young Bess. *1953*

Starring Jean Simmons, Stewart Granger, Deborah Kerr, and Charles Laughton. Directed by George Sidney. 112 minutes; VHS; color. Available from MGM Home Entertainment, 2500 Broadway, Santa Monica, CA 90404, 310-449-3000.

Based on the novel *Young Bess* by Margaret Irwin, this film tells the story of Princess Elizabeth in the household of Thomas Seymour (Granger) and his wife, the former queen Katherine Parr (Kerr). Laughton appears as Henry VIII, reprising his famous role of 1933. Lavishly staged and costumed, the film is entertaining but short on historical accuracy. The film's strength is Simmons's outstanding performance as an intelligent but vulnerable Princess Elizabeth.

Additional Motion Pictures with Tudor Characters and Settings

Anne of the Thousand Days. *1969*

Starring Richard Burton and Genevieve Bujold. Directed by Charles Jarrott. 145 minutes; VHS; color. Available from Universal Studios Home Video, 100 Universal City Plaza, Universal City, CA 91608, 818-777-1000.

Lady Jane. *1985*

Starring Helena Bonham Carter and Cary Elwes. Directed by Trevor Nunn. 140 minutes; VHS, Beta, Laserdisc; color. Available from Paramount Home Video, Bluhdorn Building, 5555 Melrose Avenue, Los Angeles, CA 90038, 213-956-3952; The Video Catalog, 7000 Westgate Drive, St. Paul, MN 55114, 800-733-6656.

A Man for All Seasons. *1966*

Starring Paul Scofield, Robert Shaw, Orson Welles, Leo McKern, Susannah York, John Hurt, and Vanessa Redgrave. Directed by Fred Zinnemann. 120 minutes; VHS, Beta, Laserdisc; color. Available from Columbia Tristar Home Video, Sony Pictures Plaza, 10202 W. Washington Boulevard, Culver City, CA 90232, 310-280-5418; Baker and Taylor Video, 501 S. Gladiolus, Momence, IL 60954, 800-775-2300; The Video Catalog, 7000 Westgate Drive, St. Paul, MN 55114, 800-733-6656.

Mary of Scotland. *1936*

Starring Katharine Hepburn, Frederic March, and Florence Eldridge. Directed by John Ford. 123 minutes; VHS, Beta, Laserdisc; black and white. Available from Turner Home Entertainment Company, Box 105366, Atlanta, GA 35366, 800-523-0823.

The Private Life of Henry VIII. *1933*

Starring Charles Laughton, Binnie Barnes, Elsa Lanchester, Robert Donat, and Merle Oberon. Directed by Alexander Korda. 97 minutes; VHS, Beta, Laserdisc; black and white. Available from HBO Home Video, 1100 6th Avenue, New York, NY 10036, 212-512-7400; Nostalgia Family Video, P.O. Box 606, Baker City, OR 97814, 800-784-8362; Prism Entertainment, 1888 Century Park East, Suite 350, Los Angeles, CA 90067, 310-277-3270.

The Sword and the Rose. *1953*

Starring Glynis Johns, Richard Todd, and James Robertson Justice. Directed by Ken Annakin. 91 minutes; VHS, Beta, Laserdisc; color. Available from Walt Disney Home Video, 500 S. Buena Vista Street, Burbank, CA 91521, 818-562-3560; Hollywood Home Entertainment, 6165 Crooked Street Road, Suite B, Norcross, GA 30092; Baker and Taylor Video, 501 S. Gladiolus, Momence, IL 60954, 800-775-3500.

APPENDIX 6

Selected Sound Recordings
of Tudor and Elizabethan Music

All the King's Men: Henry VIII and the Princes of the Renaissance. Performed by I Fagiolini and Concordia. Metronome Recordings, LC 5896.

Country Capers: Music from John Playford's "The English Dancing Master." Performed by the New York Renaissance Band. Arabesque.

English Renaissance: The Music of William Byrd and Thomas Tallis. Performed by the King's Singers. BMG Music, 09026-68004-2.

Fantasias, Ayres, and Dances: Elizabethan and Jacobean Consort Music. Performed by the Julian Bream Consort. BMG Music, 7801-2-RC.

1588: Music from the Time of the Spanish Armada. Performed by the York Waits. Saydisc.

A Golden Treasury of Elizabethan Music. Performed by various artists. Saydisc Records, CD-SAR62.

A Handfull of Pleasant Delites: Elizabethan Ballads and Dances. Performed by Nancy Hadden. ASV Ltd., CD GAU 163.

Love, Lust & Piety: English Songs from the 15th and 16th Centuries. Performed by the Pro Cantione Antiqua of London, directed by Bruno Turner, and the Early Music Consort, directed by David Munrow. Quintessence, PMC-7185.

Music from the Time of Elizabeth I. Performed by the Academy of Ancient Music, directed by Christopher Hogwood. Decca Record Company, Ltd. 433 193-2.

Music of King Henry VIII. Performed by St. George's Canzona, directed by John Sothcott. Peerless Record Company, Ltd., EXP 57.

"Musique of Violenze": Dances, Fantasias and Popular Tunes for Queen Elizabeth's Violin Band. Performed by the Parley of Instruments Renaissance Violin Consort. Hyperion Records Ltd., CDA 66929.

My Fayre Ladye: Tudor Songs and Chant. Performed by Lionheart. Nimbus Records, NI 5512.

A Renaissance Christmas. Performed by the Boston Camerata, directed by Joel Cohen. The Moss Music Group, TV-S34569.

Shakespeare's Musick: Songs and Dances from Shakespeare's Plays. Performed by the Musicians of the Globe, directed by Philip Pickett. Philips Classics, 446 687-2.

In the Streets and Theatres of London: Elizabethan Ballads and Theatre Music. Performed by the Musicians of Swanne Alley. Virgin Classics.

There Were Three Ravens. Performed by the Consort of Musicke. Virgin Classics.

The Three Ravens: Songs of Folk and Minstrelsy Out of Elizabethan England. Performed by Alfred Deller, with Desmond Dupré. Vanguard Recording Society, 299 SD.

Watkins Ale: Music of the English Renaissance. Performed by the Baltimore Consort. Dorian Recordings, DOR-90142.

APPENDIX 7

Selected Web Sites
for Tudor and Elizabethan Topics

Compiled by Donna Bronski

The Internet offers a large number of sites relating to Elizabeth I or to some aspect of Tudor or Elizabethan history. Typically, these Web sites provide basic biographical information on Elizabeth I, her family, and the leading figures of her court and reign. Quality is uneven: some sites offer interesting images and accurate, useful information; others are inaccurate, simplistic, or poorly written and designed. Many focus on their creator's particular enthusiasm—e.g., Elizabethan costume, architecture, literature, or weaponry. Most of these sites can be uncovered simply by searching for "Elizabeth I" or "Elizabethan". The sites listed below are samples of a few of the most useful and best-designed sites currently available on the Web.

Academic Info on Irish History

This annotated directory of Irish history resources on the Internet offers links to a wide variety of Irish history sites, including those describing Ireland under the Tudors and early Stuarts. Besides links to other Web pages, the site lists print sources and includes links to online texts, document archives, and historical maps of Ireland and Western Europe. Although somewhat more scholarly, this site is an excellent companion resource to **Irish History on the Web** (see below).

< http://www.academicinfo.net/histirish.html >

Astrology Charts

This rather fun—though nonscholarly—page on the **Astrology Charts** Web site is an interesting introduction to an art—astrology—that Elizabeth I and many well-educated people of her time took very seriously. The site describes the horoscopes of Elizabeth I and Sir Francis Bacon, and it provides links to other astrology pages, including sites on the topic of astrology and Shakespeare.

< http://www.sirbacon.org/links/charts.htm >

Britannia: A Brief History of Wales

This online narrative of Welsh history offers chapters on "The Act of Union," "The Welsh Bible," "Elizabethan Wales," and "Cultural Survival," all topics of interest to students of Tudor Wales. The site also contains essays on the survival of the Welsh language and culture, Welsh religion and society, and Welsh castles, as well as maps, lists of books on Welsh history, and links to related sites. Like the **Britannia: Scotland** site described below, this mini-site on the **Britannia** Web page is a brief and readable source of online information on the history of Wales and a good place to begin online research on Welsh topics.

< http://britannia.com/wales/whist.html >

Britannia: Scotland: A Brief History

This online narrative of Scottish history, a mini-site on the large **Britannia** Web page, is an excellent place to begin researching sixteenth-century Scotland on the Internet. Chapters 5 and 6 have the greatest relevance for students of Tudor history, with Chapter 5 covering the reign of Mary, Queen of Scots, and Chapter 6 focusing on the reign of James VI and I and the union of the Crowns of Scotland and England. The narrative is readable and generally accurate, and it offers a good source of basic information on Scotland's past.
<http://britannia.com/celtic/scotland/history_scotland.html>

British Monarchy Web Site

The official Web site of the British Crown traces the entire history of the British monarchy and includes a series of pages covering the Tudors and the sixteenth century. The Tudor pages contain photos of paintings and artworks from the extensive Royal Collection; brief biographies of the Tudor monarchs, including Elizabeth I; and basic historical information on the Tudor period. The rest of the site covers other periods of British history and offers general information on the monarchy, such as discussion of the coronation rite and the current succession to the throne. The site also supplies information on the current state of the British monarchy, royal palaces, the royal art collection, and, of course, the obligatory discussion of the life of the late Princess Diana.

British Monarchy Site
<http://www.royal.gov.uk/index.htm>
Tudor Pages
<http://www.royal.gov.uk/history/tudor.htm>

Complete Works of William Shakespeare

This site provides the complete text of all Shakespeare's plays and poems. The site also offers a glossary of terms, a list of famous quotations from the plays, and a chronological listing of the plays based on the best current scholarship. Also featured are a Shakespeare discussion group and numerous links to other Shakespeare-related Web sites.
<http://the-tech.mit.edu/Shakespeare/works.html>

Elizabeth I

Created by Alicia Marie Minnich, this Web site offers basic information on the life and times of Elizabeth I, as well as a short narrative history of the major figures and events of the reign. The site also provides a series of images and an annotated listing of important books on both the queen and related people and topics. An annotated listing of works of fiction set in the Tudor period and links to related Web sites are also provided. Although not a scholarly site, it makes available useful basic information and good book reviews.
<http://mail.utep.edu/~aliciam/home.html>

The Elizabethan Costuming Page

This site is ideal for anyone interested in making or learning about Elizabethan attire. The site offers pictures of sixteenth-century clothing, a brief narrative history of different types of Elizabethan clothing, and instructions on how to make various items. The site discusses clothing styles for both sexes and all classes, and it provides information on hats, shoes, accessories, and fabrics, as well as a listing of books on Elizabethan costume. Links to other costuming and more general Elizabethan sites are also provided.
<http://www.dnaco.net/~aleed/corsets/general.html>

Elizabethan England

Created by senior English literature and composition students at Springfield High School in Springfield, Illinois, this site contains illustrated student-written essays and overviews of Elizabeth I and the major figures and events of her reign. The essays cover such topics as Mary I, the defeat of the Armada, Sir Francis Drake's voyage of circumnavigation, the Tower of London, and William Shakespeare and the Elizabethan theatre. A section on everyday life includes interesting essays on Elizabethan food, fashion, entertainment, and medicine, and another set of pages covers Elizabethan art and architecture. Each essay includes a brief annotated bibliography, and the site offers a listing of links to other Tudor and Elizabethan Web sites. Although the essays are somewhat uneven in quality, this is a good site for high school students to begin their study of Elizabethan life and personalities.
<http://www.springfield.k12.il.us/schools/springfield/eliz/elizabethanengland.html>

Elizabethan Heraldry

This site offers a brief essay on the work of heralds and the practice of heraldry in Elizabethan England. It also contains heraldic descriptions and color graphics depicting the coats of arms of important and well-known peers, courtiers, and gentleman of the Elizabethan period. Links to other heraldry sites are also provided.
<http://renaissance.dm.net/heraldry/index.html>

Elizabethan Review

The *Elizabethan Review* is a peer-reviewed online journal that publishes articles on a broad range of Elizabethan topics, particularly on Shakespeare, Elizabethan literature, and the English Renaissance. The journal also offers essays, letters, notes, and book reviews. The site is a good place to find the latest research and thinking on many aspects of Elizabethan history and culture.

<http://elizreview.com>

English Heritage Web Site

English Heritage is a national body created by the British Parliament in 1984 to preserve, protect, and promote England's historical sites. English Heritage is responsible for some 400 historical properties, from Roman forts to Tudor Castles (e.g., Deal Castle built by Henry VIII) and the World War II tunnels in the white cliffs of Dover. Although primarily a tourist site with information for planning visits, this Web page offers photographs, maps, and descriptions of Elizabethan sites that will be of interest to students of Tudor history.

<http://www.english-heritage.org.uk/
dminterface/dmindex.asp>

Folger Shakespeare Library Web Site

The Folger Library in Washington, D.C., is an independent research library that opened in 1932 as a gift to the American people from Henry Clay Folger and his wife Emily Jordan Folger. The Folger holds the world's largest collection of the printed works of William Shakespeare, as well as other books, manuscripts, paintings, drawings, prints, costumes, films, and artifacts relating to Tudor England and Renaissance Europe. This site provides basic information on the library and its holdings and is a good place to start for general information on Shakespeare and his works, as well as on other aspects of Elizabethan drama and poetry.

<http://www.folger.edu>

Henry VIII

This visually interesting site offers many fine pictures and numerous links to related sites. The site covers Henry's life, religion, wives, children—and all other things relating to his long reign. This is an excellent beginning site for online research into the life and times of Elizabeth's powerful and fascinating father.

<http://members.tripod.com/~JeanneAnn/
henryviii.htm>

In Her Own Words: Elizabeth I Onstage and Online

Created by the Brown University Women Writers Project and the Rhode Island Office of Library and Information Services, this site describes and promotes a series of performances at Brown that use Elizabeth I's own words to dramatize her life and times. For students of Tudor history, the site offers the text of some of Elizabeth's speeches, a chronol-

ogy of her life, a Tudor family tree, a bibliography, and links to related Web sites.

<http://www.wwp.brown.edu/rich/
OEIhome.html>

Irish History on the Web

This site provides links to a variety of Web pages covering all periods and many aspects of Irish history, including the Elizabethan conquest of Ireland in the sixteenth century and the Anglo-Scottish settlement of Protestants in the early Stuart period. Besides links to other sites, **Irish History on the Web** offers brief narratives of Irish history, a list of suggested readings, genealogical resources, timelines, a listing of universities with Irish studies programs, and the text of relevant historical documents. This site is an excellent starting point for conducting Irish history research on the Internet.

<http://wwwvms.utexas.edu/~jdana/
irehist.html>

Late Medieval England Page—On-Line Reference Book for Medieval Studies

This page is part of the **On-Line Reference Book for Medieval Studies**, a scholarly site providing the text of primary source materials for various periods of medieval history, as well as bibliographies of books and articles on medieval topics. Teaching resources are also offered to instructors of medieval history. This site is a work in progress, but one with great potential for students of Tudor history.

<http://orb.rhodes.edu/encyclop/late/england/
index.html>

Luminarium—Elizabeth I Pages

Part of the **Luminarium—Renaissance Literature** Web site created by Anniina Jokinen, these pages offer the text of letters, poems, and speeches written or delivered by Elizabeth I. Included are the queen's speech to the troops awaiting the Armada invasion at Tilbury in 1588, the queen's coronation address, and the famed "Golden Speech" to the members of Parliament in 1601. Also available are the queen's verse translation of the Thirteenth Psalm and her surviving letters to Queen Katherine Parr, Mary I, Edward VI, James VI of Scotland, and Mary, Queen of Scots. The pages also provide images of the queen, brief biographical information, and bibliographies of books, articles, and essays on Elizabeth I and her times.

<http://luminarium.org/renlit/eliza.htm>

Luminarium—Renaissance Literature

Created by Anniina Jokinen, this site offers quotes from, the text of works of, images of, and essays and articles on a series of literary figures from the English Renaissance. Included are such Elizabethan writers and poets as Sir Philip Sidney, Edmund

Spenser, Thomas Nashe, Fulke Greville, George Gascoigne, Richard Hooker, Sir Walter Raleigh, John Lyly, Christopher Marlowe, William Shakespeare, and Mary (Sidney) Herbert. The site also includes the works of such earlier Tudor writers as Sir Thomas More, Roger Ascham, and John Foxe, and two royal authors—Henry VIII and Elizabeth I (whose **Luminarium** pages are noted separately, above).

<http://www.luminarium.org/renlit/>

The *Mary Rose*—Portsmouth

This interesting site offers information and pictures of the *Mary Rose*, one of the favorite ships of Henry VIII. The *Mary Rose* sank in Portsmouth harbor in 1545 during a naval battle with the French fleet. The remnants of the ship were raised in the early 1980s and can now be viewed, along with many of its guns and other recovered artifacts, in a specially constructed dry-dock and museum in Portsmouth. This Web site includes links to related pages and to a page, designed for children ages 7–11, offering drawings of the sinking of the *Mary Rose*. This is an important site for anyone interested in the Tudor navy or in sixteenth-century ship construction and naval weaponry.

<http://www.compulink.co.uk/~mary-rose/ Welcome.html>

Medieval and Renaissance Wedding Information Page

Compiled and annotated by Judy Gerjuoy, this interesting Web site has a bibliography of books and articles on medieval and Renaissance weddings, food, and feasts. The site also has an FAQ page and links to related sites. Besides providing information on Tudor and Elizabethan wedding ceremonies and celebrations, the articles listed cover such fascinating topics as Viking weddings and divorces.

<http://www.spu.edu/~ks/bib/bib.html>

Mr. William Shakespeare and the Internet

This annotated guide to online sources of information on William Shakespeare and his life and works is the place to begin an Internet study on *Shakespearean* topics. Besides a listing of Shakespeare Web sites, this page offers a timeline, a Shakespeare family genealogy, biographical information on Shakespeare himself, an annotated listing of Shakespeare's works, and reproductions of the front matter material from the First Folio. Well crafted and highly detailed, **Mr. William Shakespeare and the Internet** focuses on scholarly Shakespeare Web sites but also includes a listing of interesting or unusual nonscholarly sites.

<http://daphne.palomar.edu/Shakespeare/>

Renascence Editions

This site provides online editions of English literary works printed between 1477 and 1799. Although the site's creators warn that these versions are not suitable for scholarly research, they are excellent for giving students and interested readers a taste of the works of prominent Tudor and Elizabethan writers. Currently available on the site are the full text of various works of such sixteenth-century writers as Roger Ascham, Sir Francis Bacon, George Gascoigne, Mary (Sidney) Herbert, Sir Philip Sidney, and Edmund Spenser. The site also offers numerous vivid and interesting images.

<http://darkwing.uoregon.edu/~rbear/ ren.htm>

Renaissance Faire

Although intended for people who work at modern Renaissance fairs, this Web page is also of interest to students of Elizabethan history. Besides listing the dates and locations of "Renaissance faires," the site provides information on Elizabethan clothing, sixteenth-century language and word pronunciation (including colorful insults and oaths), and Queen Elizabeth and her court. The site also presents a timeline and links to such related sites as Shakespearean acting troupes and fencing masters.

<http://www.renfaire.com>

The Richard III and Yorkist History Server

Although focusing on the life and reign of Richard III (r. 1483–1485), the last Plantagenet king of England, this Web site from the American branch of the Richard III Society offers students of Tudor history information on the Wars of the Roses; the life of Henry VII, Elizabeth's grandfather and Richard's supplanter; and William Shakespeare, the author of the play *Richard III*. The site offers links to the complete text of various important sources of fifteenth-century English history and to other related medieval and Tudor Web sites.

<http://www.r3.org>

Scotweb's Scottish History Online Magazine

This Web page is the history section of the **Scotweb** site, a general information site for Scottish tourism and contemporary topics of general interest. The magazine contains readable nonscholarly articles and essays on various events and topics. Perhaps reflecting the lingering interest generated by the recent movie *Braveheart*, many of the current articles address some aspect of the career of William Wallace, the thirteenth-century Scotsman who opposed the attempts of Edward I to extend English lordship into Scotland. However, the magazine covers all periods of Scottish history, including the sixteenth century.

<http://www.clan.com/history/>

Selected Poetry of Elizabeth I

Although this Web page contains the text of only six poems written by Elizabeth I, students of Renaissance poetry will also appreciate the numerous links to other online poetry pages provided by the University of Toronto. The entire Web site can be searched by poet, first line of the poem, date, or keyword. The selections of the queen's work that are provided include a poem written in Elizabeth's French Psalter, a poem written on a wall at Woodstock, and the poems titled "The Doubt of Future Woes" and "In Defiance of Fortune." The site also links to online sources of modern poetry criticism.

<http://utl2.library.utoronto.ca/www/wtel/rp/authors/1ELIZ.html>

Shakespeare Oxford Society

This interesting Web site argues passionately that Edward de Vere, 17th Earl of Oxford, was the author of the plays attributed to Shakespeare. In brief but clear arguments, the site explains why Oxford is by far the best candidate for authorship of the plays and poetry of Shakespeare, and why the man from Stratford known as Shakespeare is not. The site also provides a good background discussion of the Shakespeare authorship controversy and discusses the cases being made by others for Sir Francis Bacon and Christopher Marlowe as the real authors of the works attributed to Shakespeare. The site also links to *The Ever Reader* <http://www.everreader.com>, the online journal of Oxfordian scholarship.

<http://www.shakespeare-oxford.com/>

Sidney Journal

The *Sidney Journal* is an international scholarly journal published by the Sidney Society, which is dedicated to discussion of the life and works of Sir Philip Sidney; his sister Mary (Sidney) Herbert, Countess of Pembroke; and other members of the Sidney circle of court writers and poets. Although only early issues of the journal's articles, essays, and book reviews are available online, the Web site is still a good source of information on the Sidneys and their literary friends, and on current books and research on the Sidneys in particular and on Elizabethan literature in general. The site also offers a Sidney discussion list and links to related Web sites.

<http://www.uoguelph.ca/englit/Sidney/>

The Six Wives of Henry VIII

This page has numerous pictures of the six wives of Henry VIII, including the king's second wife, Anne Boleyn (the mother of Elizabeth I) and the king's fifth wife, Katherine Howard (a cousin of Elizabeth I). The Web site also provides brief biographies of each wife, along with their family coat of arms. The information provided is spare but accurate, and the photo reproductions are excellent.

<http://www.larmouth.demon.co.uk.sarah-jayne/wives/wives.html>

Tudor England

This Web site created by Lara E. Eakins provides simple biographical information on all the Tudor monarchs, including Elizabeth I. Although the site is not scholarly, it is well designed and written and contains some interesting types of information, such as discussions of Tudor architecture and of the Tudors in current books and movies. The site also offers biographical information on nonroyal Elizabethans, maps, photos, and a basic bibliography. The site's links page <http://tudor.simplenet.com/links.html> connects you to a wide variety of related sources, ranging from Queen Elizabeth II's official **British Monarchy Web Site** (see above) to the History Channel Classroom, to online sources of medieval English history. The **Elizabeth I Gallery Page** <http://tudor.simplenet.com/elizabeth/gallery.html> provides 15 portraits of Elizabeth from various times in her life. If you're interested in the Tudors and their England, you'll find the information you want here.

<http://tudor.simplenet.com>

Wars of the Roses

Although fought in the late fifteenth century, the Wars of the Roses greatly influenced the political development of England in the sixteenth century. This site offers brief biographical information on most of the key figures in the English dynastic struggle between the Houses of Lancaster and York, as well as a Wars of the Roses quiz, illustrations of fifteenth-century battles, and links to related sites. Although not a scholarly site, the page offers good basic information.

<http://www.geocities.com/Area51/Cavern/5123/roses.html>

BIBLIOGRAPHY

General Works and Reference Works

Bindoff, S. T. *Tudor England*. Baltimore: Penguin Books, 1966.

Black, J. B. *The Reign of Elizabeth 1558–1603*. 2nd ed. Oxford: Oxford University Press, 1994.

Boyce, Charles. *Shakespeare A to Z*. New York: Dell Publishing, 1990.

Carpenter, Christine. *The Wars of the Roses*. Cambridge: Cambridge University Press, 1997.

Connolly, S. J., ed. *The Oxford Companion to Irish History*. Oxford: Oxford University Press, 1998.

Davies, C. S. L. *Peace, Print and Protestantism 1450–1558*. London: Hart-Davis MacGibbon, 1977.

Elton, G. R. *England Under the Tudors*. 3rd ed. London: Routledge, 1991.

Fritze, Ronald H., ed. *Historical Dictionary of Tudor England, 1485–1603*. Westport, CT: Greenwood Press, 1991.

Gardiner, Juliet and Wenborn, Neil, eds. *The Columbia Companion to British History*. New York: Columbia University Press, 1997.

Gillingham, John. *The Wars of the Roses*. Baton Rouge, Louisiana State University Press, 1981.

Goodman, Anthony. *The Wars of the Roses*. New York: Dorset Press, 1990.

Griffiths, Ralph A. and Thomas, Roger S. *The Making of the Tudor Dynasty*. New York: St. Martin's Press, 1985.

Guy, John. *Tudor England*. Oxford: Oxford University Press, 1988.

Guy, John and Morrill, John. *The Tudors and the Stuarts*. The Oxford History of Britain. New York: Oxford University Press, 1992.

Haigh, Christopher, ed. *The Reign of Elizabeth I*. Athens: University of Georgia Press, 1987.

Hoffmann, Ann. *Lives of the Tudor Age 1485–1603*. New York: Barnes and Noble, 1977.

Hurstfield, Joel. *Elizabeth I and the Unity of England*. London: The English Universities Press, 1960.

Kelly, J. N. D. *The Oxford Dictionary of Popes*. New York: Oxford University Press, 1986.

Kenyon, J. P., ed. *A Dictionary of British History*. New York: Stein and Day, 1981.

Lander, J. R. *The Wars of the Roses*. New York: Capricorn Books, 1967.

Loades, David. *The Reign of Mary Tudor*. 2nd ed. London: Longman, 1991.

MacCaffrey, Wallace. *Elizabeth I: War and Politics 1588–1603*. Princeton, NJ: Princeton University Press, 1992.

———. *Queen Elizabeth and the Making of Policy, 1572–1588*. Princeton, NJ: Princeton University Press, 1981.

———. *The Shaping of the Elizabethan Regime: Elizabethan Politics 1558–1572*. Princeton, NJ: Princeton University Press, 1968.

Morrill, John. *The Oxford Illustrated History of Tudor & Stuart Britain*. Oxford: Oxford University Press, 1996.

Neillands, Robin. *The Wars of the Roses*. London: Cassell, 1992.

O'Day, Rosemary. *The Longman Companion to the Tudor Age*. London: Longman, 1995.

Palliser, D. M. *The Age of Elizabeth: England Under the Later Tudors, 1547–1603*. 2nd ed. London: Longman, 1992.

Palmer, Alan and Palmer, Veronica. *Who's Who in Shakespeare's England*. New York: St. Martin's Press, 1981.

Ross, Charles. *The Wars of the Roses*. London: Thames and Hudson, 1987.

Routh, C. R. N. *Who's Who in Tudor England*. Chicago: St. James Press, 1990.

Seward, Desmond. *The Wars of the Roses*. New York: Viking, 1995.

Slavin, Arthur J. *The Tudor Age and Beyond: England from the Black Death to the End of the Age of Elizabeth*. Malabar, FL: R. E. Krieger, 1987.

Smith, Lacey Baldwin. *The Elizabethan World*. Boston: Houghton Mifflin, 1991.

———. *This Realm of England 1399–1688*. History of England Series. 7th ed. Lexington, MA: D.C. Heath and Company, 1996.

Williams, Penry. *The Later Tudors: England 1547–1603*. Oxford: Oxford University Press, 1995.

Youings, Joyce. *Sixteenth-Century England*. New York: Penguin Books, 1984.

Politics and the Court

Doran, Susan. *Monarchy and Matrimony: The Courtships of Elizabeth I*. London: Routledge, 1996.

Figgis, John Neville. *The Divine Right of Kings*. New York: Harper and Row, 1965.

Guy, John. *The Tudor Monarchy*. Oxford: Oxford University Press, 1997.

Hopkins, Lisa. *Elizabeth I and Her Court*. New York: St. Martin's Press, 1990.

Jones, Norman. *The Birth of the Elizabethan Age: England in the 1560s*. Oxford: Basil Blackwell, 1993.

Levin, Carole. *The Heart and Stomach of a King: Elizabeth I and the Politics of Sex and Power*. Philadelphia: University of Pennsylvania Press, 1994.

Levine, Mortimer. *The Early Elizabethan Succession Question 1558–1568*. Stanford, CA: Stanford University Press, 1966.

———. *Tudor Dynastic Problems 1460–1571*. New York: Barnes and Noble, 1973.

Loades, D. M. *Politics and the Nation 1450–1660: Obedience, Resistance and Public Order*. 4th ed. London: Fontana, 1992.

———. *The Tudor Court*. London: Batsford, 1986.

———. *Tudor Government*. Oxford: Blackwell Publishers, 1997.

———. *Two Tudor Conspiracies*. Cambridge: Cambridge University Press, 1965.

Pulman, Michael B. *The Elizabethan Privy Council in the Fifteen Seventies*. Berkeley: University of California Press, 1971.

Smith, A. G. R. *The Babington Plot*. London: Macmillan, 1936.

———. *The Government of Elizabethan England*. New York: W. W. Norton, 1967.

Somerset, Anne. *Ladies-in-Waiting*. New York: Alfred A. Knopf, 1984.

Wernham, R. B. *Before the Armada: The Emergence of the English Nation, 1485–1588*. New York: Harcourt, Brace and World, 1966.

Williams, Neville. *All the Queen's Men: Elizabeth I and Her Courtiers*. New York: Macmillan, 1972.

Williams, Penry. *The Tudor Regime*. Oxford: Clarendon Press, 1979.

Youngs, Frederic A., Jr. *The Proclamations of the Tudor Queens*. Cambridge: Cambridge University Press, 1976.

Economic and Social History

Abbott, Mary. *Life Cycles in England, 1560–1720: Cradle to Grave*. London: Routledge, 1996.

Amussen, Susan D. An *Ordered Society: Gender and Class in Early Modern England, 1560–1725*. Oxford: Basil Blackwell, 1988.

Andrews, John F., ed. *William Shakespeare: His World, His Works, His Influence*. Vol. 1 *His World*. New York: Scribner, 1985.

Appleby, Andrew B. *Famine in Tudor and Stuart England*. Stanford, CA: Stanford University Press, 1978.

Archer, Ian W. *The Pursuit of Stability: Social Relations in Elizabethan London*. Cambridge: Cambridge University Press, 1991.

Arnold, Janet. *Patterns of Fashion: The Cut and Construction of Clothes for Men and Women c.1560–1620*. New York: Drama Books, 1985.

Ashelford, Jane. *A Visual History of Costume*: Vol. 2: *The Sixteenth Century*. London: Batsford, 1983.

Ashley, Maurice. *The People of England: A Short Social and Economic History*. Baton Rouge: Louisiana State University Press, 1982.

Barry, Jonathan, ed. *The Tudor and Stuart Town: A Reader in English Urban History, 1530–1688*. New York: Longman, 1990.

Beier, A. L. *Masterless Men: The Vagrancy Problem in England 1560–1640*. New York: Metheun, 1985.

Beier, A. L. and Roger Finaly, eds. *London 1500–1700: The Making of the Metropolis*. London: Longman, 1986.

Bisson, Douglas R. *The Merchant Adventurers of England*. Newark: University of Delaware Press, 1993.

Bowden, Peter J. *The Wool Trade in Tudor and Stuart England*. New York: St. Martin's Press, 1962.

Burke, Thomas. *Travel in England from Pilgrim and Pack-Horse to Light Car and Plane*. London: B. T. Batsford, 1942.

Bush, M. L. *The English Aristocracy*. Manchester, England: Manchester University Press, 1984.

Cahn, Susan. *Industry of Devotion: The Transformation of Women's Work in England 1500–1660*. New York: Columbia University Press, 1987.

Camden, Carroll. *The Elizabethan Woman*. Rev. ed. Mamaroneck, NY: P.P. Appel, 1975.

Cantor, Leonard. *The Changing English Countryside, 1400–1700*. London: Routledge & Kegan Paul, 1987.

Carlson, Eric J. *Marriage and the English Reformation*. Oxford: Blackwell, 1994.

Challis, C. E. *The Tudor Coinage*. New York: Barnes and Noble, 1978.

Charlton, Kenneth. *Education in Renaissance England*. London: Routledge & Kegan Paul, 1965.

Chaudhuri, K. N. *The English East India Company: The Study of an Early Joint-Stock Company, 1600–1640*. New York: Reprints of Economic Classics, 1965.

Cioni, Maria L. *Women and Law in Elizabethan England*. New York: Garland, 1985.

Clair, Colin. *A History of Printing in Britain*. London: Cassell, 1965.

Clark, Peter. *English Provincial Society in Kent, 1500–1640*. Sussex, England: Harvester Press, 1977.

Clarkson, Leslie A. *Death, Disease, and Famine in Pre-Industrial England*. New York: St. Martin's Press, 1976.

Clay, C. G. A. *Economic Expansion and Social Change: England 1500–1700*: Vol. 1: *People, Land and Towns*. New York: Cambridge University Press, 1984.

Coleman, D.C. *The Economy of England 1450–1750*. Oxford: Oxford University Press, 1977.

———. *Industry in Tudor and Stuart England*. London: Macmillan, 1975.

Cressy, David. *Birth, Marriage and Death*. Oxford: Oxford University Press, 1997.

———. *Bonfires and Bells: National Memory and the Protestant Calendar in Elizabethan and Stuart England*. London: Weidenfeld and Nicolson, 1989.

———. *Education in Tudor and Stuart England*. New York: St. Martin's Press, 1976.

Daiches, David. *Edinburgh*. London: Hamish Hamilton, 1978.

Davies, Margaret G. *The Enforcement of English Apprenticeship, 1563–1642*. Cambridge, MA: Harvard University Press, 1956.

Dietz, F. C. *English Public Finance, 1485–1641*. 2nd ed. London: F. Cass, 1964.

Dovey, Zillah. *An Elizabethan Progress*. Herndon, VA: Sutton Publishers, 1996.

Emerson, Kathy Lynn. *Wives and Daughters: The Women of Sixteenth Century England*. Troy, NY: Whitston Publishing Co., 1984.

Emmison, F. G. *Elizabethan Life: Home, Work and Land*. Chelmsford, England: Essex County Council, 1976.

———. *Elizabethan Life: Morals and the Church Courts*. Chelmsford, England: Essex County Council, 1973.

Epstein, Mortimer. *The Early History of the Levant Company*. London: George Routledge and Sons, 1968.

Fisher, F. J. *London and the English Economy 1500–1700*. London: Hambledon Press, 1990.

Fletcher, Anthony. *Gender, Sex, and Subordination in England 1500–1800*. New Haven, CT: Yale University Press, 1995.

Foster, Frank F. *The Politics of Stability: A Portrait of the Rulers in Elizabethan London*. London: Royal Historical Society, 1977.

Fox, Harold G. *Monopolies and Patents*. Toronto: University of Toronto Press, 1947.

Gardner, Brian. *The East India Company: A History*. New York: Dorset Press, 1990.

Greaves, Richard L. *Society and Religion in Elizabethan England*. Minneapolis: University of Minnesota Press, 1981.

Halliday, F. E., ed. *Richard Carew of Antony: The Survey of Cornwall*. London: Andrew Melrose, 1953.

Harrison, William. *The Description of England: The Classic Contemporary Account of Tudor Social Life*. Edited by Georges Edelen. New York: Dover Publications, 1994.

Hartley, Dorothy. *Lost Country Life*. New York: Pantheon, 1979.

Haynes, Alan. *Sex in Elizabethan England*. Stroud, England: Sutton, 1997.

Heal, Felicity. *Hospitality in Early Modern England*. Oxford: Oxford University Press, 1990.

Heal, Felicity and Holmes, Clive. *The Gentry in England and Wales 1500–1700*. Stanford, CA: Stanford University Press, 1994.

Heath, James. *Torture and English Law*. Westport, CT: Greenwood Press, 1982.

Hinton, R. W. K. *The Eastland Trade and the Common Weal in the Seventeenth Century*. Hamden, CT: Archon Books, 1975.

Hoeniger, David F. *Medicine and Shakespeare in the English Renaissance*. Newark: University of Delaware Press, 1992.

Hogrefe, Pearl. *Tudor Women*. Ames: Iowa State University Press, 1975.

Holmes, Martin. *Elizabethan London*. New York: Frederick A. Praeger, 1969.

Hunt, Alan. *Governance of the Consuming Passions: A History of Sumptuary Law*. New York: St. Martin's Press, 1996.

Hurstfield, Joel. *The Queen's Wards: Wardship and Marriage under Elizabeth I*. 2nd ed. London: Frank Cass, 1973.

Hurstfield, Joel and Smith, A. G. R. *Elizabethan People: State and Society*. New York: St. Martin's Press, 1972.

Hutton, Ronald. *The Rise and Fall of Merry England: The Ritual Year 1400–1700*. Oxford: Oxford University Press, 1994.

———. *The Stations of the Sun: A History of the Ritual Year in Britain*. New York: Oxford University Press, 1996.

Jack, Sybil M. *Towns in Tudor and Stuart Britain*. London: Macmillan, 1996.

———. *Trade and Industry in Tudor and Stuart England*. London: George Allen and Unwin, 1977.

Jardine, Lisa. *Still Harping on Daughters: Women and Drama in the Age of Shakespeare*. Totowa, NJ: Barnes and Noble, 1983.

Laslett, Peter. *The World We Have Lost: England Before the Industrial Age*. 2nd ed. New York: Scribner, 1971.

———. *The World We Have Lost: Further Explored*. 3rd ed. New York: Scribner, 1984.

Lawson, Philip. *The East India Company: A History*. London: Longman, 1993.

Lipson, Ephriam. *The Economic History of England*, Vol. 2: *The Age of Mercantilism*. 6th ed. London: A. and C. Black, 1961.

MacCaffrey, Wallace. *Exeter, 1540–1640: The Growth of an English County Town*. Cambridge, MA: Harvard University Press, 1958.

Macfarlane, A. D. J. *Witchcraft in Tudor and Stuart England*. New York: Harper and Row, 1970.

Macfarlane, Alan. *Marriage and Love in England 1300–1840*. Oxford: Blackwell, 1986.

Massie, Allen. *Edinburgh*. London: Sinclair-Stevenson, 1994.

McCollum, John I., ed. *The Age of Elizabeth: Selected Source Materials in Elizabethan Social and Literary History*. Boston: Houghton Mifflin, 1960.

Mertes, Kate. *The English Noble Household: 1250 to 1600: Good Governance and Politic Rule*. Oxford: Blackwell, 1988.

Osborne, Jane. *Entertaining Elizabeth: The Progresses and Great Houses of Her Time*. London: Bishopsgate Press, 1989.

Parry, Leonard A. *The History of Torture in England*. Montclair, NJ: Patterson Smith, 1975.

Patten, John. *English Towns 1500–1700*. Hamden, CT: Archon Books, 1978.

Porter, Roy. *London: A Social History*. Cambridge, MA: Harvard University Press, 1994.

Prior, Mary, ed. *Women in English Society, 1500–1800*. New York: Methuen, 1985.

Ramsay, G. D. *English Overseas Trade During the Centuries of Emergence*. London: Macmillan, 1957.

———. *The English Woolen Industry, 1500–1750*. London: Macmillan, 1982.

Ribeiro, Aileen. *Dress and Morality*. New York: Holmes and Meier, 1986.

Rowse, A. L. *Court and Country: Studies in Tudor Social History*. Athens: University of Georgia Press, 1987.

———. *The Elizabethan Renaissance*. New York: Scribner, 1971, 1972.

———. *Eminent Elizabethans*. Athens: University of Georgia Press, 1983.

———. *The England of Elizabeth: The Structure of Society*. Madison: University of Wisconsin Press, 1978.

———. *Tudor Cornwall: Portrait of a Society*. rev. ed. New York: Scribner, 1969.

St. Clare Byrne, Muriel. *Elizabethan Life in Town and Country*. 7th ed. Gloucester, England: Alan Sutton, 1987.

Salgado, Gamini. *The Elizabethan Underworld*. Stroud, England: Alan Sutton Publishing, 1992.

Sharpe, J. A. *Early Modern England: A Social History, 1550–1760*. 2nd ed. Oxford: Oxford University Press, 1997.

———. *Instruments of Darkness: Witchcraft in England 1550–1750*. New York: Penguin, 1996.

Sheppard, Francis. *London: A History*. Oxford: Oxford University Press, 1998.

Singman, Jeffrey L. *Daily Life in Elizabethan England*. Westport, CT: Greenwood Press, 1995.

Slack, Paul. *The English Poor Law, 1531–1782*. Cambridge: Cambridge University Press, 1995.

———. *The Impact of Plague in Tudor and Stuart England*. Oxford: Clarendon Press, 1985.

———. *Poverty and Policy in Tudor and Stuart England*. London: Longman, 1988.

Smith, Charles Hamilton. *Ancient Costumes of England: From the Druids to the Tudors*. New York: Arch Cape Press, 1989.

Spufford, Margaret. *Contrasting Communities: English Villagers in the Sixteenth and Seventeenth Centuries*. Cambridge: Cambridge University Press, 1974.

Stone, Lawrence. *The Crisis of the Aristocracy 1558–1641*. abridged ed. Oxford: Oxford University Press, 1967.

———. *The Family, Sex and Marriage: In England 1500–1800*. New York: Harper & Row, 1977.

———. *Social Change and Revolution in England 1540–1640*. London: Longman, 1965.

Thirsk, Joan. *Economic Policy and Projects: The Development of a Consumer Society in Early Modern England*. Oxford: Clarendon Press, 1978.

Thomas, Keith. *Religion and the Decline of Magic: Studies in Popular Beliefs in Sixteenth and Seventeenth Century England*. Oxford: Oxford University Press, 1997.

Vale, Marcia. *The Gentleman's Recreations: Accomplishments and Pastimes of the English Gentleman, 1580–1630*. Totowa, NJ: Rowman and Littlefield, 1977.

Wagner, Anthony R. *Heralds of England: A History of the Office and College of Arms*. London: HMSO, 1967.

Warnicke, Retha M. *Women of the English Renaissance and Reformation*. Westport, CT: Greenwood Press, 1983.

Webster, Charles, ed. *Health, Medicine, and Mortality in the Sixteenth Century*. Cambridge: Cambridge University Press, 1979.

Willan, Thomas Stuart. *The Early History of the Russia Company, 1553–1603*. Manchester, England: Manchester University Press, 1956.

Williams, Norman Lloyd. *Tudor London Visited*. London: Cassell, 1991.

Williams, Penry. *Life in Tudor England*. New York: G. P. Putnam's Sons, 1964.

Willis, Deborah. *Malevolent Nurture: Witch-Hunting and Maternal Power in Early Modern England*. Ithaca, NY: Cornell University Press, 1995.

Wood, A. C. *A History of the Levant Company*. London: Frank Cass and Co., 1964.

Wrightson, Keith. *English Society 1580–1680*. New Brunswick, NJ: Rutgers University Press, 1982.

Wrigley, E. A. and Schofield, R. S. *The Population History of England, 1541–1871*. Cambridge: Cambridge University Press, 1981.

Intellectual and Cultural History

Adams, John Cranford. *The Globe Playhouse: Its Design and Equipment*. 2nd ed. New York: Barnes and Noble, 1961.

Anglo, Sydney. *Spectacle, Pageantry, and Early Tudor Policy*. 2nd ed. Oxford: Oxford University Press, 1997.

Auerbach, Erna. *Tudor Artists*. Fair Lawn, NJ: Essential Books, 1954.

Baldwin, David. *The Chapel Royal: Ancient and Modern*. London: Duckworth, 1990.

Bates, Catherine. *The Rhetoric of Courtship in Elizabethan Language and Literature*. Cambridge: Cambridge University Press, 1992.

Beckerman, Bernard. *Shakespeare at the Globe, 1599–1609*. New York: Macmillan, 1962.

Berry, Herbert. *Shakespeare's Playhouses*. New York: AMS, 1987.

Berry, Philippa. *Of Chastity and Power: Elizabethan Literature and the Unmarried Queen*. London: Routledge, 1989.

Blagden, Cyprian. *The Stationers' Company: A History*. Cambridge, MA: Harvard University Press, 1960.

Caspari, Fritz. *Humanism and the Social Order in Tudor England*. New York: Teachers College Press, 1968.

Clare, Janet. *"Art Made Tongue-Tied by Authority": Elizabethan and Jacobean Dramatic Censorship*. New York: St. Martin's Press, 1990.

Copley, Gordon J., ed. *Surrey and Sussex*. Taken from the 1789 English edition of William Camden's *Britannia*. London: Hutchinson, 1977.

Donohue, Joseph W., Jr., ed. *The Theatrical Manager in England and America*. Princeton, NJ: Princeton University Press, 1971.

Dutton, Richard. *Mastering the Revels: The Regulation and Censorship of English Renaissance Drama*. Iowa City: University of Iowa Press, 1991.

Evans, Joan. *A History of the Society of Antiquaries*. Oxford: Society of Antiquaries, 1956.

Feather, John. *A History of British Publishing*. New York: Croom Helm, 1988.

Fineberg, Nona. *Elizabeth, Her Poets, and the Creation of the Courtly Manner: A Study of Sir John Harington, Sir Philip Sydney, and John Lyly*. New York: Garland, 1988.

Fisher, John H. *The Emergence of Standard English*. Lexington: University of Kentucky Press, 1996.

Gerrard, Ernest A. *Elizabethan Drama and Dramatists: 1583–1603*. New York: Cooper Square Publishers, 1972.

Girouard, Mark. *Robert Smythson and the Architecture of the Elizabethan Era*. South Brunswick, NJ: Barnes, 1967.

———. *Robert Smythson and the Elizabethan Country House*. New Haven, CT: Yale University Press, 1983.

———. *Windsor, the Most Romantic Castle*. London: Hodder and Stoughton, 1993.

Harrison, G. B. *Elizabethan Plays and Players*. Ann Arbor: University of Michigan Press, 1956.

Helgerson, Richard. *Forms of Nationhood: The Elizabethan Writing of England*. Chicago: University of Chicago Press, 1992.

Holmes, Martin. *Elizabethan London*. New York: Frederick A. Praeger. 1969.

Bibliography

Hosley, Richard, ed. *Shakespeare's Holinshed: An Edition of Holinshed's Chronicles*. New York: Putnam, 1968.

Hotson, Leslie. *Shakespeare's Wooden O*. London: Hart-Davis, 1959.

Howard, Skiles. *The Politics of Courtly Dancing in Early Modern England*. Amherst: University of Massachusetts Press, 1998.

Inglis, Fred. *The Elizabethan Poets: The Making of English Poetry from Wyatt to Ben Jonson*. London: Evans Brothers, 1969.

Ingram, William. *The Business of Playing: The Beginnings of Adult Professional Theater in Elizabethan London*. Ithaca, NY: Cornell University Press, 1992.

Jones, Emrys, ed. *The New Oxford Book of Sixteenth Century Verse*. Oxford: Oxford University Press, 1992.

Kearney, Hugh F. *Scholars and Gentlemen: Universities and Society in Pre-Industrial Britain*. Ithaca, NY: Cornell University Press, 1970.

Kelley, Donald R. *Renaissance Humanism*. Boston: Twayne Publishers, 1991.

Knutson, Roslyn L. *The Repertory of Shakespeare's Company, 1594–1613*. Fayetteville: University of Arkansas Press, 1991.

Laroque, François. *The Age of Shakespeare*. New York: Harry N. Abrams, 1993.

Lever, J. W. *The Elizabethan Love Sonnet*. London: Methuen, 1978.

Levy, F. J. *Tudor Historical Thought*. San Marino, CA: Huntington Library, 1967.

McConica, James Kelsey. *English Humanists and Reformation Politics*. Oxford: Clarendon Press, 1965.

McCoy, Richard C. *The Rites of Knighthood: The Literature and Politics of Elizabethan Chivalry*. Berkeley: University of California Press, 1989.

McCrum, Robert, Cran, William, and MacNeil, Robert. *The Story of English*. rev. ed. Boston: Faber and Faber, 1992.

Mendyk, Stanley G. *"Speculum Britanniae": Regional Study, Antiquarianism, and Science in Britain to 1700*. Toronto: University of Toronto Press, 1989.

Mercer, Eric. *English Art 1553–1625*. Oxford: Clarendon Press, 1962.

Millar, John Fitzhugh. *Elizabethan Country Dances*. Williamsburg, VA: Thirteen Colonies Press, 1985.

Orgel, Stephen. *The Jonsonian Masque*. Cambridge, MA: Harvard University Press, 1965.

Orrell, John. *The Quest for Shakespeare's Globe*. New York: Cambridge University Press, 1983.

Patterson, Annabel. *Reading Holinshed's Chronicles*. Chicago: University of Chicago Press, 1994.

Philip, Ian Gilbert. *The Bodleian Library in the Seventeenth and Eighteenth Centuries*. Oxford: Clarendon Press, 1983.

Pomeroy, Elizabeth W. *Reading the Portraits of Queen Elizabeth I*. Hamden, CT: Archon Books, 1989.

Prior, Moody E. *The Drama of Power: Studies in Shakespeare's History Plays*. Evanston, IL: Northwestern University Press, 1973.

Robinson, John Martin. *Royal Residences*. London: MacDonald and Company, 1982.

Rossiter, A. P. *English Drama from Early Times to the Elizabethans: Its Background, Origins, and Development*. Folcroft, PA: Folcroft Library Editions, 1977.

Rowse, A. L. *Windsor Castle in the History of England*. New York: G. P. Putnam's Sons, 1974.

Senn, Werner. *Studies in the Dramatic Construction of Robert Greene and George Peele*. Bern, Switzerland: Francke, 1973.

Shakespeare, William. *Love Poems and Sonnets of William Shakespeare*. New York: Doubleday, 1957.

Simon, Joan. *Education and Society in Tudor England*. Cambridge: Cambridge University Press, 1966.

Smith, Irwin. *Shakespeare's First Playhouse*. Dublin: Liffey Press, 1981.

Speed, John. *The Counties of Britain: A Tudor Atlas*. Introduction by Nigel Nicolson. County Commentaries by Alasdair Hawkyard. New York: Thames and Hudson, 1989.

Stow, John. *A Survey of London Written in the Year 1598*. London: J. M. Dent and Sons, 1997.

Stoye, John. *English Travellers Abroad 1604–1667*. rev. ed. New Haven, CT: Yale University Press, 1989.

Strong, Roy. *The Cult of Elizabeth: Elizabethan Portraiture and Pageantry*. London: Thames and Hudson, 1977

————. *Gloriana: The Portraits of Queen Elizabeth I*. London: Thames and Hudson, 1987.

Thomson, Peter. *Shakespeare's Theatre*. 2nd ed. London: Routledge, 1992.

Thurley, Simon. *The Royal Palaces of Tudor England*. New Haven, CT: Yale University Press, 1993.

Tillyard, E. M. W. *The Elizabethan World Picture*. New York: Vintage, 1967.

Todd, Margo. *Christian Humanism and the Puritan Social Order*. Cambridge: Cambridge University Press, 1987.

Trapp, J. B. *Erasmus, Colet and More: The Early Tudor Humanists and Their Books*. London: British Library, 1991.

Vere, Edward de. *The Poems of Edward de Vere*. Chapel Hill: University of North Carolina Press, 1981.

Wilson, Derek. *The Tower*. New York: Charles Scribner's Sons, 1978.

Wilson, Jean. *Entertainments for Elizabeth I*. Totowa, NJ: Rowman and Littlefield, 1980.

Wulstan, David. *Tudor Music*. Iowa City: University of Iowa Press, 1986.

Parliamentary, Administrative, and Legal History

Bellamy, John. *The Tudor Law of Treason*. London: Routledge & Kegan Paul, 1979.

Blatcher, Marjorie. *The Court of King's Bench, 1450–1550: A Study in Self-Help*. London: Athlone Press, 1978.

Brooks, C. W. *Pettyfoggers and Vipers of the Commonwealth: The "Lower Branch" of the Legal Profession in Early Modern England*. Cambridge: Cambridge University Press, 1986.

Dean, D. M. and Jones, Norman L., eds. *The Parliaments of Elizabethan England*. Oxford: Basil Blackwell, 1990.

Elton, G. R. *The Parliament of England 1559–1581*. Cambridge: Cambridge University Press, 1986.

———. *Star Chamber Stories*. London: Methuen, 1958.

———. *The Tudor Revolution in Government*. Cambridge: Cambridge University Press, 1953.

Gleason, John H. *The Justices of the Peace in England, 1558–1640*. Oxford: Clarendon Press, 1969.

Graves, Michael A. R. *Elizabethan Parliaments, 1559–1601*. 2nd ed. London: Longman, 1996.

———. *The Tudor Parliaments: Crown, Lords and Commons, 1485–1603*. London: Longman, 1985.

Guy, John. *The Court of Star Chamber and Its Records to the Reign of Elizabeth I*. London: HMSO, 1985.

Hartley, T. E. *Elizabeth's Parliaments: Queen, Lords and Commons 1559–1601*. New York: St. Martin's Press, 1992.

Hastings, Margaret. *The Court of Common Pleas in Fifteenth Century England*. Ithaca, NY: Cornell University Press, 1947.

Hogue, Arthur R. *Origins of the Common Law*. Indianapolis: Liberty Fund, 1985.

Hurstfield, Joel. *Freedom, Corruption and Government in Elizabethan England*. London: Jonathan Cape, 1973.

Jones, W. J. *The Elizabethan Court of Chancery*. Oxford: Clarendon Press, 1967.

Lehmberg, Stanford E. *The Later Parliaments of Henry VIII, 1536–1547*. Cambridge: Cambridge University Press, 1977.

———. *The Reformation Parliament, 1529–1536*. Cambridge: Cambridge University Press, 1970.

Loach, Jennifer. *Parliament and the Crown in the Reign of Mary Tudor*. Oxford: Clarendon Press, 1986.

———. *Parliament Under the Tudors*. Oxford: Clarendon Press, 1991.

Neale, J. E. *Elizabeth I and Her Parliaments 1559–1581*. New York: St. Martin's Press, 1958.

———. *Elizabeth I and Her Parliaments 1584–1601*. New York: St. Martin's Press, 1958.

———. *The Elizabethan House of Commons*. rev. ed. Harmondsworth, England: Penguin Books, 1963.

Prest. Wilfrid R. *The Inns of Court under Elizabeth I and the Early Stuarts, 1590–1640*. London: Longman, 1972.

Smith, A. G. R. *The Government of Elizabethan England*. New York: W. W. Norton, 1967.

Smith, Lacey Baldwin. *Treason in Tudor England*. London: Jonathan Cape, 1986.

Snow, Vernon F. *Parliament in Elizabethan England: John Hooker's Order and Usage*. New Haven, CT: Yale University Press, 1977.

Stuckey, Michael. *The High Court of Star Chamber*. Holmes Beach, FL: Gaunt, 1998.

Van Caenegem, R. C. *The Birth of the English Common Law*. 2nd ed. Cambridge: Cambridge University Press, 1988.

Religious History

Acheson, R. J. *Radical Puritans in England, 1550–1660*. London: Longman, 1990.

Adair, John. *Puritans: Religion and Politics in Seventeenth-Century England and America*. Gloucester, England: Sutton Publishing, 1998.

Basset, Bernard. *The English Jesuits from Campion to Martindale*. New York: Burns and Oates, 1968.

Bettey, J. H. *The Suppression of the Monasteries in the West Country*. Gloucester, England: Alan Sutton, 1989.

Bloomfield, Edward H. *The Opposition to the English Separatists, 1570–1625*. Washington, DC: University Press of America, 1981.

Bossy, John. *The English Catholic Community 1570–1850*. New York: Oxford University Press, 1976.

Brachlow, Stephen. *The Communion of Saints*. New York: Oxford University Press, 1988.

Brigden, Susan. *London and the Reformation*. Oxford: Clarendon Press, 1989.

Bruce, F. F. *History of the Bible in English*. New York: Oxford University Press, 1987.

Burns, Edward McNall. *The Counter Reformation*. Princeton, NJ: Van Nostrand, 1964.

Collinson, Patrick. *The Elizabethan Puritan Movement*. Oxford: Clarendon Press, 1990.

———. *The Religion of Protestants: The Church in English Society 1559–1625*. Oxford: Clarendon Press, 1982.

Cross, Claire. *Church and People 1450–1660: The Triumph of the Laity in the English Church.* Atlantic Highlands, NJ: Humanities Press, 1976.

———. *The Elizabethan Religious Settlement.* Bangor, ME: Headstart History, 1992.

———. *The Royal Supremacy in the Elizabethan Church.* New York: Barnes and Noble, 1969.

Dakin, Arthur. *Calvinism.* Philadelphia: Westminster Press, 1946.

Davidson, N. S. *The Counter-Reformation.* Oxford: Blackwell, 1987.

Dickens, A. G. *The Counter Reformation.* New York: Harcourt, Brace & World, 1969.

———. *The English Reformation.* 2nd ed. University Park: Pennsylvania State University Press, 1989.

Duffy, Eamon. *The Stripping of the Altars: Traditional Religion in England 1400–1580.* New Haven, CT: Yale University Press, 1992.

Elton, G. R., ed. *The New Cambridge Modern History.* Volume II: *The Reformation.* London: Cambridge University Press, 1975.

Estep, William R. *The Anabaptist Story.* Grand Rapids, MI: William B. Eerdmans, 1975.

The First and Second Prayer Books of Edward VI. New York: E. P. Dutton, 1949.

Fitzpatrick, P. J. *In Breaking of Bread: The Eucharist and Ritual.* Cambridge: Cambridge University Press, 1993.

Foxe, John. *Fox's Book of Martyrs.* Edited by William Byron Forbush. Grand Rapids, MI: Zondervan, 1980.

Garrett, Christina. *The Marian Exiles.* Cambridge: Cambridge University Press, 1966.

Haigh, Christopher. *English Reformations: Religion, Politics, and Society Under the Tudors.* Oxford: Clarendon Press, 1993.

Haller, William. *The Elect Nation: The Meaning and Relevance of Foxe's Book of Martyrs.* New York: Harper & Row, 1963.

———. *Elizabeth I and the Puritans.* Ithaca, NY: Cornell University Press, 1964.

———. *The Rise of Puritanism.* New York: Harper and Brothers, 1957.

Holmes, Peter. *Resistance and Compromise: The Political Thought of Elizabethan Catholics.* Cambridge: Cambridge University Press, 1982.

Haugaard, William P. *Elizabeth and the English Reformation: The Struggle for a Stable Settlement of Religion.* Cambridge: Cambridge University Press, 1968.

Heal, Felicity. *Of Prelates and Princes: A Study of the Economic and Social Position of the Tudor Episcopate.* Cambridge: Cambridge University Press, 1980.

Houlbrooke, Ralph. *Church Courts and the People during the English Reformation.* Oxford: Oxford University Press, 1979.

Hudson, Winthrop S. *The Cambridge Connection and the Elizabethan Settlement of 1559.* Durham, NC: Duke University Press, 1980.

Jones, Norman L. *Faith by Statute: Parliament and the Settlement of Religion 1559.* London: Royal Historical Society, 1982.

Knappen, M. M. *Tudor Puritanism: A Chapter in the History of Idealism.* Chicago: University of Chicago Press, 1966.

Lake, Peter. *Anglicans and Puritans.* Boston: Allen & Unwin, 1988.

———. *Moderate Puritans and the Elizabethan Church.* Cambridge: Cambridge University Press, 1982.

Lunn, David. *The Catholic Elizabethans.* Bath, England: Downside Abbey, 1998.

Matthews, Walter Robert and W. M. Atkins, eds. *A History of St. Paul's Cathedral.* London: Phoenix House, 1957.

McGinn, Donald Joseph. *The Admonition Controversy.* New Brunswick, NJ: Rutgers University Press, 1949.

McGrath, Patrick. *Papists and Puritans Under Elizabeth I.* New York: Walker and Company, 1967.

McNeill, John Thomas. *The History and Character of Calvinism.* New York: Oxford University Press, 1954.

Meyer, A. O. *England and the Catholic Church under Elizabeth.* Translated by J. R. McKee. New York: Barnes and Noble, 1967.

Morey, Adrian. *The Catholic Subjects of Elizabeth I.* Totowa, NJ: Rowman and Littlefield, 1978.

O'Day, Rosemary. *The Debate on the English Reformation.* London: Metheun, 1986.

O'Day, Rosemary and Heal, Felicity, eds. *Princes and Paupers in the English Church 1500–1800.* Leicester: Leicester University Press, 1981.

O'Donovan, Oliver. *On the Thirty-Nine Articles: A Conversation with Tudor Christianity.* Exeter: Paternoster Press, 1986.

Parker, T. H. L. *Calvin: An Introduction to His Thought.* London: Geoffrey Chapman, 1995.

Primus, John Henry. *The Vestments Controversy.* Kampen, Netherlands: J. H. Kok, 1960.

Pritchard, Arnold. *Catholic Loyalism in Elizabethan England.* Chapel Hill: University of North Carolina Press, 1979.

Reynolds, E. E. *Campion and Parsons: The Jesuit Mission of 1580–1.* London: Sheed and Ward, 1980.

Roth, Cecil. *A History of the Jews in England.* 3rd ed. Oxford: Clarendon Press, 1964.

Scarisbrick, J. J. *The Reformation and the English People*. Oxford: Blackwell, 1984.

Searle, G. W. *The Counter Reformation*. London: University of London Press, 1974.

Seaver, Paul S. *The Puritan Lectureships*. Stanford, CA: Stanford University Press, 1970.

Simpson, Alan. *Puritanism in Old and New England*. Chicago: University of Chicago Press, 1972.

Thornbury, Walter. *Old London, Cheapside and St. Paul's*. London: Alderman Press, 1986.

Tittler, Robert. *The Reformation and the Towns in England: Politics and Political Culture, 1540–1640*. Oxford: Clarendon Press, 1998.

Trimble, W. R. *The Catholic Laity in Elizabethan England, 1558–1603*. Cambridge, MA: Harvard University Press, 1964.

Walsham, Alexandra. *Church Papists: Catholicism, Conformity and Confessional Polemic in Early Modern England*. Rochester, NY: Boydell Press, 1993.

Watt, Tessa. *Cheap Print and Popular Piety 1550–1640*. Cambridge: Cambridge University Press, 1991.

White, B. R. *The English Separatist Tradition*. London: Oxford University Press, 1971.

Woodward, G. W. O. *The Dissolution of the Monasteries*. London: Blandford, 1966.

Military History, Foreign Policy, and Europe

Anderson, M. S. *The Rise of Modern Diplomacy, 1450–1919*. London: Longman, 1993.

Andrews, K. R. *Elizabethan Privateering: English Privateering During the Spanish War 1585–1603*. Cambridge: Cambridge University Press, 1964.

Baumgartner, Frederic J. *France in the Sixteenth Century*. New York: St. Martin's Press, 1995.

Boynton, Lindsay. *The Elizabethan Militia, 1558–1638*. London: Routledge and Kegan Paul, 1967.

Briggs, Robin. *Early Modern France, 1560–1715*. 2nd ed. Oxford: Oxford University Press, 1998.

Crowson, P. S. *Tudor Foreign Policy*. New York: St. Martin's Press, 1973.

Cruickshank, C. G. *Elizabeth's Army*. 2nd ed. Oxford: Clarendon Press, 1966.

Dulles, F. R. *Eastward Ho: The First English Adventurers to the Orient*. Freeport, NY: Books for Libraries Press, 1969.

Elliott, J. H. *Imperial Spain, 1469–1716*. New York: St. Martin's Press, 1967.

Fernandez-Armesto, Felipe. *The Spanish Armada: The Experience of War in 1588*. Oxford: Oxford University Press, 1988.

Ffoulkes, Charles John. *Sword, Lance, and Bayonet: A Record of the Arms of the British Army and Navy*. 2nd ed. New York: Arco, 1967.

Geyl, Pieter. *The Revolt of the Netherlands, 1555–1609*. London: Cassell, 1988.

Greengrass, Mark. *France in the Age of Henri IV*. New York: Longman, 1984.

Grierson, Edward. *The Fatal Inheritance: Philip II and the Spanish Netherlands*. Garden City, NY: Doubleday, 1969.

Guill, James H. *A History of the Azores Islands*. Menlo Park, CA: n.p., 1972.

Howarth, David. *The Voyage of the Armada: The Spanish Story*. New York: Viking Press, 1984.

Israel, Jonathan I. *The Dutch Republic: Its Rise, Greatness, and Fall 1477–1806*. Oxford: Clarendon Press, 1998.

Kingdon, Robert McCune. *Myths about the St. Bartholomew's Day Massacres, 1572–1576*. Cambridge, MA: Harvard University Press, 1988.

Knecht, R. J. *The French Wars of Religion, 1559–1598*. 2nd ed. London: Longman, 1996.

Koenigsberger, H. G. *The Habsburgs and Europe, 1516–1660*. Ithaca, NY: Cornell University Press, 1971.

Lewis, Michael A. *The Spanish Armada*. New York: Macmillan, 1960.

Loades, D. M. *The Tudor Navy: An Administrative, Political, and Military History*. Brookfield, VT: Ashgate Publications, 1992.

Loomie, Albert J. *The Spanish Elizabethans: The English Exiles at the Court of Philip II*. New York: Fordham University Press, 1963.

Lovett, A. W. *Early Habsburg Spain 1517–1598*. Oxford: Oxford University Press, 1986.

Lynch, John. *Spain, 1516–1598: From Nation State to World Empire*. Oxford: Blackwell, 1992.

Martin, Colin. and Parker, Geoffrey. *The Spanish Armada*. New York: Norton, 1988.

Mattingly, Garrett. *The Armada*. Boston: Houghton Mifflin, 1959.

———. *Renaissance Diplomacy*. Baltimore: Penguin, 1964.

Morgan, E. Delmar. *Early Voyages and Travels to Russia and Persia*. New York: B. Franklin, 1963.

Neale, J. E. *The Age of Catherine de Medici*. New York: Barnes and Noble, 1959.

Nogueres, Henri. *The Massacre of Saint Bartholomew*. Translated by Claire Elaine Engel. New York: Macmillan, 1962.

Norman, A. Vesey. *A History of War and Weapons, 449 to 1660: English Warfare from the Anglo-Saxons to Cromwell*. New York: Crowell, 1966.

Oosterhoff, F. G. *Leicester and the Netherlands, 1586–1587*. Utrecht: HES, 1988.

Parker, Geoffrey. *The Dutch Revolt*. Ithaca, NY: Cornell University Press, 1977.

————. *Spain and the Netherlands, 1559–1659.* Short Hills, NJ: Enslow Publishers, 1979.

Quinn, David B. and Ryan, A. N. *England's Sea Empire, 1550–1642.* Boston: G. Allen & Unwin, 1983.

Ramsay, G. D. *The Queen's Merchants and the Revolt of the Netherlands.* Manchester, England: Manchester University Press, 1986.

Rodger, N. A. M. *The Safeguard of the Sea: A Naval History of Britain.* New York: W. W. Norton, 1998.

Rothrock, George A. *The Huguenots: A Biography of a Minority.* Chicago: Nelson-Hall, 1979.

Rowse, A. L. *The Expansion of Elizabethan England.* New York: Scribner, 1972.

Salmon, J. H. M. *Society in Crisis: France in the Sixteenth Century.* New York: St. Martin's Press, 1975.

Sedgwick, Henry Dwight. *The House of Guise.* Indianapolis: Bobbs-Merrill, 1938.

Solari, Giovanni. *The House of Farnese.* Garden City, NY: Doubleday, 1968.

Sutherland, N. M. *The Massacre of St. Bartholomew and the European Conflict, 1559–1572.* London: Macmillan, 1973.

Tracy, James D. *Holland under Habsburg Rule, 1506-1566: The Formation of a Body Politic.* Berkeley: University of California Press, 1990.

Waldman, Milton. *Biography of a Family: Catherine de Medici and Her Children.* Boston: Houghton Mifflin, 1936.

Wernham, R. B. *After the Armada: Elizabethan England and the Struggle for Western Europe, 1588–1595.* Oxford: Clarendon Press, 1984.

————, ed. *The Expedition of Sir John Norris and Sir Francis Drake to Spain and Portugal, 1589.* Aldershot, England: Gower, 1988.

————. *The Making of Elizabethan Foreign Policy 1558–1603.* Berkeley: University of California Press, 1980.

————. *The Return of the Armadas: The Last Years of the Elizabethan War Against Spain, 1595–1603.* Oxford: Oxford University Press, 1994.

Wilson, C. H. *Queen Elizabeth and the Revolt of the Netherlands.* Berkeley: University of California Press, 1970.

Scotland, Ireland, Wales, and America

Armstrong Davison, M. H. *The Casket Letters.* London: Vision, 1965.

Ashley, Maurice. *The House of Stuart: Its Rise and Fall.* London: J. M. Dent, 1980.

Bell, Robin, ed. *Bittersweet Within My Heart: The Love Poems of Mary, Queen of Scots.* San Francisco: Chronicle Books, 1992.

Berleth, Richard. *The Twilight Lords: An Irish Chronicle.* New York: Barnes and Noble, 1978.

Bingham, Caroline. *The Stewart Kingdom of Scotland 1371–1603.* New York: St. Martin's Press, 1974.

Blacker, Irwin R., ed. *The Portable Hakluyt's Voyages.* New York: Viking Press, 1965.

Bottigheimer, Karl S. *Ireland and the Irish: A Short History.* New York: Columbia University Press, 1982.

Canny, Nicholas P. *The Elizabethan Conquest of Ireland: A Pattern Established, 1565–1576.* New York: Barnes and Noble, 1976.

Cowan, Ian B. *The Scottish Reformation: Church and Society in Sixteenth-Century Scotland.* New York: St. Martin's Press, 1982.

Davies, John. *A History of Wales.* London: Penguin Press, 1993.

Donaldson, Gordon. *All the Queen's Men: Power and Politics in Mary Stewart's Scotland.* London: Batsford Academic and Educational, 1983.

————. *Scotland: James V to James VII.* New York: Praeger, 1965.

————. *The Scottish Reformation.* Cambridge: Cambridge University Press, 1960.

Durant, David N. *Raleigh's Lost Colony.* New York: Atheneum, 1981.

Edwards, Philip, ed. *Last Voyages: Cavendish, Hudson, Ralegh, the Original Narratives.* Oxford: Clarendon Press, 1988.

Edwards, R. D. *Ireland in the Age of the Tudors.* New York: Barnes and Noble, 1977.

Ellis, Steven G. *Tudor Ireland. Crown, Community and the Conflict of Cultures 1470–1603.* London: Longman, 1985.

Falls, Cyril. *Elizabeth's Irish Wars.* London: Metheun, 1950.

Fitzgerald, Brian. *The Geraldines: An Experiment in Irish Government, 1169–1601.* London: Staples Press, 1951.

Ford, Alan. *The Protestant Reformation in Ireland, 1590–1641.* Portland: Four Courts Press, 1997.

Foss, Michael. *Undreamed Shores: England's Wasted Empire in America.* New York: Scribner's, 1974.

Gibson, Charles. *Spain in America.* New York: Harper & Row, 1967.

Hakluyt, Richard. *Voyages and Discoveries: The Principal Navigations, Voyages, Traffiques, and Discoveries of the English Nation.* Various modern editions.

Harriot, Thomas. *A Brief and True Report of the New Found Land of Virginia.* Facsimile ed. Introduced by Randolph G. Adams. New York: History Book Club, 1951.

Johnson, Paul. *Ireland: A Concise History.* Chicago: Academy Chicago Publishers, 1992.

Jones, J. Gwynfor. *Early Modern Wales, 1525–1640*. New York: St. Martin's Press, 1994.

————. *Wales and the Tudor State: Government, Religious Change and the Social Order, 1534–1603*. Cardiff: University of Wales Press, 1989.

Kupperman, Karen Ordahl. *Roanoke: The Abandoned Colony*. New York: Barnes and Noble, 1993.

Lennon, Colm. *The Lords of Dublin in the Age of the Reformation*. Dublin: Irish Academic, 1989.

————. *Sixteenth–Century Ireland: The Incomplete Conquest*. Dublin: Gill & Macmillan, 1994.

Lounsburg, R. G. *The British Fishery at Newfoundland*. Hamden, CT: Archon Books, 1969.

MacCurtain, Margaret. *Tudor and Stuart Ireland*. Dublin: Gill & Macmillan, 1972.

Mackie, J. D. *A History of Scotland*. 2nd ed. New York: Dorset Press, 1985.

Maclean, Fitzroy. *A Concise History of Scotland*. New York: Beekman House, 1970.

McCarthy-Morrogh, Michael. *The Munster Plantation: English Migration to Southern Ireland, 1583–1641*. Oxford: Clarendon Press, 1986.

McGurk, John. *The Elizabethan Conquest of Ireland: The 1590s Crisis*. Manchester, England: Manchester University Press, 1997.

Meigs, Samantha A. *The Reformations in Ireland: Tradition and Confessionalism, 1400–1690*. New York: St. Martin's Press, 1997.

Mitchison, Rosalind. *A History of Scotland*. 2nd ed. London: Routledge, 1982.

Morgan, Hiram. *Tyrone's Rebellion: The Outbreak of the Nine Years War in Tudor Ireland*. Rochester, NY: Boydell Press, 1993.

Morison, Samuel Eliot. *The European Discovery of America: The Northern Voyages A.D. 500–1600*. New York: Oxford University Press, 1971.

Morton, Grenfell. *Elizabethan Ireland*. London: Longman, 1971.

Neatby, Leslie H. *In Quest of the North West Passage*. New York: Crowell, 1958.

Quinn, David B. *The Elizabethans and the Irish*. Ithaca, NY: Cornell University Press, 1966.

————. *England and the Discovery of America, 1481–1620*. New York: Knopf, 1974.

————. *Explorers and Colonies, 1500–1625*. London: Hambledon Press, 1990.

————. *Set Fair for Roanoke: Voyages and Colonies, 1584–1606*. Chapel Hill: University of North Carolina Press, 1984.

Rabb, Theodore K. *Enterprise and Empire: Merchant and Gentry Investment in the Expansion of England, 1575–1630*. Cambridge, MA: Harvard University Press, 1967.

Rowse, A. L. *The Elizabethans and America*. New York: Harper, 1959.

Sanderson, Margaret H. B. *Mary Stewart's People: Life in Mary Stewart's Scotland*. Tuscaloosa: University of Alabama Press, 1987.

Sauer, Carl Ortwin. *The Early Spanish Main*. Berkeley: University of California Press, 1969.

————. *Sixteenth Century North America*. Berkeley: University of California Press, 1971.

Silke, John. *Kinsale: The Spanish Intervention in Ireland at the End of the Elizabethan Wars*. New York: Fordham University Press, 1970.

Thomas, W. S. K. *Tudor Wales, 1485–1603*. Llandsul, Wales: Gomer Press, 1983.

Thomson, George M. *A Kind of Justice: Two Studies in Treason*. London: Hutchinson, 1970.

————. *Search for the North-West Passage*. New York: Macmillan, 1975.

Williams, Glanmor. *Renewal and Reformation: Wales c.1415–1642*. Oxford: Oxford University Press, 1993.

————. *Wales and the Reformation*. Cardiff: University of Wales Press, 1997.

Williams, Neville. *The Sea Dogs: Privateers, Plunder and Piracy in the Elizabethan Age*. New York: Macmillan, 1975.

Williamson, James A. *The Age of Drake*. New York: World Publishing, 1965.

Wilson, Derek A. *The World Encompassed: Francis Drake and His Great Voyage*. New York: Harper and Row, 1977.

Wormald, Jenny. *Court, Kirk, and Community: Scotland, 1470–1625*. Toronto: University of Toronto Press, 1981.

Biography—Elizabeth I

Bassnett, Susan. *Elizabeth I: A Feminist Perspective*. New York: St. Martin's Press, 1988.

Camden, William. *The History of the Most Renowned and Victorious Princess Elizabeth, Late Queen of England*. Edited by Wallace T. MacCaffrey. Chicago: University of Chicago Press, 1970. (Reprint of Part 1 of Camden's Latin *Annals of Elizabeth,* first published in 1615.)

Erickson, Carolly. *The First Elizabeth*. New York: Summit Books, 1983.

Haigh, Christopher. *Elizabeth I*. London: Longman, 1988.

Hibbert, Christopher. *The Virgin Queen: Elizabeth I, Genius of the Golden Age*. Reading, MA: Addison-Wesley, 1991.

Jenkins, Elizabeth. *Elizabeth the Great*. New York: Coward-McCann, 1959.

Johnson, Paul. *Elizabeth I: A Biography*. New York: Holt, Rinehart and Winston, 1974.

MacCaffrey, Wallace. *Elizabeth I*. London: Edward Arnold, 1993.

Neale, J. E. *Queen Elizabeth I: A Biography*. Chicago: Academy Chicago Publishers, 1992 (originally published 1934).

Perry, Maria. *The Word of a Prince: A Life of Elizabeth I*. Woodbridge, England: Boydell Press, 1990.

Ridley, Jasper. *Elizabeth I: The Shrewdness of Virtue*. New York: Viking, 1988.

Smith, Lacey Baldwin. *Elizabeth Tudor: Portrait of a Queen*. Boston: Little, Brown and Company, 1975.

Somerset, Anne. *Elizabeth I*. New York: Alfred A. Knopf, 1991.

Weir, Alison. *The Life of Elizabeth I*. New York Ballantine Books, 1998.

Williams, Neville. *Elizabeth the First: Queen of England*. New York: E. P. Dutton, 1968.

Other Biography

Adamson, Jack H. and H. F. Follard. *The Shepherd of the Ocean: An Account of Sir Walter Ralegh and His Times*. Boston: Gambit, 1969.

Akrigg, G. P. V. *Shakespeare and the Earl of Southampton*. Cambridge, MA: Harvard University Press, 1968.

Anderson, F. H. *Francis Bacon, His Career and His Thought*. Los Angeles: University of Southern California Press, 1962.

Archer, Stanley. *Richard Hooker*. Boston: Twayne, 1983.

Auerbach, Erna. *Nicholas Hilliard*. London: Routledge and Paul, 1961.

Bamborough, J. B. *Ben Jonson*. London: Hutchinson, 1970.

Baumgartner, Frederic J. *Henry II, King of France 1547–1559*. Durham, NC: Duke University Press, 1988.

Beckingsale, B. W. *Burghley: Tudor Statesman 1520–1598*. New York: St. Martin's Press, 1967.

Beer, Barrett L. *Northumberland*. Kent, OH: Kent State University Press, 1973.

Berlin, Norman. *Thomas Sackville*. New York: Twayne Publishers, 1974.

Bindoff, S. T. *The Fame of Sir Thomas Gresham*. London: Cape, 1973.

Bingham, Caroline. *Darnley: A Life of Henry Stuart, Lord Darnley*. London: Constable, 1995.

Blake, William. *William Maitland of Lethington*. Lewiston, NY: E. Mellen Press, 1990.

Blakiston, Georgiana. *Woburn and the Russells*. London: Constable, 1980.

Booty, J. E. *John Jewel as Apologist of the Church of England*. London: S.P.C.K., 1963.

Bouwsma, William J. *John Calvin*. Oxford: Oxford University Press, 1988.

Bowen, Catherine Drinker. *Francis Bacon: The Temper of a Man*. Boston: Little, Brown, 1963.

Bowen, Marjorie. *Mary, Queen of Scots*. London: Sphere Books Limited, 1971 (originally published 1934).

Brandi, Karl. *The Emperor Charles V*. London: Jonathan Cape, 1970.

Brewster, Eleanor. *Oxford: Courtier to the Queen*. New York: Pageant Press, 1964.

Brook, Victor J. K. *A Life of Archbishop Parker*. Oxford: Clarendon Press, 1962.

Brooks, Eric St. John. *Sir Christopher Hatton*. London: Jonathan Cape, 1947.

Buchanan, Patricia. *Margaret Tudor: Queen of the Scots*. Edinburgh: Scottish Academic Press, 1985.

Caraman, Philip. *Henry Garnet, 1555–1606, and the Gunpowder Plot*. London: Longmans, Green, and Company, 1964.

Carrafiello, Michael L. *Robert Parsons and English Catholicism, 1580–1610*. London: Associated University Presses, 1998.

Cecil, Algernon. *A Life of Robert Cecil, First Earl of Salisbury*. Westport, CT: Greenwood Press, 1971.

Cecil, David. *The Cecils of Hatfield House: An English Ruling Family*. Boston: Houghton Mifflin, 1973.

Chapman, Hester W. *The Last Tudor King: A Study of Edward VI*. New York: Macmillan, 1958.

———. *The Thistle and the Rose: The Sisters of Henry VIII*. New York: Coward, McCann & Geoghegan, 1971.

———. *Two Tudor Portraits: Henry Howard, Earl of Surrey and Lady Katherine Grey*. Boston: Little, Brown, 1963.

Chidsey, Donald Barr. *Sir Humphrey Gilbert*. New York: Harper and Brothers, 1932.

Chrimes, S. B. *Henry VII*. Berkeley: University of California Press, 1972.

Collinson, Patrick. *Archbishop Grindal 1519–1583: The Struggle for a Reformed Church*. Berkeley: University of California Press, 1979.

Connell, Charles. *They Gave Us Shakespeare: John Heminge and Henry Condell*. Boston: Oriel Press, 1982.

Coote, Stephen. *A Play of Passion: The Life of Sir Walter Raleigh*. London: Macmillan, 1993.

Coquillette, D. R. *Francis Bacon*. Stanford, CA: Stanford University Press, 1992.

Cross, Claire. *The Puritan Earl: The Life of Henry Hastings*. New York: St. Martin's Press, 1967.

Crupu, Charles W. *Robert Greene*. Boston: Twayne, 1986.

Cummins, John. *Francis Drake*. New York: St. Martin's Press, 1995.

Davis, John. *The Voyages and Works of John Davis, the Navigator*. New York: B. Franklin, 1970.

Dawley, Powel Mills. *John Whitgift and the English Reformation*. New York: Scribner, 1954.

Deacon, Richard. *John Dee*. London: Macmillan, 1968.

Devlin, Christopher. *The Life of Robert Southwell: Poet and Martyr*. New York: Greenwood Press, 1969.

Dewar, Mary. *Sir Thomas Smith*. London: University of London, Athlone Press, 1964.

Dickens, A. G. *Thomas Cromwell and the English Reformation*. New York: Harper & Row, 1969.

Doe, Paul. *Tallis*. 2nd ed. London: Oxford University Press, 1976.

Donaldson, Gordon. *Mary, Queen of Scots*. London: English Universities Press, 1974.

Duncan-Jones, Katherine. *Sir Philip Sidney: Courtier Poet*. New Haven, CT: Yale University Press, 1991.

Dunkel, Wilbur. *William Lambarde: Elizabethan Jurist 1536–1601*. New Brunswick, NJ: Rutgers University Press, 1965.

Durant, David N. *Arabella Stuart: A Rival to the Queen*. London: Weidenfeld and Nicolson, 1978.

———. *Bess of Hardwick: Portrait of an Elizabethan Dynast*. New York: Atheneum, 1978.

Edmond, Mary. *Hilliard and Oliver: The Lives and Works of Two Great Miniaturists*. London: R. Hale, 1983.

Edwards, Francis. *The Marvellous Chance: Thomas Howard, Fourth Duke of Norfolk, and the Ridolfi Plot, 1570–1572*. London: Hart-Davis, 1968.

———. *Robert Parsons: The Biography of an English Jesuit, 1546–1610*. St. Louis: Institute of Jesuit Sources, 1995.

Edwards, Philip. *Thomas Kyd and Early Elizabethan Tragedy*. London: Longmans, 1966.

Erickson, Carolly. *Bloody Mary*. Garden City, NY: Doubleday, 1978.

———. *Great Harry: The Extravagant Life of Henry VIII*. New York: Summit Books, 1980.

———. *Mistress Anne: The Exceptional Life of Anne Boleyn*. London: Macmillan, 1984.

Evans, John X., ed. *The Works of Sir Roger Williams*. Oxford: Clarendon Press, 1972.

Falls, Cyril. *Mountjoy: Elizabethan General*. London: Odhams Press, 1955.

Faulkner, Robert K. *Richard Hooker and the Politics of Christian England*. Berkeley: University of California Press, 1981.

Foster, Sir William. *The Voyages of Sir James Lancaster*. London: Hakluyt Society, 1940.

Fraser, Antonia. *King James VI of Scotland and I of England*. London: Sphere Books Limited, 1977.

———. *Mary, Queen of Scots*. New York: Delacorte Press, 1969.

———. *The Wives of Henry VIII*. New York: Alfred A. Knopf, 1992.

Freedman, Sylvia. *Poor Penelope: Lady Penelope Rich, an Elizabethan Woman*. Abbotsbrook, England: Kensal Press, 1983.

Freeman, Arthur. *Thomas Kyd, Facts and Problems*. Oxford: Clarendon Press, 1967.

French, Peter J. *John Dee*. New York: ARK Paperbacks, 1987.

Gerard, John. *The Autobiography of a Hunted Priest*. Translated by Philip Caraman. New York: Pellegrini & Cudahy, 1952.

Gore-Browne, Robert. *Lord Bothwell and Mary, Queen of Scots*. Garden City, NY: Doubleday, Doran, 1937.

Graves, Michael A. R. *Thomas Norton: The Parliament Man*. Oxford: Blackwell, 1994.

Greenblatt, Stephen J. *Sir Walter Raleigh: The Renaissance Man and His Roles*. New Haven, CT: Yale University Press, 1973.

Gresham, Perry E., with Carol Jose. *The Sign of the Golden Grasshopper: A Biography of Sir Thomas Gresham*. Ottawa, IL: Jameson Books, 1995.

Greville, Fulke, Baron Brooke. *Sir Fulke Greville's Life of Sir Philip Sidney*. Folcroft, PA: Folcroft Press, 1971.

Habsburg, Otto. *Charles V*. New York: Praeger, 1970.

Hakluyt Society. *Richard Hakluyt and His Successors*. London: Hakluyt Society, 1946.

Hamilton, A. C. *Sir Philip Sidney: A Study of His Life and Works*. Cambridge: Cambridge University Press, 1977.

Handover, P.M. *Arabella Stuart*. London: Eyre & Spottiswoode, 1957.

———. *The Second Cecil*. London: Eyre & Spottiswoode, 1959.

Hannay, Margaret P. *Philip's Phoenix: Mary Sidney, Countess of Pembroke*. New York: Oxford University Press, 1990.

Harington, Sir John. *The Letters and Epigrams of Sir John Harington*. Edited by Norman Egbert McClure. New York: Octagon Books, 1977.

Harley, John. *William Byrd: A Gentleman of the Chapel Royal*. Brookfield, VT: Ashgate Publishers, 1997.

Harvey, Nancy Lenz. *Elizabeth of York: Tudor Queen*. New York: Macmillan, 1973.

Haynes, Alan. *Robert Cecil, Earl of Salisbury, 1563–1612: Servant of Two Sovereigns*. London: Peter Owen, 1989.

———. *The White Bear: Robert Dudley, the Elizabethan Earl of Leicester.* London: Peter Owen, 1987.

Head, David. *The Ebbs and Flows of Fortune: The Life of Thomas Howard, Third Duke of Norfolk*. Athens: University of Georgia Press, 1995.

Henderson, Philip. *Christopher Marlowe*. 2nd ed. New York: Barnes and Noble Books, 1974.

Holmes, Martin. *Shakespeare and Burbage*. Totowa, NJ: Rowman and Littlefield, 1978.

Houppert, Joseph W. *John Lyly*. Boston: Twayne, 1975.

Houston, S. J. *James I*. 2nd ed. London: Longman, 1995.

Howell, Roger. *Sir Philip Sidney: The Shepherd Knight*. Boston: Little, Brown, 1968.

Hunter, G. K. *John Lyly: The Humanist as Courtier*. Cambridge, MA: Harvard University Press, 1962.

———. *Lyly and Peele*. Harlow, England: Published for the British Council and the National Book League by Longmans, 1968.

Ives, Eric W. *Anne Boleyn*. Oxford: Blackwell, 1986.

Izon, John. *Sir Thomas Stucley c. 1525–1578: Traitor Extraordinary*. London: Andrew Melrose, 1956.

Jardine, Lisa. *Francis Bacon: Discovery and the Art of Discourse*. London: Cambridge University Press, 1974.

Jenkins, Elizabeth. *Elizabeth and Leicester: A Biography*. New York: Coward-McCann, 1962.

Jones, Frederick M. *Mountjoy, 1563–1606: The Last Elizabethan Deputy*. Dublin: Clanmore and Reynolds, 1958.

Jones, Michael K. and Underwood, Malcolm G. *The King's Mother: Lady Margaret Beaufort, Countess of Richmond and Derby*. Cambridge: Cambridge University Press, 1992.

Jordan, John Clark. *Robert Greene*. New York: Octagon Books, 1965.

Jordan, W. K. *Edward VI: The Threshold of Power: The Dominance of the Duke of Northumberland*. Cambridge, MA: Harvard University Press, 1970.

———. *Edward VI: The Young King: The Protectorship of the Duke of Somerset*. Cambridge, MA: Harvard University Press, 1968.

Kamen, Henry. *Philip of Spain*. New Haven, CT: Yale University Press, 1997.

Kay, Dennis. *Shakespeare: His Life, Work, and Era*. New York: William Morrow, 1992.

Kelsey, Harry. *Sir Francis Drake: The Queen's Pirate*. New Haven, CT: Yale University Press, 1998.

Kenny, Robert W. *Elizabeth's Admiral: The Political Career of Charles Howard, Earl of Nottingham 1536–1624*. Baltimore: Johns Hopkins Press, 1970.

Knecht, R. J. *Catherine de Medici*. London: Longman, 1998.

———. *Francis I*. Cambridge: Cambridge University Press, 1982.

———. *French Renaissance Monarchy: Francis I and Henry II*. 2nd ed. London: Longman, 1996.

Lacey, Robert. *Robert Devereux, Earl of Essex*. New York: Atheneum, 1971.

———. *Sir Walter Ralegh*. New York: Atheneum, 1974.

Lamont, Stewart. *The Swordbearer: John Knox and the European Reformation*. London: Hodder and Stoughton, 1991.

Lang, Andrew. *John Knox and the Reformation*. Port Washington, NY: Kenniket Press, 1967.

Lee, Maurice. *James Stewart, Earl of Moray*. New York: Columbia University Press, 1953.

Lennon, Colm. *Richard Stanihurst the Dubliner, 1547–1618*. Dublin: Irish Academic Press, 1981.

Lever, Sir Tresham. *The Herberts of Wilton*. London: Murray, 1967.

Levi, Peter. *The Life and Times of William Shakespeare*. New York: Henry Holt and Company, 1988.

Lloyd, Christopher. *Sir Francis Drake*. London: Faber and Faber, 1979.

Loades, D. M. *John Dudley, Duke of Northumberland*. Oxford: Clarendon Press, 1996.

———. *Mary Tudor: A Life*. Oxford: Basil Blackwell, 1989.

Luke, Mary M. *The Nine Days Queen: A Portrait of Lady Jane Grey*. New York: W. Morrow, 1986.

Marshall, Rosalind K. *Queen of Scots*. Edinburgh: HMSO, 1986.

Martienssen, Anthony. *Queen Katherine Parr*. London: Seeker and Warburg, 1973.

Martin, A. Lynn. *Henry III and the Jesuit Politicians*. Geneva: Droz, 1973.

Martin, Julian. *Francis Bacon, the State, and the Reform of Natural Philosophy*. Cambridge: Cambridge University Press, 1992.

Mathew, David. *James I*. London: Eyre & Spottiswoode, 1969.

Mattingly, Garrett. *Catherine of Aragon*. Boston: Little, Brown, 1941.

MacCulloch, Diarmaid. *Thomas Cranmer*. New Haven, CT: Yale University Press, 1996.

McFee, William. *Sir Martin Frobisher*. London: J. Lane, Bodley Head, 1928.

McGinn, Donald J. *John Penry and the Marprelate Controversy*. New Brunswick, NJ: Rutgers University Press, 1966.

McGrath, Alister E. *A Life of John Calvin*. Oxford: Basil Blackwell, 1990.

McInnes, Ian. *Arabella*. London: W. H. Allen, 1968.

Melville, Sir James. *Memoirs of Sir James Melville of Hahill*. Edited by A. Francis Steuart. London: George Routledge and Sons, 1929.

Miller, Amos C. *Sir Henry Killigrew: Elizabethan Soldier and Diplomat*. Leicester: Leicester University Press, 1963.

Miles, Rosalind. *Ben Jonson: His Life and Work*. London: Routledge & Kegan Paul, 1986.

Mitchell, C. Martin. *The Shakespeare Circle: A Life of Dr. John Hall, Shakespeare's Son-in-Law*. Birmingham, England: Cornish Brothers, 1947.

Morrison, N. Brysson. *Mary, Queen of Scots*. New York: Vanguard Press, 1960.

Mozley, J. F. *John Foxe and His Book*. New York: Octagon Books, 1970.

Nicholl, Charles. *A Cup of News: The Life of Thomas Nashe*. London: Routledge and Kegan Paul, 1984.

Nolan, John S. *Sir John Norrys and the Elizabethan Military World*. Exeter: University of Exeter Press, 1997.

O'Faolain, Sean. The Great O'Neill. New York: Duell, Sloan and Pearce, 1942, reprint ed. Dufour Editions, 1997.

Ogburn, Charlton. *The Mysterious William Shakespeare*. 2nd ed. McLean, VA: EPM Publications, 1992.

Olsen, V. N. *John Foxe and the Elizabethan Church*. Berkeley: University of California Press, 1973.

Parker, Geoffrey. *Philip II*. 3rd ed. Chicago: Open Court, 1995.

Parker, T. H. L. *John Calvin*. Philadelphia: Westminster Press, 1975.

Parks, George Bruner. *Richard Hakluyt and the English Voyages*. New York: F. Ungar, 1961.

Parry, G. J. R. *A Protestant Vision: William Harrison and the Reformation of Elizabethan England*. Cambridge: Cambridge University Press, 1987.

Paul, John E. *Catherine of Aragon and Her Friends*. London: Burns & Oates, 1966.

Pearson, A. F. Scott. *Thomas Cartwright and Elizabethan Puritanism, 1535–1603*. Gloucester, MA: P. Smith, 1966.

Petrie, Sir Charles. *Don John of Austria*. New York: Norton, 1967.

Pierson, Peter. *Commander of the Armada: The Seventh Duke of Medina Sidonia*. New Haven, CT: Yale University Press, 1989.

Plowden, Alison. *Lady Jane Grey and the House of Suffolk*. London: Sidgwick & Jackson, 1985.

Prescott, H. F. M. *Mary Tudor*. New York: Macmillan, 1953.

Prouty, Charles Tyler. *George Gascoigne*. New York: B. Blom, 1966.

Quinn, David B. *Raleigh and the British Empire*. rev. ed. New York: Collier Books, 1962.

Rae, Wesley D. *Thomas Lodge*. New York: Twayne, 1967.

Rebholz, Ronald A. *The Life of Fulke Greville, First Lord Brooke*. Oxford: Clarendon Press, 1971.

Read, Conyers. *Lord Burghley and Queen Elizabeth*. New York: Alfred A. Knopf, 1960.

———. *Mr. Secretary Cecil and Queen Elizabeth*. London: Jonathan Cape, 1965.

———. *Mr. Secretary Walsingham and the Policy of Queen Elizabeth*. Hamden, CT: Archon Books, 1967.

Reid, Aileen and Robert Maniura, eds. *Edward Alleyn: Elizabethan Actor, Jacobean Gentleman*. London: Dulwich Picture Gallery, 1994.

Ridley, Jasper. *Henry VIII: The Politics of Tyranny*. London: Constable, 1984.

———. *John Knox*. Oxford: Oxford University Press, 1968.

Riggs, David. *Ben Jonson*. Cambridge, MA: Harvard University Press, 1989.

Rossi, Paolo. *Francis Bacon: From Magic to Science*. Translated by Sacha Rabinovitch. London: Routledge & K. Paul, 1968.

Rowse, A. L. *Christopher Marlowe: His Life and Work*. New York: Grosset & Dunlap, 1966.

———. *Ralegh and the Throckmortons*. London: Macmillan, 1962.

———. *Sex and Society in Shakespeare's Age: Simon Forman the Astrologer*. New York: Charles Scribner's Sons, 1974.

———. *Shakespeare's Southampton: Patron of Virginia*. New York: Harper and Row, 1965.

———. *Sir Richard Grenville of the Revenge*. London: Book Club Associates, 1977.

———. *Sir Walter Ralegh: His Family and Private Life*. New York: Harper, 1962.

———. *William Shakespeare: A Biography*. New York: Harper & Row, 1963.

Ryan, Lawrence V. *Roger Ascham*. Stanford, CA: Stanford University Press, 1963.

Saaler, Mary. *Anne of Cleves*. London: The Rubicon Press, 1995.

Sammartino, Peter. *The Man Who Was William Shakespeare*. New York: Cornwall Books, 1990.

Scarisbrick, J. J. *Henry VIII*. Berkeley: University of California Press, 1968.

Schoenbaum, S. *Shakespeare's Lives*. Oxford: Clarendon Press, 1991.

Seymour, William. *Ordeal by Ambition: An English Family in the Shadow of the Tudors*. London: Sidgwick and Jackson, 1972.

Seward, Desmond. *The First Bourbon: Henri IV, King of France and Navarre*. Boston: Gambit, 1971.

———. *Prince of the Renaissance: The Golden Life of François I*. New York: Macmillan, 1973.

Sharpe, Kevin. *Sir Robert Cotton*. New York: Oxford University Press, 1979.

Shirley, J. W. *Thomas Harriot*. New York: Clarendon Press, 1983.

Simon, Linda. *Of Virtue Rare: Margaret Beaufort, Matriarch of the House of Tudor*. Boston: Houghton Mifflin, 1982.

Smith, Lacey Baldwin. *Henry VIII: The Mask of Royalty*. Boston: Houghton Mifflin, 1971.

———. *A Tudor Tragedy: The Life and Times of Catherine Howard*. New York: Pantheon Books, 1961.

Spence, Richard T. *The Privateering Earl: George Clifford, 3rd Earl of Cumberland, 1558–1605*. Stroud, England: Alan Sutton Publishers, 1995.

Stern, Virginia F. *Gabriel Harvey*. Oxford: Clarendon Press, 1979.

Strachey, Lytton. *Elizabeth and Essex*. Oxford: Oxford University Press, 1981.

Strong, Roy. *Henry, Prince of Wales, and England's Lost Renaissance*. London: Thames and Hudson, 1986.

Sugden, John. *Sir Francis Drake*. New York: Simon & Schuster, 1990.

Swart, J. *Thomas Sackville: A Study in Sixteenth-Century Poetry*. Groningen, Netherlands: J. B. Wolthers, 1949.

Tittler, Robert. *Nicholas Bacon, 1510–1579: The Making of a Tudor Statesman*. Athens: Ohio University Press, 1976.

Tyler, Royall. *The Emperor Charles V*. London: G. Allen and Unwin, 1956.

Wagner, J. A. *The Devon Gentleman: The Life of Sir Peter Carew*. Hull, England: University of Hull Press, 1998.

Waller, Gary F. *Edmund Spenser: A Literary Life*. London: Macmillan, 1994.

Walsh, Micheline Kerney. *Hugh O'Neill: An Exile of Ireland, Prince of Ulster*. Dublin: Four Courts Press, 1996.

Warnicke, Retha M. *The Rise and Fall of Anne Boleyn*. Cambridge: Cambridge University Press, 1989.

———. *William Lambarde: Elizabethan Antiquary, 1536–1601*. London: Phillimore, 1973.

Waugh, Evelyn. *Edmund Campion*. London: Cassell, 1987.

Wedgwood, C.V. *William the Silent*. rev. ed. New Haven, CT: Yale University Press, 1960.

Weir, Alison. *The Children of Henry VIII*. London: J. Cape, 1996.

———. *The Six Wives of Henry VIII*. New York: Grove Weidenfeld, 1991.

West, Jane. *The Brave Lord Willoughby: An Elizabethan Soldier*. Edinburgh: Pentland Press, 1998.

Williams, Neville. *A Tudor Tragedy: Thomas Howard Fourth Duke of Norfolk*. London: Barrie and Jenkins, 1964.

Williams, Norman Lloyd. *Sir Walter Raleigh*. Baltimore: Penguin Books, 1965.

Williamson, Hugh Ross. *Catherine de Medici*. New York: Viking, 1973.

———. *Sir Walter Raleigh*. Westport, CT: Greenwood Press, 1978.

Williamson, James A. *Hawkins of Plymouth*. 2nd ed. New York: Barnes & Noble, 1969.

Willson, D. Harris. *King James VI and I*. New York: Henry Holt and Company, 1956.

Wilson, Derek A. *Sweet Robin: A Biography of Robert Dudley, Earl of Leicester*. London: H. Hamilton, 1981.

Winton, John. *Sir Walter Ralegh*. New York: Coward, McCann & Geohegan, 1975.

Wormald, B. H. G. *Francis Bacon: History, Politics and Science, 1561–1626*. Cambridge: Cambridge University Press, 1993.

Wormald, Jenny. *Mary Queen of Scots: A Study in Failure*. London: Collins & Brown, 1991.

Wraight, A.D. *Christopher Marlowe and Edward Alleyn*. Chichester, England: Adam Hart, 1993.

INDEX

Boldface page references denote full entries. The abbreviation (illus.) indicates a photograph, table, or other illustration, while the abbreviations (gen.) and (map) indicate a genealogical chart and a map, respectively.

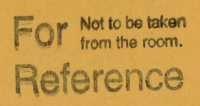